FALSER THAN
A WEEPING
CROCODILE
AND OTHER SIMILES

FALSER THAN
A WEEPING
CROCODILE
AND OTHER SIMILES

E L Y S E   S O M M E R
M I K E   S O M M E R
ILLUSTRATIONS BY TERRY COLON

DETROIT   CHICAGO   WASHINGTON, D.C.   LONDON

Falser than a Weeping Crocodile
and Other Similes

Published by Visible Ink Press,
a division of Gale Research Inc.
835 Penobscot Building
Detroit, MI 48226-4094

Visible Ink Press is a trademark of Gale Research Inc.

ISBN 0-8103-9414-6

Art Director: Arthur Chartow
Cover Design: Cynthia Baldwin
Interior Design: Mary Krzewinski, Bernadette Gornie
Illustrations: Terry Colon

Contents

crocodile tears—Pretended or insincere tears, hypocritical weeping, false sorrow. Legend has it that a crocodile sheds tears and moans in order to lure passersby into its clutches, and then, still weeping, devours them. A person who feigns deep sorrow in order to impress others or gain their sympathy is thus said to cry crocodile tears.

Introduction

After the publication of ... *As One Mad With Wine,* letters clamoring for more similes abounded like street vendors on a spring day. These letters became our mandate for another simile-scouting expedition. Once again we foraged through centuries of expressions, from the Bible to Shakespeare to recently published, broadcast, and overheard similes. And here's the result: 9,000 new similes, arranged into hundreds of new thematic categories to steer you to a phrase that will add spark to a speech or unleash your own creative wellspring—from **abandoned as a used Kleenex** under ABANDONMENT to **yellow like moldy linen** under YELLOW.

The "Similists"

As with the first book, this volume owes everything to the multitude of authors whose similes illuminate its pages. Their comparative wit is **as varied as a Cook's tour** (see DIVERSE-NESS). And as you'll discover when you check out the convenient **Author Index,** so are their backgrounds. Sharing space with eminent literati, like the poet John Dryden whose **falser than a weeping crocodile** gave us our title (see TRUENESS/FALSENESS), are luminaries from all walks of life.

Football fans will want to check out New York Giants quarterback Y.A. Tittle's **passes that swerved like a diving duck,** and Frank Gifford's comparison of pro football to **nuclear warfare with no winners, only survivors** (see FOOTBALL). Golf similes include Chi Chi Rodriguez's **I'm playing like Tarzan and scoring like Jane,** as well as several gems from that master writer of golf stories, P.G. Wodehouse (see GOLF). And if you like boxing and wrestling, you'll find items like the great Sonny Liston's "similistic" definition: **A boxing match is like a cowboy movie. There's got to be good guys and there's got to be bad guys. What people pay for is to see the bad guys get beat** (see BOXING AND WRESTLING).

Journalism and show business also yield some pungent and amusing contributions. Columnist Russell Baker provides several offerings, including his comparison of Americans' treatment of history to **a cookbook to which they turn in times of uncertainty in hopes of finding the proper recipe** (see HISTORY). Actress Zsa Zsa Gabor, who knows more about husbands than most, compares them to **fires: they go out when unattended** (see MARRIAGE).

Probably the one type of fiction writer most frequently associated with the crisp and colorful simile is the spinner of mystery yarns. You'll find many you know and some you don't represented with quick-on-the-draw comparisons. Amongst old-time favorites you'll find Raymond Chandler and Dashiell Hammett with phrases like **lithe as a whip** (see AGILITY), and **black as a politician's prospects** (see BLACK). Currently popular sleuth (and simile) inventors include James Crumley, Sue Grafton, and Jonathon Valin.

Of course, not to be outdone by the famous, or infamous, is the super-prolific Anon who compels attention with a melange of scintillating similes. Anon's "similistic" bon mots range over a wide spectrum of topics: **Making love to the same woman too frequently is like scratching a place that doesn't itch any more** comes from LOVE, **life is like a jigsaw puzzle with most of the pieces missing** from LIFE, DEFINED, and **some minds are like concrete: thoroughly mixed and permanently set** from MIND, DEFINED.

Additional anonymous contributors can also be found through the Author Index listing for the Bible and Colloquialisms, like this Spanish proverb from KISSES: **A kiss without a mustache is like an egg without salt.**

Distinguishing Similes from Metaphors

For those *...As One Mad With Wine* readers who need reinforcement, and for anyone who missed the first round of simile madness, here's a little review in rhyme to keep the difference between the simile and its cousin the metaphor sorted out:

> Similes are rhetorical tools to compare
> Two dissimilar ideas with color and flare.
> Flag the comparison with **as if, like** or **as**
> And add the element of surprise for snap and pizazz.

The metaphor is the simile's kin
But with an implicit and more subtle spin.
Instead of comparing one thing to another
Metaphorically speaking, it becomes the other.

With the above rhyme in mind, many of the similes in these pages can be multiplied by transforming them into metaphors. A woman described in a simile as **active and strong as a lioness** (see ACTIONS) would, metaphorically speaking, be referred to as a lioness.

As one simile leads to another, so our rhyme to mark the distinction between similes and metaphors brings to mind another about usage. It's actually a paraphrase of Lewis Carroll's simile on the judicious use of epithets (see WORDS, EFFECT OF). As you can see it fits the simile **as a hollow fits a circle:**

Similes, like pepper, give zest to what you write
And if you strew them sparely, you whet the appetite;
But if you lay them on too thick,
You spoil the matter quite!

As the thematic categories will lead you to specific similes to color your speech, and the **Author Index** to specific writers' and speakers' ideas, so a leisurely browse through these pages will heighten your appreciation for the simile's versatility as a tool for evoking word pictures that stir a shiver of appreciation and recognition in the reader or listener. Six permutations of the basic simile that you'll encounter while browsing are:

Poetic Similes—These offer captivating and particularly vivid images. You'll find some of the most inspirational examples in categories that feature scenery; for example, **clouds lumbered off westward like ghosts of buffalo** from CLOUD MOVEMENTS, **stars gleamed and winked like searching fireflies,** from STARS, and **the streets looked as if they were made of silver, they were so bright and glistening** from CITY/STREETSCAPES.

Alliterative Similes—The first poems written in English were not rhymes but alliterative phrases. This poetic device also energizes many similes such as **dry as dust** and **dry as a desert** (see DRYNESS) and **slick as spit** (see SMOOTHNESS). However, Delmore Schwartz's simile

alliteration is like ivy, some of it is poison, might be taken as a warning not to allow alliteration (or similes per se) to proliferate through your speech and writing **like coat hangers in a closet** (see GROWTH).

Extended Similes—Here two or more related comparisons are strung together for added emphasis, as in **Innocent as milk and built like a chocolate eclair** (see PERSONALITY PROFILES). For one of the longest extended similes ever used successfully, check out Donald Westlake's priceless portrait of a character named Gross under PHYSICAL APPEARANCE.

Snap-Crackle-Pop Similes—These are the brisk and snappy snippets that are often borrowed and quoted so much that they become commonplace—at least until they seed a fresh crop of twists and variations. Many include alliteration for extra snap as do **spread like butter on toast** (see SPREADING), **slick as nail polish** (see SMOOTHNESS), and **stout as a stump** (see FATNESS).

Ironic Similes—Irony gives the words a spin that belies the real meaning intended, as in **drinks flowed like cement,** (see AVAILABILITY/UNAVAILABILITY), **chummy as a pair of panthers** (see SOCIABILITY/ UNSOCIABILITY). A straightforward simile such as **futile as shovelling sand into the sea** (see FUTILITY) could easily take an ironic turn by changing futile to effective.

"Similistic" Quotations—Many similes work as freestanding quotations. Two such nuggets from the GOVERNMENT category are Antoine de Saint-Exupery's **an administration, like a machine, does not create. It carries on;** and Ben Franklin's **a great empire, like a great cake, is most easily diminished at the edges.** Quotable similes are scattered throughout these pages. Categories such as ECONOMICS, KNOWLEDGE, and WORLD are particularly fertile quotation sources.

Browsers who enjoyed the fascinating tidbits that elucidated and enriched many entries in *...As One Mad With Wine* will find more of the same in *Falser than a Weeping Crocodile*. For example, a comment note under the category for SPREADING points out how **spread like a stain** can be successfully linked to completely different points of reference. The addendum to Cole Porter's **fumes like Vesuvius** (see ANGER), reveals that the famous lyricist hardly ever used a simile before he worked on the musical *Kiss Me Kate*, based on the simile-happy William Shakespeare's *Taming of the Shrew*. These added notes provide many other interesting details about phrase origins, sources, and variations.

Our Comments

To help you to wring the last drop of pleasure and usefulness from this book, here are three creative tips garnered from readers who got hooked on similes through *...As One Mad With Wine:*

More Fun with Similes

1. Use the similes to play charades

Dee Mass of Memphis, Tennessee, got the idea for simile-related charades from our illustrations. "I can't draw, but I started to think about how I would illustrate some of these similes if I could draw. One thing led to another, and instead of thinking about sketches, I began to think in terms of acting out some of the ideas and having someone else guess the phrase. We've played these charades at both adult and kid's parties ever since."

2. Use the similes to personalize gift and greeting cards

Another reader, Ellen Houlihan from Los Angeles, California, wrote that though she isn't a speechwriter or any other kind of writer, she now browses through our book's various thematic categories before merely signing her name to a printed card. She found that looking beyond the obvious subject categories, and changing the frame of reference to suit her needs helped her to warm up her skill for developing her own twists and phrases. (We followed suit when we switched from epithets to similes in our rhyme about using alliteration.)

3. Expand your horizons as a reader by reading the works of the authors of similes you particularly admire.

Ben Baker from Holyoke, Massachusetts, felt that if he enjoyed someone's phrase found in *...As One Mad With Wine*, he might get even more pleasure from more in-depth reading. He reports discovering a number of first-rate authors whom he'd never read and being richly rewarded with "good reads" from these good leads. He also spotted many additional picturesque expressions.

<hr/>

Parting Shot

We'll leave you with a lyrical and thought-provoking view of the simile, taken from Poet Laureate Richard Wilbur's 1987 poem "Lying":

Odd that a thing is most itself when likened:
The eye mists over, basil hints of clove,
... And in the barnyard near the sawdust-pile
Some great thing is tormented. Either it is
A tarp torn loose and in the groaning wind
Now puffed, now flattened, or a hip-shot beast
Which tries again, and once again, to rise.
What, though for pain there is no other word,
Finds pleasure in the cruellest simile?
It is something in us like the catbird's song
From neighbor bushes in the grey of morning
That, harsh or sweet, and of its own accord,
Proclaims its many kin.

Elyse and Mike Sommer
Forest Hills, New York/Lee, Massachusetts

A User's Guide to Organization and Use

Table of Thematic Categories. Alphabetically arranged, with See: and See also: cross-references, for finding similes on particular topics.

The Entries. Similes are in alphabetical order (except for a, an, the). Parenthetical text is part of the source material included to clarify meaning and usage. Text in square brackets, and at the end of the entry, is added by editors to enhance meaning and reader enjoyment. Additional cross-references are also included.

Author Index. A source-to-idea reference, referring readers to the categories where similes by an author or source (like **Bible, The Holy**) are represented.

Table of Thematic Categories

In the following table, categories used throughout the text and synonyms that are cross-references to categories are combined in one alphabetic order.

ABANDONMENT
See also: REJECTION
Ability
See: ACCOMPLISHMENT
ABSORBABILITY
Absurdity
See: FOOLISHNESS, FUTILITY
ABUNDANCE
See also: GROWTH, SPREADING
Abuse
See: CRUELTY
Acceptability
See: BELONGING
Accessibility
See: AVAILABILITY/ UNAVAILABILITY
Accident
See: FATE
ACCOMPLISHMENT
Accumulation
See: GROWTH, SPREADING
Accuracy
See: CORRECTNESS
Accusation
See: CRITICISM
ACTIONS
See also: BEHAVIOR, CAUTION, LEAPING, MOVEMENT, VIOLENCE
Activeness/Inactiveness
See: ALERTNESS, ENERGY, MOVEMENT

Adaptability
See: BELONGING, FLEXIBILITY/INFLEXIBILITY
Adjustment
See: FLEXIBILITY/ INFLEXIBILITY, HABIT
Admiration
See: FLATTERY
Adultery
See: MARRIAGE
Advancing
See: ENTRANCES/EXITS, MOVEMENT
ADVANTAGEOUSNESS
See also: COST
ADVERSARY
ADVERTISING
ADVICE
See also: FUTILITY
Affability
See: AVAILABILITY/ UNAVAILABILITY, BEHAVIOR
AFFECTION
See also: LOVE
AGE
See also: MANKIND
Aggression
See: VIOLENCE
AGILITY
See also: MOVEMENT, SPEED, TURNING AND TWISTING, WALKING

AGITATION
See also: HEARTBEAT,
NERVOUSNESS,
TREMBLING
AGREEMENT/DISAGREEMENT
Aim
See: PURPOSEFULNESS
AIMLESSNESS
See also: BELONGING
Air
See: ATMOSPHERE
Alcohol
See: DRINKING
ALERTNESS
See also: WATCHFULNESS
Alikeness
See: SIMILARITY
Alimony
See: MARRIAGE
Aloneness
See: ABANDONMENT
Aloofness
See: RESERVE
Amazement
See: SURPRISE
Ancestors
See: PAST, THE
ANGER
See also: EMOTIONS
Animation
See: ENERGY
Ankles
See: LEGS
ANNOYANCE
ANTICIPATION
See also: HOPE
Anxiety
See: EMOTIONS,
NERVOUSNESS
APPRECIATION
ARGUMENT
Arithmetic
See: MATHEMATICS AND
SCIENCE

ARM(S)
See also: ARM
MOVEMENTS, FINGERS
ARM MOVEMENTS
See also: HAND
MOVEMENTS
ARMY
Art and Literature
See: BOOKS,
POETS/POETRY,
WRITERS/WRITING
Astonishment
See: SURPRISE
ATMOSPHERE
ATTENTION
See also: ALERTNESS,
WATCHFULNESS
Attire
See: CLOTHING
ACCESSORIES; CLOTHING,
ITS FIT
ATTRACTIVENESS
See also: DESIRABILITY
Authenticity
See: TRUENESS/FALSENESS
Authorship
See: POETS/POETRY,
WRITERS/WRITING
AVAILABILITY/UNAVAILABILITY
Avarice
See: GREED
Awareness
See: REALIZATION
AWKWARDNESS
See also: MOVEMENT
Badness
See: CRUELTY
Balance
See: REGULARITY/
IRREGULARITY
BALDNESS
Bargains
See: ADVANTAGEOUSNESS
Beaches
See: OCEAN/OCEANFRONT

BEARDS

Bearing
See: FACIAL EXPRESSIONS, MISCELLANEOUS; LYING; POSTURE; SITTING; STANDING; WALKING

Beauty
See: BEAUTY, DEFINED; FACE(S); PHYSICAL APPEARANCE

BEAUTY, DEFINED

Beginnings/Endings
See: BIRTH, ENTRANCES/EXITS, PASSION

BEHAVIOR
See also: LIES/LIARS, MANKIND, PROPRIETY/IMPROPRIETY

BELIEF
See also: GOVERNMENT, MORALITY, RELIGION

BELIEVABILITY

BELONGING

Benefits
See: ADVANTAGEOUSNESS

Bereavement
See: SADNESS

BEWILDERMENT
See also: EMOTIONS

Bible
See: BOOKS

BIGNESS
See also: FATNESS, TALLNESS

Biography
See: BOOKS, WRITERS/WRITING

BIRDS
See also: SINGING

BIRTH
See also: ENTRANCES/EXITS

BITTERNESS
See also: LOVE

BLACK
See also: FACIAL EXPRESSIONS, SERIOUS; GLOOM

BLINDNESS
See also: EYE EXPRESSIONS, BLANK

BLOOD
See also: VIOLENCE

Blooming
See: GROWTH

BLUE

BLUSHES
See also: FACIAL COLOR, RED, SHYNESS

BODY
See also: AGILITY, AWKWARDNESS, BODY ORGANS, FATNESS, MUSCLES, STOMACH

BODY ORGANS
See also: TONGUE

Bonds
See: CONNECTIONS

BOOKS

Boredom/Boring
See: DULLNESS

Boundlessness
See: CONTINUITY

BOXING AND WRESTLING

BREASTS
See also: BODY ORGANS

BREATHING

BREVITY

BRIGHTNESS
See also: GLITTER AND GLOSS, LIGHTING

Brittleness
See: FRAGILITY

BROWN

Brutality
See: CRUELTY, VIOLENCE

Burst
See: DISINTEGRATION, SUDDENNESS

Business
    See: ADVERTISING
Calmness
    See: PEACEFULNESS
Candor
    See: HONESTY,
    TRUENESS/FALSENESS
Carefulness
    See: CAUTION,
    CORRECTNESS
CARELESSNESS
Cares
    See: PROBLEMS/
    SOLUTIONS
CAUSE/EFFECT
CAUTION
    See also: BEHAVIOR
Censorship
    See: CONTROL, CRITICISM
Cessation
    See: PAUSE
Change
    See: ENTRANCES/EXITS
CHARACTER
    See: REPUTATION
**CHARACTERISTICS,
    NATIONAL**
Charm
    See: ATTRACTIVENESS,
    BEHAVIOR
Cheapness
    See: COST
CHEEKS
    See also: BLUSHES, FACIAL
    COLOR
CHEERFULNESS
    See also: BRIGHTNESS,
    GAIETY
CHILDREN
    See also: PARENTHOOD
CHIN
    See also: CHEEKS
CHOICES
Cities
    See: CITY/STREETSCAPES

CITY/STREETSCAPES
Civilization
    See: SOCIETY
CLARITY
CLEANLINESS/UNCLEANLINESS
Cleverness
    See: ALERTNESS
Cliche
    See: MAXIMS, PROVERBS
    AND SAYINGS;
    ORIGINALITY/UNORIGINALITY
Clinging
    See: RELATIONSHIPS
Clothing
    See: CLOTHING
    ACCESSORIES; CLOTHING,
    ITS FIT
CLOTHING ACCESSORIES
CLOTHING, ITS FIT
Cloud(s)
    See: CLOUD MOVEMENTS
CLOUD MOVEMENTS
    See also: RAIN
Clumsiness
    See: AWKWARDNESS
Coldness
    See: RESERVE
COLLAPSE
    See also: DISINTEGRATION
Colors
    See: BLACK, BLUE,
    BRIGHTNESS, BROWN,
    GREEN, PALLOR, PINK,
    RED, WHITE, YELLOW
COMMONPLACE
    See also: FAMILIARITY
Compactness
    See: BREVITY
Compassion
    See: PITY
Compatibility/Incompatibility
    See: BELONGING
Competence
    See: ACCOMPLISHMENT

COMPETITION
Complacency
    See: CONTENTMENT
Complaints
    See: CRITICISM
COMPLEXION
    See also: WRINKLES
COMPLEXITY
Compliments
    See: FLATTERY
Composition
    See: MUSIC
Comprehensibleness
    See: CLARITY
Conciseness
    See: BREVITY
Condemnation
    See: CRITICISM
Confidence
    See: TRUST/MISTRUST
Confusion
    See: BEWILDERMENT
CONNECTIONS
CONSCIENCE
    See also: REGRET
Conspicuousness
    See: OBVIOUSNESS,
    VISIBILITY
Constancy
    See: LOYALTY/
    DISLOYALTY
Contagion
    See: SPREADING
CONTEMPT
CONTENTMENT
CONTINUITY
CONTROL
CONVERSATION
Conviction
    See: BELIEF
Cookery
    See: FOOD AND DRINK
Corpulence
    See: FATNESS

CORRECTNESS
    See also: TRUENESS/
    FALSENESS, REPUTATION
CORRESPONDENCE
    See also: WRITERS/
    WRITING
COST
    See also:
    ADVANTAGEOUSNESS
Counsel
    See: ADVICE
Courtesy
    See: BEHAVIOR
Craziness
    See: MADNESS
Credibility
    See: BELIEVABILITY
CREDIT
CRIME
CRITICISM
Criticism, Dramatic/Literary
    See: POETS/POETRY,
    WRITERS/WRITING
CROWDS
CRUELTY
CRYING
    See also: GROANS AND
    WHISPERS; SCREAMS
CURIOSITY
CURSES
Custom
    See: HABIT
Dampness
    See: DISCOMFORT
DANCING
    See also: AGILITY
DANGER
DAY
    See also: NIGHT,
    SLOWNESS
Death
    See: DEATH, DEFINED;
    DEATH, FINALITY OF;
    ENTRANCES/EXITS;
    SUDDENNESS;

TIMELINESS/UNTIMELINESS
DEATH, DEFINED
DEATH, FINALITY OF
Debt
   See: CREDIT
Deception
   See: TRUENESS/FALSENESS
Decisions
   See: CHOICES
Decorativeness
   See: ATTRACTIVENESS
DECREASE
Deeds
   See: ACTIONS
Dejection
   See: EMOTIONS, GLOOM
Delay
   See: LINGERING
Deliberateness
   See: PURPOSEFULNESS
Democracy
   See: GOVERNMENT
Denial
   See: BEHAVIOR
Density
   See: ABUNDANCE
Departure
   See: EXITS
Depletion
   See: DECREASE
Depression
   See: GLOOM
Desertion
   See: ABANDONMENT
DESIRABILITY
   See also: PLEASURE
Desolation
   See: ABANDONMENT
Destitution
   See: POVERTY
Destruction/Destructiveness
   See: DISINTEGRATION
Deterioration
   See: DISTINTEGRATION

Determination
   See: PURPOSEFULNESS
Devotion
   See: LOYALTY/
   DISLOYALTY
Diction
   See: SPEECH PATTERNS
Dictionaries
   See: BOOKS
DIFFERENCES
Difficulty
   See: FUTILITY
Dilemmas
   See: PROBLEMS/
   SOLUTIONS
Diplomacy
   See: TACT
Directness
   See: STRAIGHTNESS
Disagreement
   See: AGREEMENT/
   DISAGREEMENT,
   ARGUMENT
DISAPPEARANCE
   See also: DISPERSAL,
   ELUSIVENESS
DISAPPOINTMENT
Disapproval
   See: CONTEMPT
DISCOMFORT
DISCONTENT
   See also: GLOOM
Discord
   See: AGREEMENT/
   DISAGREEMENT
Discretion
   See: CAUTION, TACT
Discrimination
   See: STYLE
Dishonesty
   See: BELIEVABILITY, CRIME,
   LIES/LIARS
Disillusionment
   See: DISAPPOINTMENT

DISINTEGRATION
Disloyalty
    See: LOYALTY/
    DISLOYALTY
DISPERSAL
Disposability
    See: TRANSIENCE
Dissatisfaction
    See: DISCONTENT
Dissension
    See: AGREEMENT/
    DISAGREEMENT,
    ARGUMENT
Dissimilarity
    See: DIFFERENCES
Distinctiveness
    See: ORIGINALITY/
    UNORIGINALITY
DIVERSENESS
    See also: DIFFERENCES
Divorce
    See: MARRIAGE
DOCTORS
    See also: PROFESSIONS
Doubt
    See: TRUST/MISTRUST
DREAMS
    See: HOPE
DRINKING
    See also: FOOD AND
    DRINK
DRYNESS
DULLNESS
Ears
    See: FACIAL DETAILS
Eating and Drinking
    See: FOOD AND DRINK
ECONOMICS
Education
    See: KNOWLEDGE
Effect
    See: CAUSE/EFFECT
Elasticity
    See:
    FLEXIBILITY/INFLEXIBILITY

Elegance
    See: STYLE
Eloquence
    See: SPEECHMAKING
ELUSIVENESS
Embarrassment
    See: SHYNESS
EMBRACES
    See also: KISSES, SEXUAL
    INTERACTION
EMOTIONS
    See also: CHEERFULNESS,
    GLOOM, LOVE,
    NERVOUSNESS, SADNESS
Empathy
    See: PITY
Emptiness
    See: ABANDONMENT,
    EMOTIONS
Endurance
    See: CONTINUITY
Enemy
    See: ADVERSARY
ENERGY
Enjoyment
    See: PLEASURE
Enthusiasm
    See: ENERGY
ENTRANCES/EXITS
    See also: EXITS
ENTRAPMENT
Erectness
    See: POSTURE
ERRORS
Eternity
    See: CONTINUITY
Evasiveness
    See: ELUSIVENESS
Evenness
    See: STRAIGHTNESS
EVIL
    See also: CRUELTY
Exactness
    See: CORRECTNESS

EXCITEMENT
See: AGITATION, ENERGY
Exercise
See: MOVEMENT
EXITS
See also:
ENTRANCES/EXITS
Expansion
See: GROWTH
Expectation
See: ANTICIPATION, HOPE
Expensiveness
See: COST
EXPERIENCE
See also: KNOWLEDGE
Explosion
See: SUDDENNESS
EYE(S)
See also: EYES, BRIGHT;
EYEBROWS; EYE COLOR;
EYE EXPRESSIONS,
MISCELLANEOUS;
EYELASHES; EYELIDS; EYE
MOVEMENTS
EYES, BRIGHT
EYEBROWS
EYE COLOR
See also: BLACK, BLUE,
BROWN, GRAY, GREEN
**EYE EXPRESSIONS,
MISCELLANEOUS**
EYELASHES
EYELIDS
EYE MOVEMENTS
FACE(S)
See also: CHEEKS; FACIAL
COLOR; FACIAL DETAILS;
FACIAL EXPRESSIONS,
BLANK; FACIAL
EXPRESSIONS,
MISCELLANEOUS; FACIAL
EXPRESSIONS, SERIOUS;
FACIAL SHAPE; LIPS;
WRINKLES

FACIAL COLOR
See also: BLUSHES,
COMPLEXION, PALLOR,
RED, WHITE
FACIAL DETAILS
**FACIAL EXPRESSIONS,
BLANK**
See also: EYE
EXPRESSIONS,
MISCELLANEOUS
**FACIAL EXPRESSIONS,
MISCELLANEOUS**
See also: EYE
EXPRESSIONS,
MISCELLANEOUS
**FACIAL EXPRESSIONS,
SERIOUS**
See also: EYE
EXPRESSIONS,
MISCELLANEOUS
FACIAL SHAPE
FACTS
Failure
See: COLLAPSE,
DISINTEGRATION
Faith
See: BELIEF, RELIGION
Faithfulness/Faithlessness
See: LOYALTY/
DISLOYALTY
Falling
See: COLLAPSE
Falseness
See: TRUENESS/FALSENESS
Fame
See: GREATNESS
FAMILIARITY
See also: COMMONPLACE
Family
See: RELATIONSHIPS
Fascination
See: ATTRACTIVENESS
Fashion
See: STYLE

FATE
See also: HELPLESSNESS
FATNESS
Faultfinding
See: CRITICISM
Fear
See: EMOTIONS, NERVOUSNESS
Feelings
See: EMOTIONS, PHYSICAL FEELINGS
Feet
See: LEGS
FEROCITY
See also: SCREAMS
Fertility
See: GROWTH
Fickleness
See: LOYALTY/ DISLOYALTY
Fiction
See: STORIES
Fighting
See: ARGUMENT
Finance
See: ECONOMICS
FINGERS
Fire and Smoke
See: TOBACCO
FIRMNESS
See also: FLEXIBILITY/ INFLEXIBILITY
Fitting
See: BELONGING
FLATTERY
Flavor
See: FOOD AND DRINK
Flaws
See: ERRORS
FLEXIBILITY/INFLEXIBILITY
See also: HABIT
Flight
See: EXITS
Flimsiness
See: FRAGILITY

FOG
FOOD AND DRINK
FOOLISHNESS
See also: FUTILITY
FOOTBALL
FOREHEAD
FORGIVENESS
Forlornness
See: ABANDONMENT
FORMALITY/INFORMALITY
FRAGILITY
Fraud
See: CRIME
Freckles
See: FACIAL DETAILS
FRESHNESS
Friendliness
See: SOCIABILITY/ UNSOCIABILITY
Friendship
See: LOVE, SOCIABILITY/ UNSOCIABILITY
FRIENDSHIP, DEFINED
FROWNS
See: FACIAL EXPRESSIONS, MISCELLANEOUS; STARES
FRUSTRATION
See also: EMOTIONS
Fun
See: PLEASURE
Furniture and Furnishings
See: ROOMS
FUTILITY
FUTURE
GAIETY
See also: CHEERFULNESS, LAUGHTER
Gait
See: WALKING
Genius
See: GREATNESS
GENTLENESS
Gestures
See: HAND MOVEMENTS

9

Glimmer
    See: GLITTER AND GLOSS
GLITTER AND GLOSS
    See also: BRIGHTNESS,
    LIGHTING
GLOOM
    See also: BEHAVIOR;
    FACIAL EXPRESSIONS,
    SERIOUS; SADNESS
Glossiness
    See: GLITTER AND GLOSS
Gluttony
    See: GREED
God
    See: FORGIVENESS,
    RELIGION
GOLF
GOVERNMENT
Gracefulness
    See: AGILITY
Graciousness
    See: BEHAVIOR
GRAY
    See also: GLOOM, HAIR
    COLOR, WEATHER
GREATNESS
GREED
GREEN
Grief
    See: SADNESS
GRINS
    See also: LAUGHTER
GROANS AND WHISPERS
    See also: SIGHS
GROWTH
    See also: SPREADING
Grumbling
    See: CRITICISM
Guilt
    See: CONSCIENCE
HABIT
    See also: BEHAVIOR,
    FLEXIBILITY/INFLEXIBILITY
Hair
    See: BEARDS; HAIR

COLOR; HAIR, CURLY;
    HAIR STYLES; HAIR
    TEXTURE; MUSTACHES
HAIR COLOR
    See also: BLACK, BROWN,
    GRAY, RED, WHITE
HAIR, CURLY
    See also: HAIR STYLES
HAIR STYLES
HAIR TEXTURE
Hand(s)
    See: FINGERS, HAND
    MOVEMENTS,
    HANDSHAKE
HAND MOVEMENTS
    See also: HANDSHAKE
HANDSHAKE
HANDWRITING
Happiness
    See: CONTENTMENT,
    PLEASURE
Hardness
    See: FIRMNESS,
    TOUGHNESS
Hard-heartedness
    See: CRUELTY
HARMLESSNESS
HARSHNESS
    See also: VOICE, HARSH
Haste
    See: SPEED
Hastiness
    See: CARELESSNESS
HATRED
Head(s)
    See: HEAD MOVEMENTS
HEAD MOVEMENTS
Heart(s)
    See: AGITATION,
    HEARTBEAT
HEARTBEAT
    See also: AGITATION
Heartiness
    See: EMOTIONS

Heat
  See: WEATHER
HEAVINESS
HELPLESSNESS
HISTORY
  See also: PAST, THE
Home
  See: ROOMS
HONESTY
Honor
  See: REPUTATION
HOPE
HOSPITALITY
Houses
  See: ROOMS
Hovering
  See: LINGERING
Howls
  See: SCREAMS
Humanity
  See: MANKIND
Humor
  See: LAUGHTER
Hurrying
  See: SPEED, RUNNING
Husbands
  See: MARRIAGE
Icicles
  See: SNOW
Ideals
  See: BELIEF
Idleness
  See: SITTING
Imitation
  See: SIMILARITY
Immediacy
  See: SPEED
Immobility
  See: LYING, POSTURE,
  SITTING, STANDING
Impassiveness
  See: RESERVE
Impatience
  See: RESTLESSNESS

Impermanence
  See: FRAGILITY,
  TRANSIENCE
Impetuousness
  See: BEHAVIOR,
  NATURALNESS
Impossibility
  See: FUTILITY,
  OPPORTUNITY
Impropriety
  See: PROPRIETY/
  IMPROPRIETY
Inaccuracy
  See: ERRORS
Inappropriateness
  See: BELONGING
Incorrectness
  See: ERRORS
Increase
  See: GROWTH
Indecision
  See: CHOICES
Indifference
  See: RESERVE
Indistinctness
  See: VAGUENESS
Individuality
  See: ORIGINALITY/
  UNORIGINALITY
Ineffectiveness
  See: FUTILITY
Inexorability
  See: STEADINESS
Inexpensiveness
  See: COST
Infatuation
  See: LOVE
Inflation
  See: ECONOMICS
Informality
  See: FORMALITY/
  INFORMALITY
Information
  See: KNOWLEDGE

Inheritance
See: PAST, THE
Innocence
See: HARMLESSNESS
Inquisitiveness
See: CURIOSITY
Insanity
See: MADNESS
Inseparability
See: RELATIONSHIPS
Insight
See: WISDOM
Instinctiveness
See: NATURALNESS
Intangibility
See: ELUSIVENESS
Intemperance
See: DRINKING
Intensity
See: STARES
Intimacy
See: RELATIONSHIPS
Irregularity
See: REGULARITY/
IRREGULARITY
IRRITABLENESS
See also: NERVOUSNESS
Journalism
See: PROFESSIONS,
WRITERS/WRITING
Jowls
See: CHEEKS
Joy
See: CONTENTMENT,
PLEASURE
Judgments
See: OPINION
Jumping
See: LEAPING
KINDNESS
See also: GENTLENESS,
SWEETNESS
KISSES
Knees
See: LEGS

KNOWLEDGE
Knuckles
See: FINGERS
Landscapes
See: PONDS AND
STREAMS; ROAD SCENES
LANGUAGE
See also: SPEAKING
LAUGHTER
See also: GAIETY, GRINS
Law
See: LAWYERS
Lawbreaking
See: CRIME
LAWYERS
See also: PROFESSIONS
Leaping
LEAVES
LEGS
Letter-writing
See: CORRESPONDENCE
LIES/LIARS
Life
See: LIFE, DEFINED;
MANKIND
LIFE, DEFINED
LIGHTING
See also: BRIGHTNESS
Likeness
See: SIMILARITY
Limbs
See: LEGS
LINGERING
LIPS
Literature
See: BOOKS,
WRITERS/WRITING
Liveliness
See: ENERGY
Loneliness
See: ABANDONMENT
Looks
See: STARES

LOOSENESS
LOVE
LOYALTY/DISLOYALTY
See also: LOVE
Lucidity
See: CLARITY
Lunacy
See: MADNESS
Lushness
See: ABUNDANCE
LYING
See also: POSTURE,
SITTING, STANDING
MADNESS
Malice
See: CRUELTY
MANKIND
See also: HELPLESSNESS
Manners
See: BEHAVIOR,
PROPRIETY/IMPROPRIETY
MARRIAGE
See also: RELATIONSHIPS
MATHEMATICS AND
SCIENCE
Matrimony
See: MARRIAGE
MAXIMS, PROVERBS AND
SAYINGS
Meanness
See: CRUELTY
MEEKNESS
See: MODESTY
MEETINGS
Melancholy
See: GLOOM
MEMORY
See also: PAST, THE
MEN AND WOMEN
See also: LOVE, MARRIAGE,
SEXUAL INTERACTION
Merriment
See: GAIETY
Method
See: PURPOSEFULNESS

Mind
See: MIND, DEFINED
MIND, DEFINED
Mirth
See: GAIETY
Misery
See: GLOOM
Mist
See: FOG
Mistakes
See: ERRORS
Mixture
See: CONNECTIONS
Moans
See: GROANS AND
WHISPERS
MODESTY
Monarchy
See: GOVERNMENT
Money
See: COST, GREED
Monotony
See: DULLNESS,
REPETITION
Moodiness
See: GLOOM
MORALITY
See also: BELIEF
Motherhood
See: CHILDREN,
PARENTHOOD
Mothers-in-law
See: PARENTHOOD
MOTIVATION
See also: PURPOSEFULNESS
Mouth
See: CHIN; CHEEKS;
MOUTH, OPEN/SHUT
MOUTH, OPEN/SHUT
MOVEMENT
See also: LEAPING,
RUNNING, TURNING AND
TWISTING, WALKING
Murder
See: CRIME

MUSCLES
MUSIC
   See also: SINGING
MUSTACHES
   See also: BEARDS
Nails
   See: FINGERS
NAMES
Nations
   See: CHARACTERISTICS,
   NATIONAL; GOVERNMENT
NATURALNESS
Nature
   See: LEAVES;
   OCEAN/OCEANFRONT;
   PONDS AND STREAMS;
   RAIN; SNOW; STARS;
   WEATHER
Neatness
   See: CLEANLINESS/
   UNCLEANLINESS
NECK
   See also: CHEEKS, CHIN
Neglect
   See: ABANDONMENT,
   REJECTION
Negligence
   See: CARELESSNESS
NERVOUSNESS
   See also: TREMBLING
Newness
   See: FRESHNESS,
   TIMELINESS/UNTIMELINESS
NEWS
   See also: KNOWLEDGE
NIGHT
NOISE
Nonsense
   See: FOOLISHNESS
NOSES
   See also: FACIAL DETAILS
Nourishment
   See: FOOD AND DRINK
Novels
   See: BOOKS

Numbness
   See: RESERVE
Oath
   See: PROMISE
Obesity
   See: FATNESS
OBJECTS, MISCELLANEOUS
Oblivion
   See: BLINDNESS
Obscurity
   See: VAGUENESS
Obsolescence
   See: TIMELINESS/
   UNTIMELINESS
OBVIOUSNESS
   See also: CLARITY,
   VISIBILITY
OCEAN/OCEANFRONT
Occupations
   See: DOCTORS, LAWYERS,
   PROFESSIONS
Opaqueness
   See: VAGUENESS
OPEN/SHUT
Opera
   See: MUSIC
OPINION
Opportuneness
   See: TIMELINESS/
   UNTIMLINESS
OPPORTUNITY
Optimism
   See: CHEERFULNESS
Oratory
   See: SPEECHMAKING
Order/Disorder
   See: CLEANLINESS/
   UNCLEANLINESS
Ordinariness
   See: COMMONPLACE
ORIGINALITY/UNORIGINALITY
Out Of Place
   See: BELONGING
PALLOR
   See also: FACIAL COLOR,

GRAY, RED, WHITE
Parental Love
    See: PARENTHOOD
PARENTHOOD
PASSION
    See also: LOVE
PAST, THE
    See also: HISTORY
Patriotism
    See: BELIEF
Paunchiness
    See: FATNESS, STOMACH
PAUSE
    See also: CAUTION
PEACEFULNESS
Pennants
    See: OBJECTS,
    MISCELLANEOUS
People, Interaction
    See: CROWDS,
    RELATIONSHIPS
Perceptiveness
    See: ALERTNESS
Permanence
    See: CONTINUITY
Perplexity
    See: BEWILDERMENT
Persistence
    See: PURPOSEFULNESS
Personal Traits
    See: DULLNESS
PERSONALITY PROFILES
PHYSICAL APPEARANCE
    See also: ATTRACTIVENESS,
    FATNESS,
    UNATTRACTIVENESS
PHYSICAL FEELINGS
Physicians
    See: DOCTORS
PINK
    See also: CHEEKS, FACIAL
    COLOR
PITY
PLACES
    See also: CITY/

STREETSCAPES
Plainness
    See: SIMPLICITY
Planning
    See: PURPOSEFULNESS
PLEASURE
    See also: GAIETY
Plenty
    See: ABUNDANCE
POETS/POETRY
    See also: WRITERS/
    WRITING
PONDS AND STREAMS
POPULARITY
Possibility
    See: OPPORTUNITY
POSTURE
    See also: STRAIGHTNESS
POVERTY
    See also: ECONOMICS
Powerlessness
    See: HELPLESSNESS
Praise
    See: FLATTERY
Prayer
    See: RELIGION
Precariousness
    See: DANGER
Precision
    See: CORRECTNESS
Predicament
    See: DANGER,
    PROBLEMS/SOLUTIONS
PREPAREDNESS
PRESENT, THE
Preservation
    See: PROTECTIVENESS
Prevention
    See: PROBLEMS/
    SOLUTIONS
Price
    See: COST
PROBLEMS/SOLUTIONS
Procrastination
    See: LINGERING

Profanity
   See: CURSES
PROFESSIONS
   See also: DOCTORS,
   LAWYERS
Profusion
   See: ABUNDANCE
Progress
   See: GROWTH
Proliferation
   See: SPREADING
PROMISE
PROMPTNESS
Pronunciation
   See: SPEECH PATTERNS
PROPRIETY/IMPROPRIETY
Prose
   See: POETS/POETRY,
   WRITERS/WRITING
PROTECTIVENESS
   See also: WATCHFULNESS
PROTRUSION
   See also: BELONGING,
   OBVIOUSNESS, VISIBILITY
Proverbs
   See: MAXIMS, PROVERBS
   AND SAYINGS
Prudence
   See: CAUTION
Psychology
   See: PROFESSIONS
Public Opinion
   See: OPINION
PURITY
PURPOSEFULNESS
PURSUIT
Puzzlement
   See: BEWILDERMENT
Questions/Answers
   See: PROBLEMS/
   SOLUTIONS
Quickness
   See: RUNNING, SPEED
RAIN
   See also: WEATHER

Ranting
   See: SCREAMS
Rapidity
   See: SPEED
Rarity
   See: ORIGINALITY/
   UNORIGINALITY
Rashness
   See: SPEED
Readers/Reading
   See: BOOKS
Readiness
   See: PREPAREDNESS
REALIZATION
REALNESS/UNREALNESS
REAPPEARANCE
RED
   See also: BLUSHES,
   CHEEKS, LIPS
Reduction
   See: DECREASE
REGRET
   See also: CONSCIENCE
REGULARITY/IRREGULARITY
REJECTION
   See also: ABANDONMENT
RELATIONSHIPS
   See also: MARRIAGE;
   PARENTHOOD
Reliability/Unreliability
   See: FIRMNESS,
   STEADINESS
Relief
   See: EMOTIONS
RELIGION
   See also: BELIEF
Remedy
   See: PROBLEMS/
   SOLUTIONS
Remembrance
   See: PAST, THE
Remorse
   See: REGRET
Remoteness
   See: RESERVE

REPETITION
See also: CONTINUITY,
DULLNESS
REPUTATION
RESERVE
See also: EMOTIONS
RESTLESSNESS
Restraint
See: EMOTIONS
Results
See: CAUSE/EFFECT
Retreat
See: EXITS
Return
See: PAST, THE;
REAPPEARANCE
Revelry
See: GAIETY
Revenge
See: BITTERNESS
Rhetoric
See: SPEECHMAKING
Riches
See: ABUNDANCE
RICHNESS
Ridiculousness
See: FOOLISHNESS
Rightness
See: CORRECTNESS,
TRUENESS/FALSENESS
RISING
See also: STANDING
RISK
See also: DANGER
Rivers
See: PONDS AND
STREAMS
ROAD SCENES
ROARS
See also: SCREAMS
Rocking and Rolling
See: MOVEMENT,
UNSTEADINESS,
VIBRATION

Romance
See: LOVE
ROOMS
RUNNING
See also: MOVEMENT,
SPEED
Ruthlessness
See: CRUELTY
SADNESS
See also: EMOTIONS,
GLOOM
SAFETY
See also: DANGER, RISK
Satisfaction
See: CONTENTMENT
Sayings
See: MAXIMS, PROVERBS
AND SAYINGS
Scandal
See: REPUTATION
Scars
See: FACIAL DETAILS
Scattering
See: DISPERSAL
Science
See: MATHEMATICS AND
SCIENCE
SCREAMS
See also: ROARS
Scrupulousness
See: CORRECTNESS
Seascapes
See: OCEAN/
OCEANFRONT, PONDS
AND STREAMS
Self-consciousness
See: DISCOMFORT,
NATURALNESS
Sensations
See: EMOTIONS
Serenity
See: PEACEFULNESS
Sermons
See: SPEECHMAKING

Sex
    See: ATTRACTIVENESS,
    SEXUAL INTERACTION,
    RELATIONSHIPS

SEXUAL INTERACTION

Shame
    See: BLUSHES

Shining
    See: BRIGHTNESS; GLITTER
    AND GLOSS

Shock
    See: CAUSE/EFFECT,
    SURPRISE

Shouts
    See: SCREAMS

Shrieks
    See: SCREAMS

Shut
    See: OPEN/SHUT

SHYNESS

Sideburns
    See: BEARDS

SIGHS
    See also: GROANS AND
    WHISPERS

SILENCE

Silliness
    See: FOOLISHNESS

SIMILARITY

Similes
    See: MAXIMS, PROVERBS
    AND SAYINGS

SIMPLICITY

SINGING
    See also: MUSIC

SITTING

Skepticism
    See: TRUST/MISTRUST

Skills
    See: ACCOMPLISHMENT

Skin
    See: BALDNESS,
    COMPLEXION, FACIAL
    COLOR, FACIAL DETAILS,
    PALLOR, WRINKLES

Sky
    See: SKY COLOR

SKY COLOR

Sleep
    See: SNORES

Sloppiness
    See: CARELESSNESS

SLOWNESS
    See also: MOVEMENT

Smell
    See: SWEAT

Smiles
    See: BRIGHTNESS; FACIAL
    EXPRESSIONS,
    MISCELLANEOUS; GRINS;
    LAUGHTER

Smoking
    See: TOBACCO

SMOOTHNESS

SNORES

Snow
    See also: WEATHER

SOCIABILITY/UNSOCIABILITY
    See also: BEHAVIOR

SOCIETY

Solidity
    See: FIRMNESS,
    STEADINESS

SOUL

SPEAKING
    See also: SPEECH
    PATTERNS

SPEECHMAKING

SPEECH PATTERNS

SPEED
    See also: RUNNING

Spoilage
    See: DISINTEGRATION

Spontaneity
    See: NATURALNESS

Sports
    See: BOXING AND
    WRESTLING, FOOTBALL,
    GOLF

SPREADING
See also: GROWTH
STALENESS
See also:
TIMELINESS/UNTIMELINESS
STANDING
See also: POSTURE
STARES
STARS
Starting and Stopping
See: PAUSE
Statistics
See: FACTS
STEADINESS
See also: FIRMNESS
Stiffness
See: AWKWARDNESS,
PHYSICAL FEELINGS
Stillness
See: PEACEFULNESS
STOMACH
See also: FATNESS
Stop
See: PAUSE
STORIES
See also: BOOKS,
WRITERS/WRITING
STRAIGHTNESS
See also: POSTURE
Streams
See: PONDS AND
STREAMS
Streetscapes
See: CITY/STREETSCAPES
Strength
See: MUSCLES,
TOUGHNESS
STRUGGLE
See also: BEHAVIOR,
FUTILITY
Stupidity
See: DULLNESS,
FOOLISHNESS
Sturdiness
See: FIRMNESS

STYLE
Subtlety
See: TACT
Success/Failure
See: GROWTH; PAST, THE
SUDDENNESS
See also:
ENTRANCES/EXITS,
SURPRISE
Sun
See: SUNSET
SUNSET
SURPRISE
See also: SUDDENNESS
Suspicion
See: TRUST/MISTRUST
Swearing
See: CURSES
SWEAT
SWEETNESS
See also: PLEASURE
Symmetry
See: REGULARITY/
IRREGULARITY
Sympathy
See: PITY
TACT
Talent
See: ACCOMPLISHMENT
TALLNESS
TEARS
See also: CRYING
Tedium
See: DULLNESS,
REPETITION
Tenderness
See: AFFECTION,
GENTLENESS, LOVE
Tension
See: NERVOUSNESS
Thickness
See: ABUNDANCE
Thighs
See: LEGS

Threats
See: VIOLENCE

Throat
See: NECK

Thunder and Lightning
See WEATHER

Tightness
See: FIRMNESS

Time
See: DAY, NIGHT,
SLOWNESS, SPEED

TIMELINESS/UNTIMELINESS
See also: STALENESS

TOBACCO

TONGUE

TOUGHNESS

Trading
See: ADVANTAGEOUSNESS

Traffic
See: ROAD SCENES

Trail
See: PURSUIT

Tranquility
See: PEACEFULNESS

TRANSIENCE
See also: BREVITY

TRAVEL

Trees
See: LEAVES

TREMBLING
See also: VIBRATION

Triteness
See: STALENESS

Troubles
See: PROBLEMS/
SOLUTIONS

TRUENESS/FALSENESS

TRUST/MISTRUST

Truth
See: HONESTY

TURNING AND TWISTING

Umbrellas
See: OBJECTS,
MISCELLANEOUS

UNATTRACTIVENESS
See also: UNDESIRABILITY

Unavailability
See: AVAILABILITY/
UNAVAILABILITY

Unawareness
See: BLINDNESS

Uncertainty
See: FATE

Uncomfortableness
See: DISCOMFORT

Unconsciousness
See: NATURALNESS

Undemonstrativeness
See: RESERVE

Understandability
See: CLARITY

Understanding
See: KNOWLEDGE

UNDESIRABILITY

Unexpectedness
See: SUDDENNESS,
SURPRISE

Unfriendliness
See: SOCIABILITY/
UNSOCIABILITY

Unhappiness
See: DISCONTENT, GLOOM

Uniqueness
See: ORIGINALITY

Unkindness
See: CRUELTY

Unnaturalness
See: NATURALNESS

Unobtrusiveness
See: OBVIOUSNESS

Unpredictability
See: SURPRISE

Unprofitability
See: ADVANTAGEOUSNESS

Unreality
See: REALNESS/
UNREALNESS

Unresponsiveness
See: RESERVE

UNSTEADINESS
See also: MOVEMENT
Untimeliness
See: TIMELINESS/
UNTIMELINESS
Untruth
See: LIES/LIARS
Unwelcomeness
See: UNDESIRABILITY
Uprightness
See: POSTURE,
STRAIGHTNESS
Up-to-datedness
See: TIMELINESS/
UNTIMELINESS
VAGUENESS
Variety
See: DIVERSENESS
Vehicles
See: ROAD SCENES
VEHICLES, OPERATION OF
VIBRATION
See also: TREMBLING
Vigilance
See: ALERTNESS,
WATCHFULNESS
VIOLENCE
See also: BEHAVIOR
Virtue
See: ACCOMPLISHMENT,
MORALITY, PURITY
VISIBILITY
See also: CLARITY,
OBVIOUSNESS,
PROTRUSION
Vividness
See: BRIGHTNESS
Vocation
See: PROFESSIONS
Voice(s)
See: CRYING; GROANS
AND WHISPERS; SINGING;
VOICE, EFFECT OF; VOICE,
HARSH; VOICE,
MONOTONOUS; VOICE,

MUSIC-RELATED; VOICE,
SOFT; VOICE, WEAK
VOICE, EFFECT OF
VOICE, HARSH
See also: HARSHNESS
VOICE, MONOTONOUS
VOICE, MUSIC-RELATED
VOICE, SOFT
VOICE, WEAK
WALKING
See also: AWKWARDNESS,
CAUTION, MOVEMENT,
RUNNING
WAR
See also: ARMY
WASTE
WATCHFULNESS
See also: PROTECTIVENESS
Water
See: OCEAN/
OCEANFRONT; PONDS
AND STREAMS
Weakness
See: HELPLESSNESS
WEATHER
See also: FOG, RAIN,
SNOW
Weddings
See: MARRIAGE
Weight
See: HEAVINESS
Welcomeness
See: DESIRABILITY
Whispers
See: GROANS AND
WHISPERS
WHITE
See also: COMPLEXION,
PALLOR
Wildness
See: FEROCITY
Wind
See: WEATHER
WISDOM
See also: KNOWLEDGE

21

Wit

WIT
  See also: WISDOM
Wives
  See: MARRIAGE
Word(s)
  See: SPEAKING; WORDS,
  DEFINED; WORDS, EFFECT
  OF; WRITERS/WRITING
WORDS, DEFINED
WORDS, EFFECT OF
Work
  See: DOCTORS, LAWYERS,
PROFESSIONS
World
Worry
  See: AGITATION
WRINKLES
  See also: COMPLEXION,
  FOREHEAD
WRITERS/WRITING
  See also: POETS/POETRY
Yells
  See: SCREAMS
YELLOW

The Similes

ABANDONMENT
See also: REJECTION

Abandoned as a used Kleenex —Anon

Abandoned, like the waves we leave behind us —Donald G. Mitchell

Cast off friends, as a stripper her clothes —Anon

Cast off his friends, as a huntsman his pack —Oliver Goldsmith

(My youth has been) cast aside like a useless cigar stump
    —Anton Chekhov

Chuck me in the gutter like an empty purse —Edith Wharton

Deserted as a playwright after the first night of an unsuccessful
    play —W. Somerset Maugham

Deserted as a cemetery —Anon

Desolate ... as the dark side of the moon —Pat Conroy

Discard like a withered leaf, since it has served its day
    —John Gould Fletcher

(What have we come to when people ... could be)
    discarded ... like an old beer can —May Sarton

Discarded ... like used bandages —Louis MacNeice

Discard like a bad dream —Anon

Divest himself of his profoundest convictions and his beliefs as
    though they were a pair of old shoes whose soles had come
    loose and were flapping in the rain —Irving Stone

Feeling quite lost ... like a fly that has had its head taken off
    —Luigi Pirandello

Abandonment

Felt stranded, as if some solid security has left him, as if he had, recklessly and ruthlessly, tossed away the compass which for years had kept him straight and true —Carolyn Slaughter

Leaving me alone like a shag on a rock —John Malcolm

Left like balloons with the air let out —Gloria Norris

Left high and dry like a shipwreck in a drained reservoir —Thomas McGuane

Neglected as the moon by day —Jonathan Swift

People had fallen away like veils —Susan Richards Shreve

Put off [as religious faith] quite simply, like a cloak that he no longer needed —W. Somerset Maugham

Shed [adult reality for past] like a snake sheds an old and worn skin —Guy Vanderhaeghe
> Vanderhaeghe used the snake comparison to describe someone shedding the reality of the present for the past.

Stood like a forgotten broom in the corner —Eudora Welty

ABILITY
See: ACCOMPLISHMENT

Absorbability

ABSORBABILITY

Absorbed them [the influences of women around whom author grew up] as I would chloroform on a cloth laid against my face —Vivian Gornick

Absorbent as a sponge —Anon

Absorbent as blotting paper —Anon

Absorbent as cereal soaking up cream —Anon

It [a huge Christmas tree] soaked up baubles and tinsel like melting snow —Truman Capote

ABSURDITY
See: FOOLISHNESS, FUTILITY

24

FEELING QUITE LOST...LIKE A FLY THAT HAS
HAD ITS HEAD TAKEN OFF

ABUNDANCE
See also: GROWTH, SPREADING

Abound like street vendors on a spring day —Anon

Abound like blades of grass —George Sandys

Abundant as the light of the sun —Thomas Carlyle

Abundant as the salt in the sea —Anon

Abundant as air —Anon
> Modern day life has added "Abundant as polluted air and water."

Abundant as June graduates in search of jobs —Anon

Abundant as poverty —Anon

Ample as the wants of man —Henry Wadsworth Longfellow

As full as a fruit tree in spring blossom —Janet Flanner
> The simile refers to a letter filled with good news.

As stuffed (with idle hopes and false illusions) as any Whitsun goose crammed with bread and spices —George Garrett

As stuffed with ideas as a quilt is with batting —Anon

Bountiful as April rains —William Cowper

Bountiful as the showers that fall into the Spring's green bosom —James Shirley

Bulging like a coin purse fallen on the ground —W. D. Snodgrass

[Dreams] came like locusts —Isaac Bashevis Singer

(The big racket money) comes in like water from a pipe in your bathroom, a steady stream that never stops flowing —Raymond Chandler

Ladled out fines like soup to breadline beggars —Bernard Malamud
> In Malamud's novel, *The Natural*, the simile refers to fines issued by a baseball coach to rule-breaking players.

Lush as a Flemish oil painting —Anon

Numerous as a bank or trust company's vice-presidents
—*New York Tribune*, January 6, 1921

With the lean-and-mean management style in vogue since the mid-eighties, this long-enduring simile may well be headed for obsolescence.

(Children appearing here and there ...) numerous as fireflies
—Alice McDermott

Overdo ... like a host who stuffs his guests with too many hors d'oeuvres —Tom Shales, Public Radio, January 10, 1986
The simile referred to the directorial touches used in a movie, *The Color Purple*.

Plentiful as blackberries —William Shakespeare

Plentiful as New Year's Eve predictions and resolutions
—Elyse Sommer

Plentiful as oak leaves, as plentiful as the fireflies that covered the lawn at evening —Ellen Gilchrist

Plentiful as tabby cats —W. S. Gilbert

Stuffed like a Strasbourg goose —Anon
Strasbourg geese are over-fed and under-exercised in order to obtain the largest possible liver for making pâté. Being stuffed like a Strasbourg goose is linked to any kind of excess.

They're like plums on a tree —H. E. Bates
Bates compared the abundance of plums on a tree to an abundance of admirers.

Thick as autumnal leaves —John Milton

Thick as fleas —American colloquialism, attributed to New England
Some variations from the American South: "Thick as fleas on a fat pup," or "Thick as flies on flypaper."

Thick as hail —William Shakespeare

(You have fallen into ripeness) thick as honey —Marge Piercy

Thick as Japanese beetles —Herman Wouk
Wouk's simile from *Inside, Outside* refers to the behavior of people working for the president of the United States.

(Eyelashes) thick as June grass —Elizabeth Spencer

Thick as summer stars —William Blake

Abundance

Thick as buttercups in June —Henry James

Thick as ... freckles —George Garrett
> In his novel, *Death of the Fox*, Garrett refers specifically to the freckles of Sir Francis Drake.

Thick as the green leaves of a garden —Henry James

ABUSE
See: CRUELTY

ACCEPTABILITY
See: BELONGING

ACCESSIBILITY
See: AVAILABILITY

ACCIDENT
See: FATE

Accomplishment

ACCOMPLISHMENT

Accomplishment and authority hang on him like a custom-tailored suit —Alvin Boretz (play-in-progress)

Encased in talent like a uniform —W. H. Auden

He uses irony as a surgeon uses a scalpel ... with the same skill and to the same effect —Anon

Like a hog he does no good till he dies —Thomas Fuller

Rise to the occasion like a trout to the hook —Anon

Skilled and coordinated as an NFL backfield —James Mills

Something positive had been accomplished, like wrapping up a package in smooth paper, firm, taut, with a tight knot —Belva Plain

(Slowly he crept upon the heart of Manhattan, his) talent poised like a knife —Scott Spencer

To watch him is like watching a graceful basketball player sink shot after shot —Anon

ACCUMULATION
See: GROWTH, SPREADING

ACCURACY
See: CORRECTNESS

ACCUSATION
See: CRITICISM

ACTIONS
See also: BEHAVIOR, CAUTION, LEAPING, MOVEMENT, VIOLENCE

Acting without thinking is like shooting without aiming
—B. C. Forbes

The actions of men are like the index of a book; they point out what is most remarkable in them —Heinrich Heine

Actions of the last age are like almanacs of the last year —Sir John Denham

[Meaningless] actions that seemed like a charade played behind thick glass —Franz Werfel

All action is involved in imperfection, like fire and smoke —*Bhagavad-Gita*

Driven to make a move, like a dilatory chess player prodded on by an impatient opponent —Harvey Swados

Evil deeds are like perfume, difficult to hide —George Herzog

A good deed will stick out with an inclination to spread like the tail of a peacock —Bartlett's *Dictionary of Americanisms*

Our deeds are like children born to us; they live and act apart from our own will —George Eliot

Our least deed, like the young of the land crab, wends its way to the sea of cause and effect as soon as born, and makes a drop there to eternity —Henry David Thoreau

Reprehensible actions are like overstrong brandies; you cannot swallow them at a draught —Victor Hugo

The acts of my life swarm down the street like Puerto Rican kids —William Meredith

Trying to shake off the sun as a dog would shake off the sea
    —James Dickey

The vilest deeds like poison weeds bloom well in prison air
    —Oscar Wilde

ACTIVENESS/INACTIVENESS
See: ALERTNESS, BEHAVIOR, BUSINESS, ENERGY, MOVEMENT

ADAPTABILITY
See: BELONGING, FLEXIBILITY/INFLEXIBILITY

ADJUSTMENT
See: FLEXIBILITY/INFLEXIBILITY, HABIT

ADMIRATION
See: FLATTERY

ADULTERY
See: MARRIAGE

ADVANCING
See: ENTRANCES/EXITS, MOVEMENT

ADVANTAGEOUSNESS
See also: COST

Beneficial ... like water to a garden —Anon

Benefits, like bread, soon become stale —Caroline Forne

Benefits, like flowers, please most when they are fresh
    —George Herbert

Free [things] ... free as a well to get into, but like a rat trap, not
    exactly free to get out of —Josh Billings
        Billings wrote in a phonetic dialect. Here's the dialect
        version of the above: "I hav found a grate menny things in
        this wurld that was free—free az a well tew git into, but
        like a rat trap, not ekzackly free tu git out ov."

A good deal ... like trading an apple for an orchard —Anon
        The opposite of this is a German proverb: "Like trading
        the hen for the egg."

Like parenthood, you bid [at an auction,] then see what you've got
    —John Ciardi

Privileges she could list as a prisoner might count out the days of his sentence —Margaret Sutherland

ADVERSARY

An adversary as easily wiped out as writing on a chalkboard —Elyse Sommer

Being in the same room with the two men was like dropping in on a reunion of Capulets and Montagues —P. G. Wodehouse

A dead enemy is as good as a cold friend —German proverb

Fill me with strength against those who ... like water held in the hands would spill me —Louis MacNeice

ADVERTISING

Commercials on television are similar to sex and taxes; the more talk there is about them the less likely they are to be curbed —Jack Gould, *New York Times*, October 20, 1963

Doing business without advertising is like winking at a girl in the dark. You know what you are doing, but nobody else does — Stewart Henderson Britt, *New York Herald-Tribune*, October 30, 1956

A good ad should be like a good sermon: It must not only comfort the afflicted, it also must afflict the comfortable —Bernice Fitz-Gibbon

ADVICE
See also: FUTILITY

Advice after an evil is done is like medicine after death —Danish proverb
   It's quite common to substitute the word 'mischief' for 'evil.'

Advice is like kissing: it costs nothing and is a pleasant thing to do —Josh Billings

Advice is like snow; the softer it falls ... the deeper it sinks into the mind —Samuel Taylor Coleridge

Advice, like water, takes the form of the vessel it is poured into —*Punch*, August 1, 1857

Advice

The advice of old age gives light without heat, like winter sun
—Marquis de Luc de Clapiers Vauvenargues

Advice is like castor oil, easy enough to give but dreadful uneasy to take —Josh Billings

Good advice is like a tight glove; it fits the circumstances, and it does not fit other circumstances —Charles Reade

His (Ariel Sharon's) advice on that subject (Lebanon 1984-1985) ... was akin to a man with seven traffic accidents opening a driving school —Abba Eban, *New York Times*, February, 1986

It [excellent advice] is a good deal like giving a child a dictionary to learn a language with —Henry James

A proposal is like a flashlight. It's completely useless in the spotlight, but in the shadows it can do lots of good —Professor Steven Carvell, *Wall Street Journal*, December 11, 1986
> Professor Carvell's simile was specific to a proposal for investment research.

Telling a runner he can't run ... is a bit like being advised not to breathe —Thomas Rogers on runner Fred Lebow's being so advised for medical reasons, *New York Times*, 1986

To heed bad advice is like eating poisoned candy —Anon

To listen to the advice of a treacherous friend, is like drinking poison from a golden cup —Demophilus

AFFABILITY
See: AVAILABILITY

Affection

AFFECTION
See also: LOVE

Affectionate as a miser toward his money —Anon

(She had an) affection for her children almost like a cool governess —D. H. Lawrence

Affection is the youth of the heart, and thought is the heart's maturity —Kahlil Gibran
> Gibran completed the simile with "But oratory is its senility."

AN ADVERSARY AS EASILY WIPED OUT AS
WRITING ON A CHALKBOARD

Affection

Affection, like melancholy, magnifies trifles —Leigh Hunt

Affection, like spring flowers, breaks through the most frozen ground at last —Jeremy Bentham

Affection, like the nut within the shell, wants freedom —Dion Boucicault

Affection or love ... intended for someone else and spilled accidentally like a bottle of ink under a dragging sleeve —Diane Wakoski

Affections are like slippers; they will wear out —Edgar Saltus

The affections, like conscience, are rather to be led than driven —Thomas Fuller

Her cowlike, awkward affection surrounding him like a moist fog —Hank Searls

The human affections, like the solar heat, lose their intensity as they depart from the center —Alexander Hamilton

My affection has no bottom, like the Bay of Portugal —William Shakespeare
> The shorter, more commonly used "Affection is like a bottomless well" was more than likely inspired by this comparison from *As You Like It*.

She was like a cat in her fondness for nearness, for stroking, touching, nestling —Katherine Anne Porter

Age

AGE
See also: MANKIND

Old as Methuselah —Seventeenth century proverb
> This has inspired many variations including another cliche, "As old as the hills," generally attributed to Sir Walter Scott's *The Monastery* and Dickens' *David Copperfield*.

I feel age like an icicle down my back —Dyson Carter

A man of fifty looks old as Santa Claus to a girl of 20 —William Feather

A man's as old as his arteries —Pierre J. G. Cabanis

34

Most old men are like old trees, past bearing themselves, will suffer no young plants to flourish beneath them —Alexander Pope

My age is as a lusty winter, frosty but kind —William Shakespeare

Old age is a tyrant which forbids the pleasures of youth on pain of death —François, Duc de La Rochefoucauld

Old age is false as Egypt is, and, like the wilderness, surprises —Babette Deutsch

Old age is like an opium-dream. Nothing seems real except what is unreal —Oliver Wendell Holmes, Sr.

Old age is like a plane flying through a storm. Once you're on board there's nothing you can do —Golda Meir, quoted on being over 70 by Oriana Fallaci, *L'Europe,* 1973

Old age is like being engaged in a war. All our friends are going or gone and we survive amongst the dead and dying as on a battlefield —Muriel Spark

Old age is like everything else. To make a success of it, you've got to start young —Fred Astaire

Old age is rather like fatigue, except that you cannot correct it by relaxing or taking a vacation —B. F. Skinner and M. E. Vaughan

Old age is rather like another country. You will enjoy it more if you have prepared yourself before you go —B. F. Skinner and M. E. Vaughan

Old age took her [Queen Elizabeth] by surprise, like a frost —Anon

Old as a garment the moths shall eat up —*The Holy Bible/Isaiah*

Old as a hieroglyph —John Berryman

Old as civilization —Morley Safer, "60 Minutes" segment on torture, November 9, 1986

Old as death —Elizabeth Barrett Browning

Old as God —Delmore Schwartz

Old as the sun —Slogan, Sun Insurance Co.

Old as history —Slogan, Anheuser-Busch beer

(I'm as) old as my tongue and a little older than my teeth —Jonathan Swift

Age

(Made her feel) older than coal —Joseph Wambaugh

The old man is like a candle before the wind —Hilda Doolittle

An old man, like a spider, can never make love without beating his own death watch —Charles Caleb Colton

The old man who is loved is winter with flowers —German proverb

(The Jewish women were as ...) old as nature, as round as the earth —Thomas Wolfe

(The problem now is as) old as realism —Max Apple

Old as stone —Marge Piercy

Old as the most ancient of cities and older —Saul Bellow

AGGRESSION
See: VIOLENCE

Agility

AGILITY
See also: MOVEMENT, SPEED, TURNING AND TWISTING, WALKING

(A small, shrivelled old man ...) agile and quick like one of those whiskered little monkeys at the Zoo —Aldous Huxley

Agile as a fish —William Humphrey

Agile as a monkey —Alexandre Dumas, père

Agile as squirrels —Luigi Pirandello

(Moved) as lightly as a bubble —Hans Christian Andersen

As nimble as a cow in a cage —Thomas Fuller

Deft as spiders' catenation —C. S. Lewis

Frisky and graceful as young lambs at play —George Garrett

Graceful as joy —Babette Deutsch

Graceful as a panther —Raymond Chandler

Graceful as a première danseuse —Natascha Wodin

Graceful as a Stillson wrench —Diane Wakoski

Graceful as the swallow's flight —Julian Grenfell

Graceful figure ... which was as tough as hickory and as flexible as a whip —Thomas Wolfe

He could leap like a grasshopper and melt into the tree-tops like a monkey —G. K. Chesterton

Light-footed as a dancer waiting in the wings —Vita Sackville-West

(Her tiny body as) limber as a grass —Jean Stafford

Lithe as a swan —Richard Ford

Lithe as a whip —Raymond Chandler

Nimble as a cat —Anon
> Herman Melville used this to begin chapter 68 of *Moby Dick* but it probably dates back well before that.

Nimble as a deer —Geoffrey Chaucer

Quick as a wrestler —Edward Hoagland

Sprang [out of his bed] like a mastiff —T. Coraghessan Boyle

Springy as a trampoline —Marge Piercy

Spry as a yearling —Eugene O'Neill

Step as elastic as a cat's —Jo Bannister

Supple as a cat —Irwin Shaw
> This is a variation of the often used "Agile as a cat" and "Agile as a cat, and just as sly."

Supple as a red fox —Maxine Kumin

Swift and light as a wild cat —D. H. Lawrence

There was something breath-taking in the grace of his big body which made his very entrance into a room like an abrupt physical impact —Margaret Mitchell
> Mitchell is describing Rhett Buttler, the hero of her epic *Gone With the Wind*.

AGITATION
See also: HEARTBEAT, NERVOUSNESS, TREMBLING

Agitated with delight as a waving sea —*Arabian Nights*

Agitation ... like insects coming alive in the spring —William Goyen

Calm as a tornado —Anon

Composed as an egg gatherer in a rattlesnake pit —Harry Prince

Disturbing as decay in a carcass —Julia O'Faolain

Feel like he had a mouse water skiing in his stomach
     —Joseph Wambaugh

Feel my insides slipping away as if they are on a greased slide
     —W. P. Kinsella

Felt as if his heart was beating itself to death in some empty hollow
     —Oscar Wilde

Felt her heart make little leaps, as though it might creep onto her
     tongue and expose something —Leigh Allison Wilson

Felt his heart quicken, as a horse quickens at the faint warning touch
     of the spur —Ben Ames Williams

(Arrived in the library with every nerve twittering) felt like a tree full
     of starlings —M. J. Farrell

Froze my heart like a block of ice —T. Coraghessan Boyle

Hearts drumming like wings —Paul Horgan

Her heart leaped like a fish —Katherine Mansfield

Her heart ... plucking inside her chest like a bird in a bag
     —Brian Moore

His heart pumping like a boiler about to blow —Ira Wood

Her heart ... thundering like ten hearts —Sharon Sheehe Stark

Her stomach leaped up inside her like a balloon —William Styron

His heart beat so hard he sometimes fondled it with his hands as
     though trying to calm a wild bird that wanted to fly away
     —Bernard Malamud

His heart chilled like a stone in a creek —John Farris

His heart ... like a madly bouncing ball, beating the breath out of
     his body —Helen Hudson

His heart moving so fast it was like one of those motorcycles at fairs that the fellow drives around the walls of a pit
—Flannery O'Connor

His heart racing like a quick little animal in a cage
—T. Coraghessan Boyle

His heart sinks like a soap in a bucket —Robert Coover

His heart thundered like horses galloping over a wooden bridge
—Gerald Kersh

His heart whammed like a wheezing steam engine
—Bernard Malamud

His soul seething within him like a Welsh rabbit at the height of its fever —P. G. Wodehouse
See also: SOUL

I could hear my heart, like somebody hammering on a tree
—John D. MacDonald

It seemed like something snapped inside of me, something like a suspender strap —John Steinbeck

(Scandal and chaos ...) kicked up like chicken feathers
—Pat Ellis Taylor

My heart behaved like a fresh-caught trout
—Lael Tucker Wertenbaker

My heart felt like a rabbit running wildly around inside my rib cage
—James Crumley

My heart jumped like a fox —Scott Spencer

My heart leaped like a big bass after a willow fly —Borden Deal

My heart pounded like a drowning swimmer's —Frank Conroy

My heart pounded ... like the hoofbeats of a horse
—Charles Johnson

My heart stopped as if a knife had been driven through it
—Rudyard Kipling

My heart turned over like a dirtbike in the wrong gear
—T. Coraghessan Boyle

My heart would flutter like a duck in a puddle, and if I tried to outdo it and speak, it would get right smack up in my throat and choke me like a cold potato —Irving Stone

My stomach plunged like an elevator out of control —T. Coraghessan Boyle

Nerves melt like jellyfish —Derek Walcott

Placid as a riptide —Joseph Wambaugh

The pressure was building in me like beer on a full bladder —T. Coraghessan Boyle

Seemed to smoulder like a tar-barrel on the point of explosion —Lawrence Durrell

The sense of horror and failure had clutched his spine like the wet, wrinkled hand of a drowned woman —William Styron

Set my heart to rocking like a boat in a swell —Edna St. Vincent Millay

She explodes like a chestnut thrown on the fire —Colette

AGREEMENT/DISAGREEMENT

About as far apart as an atheist and a born-again Christian —Anon

Acquiesced like an old man acquiescing in death —Wilfrid Sheed

(Nobody can be as) agreeable as an uninvited guest —Frank McKinney
> Humorists like McKinney are notable phrase converters. This simile may be a case in point, evolving from William Wordsworth's sonnet *To a Snowdrop,* which describes a flower bending its forehead "As if fearful to offend, like an unbidden guest."

See also: BEHAVIOR

Agree like a finger and a thumb —Anon

Agree like two cats in a gutter —John Heywood's *Proverbs*

Agree like cats and dogs —John Ray's *Proverbs*
> This sarcastic twist to the more commonly used "Fight like cats and dogs" dates back to the nineteenth century.

Agree like pickpockets in a fair —John Ray's *Proverbs*

Agree like the clocks of London —Richard Brinsley Sheridan

As coals are to burning coals, and wood to fire, so is a contentious
man to kindle strife —*The Holy Bible/Proverbs*

As far apart as the atheists who claim there is no soul, and the
Christian Scientists who declare there is no body —Anon

Co-operate about as much as two tomcats on a fence
—Raymond Chandler

Far apart as the poles —Anon

Flock together in consent, like so many wild geese
—William Shakespeare

Like the course of the heavenly bodies, harmony in national life is a
resultant of the struggle between contending forces
—Judge Louis D. Brandeis

Sentiments as equal as if weighed on a golden scale —Janet Flanner

We are made for cooperation, like feet, like hands, like eyelids, like
the row of the upper and lower teeth. To act against one another
is contrary to nature —Marcus Aurelius

AIM
See: PURPOSEFULNESS

AIMLESSNESS
See also: BELONGING

Aimless as an autumn leaf borne in November's idle winds
—Paul Hamilton Hayne

Chuckled aimlessly, like an old man searching for his spectacles
—James Crumley

The crowd scurried aimlessly away like ants from a disturbed crumb
—O. Henry

Drift about ... aimlessly as a ghost —Lawrence Durrell

Drifted like winter moons —Richard Wilbur

Drifting like breath —Robert Penn Warren

Drifts like a cloud —Dante Gabriel Rossetti

Aimlessness

He was without subject matter, like a tennis player in the Arctic or a skier in Sahara's sand —Delmore Schwartz

Kept going ... like a car without a driver —Cornell Woolrich
> Woolrich's description of aimlessness is a variant of "Aimless as a ship without a rudder;" in fact, in his story, *Dawn to Dusk*, Woolrich used the two similes together.

Lived from day to day as if the years were circular
—Alice McDermott

Never really taking hold of anything, he slides in and out of jobs like a wind-up toy sledding about until the inevitable slowdown —Alvin Boretz, film treatment

Ran out of motives, as a car runs out of gas —John Barth

Walking in aimless circles like children during a school fire drill
—James Crumley

Wandered about at random, like dogs that have lost the scent
—Voltaire

AIR
See: ATMOSPHERE

ALCOHOL
See: DRINKING

Alertness

ALERTNESS
See also: WATCHFULNESS

Alert as a bird in the springtime —George Moore

Alert as a bloodhound at dinnertime —T. Coraghessan Boyle

Bright as a bee —Julia O'Faolain

Bright as a cigar band —Rita Mae Brown

Bright as a salesman in a car showroom —Donald Seaman

Bright-eyed as hawks
—Walt Whitman, on the pioneer cowboys of the West

(It helps to have a friend at City Hall with) an ear like a redskin, always to the ground —Arthur A. Cohen

Ears ... as sensitive as two microphones —Robert Culff

Ears quick as a cat's —Frank Swinnerton

His brain [when free of restraint] skips like a lambkin
—Calder Willingham

His mind ... was crrckling like a high-tension wire
—Cornell Woolrich

Keen as a hawk's eye —Barbara Howes

Keen as robins —Frank Swinnerton

(His alertness is nearly palpable,) keenness trembling within him like
his pilot light —Philip Roth about Primo Levi, *New York Times
Book Review*, October 12, 1986

On the watch [for recurring problem] like a captain at sea, riding the
unknown forces which may produce the known disaster all over
again —Paul Horgan

Quest about like a gun-dog —Lawrence Durrell

Saw like Indian scouts and heard like blind people ... and smelt like
retrievers —Wilfrid Sheed

Sharp-eyed as a lynx —Sir Walter Scott

Wait like a set trap for a mouse —Anon

Wide awake as a lie detector —Wallace Stegner

Wide awake, brain cells flashing like free-game in a pinball machine
—T. Coraghessan Boyle

ALIKENESS
See: SIMILARITY

ALIMONY
See: MARRIAGE

ALONENESS
See: ABANDONMENT

ALOOFNESS
See: RESERVE

AMAZEMENT
See: SURPRISE

ANCESTORS
See: PAST, THE

Anger

ANGER
See also: EMOTIONS

Angry as a hornet —George Garrett
A variation by movie critic Rex Reed: "Angry as a ruptured hornet."

Angry as a wasp —John Heywood's *Proverbs*

Angry as a bear with a sore head —Stanley Weyman
Some variations of this popular simile are "Angry as a grizzly bear with a bad tooth" and "Cross as a bear with a sore head."

Angry words fan the fire like wind —Epigram

Bounced with indignation, as if she had robbed him of his reputation, of the esteem of honest people, of his humor, of something rare that was dearer to him than life
—Guy de Maupassant

(He was) burning like a boiler —Saul Bellow

Carried on as though he had uremic poisoning —Rita Mae Brown

Cold, vicious rage that covered every inch of me like a rank sweat
—Jonathan Valin

Come boiling out like bloodhounds —Richard Ford

Could feel her fury buzzing and burrowing into the meat under my skull like a drill bit —Stephen King

Die in a rage, like a poisoned rat in a hole —Jonathan Swift

A draft of anger and deep hurt trailing her like a cheap perfume
—Paul Kuttner

Feel as though I had swallowed a hand grenade
—Erich Maria Remarque

Feeling mean ... like a bull gator —Robert Campbell

A feeling of rage cut him as with a sharp knife and took possession of him —Mikhaïl P. Arzybashev

Felt furious and helpless as if she had been insulted by a child
—Flannery O'Connor
See also: HELPLESSNESS

A fit of anger is as fatal to dignity as a dose of arsenic to life
—Josiah Gilbert Holland

Fumed like champagne that is fizzy —Bliss Carman

Fumes like Vesuvius —Cole Porter, from "I've Come to Wive It
Wealthily in Padua," one of the lyrics from *Kiss Me Kate*, the
musical adaptation of Shakespeare's *Taming of the Shrew*.
Since Porter rarely used similes, it's natural to wonder if
working on a play by as prolific a simile creator as
Shakespeare inspired not just this but the several other
similes in this one song.

Fuming anger like a toaster with crust jammed against its heating coil
—Ira Wood

Furious ... like a wounded bull in an arena —Dumas, Père

Fury pervading her like a bloat —Lynne Sharon Schwartz

Fury was running all through his blood and bones like an electric
flood —Robert Campbell

Gall ... like a crown of flowering thorn —W. D. Snodgrass
The poem from which this simile is extracted is about a
dead marriage and the narrator's regret that his love has
become a galling thing. He follows up the flowering thorn
comparison with: "My love hung like a gown of lead that
pulled you down."

Getting angry is like worshipping idols —L'Olam Midrash

Growling like a fox in a trap —William Diehl

Heaven has no rage like love to hatred turned, nor hell a fury like a
woman scorned —William Congreve

Her rage ... dammed up regularly as water —Louise Erdrich

Her resentment was like a coagulant ... she felt sullen, dull, thick
—Nancy Huddleston Packer

He's like a scalded cat —William Alfred

Anger

He was like the mule in the story that kept running into the trees; he wasn't blind, he was just so mad he didn't give a damn —Rex Stout

Hissed like an angry kettle —Herbert Lieberman

(Barcaloo's rage took about five seconds to boil up.) It was like dropping cold water into a pot of hot iron —Robert Campbell

Let it [anger at wife] all come out of him, like air from a tire —Bruce Jay Friedman

Like ice, anger passes away in time —Anon

Mad as a bobcat —James Kirkwood

Mad as a buck —William Shakespeare

Mad as a bull among bumblebees —Anon

Mad as a cat that's lost a mouse —O. Henry

Mad as all wrath —Anon

Mad as a vexed sea —William Shakespeare
Like many Shakespearean phrases, this one has fallen into common usage with 'vexed' usually changed to 'angry.'

Mad as a wet hen —American colloquialism
A variation from George Garrett's novel, *The Finished Man:* "Mad as a doused rooster."

Mad as hops —American colloquialism
In *Picturesque Expressions*, Laurence Urdang speculates that this is a twist on being 'hopping' mad.

On the warpath [against world's injustices] like a materialistic Don Quixote —Clarence Day

Outrage which was like sediment in his stomach —Paule Marshall

Outrage ... worked like acid in his temper —Frank Swinnerton

Puffed up with rage like a squid (my psyche let out angry ink) —Saul Bellow

ANIMATION
See: ENERGY

ANKLES
See: LEGS

ANTICIPATION
See also: HOPE

Anticipation went through me like a ripple of discordant notes
        —A. E. Maxwell

Lay in waiting like a giant crab —August Strindberg
            In Strindberg's play, *The Stranger,* a character named Mrs.
            X thus compares the woman who wants her husband.

Like chill dawn waiting for sunrise, I am waiting for you
        —Rainer Maria Rilke

Wait, breathless as a bride —George Garrett

Waited ... keenly as fisherman waiting for a bite —Lawrence Durrell

Waiting for her like a king awaiting the arrival of a courtier
        —Harvey Swados

Waiting [without thought or action] like a radio set equipped with a
        receiver only, for a signal from a distance which he wasn't even
        certain would be transmitted —Kenzaburo Oë

Wait ... like a dog expecting to be taken for a walk
        —Rosamund Pilcher

Wait ... like a pair of sea captains' wives in their widow's walks
        —Thomas McGuane

ANXIETY
See: EMOTIONS, NERVOUSNESS

APPRECIATION

Applause ... like pebbles being rattled in a tin —Francis King
        See also: NOISE

Cherish like a secret —D. H. Lawrence

Poorly appreciated ... like a fine landscape in dull weather
        —Arthur Schopenhauer

She looked on him as a kind of gigantic treat, a prize won in a
        lottery —Anita Brookner

Ungrateful as children, who can never pay their debt of gratitude because they owe so much —Honoré de Balzac

An ungrateful man is like a hog under a tree eating acorns, but never looking up to see where they come from —Timothy Dexter

ARGUMENT

Argued like a lawyer —Edith Wharton
See also: LAWYERS

Argue like geese —Ben Hecht

Arguing like sparring fish in a tank —Graham Swift

Arguing with Owen was like fencing with a bag of wool —Julia O'Faolain
See also: FUTILITY

The argument broke open, porous as cheese —Julia O'Faolain

Arguments are like the grinding of rusty blades —Elizabeth Hardwick

Can't help arguing like I can't help the man in the moon —Louise Erdrich

Clash like the coming and retiring wave —Alfred, Lord Tennyson

Clash, like waves of the sea —John Hall Wheelock

Contention is like fire, both burn so long as there is any exhaustible matter to contend with —Thomas Adams

Grabbed the argument as if it were a beachball we were tossing between us —Dorothy B. Francis

Her argument clung to its point like a frightened sharp-clawed animal —Edith Wharton

His argument is as thin as the homeopathic soup that was made by boiling the shadow of a pigeon that had been starved to death —Abraham Lincoln

Her arguments are like elephants. They squash you flat —Rumer Godden

Protesting like children at nap time —George Garrett

Split [in disagreement] like an egg —Paige Mitchell

Talking to Oscar [Levant] is like fighting a man who has three fists instead of the regulation two —Alexander Woolcott

True disputants are like true sportsmen, their whole delight is in the pursuit —Alexander Pope

Words ... flew between them like sparks between steel striking steel —Edna Ferber

The words [during an argument] whipped away like weightless leaves —Lael Tucker Wertenbaker

ARITHMETIC
See: MATHEMATICS AND SCIENCE

ARM(S)
See: ARM MOVEMENTS, FINGERS

ARM MOVEMENTS
See also: HAND MOVEMENTS

Arms extended over his head, fists clenched, like a soccer player running mad with triumph —Daniel Curley

Arms spread out like wasps —James Patterson

Arms upraised like two giant branches —Harvey Swados

Arms waggled like duck wings —Martin Cruz Smith

Arms working like a windmill —Mike Fredman

Crook his arm like an usher at a wedding —Susan Neville

Crooking her arms like broken branches —Bernard Malamud

Folded her arms like hemp cord —Leigh Alison Wilson

Opened your arms like cupboard doors —Marge Piercy

Raised his arms like a fight announcer —Harvey Swados

Spreading their arms wide like galleons in full sail —Lawrence Durrell

Waving his arms like a deranged pelican —George Garrett

Waved ... like a queen in a passing coach —William McIlvanney

ARMY

An army, like a snake, goes on its belly —Frederick the Great

Military intelligence has about as much to do with intelligence as military music has to do with music. —John Le Carré

Soldiers in peace are like chimneys in summer —John Ray's *Proverbs*
    The word 'chimneys' has been modernized from 'chimnies.'

ART AND LITERATURE
See: BOOKS, MUSIC, POETS/POETRY, WRITERS/WRITING

ASTONISHMENT
See: SURPRISE

ATMOSPHERE

Air ... full of unspoken words, unformulated guilts, a vicious silence, like the moments before a bridge collapses —John Fowles

The atmosphere (of the room) was as vapid as a zephyr wandering over a Vesuvian lava-bed —O. Henry

Evil which hung in ... air like an odorless gas —Ross Macdonald

(The circle in which I moved was a self-contained world ...) it was like being in the treacly, supersaturated air of a hothouse filled with luxuriant vegetation, or in an aquarium with its own special heating unit and food supply, its own species of plankton —Natascha Wodin

(The whole place seemed restless and troubled and) people were crowding and flitting to and fro, like shadows in an uneasy dream —Charles Dickens

Sensed a wrongness around me, like an alarm clock that had gone off without being set —Maya Angelou

They [women who run shops in a town] have given the Square a fussy, homespun air that reminds you of life pictured in catalogs —Richard Ford

Thick and sultry the atmosphere steams like an island in the Pacific —T. Coraghessan Boyle

ATTENTION
See: ALERTNESS, WATCHFULNESS

ATTIRE
See: CLOTHING ACCESSORIES; CLOTHING, ITS FIT

ATTRACTIVENESS
See also: DESIRABILITY

Adorable as a baby —Anon
> Babies have long been linked with adjectives that equate appealing (or peaceful) qualities. This commonly used form may have its origins in Swinburne's "Adorable as is nothing save a child."

Alluring as a ripe peach —Guy de Maupassant

Appealing as power to a politician —Anon

Appealing as something for nothing —Anon

Appealing as sunlight after a storm —Anon

An appeal shone from her as light from a twisted filament
    —John Updike

Charm rolled off him like a halo off an angel —James Kirkwood
> In the television movie adaptation of Kirkwood's *There Must Be a Pony* the character played by Elizabeth Taylor uses this simile to characterize the man played by Robert Wagner.

Cute as a bug's ear —Bobbie Ann Mason

Dazzle like an impressionistic painting in which every brush stroke tells and contains something germane to the whole
    —V. S. Pritchett on George Meredith

(The novel is often as) disarming as a work of folk art —Bethami Probst, *New York Times Book Review*, April 12, 1987

Interesting, like a plot in the mystery books —Louise Erdrich

Inviting as a down comforter —Anon

Look like something that ought to be eaten for dessert —Irwin Shaw

More alluring than an invitation to visit rich and charming friends on the Côte d'Or —Ogden Nash

Attractiveness

Seductive as Cleopatra —Louis Bromfield

She's like a mound of nectarines —Saul Bellow

AUTHENTICITY
See: TRUENESS/FALSENESS

AUTHORSHIP
See: POETS/POETRY, WRITERS/WRITING

**Availability/
Unavailability**

AVAILABILITY/UNAVAILABILITY

About as hard to get as lion shit in Africa —Stephen Longstreet

Accessible as a candidate looking for another hand to shake
    —Mike Sommer

Accessible as a hooker plying her trade —Anon

As unattainable, as desirable, as beauty —Margaret Sutherland
    See also: DESIRABILITY

(Drinks here) flow like cement —John Mortimer, Public Television
    series, "Paradise Postponed," 1986

Has been handed round like snuff at a wake —Ellen Currie
        The descriptive frame of reference is a promiscuous girl.

Inaccessible as time —Alice McDermott
        In her novel, *That Night*, the author talks about old
        neighborhoods from which parents have moved away and
        now say "You can't go there anymore" as if change made
        a place inaccessible as time.

Laying around like pop-corn —Clifford Odets
        In his play "Golden Boy" Odets follows this up with "You
        think good boys are laying around like pop-corn?"

Like an apple hanging on a tree, waiting for somebody to come
    along and pick it —Lee Smith

Like Meissen china in a glass case, the admiration [for an appealing
    but inaccessible woman] had to be kept at a distance
    —Jilly Cooper

Lived high up [in an apartment complex] ... as accessible as a bald
    Rapunzel —William McIlvanney

Unobtainable as a taxi when it rains —Anon

Untouchable as God —Erich Maria Remarque

AVARICE
See: GREED

AWARENESS
See: REALIZATION

AWKWARDNESS
See also: MOVEMENT

Awkward as a bull in a china shop —Anon
> This still popular simile endures with many substitutions for the bull such as "A blind dog," "A gorilla," "A monkey." Often, instead of a substitute comparison, a different context can lift a simile like this beyond the cliche; for example, "Like wild bulls in a china shop ... are my awkward hands of love" from poet Delmore Schwartz's journals and notes.

Awkward as learning newly learned —Adrienne Rich

Awkward in her movements, as if she had been in solitary for years
—Ross Macdonald

Awkward ... like a guest at a party to whose members he carried bad news he had no right to know, no right to tell
—Hortense Calisher

Awkward like a leaden ballet dancer lifting a fat partner
—Ed McBain

Awoke as stiff as if I'd been spray-starched —Jonathan Kellerman

Blunder and fumble like a moth ... a rabbit caught in the glare of a torch —William Faulkner

Bumbled up to him like a mole —Wilfrid Sheed

Clumsy as two kids on their first date —Anon

Clumsy ... like a leaky old engine with the driving belt slipping and steam escaping from every joint —Christopher Isherwood

Feel awkward like a boy on a date with an older girl
—Bobbie Ann Mason

Graceless as a pelican on the ground —George Garrett

Had about as much grace as a hippopotamus in a bubble bath —Harry Prince

Has the grace of an arthritic elephant on roller skates —Corey Sandler

Moved thickly, like a clumsy, good-tempered horse —William Faulkner

Moving stiffly like a man in a body cast —Martin Cruz Smith

She ran on like a clumsy goat, trampling and trespassing on land that was preserved —Daphne du Maurier

Stiff as a gaffer —Richard Wilbur

Stiff as a line in Euclid —Saul Bellow

Stiff as a poker grew —Wallace Irwin

Stumbling about like a drunken bear —James Crumley

Uncoordinated as a rag doll —Dorothea Straus

Unwieldy as a pregnant elephant —Anon

BADNESS
See: CRUELTY

BALANCE
See: REGULARITY/IRREGULARITY

BALDNESS

Bald as a ballpeen hammer —Thomas Lux

Bald as a brass knob —Beverly Farmer

Bald as a nun —Patrick White

Bald and wrinkled as a lizard —Sarah Bird
See also: WRINKLES

Bald as a balloon —Percival Wilde

Bald as a barefaced lie —Anon

Bald as a bearing —Loren D. Estleman

MASSIVE SIDEBURNS HUNG LIKE STIRRUPS ON
EITHER SIDE OF HIS FACE

Bald as a billiard ball —Anon
> Of the many objects comparatively linked with baldness, the billiard or cue ball probably ranks at the very top.

Bald as a brick —Raymond Chandler

Bald as an egg —Anon

Bald as a football —William Boyd

Bald as an orange —Thomas Bailey Aldrich

Bald as a winter tree —William Morris

Bald as convicts —George Garrett

Bald as peeled onion —Margaret Laurence

Bald as the beach —William Diehl

Bald as the palm of your hand —Richard Harris Barham

Bald as time —Richard Prome

Bald head shining like a polished stone —George Garrett

The gleaming skull [of bald-headed man] shone like a supernatural sun —Sholem Asch

Had gone completely bald very young as though to get that over with as soon as possible —Helen Hudson

Hair beginning to recede like the polar ice cap in warm weather —Jean Thompson

Head as smooth as a knob
—Russell Baker, *New York Times,* May 17, 1986

He had a bald patch on the top of his head which made him look rather like a monk —Guy De Maupassant

He was bald, his back hair was thick and projected like one of those large tree mushrooms that grow on the mossy side of a trunk —Saul Bellow

His bald head coming to a point, like an egg —Richard Llwellyn

His bald head shone ... like an agitated moon
—Erich Maria Remarque

His head [bald, with ring of grey-brown hair] was like the brown
    edges of a leaf in fall, a sign that the tree, however tall and
    green from a distance, was being eaten away at the edges, dying
    from the outside in —Jay Parini

His strong, bald head had a dull glow, like old ivory —Ivan Bunin

No more hair than a stone —John MacDonald

A semi-circular fringe of white hair surrounding his bald pate like a
    broken halo —Margaret Millar

BARGAINS
See: ADVANTAGEOUSNESS

BEACHES
See: OCEAN/OCEANFRONT

BEARDS

Bearded as Abraham —George Garrett

Bearded like a black sky before a storm —George Garrett

Beard not clipped, but flowing like a bridal veil —Sinclair Lewis

Beards like Spanish moss —T. Coraghessan Boyle

Beard stiff and jutting like a Michelangelo prophet —Harvey Swados

Bristly gray beard ... as rusted as old iron —Paige Mitchell

Flecks of premature gray in his beard, like the first seeds of age
    beginning to sprout in him —Ross Macdonald

Gray beard like a goat's chin tuft —Ernest Hemingway

A heavy black beard that grew high on his cheeks like a mask
    —James Crumley

His beard is like a bird's nest, woven with dark silks
    —Bobbie Ann Mason

His red beard looked like a toy doctor's beard stuck on a child's face
    —Gloria Norris

His sideburn, shaped like the outline of Italy, juts out onto his jaw
    —Bobbie Ann Mason

Beards

Long beard was spread out like a little blanket on his chest
—Willis Johnson

Massive sideburns hung like stirrups on either side of his face
—Ross Macdonald

A neat little beard, like a bird's nest, cupped his chin
—Bobbie Ann Mason

A shadow of beard lay over his bony cheeks like soot on a chimney
sweep —W. T. Tyler

Sideburns like brackets —Max Shulman

Sideburns stood like powerful bushy pillars to the beard
—Saul Bellow

A small goatee stuck to his chin like a swab of surgical cotton
—Dorothea Straus

A two-day growth of beard that made him look like a cactus
—Sue Grafton

Whiskers grew like small creeper upon a scorched face
—Frank Swinnerton

BEARING
See: FACIAL EXPRESSIONS, MISCELLANEOUS; LYING; POSTURE;
SITTING; STANDING; WALKING

BEAUTY
See: BEAUTY, DEFINED

Beauty, Defined

BEAUTY, DEFINED

As fair as day —William Shakespeare

Beauty as definite as that of a symphony by Beethoven or a picture
by Titian —W. Somerset Maugham

Beauty can pierce one like a pain —Thomas Mann

Beauty in a modest woman is like a distant fire or a sharp-edged
sword: the one does not burn, the other does not cut, those who
do not come near it —Miguel de Cervantes

Beauty is a fading flower —*The Holy Bible/Isaiah*

Beauty is like an almanac; if it lasts a year, it is well
——Thomas Adam

Beauty is like summer fruits which are easy to corrupt and cannot
last ——Francis Bacon
> Transposed for modern style from ''Beauty is as summer
> fruits.''

Beauty ... is like the morning dew ——Samuel Daniel

Beauty is like the surf that never ceases ——Struthers Burt

Beauty is the virtue of the body, as virtue is the beauty of the soul
——Ralph Waldo Emerson

Beauty, like supreme dominion, is best supported by opinion
——Jonathan Swift

Beauty, like truth and justice, lives within us ——George Bancroft

Beauty, like wit, to judges should be shown ——Lord Lyttleton

The beauty of a lovely woman is like music ——George Eliot

Beauty passes like a breath ——Alfred, Lord Tennyson

Beauty's a flowwr ——William Shakespeare

Beauty vanishes like vapor ——Harriet Prescott Spofford

Beauty without grace is the hook without the bait
——Ralph Waldo Emerson

Beauty without modesty is like a flower broken from its stem
——Anon

Beauty without virtue is a rose without fragrance
——German and Danish proverbs

Glorious beauty is a fading flower ——*The Holy Bible/Isaiah*

Women's beauty, like men's wit, is generally fatal to the owners
——Lord Chesterfield
> Had Chesterfield lived to become attuned to nonsexist
> language he might have eliminated the gender references
> as follows: ''Beauty, like wit, is generally fatal to the
> owners.''

BEGINNINGS/ENDINGS
See: BIRTH, ENTRANCES/EXITS, PASSION

Behavior

BEHAVIOR
See also: LIES/LIARS, MANKIND, PROPRIETY/IMPROPRIETY

Accepted the crisp bills with a certain famished delicacy like an aristocrat determined not to slaver at the sight of food
—John Farris

Accumulated [information] like a nest-building bird
—Louis Auchincloss

Act badly ... like a man hitting a woman in the breast
—George Bernard Shaw

Acted bored but patient, as though an enthusiastic acquaintance had just shown him the picture of a new grandchild —Joel Swerdlow

Allowed himself to be absorbed (into the softly palpitating life about him,) like a tired traveler sinking, at his journey's end, into a warm bath —Edith Wharton

Ate like Satan, and worked like a gnat —A. E. Coppard

Attention-getting behavior ... like I was screaming at the universe [to fulfill my ambitions] —Mel Brooks, *Playboy*, April, 1973

Battled failure like the seven plagues —Anon

Behave ... like a sort of love-crazed sparrow —Roald Dahl

Behavior is a mirror in which everyone shows his image
—Johann Wolfgang von Goethe

Bluster like the north wind —Mrs. Centlivre

Butters it [the truth] over like a slice of bread
—Erich Maria Remarque
    In his novel, *All Quiet on the Western Front,* Remarque uses the simile to explain that man is "Essentially a beast" but covers up this truth "With a little decorum."

(All he was doing was) calling attention to himself, rather like those movie stars who go around wearing dark glasses on cloudy days
—Loren D. Estleman

Carrying on like a revivalist facing a full tent —Robert Traver

Charm was put forward like a piece of acting in a theatre
   —Hugh Walpole

Clutched at her throat like one stifled for want of air
   —Anzia Yezierska

Crawl into (his secret life) and nestle there, like the worm in the
   rose —Mary McCarthy

Dangled herself [before men] ... like a drum majorette
   —Margaret Millar

Deny like a piano player in a bordello who claimed he didn't know
   what went on upstairs —Ed McBain

Flinched as if someone had thrown a baseball directly at his face
   —Graham Masterton

Flinched back like a box turtle into its shell —F. van Wyck Mason

Flirtatious as a Southern belle —Alice McDermott

For the promise of favor he will kneel down and lick boots like a
   spaniel —George Garrett

Glancing around him like a hunting dog nosing for a spoor
   —Kenzaburo Oë

Go forward like a stoic Roman —Edwin Arlington Robinson

Gripped life like a wrestler with a bull, impetuously
   —Stephen Vincent Benét

He had a way of ... suddenly pouncing on something [someone says]
   that interested him, like a heron spearing a fish —Antonia White

Her not doing it was like the Baskerville hound that didn't bark
   —William Dieter

In public, they act like flat-chested old maids preaching temperance
   —Charles Simic

Intruded upon my vision like a truck on an empty road
   —Mary Gordon

I talk half the time to find out my own thoughts, as a schoolboy
   turns his pockets inside out to see what is in them
   —Oliver Wendell Holmes, Sr.

Jerked at the [fishing] net like a penitent —T. Coraghessan Boyle

Like a nun withdrawing, or a child exploring a tower, she went upstairs —Virginia Woolf

Lived and behaved like that sandpiper [in my poem] ... just running along the edges of different countries, looking for something —Elizabeth Bishop, acceptance speech at University of Oklahoma, 1976, on receiving Books Abroad/Neustadt International Prize for Literature

Looked round ... desperately like someone trying to find a way of crossing a muddy path without getting her shoes soiled —Franz Werfel

Lurking like a funeral director at a christening —W. P. Kinsella

Many talk like philosophers, and live like fools —H. G. Bohn's *Handbook of Proverbs*
    See below for variations on the same theme.

Men's behavior should be like their apparel, not too straight ... but free for exercise or motion —Francis Bacon

Nodded judiciously like someone making a mental note —Lynne Sharon Schwartz

Pedestrians in the East behave like lemmings rushing dispassionately to their deaths —W. P. Kinsella

People loll upon the beaches ripening like gaudy peaches —Ogden Nash

Play with ... like a clever cat with a rubber mouse —Maureen Howard

(She) poured out feelings and thoughts that most people keep to themselves like a prodigal flinging gold pieces to a scrambling crowd —W. Somerset Maugham

Pushed me across [stage] like a broom —Edith Pearlman

Pull rank like a little red wagon (if it'd get her a place in the shade) —Tom Robbins

(Mary) pulled nerves like string in a blanket —Louise Erdrich

Pushing and jostling like a stormy sea —Stephen Vincent Benét

Raving, but soundlessly ... so that she looked like a film of herself without a sound-track —Lawrence Durrell

Recoiled ... like a man walking in his sleep, awakened from a frightful dream —Charles Dickens

Rose like a trout to the fly or a pickerel to the spoon —Mary McCarthy

> The simile as used in the short story, *Yellowstone Park,* describes a character who's an easy prey for any appeal for money to be spent for educational purposes.

(A day after helping the Giants to their victory over the Raiders in Los Angeles, Lional Manuel, the third-year wide receiver) sauntered through the locker room like an explorer just back from a glorious expedition —William R. Rhoden, *New York Times,* September 23, 1986

(She sat in bed,) sharpening her charms and her riddles like colored pencils —Yehuda Amichai

She went toward the sitting room seeking him like a cold animal seeking the fire —Margaret Mitchell

Shook himself like an angry little dog coming out of the water —Barbara Pym

Shrugged their shoulders as if to shake off whatever chips of responsibility might have lodged there —Helen Hudson

Spoke like a fool, and acted like a fiddler —Saul Bellow

Stuffed his own emptiness with good work like a glutton —Flannery O'Connor

Swallowed his temper but it left a sour taste in his stomach like heartburn —Donald McCaig

Swallowing hard like a stiff-necked goose —Paige Mitchell

Talk like a saint and behave like a fool —Jerome K. Jerome

Talks like a prophet and acts like a comedian —Amos Oz

Thought and action ... were simultaneous in her, rather like thunder and lightning —Leigh Allison Wilson

Took them [spectacles] off, polished the lenses, and held them to the light like a spinster checking her crystal —Donald MacKenzie

> Were MacKenzie writing the novel from which this is culled, *Postscript to a Dead Letter,* today he might well use a new bride or a proud homeowner instead of spinster, which has fallen into disfavor.

Toys with ... as with a yo-yo —Benjamin Netanyahu, Israeli representative to the United Nations, *New York Times*, November 23, 1986

> This simile was used in connection with an article on Syrian terrorism. Typically, the simile was highlighted as a blurb!

Treat us like mushrooms ... keep us in the dark and throw shit at us —Loren D. Estleman

Used tranquilizing drugs ... like the inhabitants of besieged medieval cities who, surprised by death, went back to bed, trying to fall asleep by telling themselves that the threatening flames were only a nightmare —Marguerite Yourcenar

Using a ... flippant tone, as if he were talking about people in a play, or watching the ceiling at the dentist's —Ross Macdonald

Wore abuse like widow's weeds —Lael Tucker Wertenbaker

BELIEF
See also: GOVERNMENT, MORALITY, RELIGION

Belief is as necessary to the soul as pleasures are necessary to the body —Elsa Schiaparelli

Belief, light as a drum rattle, touches us —A. R. Ammons

Communism is like Prohibition, it's a good idea but it won't work —Will Rogers

Conservatives, like embalmers, would keep intact the forms from which the vital principle has fled —John Lancaster Spalding

Convictions ... the deeper you went the filmier the convictions got, until they were like an underwater picture, shifting, dreamy, out of focus —Wilfrid Sheed

Fascism would sprout to life like a flower through a coffin's cracks, watered by the excreta of the dead —Dylan Thomas

Faith is like a lily lifted high and white —Christina Georgina Rossetti

Faith, like a jackal, feeds among the tombs, and even from these dead doubts she gathers her most vital hope —Herman Melville

Faith ... stronger than a bank vault —Jimmy Breslin

His religious ethics fell like drowned fences —Graham Masterson

Ideals are like comets, revisit the earth periodically after long cycles of years—always excepting the enormous ideas that so many sublime donkeys envision of themselves —*Punch*, 1850

Ideals are like the stars: we never reach them, but like the mariners of the sea, we chart our course by them
—Carl Schurz speech, Faneuil Hall, Boston, April 18, 1859

(He was fast in the clutches of his theory). It seemed to guide him like some superior being seated at the helm of his intelligence
—Edith Wharton

(Fanaticism is a pain). It's like talking to a rock trying to talk to a fanatic —Robert Campbell

Living up to ideals is like doing everyday work with your Sunday clothes on —Ed Howe

Love of country is like love of woman ... he loves her best who seeks to bestow on her the highest good —Felix Adler

A man's ideal, like his horizon, is constantly receding from him as he advances toward it —W.G.T. Shedd

(Like many another big boss,) nationalism is largely bogus ... like a bunch of flowers made out of plastics —J. B. Priestly

One by one, like leaves from a tree, all my faiths have forsaken me
—Sara Teasdale

Our dogmas have been greatly enlarged to make them fit in with all sorts of necessities, so that they are like a patched coat, well-worn, and comfortable to wear. Our religion is as variegated as a Harlequin's dress —Anatole France

Patriotism is a kind of religion: it is the egg from which wars are hatched —Guy de Maupassant

Patriotism is as fierce as a fever, pitiless as the grave, blind as a stone and irrational as a headless man —Ambrose Bierce

(I think) patriotism is like charity—it begins at home —Henry James

Principles are like mountains; they rise very near heaven, but when they stand in our way, we drive a tunnel through them
—Cardinal Rampolla

Belief

Skepticism [in preference to superstition] ... it seems to be like a choice between lunacy and idiocy, death -by-fire or -by-water —Henry James, letter to Thomas Sergeant Perry, November 1, 1863

The theory towered up ... like some high landmark by which travelers shape their course —Edith Wharton

We naturally lose illusions as we get older, like teeth —Sydney Smith

A wise conviction is like light —Sir Arthur Helps

Believability

BELIEVABILITY

As full of shit as a Christmas goose —American colloquialism

Believable as a declaration of eternal love from a call girl —Elyse Sommer

Believable as a forced confession —Anon

Believable as the testimony of a proven perjurer —Anon

Giving up credibility in a free society is like giving up force in a totalitarian society —Mario M. Cuomo, commenting on President's Special Review Board findings on Reagan Administration's involvement in Iran-Contra affair, *New York Times*, March 1, 1987

It's [my growing cold towards him] unbelievable ... as if I had suddenly waked and found this lake dried up and sunk in the ground —Anton Chekhov
> The comparison from Chekhov's play, *The Sea Gull*, refers to the relationship between two of the characters, Nina and Trepleff.

Like a man who dreams he sees a friend run on him sword in hand, felt not pain so much as a wild incredulity —Dorothy Canfield Fisher

Shadowy and plausible as a ghost —W. D. Snodgrass

Some circumstantial evidence is very strong, as when you find a trout in milk —Henry David Thoreau

That this feeble, unintelligent old man was possessed of such power ... seemed as impossible to believe as that he had once been a pink-and-white baby —F. Scott Fitzgerald

To tell a soldier defending his country that "This is the war that will end war" is exactly like telling a workman, naturally rather reluctant to do his day's work, that "This is the work that will end work" —G. K. Chesterton
See also: ARMY

Unimaginable as hate in heaven —John Milton
The word 'heaven' has been modernized from 'heav'n' as it appeared in *Paradise Lost.*

Unthinkable as an honest burglar —H. L. Mencken

The whole idea was fantastic, like a polar bear in the Sahara desert —Ken Follett

BELONGING

As much at home ... as a fish in water —Honoré de Balzac
An enduring comparison, as illustrated by a 1986 quote from the *New York Times:* "We belong ... like fish in water. We're in our environment."

As much out of his element as an eel in a sand bag —H. G. Bohn's *Handbook of Proverbs*

As well adapted to the purpose as a one-pronged fork for pitching hay —Herman Melville

(She had) clicked into place [as teacher in school] like a well-hung door closing evenly —Barry Targan

Felt as well placed in the world as a fresh loaf of bread —Laurie Colwin

Fit [poor fit] like a breeching on a pig —Anon

Fit like a duck's foot in the mud —Anon

Fit ... like a tongue into a groove —Jonathan Valin
In the novel, *Life's Work*, the simile refers to the way a man's body fits into a chair.

Fits as a hollow fits a circle —Anon

Fits him as easily as his skin —Thomas Hughes

Fits like the skin on a sausage —Anon

Fitted (into their scheme of life) as a well-made reel fits the butt of a good rod —Henry Van Dyke

Fitted in like a Marine in a parade —William Beechcroft

Fitted (its new home) like a coin in a slot —George Garrett

Fitting comfortable and heavy like a gun in a holster
    —George Garrett

Like a barber's chair, fit for everyone —Thomas Fuller

Like Miniver Cheevy, he had been born too late —Joseph Heller
    See also: TIMELINESS/UNTIMELINESS

Looking as lost as a shipwrecked mariner —Yisrael Zarchi

[Feel] misplaced ... as if she had been expelled from a dream in
    which she would have dearly loved to remain —Milan Kundera

Part of the landscape, like a tree —John Updike

Swam as happily in society as a fish swam in schools
    —Susan Fromberg Schaeffer

BENEFITS
See: ADVANTAGEOUSNESS

BEREAVEMENT
See: SADNESS

BEWILDERMENT
See also: EMOTIONS

As confounding as the groom who drives into a stop sign on the
    way to his wedding —Amy Hempel

As puzzling as a page in an unknown language —Henry James
        In James's story, *The Pupil*, the personality of one of the
        characters serves as a frame of reference for the
        comparison.

Bewildering like a fruitless spring —Jean Garrigue

Confounded utterly, like an orphan in solitary confinement
    —Jean Stafford

Confused, like a mourner who has wandered into the wrong funeral
    parlor —James Crumley

He's as mixed up as the tweetieth century —Clifford Odets

Inexplicable as the birth of a star —Stephen Vincent Benét

[Speaking candidly] muddled her like wine, or like a first breath of freedom —Kate Chopin

Mysterious as the sea —Robert Traver

So confused he's like a hypnotized rabbit —Derek Lambert

Wrinkled his long nose uncertainly, like a hound robbed of the scent by heavy rain —Donald Seaman

BIBLE
See: BOOKS

BIGNESS
See also: FATNESS, TALLNESS

Ample as a fat man's waistline —Anon

As large as life —Maria Edgeworth

As large as life and twice as natural —Anon
> While this is most commonly attributed to Lewis Carroll, who used it in *Through the Looking Glass* in 1873, Stevenson's *Proverbs, Maxims and Famous Phrases* includes an earlier (though likely not the earliest) source, Cuthbert Bede's 1853 work, *Verdant Green.*

Big as a braggart's mouth —Anon

Big as a den bear —Richard Ford

Big as a draft animal —William Brammer

Big as all out of doors —Anon

[A man] big as an express train —T. Coraghessan Boyle

(Bombers) big as bowling alleys —Marge Piercy

A big man, filling the chair like a great mound of wheat —H.R.F. Keating

Great as man's ambitton —Dame Edith Sitwell

Huge as a planet —Lord Byron

Huge as mountains —Walter Savage Landor

Bigness

Immense as whales —Sir William Davenant

Large as a log of maple
  —Refrain from "Yankee Doodle," early American folk song

(My disappointment) large as capsized tugs —Richard Eberhart

A large business organization is like a damn big dragon. You kick it
  in the tail, and two years later, it feels it in the head
  —Frederick Kappell, *Look*, August 28, 1962
      Kappell, chairman of American Telephone and Telegraph,
      began his comparison with "The Bell System is ... "
      instead of the more general phrase used here.

A list big as a comedian's gag file —Anon

Over-sized like a clown's shoes —Anon

She's big as a damned barn and tough as knife metal —Ken Kesey
  See also: TOUGHNESS

She was big as three women —Ernest Hemingway

Vast as water —Madeleine L'Engle

Vast like the inside of a Pharaoh's tomb —Arthur A. Cohen
      In Cohen's novel, *In the Days of Simon Stern*, the
      comparison describes New York's Madison Square
      Garden.

BIOGRAPHY
See: BOOKS, WRITERS/WRITING

Birds

BIRDS
See also: SINGING

(Birds) twitter louder than a flute —Phyllis McGinley

Birds ... white as scraps of paper —Willa Cather
  See also: WHITE

Crows whirled lazily in the sky like flakes of black ash rising from a
  fire —Guy Vanderhaeghe

A dove ... glistening like a pearl —Hans Christian Andersen

The eagles were reveling in the air like bank robbers who had
  broken into the vault —Edward Hoagland

A flight of egrets ... flying low, and scattered ... like a ripple of white notes, sweet and pure and springlike, which an unseen hand drew forth, like a divine arpeggio, from an unseen harp —W. Somerset Maugham
See also: MUSIC

A flock of white swans flew like a long white veil over the water —Hans Christian Andersen

The fluttering, honking formation of birds was like a ship borne by the wind into the high invisible distance —Bernard Malamud

Geese ... blackening the sky like a shake of pepper —Diane Ackerman

Gulls cry like hurt children —George Garrett

Gulls ... settling and stirring like blown paper —Sylvia Plath

A handful of thrushes set down in an oak tree, like a flurry of leaves —Linda Bierds
     This simile marks the closing of Bierds' poem, *Mid-Plains Tornado.*

(That great) hawk circling like a black planet —Ellen Gilchrist

Hens ... like dowager women, plump and impeccably arrayed in brown and grey —Rolf Yngve

His wings [Jonathan Livingston Seagull's] were smooth and perfect as sheets of polished silver —Richard Bach

Hummingbird ... with a beak that looked as long as a darning needle and about as sharp —A. E. Maxwell

A jaybird ... flying in a feathered flash of blue and white like a swift piece of the sky —George Garrett

The parrots shriek as if they were on fire —Ted Hughes
     In a poem entitled *The Jaguar*, the parrots not only shriek but "Strut like cheap tarts to attract the stroller with the nut."
See also: SCREAMS

The pigeons lolloped from illusory pediment to window-ledge like volatile, feathered madmen, chattering vile rhymes and laughing in hoarse, throaty voices —Angela Carter

Pigeons ... settled into trees that shone with them like soft blue and gray fruit —Marge Piercy

71

Birds

Pigeons ... with spreading wings like falling snow —Émile Zola

Soared high above the other birds, climbing like a dart
—R. Wright Campbell

Birth

BIRTH
See also: ENTRANCES/EXITS

Birth and death are like two ships in a harbor. There is no reason to
rejoice at the ship setting out on a journey [birth] not knowing
what she may encounter on the high seas, but we should rejoice
at the ship returning to port [death] safely —Amora Levi

Into the world we come like ships launch'd from the docks, and
stocks, and slips, for fortune fair or fatal! —Edward Fitzgerald

Once upon a time we were all born, popped out like jelly rolls
—Anne Sexton

Passed like an envelope through a letter box [about an easy birth]
—Anaïs Nin

The solemnity of birth, like that of death, is lost in repulsive or
merely commonplace details for those who are in attendance
—Marguerite Yourcenar

Bitterness

BITTERNESS
See also: LOVE

Bitter and sharp as a pulled leek with earth still clinging to it
—George Garrett

Bitter as a broken friendship —Anon

Bitter as acorns —Ann Tyler

Bitter as a day of mourning —Joseph Conrad

(My youth was) bitter as a hard green fruit —Marilyn Hacker

Bitter as alum —Reynolds Price

(The air was) bitter as a stiffed hooker —Loren D. Estleman

Bitter as a tear —Algernon Charles Swinburne

Bitter as blood —Algernon Charles Swinburne

Bitter as coffee that's set too long —Rebecca Rule
A variation: "Bitter as warmed up coffee."

GEESE... BLACKENING THE SKY
LIKE A SHAKE OF PEPPER

(His voice was) bitter as dregs —Stephen Crane

Bitter as gall —John Webster

Bitter as self-sacrifice —Elizabeth Barrett Browning

Bitter as soot —Laurence Sterne

Bitter as the breaking down of love —Algernon Charles Swinburne

Bitter to me as death —William Shakespeare

Bitter as wormwood —*The Holy Bible/Proverbs*

Bitterness ... kept coming back like a taste in the mouth after eating something bad —Rachel Ingalls

Embittered in mind, as a bear robbed of her whelps —*The Holy Bible/Samuel*

A flood of bitterness that washes over me every seven minutes like plagues visited upon a speeded-up pharaoh —William H. Gass

BLACK
See also: FACIAL EXPRESSIONS, SERIOUS; GLOOM

(Hair) black and gleaming as a new galosh —Loren D. Estleman

(The newel post) black and shiny as a skull —W. P. Kinsella

Black as a black poodle's nose —Babette Deutsch

Black as a baker's shovel —Isaac Bashevis Singer

[A hall] black as a billy goat's belly —Ruth Chatterton

Black as a bull-moose in December —Henry Van Dyke

Black as a child's midnight waking —Marge Piercy

Black as a crow —Petronius
     An ancient simile that's still going strong, with "Black as a raven" from *The Holy* Bible the most frequently used variant.

Black as a funeral procession —Diane Ackerman

[Darkening sky] black as a giant tortoise —Stefan Zweig

Black as a heavy smoker's lungs —Elyse Sommer

Black as a manic depressive's thoughts —Elyse Sommer

(The room was) black as an honest politician's prospects
—Dashiell Hammett

Black as an undertaker's hat —Donald Seaman

Black as a pine at night —Stephen Vincent Benét

(Locks) black as a raven —*The Holy Bible/Song of Solomon*

Black as a stack of black cats in the dark —H. W. Thompson

Black as a tar-barrel —Lewis Carroll

Black as black —W. B. Yeats

(Eyes ...) black as bottomless water —Ellen du Pois Taylor

(Eyes) black as caverns —T. Coraghessan Boyle

(Black coats were) black as coffins —Rebecca West

Black as despair —John Phillips

Black as dusk —William Styron

Black like an oven (our kin was ...) —*The Holy Bible/Lamentations*

Black as fate —Dame Edith Sitwell

Black as hell —William Shakespeare
> Shakespeare, the master of so many similes, can be credited for a fair share of the best-known "Black as" comparisons. Besides this one from *Hamlet,* they include "Black as ink," "Black as ebony," and "Black as jet."

Black as midnight without a moon —Anon

Black as murder —Thomas Dekker

Black as perjury —Anon

(Our hands were) black as potatoes dug from the ground
—T. Coraghessan Boyle

Black as some charred rafter —W. D. Snodgrass

Black as sorrow —Sir Philip Sidney

Black as the ace of spades —Anon

Black as the devil's hind foot —T. C. Haliburton

Black as the devil's heart —Ariel Dorfman

Black as the head of a hanged man —F. D. Reeve

(Black holes,) black as the moments before birth and after death —T. Coraghessan Boyle

Black as thunder —William Makepeace Thackeray

(Their visages) blacker than coal —*The Holy Bible/Lamentation*

(Deep and) black like an abyss —Aharon Megged

Black ... like a subway tunnel —William Faulkner

It [a room] was black as the inside of a cat —Davis Grubb

The sky was as black as a monsoon —Dominique Lapierre

BLINDNESS
See also: EYE(S)

Blind as a bat —Anon
> Attribution for this enduringly popular cliche dates back to the seventeenth century and a somewhat longer old English version from John Clarke's *Paromiologia:* "Blind as a bat at noone." Less used variants are "Blind as a beetle" and "Blind as a buzzard."

Blind as a flame of fire —Algernon Charles Swinburne

Blind as a fool's heart —Robert Browning

Blind [about understanding love and hate] as a newborn child —Marguerite Duras

Blind as a newt —Leigh Allison Wilson

Blind as a night fog —Daniel Berrigan

Blind as a stone —Anon
> This still commonly used expression dates back to the fourteenth century, even before Chaucer used it in *Canterbury Tales:* "Blind as is a stoon."

(Eyes staring,) blind as glass —Rose Tremain

Blind as Hell —William Habbington

Blind as ignorance —Francis Beaumont and John Fletcher

Blind as inexperience —Victor Hugo

Blind as love —Percy Bysshe Shelley

Blind as maggots —Mark Helprin

Blind as night —Beryl Markham

(Bright and) blind as the moon in the blank mid-morning sky
    —F. D. Reeve

Blind as the waves of the sea —Eva Gore-Booth

Oblivious of ... as an ant or a flea might be to the sound of the
    avalanche on which it rides —William Faulkner

BLOOD
See also: VIOLENCE

Bleeding like a stuck pig —Anon

Bleed, like a can of cherries —D. H. Lawrence

Blood ... hot and sticky like spilled wine —Harvey Swados

Blood is like a parachute. If it's not there when you need it, you'll
    probably never need it again
    —Slogan for blood donor drive, June, 1987

Blood spouting ... as generously as water from a fountain
    —Jack London

Blood like turpentine —George Garrett

Blood spurting out of his noseholes like tomato puree —Jay Parini

Bloodthirsty as a tick —Diane Ackerman

Blood ... which flows like a scream through the woods
    —Charles Simic

Bubbled blood like a little red spring —William Goyen

Face bloody as raw pork —Nelson Algren

[Man in hopes of improving world] scatters blood like a fish leaping
    from a lake —Janet Flanner

Stale, coppery smell [of blood] like the taste of pennies on the
    tongue —Jonathan Valin

BLOOMING
See: GROWTH

BLUE

Blue and delicate as spring sky reflected in an old window
—Elizabeth Spencer

(Eyes) blue as chicory in bloom —Ed McBain

(Sky ...) blue as a robin's egg —Lee Smith

Blue as a brochure sea —William McIlvanney

Blue as a jay bird's wing —Ellen Glasgow

(Eyes as) blue as a peacock's neck —Flannery O'Connor

(Sky ...) blue as a staring Northern eye —Elizabeth Enright

Blue as autumn mist —Thomas Hardy

(Eyes as) blue as corn-flowers —Lawrence Durrell

(Sea and sky are a matched set,) blue as delftware
—T. Coraghessan Boyle

(Eyes) blue as heaven —Lord Byron
> Other famous poets to link heaven and the color blue
> include Christina Rossetti with "Saphires shining blue as
> heaven" and Percy Bysshe Shelley with "Blue as the
> overhanging heaven." For everyday usage there's "Blue as
> the sky."

Blue as hyacinths —Richard Ford

Blue as melancholy —Anon

(Sky) blue as the core of a match flame —George Garrett

Blue as the decks of the sea —Dame Edith Sitwell

Blue as the glimpses of sea beyond —John Greenleaf Whittier

Blue as the nose that graduate drunkards wear —Don Marquis

Blue as the sky —American colloquialism, attributed to New England

Blue as with the cold —Israel Zangwill

Blue like a corpse —Nikolai V. Gogol

Blue [of a repelling place] ... like the color of the lips of an
	asthmatic plumber dying of lead poisoning who has put himself
	out of his misery with cyanide —Gerald Kersh

Blue like the last thundercloud of a tempest dispersed
	—Alexander Pushkin

Pale blues like old people's eyes —Edna O'Brien

BLUSHES
See also: FACIAL COLOR, RED, SHYNESS

Blood gushed crimson to her cheek ... as though red wine had been
	poured into a crystal glass —Stefan Zweig

The blood showed clearly [on his face] like wine stains a pearly glass
	—Elinor Wylie

Blushed like a beetroot —Anatoly Rybakof

Blushed like a brick —Samuel Hopkins Adams

Blushed like a rose —Isak Dinesen

Blushed, like a wave of illness —Nadine Gordimer

Blushes rising like the tide —Lael Tucker Wertenbaker

Blushing like a strawberry —Marcel Proust

Blushing like a tomato —E. V. Lucas

Blushing pink as dawn —George Garrett

Blush like a black dog —John Ray's *Proverbs*

Blush like a geranium —Harry Graham

A blush that felt like a gasoline fire —R. V. Cassill

Color came to his face like blood on a galled fish
	—Loren D. Estleman

The color flew in her face like a flag —D. H. Lawrence

A deep flush enveloped him like darkness —Heinrich Böll

A delicate flush of pink ... like the flush in the face of the
	bridegroom when he kissed the lips of the bride —Oscar Wilde

(I could feel my) face flaming as red as all the tomatoes in the world —H. C. Witwer

A faint blush, like the shadow of a rose in a mirror of silver came to her cheeks —Oscar Wilde

Felt shame flooding his cheeks like a hot geyser —Mark Helprin

His face went red as a peony —Julia O'Faolain

His neck flushing red even to his ears, like some overgrown schoolboy who had been made to recite when he didn't know his lesson —John Yount

Red as a barn —Susan Fromberg Schaeffer

Red crawling across her face like a stain —Harvey Swados

Ruddiness spreading across her cheeks like a wound —Joseph Koenig

Turned all colors—as a peacock's tail, or sunset streaming through a Gothic skylight —Lord Byron

Turned as red as a winter apple —American colloquialism
> The comparison of blushing cheeks to apples is common in everyday language as well as literature. An example of the latter: "Color like an apple" from Truman Capote's short story, *Children on Their Birthdays*.

Turned red as ... a nectarine, as a dahlia, as the most divinely red thing in the world —Colette

BODY
See also: AGILITY, AWKWARDNESS, BODY ORGANS, FATNESS, MUSCLES, STOMACH

(Had a) body like a stack of lumpy pillows —Robert Campbell

Body like dry bone —Robert Silverberg

Body ... long like a weasel's —Anton Chekhov

Body ... shaped like a sack half full of cement —Sterling Hayden

Body ... silvery like a white rose —Isak Dinesen

The body turns empty as the shell of an insect, or like something inflatable but flattened —Jayne Anne Phillips

Body warm and flat as beer that's been standing —Marge Piercy

Buddha-like body still as an onyx boulder —Ralph Ellison

Build like a sack of angle irons —Loren D. Estleman

Built like a bowling pin —Clive Cussler

(She's hard to fit, being) built like a cement root cellar
    —Louise Erdrich

Built like a Coke machine —Joseph Wambaugh

Built like a crate —William Diehl

Built like a fire plug —Pat Conroy

Built like a greyhound —Miles Gibson

Built like a hammer —Lee K. Abbott

Built like a Russian weightlifter —William Diehl

Built like a skyscraper —Slogan, Shaw-Walker steel filing cabinets

Built like a snowman. A small round head atop a large round body
    with no neck in between —Rick Borsten

Built like a vault —Anon

Built like refrigerators —Jonathan Valin

Built solid, firm and square, like an unencumbered pine
    —Sylvia Berkman

Built square, like a van —William Beechcroft

Built with curves like the hull of a racing yacht —Ernest Hemingway
        A quick simile is about as much space as a master of
        conciseness like Hemingway devotes to physically
        describing a character. The woman with the racing yacht
        curves is Lady Brett from *The Sun Also Rises.*

Chest like a nail keg —Peter Matthiessen

Chest like an oak wine cask —Ira Wood

Chest like an oyster barrel —Ogden Nash

Chests and bellies like a pair of avalanches —T. Coraghessan Boyle

Chunky, heavy, like a Samoan swimmer —Herbert Gold

Corded and tough as a short piece of tallowed cable —George Foy

The simile in Foy's novel, *Coaster*, applies to a sailor.

Delicate and softly rounded as a painting by Boucher
—F. van Wyck Mason

(Against the light of the lamp,) the delicate erotic lines of her slender
body came up like a photographic print in a developing tray
—Brian Moore

Even her hipbones [like rest of angular body] jutted out as if her
skirt was draped on a coathanger —Richard Maynard

A figure like a beer barrel —Oscar Wilde
A variation by Charles Johnson: "Broad as a beer barrel."

Figure like a sack of flour —Josephine Tey

A figure like a two-armed Venus de Milo who had been on a
sensible diet —David Niven
Being an actor as well as a writer, Niven undoubtedly had
a special appreciation for any device which would capture
audience attention the minute the curtain rises; and so this
simile from the first sentence of his autobiography, *The
Moon's a Balloon*.

Figure ... so delicate that she moved like a shadow
—Inez Haynes Irwin

(She had) a figure that was like a swift unexpected blow to the
diaphragm —that to linger on makes the beholder feel obscene
—Frederick Exley

A fine small body, like a miniature dog bred for show
—Maureen Howard

(He was) flat and wide as a gingerbread man —Charles Portis

Flat-chested and straight as a board —MacDonald Harris

Graceful figure, which was as tough as hickory and as flexible as a
whip —Thomas Wolfe

(Kaplan was examining the) midriff bulge that ballooned out over his
belt like an inflated inner tube —William P. Kennedy
The simile marks the opening of Kennedy's espionage
novel, *The Masakado Lesson*.

(Was halfway through the process of turning from muscular to fat, so
that at present he was) of uncertain consistency, like a cheap
mattress —Richard Francis

Round and curved as a marble statue —George Garrett

A small boned body as easy to fragment as a young grouse's
    —Penelope Gilliatt

A small, plump woman, with her waist cinctured in sternly, like a
    cushion with a noose around it —John Cheever

Spine ... like an iron rod —Angela Carter

Square as a wooden block —T. Coraghessan Boyle

Square like a block of stone —Willis Johnson

(She no longer had her slim waist or rounded bosom but was)
    square like a stack of firewood —Isak Dinesen

(A massive woman ...) square, rather like a great piece of oak
    furniture —Willa Cather

Still had an athlete's frame ... but the flesh had sagged on the
    hanger, like an old suit with change left in the pockets
    —Jonathan Valin

Straight as a mast, muscled like a gorilla
    —Maxwell Anderson and Laurence Stallings

A strong, supple body, like a tigress —Anthony Powell

BODY ORGANS
See also: TONGUE

Balls like a gorilla —James Crumley

A cunt that looks like candy and smells like an English garden
    —Norman Keifetz

Genitals like rockets —Saul Bellow

Hard long testicles like a pair of furry avocados —Carlos Fuentes

Her frilly cunt had lipped open like a dogwinkle shell —John Farris

His dick looked like a hot dog in a long, furry bun —Sue Grafton
            In her mystery novel, *"C" Is for Corpse*, Grafton follows
            this simile with another: "And he wagged it at me like a
            guy who's just stepped out of a phone booth to open his
            raincoat."

A liver [from excessive drinking] like an old boot —J. B. Priestly

(Just me telling about it, made your) pecker hard as a pole
—R. Wright Campbell

Penises as flaccid as ruined breasts —James Crumley

Penis ... like a hard, live bedpost —Alice Walker

Penis like an upraised club —John Farris

A prick like a balloon —Gerald Kersh

Prostate like an Idaho potato —dialogue spoken by Marlon Brando in
The Last Tango in Paris, 1972

Prostate ... as round and elastic as a handball —Walker Percy
The prostate comparison is made by the doctor-narrator of
Percy's *Love in the Ruins* about an old male patient.

BONDS
See: CONNECTIONS

BOOKS

All the juice of a book is in an unpublished manuscript, and the
published book is like a dead tree—just good for cutting up and
building your house with —Christina Stead

Bad books are like intoxicating drinks; they furnish neither
nourishment, nor medicine —Tryon Edwards

The *Bible* among books is as a diamond among precious stones
—John Stoughton

A book is a friend whose face is constantly changing —Andrew Lang

A book is a mirror: if an ass peers into it, you can't expect an
apostle to look out —Georg Christoph Lichtenberg

A book is like a garden carried in the pocket —Arab proverb

A book, like a child, needs time to be born —Heinrich Heine

A book, like a grape-vine, should have good fruit among its leaves
—Edward Parsons Day

A book, like a landscape, is a state of consciousness varying with
readers —Ernest Dimnet

A book may be as great a thing as a battle —Benjamin Disraeli

Books are like individuals; you know at once if they are going to create a sense within the sense ... or if they will merely leave you indifferent —George Moore

Books ... arranged carefully according to size, like schoolchildren lined up for recess —Helen Hudson

Books, like friends, should be few and well chosen —Thomas Fuller

Books, like men their authors, have no more than one way of coming into the world, but there are ten thousand to go out of it and return no more —Jonathan Swift

Books like proverbs receive their value from the stamp and esteem of ages through which they have passed —Sir William Temple

Books ... as little read as tombstones —Frank Swinnerton

The [thick] book was just like a warm, thick eiderdown that she could pull over herself, snuggle into —Alice Munro

A book without an index is as incomplete as a eunuch —Theodore Stanton

A classic ... is a successful book that has survived the reaction of the next period or generation. Then it's safe, like a style in architecture or furniture —F. Scott Fitzgerald

Dictionaries are like watches: the worst is better than none, and the best cannot be expected to go quite true —Samuel Johnson

Disliking a classic like disliking a nation one visits, it's the result of a blind spot, which goes away and leaves one embarrassed —Edward Hoagland

Each new book is as a ship that bears us away from the fixity of our limitations into the movement and splendor of life's infinite ocean —Helen Keller

Every book is like a purge, at the end of it one is empty ... like a dry shell on the beach, waiting for the tide to come in again — Daphne du Maurier, *Ladies Home Journal*, November, 1956

The harmonies of bound books are like the flowers of the field —Hilaire Belloc

Books

It is with books as with new acquaintances. At first we are highly
delighted, if we find a general agreement ... with closer
acquaintances differences come to light; and then reasonable
conduct mainly consists in not shrinking back at once
—Johann Wolfgang von Goethe

It is with books as with men: a very small number play a great part
—Voltaire

Like the fortune teller who sees a long journey in the cards or death
by water, they [books] influence the future —Graham Greene

Most books, like their authors, are born to die —Joshua Swartz

A new book, like a young man, has a reputation to acquire
—Clarence Walworth

A new book ... not one of a number of similar objects, but like an
individual man, unmatched —Marcel Proust

Novels are useful as bibles, if they teach you the secret that the best
of life is conversation and the greatest success is confidence
—Ralph Waldo Emerson

An old book, like an old man, is bound to have a good character
already established, and must expect to be looked upon with
suspicion if it has not —Clarence Walworth

The reading of good books is like a conversation with the finest men
of past centuries —Rene Descartes

A room without books is like a body without a soul —Cicero
> A twist to this, variously attributed to Hannah More and
> Henry Ward Beecher, is "A house without books is like a
> room without windows."

Such books are like frowzy old broads who have been handled by a
thousand men —Peter De Vries
> The books being compared to frowzy old broads are
> telephone directories in phone booths.

There is no frigate like a book —Emily Dickinson
> Dickinson's simile serves as both title and first line for one
> of her best known poems.

Volumes [of books produced in America] by the dozens like
doughnuts, big and soft and empty at the core —Helen Hudson

BOREDOM/BORING
See: DULLNESS

BOUNDLESSNESS
See: CONTINUITY

BOXING AND WRESTLING

A boxing match is like a cowboy movie. There's got to be good guys and there's got to be bad guys. What people pay for is to see the bad guys get beat —Sonny Liston, quoted from his obituary, *New York Times*

Fell on his face, kicking and heaving like a wounded leopard —Gerald Kersh

Fired himself across the ring like a stone from a catapult —Gerald Kersh

Got up the third time with blood like a livid splash of ripe fruit all over his face —H. E. Bates

He (Joe Louis) punches like he had a baseball bat in his both hands —Irwin Shaw

His nostrils [Joe Louis'], like the mouth of a double-barreled shotgun, took a quiet lead and let him have both barrels —Bob Considine, International News Service report on Louis-Schmeling fight, June 22, 1938

(Sharkey) kept coming in like the surf —Anon comment about the 1899 Jeffries-Sharkey fight

Their long, stiff jabs made their gloves dip and seem heavy, like big red balloons —Richard Ford

They clung together, spinning round and round like two twigs in a whirlpool —Gerald Kersh

Went down like a letter in a mail chute —Anon

When he (Jake La Motta) was in the ring, it was like he was in a cage fighting for his life —Ray Arcel, boxing trainer, quoted in Ira Berkow's Sports of the Times column, *New York Times*, August 20, 1986

Wrestled together, interlaced like snakes —Honoré de Balzac

BREASTS

See also: BODY ORGANS

Bosom like a Spanish balcony —Colette

Bosom like the prow of a ship —M. J. Farrell

Bosoms ... large, like mounds of earth on the banks of a dug-up
canal —R. K. Narayan

Bosoms like cheese-wheels —David Huddle

Bosoms like vast, half-filled hot-water bottles —M. J. Farrell

Bosoms set like two great prows of battleships —Brian Donleavy

Breasts as large and round as a bald man's head —James Crumley

Breasts hard as stone, project like a bulwark —Erich Maria Remarque

A breast divided into segments like a peeled orange, or a pair of
thighs that converge into a single swollen knee —Kingsley Amis

Breasts heaving like a flight deck —Rita Mae Brown

Breasts ... hung like water-filled balloons from her chest
—Bernard Malamud

Breasts lie flat on her ribs like soft purses —Rose Tremain

Breasts, like a nursing mother's —Katherine Anne Porter

Breasts like a pair of piggies —Vladimir Nabokov

Breasts like armaments —T. Coraghessan Boyle

Breasts ... like bread loaves hot from the oven
—Francine du Plessix Gray

Breasts like ... clusters of the vine —*The Holy Bible/Song of Solomon*

Breasts ... like dried apples —Annette Sanford

Breasts like dunes —John D. MacDonald

Breasts ... like empty purses except when they filled briefly and fed
another child —H. E. Bates

Breasts like giant cabbages —W. Somerset Maugham

Breasts like overripe squash —Patricia Henley

Breasts like pennants —Irwin Shaw

Breasts like small hard apples —Francine du Plessix Gray

Breasts like smooth and ivory-colored hills —Marguerite Young

Breasts ... sag from her chest like two plump gourds
  —Susan Yankowitz

Breasts sagging like overripe fruit —George Garrett

Breasts ... shaped like crescent moons —Ira Wood

Breasts swaying like party balloons —Jilly Cooper

Breasts swelling ... like rising bread —Marge Piercy

Breasts that drop, big as barrels —Dylan Thomas

Breasts were like long white grapes in the hot sun —D. H. Lawrence

Breasts, which were like apples cut in half —Colette

Breasts ... whose fruits are dark as plums —C. J. Koch

Bursts like creamy milk-fed veal —Susan Lois
  The character who thus pronounces and describes a
  woman's breasts in a novel entitled *Personals* is a kosher
  butcher.

Chest like a promontory —Daphne Merkin

Cleavage deep as the jungle —T. Coraghessan Boyle

Enormous breasts that seemed to rise up and nearly out of her gown
  with every deep breath, defying physical laws, like a half-finished
  bridge —William Brammer

Full breasts soaring all over the place like billowing pennants in a
  strong wind —Joseph Heller

Her boobs, in a crocheted halter top, sagged down like flesh melons
  bursting through the bottom of a string bag —Sue Grafton

Her bosom heaved like an opera singer's —Ruth Prawer Jhabvala

Her breasts are tiny and hang from her chest like a pair of prunes
  —Milan Kundera

(An ample woman,) her breasts hung like calabashes inside her grey
  dress —Thomas Keneally

Her breasts looked like two five-pound flour sacks from which some
  of the contents had spilled —Sue Grafton

Breasts

Her large heavy breasts seemed to lift like wings —James Crumley

Her nipples preceded her like scouts —Yehuda Amichai

Her small girlish breasts already sagged like little pockets on her white chest —Jonathan Valin

Her tits were swelled up like two big muffins with a glob of pink frosting in the center of each —Will Weaver

His bared breast glistened soft and greasy as though he had sweated out his fat in his sleep —Joseph Conrad

Jutting breasts like hills —Robinson Jeffers

Little mounds had appeared like soft marshmallows through her sweater —Carol Ascher

Long pointed breasts rearing like the muzzles of two Afghans —James Crumley

The nipple [of mother nursing child] looked like the end of a Tootsie Roll —Bobbie Ann Mason

Nipples ... flat and wide as poker chips —Sue Miller

Nipples large as cookies —Ira Wood

Nipples ... like buds of peonies —Amy Lowell

Nipples like two dark eyes —David Michael Kaplan

Nipples shaped like discs of milk chocolate —Ira Wood
  Wood's novel, *The Kitchen Man*, brims with food-related images.

Nipples ... small as buttons —Miles Gibson

Nipples standing out like two overgrown M&Ms —T. Glen Coughlin

The profile of her body stood forth like the prow of a clipper ship —Calder Willingham

She had fenders like a GMC truck —Loren D. Estleman

They [breasts] were wide mounds growing like muscles across her chest —Will Weaver

Tits like twin cannons —Robert Campbell

A woman without breasts is like a bed without pillows —Anon

BREATHING

Alimentary canal ... working like a derrick without a soul
—Tess Slesinger

Breath ... as black as funerals —Miles Gibson
See also: BLACK

(His) breath came heavily, like puffs of wind over a stormy sea
—Walter De La Mare

Breath came like puffs from a steam locomotive —Gerald Tomlinson

Breath clear and sweet like a child's —Flannery O'Connor

Breathed as if she had a fever —Mark Helprin

Breathed deeply like a swimmer coming up for air —George Garrett

(He) breathed like a prisoner set free —Willa Cather

Breathe hard like a horse when you take the saddle off —O. Henry

Breathe like a chugging train —Tony Ardizzone

Breathe like a second-hand bicycle pump —O. Henry

Breath [from snoring] grating like bark stripped from a tree
—T. Coraghessan Boyle

Breathing as rapidly as an exhausted dog —Derek Lambert

Breathing as softly as a butterfly —Ellen Glasgow

Breathing as though stream engines were working his lungs
—Pat Conroy

Breathing like a hard-run horse —James Crumley

Breathing like almost any sort of man who has just been chased for
a mile or so uphill by a bull in the pink of condition
—Kingsley Amis

Breathing like an escape valve —Joseph C. Lincoln

Breathing like a tire pump —Dashiell Hammett

Breathing like the friction of rusted gears —T. Coraghessan Boyle

Breathing like two hippos with a chest cold —Jane Wagner
This line, spoken by the character Paul (interpreted by Lily
Tomlin), describes his participation at his wife's labor.

Breathing

Breathing, quick and hoarse like a dog's panting —Albert Camus

Breathing ... slow and rhythmical, like the bellows at a forge rising and falling —Henri-Pierre Roche

Breathing [an overweight man's] sounded like someone sitting down on a leather couch —Sue Grafton

Breathing with irregularity, like an overworked horse. Breathing deeply like a man asleep —George Garrett

Breath is like the gentle air of spring —Henry Wadsworth Longfellow

Breath ... like the steam of apple-pies —Robert Greene

Breath popping like steam valves in old boilers —Denis Johnson

(Rankin's) breath rushed out like an undertow beneath the words —Richard Moran

Breath sweet as May —Christina Rossetti

The breath was pumped from their bodies as though from machines —Vicki Baum

Breath [of dying woman] whistled like the wind in a keyhole —Edith Wharton

Each breath was expelled in a puff, as if one were blowing a trumpet, Dizzy Gillespie fashion —Stephen King

Each breath was like a hill to climb —Barbara Reid

Gasped for breath like a wounded animal —Vicki Baum

Gasped the air deeply, like a diver escaping from a watery grave —Jan Kubicki

Gasping like a fish stranded on a sandbank —F. van Wyck Mason
An extension of "Gasped like a stranded fish."

Gulped in air through her mouth, straining like a nearly drowned man dragged out of the water —William Moseley

Gulping in air like a swimmer exhausted from fighting a heavy surf —Margaret Millar

Hack and wheeze like an overworked horse —T. Coraghessan Boyle

Her breath seems to flow like the water in a frozen stream —Rochelle Ratner

His breath [as he kissed her hand] was between her fingers like a web on summer grass —Ellen Gilchrist

His breath was staccato, like obstructed sobs
    —Nancy Huddleston Packer

Holds her breath like a seal —John Berryman

Huff like windy giants —W. D. Snodgrass

Let out a long, whistling breath like a deflating tire
    —Cornell Woolrich

Lungs ... blowing like leathern bellows —Frank Ross

(Stearn's) lungs fluttered like a sparrow's heartbeat —Z. Vance Wilson

(I was panting and) my breath came like fire —Louise Erdrich

Pant like a fat man running for a bus —Lawrence Durrell

Panting like a steamboat —Joyce Cary

Puffed like a leaky steam pipe —O. Henry

Puffing like a blown shire horse —Donald Seaman

A rasping gasp as though he were swallowing his false teeth
    —W. P. Kinsella

Sharp intake of breath, like a toy balloon suddenly deflated
    —Ralph Ellison

Snort [while asleep] like a timid locomotive —MacDonald Harris

Sound of breathing ... like the soft crackle of tissue paper
    —Frank Swinnerton

Sucked air like a drowning fish —Miles Gibson

Took as much breath as if I'd heaved a shot put —Larry McMurtry

Wheezing ... like a horse with a progressive lung disease
    —T. Coraghessan Boyle

BREVITY

As compact as a drop of pure water —Richard E. Shepard, *New York Times*, November 3, 1986
        The simile attempts to explain the mystery of the Flamenco
        Puro dance troop's creative wellsprings.

Brevity

Brief as a classified ad —Anon

Brief as a drop of dew —Cale Young Rice

Brief as a grouch's smile —Anon

Brief as a sinner's prayer —Anon

Brief as a twinge —Margaret Atwood

Brief as the Z column in a pocket dictionary —Irvin S. Cobb
> Or, to be even more specific, "Brief as the Z column in this dictionary."

Brief as youth in retrospect —Elyse Sommer

(Smiled) briefly, on and off like a light switch —Gavin Lyall

Concise as a telegram —Elyse Sommer

Short as any dream —William Shakespeare

Short, clear as a bird-note, trailing away —E. B. White

Brightness

BRIGHTNESS
See also: GLITTER AND GLOSS, LIGHTING

Blazing like the windows of the city —James Dickey

(He possessed a brainful of information,) bright and beautiful as diamonds swaddled in midnight-blue velvet —W. P. Kinsella

Bright and light as the crest of a peacock —Alfred, Lord Tennyson

Bright and pleasing as a child's rattle —Virginia Woolf

Bright as a beach in the moonlight —Alfred Austin

(An image came to me across the years,) bright as a coin from the mint —Norman Mailer

Bright as a frog's eyes —Hart Crane

Bright as all between cloudless skies and windless streams —Percy Bysshe Shelley

Bright as a nettle rash —Diane Ackerman

(Laugh ...) bright as a new ensign's buttons —Frederic Wakeman

Bright as a newly painted toy —Hugh Walpole

Bright as an icon —Margaret Atwood

Bright as any glass —Geoffrey Chaucer

Bright as any meteor ever bred by the North Pole —Lord Byron

Bright as a parakeet —Dame Edith Sitwell

(Every day) bright as a postcard —Karl Shapiro

Bright as a roomful of crystal chandeliers —Anon

Bright as a splinter from a glazier's table —Beryl Markham

(A face) bright as a waterdrop —Padraic Fallon

Bright as day —Geoffrey Chaucer

Bright as foil —Molly Giles

Bright as freedom —Marge Piercy

Bright as joy —Hartley Coleridge

Bright as light —Alfred, Lord Tennyson

Bright as moonlight over snow —Wallace Stegner

Bright as Spring —Walter Savage Landor

(Eyes as) bright as the Dipper —Stephen Vincent Benét

Bright as the fullest moon in blackest air —*Arabian Nights*

Bright as the promises of a new administration —Elyse Sommer

Bright as the promise of life on commencement day —Elyse Sommer

Bright as the promise of a cloudless day —C. P. Wilson

Bright as the raindrops and roses in June —Dame Edith Sitwell

Bright as the world was in its infant years —John Banks

Bright as truth —Barry Cornwall

Bright like a brimming bowl of jewels —Peter De Vries

Bright, like a flash of sunlight —Edward Bulwer-Lytton

Bright (eyes) like agate —D. H. Lawrence

Bright like blood —Algernon Charles Swinburne

Brightness ... bright as dipper —Stephen Vincent Benét

Brilliant as a postage stamp —Lawrence Durrell

(Eyes) brilliant as fire —Nadine Gordimer

[Oranges and grapefruits] brilliant as planets —Cynthia Ozick

Brilliant as the stars —Ouida

Brilliant as the sun —Slogan, Lustberg-Nast, Lustray shirts

Brilliant like a Chinese porcelain —W. Somerset Maugham

Brilliantly, gaudily colored as a Gypsy camp —Kate Simon

Dazzled the eyes like a second noonday sun —Edna Ferber

Growing brighter and brighter like a forest after a rain
    —Denis Johnson

Lights up like a Star Wars pinball machine —Marge Piercy

[Face] light up like a bonfire of joy —Carl Sandburg

Vivid as sun through a thin brown bottle —Reynolds Price

Vivid as the granules of paint in a Dubuffet —John Updike

BRITTLENESS
See: FRAGILITY

BROWN

(Wine) as brown as November leaves —Wilbur Daniel Steele

[Pupils of eyes] brown and shiny like melting chocolate
    —Margaret Millar

Brown as a berry —Geoffrey Chaucer
        The old English original read "Broun as is a berye."

(His face was) brown as an old boot —Christopher Isherwood
    See also: TOUGHNESS

Brown as an old daguerreotype fading —Robert Penn Warren

Brown as a nut —Henry Wadsworth Longfellow

(Cheeks) brown as oak-leaves —Henry Wadsworth Longfellow

(Hair) brown as a pecan shell —Reynolds Price

Brown as cinnamon —Truman Capote

Brown as onion soup —Saul Bellow

Brown as rust —George Garrett

(A tan) brown as seven-grain bread —Patricia Henley

(A girl as) brown as the ground —Cynthia Ozick

Brown as tobacco spit brew —Truman Capote

Brown ... like the color of the basket —H. E. Bates

A dreggy brown, like bad coffee —Irvin S. Cobb

Pale brown, like canvas —Mary McCarthy

BRUTALITY
See: CRUELTY, VIOLENCE

BURST
See: DISINTEGRATION, SUDDENNESS

BUSINESS
See also: ADVERTISING

As oxygen is the disintegrating principle of life, working night and day to dissolve, separate, pull apart and dissipate, so there is something in business that continually tends to scatter, destroy and shift possession from this man to that. A million mice nibble eternally at every business venture —Elbert Hubbard

Business is like a man rowing a boat upstream. He has no choice; he must go ahead or he will go back —Lewis E. Pierson

Business is like oil. It won't mix with anything but business —J. Grahame

Business ... is very much like religion: it is founded on faith —William McFee

Business policy flows downhill from the mountain, like water —Anon

A business without customers is like a computer without bytes —Anon

As the entries that follow show, this concept lends itself to many additional twists.

A business without customers is like a stage without light —Anon

A business without orders is like a room without windows —Anon

Buying and selling like a Rockefeller —Arthur A. Cohen

A corporation is just like any natural person, except that it has no pants to kick or soul to damn —Ernst and Lindley
> Playwrights Ernst and Lindley wrote this simile to be spoken by a judge in their 1930s play *Hold Your Tongue.*

Corporate politics is like the days of Andrew Jackson, the spoils system —Rita Mae Brown

Customers drop away like tenpins —Anon

Inventory that just sits there like it's nailed to the floor —Anthony E. Stockanes

Nowadays almost every business is like show business, including politics, which has become more like show business than show business is —Russell Baker

Orders fell like stones —Anon

(Being in the microcomputer business is) risky, like going 55 miles an hour three feet from a cliff. If you make the wrong turn you're bankrupt so fast you don't know what hit you —George Morrow, quoted in *New York Times*, March 11, 1986 when his company went bankrupt
See also: DANGER

Some businesses are like desert flowers. They bloom overnight, and they're gone —George Morrow, quoted *New York Times*, March 11, 1986
> The first two words are transposed from "Computer companies" to generalize the comparison.

The tide of business, like the running stream, is sometimes high and sometimes low, a quiet ebb, or a tempestuous flow, and always in extreme —John Dryden

Tradespeople are just like gardeners. They take advantage of your not knowing —Agatha Christie

DISCREET...AS IF YOU'RE TRYING TO
TAIL YOURSELF

CALMNESS
See: PEACEFULNESS

CANDOR
See: HONESTY, TRUENESS/FALSENESS

CAREFULNESS
See: CAUTION, CORRECTNESS

CARELESSNESS

Carelessness

Act with the calm forethought of a beheaded chicken
—Herman Wouk
> In his novel, *Inside, Outside*, Wouk used the comparison to
> describe the behavior of political characters.

Careless as a child at play —William Winter

Careless as saints who live by faith alone —George Garrett

[Charles de Gaulle] has been abysmally careless, like a man running
a bus over mountains, who forgot to equip it with good brakes
—Janet Flanner

Ignore caution like a gambler with a hot tip —Anon

CARES
See: PROBLEMS/SOLUTIONS

CAUSE/EFFECT

Cause/Effect

Affect me [with revulsion] like the smell of a cheap cigar left
smoldering in an ashtray —Jonathan Valin
> In Valin's novel, *Final Notice*, the descriptive frame of
> reference for the simile is a tattoo.

The certainty [of his desire] landed in the bottom of my stomach like
a flatiron —Mary Gordon

The change [in living accommodations] would be like going from
Purgatory to Paradise —Louisa May Alcott

The conviction that I am loved and loving affects me like a military
bracing —John Cheever

The effort made him choke like a tiger at a bone —Robert Frost

Every gesture ... aroused a beat chant like the beat of the heart of the desert —Anaïs Nin

(This city) exacerbates loneliness in me the same way that water makes Alka-Seltzer fizz —Pat Conroy

The general effect was exactly like a microscopic view of a small detachment of black beetles in search of a dead rat
—John Ruskin

Has a disruptive effect ... like a torpedo coming down Main Street
—Anon politician on Gramm-Rudman Law, February, 1986

Has as little effect on me as water on a duck's back
—American colloquialism, attributed to South
    A variation: "As water rolling off a duck's back."

Her absence felt like a presence, an electrical charge of silence in the house —John Updike

His death served to remind me, like a custard pie in the face, that life is sometimes like one big savage joke —Sue Grafton

(A blast of Prince [music] ...) hit me like a feather boa with a length of lead pipe in it —Jonathan Valin

Its [melancholy] effect upon you is somewhat similar to what would probably be produced by a combined attack of toothache, indigestion and a cold in the head —Jerome K. Jerome

It [forcing an old priest into retirement] was just like ripping an old tree out of the ground —W. P. Kinsella

The kind whisper went to my heart like a dagger —Charlotte Brontë

Offering a flight attendant a $20 bill for a $2 drink is like spitting on an Alabama state trooper
—Louis D. Wilson, *Wall Street Journal*, June 30, 1986

Pain and poverty and thwarted ambition ... can break the virtues like brittle bones —George Garrett

Seeing her again ... was like rediscovering a half-forgotten landmark
—Ann Petry

[When a tired-looking woman smiles] some of the years of hard living fall away like happy tears —James Crumley

CAUTION

See also: BEHAVIOR

Cagey as a feral cat —John Yount

Careful as a cat walking on eggshells
    —American colloquialism, attributed to New England

Carries it [a plant] as if it's made of Steuben glass —Ann Beattie

Carry ... like a hot tureen —Eudora Welty

Caution flowed over the [telephone] wire like a wave
    —Robert M. Coates

Caution, like that of a wild beast that is fierce but feeble or like that
    of an insect whose little fragment of earth has given way, and
    made it pause in a palsy of distrust —George Eliot

Cautious as a burglar walking over a tin roof in cowhide boots
    —Wallace Irwin

Cautious as a good housekeeper —Honoré de Balzac

Cautious as a tightrope walker with a severe itch —Anon
        This is yet another perversion of the popular "Busy as a
        one-armed paperhanger" comparison.

Cautious as his gray suit —John Dancy, NBC-TV, about Robert Gates
    at CIA confirmation hearings, April, 1987

Cautiously, like a man handling sixteenth-century lace —Roald Dahl

Choosy as a stud in a harem —Mike Sommer

Discreet ... as if you're trying to tail yourself —William McIlvanney

Going as if he trod upon eggs —Robert Burton

Like a weight-watcher at the feast of San Gennaro, I just nibbled a
    bit —Leonard M. Heine, Jr., commenting on his cautious stock
    purchases when others were investing freely, quoted *Wall Street
    Journal* column by Vartanig G. Vartan, January 19, 1987

Peeped out carefully like a mole from its hole —Derek Walcott

Picked up the pieces as carefully as if they were cuttings from the
    Koh-i-noor —Israel Zangwill

Picking his words like a man making his way through a minefield
    —Donald Seaman

Progressed like a man tracing and following a chalk line
  —Frank Swinnerton

A prudent man is like a pin; his head prevents him from going too
  far —Anon

Should be used with discretion, like cayenne pepper —Anon

So wary that he sleeps like a hare, with his eyes open
  —Thomas Fuller

Timid as hares —Anton Chekhov

To take all you want is never as good as to stop when you should
  —Lao Tzu

(We must) treat him like Dresden china —Nikolai V. Gogol

Wary as a blind horse —Thomas Fuller

Wary as a pickpocket's confidence that the policeman on the beat
  will stay bought —H. L. Mencken
        This is slightly changed from Mencken's original words
        which identified the pickpocket as an American.

Watched what he said as carefully as if he were in court
  —John Updike

CENSORSHIP
See: CONTROL, CRITICISM

CESSATION
See: PAUSE

CHANGE
See: ENTRANCES/EXITS

CHARACTER
See: REPUTATION

CHARACTERISTICS, NATIONAL

America is more a ratatouille than a melting pot
  —Ken Holm, *New York Times Magazine*, October 12, 1986
        The food image is particularly appropriate to Holm's
        article about mixing Eastern and Western ingredients
        when cooking.

America is rather like life. You can usually find in it what you look for —E. M. Forster

As American as a catcher's mit —George Jean Nathan

As American as a Norman Rockwell painting —Max Shulman

As American as a sawed-off shotgun —Dorothy Parker about Dashiell Hammett, *New Yorker*, April 15, 1931

As American as cheesecake —Samuel Yellen

As American as corn on the cob —Anon

As American as jazz —Anon

As American as shopping malls —Anon

As American as the dream of being a millionaire —Anon

As American as the two-car garage —Anon

As British as roast beef —Anon

As English as tea and scones —Elyse Sommer
>The variations to this are virtually limitless; to cite just a few: "As English as the changing of the guards at Buckingham Palace," "English as clotted cream," "As English as Picadilly," "As English as Trafalgar Square."

As in sex, the Japanese do not care for extended encounters: "in and out" is their motto in love and war —James Kirkup

Bullied and ordered about, the Englishman obeys like a sheep, evades like a knave, or tries to murder his oppressor —George Bernard Shaw

Countries are like fruit; the worms are always inside —Jean Giradoux

Energy in a nation is like sap in a tree, it rises from the bottom up —Woodrow Wilson, October 28, 1912 speech

Frenchmen are like grains of gunpowder, each by itself smutty and contemptible, but mass them together and they are terrible indeed —Samuel Taylor Coleridge

A French woman dips into love like a duck into water, 'tis but a shake of the feathers and wag of the tail and all is well again; but an English woman is like a heedless swan venturing into a pool who gets drowned —Washington Irving

Friendship in France as impossible to be attained as orange-trees on the mountains of Scotland —Lady Mary Wortley Montague letter to Lady Pomfret, July 12, 1744

(In America ... people claim and disown 'identities') as easily as they slap on bumper stickers —Philip Roth

Nations, like individuals, have to limit their objectives or take the consequences —James Reston

Nations, like men, die by imperceptible disorders —Jean Giraudoux

Nations, like men, have their infancy
   —Henry St. John, Viscount Bolingbroke

A quiet Irishman is about as harmless as a powder magazine built over a match factory —James Dunne

Soviet action is like a riddle wrapped inside an enigma
   —Winston Churchill

The wheels of American foreign relations turn like the wheels of an ox cart —Clive Cussler

CHARM
See: ATTRACTIVENESS, BEHAVIOR

CHEAPNESS
See: COST

CHEEKS
See also: BLUSHES, FACIAL COLOR

Cheekbones glistening as if they'd been oiled —T. Coraghessan Boyle
   See also: SWEAT

Cheekbones like bunyons —Steve Stern

Cheekbones, like little gossamer-covered drums —Eudora Welty

Cheeks ... always a bright inflamed red, as if they'd been scoured —Jean Thompson

Cheeks ... big as a balloon —Njabulo Ndebele

Cheeks bright as a wooden doll's —Derek Lambert

Cheeks bulging like a trumpeter's —George Garrett

Cheeks glowing like one of those apples in an expensive fruit shop —Patrick White

Cheeks had turned to blotches of dull red, like some pigment which has darkened in drying —Edith Wharton

Cheeks had risen like puffy omelettes [from weight gain] —Phyllis Bottome

Cheeks ... just tinged, like the snow apple —Helga Sandburg

Cheeks ... like a raspberry patch —Truman Capote

Cheeks ... like caves —John Rechy

Cheeks like poppies —John Galsworthy

Cheeks ... pale as a winter snow upon which a few drops of blood have fallen —Arthur A. Cohen

Cheeks ... round and ruddy as marzipan fruit —Sylvia Plath

Cheeks ... sweet as flowers —*The Holy Bible/Song of Solomon*

Cheeks the luscious pink of ripening strawberries —W. P. Kinsella

Jowls ... hanging like wineskins —Z. Vance Wilson

Red cheeks glistened like polished apples —Anon

Spots of rouge on her cheekbones like a couple of roses pressed into the pages of a book —George Garrett

CHEERFULNESS
See also: BRIGHTNESS, GAIETY

All smiles ... as if ready for a thousand little curtseys —André Malraux

(She was) as bubbly as a magnum of champagne —Harry Prince

[A movie] as heart-warming as an approaching headache —Vincent Canby, *New York Times*, March 21, 1986

[A young girl] blithe and airy as a wind-swept leaf —Sylvia Berkman

Blithe as a boy —Pamela Hansford Johnson

[A sunlit room] bright and bouncing as a newly bathed baby —John Braine

Bright as a chirping bird —Stephen Longstreet

Buoyant as a bride —Thomas McGuane

Cheerful as a grove in spring —William Wordsworth

Cheerful as the rising sun in May —William Wordsworth

(Smile ... as) cheerful as the winter solstice —William McIlvanney

A cheerful face is nearly as good for an invalid as healthy weather
    —Benjamin Franklin

Cheerfulness is like money well expended in charity; the more we
    dispense of it, the greater our possessions —Victor Hugo

Cheerfulness opens, like spring, all the blossoms of the inward man
    —Jean Paul Richter

Encouraging as a round of applause —Anon

(I am) gay as morning, light as snow —Dorothy Parker

Optimistic as a sweepstake ticket buyer —Anon

Optimistic as a company spokesperson —Anon

Positive as good news —G. K. Chesterton

Positive as the forecast in a Chinese fortune cookie —Elyse Sommer

Radiant like a work of art, full of strange rays —Iris Murdoch

(She's always happy. She) shies away from misery like a petrified
    horse —Carolyn Slaughter

Sunny and open as a May morning —Willa Cather

CHILDREN
See also: PARENTHOOD

A baby is like a beast, it does not think —Aeschylus

Childhood is like a mirror, which reflects in after life the images first
    presented to it —Samuel Smiles

Childhood ... like so many oatmeal cookies —Frank O'Hara

Childhood shows the man, as the morning shows the day
    —John Milton

Children are like beggars; often coming without being called
—Proverb

Children are like leaves on a tree —Marcus Aurelius

Children are like puppies: you have to keep them near you and look
after them if you want to have their affection —Anna Magnani

Children are like pancakes: You should always throw out the first
one —Peter Benchley

Children [in families] are like rival pretenders to a throne and their
main object in life is to eliminate their competitors
—Milton R. Sapirstein

Children in a family are like flowers in a bouquet: there's always
one determined to face in an opposite direction from the way the
arranger desires —Marcelene Cox

Children like apples ... good enough to eat —Donald Culross

Children ... like robins, pink-cheeked and rosy —Lawrence Durrell

Children ... they string our joys, like jewels bright, upon the thread
of years —Edward A. Guest

The faces of the kids ... suddenly deprived by fear of their
childhood, looked like ancient agonized adults —Herbert Gold

A happy childhood can't be cured. Mine'll hang around my neck like
a rainbow —Hortense Calisher
> This is the opening for the novel, *Queenie*, in which the
> author is much sparer with her similes than she is in her
> short stories.

Ladies touch babies like bankers touch gold —James Ferry
> One of two similes from a little rhyme within a short story
> entitled *Dancing Ducks*.

Life without children is like a tree without leaves —Milan Kundera

A little girl without a doll is almost as unfortunate and quite as
impossible as a woman without children —Victor Hugo

Maternal testimony notwithstanding, babies are like biscuits in a pan
—Ellery Sedgewick

My childhood clings to me like wet paint —Daphne Merkin

In *Enchantment,* a novel about a young woman's search for self-discovery, the simile concludes: "Blotching the picture of who I am in the present."

With children as with plants ... future character is indicated by their early disposition —Demophilus

CHIN
See also: CHEEKS

A chin like an infant's elbow —Penelope Gilliatt

Chin like the butt end of a ham —Ross Macdonald

(A small) chin like half a rubber ball —Robert Campbell

Chin line ... shaped like a persimmon —Susan Minot

Her chin rising and falling upon her heaving bosom like the figurehead of a vessel upon a heavy harbor swell —Arthur Train

Chin stood out like the knuckles in a clenched hand —Max Apple

Chin was blue as if it had been shot full of gunpowder —Joyce Cary

Jaw as rigid as a shovel —John Yount

A jaw like a park bench —Raymond Chandler

Jaw like the head of an ax slipped through at the last second like a curl of smoke —R. Wright Campbell

A jaw like the share of a plow —Sterling Hayden

Jawline like granite —William Diehl

Jaw set like a rock —Donald Seaman

(He popped a mint into his mouth and) snapped his jaws shut like a shark —Harvey Swados

Their shaven jowls looked like the hide of a fresh-scalded, fresh-scraped hog —William Humphrey

CHOICES

Alternatives faced one like knives —Hortense Calisher

Choices

Feel like a piece of flux caught between two magnets —William Diehl
> In Diehl's novel, *Hooligans,* the two magnets represent the choice between two life-styles.

Indecisive as a young boy in an ice cream parlor —Ira Berkow discussing George Steinbrenner's choices of field leaders for Yankees, *New York Times*/Sports of the Times, September 20, 1986

I would sooner smarm like a fart-licking spaniel than starve in a world of fat poems —Dylan Thomas

It [making a choice] seems like a choice between lunacy and idiocy, death by fire or by water —Henry James, letter to Thomas Sergeant Perry, November 1, 1863

Like a kid jumping off the barn ... once they decide to go, they go —John D. MacDonald

Sudden resolutions, like the sudden rise of the mercury in the barometer, indicate little else than the changeableness of the weather —Julius Charles Hare

Took all things of life for her to choose from and apportion, as though she were continually picking presents for herself from an inexhaustible counter —F. Scott Fitzgerald

CITIES
See: CITY/STREETSCAPES

City/Streetscapes

CITY/STREETSCAPES

Alleys open and fall around me like footsteps of a newly shod horse —Frank O'Hara

The ancient oaks ... arched over the avenue like a canopy —John Kennedy Toole

The asphalt shines like a silk hat —Derek Walcott

Bars were strung along the street like bright beads —Margaret Millar
> In her novel, *Experiment in Springtime,* Millar strings the actual names of the bars to this simile.

A big limestone church hangs like a gray curtain under the street lamp —John Updike

The black night falls like a shroud over the whole town —Lu Hsün
    See also: NIGHT

A brutally ugly, utilitarian place, like a mill town without the mill
    —Jonathan Valin

The city seems to uncurl like some hibernating animal dug out of its
    winter earth —Lawrence Durrell

The city unwrinkles like an old tortoise —Lawrence Durrell

Far below and around lay the city like a ragged purple dream
    —O. Henry

In the distance, the city rose like a cluster of warts on the side of
    the mountain —Flannery O'Connor

The noon sun put a glaze on them [the sidewalks], so that the
    cement burned and glittered like glass —Carson McCullers

The passing scene spread outside the windows like a plentiful, prim
    English tea —Dorothea Straus

People [on crowded sidewalk] ... jostling along like sheep in a pen
    that has no end —Maeve Brennan
    See also: CROWDS

The public streets, like built canals of air —David Denby

Raw grass sprouted from the cobbles like hair from a deafened ear
    —Philip Levine

The shadows of the palms lay like splash marks of dark liquid on
    the pavement —Ross Macdonald

The shop fronts stood along that thoroughfare with an air of
    invitation, like rows of smiling saleswomen
    —Robert Louis Stevenson

A steep lane, like a staircase —Émile Zola

The street as gray as newspapers —Marge Piercy
    See also: GRAY

The street lay still as a photograph —Jack Finney

The street shone ... like a fire in a forest —Robert Louis Stevenson

The streets looked as if they were made of silver, they were so
    bright and glistening —Oscar Wilde

111

The streets (of Bethany, Massachusetts), sparkled like high-gloss picture postcards sold in drugstores of small New England villages —Susan Richards Shreve

Streets tangled like old string —W. H. Auden

Street ... that neither stank or sparkled but merely had a look of having been turned, like the collar on an old shirt —Hortense Calisher

The town, like an upturned sky, swollen with human lights —Albert Camus

The town [seen from a distance] looked small and clean and perfect, as if it were one of those miniature plastic towns sitting beside a child's electric railroad —Ann Tyler

A view (of Brewer) spread out below like a carpet —John Updike

Village ... jumbled and colorful like a postcard —George Garrett

Wide, smooth, empty sidewalks looked like long canals of grey eyes —Ayn Rand

CIVILIZATION
See: SOCIETY

CLARITY

(The scents of the garden descended upon him, their contours) as precise and clear as the colored bands of a rainbow —Patrick Suskind

As sharp as the last daybreak —Joy Williamson
From a book jacket blurb about Tess Gallagher's ability to portray aging people's vision of irremediable loss in the novel, *The Lovers of Horses*.

As unreadable as a piece of modern sculpture —Frank Swinnerton

(The image) blurred ... like something familiar seen beneath disturbed though clear water —William Faulkner

(The consonants) blur together like ink on a wet page —Sue Grafton

Clear and diminished like a scene cut in cameo —Edna St. Vincent Millay

Clear as a bell —John Ray's *Proverbs*
> One could compile a small book of just "Clear as" similes. The bell comparison along with "Clear as a whistle" and "Clear as crystal" are probably most frequently used and familiar.

[A theory synthesized from suppositions] clear as a case history written in a book —Jean Stafford

Clear as a cloudless hour —Algernon Charles Swinburne

Clear as a cube of solid sunshine —Anon

[Eyes) clear as a fountain —Walter Savage Landor

Clear as a graph —Anon

Clear as a lake —Samuel Taylor Coleridge

Clear as a legal confession of murder —John Cheever

Clear as an oboe solo —Diane Ackerman

Clear as A on the piano in the middle of all the tuning instruments of an orchestra —Sylvia Plath

Clear as a tear —Sylvia Plath

Clear as cold water —Mark Helprin

(The morning was) clear as glass —Mark Helprin

Clear as infant's eyes —John Keats

(The creek flashed) clear as quartz —Ella Leffland

Clear as righteousness —Algernon Charles Swinburne

Clear as the A, B, C —George Washington

Clear as the day —Miles Coverdale
> "Clear as" comparisons linked with the day, time of day, and the sun at different times of the day include "Clear as noon" (shortened from the once popular "Clear as noon-day") and "Clear as the sun" (both attributed to Roger North); "Clear as is the summer's sun" (William Shakespeare); "Clear as the mid-day sunshine" (Nathaniel Hawthorne); "Clear as day-light" (Arnold Bennett).

Clear as the figures at the bottom of a Profit and Loss Statement —Anon

Clear as the lines in a wet leaf —Charles Johnson

Clear as the note of doom —Lord De Tabley

(The men were naked and) clear as the point of a sword in the sun —George Garrett

(The sky is as) clear as the song of a boy —Beryl Markham

Clear as the twanging of a harp —Alfred, Lord Tennyson

Clear as wind —Alfred, Lord Tennyson

Clear, like accusation —Paul Horgan

[Voice in the "silent dead of night"] distinct as a passing footstep's fall —Henry Wadsworth Longfellow

Distinctly as white lace on velvet —Thomas Hardy

(Shouldn't the soul of a man be as) limpid and cutting as a diamond —John Cheever

(The air is) lucid and lonely as wind chimes —Sharon Sheehe Stark

(The poet's work was about as) lucid as a polygraph chart —Joseph Wambaugh

Lucidity is positively flowing over me like the sweet oils of Persia —Lorraine Hansberry

Precise as a portrait photo —Natascha Wodin

To read him (Descartes) was like swimming in a lake so clear that you could see the bottom —W. Somerset Maugham

(Lake) transparent as liquid chrysolite —T. H. White

Transparent as a white cloud in the moonshine —Hans Christian Anderson

Transparent like some holy thing —Thomas Moore

CLEANLINESS/UNCLEANLINESS

Clean and smooth as a peeled onion —O. Henry

Clean and well-kept as a cemetery —Karl Shapiro

(Her face) clean and white as a handkerchief —John Ashbery

Clean as a Band-Aid —Max Apple

SHOES GLEAMING LIKE BEER BOTTLES

Clean as a bleached bone —Wallace Stegner

Clean as a convent cell —Vita Sackville-West

Clean as a hound's tooth
—American colloquialism, attributed to New England

(His heart felt) clean as a new green leaf —Stephen Vincent Benét

Clean as a New England kitchen —Anon

Clean as a newly laundered sheet —Rosamund Pilcher
Pilcher uses the "Clean as a sheet" simile to describe the
smoothness and cleanliness of sand when the tide is out in
a story entitled *The White Birds.*

Clean as a new pin of every penny of debt —Sir Walter Scott

Clean as a penny —William Robertson
A much used simile to describe anyone who is neatly and
cleanly dressed.

Clean as a pig's whistle
—American colloquialism, attributed to New England
Just plain "Clean as a whistle," is said to stem from the
fact that it takes a clean dry whistle to produce a good
sound.

Clean as a piglet bathed in milk —Mary Gordon

Clean as a rose is after rain —James Whitcomb Riley

Clean as a toilet bowl —Lincoln Kirstein

(The woman was as) clean as a white rose in the morning gauze of
dew —Carl Sandburg

Clean as driftwood —Robert Hass

(Legs) clean as marble —Beryl Markham

Clean as new grass when the old grass burns —Carl Sandburg

Clean as water pouring from a silver tap —Tennessee Williams

Dirty as a glass roof in a train station —Leonard Cohen

Dust balls sail like galleons [on a carpet] on the dry sea
—Robert Irwin

Fingernails ... like watch crystals —Walker Percy

Immaculate as a laboratory —Ben Ames Williams

Spotless as naked innocence —John Smith

The water's (of swimming pool) like bouillabaisse. It's got more
things in it than Macy's window —Noël Coward

CLEVERNESS
See: ALERTNESS

CLICHE
See: ORIGINALITY, MAXIMS AND SAYINGS

CLINGING
See: RELATIONSHIPS

CLOTHING
See: CLOTHING ACCESSORIES; CLOTHING, ITS FIT

CLOTHING ACCESSORIES

Boots that shone like a well-rubbed table —Stephen Vincent Benét

A collar that looked like a pancake flapping around my head
and ... made me look like a pregnant penguin —Elizabeth Taylor

Glasses as thick as the bottom of a pop bottle —George Garrett

Handkerchief hoisted like a brave little flag from his breast pocket
—Vicki Baum

Hat big as an Easter cake —Joyce Cary

A hat ... perched right on top of her head, like a mushroom
—Roald Dahl

Impenetrably black sunglasses like Batman's mask —John Rechy

Shoes gleaming like beer bottles —Loren D. Estleman

Shoes ... shined up like patent leather —George Garrett

Shoes sticking out like tongues beneath the long black robe
—Helen Hudson

Silk, like wrinkled skins on scalded milk
—Oliver Wendell Holmes, Sr.

Socks which fell like a couple of woolen concertinas over his dusty
shoes —John Mortimer

Straw hat with a bow on it like the sails of a windmill
      —L. P. Hartley

A ten-gallon hat like a walking mushroom —Truman Capote

Tie ... loose and awry like a long lazy tongue ... wore a costume as distinctive as a ballet dancer's tutu —Van Wyck Mason

Ties pulled loose from their collars, like weary gamblers
      —Graham Swift

CLOTHING, ITS FIT

Bathing suit so tight that it seemed any moment she would burst out of it like a cooked frankfurter —George Garrett

A blanket wrapped around her body as tight as a cigar
      —Scott Spencer

(Clothes which) clung like refractory cobwebs —Patrick White

A coat which seems to fit her as her life fits, barely, inadvertently, not at all —Herbert Morris

Everything she wears fits like a saddle on a sow —Harold Adams

(Her bathing suit that) fit her like a sack —Flannery O'Connor

Fit like a saddle fits a sow —Anon
         An alliterative putdown for the way a person is dressed. It dates back to sixteenth century England and became an American colloquialism shortly after it crossed the ocean.

[A dress] fits like the skin of a grape —Charles Raddock describing Jacqueline Susann's outfit in a play, *Between the Covers.*
         Raddock's scathing review commented that the lines of the dress were the play's only good lines.

Fits you like flannel washed in hot suds —O. Henry

Fitted her like a duck's foot in the mud
      —American colloquialism, attributed to New England

Her coat fit her like a cheese box —Mary Gordon

Her garments seeming to flutter round her like draperies
      —Barbara Pym

Her halter top that cradled her breasts like a hammock
      —Phyllis Naylor

Her sleeves dropped like a sigh —Anaïs Nin

Her slip was stretched over her breast, as firmly and simply as linen over an embroidery frame —Boris Pasternak

Her stockings hung about her ankles like Hamlet's when he exposed himself to Ophelia and called her a whore —Leonard Michaels

His [shirt] collar was so tight, it felt like a string cutting his neck —Dan Wakefield

His jacket hung on him like a scarecrow —Ross Macdonald

His pants hung as full as an Arab tent from his global stomach —William Diehl

His shirt fit him like a sail at the back —Philip Gerard

His short-sleeved shirt and short pants fit him like a dirty sack —James Crumley

(The uniform) hung slack like a castoff on a scarecrow —Paige Mitchell

Jeans fit like a rubber glove —W. P. Kinsella

The jeans fitted like hand-me-ups from a younger, thinner sister —Margaret Millar

(A healthy blonde with) jeans so tight her hipbones looked like towel hooks —Erma Bombeck

[Pants] tight ... like elastic bandages —Ann Petry

Jeans that made his legs look like tree trunks. The bright green fishnet shirt he wore made him look even more like a tree —Ann Beattie

Legs ... hung straight and rigid as if she had iron shinbones and ankles —William Faulkner

She wears her clothes as if they were thrown on her with a pitchfork —Jonathan Swift

Snugger than the bark to a dead maple —Anon

(A yellow) tee shirt that clings to her arms, breast and round belly like the skin of a sausage —Russell Banks

They [too-large trousers] make you look like an elephant that has lost weight —Penelope Gilliatt

Tight blue jeans that grip her behind like two hands
    —Charles Bukowski

Tight ... like a lobster shell —W. S. Gilbert

Trousers and jacket droop like a tailor's nightmare
    —T. Coraghessan Boyle

Trousers ... as wrinkled at the crotch as if he'd had them pressed
    that way —Harvey Swados

The trousers fitted her legs closely, but she could come out of them
    as though she were peeling a banana —MacDonald Harris

CLOUD(S)
See: CLOUD MOVEMENTS

CLOUD MOVEMENTS
See also: RAIN

Black clouds lumbered off westward like ghosts of buffalo
    —W. P. Kinsella

A billow of woolly clouds ... like milk spilt on a table, commenced
    to cascade down the mountain side —F. van Wyck Mason

Clouds floating around [in the sky] ... like suds in a pan
    —Helen Hudson

Clouds ... gathered like great boneless birds —Hugh Walpole

Clouds hastening like messengers through heaven
    —John Hall Wheelock

Clouds rising like a tide of ink just beneath the moon —John Farris

Clouds rose up from the meadows like soft creamy wings seeking the
    bodies of gigantic birds —Rita Mae Brown

Clouds sailing ... like a flock of birds taking flight to distant lands
    —Hans Christian Andersen

Clouds that hung, like banners —Edgar Allan Poe

Clouds that swam like lonely white fish in the sky —Robie Macauley

Clouds would part like windows, as though to air the sky
    —Boris Pasternak

Gray clouds ballooned down like the dirty underside of a great circus tent —Brian Moore

Inky clouds, like funeral shrouds, sail over the midnight skies —W. S. Gilbert
> Gilbert contributed many a simile to the famous Gilbert and Sullivan operettas, like this one from *Ruddigore*.

Rain clouds scudded past like big ships sailing out of harbor —Brian Moore

Lonely clouds were floating above, like guests strolling above the sky —Yehuda Yaari

A rolling cloud boiled onto the horizon like black liquid —Dorothy Francis

The sailing clouds went by, like ships upon the sea —Henry Wadsworth Longfellow

There's a feathery little cloud floatin' by like a lonely leaf on a big blue stream —Oscar Hammerstein, II, lyrics for "Two Little People" from *Carousel*

Troops of small feathery white clouds ranged over the sky, like grazing herds of the gods —Thomas Mann

CLUMSINESS
See: AWKWARDNESS

COLDNESS
See: RESERVE

COLLAPSE
See also: DISINTEGRATION

Caved in like a sinkhole —Jonathan Valin

Caving in like a mud dam —Kurt Rheinheimer

(Periods in one's life that once seem important until you look back on them) collapsed as flat as packing cartons —Jonathan Penner
> In a short story entitled *Emotion Recollected in Tranquility*, the author tied collapsed packing carton comparison to the collapse of part of one's life.

Collapsed like an elephant pierced by a bullet in some vital spot —Kingsley Amis

Collapsed like a rotten tree —Erich Maria Remarque

Collapsed like a rump-shot dog —T. Coraghessan Boyle

(Half a dozen career daydreams) collapsed like a telescope —Thomas McGuane

Collapsed like a wounded soldier in the mud —Z. Vance Wilson

Collapsed to the floor like a tent that has had all the guy ropes and poles removed at the same time —Jimmy Sangster

Collapsed upon the sea as if his body had telescoped into itself, like a picnic beaker —Joyce Cary

(His body) collapsed vertically like a punctured concertina —Frank Ross
> An older, simpler variation by Irving Cobb: "Fold up like a concertina."

(One day would) collapse like a peony —Jilly Cooper

Collapse like a sack of meal —Anon
> The sack of meal as a comparison linked to falling, collapsing or toppling has seeded so much use and extension that one can only list some of its in-print appearances: "Went over like a sack of meal" (Frank O'Connor); "Fall heavily, like a sack of meal" (S. J. Perelman); "Went down ... like an empty sack" (John M. Synge); "Dropped, like a flour sack falling from a loft" (Gerald Kersh). Most commonly overheard in everyday conversation is "Collapse like an empty paper bag."

Collapse like a snowman in the sun —Anon

Collapse like a tent when the pole is kicked out from under it —Loren D. Estleman

Collapse ... like empty garments —Joyce Cary Collapse like sandcastles against the ocean tide —Anon

Collapse like a punctured blister —Mike Sommer

Collapse like the cheeks of a starved man —Charles Dickens

Collapsing like a cardboard carton thrown on a bonfire —Margaret Atwood

Comes apart [no longer able to control laughter] like a slow-ripping seam —Sharon Sheehe Stark

Crashed on the leather sofa, going down like a B-52 with a bellyful of shrapnel —Jonathan Kellerman

[Souvenirs of a romance] crumble like flowers pressed in dictionaries —Judith Martin

Crumble like tinder —Anon

(A small white house that was) crumbling at the corners like stale cake left out on a plate —Jonathan Valin

Crumbling like one of those dry sponge cakes —Francis King

Crumpled like caterpillars on mulberry leaves —James Purdy

(She) crumpled like paper crushed in a fist and began to cry —Harold Adams

Crumpled up as if he were a paper flower —Ruth Prawer Jhabvala

Crumples like a used-up piece of paper —Daphne Merkin

[Gulls] downed ... like a tumbled kite —John Hall Wheelock

(The bird) dropped like an arrow —Leo Tolstoy

Dropped like an elephant's trunk —Eudora Welty

Dropped like one hit in the head by a stone from a sling —Eudora Welty

Drops like a piece of flotsam —T. Coraghessan Boyle

Falling as gently and slowly as a kite —Elizabeth Hardwick

Fall over like a frozen board —William H. Gass

Fall to the floor like misfired cannon balls —John Updike

(She's welcome to climb with man if she wishes ... and) fall with a crash like a trayful of dishes —Amy Lowell

Fell as low as a toad —American colloquialism, attributed to Midwest

(Accents of peace and pity) fell like dew (upon my heart) —Percy Bysshe Shelley

Fell ... like insects knocked off by a gardener's spray —Derek Lambert

Fell like one who is seized with sleep —Dante Alighieri

Collapse

Fell slowly forward like a toppling wall —Stephen Crane

Fell to her knees like a nun seeking sudden forgiveness
—James Crumley

Flopped like the ears of a dog —Edgar Allan Poe

Folded up like a pocket camera —George Ade

Fold up like a cheap camera —Anon

[First baseman] goes down slow as a toppling tree —W. P. Kinsella

Going under [dying] like shipwrecked sailors —Thomas Keneally

(Let life face him with a new demand on his understanding and
then watch him) go soggy, like a wet meringue
—D. H. Lawrence

He dropped like a bullock, he lay like a block —Rudyard Kipling

(When I tell him he must go, he suddenly) hits the floor like a
toppled statue —Louise Erdrich

Hit the floor like an anvil —Joseph Wambaugh

(Slumped to the floor and) lay there like a punctured balloon
—Myron Brinig
> Some variations on the balloon comparison: "I was going
> down ... like a child's balloon as it gradually lets out air"
> (Eugene Ionesco's play, *The Stroller in the Air*); "Ripples to
> the pavement like a deflated balloon" from T.
> Coraghessan Boyle's novel, *Water Music*.

Like an emptying tube, after a couple of minutes he collapses
—Erich Maria Remarque

Over she went ... like a little puff of milkweed —Eudora Welty

Pitched forward like a felled tree —Oakley Hall

(His heaving bulk suddenly) sagged, like a sail bereft of wind
—Jan Kubicki

[Old man] scrunched like an old gray fetus —Grace Paley

Thudded like a bird against the glass wall —Ross Macdonald

Topple over like a doll with a round base —Wilfrid Sheed

Tumble down like a house of cards —George Du Maurier

The many twists on tumbling, falling or collapsing cards as comparisons include Robert Browning's ''Fell like piled-up cards'' and Edith Wharton's ''Collapsed like a playing card.''

Tumbled down like the Tower of Babel —Bernard Malamud

We fell to the carpet like leaves circling in a light wind
—James Crumley

Went down like a ninepin —Edith Wharton
This still popular simile to describe a sudden fall was probably in use before its appearance in Wharton's story, *The Pelican*.

Went down like a plumb line —Lawrence Durrell

Went down like a pole-axed steer —Donald Seaman

Went over [after being hit] like a paper cut-out and lay just as flat as one —Cornell Woolrich

COLORS
See: BLACK, BLUE, BRIGHTNESS, BROWN, GREEN, PALLOR, PINK, RED, WHITE

COMMONPLACE
See also: FAMILIARITY

As corny as Kansas in August ... as normal as blueberry pie —Oscar Hammerstein II, from lyric for *South Pacific*.
Another famous simile from the same score: ''High as a flag on the Fourth of July.''

As daily as bread —Thomas Lux

Common as adultery, and hardly less reprehensible
—Lord Altringham
Societal changes have seeded ''Common as divorce'' and ''Common as sex before marriage.''

Common as bag ladies on city streets —Anon

(Angels were as) common as birds or butterflies —Donald Justice

Common as dentists who molest female patients —Loren D. Estleman

Common as dirt —American colloquialism attributed to New England

A popular variation: "Common as mud."

Common as frozen dinners —Anon
Another up-and-coming one from our fast food age:
"Common as microwave dinners."

Common as get out —William Hazlitt
This has become known and used as "Common as all get-out."

Common as graduation parties in June —Anon

Common as hot spells in July and snowflakes in winter
—Elyse Sommer

Common as pig's tracks —H. W. Thompson
American folklore has simplified this to "Common as dirt."

Common ... as potatoes —Hugh Walpole

Common as the highway —John Ray's *Proverbs*

Common as the New York cockroach
—Erik Sandberg-Diment, writing about the increased use and availability of personal computer clones of the original IBM model, *New York Times*, December 12, 1986
New Yorkers might well argue that they have no exclusiveness when it comes to cockroaches.

(Charles's conversation was) commonplace as a street pavement
—Gustave Flaubert

Commonplace as birth —Anon

Commonplace as slumber —Phyllis McGinley

Ordinary as walking a straight line —Lee K. Abbott

Taken for granted like a nose bob —Alistair Cooke, *New York Times* interview, referring to the television teleprompter, January 1, 1985

Traditional as a seven-layer wedding cake —Jonathan Valin

COMPACTNESS
See: BREVITY

COMPASSION
See: PITY

COMPATIBILITY/INCOMPATIBILITY
See: BELONGING

COMPETENCE
See: ACCOMPLISHMENT

COMPETITION

As competitive as two dogs after a bitch in heat —Anon

Asking him to compete fairly is like asking a hungry lion to leave the lambs alone —Mike Sommer

Competition is like sugar sprinkled on cobbler pie —Elmer Kelton

A non-competitive businessman is like an honest crook —Elyse Sommer

Playing tennis without keeping score is like apple pie sans la mode —Anon

COMPLACENCY
See: CONTENTMENT

COMPLAINTS
See: CRITICISM

COMPLEXION
See also: WRINKLES

A blotchy complexion like salami —Jilly Cooper

The cluster of red veins, like Rorschach patterns, sticking out on his cheeks —Henry Van Dyke

Complexion ... as red as a boiled shrimp —Kenzaburo Oë

Complexion ... as smooth as white mushrooms —Bobbie Ann Mason

Complexion dark as cholera —Cynthia Ozick

Complexion like a choir boy's —Robert Campbell

A complexion like the blossoms of apples —W. B. Yeats

A complexion like the moon at short range —Harry Prince

Complexion ... like the skin on porridge —Frank Swinnerton

Complexion like twelve-year-old Scotch going down
—Loren D. Estleman

Complexion the color of porridge —Christopher Isherwood

Complexion, which had become pale in the dimness of the
house ... shone as if it had been varnished
—Guy de Maupassant

Face glistened as if it were covered with scar tissue from a newly
healed burn —Kenzaburo Oë

Face ... pock-marked like a wall against which men had stood to
take the bullets of a firing squad —Penelope Gilliatt

Her complexion in its pallor showed clear as a lily petal
—Ethel Cook Eliot

His face had an unnatural smoothness as though it were massaged
and nourished with cold creams —W. Somerset Maugham

Suntan that looks likkeit was done on a rotisserie —Tom Wolfe
Wolfe is describing actor Cary Grant.

The thin veins on his massive cheeks were like the engraving on
gilt-edged securities —Ludwig Bemelmans

A tracery of red veins, distinct as mapped rivers and tributaries,
showed on his cheeks —Anne Tyler

COMPLEXITY

(He was) as complex as the double helix and sometimes as simple as
a paramecium —Mike Sommer

As complicated and unavailing as a cut-out paper snowflake
—Eudora Welty

As complicated as a full-born, rollicking infidelity right in their own
homes —Richard Ford

As complicated as the flush valve on a water closet —Anon

[A family's history] convoluted as a Greek drama —Gail Godwin

(Character is as) detailed, as intricately woven as the intricate
Oriental carpets and brocades in Freud's office
—Vincent Canby, *New York Times*, September 24, 1986

SUNTAN THAT LOOKS LIKE IT WAS DONE
ON A ROTISSERIE

The Oriental carpet and brocade comparison was particularly apt for Canby's review of *Nineteen-Nineteen*, a movie about two Freud patients, with many scenes in Freud's heavily carpeted Vienna office.

The detail was astonishing, like the circuits on a computer chip
—James Morrow

(By marriage she had to assume a whole new family of blood kin) elaborate as a graph —George Garrett

(Their relationship seemed as) intricate as a DNA blueprint
—Joseph Wambaugh

To say Freud was complex is like saying Tolstoy could write —Anon

COMPLIMENTS
See: FLATTERY

COMPOSITION
See: MUSIC

COMPREHENSIBLENESS
See: CLARITY

CONCISENESS
See: BREVITY

CONDEMNATION
See: CRITICISM

CONFIDENCE
See: TRUST/MISTRUST

CONFUSION
See: BEWILDERMENT

CONNECTIONS

Attached [to an idea] like a slug to its shell —Paige Mitchell

Bonds (of family) as immutable as a tribal code —Anon

Bonds frail as spider webs —George Garrett
   See also: FRAGILITY

The bonds which I had thought bound me ... turned out to be as flimsy and insubstantial as a kindergartner's paper chain
—Harvey Swados

Bound as the sun to the world's wheel
    —Algernon Charles Swinburne

Bound together as two trees with interwoven roots —Edith Wharton

Bound together ... like stepsisters with completely different
    backgrounds forced to live together under the same roof
    —Margaret Millar
        The comparison as used in the mystery novel, *Beyond This
        Point Are Monsters,* is applied to cities which are different
        in sight and sound but bound together by geography and
        economics.

(Different professional groups in an organization) bundled together, as
    carrots or sticks of asparagus are bundled together
    —Frank Swinnerton

Closely connected ... as a mother with her baby's belly button
    —Bertold Brecht

Connect like a recurring musical leitmotif —Anon

Drawn together and held like snowflakes in a glass glove
    —Arthur A. Cohen

(Lives and limbs) entwined like the roots of trees —John Logan

Held together as backbone holds together the ribs and limbs and
    head to a body —H. G. Wells

Holds together like a quilt —James Dickey

Joined together as in a wedding of rivers —George Garrett

Linked [together] like mountain climbers —Frank Swinnerton

Linked together by bonds as deep and mysterious as those which tie
    the mother to her young —Harvey Swados

Lives crossing like swords —Paige Mitchell

Mixes like alphabet soup —Diane Ackerman

Roped together like climbers on a rockface —Lawrence Durrell

CONSCIENCE
See also: REGRET

A bad conscience is a kind of illness, in the sense that pregnancy is
    an illness —Friedrich Nietzsche

Conscience

A clear conscience is like a wall of brass —Latin proverb

Conscience as big as the Alps —Walter Goodman, *New York Times* movie review, May 27, 1987

Conscience ... a terrifying little sprite, that bat-like winks by day and wakes by night —John Wolcott

Conscience is God's presence in man —Anon

Conscience is like a sun-dial; if you let truth shine upon it, it will put you right —Hamilton Bower
> The author expanded upon the simile as follows: "But you may cover it over so that no truth can fall upon it, or you may let false light gleam upon it and then it will lead you astray."

(His) conscience rose like a shining light —Honoré de Balzac

Conscience wide as hell —William Shakespeare

Gets little attacks of conscience, like hot flashes —Jonathan Valin

Going through life with a conscience is like driving your car with the brakes on —Budd Schulberg

A healthy conscience is like a wall of bronze —Erasmus

He that has a scrupulous conscience, is like a horse that is not well wayed [well-taught]; he starts at every bird that flies out of the hedge —John Selden
> The word 'hath' from the original simile has been modernized to 'has.'

The sting of conscience, like the gnawing of a dog at a bone, is mere foolishness —Friedrich Nietzsche

Weather-beaten conscience ... as elastic as his heart —Arthur Train

CONSPICUOUSNESS
See: OBVIOUSNESS, VISIBILITY

CONSTANCY
See: LOYALTY/DISLOYALTY

CONTAGION
See: SPREADING

CONTEMPT

As the air to a bird or the sea to a fish, so is contempt to the contemptible —William Blake

Contempt is a kind of gangrene, which if it seizes one part of a character, it corrupts all the rest by degrees —Samuel Johnson

(His voice had turned idle,) contemptuous, uncaring, like a king throwing a handful of coppers at the feet of children —Borden Deal

Disdain as a gourmet disdains TV dinners —Anon

Disdain as a lover of literature disdains a potboiler —Anon

(He started) handling my exam paper like it was a turd —J. D. Salinger

(A waiter who) looked as if he had been cornstarched in arrogance —Pat Conroy

More haughty than the devil —William Shakespeare

Scorn will curl suddenly round silent corners like bell-less bicycles —W. R. Rodgers

Sneered, like a waiter in a French restaurant who has just taken an order for a Chardonnay that he disdains —Ira Berkow, *New York Times*, September 29, 1986, about Jim Rice, a baseball hitter

They treat me like a snakebit cowpoke just in from the range —Thomas Zigal

Watch ... distastefully, as though she were a cigar being smoked in the presence of a lady without permission —Penelope Gilliatt

CONTENTMENT

(There she lay) as complacently feminine as a turtle-dove —Christopher Isherwood

Content as a Parsee priestess who had duly paid her morning devotions to the deity —Israel Zangwill

Content as a tick sitting quietly on a tree and living off a tiny drop of blood plundered years before —Patrick Suskind

(She wanted us to be as) content as trees in a rain forest —Max Apple

Contentment

Contented as a baby on a schedule —Hollis Summers

Contented as a cobra full of warm milk —Rupert Hughes

Content ... like a little white kitty in a basket —Eudora Welty

Feel rewarded, like a gardener who's cutting roots
    —Margaret Sutherland

Hummed ... like a cook with things coming out right
    —William Beechcroft

(She prospered and could expect to prosper more ... but) like
    someone in exile, uncertain of deliverance, she was restless and
    dissatisfied —Robert Henson

Looked about as satisfied as a millionaire's mistress
    —William Beechcroft

Mood of complacency ... like a man who, having been under dire
    threat of burglary, suddenly increases his insurance and changes
    all the locks on his house and is convinced that these
    emergencies will make him for ever immune —H. E. Bates

Pleased as a cat with two tails
    —American colloquialism, attributed to New England
        A common variation: "Proud as a dog with two tails."

Psyche ... topped up like the tanks of the automobiles
    —Frank Conroy
        The simile from Conroy's novel, *Stop-Time*, refers to more
        than one automobile because the scene is in a gas station.
        Removed from this context, "Topped up like the tank of an
        automobile" would have the same meaning.

Satisfying as getting a refund on your income tax —Anon

Sitting pretty, like a batter with three balls and no strikes against
    him —James Thurber

Take it (killing and bloodshed) in like the sun shines and the rain
    falls —Eileen O'Casey

Wears contentment like a wreath —Barbara Howes

CONTINUITY

Continuity

As never ending as a brook —Anon

Bottomless as Hell —Ben Jonson

Bottomless as the foundation of the Universe —Thomas Carlyle

Boundless as the sea —William Shakespeare

Boundless as the wind —Jonathan Swift

(Restaurants) come and go steadily as Bedouin tribesmen
    —Ed McBain

A constant figure in her life, like a white knight or a black mammy
    —Julia Whedon

Continued as on an endless escalator —Eleanor Clark

Continuous as an endless circle —Anon

Continuous as the beat of death —Amy Lowell

Continuous as the stars that shine and twinkle on the Milky Way
    —William Wordsworth
          A variation: "Infinite as the stars'

Endless as prairies —Margaret Atwood

Endless as the line around a circle —Anon

Eternal as mediocrity —James G. Huneker

(She was, for him,) eternal like the seasons —Dorothea Straus

Go on like an eternal flame —Lyn Lifshin

Had gone on like a bad sleep —Jean Stafford

Keeps rolling along like the Big River —John Gross

Lived on like names in a legend —John Hall Wheelock

Numberless as the sands of the desert —American colloquialism
          An equally popular variation is "Numberless as the fish in
          the sea."

Steadily as a shell secretes its beating leagues of monotone
    —Hart Crane

Timeless as a churchyard —Sharon Sheehe Stark

CONTROL

Abstinent as a reformed sinner —Anon

Censorship is like an appendix. When it is inert it is useless; when active it is extremely dangerous —Maurice Edelman

Censorship, like charity, should begin at home —Clare Booth Luce
The combinations for this comparison are virtually limitless.
See also: BELIEFS, CRITICISM, PEACE

Censure is like the lightning which strikes the highest mountains —Baltasar Gracian

Censurious ... as a superannuated sinner —William Wycherly

Circumscribed like a dog chained to a tree —Beth Nugent

(Always trying to) confine things into the shape of a phrase, like pouring water into a sewer —Vita Sackville-West

(Ordered lives) contained like climbers huddled to a rock ledge —W. D. Snodgrass

Feel like a dog on a short leash —Joanne Kates, *New York Times*/Hers, September 18, 1986

He kept it [emotional feeling] rigidly at the back of his mind, like a fruit not ripe enough to eat —H. E. Bates

He that has no rule over his own spirit is like a city without walls —*The Holy Bible/Proverbs*
'Hath' has been modernized to 'has.'

Imprison like a stone girdle —Anon

Irrepressible, like flame catching kindling —George Garrett

I wear my chains [of sexual and social roles] like ornaments, convinced they make a charming jingle —Phyllis McGinley

Manageable as chess pieces —George Meredith

[My wife's society] oppressed me like a spell —Edgar Allen Poe
In another version of the tale *Morelia*, Poe kept the comparison but changed the frame of reference to the mystery of the wife's manner instead of her company.

Suffocating as the interior of a sepulchre —Anon

The restriction is like saying to an avid reader he can't see a book for nine months —Kent Hannon on ruling restricting basketball practice for players who don't have C average, *New York Times*, July 21, 1986

To be with her was like living in a room with shuttered windows —Edith Wharton

Uncontrollable as a swift tide with a strong undertow —Anon

Uncontrollable as the wind —Robert Traver

CONVERSATION

Conversation ... like dialogue from a play that had run too long and the acting had gone stale —John McGahern

Conversation ... rapid and guttural as gunfire —Harvey Swados

The conversations ... behaved like green logs, they fumed but would not fire —Truman Capote

Conversation should be like a salad, composed of various ingredients, and well stirred with salt, oil, and vinegar —Joaquin Setanti

Conversation ... should flow, like waters after summer showers, not as if raised by mere mechanic powers —William Cowper

Conversation ... sweet as clover —Ogden Nash

The conversation was just like clockwork. It recurred regularly, except that there was no need to wind anything up
—Walter De La Mare

Conversed in whispers ... like doctors consulting on a difficult case
—Jean Stafford

Conversed like tennis players, back and forth, stroke for stroke
—Jessamyn West

Converse with himself, like a prisoner alone in his cell or like a wayfarer lost in a wilderness —Joseph Conrad

Cutting off the small talk with an opening question like a serve
—Elizabeth Spencer

Discourses on subjects above our comprehension ... it's like listening to an unknown language —Henry Fielding
See also: BEWILDERMENT

A false and most unnatural kind of chatting, like fighters meeting at a weigh-in —Norman Mailer
> Mailer was describing the beginning of an interview with Mike Wallace.

From time to time ... talk becomes effective, conquering like war, widening the boundaries of knowledge like an exploration —Robert Louis Stevenson

Gabbing like college girls with the handsomest boy on campus waiting at the curb in big convertibles —Richard Ford

Good communication is as stimulating as black coffee, and just as hard to sleep after —Anne Morrow Lindbergh

Good conversation, like any game, calls for equals in strength —Jacques Barzun

Good conversation unrolls itself like the spring or like the dawn —W. B. Yeats

A good talk is like a good dinner: one assimilates it —Jerome K. Jerome

Good talk is ... like an impromptu piece of acting where each should represent himself to greatest advantage —Robert Louis Stevenson

Good talk is like good scenery—continuous, yet constantly varying, and full of the charm of novelty and surprise —Randolph S. Bourne

He [the inveterate punster] followed conversation as a shark follows a ship, or, to shift the metaphor, he was like Jack Horner and stuck in his thumb to pull out a pun —Stephen Leacock

(For a person accustomed to obsequiousness and flattery) his conversation is by much too strong, like mustard in a child's mouth —Hester Lynch Thrale
> Thrale thus targeted Samuel Johnson's brusque manner.

(She) hit on the commonplace like a hammer driving a nail into the wall. She plunged into the obvious like a clown in a circus jumping through a hoop —W. Somerset Maugham
> Maughams's biting simile describes a dull conversationalist in his story, *Winter Cruise*.

In conversation ... like playing on the harp; there is much in laying the hands on the strings to stop their vibration as in twanging them to bring out the music —Oliver Wendell Holmes, Sr.

In married conversation as in surgery, the knife must be used with care —Andre Maurois, February, 1955
    See also: MARRIAGE

The joke went on and on ... scaring away any other kind of conversation like a schoolyard bully —William H. Gass

Like the alternating patches of sun and shade that fell on the windshield as the clouds skidded overhead, the conversation inside the pickup went by fits and starts —Phyllis Naylor

(Their habit was to engage in this) mock banter, where they slipped truths into their jokes ... like filling cream puffs
    —David R. Slavitt

Natural talk, like ploughing, should turn up a large surface of life, rather than dig mines —Robert Louis Stevenson
        Stevenson elaborated on his simile as follows: "Masses of experience, anecdote, incident, crosslights, quotation, historical instances, the whole flotsam and jetsam of two minds forced in and upon the matter at hand from every point of the compass, and from every degree of mental elevation and abasement, these are the materials with which talk is fortified, the food on which the talkers thrive."

CONVICTION
See: BELIEFS

COOKERY
See: FOOD AND DRINKS

CORPULENCE
See: FATNESS

CORRECTNESS
See also: TRUENESS/FALSENESS, REPUTATION

Accurate as a hole in one —Anon
    See also: GOLF

Accurately as a geometrician —V. S. Pritchett

As scrupulous as a well-trained tailor —Robert Penn Warren

Exact as a blueprint —Anon

Exact as the technical jargon of a trade —Aldous Huxley

More exacting than a pasha with thirty wives —Guy de Maupassant

Proper as a butler —Charles Simmons

Respectable as Jane Austen —Marge Piercy

Right as a well-done sum —Sylvia Plath

CORRESPONDENCE
See also: WRITERS/WRITING

Correspondences are like small clothes before the invention of suspenders; it is impossible to keep them up —Sydney Smith

Letters are like bodies, and their meaning like souls
    —Abraham Ibn Ezra

A letter that was like a poem. It was ... like listening to French it was so beautiful —Philip Roth

A lifelong sustained correspondence like a lifelong unbroken friendship or happy marriage, requires explaining: all the cards are stacked against it —Max Lerner

Little letters cozy and innocent as a baby's layette —Truman Capote

A mess of a letter ... it dribbles and mouths all over the place like Maurice Chevalier —Dylan Thomas

Printed [condolence] cards should be abolished; they're like canned music —Gwen Schwartz-Borden, director Bereavement Center, Family Service Association of Nassau County, quoted in *New York Times* article on bereavement notes, November 24, 1986

The time is coming when letter writing with pen and ink and sent as a personal message from one person to another will be as much of a rarity as the gold pocket watch carried on a chain —Andy Rooney

A woman's love letters are like her child. They belong to her more than to anybody else —Edith Wharton

Writing to you is like corresponding with an aching void
    —Groucho Marx

Your letters ... they're like telegrams —Dorothy Parker

COST
See also: ADVANTAGEOUSNESS

As cheap as pearls are costly —Robert Browning

Charge like a brain surgeon —Saul Bellow

Cheap as dirt —F. E. Smedley

Cheap as excuses —Anon

Cheap as lies —William Shakespeare

Cheap as old clothes —Horace Walpole

Cheap as old clothes used to be —Elyse Sommer
> An update of Horace Walpole's simile above, inspired by a change in both economic conditions and the upgraded status of old clothes.

Expensive as building an atomic reactor —Robert Traver

Expensive as Manhattan real estate —Anon

Expensive as sin —Anon

COUNSEL
See: ADVICE

COURTESY
See: BEHAVIOR

CRAZINESS
See: MADNESS

CREDIT

Credit buying is much like being drunk. The buzz happens immediately ... the hangover comes the day after
—Dr. Joyce Brothers

Credit is like a looking glass ... once cracked [it] can never be repaired again —Sir Walter Scott
> An anonymous rhymed version of this is "Credit, like a lookin-glass, broken once, is gone, alas!" and, from John Ray's *Proverbs* there's "Credit lost is like Venice glass broken."

Credit is like chastity, they can both stand temptation better than suspicion —Josh Billings

Credit

Creditors buzz like locusts —Anaïs Nin

Debts are like children: the smaller they are the more noise they make —Spanish proverb

The first step in debt is like the first step in falsehood, involving the necessity of going on in the same course, debt following debt, as lie follows lie —Samuel Smiles

It's [borrowing] like anticipating one's income, and making the future bear the expenses of the past
—Bartlett's Dictionary of Americanisms

Just as in the relations between creditor and debtor there is always an element of the disagreeable that can never be overcome, for the very reason that the one is irrevocably committed to the role of giver and the other to that of receiver; so in a sick person, a latent feeling of resentment at every obvious sign of consideration is always ready to burst forth —Stefan Zweig

Lending to the feckless is like pelting a stray dog with dumplings —Arab proverb

Crime

CRIME

Crime, like virtue, has its degrees —Jean Racine

Crimes, like lands, are not inherited —William Shakespeare

Crimes, like virtues, are their own rewards —George Farquhar

Murder, like a snowball rolling down a slope, gathers momentum as it goes —Cornell Woolrich

Murder, like talent, seems occasionally to run in families
—G. H. Lewes

Outlaws, like lovers, poets and tubercular composers who cough blood onto piano keys, do their finest work in the slippery rays of the moon —Tom Robbins

Passing statues creating new crimes is like printing paper money without anything back of it; in the one case there isn't really any more money than there was before and in the other there isn't really any more crime either —Arthur Train

Trying to find out what ultimately drove a criminal to murder is as
fruitful as trying to determine what drove fate to choose its
victims —Lucinda Franks, reviewing two books about a murder
case, *New York Times Book Review*, March 1, 1987
See also: FUTILITY

CRITICISM

(They were) as critical as a fan-club —William McIlvanney

Blaming X [one group of an industry] for the decline of business is
like blaming the iceberg for the demise of the Titanic
—Bill Soutar, *Publisher's Weekly*, 1985
Soutar was speaking specifically about poor business in his
field of soft cover book distribution.

Criticism is like champagne: nothing more execrable if bad, nothing
more excellent if good —Charles Caleb Colton

Criticism, like rain, should be gentle enough to nourish a man's
growth without destroying his roots
—Frank A. Clark, *Reader's Digest*, September, 1971

Criticizing, like charity, should begin at home —B. C. Forbes

Impersonal criticism is like an impersonal fist fight, or an impersonal
marriage, and as successful —George Jean Nathan

Like people rummaging in boxes for a knife, everyone searched deep
in his memory for a grievance —Marguerite Yourcenar

Long harangue [of complaints] ... it was like a three-hour movie with
no intermission —Elizabeth Spencer
See also: SLOWNESS

Muttering thin complaints like little children called from play
—James Crumley

Rattling off her woes like mea culpas —Rita Mae Brown

Safe from criticism as a stutter or a squint —Henry James

(Mothers) scolded in voices like amplified hens —Rumer Godden
See also: VOICES, HARSH

Shot grievances like beads across an abacus —Cynthia Ozick

143

Criticism

Sounded like a cranky old man who needs a stray Airedale to kick
—*New York Times* editorial criticizing New York Mayor Edward Koch for his remark about the Soviet government's arrest of an American journalist, September 17, 1986

Squeaking like little pigs coming out of the barn door
—Congressman Dale Lotta (Ohio), April 9, 1987

CRITICISM, DRAMATIC/LITERARY
See: WRITERS/WRITING, POETS/POETRY

Crowds

CROWDS

About as much privacy as a statue in the park —Anon

As lacking in privacy as a goldfish —Anon

Bunched and jammed together as solidly as the bristles in a brush
—Mark Twain

Came crowding like the waves of ocean, one on the other
—Lord Byron

Clustering like a swarm of bees —Amy Lowell

Crowded like a view of Venice —Frank O'Hara

Crowded [stores] like tightly woven multi-colored carpet of people
—Richard J. Meislin, *New York Times*

The crowd in the lobby [of a hotel] was frozen in poses like the chorus at the curtain of a musical comedy —Vicki Baum

The crowd scattered in all directions, like a flock of chickens among which a stone had been thrown —Aharon Megged

Feel like a pressed flower —Edith Wharton

Flocking ... like geese —Sharon Sheehe Stark

(The public was) flowing in like a river —Enid Bagnold

Huddle together like birds in a storm —Robert Graves

Jostled like two steers in the stock yards —A. R. Guerney, Jr.

Loaded up like a garbage truck —Paige Mitchell

Man ... still, like a hen, he likes his private run —W. H. Auden

Men milled everywhere, like cattle in a lightning storm
    —James Crumley

Mobs in their emotions are much like children, subject to the same tantrums and fits of fury —Euripides

No more privacy than a traffic cop —Anon

[People] packed as closely as herring in a barrel —Sholom Aleichem

Packed like a cattle pen —Paige Mitchell

The people bunched like cattle in a storm —James Crumley

People [on train] ... hanging from straps like sides of beef on a hook
    —Julio Cortzar

People [at a party] ... packed tight as a rugby scrum
    —Nadine Gordimer
        If Gordimer's story *The Smell of Death and Flowers* had
        been set in America, it might have had a football lineup for
        the rugby scrum.

People streaming from the plane like busy insects on the march
    —Sylvia Berkman

Stood packed like matches in an upright box —William Faulkner

Swarm like bees —Anon

Swarm like summer flies —William Shakespeare

(Apartments) tenanted tight as hen-houses —Barbara Howes

(Surrounded by militia ...) thick as aphids —Derek Lambert

CRUELTY

(He's always been) a bigger shit than two tons of manure
    —William McIlvanney

Cruel and cold as the judgment of man —Lord Byron

Cruel as death —James Thomson
        This is from a double simile, the second part being
        "Hungry as the grave."

Cruel as love or life —Algernon Charles Swinburne

Cruel as old gravestones knocked down and scarred faceless
    —James Wright

Cruelty

(Nothing so) cruel as panic —Robert Louis Stevenson

(She knew well the virtues of her singular attractiveness, as) cruel as shears —George Garrett

Cruel as winter —Lewis J. Bates

Crueller than hell —Algernon Charles Swinburne

Cruel, like the ostriches in the wilderness —*The Holy Bible*
> The ostrich reference appears both in *Lamentations* and the *Book of Job.*

Cruelty on most occasions is like the wind, boisterous in itself, and exciting a murmur and bustle in all the things it moves among —Walter Savage Landor

Evil, like good, has its own heroes
—François, Duc de La Rochefoucauld

Had a personality like a black hole —Jonathan Valin
> In his novel, *Natural Causes*, from which this is taken, Valin expands upon the simile with "He sucked in everything around him and gave nothing back in return."

A heart like a snake —Michael V. Gazzo

Her coarseness, her cruelty, was like bark rough with lichen
—Virginia Woolf

He's like a cobra. No conscience —William Diehl

Mean as a man who'd make knuckle-bones out of his aunt —Anon

Mean as a snake —John D. MacDonald

Mean as cat shit —James Kirkwood

Mean as cat's meat —Somerset Maugham, quoted in *New York Times Magazine* article by Thomas F. Brady, January 24, 1954

(That old scoundrel's) mean as ptomaine —Richard Ford

Mean as the man who tells his children that Santa Claus is dead
—Anon

Merciless as ambition —Joseph Joubert

Merciless as bailiffs —Erich Maria Remarque

Ordered her about like a convict —Nicholas Monsarrat

Ruthless as a Gestapo thug —Raymond Chandler

Ruthless as any sea —Beryl Markham

So mean he would steal a dead fly from a blind spider —Anon

Spiteful as a monkey —Frank Swinnerton

Spiteful as the devil —Walter Savage Landor

Treat us like mud off the bottom of the Hudson River
     —Rebecca West

Use men ruthlessly like pawns —Honoré de Balzac

Walk all over [another person] like a carpet —Elyse Sommer

Whipping and abuse are like laudanum; you have to double the dose
     as the sensibilities decline —Harriet Beecher Stowe

Wickedness burns like fire —*The Holy Bible/Isaiah*
          The above has been modernized from "Wickedness
          burneth as the fire."

Would cut me down like a piece of grass —Jimmy Sangster

CRYING
See also: GROANS AND WHISPERS, SCREAMS

Bawling like sick monkeys —Henry Miller

Cried naggingly, half-heartedly, like the grinding of a non-starting
     engine that has drained its battery —John Updike

Cries out like an Arab, high wails like a dog or human in terrible
     pain. It rises and falls like sirens going by —Robert Campbell

Cry, hopelessly and passively, like a child in a dentist's waiting room
     —William Faulkner

Cry like a rain-water spout in a shower —Charles Dickens

Crying ... muffled, like faraway nighttime waves —Z. Vance Wilson

Crying out like an abandoned infant —T. Coraghessan Boyle

(Gave a) cry like a startled sea gull —Oscar Wilde

Her eyes [when she wept] were like syphon bottles under pressure
     —Erich Maria Remarque

Her sob broke like a bubble on a pink geranium
—John Malcolm Brinnin
See also: DISINTEGRATION

Kept on crying ... like persistent rain —Elizabeth Spencer

Like a waterpot I weep —*A Broken-Hearted Gardener,* anonymous nineteenth century verse

A sad crying, like the birds going south for the winter to come —Ray Bradbury

The shrill cry of the new-born ... like the sound of the blade of a skate on ice —Angela Carter

Sobbed ... like an abandoned child —Maurice Hewlett

A sob broke the surface like a bubble of air from the bottom of a pond —Sue Grafton

Sobs ... died off softly, like the intermittent drops that end a day of rain —Edith Wharton

Sobs laboring like stones from her heaving breast —James Crumley

Sobs rippled like convulsions through her slim body —James Crumley

Thin cry [of a bluebird] like a needle piercing the ear
—Theodore Roethke

Wailed like an uneasy animal in pain —Kenneth Grahame

Weeping like a calf —François Maspero

Weeping raw as an open sausage —A. D. Winans

Wept like a fountain —Erich Maria Remarque

Wept like a gutter on a rainy day —Guy de Maupassant

Wept like a woman deceived and forsaken by a lover
—George Garrett

Whimpers like a hurt dog —Robin McCorquodale

Whine, as unctuous as old bacon grease —James Crumley

(The twangy voice was beginning to) whine like a loosening guitar string —François Camoin

CURIOSITY

Aloof curiosity like that of sixth-formers watching a sword-swallower
—Frank Swinnerton

Curious as a monkey —Anon

Curious as a two-year old —Anon

Curiosity ... like thirst —Alice McDermott

Inquisitive as a goat —Erich Maria Remarque

Inquisitive as an X-ray —Anon

Inquisitive as a reporter smelling a scoop —Elyse Sommer

Pick and pry like a doctor or archaeologist —Sylvia Plath

Poking his nose everywhere like a dog smelling out a trail
—American colloquialism

Suppressed her curiosity as if squashing a cockroach —Marge Piercy

CURSES

The captain broke loose [with oaths] upon the dead man like a
thunderclap —Jack London

Cried out a Foreign Legion of four-letter words like little prayers
—George Garrett

Cursed like a sailor's parrot —Katherine Anne Porter

Cursed like highwaymen —Stephen Crane

Curse like a drunken tinker —George Garrett

Curses are like young chickens, they always come home to roost
—Robert Southey

Curses, like processions; they return to the place from which they
have come —Giovanni Ruffini
        Probably taken from old Italian proverb.

Curses so dark they sounded like they were being fired all the way
from a ghetto of hell —Ken Kesey

Cursing and crying like some sort of fitting had busted in her mind
and this whole stream of words gushed out —Hilary Masters

Cursing like a jay —T. Coraghessan Boyle

Erupted like a volcano of profanity —Sholom Aleichem

Felt them [curse words] at the back of his tongue like dangerous little bombs —Thomas Williams

Made curses fly up like a covey of quail —George Garrett

Swear like men who were being branded —Stephen Crane

Swore like a trooper —D. M. Moir

To hear R curse was like hearing the Almighty tear through his own heavens and blow up the stars left and rightly
—Marianne Hauser

CUSTOM
See: HABIT

DAMPNESS
See: DISCOMFORT

DANCING
See also: AGILITY

As light on your feet as a fairy —Rita Mae Brown

Danced like a faun —O. Henry
O. Henry was well known for perverting and extending existing sayings. This one can be traced to Robert Lowell's "Dancing like naked fauns too glad for shame."

Danced like a wave —Dame Edith Sitwell

Danced like a wet dream —Martin Amis

Danced like sandflies —Margaret Atwood

Danced like something dark and slithery from the Argentine —P. G. Wodehouse

(People) danced, moving their bodies like thick rope —Susan Richards Shreve

Dancers swaying like wet washing in a high wind —Lawrence Durrell

Dances like a Mack truck —Cornell Woolrich

Dances like an angel —Joseph Addison

(Sometimes I think that) dancing, like youth, is wasted on the young —Max Lerner

Dancing with her must be a good deal like moving the piano or something —Ring Lardner

(Helga Danzing danced just the way she looked: big, clumsy, almost impossible to lead,) dancing with her was like pushing a weight uphill —Abraham Rothberg

(You've got) a foot movement like a baby hippopotamus trying to side-step a jab from a humming-bird ... and your knees are about as limber as a couple of Yale pass-keys —O. Henry

Pirouetting like a Baryshnikov —T. Coraghessan Boyle

Sailed like a coquettish yacht convoyed by a stately cruiser —O. Henry

You dance like there's a stone in your shoe —John Updike

DANGER

(His presence was) a foreboding, or dismal signal, like drawn blinds —Elizabeth Taylor

Dangerous as a gift from an enemy —Anon
          A twist on the Danish proverb "Gifts from enemies are dangerous."

Dangerous as cocaine —Pietro Mascagni
          The danger being described is modern music.

(I feel so many) dangers gathering round, like shadows —Davis Grubb

Feel as though I'm dancing on a volcano —Rita Mae Brown

Felt as if they were about to dive onto a postage stamp from the top of the Eiffel Tower —Fred Taylor

(One's life) hangs perilously in danger, like ripe fruit on a thin branch —Stephen Longstreet

Hazardous as sand traps for golfers —Anon

It [the need to risk] was like statistics or gambling; you had to compute probabilities —Mary McCarthy

151

In her novel, *A Charmed Life*, McCarthy expands on her simile with this sentence: "And there was always the unforeseen, the little thing you overlooked that would catch you up in the end."

The menace (of insanity) is like a warder, restricting my freedom of mind —Richard Maynard

(His) menaces ... idle as the wind —W. S. Gilbert

Menacing as a fury —Natascha Wodin

Ominous and dark as the hour before a storm —Gerald Kersh

Ominous, like waves in a gathering mid-Atlantic storm —Anon

Rode precariously, like high-wire artists —Ross Macdonald

Safe as a cow in a stockyard —Anon

Safe as a mouse in cheese —John Ray's *Proverbs*

The safe earth ... grew narrow as a grave —Phyllis Bottome

There was a feeling like a concussion in the air —Eudora Welty

This faint shadow [of danger] lay upon his life ... as discreetly as the shadow of cancer lies among cells —Thomas McGuane

Trying to maintain good relations with a Communist is like wooing a crocodile —Winston Churchill

DAY
See also: NIGHT, SLOWNESS

The afternoon droops like a hot candle —Malcolm Cowley

The afternoon sways like an elephant —Babette Deutsch
This begins a poem entitled *July Day*.

The beauty of the morning called to her like a signal bell —R. V. Cassill

Dawn came like a blanket of flowers —T. Coraghessan Boyle

The dawn came up like a Have-a-Nice-Day emblem —Tom Robbins

A day as fresh as spring itself —Wallace Stegner

(The next) day dawned like a yawning hole —Robert Barnard

The day drooped like a flag —Katherine Mansfield

The day goes by like a shadow over the heart (with sorrow where
all was delight) —Stephen Foster
> From Stephen Foster's famous "My Old Kentucky Home"
> with 'over' substituted from 'o'er' as in the original.

The day is flat and intense, like a photograph of itself
—Marge Piercy

The day [Sunday] is like wide water, without sound
—Wallace Stevens

Day like a bated breath —Sharon Sheehe Stark

A day like an endless empty sea —Delmore Schwartz

Days and nights were shuffling like lame and overweight cattle
—Don Robertson

Days are scrolls: write on them what you want to be remembered
—Bahya

Days ... arrive like crows in a field of stubble corn —Robert Hass

The days dripped away like honey off a spoon —Wallace Stegner

Days ... followed one another in an undistinguished series, growing
and then fading like the leaves on a tree —Stefan Zweig

The days go by, like caterpillars do —Johnny Mercer, opening stanza
from 1947 song, "Lazy Mood"

The days go by like film, like a long written scroll
—Maxwell Anderson

Days ... like a lengthening shadow —*The Holy Bible/Psalms*

The days, like the leaves, seemed to fly from the trees, as if this
year was intent on its own destruction
—Susan Fromberg Schaeffer

The day smelled like clear water —Joan Chase

The days pass by like a wayward tune —W. B. Yeats

Days pass like papers from a press —Wallace Stevens

The days slipped by ... like apple parings under a knife
—Stephen Vincent Benét

The days walking along higher and higher, like the way teachers line you up to have pictures taken —Lee Smith

The days were truly endless and seemed like a single black night —Barbara Reid

The day was dry, rather misty; like a day pictured in a Japanese print —Frank Swinnerton

The day was still, like a very glazed photograph —M. J. Farrell

Feel the pull of the long day, like a road he dragged behind him —Sharon Sheehe Stark

A fine morning makes you want to bust open like a pea pod —Joe Coomer

The gray winter morning descends like the huge lead-coated balloon —Jerry Bumpus

The middle of the day, like the middle of certain fruits, is good for nothing —Walter Savage Landor

Morning came like a stone breaking —Madison Smartt Bell

The morning crept out of a dark cloud like an unbidden guest uncertain of his welcome —W. Somerset Maugham

Morning ... gray like a mouse —Jessamyn West

Morning hours of inactivity ... like a beautiful sculpture-lined bridge across which I stroll from night into day, from dream into reality —Milan Kundera

(Night had died, and the) morning lay like a corpse. Like sadness, going from one end of the world to another, without a sound —Aharon Megged

My days are like a lengthening shadow —*The Holy Bible/Psalms*

One of those days that come as a surprise in the middle of winter, like a gift sent on no anniversary, so that the pleasure takes us unaware —Jean Stafford

Our days run as fast away as does the sun —Robert Herrick

Over the garden, day still hung like a pink flag —Elizabeth Bowen

The workday is finished, dead as the calendar page that bore its number —Beryl Markham

DEATH
See: DEATH, DEFINED; DEATH, FINALITY OF; ENTRANCES/EXITS;
SUDDENNESS; TIMELINESS/UNTIMELINESS

DEATH, DEFINED

Death is a black camel, which kneels at the gates of all
    —Abd-el-Kader

Death is like a fisherman who catches fish in his net and leaves
    them for a while in the water; the fish is still swimming but the
    net is around him, and the fisherman will draw him up when he
    thinks fit —Ivan Turgenev

Death is like thunder in two particulars: we are alarmed at the sound
    of it and it is formidable only from that which preceded it
    —Charles Caleb Colton

Death is simply a shedding of the physical body, like the butterfly
    coming out of a cocoon —Elisabeth Kuebler-Ross

Death, like an overflowing stream, sweeps us away
    —Abraham Lincoln

Death, like birth, is a secret of nature —Marcus Aurelius

Death, like life, is an affair of being more frightened than hurt
    —Samuel Butler

Dying is an art, like everything else —Sylvia Plath

Dying is something ghastly, as being born is something ridiculous
    —George Santayana

If a person has reached the "age of strength" [eighty years old] a
    sudden death is like dying from a kiss —*Babylonian Talmud*

Like the dew on the mountain, like the foam on the river, like the
    bubble on the fountain, you are gone, and for ever
    —Sir Walter Scott
        The above, taken from Scott's famous *The Lady of the Lake*,
        substitutes "You are gone" for the old English "Thou art
        gone."

The stroke of death is as a lover's pinch, which hurts, and is desired
    —William Shakespeare
        'Desired' has been modernized from 'desir'd.'

155

Death, Defined

(I) think of death as a sort of deleterious fermentation, like that which goes on in a bottle of Chateau Margaux when it becomes corked —H. L. Mencken

Death, Finality of

DEATH, FINALITY OF

As the cloud is consumed and vanished away: so he that goes down to the grave comes up no more —*The Holy Bible/Job*
    'Goes' is a modernization of the biblical 'goeth.'

Dead and as far away as yesterday —W. S. Gilbert

Dead as a dead mackerel —C. W. Grafton

Dead as a dodo bird
    —American colloquialism, attributed to New England

Dead as a doornail —English phrase
    Though often attributed to Shakespeare, this simile has been recorded in fourteenth century manuscripts, including those of William of Palerne and William the Werewolf.

Dead as a fried oyster —S.J. Perelman
    This is one of five different twists on the familiar "Dead as a doornail" from Perelman's spoof on cliches, *Somewhere a Roscoe.* The others used are "Dead as an iced catfish," "Dead as a stuffed mongoose," "Dead as a smoked herring," and "Dead as vaudeville." Perelman is said to have been inspired by one Robert Leslie Bellem.

Dead as a hammer —Scottish saying

Dead as a herring —Samuel Butler
    While Butler is usually credited with first using this simile, similar mention was made in a 1603 work entitled "The Bachelor's Banquet."

Dead as a turd —Stephen King

Deader than a roast turkey on Thanksgiving —Joan Hess

Dead as last year's leaves —W. S. Gilbert

DEBT
See: CREDIT

DECEPTION
See: TRUENESS/FALSENESS

DECISIONS
See: CHOICES

DECORATIVENESS
See: ATTRACTIVENESS

DECREASE

Contract, like the pupil of an eye that confronts the sun
—John Hall Wheelock

(My avarice) cooled like lust in the chill of the grave
—Ralph Waldo Emerson

Decrease like a cigar: the harder you puff on it, the shorter it gets
—Anon
    The cigar has also been likened to an actor; e. g., "An actor
    decreases like a cigar; the more you puff him, the smaller
    he gets."

Decrease like a lemon drop; the more you lick it, the less it becomes
—Anon

Decrease like hair after each decade —Mike Sommer

Devour [information] like baseball addicts devour box scores
—David E. Sanger, *New York Times*, December 14, 1985

Diminished and flat, as after radical surgery —Sylvia Plath

(All my efforts) diminish like froth —Erich Maria Remarque

Drain (as a day's happenings) like water running out of a tub
—André Dubus

Energy ... draining out like sand —May Sarton

Gobble up cash the way electronic equipment gobbles up batteries
—Anon

Goes down like an ebbing tide —Henry James
    James let the hero of his play, *Guy Domville*, use the ebbing
    tide comparison to explain the nature of his ignorance.

Go through [as bottle of pills] like a bull breaks a fence —Anon

Pared like a carrot —John Russell

157

This is often used to mean humiliation.

(The conversation was already) petering out like a smoldering cigarette end —Stefan Zweig

Receding like a threatened headache which hasn't materialized —William McIlvanney

Shrinking as violets do in summer —Thomas Moore
The original ended with "As violets do in summer's rays."

Shrinking like aches —Charles Wright

Shrivel up like the tendrils of a creeper when thrown on a bonfire —Francis King

Shrunken as a beggar's heart —Stephen Vincent Benét

Use up as fast as a ten dollar bill in the supermarket —Anon

Use up, like a cake of soap —Elyse Sommer

Wore off [feeling of self-confidence] quicker than champagne —Edith Wharton

DEEDS
See: ACTIONS

DEJECTION
See: EMOTIONS, GLOOM

DELAY
See: LINGERING

DELIBERATENESS
See: PURPOSEFULNESS

DEMOCRACY
See: GOVERNMENT

DENIAL
See: BEHAVIOR

DENSITY
See: ABUNDANCE

DEPARTURE
See: EXITS

DEPLETION
See: DECREASE

DEPRESSION
See: GLOOM

DESERTION
See: ABANDONMENT

DESIRABILITY
See also: PLEASURE

Beckoning ... like summer welcoming the swallows —Ariel Dorfman

Cherish like a secret —D. H. Lawrence

Dear as a pardon —Diane Ackerman

Dear as a remembered kiss after death —Alfred, Lord Tennyson

Dear as the mother to the son —Alfred, Lord Tennyson

(She was ...) desirable ... like a dessert. Afterward you discarded the empty plate and forgot it —Derek Lambert

(Enigmatic remarks, as elusive and as) eagerly gobbled up as currants in a bun —Robert Culff

Like a box of chocolates ... seductive and satisfying
—*Publishers Weekly* comment on a short novel
The simile expanded on the box of chocolates appeal with "Readers will want to devour it in one sitting."

Welcome as a corpse is to a coroner —Mark Twain

Welcome as a dandelion in the bosom of winter —Josh Billings

Welcome as a free tickets to a hit show —Anon

Welcome as a letter from home —Anon

Welcome as a visit from an old friend —Anon

Welcome as happy tiding after fears —Thomas Otway

Welcome as sunshine after rain —Anon
A possible inspiration for this: "Love comforteth like sunshine after rain" from Shakespeare's *Venus and Adonis.*

Welcome as the best dish in the kitchen
—H. G. Bohn's *Handbook of Proverbs*

Welcome as the flowers in May —John Ray's *Proverbs*

159

Welcomed it as a Bedouin in the desert welcomes the flies that are the herald of an oasis —Richard Selzer

DESOLATION
See: ABANDONMENT

DESTITUTION
See: POVERTY

DESTRUCTION/DESTRUCTIVENESS
See: DISINTEGRATION

DETERIORATION
See: DISINTEGRATION

DETERMINATION
See: PURPOSEFULNESS

DEVOTION
See: LOYALTY/DISLOYALTY

DICTION
See: SPEECH PATTERNS

DICTIONARIES
See: BOOKS

DIFFERENCES

Alike as the gap between Little League and Major League —Anon

Alike as an oil portrait and a polaroid snapshot —Anon

Alike as a cliche and a sonnet
   —Rod MacLeish, National Public Radio, December 29, 1986
      In his obituary on mystery writer John MacDonald, MacLeish used the simile to point out the difference between MacDonald's Travis McGee character with Raymond Chandler's Philip Marlowe.

Alike as a mom and pop grocery store and a multi-national corporation —Anon

Alike as an abacus and a computer —Anon

Alike as an elephant and a giraffe —Anon

Alike as grains of sand —Anon

Alike as human faces —Anon

WELCOMED IT AS A BEDOUIN IN THE DESERT
WELCOMES THE FLIES THAT ARE
THE HERALD OF AN OASIS

Differences

Alike as six pebbles on the beach —Eudora Welty

Alike as the gap between doing a gig at a neighborhood wedding and being on prime time TV —Anon

Alike as an apple is to a lobster —John Ray's *Proverbs*
> A variation on the same theme, also from John Ray's *Proverbs* is "As alike as an apple is to an oyster." Other entries in this section merely hint at the endless twists possible.

As like this as a crab's like an apple —William Shakespeare
> Here we have the above simile turned around, with the apple the comparison.

(In this world it is rarely possible to settle matters with an "either, or," since there are) as many gradations of emotion and conduct as there are stages between a hooked nose and one that turns up —Johann Wolfgang von Goethe

Different as a moonbeam from lightning, as frost from fire —Emily Brontë

(You and I are as) different as chalk and cheese —John Ray's *Proverbs*

Opposite as yea and nay —Francis Quarles

(Two faces) different as hot and cold —Dannie Abse

Different as three men singing the same chorus from three men playing three tunes on the same piano —G. K. Chesterton

Different as yin from yang —Harry Prince

Everything has in fact another side to it, like the moon —G. K. Chesterton

Sharply defined as salt and pepper —Anon

The difference between vivacity and wit is the same as the difference between the lightning-bug and lightning —Josh Billings

Various as the fancies of men in pursuit of a wife —James Ralph

DIFFICULTY
See: FUTILITY

DILEMMAS
See: PROBLEMS/SOLUTIONS

DIPLOMACY
See: TACT

DIRECTNESS
See: STRAIGHTNESS

DISAGREEMENT
See: AGREEMENT/DISAGREEMENT, ARGUMENT

DISAPPEARANCE
See also: DISPERSAL, ELUSIVENESS

[Food being served, vegetables] disappeared like leaves before locusts
—Charlotte Brontë

Disappeared like raindrops which fall in the ocean —John T. Morse,
about the loss of many of Oliver Wendell Holmes, Sr.'s similes
and other witticisms

Disappeared [huntsmen and hounds into a bewitched forest] like soap
bubbles —Anne Sexton

Disappeared ... like sparks dropped into wet grass —James Crumley

Disappearing like the fastest fairy who ever lived —Brian Donleavy
See also: SPEED

Disappearing, like water poured out of a wide-necked bottle
—Diane Wakoski

Disappear like a moon entering a cloud bank —Bernard Malamud

Disappear like quicksilver in the cracks —Booth Tarkington

Disappear like socks in the laundry —Elyse Sommer

Disappear like the dew on the mountain —Anon

Drift away into infinity, like a child's balloon at a circus
—Robert Penn Warren

Everybody peeled away like an onion —Official of a New York
company on reason for his firm's bankruptcy, *New York Times*,
December 12, 1986

(The vision of her early loveliness) faded from reality like dew licked
up by the sun —Elinor Wylie

Disappearance

Faded like a cloud which has outswept its rain
    —Percy Bysshe Shelley

Faded ... like dew upon the sea —Oliver Wendell Holmes, Sr.

(The restlessness in him) faded like fog before sunshine
    —Pearl S. Buck

(Light would ...) fade like a slow gray curtain dropping
    —Nelson Algren

Fades like the lustre of an evening cloud —William Wordsworth

[Awareness of children] fading like old ink —Margaret Atwood

(The season) fading like woodwind music —George Garrett

Fading like young joy —Dame Edith Sitwell

Fall away like forgiven sins —Miller Williams

(All your joys start) falling like sand through a sieve —Lorenz Hart
        Hart's lyric for "A Lady Must Live" from *America's
        Sweetheart* omitted the letter 'g' in 'falling.'

Fell away like a wall —Dudley Clendinen, *New York Times*, March
        31, 1985, about a publisher's declining advertising revenues

(Childhood and youth, friendship and love's first glow, have) fled
        like sweet dreams —Percy Bysshe Shelley

(Any thought I had for such an enterprise) fled like thunder
    —Richard Ford

Flown like a thought —John Keats

Fluttered away like flakes of snow —Louis Bromfield

[Ceremonial occasions] glide swift into shadow, like sails on the seas
    —John Greenleaf Whittier

(He was) gone again, gone like some shadow the fire had made
    —Davis Grubb

Gone as a dream is gone from a dreamer wakened with a shout
    —Lord Dunsany
        'Wakened' has been modernized from 'waked.'

Gone ... as if they had evaporated —Dorothy Canfield Fisher

164

(That moment is) gone forever, like lightning that flashed and died, like a snowflake upon the river, like a sunbeam upon the tide —Percy Bysshe Shelley

Gone from my gaze like a beautiful dream —George Linley

Gone, like the life from a busted balloon —Palmer Cox

(I am) gone like the shadow when it declines
    —*The Holy Bible/Psalms*
        The biblical 'declineth' has been modernized.

Go out ... just like a candle —Lewis Carroll

(The Contessina could no longer see him;) it was as though he had slipped from her vision, and the crack had closed above him forever —Elizabeth Bowen

(Maybe he wanted her to) lift up, blow away somewhere, like a kite —Margaret Atwood

Like a match struck on a stove ... faded and was gone —James Agee

Like a passing thought she fled —Robert Burns
        Burns' line has found its way into daily language as "Vanish like a passing thought."

Like a shadow, glided out of view —William Wordsworth

Like swallows in autumn they fled, and left the house silent —John Hall Wheelock

Lost like stars beyond dark trees —Dante Gabriel Rossetti

(Her patience) melted like snow before a blow-torch —Julia O'Faolain

(Money) melting away like butter in the sun —Bertolt Brecht

Off and away like a frightened fish —Ogden Nash

Pass as if it had never existed, like a fart in a gale of wind —Richard Russo

Pass away like clouds before the wind —William Wordsworth

Passed like a ghost from view —John Greenleaf Whittier

(The wild part of her had) perished like burned grass —Ellen Glasgow

(Life was) receding ... as the sea abruptly withdraws, abandoning a rock it has caressed too long —Françoise Sagan

Receding like a bad dream —Anon

(He felt the distress and suspicions of the previous night) receding like a tempest —George Santayana

[Sounds] receding like the image of a man between two mirrors —Frank Conroy

Sank like lead into the sea —Brian Moore

Sank to the bottom as a stone —*The Holy Bible/Exodus*

Scuttle away ... like moths —W. D. Snodgrass

(The cares that infest the day,) shall fold their tents, like the Arabs, and as silently steal away —Henry Wadsworth Longfellow

Shrank away like an ill-treated child —W. H. Auden

Shrank like an anemone —Derek Lambert

Slip away like water —Edna St. Vincent Millay

[Thoughts] slipped away ... like bushes on the side of a sheer precipice —Edith Wharton

Slipping silently away like a thief in a London fog —Jack Whitaker, ABC-TV, about the Goodyear blimp disappearing in the mist above the US Open golf tournament in San Francisco, June 20, 1987

(He had simply) vanished, like Gauguin —Lynne Sharon Schwartz

Vanished like midnight ghosts —Charles Lindbergh
    Lindbergh used the simile in 1927 to describe the flight of
    a French plane, L'Oiseau Blanc.

Vanished like some little bird that has been flushed out of the shrubbery —Mikhail Lermontov

Vanished like the last of the buffalo hunters —George Garrett

Vanished [out of his mind] like the mist before the rising sun —H. G. Wells

[The impression made upon people by a tragedy] vanishes as quickly as a delicious fruit melts in the mouth —Honoré de Balzac

Vanishes as rapidly as a road runner in a cartoon
—*New Yorker*, August 26, 1985
> In the "Talk of The Town" column, this referred to the
> speed with which a book, once finished, disappears from a
> writer's mental picture.

(Beauty) vanishing like a long sigh —George Garrett

Vanish like a changing mood —John Hall Wheelock

Vanish like a cocktail before dinner —Anon

Vanish like a dew-drop in a rose —Gerald Massey

Vanish like a ghost before the sun —P. J. Bailey

Vanish like an echo —Johann Wolfgang von Goethe

Vanish like birds in winter —George Garrett

Vanish like lightning —Henry Taylor

Vanish like plunging stars —Don Marquis

Vanish like raindrops which fall in the sea —Anon

Vanish like smoke —Percy Bysshe Shelley

Vanish like the Witch of the North —George Garrett

Vanish like white soft crowns of dandelions in the wind
—George Garrett

Vanish like writing in the sand —Anon

(My awe of Cruikback) went away like a mist in a high wind
—Gerald Kersh

DISAPPOINTMENT
See also: FACIAL EXPRESSIONS

Disappointed as a dieter who can't lose more than an ounce —Anon

Disappointed as a ghost without a house to haunt —Anon

Disappointed ... as if he'd seen his favorite teacher drunk
—Mary Gordon

Disappointing as discovering the charming man you met at a party is
gay —Anon

Disappointment

Disappointing, like signing up for a French gourmet cooking course and learning how to make French toast
—Nina Totenberg, Public Radio

Disappointment ... had fallen upon him like a blow struck by some unseen hand —Sherwood Anderson

Disappointment worked through me like a poison —Robertson Davies

Disillusioned ... as a betrayed lover —Calder Willingham

Had a look of profound disappointment ... like a child who sees a treat wafted away from him —Mary McCarthy

DISAPPROVAL
See: CONTEMPT

Discomfort

DISCOMFORT

Comfortable as a toothache —Mark Twain

(Kiss) comfortless as frozen water to a starved snake
—William Shakespeare

Comfortless as salt —Sylvia Plath

Damp like a vault —Maurice Hewlett

Felt like a door-to-door salesman, pushing unwanted sets of nature encyclopedias complete with fake walnut case —Sue Grafton

Indigestible as Christmas dinner —Patricia Ferguson
See also: FOOD AND DRINK

I've a head like a concertina, I've a tongue like a button-stick, I've a mouth like an old potato —Rudyard Kipling
Kipling's triple simile to describe a hangover, continues as follows: "And I'm more than a little sick, but I've had my fun."
See also: DRINKING

Self-conscious as a stammer —Delmore Schwartz

(Joel's fingers are cold.) The apartment is like a football game in the rain —Margaret Atwood

Uncomfortable as running a marathon in high-heeled pumps —Anon

Uncomfortable as trying to sleep standing up —Elyse Sommer

An uncomfortable feeling, like finding oneself in the same cell, and for the same crime, as a man one repudiated on every ground —John Fowles

Uneasy as a dog in a vet's waiting room —Anon

Nothing unsettles man like a bed of stinging nettles —W. S. Gilbert

DISCONTENT
See also: GLOOM

Disgruntled as an under-tipped taxi driver —Anon

Dissatisfaction with himself had settled over him ... as congruently as a second skin —François Camoin

Discontent follows ambition like a shadow —Anon

Discontent ... had come over her like a blighting wind —George Eliot

Discontent is like ink poured into water, which fills the whole fountain full of blackness —Owen Feltham

Discontent like alum in the mouth —Wallace Stegner

His whole wounded life choked him at the throat like a death agony —Émile Zola

Like jellyfish that lie beneath the warm ocean waters here [Hilton Head] there is discontent beneath the surface bonhomie (of the governors' annual conference)
—David Shieman, *Wall Street Journal*, August 26, 1986

Looking as unhappy as an aging, wet and exhausted salesman whose luck had played out at last —Howard Frank Mosher

Men who are unhappy, like men who sleep badly, are always proud of the fact —Bertrand Russell

Unhappiness burns like leaves —F. D. Reeve

Unhappiness inhabited me as if it were another person and it had the power to pull memories from me, as if from an open file —Scott Spencer

Unhappiness ... it is like climbing up a bare wall. It is like being shut up in a cellar all your life —Vicki Baum

Unhappy as a baseball player who can't get to third base —Anon

Unhappy as a character in a soap opera —Elyse Sommer

When people abhor what they cannot comprehend, they are like those burning with fever, to whom the choicest food is unpalatable —Kahlil Gibran

DISCORD
See: AGREEMENT/DISAGREEMENT

DISCRETION
See: CAUTION, TACT

DISCRIMINATION
See: STYLE

DISHONESTY
See: BELIEVABILITY, CRIME, LIES/LIARS

All frauds, like the wall daubed with untempered mortar ... always tend to the decay of what they are devised to support —Richard Whately

As honest a man as any in the cards, when the kings are out —Thomas Fuller

At length corruption, like a general flood ... shall deluge all —Alexander Pope

Borrowed thoughts, like borrowed money, only show the poverty of the borrower —Marguerite, Countess Blessington

Corruption is like a ball of snow ... once set a-rolling it must increase —Charles Caleb Colton

Crooked as a worm writhing on a hook —Herman Wouk
> The people who are likened to worms are characters from Wouk's political novel, *Inside, Outside.*

(Pompous and braggadocian, he seemed to the children as flat and) false as his teeth —Ferrol Sams

(She was) false as water —William Shakespeare

Falser than vows made in wine —William Shakespeare

Fraudulent as falsies —Helen Hudson

He that builds his house with other men's money is like one that
gathers himself stones for the tomb of his burial
—*The Holy Bible/Apocrypha: Ecclesiasticus*
        The word 'builds' has been modernized from 'buildeth'
        and 'gathers' from 'gathereth.'

It is as difficult to appropriate the thoughts of others as it is to
invent —Ralph Waldo Emerson

Permit memory to paint it [a long-ago life style] falsely, like the face
of some old whore who could wish to be taken as young and
innocent —George Garrett

Plays you as fair as if he'd picked your pocket —John Ray's *Proverbs*

Robbers are like rane, tha fall on the just and the unjust
—Josh Billings
        In Billings' phonetic dialect the word 'rane' is 'rain' and
        'tha' is 'they.'

Sneaky as a rat in a hotel kitchen —William Alfred

There is something in corruption which, like a jaundiced eye,
transfers the color of itself to the object it looks upon
—Thomas Paine

To rob a friend even of a penny is like taking his life
—Johann B. Nappaha

DISILLUSIONMENT
See: DISAPPOINTMENT

DISINTEGRATION

(Shirley's childless marriage had) become unstuck like a piece of old
and grubby sticking plaster —Gillian Tindall

Blown aside like thistledown —John Fowles
        Fowles used this simile once to describe the eventual
        collapse of a political party and another time to describe a
        mood. Some similes obviously transfer to different points
        of reference more easily than others.

Broke like a sea-bubble on the sand —James Montgomery

(Perhaps the hope will die stillborn,) broken up like wreckage by the
tides of events —Lawrence Durrell

Dishonesty

Disintegration

171

Disintegration

Come apart like wet kleenex —Anon

(When I hit him he) comes apart like a perfect puzzle or an old flower —Philip Levine

Comes apart like meat being carved —G. K. Chesterton

(He started) coming apart like seedpod —Sharon Sheehe Stark

Cracking and fading like an old photograph —George Garrett

Crumbled like crackers into alphabet soup —Dave Anderson, *New York Times*/Sports of the Times, November 24, 1986
> The comparison referred to disintegration of a once great heavyweight champion division.

Crumble like old cheese —Anon

Crumble like soda crackers —Dashiell Hammett

(Their argument) crumbles like dry rice paper —Nicholas Proffitt

(The old voice) crumpled ... like a fragile leaf —Lawrence Durrell

Crumple ... like a leaf in the fire —James Joyce

Crumple up like wet and falling roses —D. H. Lawrence

(The house was) old and decayed like the pitted trunk of a persimmon —Yasunari Kawabata

Disintegrate like a bubble at a touch —Anon

Disintegrate like a crumbling monument —Anon

(Words came to my lips and) dissipated like the wisps of children's breaths in the cold air outside —Kent Nelson

Dissolved and grew flimsy like the world after champagne —Graham Swift

[A committee] dissolved like a summer cloud —Edith Wharton

Dissolved like spit in the wind —Wallace Stevens

Dissolve like vague promises —Elyse Sommer

(Floats on water) dissolving like a paper plate —Margaret Atwood

(The white sky) empties of its promise, like a cup —Sylvia Plath
(The shadows under the trees and bushes) evaporated like puddles after a shower —Stephen King

172

Evaporated like a drop of dew —Ruth Prawer Jhabvala

Evaporate ... like hoar frost before the morning sun
    —W. Somerset Maugham
        Maugham's simile from *The Summing Up* refers to the way
        changing tastes affect perceptions of an art work's beauty.

Fall apart and scatter like a smashed string of beads
    —Yaakov Churgin

Falling intoodecay like a layer of mulch —Jean Thompson

(Furniture) falling to pieces like dry fruitcake —William H. Gass

Fizzles out like a wet firecracker —John Wainwright

Goes up in smoke like so much tissue paper —Elizabeth Spencer

Go sour [as a project] like milk abandoned in the far corner of the
    refrigerator —Marian Sturm

Melt away like salt in water —Sholom Aleichem

Melt away like Turkish delights —Frank O'Hara

Melted away like a snail —Elizabeth Spencer

[Members of a social set] melted away, like snow drops over a
    bonfire —Ayn Rand

Melted [in response to compliments] like butter on the Sahara
    —Tony Ardizzone

Melted like wax —*The Holy Bible*

(The day is) melting away like snow —Plautus
        This has been used in poetry and daily language since 200
        B.C., and is still going strong.

Melts away like moonlight in the heaven of spreading day
    —Percy Bysshe Shelley

(Your mind now) moldering like a wedding-cake —Adrienne Rich

Rot and shred and peel away like old wallpaper —George Garrett

[Resolutions] thinned away like smoke, into nothingness —Aldous
    Huxley

Rotted through like old shoe leather —Marge Piercy

Rotting like autumn leaves —Marguerite Yourcenar

Disintegration

Shredded away like leaf tobacco —Saul Bellow

(The snake slides again and again until all passed is left behind to) shrivel like a ghost without substance —Daniela Gioseffi

(The remembrance had been brought to mind so often that it was) tarnished and dull, like a trinket not worth looking at —Beryl Markham

(Her muscles came) undone like ribbons —Sharon Sheehe Stark

Wear out like a worn battery —Anon
> This makes a good update for "Wears out like a run-down gramophone record."

Went to pieces like a cheap umbrella in a gale —Anon
> This is updated from the original "Like a fifty cent umbrella," something today only obtainable at a rummage sale.

Will dissolve faster than an Alka-Seltzer under a waterfall —Barry Farber, WNYC radio, commenting on the endurance of communism.

Wither like the flower of the field —Miguel de Cervantes

Withered like grass —*The Holy Bible/Psalms*

Wither like a blighted tree —Barbara Howes

Withers like the face of an aged woman —Beryl Markham

DISLOYALTY
See: LOYALTY/DISLOYALTY

Dispersal

DISPERSAL

Diffused charm around like an indispensable perfume —Jules Janin, about the woman who served as the role model for *The Lady With the Camellias* by Alexandre Dumas, Fils

(Consciousness) disperses itself like pollen on a spring day —Carlos Fuentes

Dispersed like a broken family —Beryl Markham

Disposed of like a branch or potato sack —Graham Swift

Here and there like teeth in an old man's mouth —Maxim Gorky

Like the chaff of the summer threshing floors ... the wind carried them away —*The Holy Bible*

Scatter and divide like fleecy clouds self-multiplied
    —William Wordsworth

Scattered as the seeds of wild grass —Beryl Markham

Scattered [audience across vacant seats in a theatre] as widely as out-fielders when the champion batter steps to the plate —O. Henry

[Shadows of doubts and weaknesses] scattered, like a cloud in morning's breeze —John Greenleaf Whittier

(The rage that had been silent ... fired and) scattered like bullets
    —Belva Plain

Scattered (across the map of the land) like carelessly dropped pennies
    —George Garrett

Scattered, like chaff in a high wind —Donald Seaman

Scatter like confetti —Derek Lambert
        An extension is "To scatter like confetti at a tickertape parade."

Scattered like dusts and leaves, when the mighty blasts of October seize them —Henry Wadsworth Longfellow

Scattered like foam along the wave —George Croly

Scattered like foam on the torrent —Percy Bysshe Shelley

Scattered like mown and withered grass
    —Johann Wolfgang von Goethe

Scattered like rabbits to a gunshot —Lawrence Durrell

(Spite, malice and jealousy) scattered like spent foam —Iris Murdoch

Scatter like a bucket of water —Erich Maria Remarque

Scatter like balls on a billiard table —Tom Shales, movie review, WNYC Morning Edition Public Radio, March 20, 1987
        In the movie Shales reviewed, it was babies who were thus scattered about.

(The sparrows) scatter like handfuls of gravel —William H. Gass

Dispersal

Scatter like mist before the wind —Kenzaburo Oë
> The descriptive reference point is a feeling of contentment.

Scatter like pigeons across grass —Anon

(His foes are) scattered like chirping sparrows
    —Stephen Vincent Benét

Thrown away like used paper cups —Anon

DISPOSABILITY
See: TRANSIENCE

DISSATISFACTION
See: DISCONTENT

DISSENSION
See: AGREEMENT/DISAGREEMENT, ARGUMENT

DISSIMILARITY
See: DIFFERENCES

DISTINCTIVENESS
See: ORIGINALITY/UNORIGINALITY

Diverseness

DIVERSENESS
See also: DIFFERENCES

He [Shakespeare] was as many-sided as clouds are many-formed
    —Robert G. Ingersoll

(We had come up to the farm for our four summer weeks, and
    Maine was all before us) as various and new as the flow of the
    heavy tides —Barry Targan

As various as a Cook's tour —Delmore Schwartz

As various as a duck-billed platypus —Jean Stafford

Diverse as a smorgasbord table —Anon

Diverse as weather, changeful as the wind —Robert Hillyer

(She) had as many registers as a fine old organ —Vicki Baum

Like a Russian doll nesting ever smaller dolls inside of it, I house an
    infinity of selves —Daphne Merkin

Multi-faceted like a crystal chandelier —Anon

Varied as the expressions of the human face —George H. Ellwanger
With this book as an example, one might add "And as
varied as the similes to describe those expressions."

DIVORCE
See: MARRIAGE

DOCTORS
See also: PROFESSIONS

As with eggs, there is no such thing as a poor doctor; doctors are
either good or bad —Fuller Albright
The author of this simile is a doctor.

A breast or a foot is examined [by doctors lacking in empathy] like a
pack of cigarettes
—Hildegarde Knef, quoted in interview with Rex Reed

Carrying his little black bag like a small sample cut from the shadow
of death —Helen Hudson
This observation from Hudson's novel, *Meyer Meyer*, is
made by the main character about his doctor/brother-in-
law.

Commonly, physicians, like beer, are best when they are old; and
lawyers, like bread, when they are young and new
—Thomas Fuller

A doctor knows the human body as a cabman knows the town; he
is well acquainted with all the great thoroughfares and small
turnings; he's intimate with all the principle edifices, but he
cannot tell you what is going on inside of any one of them
—*Punch*, 1856

The fame of a surgeon is like the fame of an actor; it exists only as
long as they live, and their talent is no longer appreciable after
they have disappeared —Honoré de Balzac

Physicians are like kings; they brook no contradiction —John Webster

DOUBT
See: TRUST/MISTRUST

DREAMS
See: HOPE

DRINKING

See also: FOOD AND DRINK

Alcohol is like love. The first kiss is magic, the second is intimate, the third is routine —Raymond Chandler

A case of beer lying at his feet like the family dog —Jonathan Valin

Drank like a camel —Robert Graves

Drank like a fire engine —Ernest William Hornung

Drink like a fish —Anon
> There's a whole laundry list of "Drink like" and "Drunk as" similes. Those linking drinking with fish predominate with "Drunk as a lord" and "Drunk as owls" or "Boiled as owls" following close on the fishes' fins. A nice twist by Mary Peterson Poole: "It's all right to drink like a fish, if you drink what a fish drinks."

(He could) drink like a suction-hose —Thomas Burke

Drinks cognac like soda water —Isaac Bashevis Singer

Drunk as a cooter brown —Richard Ford

Drunk as an autumn wasp —Jonathan Gash

Drunk as a wheelbarrow —George Garrett

Drunk as dancing pigs —James Crumley

Drunk as puffed-up pigeons —Edward Hoagland

Drunk like wedding guests —Charles Simic

Feel the vodka melting into his bloodstream, like snow —Richard Lourie

Half as sober as a judge —Charles Lamb

Lit up like a Christmas tree —Anon
> Similes linking "Lit up" with a variety of comparative references became part of the American language around 1902. Here are some offshoots of the above: "Lit up like a cathedral," "Lit up like a church," "Lit up like Main Street," "Lit up like a skyscraper," and "Lit up like Times Square."

Pissed as a skunk —Martin Cruz Smith

Pissed as a newt —American colloquialism

This means to be very drunk.

Smell ... like a tap-room —Anton Chekhov

Smells like a still —Cornell Woolrich

Some men are like musical glasses: to produce their finest tones you
must keep them wet —Samuel Taylor Coleridge

Taught himself to drink as he would have taught himself Greek; like
Greek it would be the gateway to a wealth of new sensations,
new psychic states, new reactions in joy or misery
—F. Scott Fitzgerald

(I have been) tight as a tick —Tallulah Bankhead

A hangover like a herd of elephants —Graham Masterton

(He was) so knocked out with liquor that he vomited like a whale,
urinated like a dog, exposed himself like a jackass, and wallowed
in his muck like a pig —St. Kitts' government newspaper, *The
Democrat*, about leader of opposition, 1981

The stuff [liquor] was like insulin to a diabetic; he didn't need much
of it at a time, but if he needed little he needed it often
—Howard Nemerov
    The simile describes the drinking habits of a character in
    Nemerov's short story, *Unbelievable Characters*.

Woke up with his head like a big split millstone —John Dos Passos

When drunk, his color sank to a clammy white from which it rose
like a thermometer as he sobered up —Mary Ward Brown

His head still felt like a sandbag full of maggots —Sterling Hayden

Whiskey ... went through me like a rope of fire —Louise Erdrich

Whiskey ... burned his stomach like hellfire —Paige Mitchell

The spirit of the wine was rising like smoke to his head
—George Garrett

The bourbon was warm in her stomach ... like a core of heat
—Jayne Anne Phillips

DRYNESS

Arid as the sands of the Sahara —Joseph Conrad
    The everyday cliche is "Dry as the Sahara."

Dryness

(I'll) drain him dry as hay —William Shakespeare

Dries up like snakeskin —Kate Grenville

(Her words were) dry as the rustle of old leaves
—William Beechcroft

Dry and cracking like the bindings on rare books —Diane Wakoski

(His throat was) dry as a desert —Colin Forbes

(Heart) dry as an autumn leaf —Nelson Algren

(You'll sweat until you're as) dry as an old gourd —George Garrett

Dry as ashes —Fisher Ames
> Variations of this much-used cliche include "Dry as dust"
> as well as frame-of-reference switches such as "White as
> ashes."

(His sensitive palate as) dry as a bread crust —W. S. Gilbert

Dry as a spinster on a Saturday night —line from "St. Elsewhere"
television drama, broadcast December 16, 1986

(I was) dry as a stick —Thomas Gray
> Gray used this in combination with two other similes: "I
> was dry as a stick, hard as a stone, and cold as a
> cucumber."

(Her voice was) dry as burned paper —Susan Fromberg Schaeffer

(My heart felt as) dry as dirt —Bernard Malamud

(Their intellectuality is as) dry as dung that's lain on a dusty road
for weeks —Louis Adamic
> A shorter version seen in a poem by W. D. Snodgrass:
> "Parched as dung."

Dry as faded marigold —Stephen Vincent Benét

Dry as last year's crow's nest —Anon

Dry as poverty —John Ashbery

Dry as woodash —Marge Piercy

[Feeling of teeth against lips] dry as sandpaper —William Faulkner

(Hair) dry as spun glass —Elizabeth Spencer

(He was dry-looking, as) dry as talc —Marianne Wiggins

Dry as the white dunes under sunlight —Marge Piercy

Dry up faster than a pressed corsage —Reynolds Price

Parched like an open mouth —Charles Simic

DULLNESS

About as exciting as broccoli —Fred Barnes, "McLaughlin Group"
    television broadcast, December 29, 1986

About as exciting as a ride on a stone camel —Anon

As much personality as a paper cup
    —Raymond Chandler about the city of Los Angeles
        In his essay *The Country Behind the Hill*, critic Clive James
        explains that this was intended as a positive simile,
        reflecting Chandler's fascination with the city's seediness.

Bland as a Bloody Mary without tabasco —Anon

Bland as a martini without a twist of lemon —Anon

Bland as hominy grits —Frederick Exley

Blunt as ignorance —Samuel Rowley

(The place was) dead as a ghost-town cemetery —Douglas Adams
        In his novel, *The Fourth Widow*, Adams extends the simile
        as follows: "And nowhere near as pretty."

(The place seemed to be as ...) dead as a Pharaoh
    —Raymond Chandler

Dreary as an empty house —Gustave Flaubert

Dreary as an old dishrag —Anon, capsule movie review in *New York
    Times* television listings

Dreary as a Russian love story —William Diehl

Dry as the Congressional Record —James J. Montague

(Lies ...) dull and senseless as a stone —Elizabeth Barrett Browning

Dull as a jail cell —Ira Wood

(A day as) dull as a lead nickel —John Wainwright

(A brown macrame wall hanging) dull as dirt —Patricia Henley

Dull as pig shit —Ethel Merman, about her friend Benay Venuta's Jewish society friends

Dull as brushing your teeth —Anon

Dull as ditch-water —Charles Dickens
> An everyday expression modernized to "Dull as dishwater."

(When he is gone, the world will be) dull as Mars —Lorrie Moore

(The road north is ...) dull like a camel plodding through the desert —Anon

Dull ... like a cookbook written by someone who doesn't like food —Pat Conroy

An eternal sameness, like a blank wall —Robert Silverberg

Flat and insipid as a pancake —Anatole France
> Anatole France loved proverbs, and so this extension of familiar wisdom.

[About an experience someone is relating] flat as the telling at breakfast of an ecstatic dream —Stella Benson

Had the personality of a dried-out fart —Anon

Interesting as boiled potatoes —Anon

Interesting as staring at a blank wall —Anon

Interesting as watching paint dry —Dee Weber

Life as humdrum as that of a country curate —W. Somerset Maugham

Life ... devoid of incident as the longest of Trollope's novels —O. Henry

Life here is as calm as a gold-fish tank with one half-animate inmate: me —Julia O'Faolain

Life is as tedious as a twice-told tale —William Shakespeare

Looked dreary, like a theater before anybody comes —Mark Twain

Looked like she had the IQ of a well-mannered houseplant —A. E. Maxwell

Mind ... slept and snored like a full dog by the fire
   —George Garrett

Monotonous as a sailor's chantey —Raymond Chandler

Monotonous like water dripping on sandstone —John MacDonald

My life is as flat as the table I write on —Gustave Flaubert

A new idea made its way into her mind with much difficulty, as if
   it had to traverse the meshes of a choked sieve —Stefan Zweig

Numb as a potato —Daniel Asa Rose

Obtuse as an ocelot —Gregory McDonald

Personality like a cup of yogurt —Pat Conroy

Persons without minds are like weeds that delight in good earth;
   they want to be amused by others, all the more because they are
   dull within —Honoré de Balzac

Seemed dull ... as simple as a three-headed treasure-guarding troll
   —Anon

(The people who surrounded him) seemed like white bread,
   inexcusably bland —Phillip Lopate

Shadowy and uninteresting as an event in an outdated and long-
   unread novel —Gillian Tindall
        The frame of reference for the comparison is a brief, long-
        ago marriage.

There are some things so dull they hypnotize like the pendulum of a
   clock —Karl Shapiro

Tiresome as virtue —Edith Wharton

Too dull—no stir, no storm, no life about it ... like being part dead
   and part alive, both at the same time —Mark Twain
        The condition thus described in Twain's story, *Captain
        Stormfield's Visit to Heaven*, is that of running a grocery
        store.

Unconscious as a face of stone —H. W. Hudson

(His friends were as) uninteresting as the dead —Rumer Godden

Void of life as a block of ice —Patricia Henley

Eating and Drinking

EATING AND DRINKING
See also: FOOD AND DRINK

Ate as if there were a hidden thing inside him, a creature of all jaws with an infinite trailing ribbon of gut —T. Coraghessan Boyle

Ate like a cart-horse —H. E. Bates

Ate like a famished wolf —Louisa May Alcott

Ate like a trucker —Jonathan Kellerman

Ate silently like two starving peasants —James Crumley

Ate slowly, thoughtfully, as if fixing the taste of each spoonful in her mind —Paule Marshall

Bit off an end of it [a candy bar] like a man biting off a chew from a plug —Peter De Vries

The bread slices collapsed like movie-set walls beneath her bite —Tom Robbins

Chewed ... in odd little spasms, as if seeking a tooth that wouldn't hurt —Paul Horgan

Chews his granola like a Clydesdale —Ira Wood

Chomping popcorn [in a movie theatre] like their upper teeth are mad at their lower —Tonita S. Gardner, *It's All a Matter of Luck*, 1986

Diets, like clothes, should be tailored to you —Joan Rivers

Down poured the wine like oil on a blazing fire —Charles Dickens

Eat breakfast like a king, lunch like a prince and dinner like a pauper —Anon
See also: ADVICE

Eating [voraciously] ... like a blowfly on a shit pile —Steve Heller

Eating like three men —Louis Adamic

Eating quickly and silently, like a bunch of taxi drivers eager to get back to the job —Daphne Merkin

184

Eating quickly and abstractedly, like a man whose habits of life have made food less an indulgence than a necessity —Elizabeth Bowen

Eat like wolves —William Shakespeare

Eats like a well man and drinks like a sick —Benjamin Franklin

Eats ... like stolen fruit —Ralph Waldo Emerson

Gulped the tea and felt it like sleep in her body —Frank Tuohy

He's like a camel as far as serious liquid refreshment is concerned
—Iris Murdoch
See also: DRINKING

Lap up the gravy just like pigs in a trough —Lewis Carroll

Mouth moving as rapidly as the treadle on Granny's sewing machine
—William H. Gass

Nibble ... in quick little bites like a squirrel with a nut
—George Garrett

Sip [a drink] ... as though he tasted martinis for a living
—Sue Grafton

(He had) stuffed as full as an egg —Anonymous English ballad,
"The Cork"

Swallowed it [a small sandwich] like a communion wafer
—T. Coraghessan Boyle

ECONOMICS

Balancing the budget is a little like protecting your virtue—you just
have to learn to say no —Ronald Reagan

Capital is dead labor, that, vampire-like, only lives by sucking living
labor —Karl Marx

The Dow-Jones is floating up like a hot-air balloon
—François Camoin

Economics is like being lost in the woods. How can you tell where
you are going when you don't even know where you are?
—Anon

Feeding more tax dollars to government is like feeding a stray pup. It
just follows you home and sits on your doorstep asking for more
—Ronald Reagan

Financial statements are like a bikini. What they reveal is interesting; what they conceal is vital —William W. Priest, Jr., Managing Director BEA Associates, "Wall Street Week" television program, January 9, 1987

Forecasting economic averages is like assuring the non-swimmer that he can safely walk across the river because its average depth is only four feet —Milton Friedman

Inflation, like DC-10s, and Three Mile Islands, and Cold Wars is bad for your mental health —Ellen Goodman

It [the economy] looks more resistant to shoves and shocks than it once was. Like a clown on a roly-poly base, it swings back and forth but does not topple over —Leonard Silk, *New York Times*/Economic Scene, September 17, 1986

A little inflation is like a little pregnancy, it keeps on growing —Leo Henderson

Poverty is a temporary fault, but excessive wealth is [like] a lasting ailment —Kahlil Gibran

A recession is like an unfortunate love affair. It's a lot easier to talk your way in than it is to talk your way out —Bill Vaughan, *Reader's Digest*, July, 1958

Right now being an arbitrageur is kind of like being a fire hydrant at a dog show, you sure get a lot of attention —Anonymous arbitrageur, quote *Wall Street Journal*, 1987
      The fire hydrants comparison was made in connection with the image problems resulting from arbitrage scandals.

Signs of reviving inflation are as abundant as are skeptics who read each rise in inflationary barometers as an aberration —John C. Borland, *New York Times*, September 28, 1986

The stock market climbed like the horses of Apollo —Hortense Calisher

Takeovers on a scale that would make 19th-century pirates look like croquet players —-Harry A. Jacobs (senior director of Prudential-Bache Securities), commenting on increase in company takeovers and other economic ills, as quoted in Leonard Silk's column, *New York Times*/Economic Scene, February 4, 1987

Tax loopholes are like parking spaces, they all seem to disappear by the time you get there —Joey Adams

To some economists, inflation is like those trick birthday candles, the ones that are impossible to blow out
—Joel Popkin, *New York Times*, August 17, 1986

Turning national economic policy around is like turning the Queen Mary around in a bathtub —E. Gerald Corrigan, chairman of Federal Reserve Bank of New York, at Japan Society dinner, *New York Times*, April 17, 1987

The wife economy [wherein husbands assume full economic responsibility for wives] is as obsolete as the slave economy
—Elizabeth Hardwick
See also: MARRIAGE

EDUCATION
See: KNOWLEDGE

EFFECT
See: CAUSE AND EFFECT

ELASTICITY
See: FLEXIBILITY/INFLEXIBILITY

ELEGANCE
See: STYLE

ELOQUENCE
See: SPEECHMAKING

ELUSIVENESS

As slippery as an eel —Dutch proverb
> This has given rise to extensions such as, "Slippery as an eel dipped in butter" by F. van Wyck Mason.

(Love is) as slippery as greased pigskin —Delmore Schwartz
See also: LOVE

Avoided [another person] like a vampire avoids sunburn
—Joseph Wambaugh

(He was) difficult as a serpent to see —D. H. Lawrence
> The elusive creature being described is a fox sliding along in deep grass.

(The feeling persisted, insidious and) difficult to trace as perfume
—Harvey Swados

187

Elusive as a collar button —Jim Murray
> Murray, sports columnist for the *Los Angeles Herald*, applied this simile to football player Mike Garrett.

Elusive as a dream —William Diehl
> "Fugitive as dreams," used by Tom MacIntyre in a short story *Epithalamion*, illustrates the possibility for change through word substitutions.

Elusive as a wet fish —Anon

Elusive as buried treasure —Anon

Elusive as the cure for cancer —Anon

Elusive as the cure for aging —Anon

Elusive as the source of a rumor —Anon

Elusiveness, like a thought that presents itself to consciousness and vanishes before it can be captured by words
—W. Somerset Maugham

Evaded me, much like the myth of Tantalus —Marguerite Young

Evasion, like equivocation, comes generally from a cowardly or a deceiving spirit, or from both —Honoré de Balzac

Hard to hold as a flapping sail in a raging wind —Gerald Kersh
> The hold to which Kersh alludes is the grip of one wrestler on another in the story entitled *Ali the Terrible Turk*.

Intangible as a beautiful thought —W. Somerset Maugham

Intangible as love and fear —André Dubus

(A vision swarming through the mind as sudden and) irretrievable as smoke —William Styron

It [information] got away from me so easily, like the tail of a kite, when the kite's already out of your hands —Cornell Woolrich

It [trying to tie up a boxing opponent] was just like trying to hold onto a buzz-saw —Ernest Hemingway

Like fish in an aquarium, they [two girls] flashed in and out of sight —Frank Tuohy

Like sand from a clenched fist, he was slipping through her fingers —Ben Ames Williams

(She was so marvelous that, when he tried to think of her, her
    description) rolled away from him like a dropped coin
    —Mark Helprin

(She) seemed like a shadow within a shadow —D. H. Lawrence
        Lawrence is describing one of the two main female
        characters in *The Fox*, a woman the male character desires
        but doesn't understand.

She was like a rubber ball; he couldn't get a grip —Beryl Bainbridge

Slipped by like a mouse —Anton Chekhov

[Something said] slipped out of me like a cork from the deep
    —Reynolds Price

Slipped through [guards] like a fox through a barnyard
    —Clive Cussler

Slippery as shadows in day's foam —Delmore Schwartz

They might as well be looking for a shoe in a swamp
    —Clive Cussler

EMBARRASSMENT
See: SHYNESS

EMBRACES
See also: KISSES; SEXUAL INTERACTION

Almost completely covered by MaButhelezi's big arms, like a blanket
    of flesh —Njabulo Ndebele

Clasped each other like a pair of abandoned children
    —Natascha Wodin

Clinch like lovers at the final fade out —George Garrett

Curled up together like a pair of old dogs —Jean Thompson

Drawing her toward him he held her and squeezed her out like a bit
    of old washing —Edna O'Brien

Drew her to him, crushing her like a pale flower to his breast
    —Peter De Vries

Drew the child to her as if she were a springing young tree
    —Elizabeth Taylor

Embraced Himiko [name of a character] like a bear hugging an enemy —Kenzaburo Oë

Embraced him like a hot, wet towel —William H. Hallhan

Embraced like bears —Madison Smartt Bell

Embrace like penpals —Ira Wood

Embraces are keen like pain —Algernon Charles Swinburne

Her embrace was clumsy like a bad dancer's —John Braine

Her long thin arms came up to wind about him and inexorably, like tight thin wires, to hold him down —H. E. Bates

His arm around her felt as if she'd been born with it there —William McIlvanney

His arms are like a cradle in which she is warm and safe —Alvin Boretz, television program, 1986

Hold hands like teenagers, fingers meshed like the teeth of rusty gears —Ira Wood

Lay locked like human vines —Charles Bukowski

Let our arms clasp like ivy —John Donne

Locked in a profound embrace ... like Ahab and the whale —A. R. Guerney, Jr.
> Guerney's simile refers to the guests in his play *The Perfect Party.*

Marg's long tanned body entwined Fencer's like a constricting serpent —Robert Stone

Pressed herself upon me like someone pressing upon a bruise —Lawrence Durrell

She vibrated in his arms like a tuning fork —Andrew Kaplan

Snuggled up together like spoons in bed —Phyllis Naylor

They'd lie together, like a four-armed creature fearful of amputation —Julia O'Faolain

Was so huge and soft it was like embracing a cloud and sinking down —Lee Smith

SNUGGLED UP TOGETHER LIKE SPOONS IN BED

EMOTIONS

See also: CHEERFULNESS, GLOOM, LOVE, NERVOUSNESS, SADNESS

Compulsion is a mirror in which he who looks for long will see his inner self endeavoring to commit suicide —Kahlil Gibran

Emotional antagonisms that lay in us like surly dogs at the end of a chain, ready to leap up and growl at a step —Wallace Stegner

Emotional ... like a third-rate opera singer —Fred Mustard Stewart

Emotions buzzed and throbbed ... like a pent-up bee
—Elizabeth Bowen

Emotions got cut off ... like a broken string of beads
—Susan Fromberg Schaeffer

Emotions ... swarm in my head like a hive of puzzled bees
—Gertrude Atherton

Emotions to be appropriate ... may be measuring them like potatoes, but it is better than slopping them about like water from a pail
—E. M. Forster

Emotion akin to a physical blow —Henrietta Weigel

Fear and anger boiled up in my head like liquid air
—Ross Macdonald

Feeling full of wonder and illusion—like a Columbus or a pilgrim seeing the continent of his dreams take shape in the dusk for the first time —Richard Ford
> The feelings thus described are experienced as a plane comes in for a landing.

Feelings bubbled in him like water from an underground spring
—Paige Mitchell

Feelings ... call, like a buzzing of flies in autumn air
—Wallace Stevens

Feelings cross our flesh along nets of nerves, like a pattern of lightning flashes —Marguerite Yourcenar

Feelings here slice right through like speed skates —Jill Robinson
> Robinson thus described the work of poet Amy Rothholz, building on her simile with, "Racing by with fierce, original passion." The poet's publisher extracted the simile from Robinson's review to feature in an ad for the book.

Feelings ... jumbled together like ravelled wool —Frank Swinnerton

Feel mushy and wet, like a pile of leaves after they have been rained on —Daphne Merkin

Feels herself curling up like a jaundiced leaf —Alice Munro

Feel the magic building like a gathering storm —W. P. Kinsella

Felt as small and vulnerable as a calf on its first day of life
      —Linda West Eckhardt

Felt crazy, stupid, as though, having believed a burglar was rummaging through the house, I had found only the family cat
   —Kent Nelson

Felt ... inadequate, as if I were a new understudy taking on a role that had been played before, and much more effectively
   —Alice McDermott

Felt like a lifeline thrown out to someone
   —Mike Feder, *New York Times*, September 7, 1986
         Feder, a cafe story teller, thus explained how he began his career by telling stories about his day's experiences to his housebound mother.

Felt like a man in a Rembrandt, tinged brown with sorrow and wisdom —Laurie Colwin

Felt like a man reprieved from the gallows —Wilfrid Sheed

Felt like a man who had had a tooth out that had been hurting him for a long time —Leo Tolstoy

Felt like an emotional invalid, like a balloon without the helium
   —T. Coraghessan Boyle

(After my husband died I) felt like one of those spiraled shells washed up on the beach ... no flesh, no life —Lynn Caine

Felt shut off like a turtle inside her skin —Laura Furman

Felt worry and joy flinging her about like a snowflake —Mary Hedin

A foul feeling, like looking over the edge of the world —Jean Rhys

Guilty and elated, as though I'd successfully committed a small theft
   —Christopher Isherwood

Half smiles, half tears, like rain in sun —John Greenleaf Whittier
      See also: SMILES

Emotions

Heart expanded like bellows —Laurie Colwin

His senses nagged at him like pampered babies —Stephen Crane

Inhibitions gave way like an earth dam collapsing in front of a winter flood —Graham Masterson

Isolation, frustration and sometimes fear run like a leitmotif through our lives —Philip Taubman, *New York Times Magazine,* September 21, 1986

It [his emotion for a woman] struck him like sickness —H. E. Bates

Love and emptiness in us are like the sea's ebb and flow —Kahlil Gibran

My emotions flowered in me like a divine revelation —André Gide

My heart is like wax; it is melted in the midst of my bowels —*The Holy Bible/Psalms*

Old feelings gather fast upon me like vultures round their prey —Emily Brontë

Our feelings have edges and spines and prickles like cactus, or porcupines —Laurie Colwin
> Colwin is likening the cactus/porcupine edges and spines to the feelings of two lovers.

Our feelings penetrate us like a poison of undetectable nature —Anaïs Nin

Pride and anger seemed like overblown spent clouds of thunder —John Greenleaf Whittier

Profound feelings ... swept through and racked his being like gusts of fire —George Garrett

(A feeling of) relief circles us like a spring breeze —Richard Ford

Relief courses through me like cool water —Marge Piercy

Relief had come in like a warm and welcome flood —Carlos Baker

Relieved [after things have been put right] ... like they lifted a concrete block out of my belly —John Updike

Rolled in self-pity and self-hatred like a hot sulfur spring —Marge Piercy

Self-hatred living in him like a sick dog in a cellar
—Bernard Malamud

Sensations gave like snowslides in him —Larry Woiwode

Sensations ... whirling about him like snowflakes —Willa Cather

(My feelings) snapped like a glass pipette —Diane Wakoski

Stirred an emotion ... like the birth of a butterfly within a cocoon
—Adela Rogers St. Johns

Sudden relief, like a rush of tears, came to her —Nadine Gordimer

(Their hearts were open and) sweet sensations flowed in them like
honey —Ruth Prawer Jhabvala

Temperament, like liberty, is important despite how many crimes are
committed in its name —Louis Kronenberger

Temper like a bed of banked coals waiting to be fired into roaring
flame by a spill of brandy —Davis Grubb

They [true feelings] gathered around me like a mist, whose shape can
be seen as it approaches, but not when it is on you
—L. P. Hartley

Too moved to even applaud ... as if the air had been sucked out of
the room —Samuel G. Freedman, *New York Times*, September 7,
1986
> The performer who thus moved his audience was a cafe
> story teller.

Treats his emotions ... as vermin to be crushed in traps or poisoned
with bait —Marge Piercy

Truth and jealousy, like a team of plow horses, came crashing into
the fragile barn of his illusions —Louis Auchincloss

A vague uneasy stirring plagued her like some mental indigestion
—Josephine Tey

A warm feeling like cocoa on a cold night —Jean Stafford

Wore his confidence like a tailored suit —Donald McCaig

Wore sorrow and anger like a worn-out coat and would not throw it
away —Belva Plain

The young soldier's heart was ... like fire in his chest
—D. H. Lawrence

EMPATHY
See: PITY

EMPTINESS
See: ABANDONMENT, EMOTIONS

ENDURANCE
See: CONTINUITY

ENEMY
See: ADVERSARY

ENERGY

Energy

Adrenaline bubbling in my veins like grease in a deep fryer
—T. Coraghessan Boyle

Adrenaline flooded through me like water through a storm drain
—Sue Grafton

Adrenaline flowing like electricity —W. P. Kinsella

Alger-like energy —Hortense Calisher

As brisk as a bee in a tar-pot —Thomas Fuller
The condensed version of this, "Brisk as a bee," can be
traced back to Boswell's *Life of Dr. Johnson*, where it was
used to describe someone's conversational style. A
variation (also from Fuller's collection of aphorisms) is,
"As brisk as a body louse."

Bracing as an Alpine breeze —Israel Zangwill

(Suddenly this spring he's) bursting with energy, like the daffodils on
the White House lawn —James Reston about Ronald Reagan,
New York Times, March 30, 1986

Electricity dripping from me like cream —Diane Wakoski

Energetic and tireless ... like a shouting insect, some kind of queen
aunt —J. B. Priestly

Energetic ... an explosion of vitality, rather like a teapot set not to
boil over but to bubble and steam —Charles Johnson

(Feeling as) energetic as a licensed jester —Clarence Major

Energy burned off him like a light —Pat Conroy

(Quick, incisive) energy like quicksilver in the veins —Joan Chase

Energy ... like the biblical grain of mustard-seed, will remove mountains —Hosea Ballou

Energy sings like a tea kettle —Marge Piercy

Energy ... thin and sharp like gravy —Diane Wakoski

Full of pep as an electric fan —Anon

(Little Billie was full of piss and vinegar and) full of sap as a maple tree —Robert Penn Warren
> In Warren's long poem, *The Ballad of Billie Potts*, the maple tree comparison is followed by another simile: "And full of tricks as a lop-eared pup."

Full of vitality ... like a lighted candle —Rachel Ingalls

Had a brisk air of bristle, like a terrier bitch —Angela Carter

He's like 220 pounds worth of Duracell batteries —Mike Jameson, commenting on the untiring energy of boxer Mike Tyson, quoted in *Newsday* column by Paul Ballot, December 27, 1986

Hum with unspent power, like a machine left to run —Mary Gordon

(He is) just like a blob of mercury —Alice James writing from Europe about her brother William to her father and her brother Henry in America, 1889

Like an old volcano, which has pretty nearly used up its fire and brimstone, but is still boiling and bubbling
—Oliver Wendell Holmes, Sr.

Like the grass and trees and other growing things, they were quivering and glistening with vitality —Dorothy Canfield Fisher

Refreshing, like rain at the end of a muggy day —Jay McInerney

Rings with vitality, like ax-strokes on oak —Dorothy Canfield Fisher

Sparks and twinkles like a jarred lightning bug
—Sharon Sheehe Stark
> The comparison refers to a lively four-year-old girl in a story entitled *The Johnstown Polka*.

Vigorous as a run-over cat —Marge Piercy

Vitality ... like a hot flame that burnt him with an unendurable fury
—W. Somerset Maugham

(She had a) vitality that warmed you like a blazing fire
—W. Somerset Maugham

Warm with life as the waters of a tropic sea —Beryl Markham

ENJOYMENT
See: PLEASURE

ENTHUSIASM
See: ENERGY

ENTRANCES/EXITS
See also: EXITS

(A large man in white) appeared like a cuckoo out of a clock
—Madison Smartt Bell

(Children don't) appear and disappear like toadstools in a lawn
—Miles Gibson

Barged in ... like a Rugby forward —Frank Swinnerton

Blew in like a boisterous breeze —Cole Porter, from "You've Got
That Thing," one of the lyrics for the 1929 musical *Fifty Million
Frenchmen*

Came and went, like bees after honey —Wright Morris

Came as silent as the dew comes —Henry Wadsworth Longfellow

Came in like a swan swimming its way —Virginia Woolf

Came like swallows and like swallows went —W. B. Yeats

Came like water —Edward Fitzgerald
This is from Fitzgerald's classic translation of Omar
Khayyam's *Rubaiyat*.

Comes and goes, like hearts —Elizabeth Bishop

Coming in like a kite on a string —Clive Cussler
In his novel, *Cyclops*, Cussler used the simile to describe
the entrance of a vessel.

Entered like a wind —Ruth Suckow
For added emphasis there's "Come in like a high wind" as
used by Aharon Megged in his novel, *Living on the Dead*.

Enter ... tiptoeing like somebody trying to sneak in late to a funeral
—George Garrett

Flitted in and out of the house like birds —Anne Tyler

Hopped in, light as a bird —Harvey Swados

Light upon the scene like a new-made butterfly —George Garrett

Like hoodlums come ... with neither permits nor requests
—Carl Sandburg

Like Santa Claus he came and went mysteriously —Frank O'Connor

Materialize ... like a policeman presiding over an accident
—Wilfrid Sheed

Plunged into it like a rabbit into its hole —Ben Ames Williams

Popped up here and there like bubbles in a copperful of washing
—Frank Swinnerton

Rolling through the front door like a drunken bear —James Crumley

Rushed into the room like a cannon-ball —Romain Gary

Rush in like a gust of wind —Anon

Slinking in like a little ailing cat —Jean Stafford

Slipped in like a cat or the wind —John J. Clayton

Strode in like a conquering prince returning to his lands
—Alice Walker

Sweep in here like Zeus from Olympus, with his attendant nymphs
and swains —Brian Clark

Swept vivaciously in ... like a champion ice-skater
—Frank Swinnerton

Was into the living-room ... and out again with such speed that she
might have been one of the mechanical weather-people in a
child's snow-globe or a figure on a medieval clock, who zooms
across a lower balcony as the face shows the hands on the hour
—Rachel Ingalls

ENTRAPMENT

About as much chance of escape as a log that is being drawn slowly
toward a buzz saw —Arthur Train

Captured like water in oil —John Updike

Caught in [as a war] like meat in a sandwich —Robert MacNeil, Public Television broadcast, December, 1986

Caught like a forest in a lazing fire —Delmore Schwartz

(What wouldn't I give to see old Cy Lambert) caught like a monkey with his fist in the bottle —Louis Auchincloss

(The feeling came over her that she was) caught like a mouse in the trap of life —Ellen Glasgow

(I went to the war; got) clapped down like a bedbug —Clifford Odets

[Group of people] closed in upon her, like dogs on a fox —Jean Stafford

[Four walls of room] close in upon you like the sides of a coffin —O. Henry

[Many people at a party] engulfed him like an avalanche —Robert Silverberg

Feel like ... a shabby blackbird baked alive in a piecrust —George Garrett

Felt like a muskrat trapped in a weir —Sterling Hayden

Felt like a worm on a hook —Shelby Hearon

Gripped him like an empty belly —Cutcliffe Hyne

Held fast by circumstances as by invisible wires of steel —Ellen Glasgow

It [emotional trap] held him as with the grip of sharp murderous steel —Henry James

My heart chokes in me like a prison —Anzia Yezierska
> Another example of a simile used to launch a work of fiction, in this case a short story entitled *Wings*.

Pinned to ... like a butterfly to a cork —F. van Wyck Mason
> The butterfly image as used by Margaret Millar: "As easily trapped as a butterfly."

Struggling and captive like a newborn infant —Julia O'Faolain

Stuck with them [undesirable companions] like falling into a barrel of
    blackstrap molasses —Elizabeth Spencer

Thrashed about ... like a whale trying to pull free from a harpoon
    —William H. Hallhan

Trapped like a fish between two cats —Spanish proverb

Trapped like a peasant between two lawyers —Anon

Trapped [in traffic] like a fly in a spider's web —Donald Seaman

Felt trapped ... like a man in a cage with a sick bear and his keeper
    —Ross Macdonald

Trapped like a rabbit on a country road —Beryl Bainbridge

ERECTNESS
See: POSTURE

ERRORS

A flaw ... would surface like an aching wisdom tooth
    —James Lee Burke

The defects of the mind, like those of the face, grow worse as we
    grow old —François, Duc de La Rochefoucauld

Delusions, errors and likes are like huge, gaudy vessels, the rafters of
    which are rotten and worm-eaten, and those who embark in
    them are fated to be shipwrecked —Buddha

Errors, like straws, upon the surface flow; he who would search for
    pearls must dive below —John Dryden

Flaunt their folly, like a washline of dirty and patched clothes
    —George Garrett

Gone astray like a lost sheep —*The Holy Bible*

Great blunders are often made, like large ropes, of a multitude of
    fibers —Victor Hugo

Illusion forms before us like a grove —Barbara Howes
        This simile is the first line and leitmotif in Howes' poem,
        The Triumph of Death.

201

(Is somehow) impure, as sacrilegious as a Coca-Cola machine in a cathedral —Tony Ardizzone

A mistake is like a mule, not always distinguishable from a horse in front, but known beyond doubt by acquaintance with its kicking qualities —*New York Sun*, 1918

Wrong as two left shoes —Arthur Baer

ETERNITY
See: CONTINUITY

EVASIVENESS
See: ELUSIVENESS

EVENNESS
See: STRAIGHTNESS

EVIL
See: CRUELTY

EXACTNESS
See: CORRECTNESS

EXCITEMENT
See: AGITATION, ENERGY

EXERCISE
See: MOVEMENT

EXITS
See also: ENTRANCES/EXITS

Bustled off ... like a rolling whirlwind —Yukio Mishima

Crept away, after the fashion of a whipped dog —H. E. Bates

Fled ... like dammed water broken free —Z. Vance Wilson

Fled like quicksilver —William Shakespeare

Flits like a silky bat out of the room —Rose Tremain

Galloping out like a runaway horse —Donald Seaman

Go out like a candle, in a snuff —John Ray's *Proverbs*
> A commonly used version found in a short story entitled *The Beldonald Holbein* by Henry James is to "Go out like a snuffed candle."

I'm off like a dirty shirt
    —John Crier speaking in the movie *Pretty in Pink*

Jumped out of that house like fleas off a dead dog
    —Rita Mae Brown

Leave the room as a burglar might escape from the scene of a
    carefully planned crime —James Stern

Like a rabbit that had been fired at, bolted from the room
    —John Galsworthy

Like March, having come in like a lion, he purposed to go out (of
    her life) like a lamb —Charlotte Brontë
        Often a familiar simile gains freshness from the way it is
        applied, as illustrated by this example from *Shirley*.

Made like an arrow for the door —Christopher Isherwood

Made tracks like a jumped fawn —Thomas Zigal

Running away like sheep —Stephen Vincent Benét

Scuttled away as if he'd found a maggot in his meatball
    —Joseph Wambaugh

Slide away like a whisper down the wind —Richard Ford

Spook like cattle on a drive —Clinton A. Phillips, dean of faculty at
    Texas A & M University, quoted on departure of some academics
    for better opportunities, *New York Times*, December 21, 1986

Stumping to the door ... like an ancient mariner who had lost his
    temper —Frank Swinnerton

Took off like a big-assed bird —American colloquialism
        Another expression spread by the American army.

Took off like a goosed duck —Harold Adams

Took off like a scalded cat —May Swenson

Turned and left, like a key from a lock —Desmond O'Grady

EXPANSION
See: GROWTH

EXPECTATION
See: HOPE

EXPERIENCE
See also: KNOWLEDGE

Experience

Experience is ... a kind of huge spider-web of the finest silken
threads suspended in the chamber of consciousness, and catching
every air-borne particle in its tissue —Henry James

Experience is like medicine; some persons require larger doses of it
than others, and do not like to take it pure, but a little disguised
and better adapted to taste —Lord Acton

Experience, like a pale musician, olds a dulcimer of patience in his
hand —Elizabeth Barrett Browning

Experience seems to be like the shining of a bright lantern. It
suddenly makes clear in the mind what was already there,
perhaps, but dim —Walter De La Mare

A new element in her experience; like a chapter in a book
—Henry Van Dyke

The solitary and unshared experience dies of itself like the violations
of love —Archibald MacLeish

To most men, experience is like the stern light o a ship, which
illumines only the track it has passed —Samuel Taylor Coleridge

EYE(S)
See also: EYES, BRIGHT; EYEBROWS; EYE COLOR; EYE
EXPRESSIONS, MISCELLANEOUS; EYELASHES; EYELIDS; EYE
MOVEMENTS

Eye(s)

Eyes glazed and almost lightless like the little button eyes of a doll
—George Garrett

Eyes ... large and gray, and baleful, like glass on fire
—Norman Mailer

Eyes large as fifty-cent pieces, but pale, like dusty stones
—Ludwig Bemelmans
Bemelmans' subject is William Randolph Hearst.

Eyes ... large as saucers —E. N. Slocum, line from lyric of a song written in 1868 entitled "On the Beach at Cape May"

Eyes like a codfish —Frank Swinnerton

Eyes like a couple of wells —William Diehl

Eyes ... like an Arizona sunset, and they were supported on pouches as large and shapeless as badly packed duffle bags —Jimmy Sangster

Eyes like a pinwheel —Ann Beattie

Eyes ... like a spaniel's —Ouida

Eyes like a starless winter night —clear, black, bleak—A. E. Maxwell

Eyes ... like chestnuts floating on twin pools of milk —William Styron

Eyes like cold cavities in his head —Natascha Wodin

Eyes ... like crickets in daylight —Rochelle Ratner

Eyes like crosses burning on a lawn —Rochelle Ratner

Eyes like currants in a half-cooked suet pudding —Robert Graves
        A simple variation from a short story by Katherine Mansfield: "Little eyes, like currants."

Eyes like dark searchlights —Ross Macdonald

Eyes like dusty lapis lazuli —S. J. Perelman

Eyes like forest pools —W. Somerset Maugham

Eyes ... like forget-me-nots —Mazo De La Roche

Eyes ... like ground owls, deep in their burrows —Harold Adams

Eyes like holes burned with a cigar —William Faulkner

Eyes ... like holes were poked in a snowbank —Raymond Chandler

Eyes like jelly —Hanoch Bartov

Eyes like licked stones —Virginia Woolf

Eyes like licorice gumdrops —Robert Campbell

Eyes ... like lustrous black currants —Frank Swinnerton

Eyes, like marigolds, had sheathed their light —William Shakespeare

In Shakespeare's time 'sheathed' was written as 'sheath'd.'

Eyes like mice peeking into my pockets —Robert Campbell

Eyes like oiled black olives —Frank Tuohy

Eyes ... like old pictures of Rachmaninoff's eyes —Henry Van Dyke

Eyes like onions —Donald Barthelme

Eyes ... like pale marble in a field of red —Linda West Eckhardt

Eyes ... like peas —T. Coraghessan Boyle

Eyes ... like pebbles at the bottom of a mountain trout pool, fixed and icy —Donald MacKenzie

Eyes like pebbles, the kind of pebbles which kids call aggies —Ludwig Bemelmans

Eyes like pebbles unwashed by the sea —Kathleen Farrell

Eyes ... like pools of oil —T. Coraghessan Boyle

Eyes ... like punctuation marks —Geoffrey Wolff

Eyes ... like rubber knobs, like they'd give to the touch —William Faulkner

Eyes like searchlights —Donald McCaig

Eyes ... like shrewd marbles —Harvey Swados

Eyes like the brown waters of a woodland stream —Henry Van Dyke

Eyes like the deep, blue boundless heaven —Percy Bysshe Shelley

(Watery gray) eyes, like the thick edges of broken skylight glass —Willa Cather

Eyes ... shiny and flat as mirrors —Shirley Ann Grau

Eyes ... small and dark and liquid, like drops of strong coffee —Margaret Millar

Eyes ... small and nacreous like painted ornaments —Jean Stafford

Eyes ... small and dirty like the eyes of a potato —Ross Macdonald

Eyes ... small and hard and shiny like dimes —Ross Macdonald

Eyes soft as a leading lady's, round as a doe's
   —T. Coraghessan Boyle

Eyes, speckled and hard as pebbles at the bottom of a stream
   —John Yount

Eyes spoked and rimmed with black, like a mourner's rosette
   —Edith Pearlman
      The simile is particularly appropriate as the writer is
      describing a character who is a widow.

Eyes that looked like imitation jewels —Henry James

Eyes the size of melons —Mary Hood

Eyes were small, so that with the mascara and the shadows painted
   on their lids they looked like flopping black butterflies
   —Eudora Welty

Her eyes looked awful [from too much liquor] as though they had
   been boiled —Christopher Isherwood

Her eyes lost in the fatty ridges of her face, looked like two small
   pieces of coal pressed into a lump of dough —William Faulkner

His eyes behind his glasses kind of all run together like broken eggs
   —William Faulkner

His eyes stood in his head like two poached eggs
   —Erich Maria Remarque

Large eyes like dark pools —Erich Maria Remarque

Little eyes like cigarette-ends —Charles Bukowski

Looked like cat's eyes do, like a big cat against the wall, watching us
   —William Faulkner

Lynx-like eyes —O. Henry

EYES, BRIGHT

(Stood there ... his) black eyes burning like anthracite
   —Stephen Vincent Benét

Burning eyes like flaming wells —Anzia Yezierska

Eyes as bright as sunlight on a stream —Christina Rossetti

Eyes blazed like molten nuggets —Robert Silverberg

Eyes like burning torches —*Arabian Nights*

Eyes like flashlights —Elizabeth Spencer

Eyes as glowing as the summer and as tender as the skies
—James Whitcomb Riley

Eyes ... blazed with a sudden burst of terror, like an explosion of
the heart —Robert Campbell

Eyes blazing like bonfires —Miles Gibson

Eyes bright as dance floors —Scott Spencer

Eyes bright as squirrels' —John Galsworthy

Eyes bright as the lights in a valuable stone —Norman Mailer

Eyes fired up for a moment like pieces of coal. The laughter in them
[eyes] was like two melting ice cubes gleaming in a dish
—Alice Walker

Eyes gleam like those of a popular salesman about to hear an old,
familiar joke —Hilary Masters

Eyes glittered like a wildcat's —Honoré de Balzac

Eyes glittered like razors —Jonathan Valin

Eyes ... glittering and unsteady, like a dog's when it is looking out
of a car window —Frank Tuohy

(His dark) eyes glowed like brandy —Rita Mae Brown

Eyes glowed ... like fire in a cave —Nathaniel Hawthorne

Eyes glowed like two tiny electric bulbs —William Faulkner

Eyes ... like black marbles lying in dust, dark and gleaming and
sharp, with light —Paul Horgan

Eyes like chips of broken glass that catch the light
—Joyce Carol Oates

Eyes, like cinders, all aglow —Lewis Carroll

Eyes like glow-worms —William Shakespeare

Eyes [animal] shining like wind-whipped embers on a pitch-black
night —Jesse Stuart

Eyes shone brighter than the stars —Dante Alighieri

EYEBROWS OVERHUNG HIS EYES
LIKE MUSTACHES

Eyes sparkled as if he'd just heard a joke or told one
—Jonathan Valin

Eyes sparkled like rusty wet bolts —Abraham Rothberg

Eyes that could snap and crackle points of fire like those which
sparkle from a whirling sword —Jack London

Eyes, they glow like tiger's eyes —James Baldwin

Eyes which possessed a warm, life-giving quality like the sunlight
—Willa Cather

Ferocious eyes, much too shiny, like something boiling in a pot
—Cynthia Ozick

Glittering eyes like rats hurrying this way and that —Louis Bromfield

Her eyes gave the impression of being lighted from within ... as if
she had been endowed with her own small sun —Paule Marshall

His eyes shone with certainty, like glints of shellac —Paul Theroux

The light of her eye, like a star glancing out from the blue of the
sky —John Greenleaf Whittier

Lights shone in his eyes like travelers' fires seen far out on the river
—Eudora Welty

Sparks burning in them [black eyes] like fire at the end of a tunnel
—Paige Mitchell

EYEBROWS

Black eyebrows going up like a pair of swallows —V. S. Pritchett

A brow like a thunderclap —Peter DeVries

Brows and lashes smudged like charcoal across her face —Kay Boyle

Brows like bended bows —Thomas Campion

Brows ... like charcoal arches —Aharon Megged

Brows like strung bows —Ruth Prawer Jhabvala

Brows were joined above the nose like the hilt of a large dagger
—Saul Bellow

Dark eyebrows like sudden brushstrokes above the deep dark eyes
—Sylvia Berkman

(Raising an) eyebrow built like a wooly worm —James Crumley

Eyebrows arched like skipping ropes —Henry James

Eyebrows as big as mustaches —Jilly Cooper

Eyebrows curved like big rainbows above her eyes —J. P. Donleavy

Eyebrows drawn so closely together that they seemed like a hedge blocking her view —Carolyn Slaughter

Eyebrows lifted in pink crescents upturned like the dogwood's first leaves in spring —Eudora Welty

Eyebrows ... like birds of prey —T. Coraghessan Boyle

Eyebrows like commas —John Fowles

Eyebrows like frost —James Dickey

Eyebrows like hanging gardens —Max Shulman

Eyebrows like peaked black thread —Jean Stafford

Eyebrows like unclipped hedges —Daphne Merkin

Eyebrows looking like a big iron-grey caterpillar lying along the edge of a cliff —William Faulkner

Eyebrows overhung his eyes like mustaches —John Steinbeck

Eyebrows raised, like hoods on baby-carriages —Eudora Welty

Eyebrows rising like fans —Martin Cruz Smith

Eyebrows thick and full like fur frames —Paige Mitchell

Eyebrows were thick, tough as strips of bark —Truman Capote

A great deal of brow in a face is like a great deal of horizon in a view —Victor Hugo

His brows ... brindled with grey and tufted like the pelt of a beast. They looked like structural beams, raised into a position that would support the weight of his knowledge and authority —John Cheever

His eyebrows punctuate his speech like hands —Ira Wood

Knitted his brows like sharply molded steel —D. H. Lawrence
　　　　The text of *Women in Love*, where this appeared, used the English spelling 'moulded' instead of 'molded.'

Eyebrows

(When she was excited she liked to) raise first one thin eyebrow and then the other so that they almost leapt off her face like antennae —Molly Giles

Thick, black eyebrows like the wings of a swallow —Maxim Gorky

Eye Color

EYE COLOR
See also: BLACK, BLUE, BROWN, GRAY, GREEN

Black eyes like plum pits —Bernard Malamud

Black eyes turned shiny like the sun —Shirley Ann Grau

Blue eyes like transparent agate marbles, hard and polished and just about indestructible —Sylvia Plath

Blue eyes ... round and open like two lakes —Aharon Megged

Blue eyes that sat in his lined face like a piece of sky
    —Erich Maria Remarque

Brown eyes like quicksand —Diane Ackerman

Eyes ... black and burning as coal —Lord Byron
        Byron's "Black as coal" comparison from *Don Juan* has been much used, and with many new twists, several of which can be found here. The "Black as coal" comparison has also been linked with many other descriptive references.

Eyes ... black as bullets and as fierce —Belva Plain

Eyes ... blue and guileless as a doll's —David Brierley

Eyes ... brown and irisless, like those of an old dog
    —William Faulkner

Eyes ... deepened to the color of caramel, like sugar coming to a boil
    —Louise Erdrich

Eyes faded to a brittle, metallic gray, like chips of slate
    —James Crumley

Eyes ... light, blue, like colorless water reflecting a blue sky
    —Jessamyn West
        In the short story, *The Calla Lily Cleaners & Dyers*, from which this is taken, the simile is extended as follows: "And his face being so suntanned they were more like vacancies in his head than eyes."

Eyes, like bitter chocolate —Margaret Millar
> A more recent example of this simile appears Ira Wood's novel *The Kitchen Man* which is as chockfull of food imagery as a refrigerator after a weekly shopping trip.

Eyes ... like black buttons or raisins sunk in dough —Nina Bawden

Eyes ... like blue cake-icing —Truman Capote

Eyes like blue-painted glass —Flannery O'Connor

Eyes like chocolate fudge still warm from the pan —Elizabeth Spencer

Eyes like the sky on a misty summer morning —Piers Anthony

Eyes ... like those of a rabbit, not frightened, but utterly impenetrable —Graham Masterton

Eyes pale as the moon —Grace Paley

Eyes redder than burning coals —Gustave Flaubert

Eyes so pale they were like openings on the sky —Wright Morris

Eyes the color of water vapor —T. Coraghessan Boyle

Eyes ... they didn't have much color ... like, whoever was putting the color into them got a phone call in the middle and just quit —Lee Smith

Eyes ... warmly blue as the glint of summer sunshine on an iceberg drifting in Southern seas —O. Henry

Gray eyes ... watery like the winter sky —Frank Tuohy

Large, brown eyes like mushroom caps —Helen Hudson
> In her novel, *Meyer Meyer*, Helen Hudson returns to this simile with another: "Her dull mushroom eyes seemed to have grown smaller, as though they had been sautéed too long."

Light-blue eyes ... like bits of glass —Jean Rhys

Pale eyes like pools of phlegm —Richard S. Prather

Sharp blue eyes, each like a pin —Robert Browning

Small green eyes, like grapes about to burst —Mary McCarthy

Eye Color

Soft brown eyes, like those of a mild-tempered dog
    —Frank Swinnerton

Toffee-colored eyes like a spaniel's —T. H. White

Wet blue eyes, like eyes in a clear aspic —Jonathan Valin

Eye Expressions, Miscellaneous

EYE EXPRESSIONS, MISCELLANEOUS

Excitement widened her eyes like periods at the end of billboard
    sentences —Tom Robbins

Expressionless blue eyes ... like a pair of glass marbles
    —Frank Swinnerton

Eyes ... alive, like blue tigers —Cynthia Ozick

Eyes ... as cold and lacking in interest as the eyes of a tortoise
    —Nadine Gordimer

Eyes as dead as stale oysters —Raymond Chandler

Eyes as deep and storyless as the sea —Terry Bisson

Eyes as doleful and red-rimmed as an old hound's —Robert Traver

Eyes, as hard and cold as a frozen lake —Ellen Glasgow

Eyes ... as innocent as if they had entered their sockets a half-hour
    ago —Ben Hecht

Eyes ... as opaque as jelly beans —Joan Hess

Eyes ... as shy as a wild stag's —Mary Lee Settle

Eyes, bland and sad as a dog's —George Garrett

Eyes ... blank, clouded with anger or grief, like the sky before a
    snowstorm —James Crumley

Eyes blind as woodknots —Daniel Berrigan

Eyes clear and cool as rainwater —George Garrett

Eyes clear and candid as a winter sky at dawn —Harvey Swados

Eyes clear as water —John Steinbeck

Eyes clear as window glass —Ward Just

Eyes ... cloudless as a sky in spring —George Garrett

Eyes ... cold as a crocodile's —Peter Benchley

Eyes cold as grey agate —Margaret Mitchell

Eyes cool as coins —Margaret Millar

Eyes ... dark and cold ... like water under ice —Mary Hedin

Eyes ... dark and empty, like open graves —Donald Seaman

Eyes ... dead and cold, like marbles swimming in glass
      —Paige Mitchell

Eyes ... expressionless as ice cubes —Clive Cussler

Eyes, fishy and staring like headlights —Harvey Swados

(When he is excited or amused ... his) eyes flare like two cigarette
      lighters —Bryan Miller, *New York Times* story about Yves
      Montand, June 24, 1987

Eyes flat and vicious like the eyes of a mean dog crouched over a
      bone —George Garrett

Eyes frightened as if she expected any moment the stunning blow of
      a fist —George Garrett

His eyes glaze over like eggs up —Ira Wood

Eyes ... grow blank as a dropped blind —Edith Wharton

Eyes ... hard as almond shells with a kernel of light
      —Rumer Godden

Eyes hard as buttons —Louise Erdrich

(Her inky) eyes have the look of someone who has been in prison a
      long time and knows they can send her back —Sharon Olds

Eyes in which intelligence and comprehension burned like two fixed
      stars —Edith Wharton

Eyes keen as talons —T. Coraghessan Boyle

Eyes, like a stern judge's, seemed to pierce the heart of all questions
      —Honoré de Balzac

Eyes like flint-stones —Donald Seaman

Eyes like glacier lakes —Donald McCaig

Eyes like marbles, hard and glazed —Borden Deal

Eyes like needles —Lord Byron

Eyes like smoking tragedies —Edna O'Brien

Eyes ... like the eyes in the statues blank and unseeing and serene —William Faulkner

Eyes ... like the eyes of a dying man who looks everywhere for healing —James Baldwin

Eyes ... like the eyes of the dead that noon has closed with love's last kiss —Johann Wolfgang von Goethe

(Looked back at him, his black) eyes like two drill bits —Nicholas Proffitt

Eyes like two steel spies —Flannery O'Connor

Eyes looked like the prelude to a scream —Raymond Chandler

Eyes observant and curious like those of a man caught in a great catastrophe which it is his duty to record —Graham Greene

(Lying motionless on his back,) eyes staring up at the ceiling like a doll's —Joseph Heller

Eyes ... steely as a bird's —Jean Garrigue

Eyes swollen with rage; they look like hard-cooked eggs —T. Coraghessan Boyle

Eyes that looked as if they might warm up at the right time and in the right place —Raymond Chandler

Eyes that looked as if they were trying to see beyond the horizon —William McIlvanney

Eyes went flat with terror, like a rabbit caught by a car's headlights —Andrew Kaplan

Eyes widened with fear, like a cat facing headlights in the night —Z. Vance Wilson

Eyes ... wide open like a deer's —Colette

Fury flashing from her eyes like New Year's Eve sparklers —Dorothea Straus

Hard eyes ... like little metal studs (pinned into the white faces of young men) —John Updike

His eyes [Mike Wallace's] grew flat as the eyes of a movie Apache who has just taken a rifle bullet to the stomach
—Norman Mailer
> The Apache comparison underscores Mailer's repeated references to Mike Wallace's resemblance to an Indian.

Little eyes lit up like a cat's in a room full of yarn —Thomas Zigal

Look in his eyes like a glutted steer in a feedlot —Mary Hood

Mischief crackling like static electricity in her eyes —W. P. Kinsella

Tired, kindly eyes, like the eyes of a monkey —Elizabeth Bowen

Wide amazed eyes like an expensive china doll —George Garrett

Wide penetrating eyes, like black raisins —Rex Reed
> The eyes Reed is comparing to black raisins belong to Sophia Loren.

EYELASHES

(She was an artist of the face,) drawing her long lashes out like licorice —Jay Parini

Eyelashes like the wicks of many extinguished candles
—Frank Swinnerton

Eyelashes long as shish kebab —Rex Reed
> The owner of the long lashes is Carol Channing.

Eyelashes ... long, like flies' legs —Aharon Megged

Eyelashes stiff as bird-tails —Eudora Welty

Eyelashes ... thick and furry as tarantula legs —James Crumley

[Eyes] lash-fringed like Spanish lace —Davis Grubb

Lashes as thick and dark as raven feathers —Jonathan Kellerman

Lashes bunched together like star points —Jill Ciment

Lashes thick and black as if painted with a black tar-like material
—Joyce Carol Oates

Long lashes fluttered like the feelers of a beetle on its back
—Truman Capote
> The lashes thus described belong to Mae West

Thick lashes, soft as paintbrushes —Louise Erdrich

217

Eyelids

Eyelids drooped as though the lashes weighed intolerably
    —Truman Capote

Eyelids fluttering, as if assailed by gnats —Leonard Michaels

Eyelids heavy as if from too much dreaming. His dreaming lay like
    the edges of a deep slumber on the rim of his eyelids
    —Anaïs Nin

Eyelids ... hung askew over her cloudy gray eyes [too weak to be
    raised or lowered] like broken blinds in the windows of a
    condemned house —Gerald Kersh

Eyelids like thin gray leather —Ken Kesey

Eyelids pale like a chicken's —V. S. Pritchett

Eyelids translucent as crepe —Jayne Anne Phillips

Eyelids which looked like walnut shells —Julia O'Faolain

Eyes ... double-lidded like the eyes of the black bull snake
    —Will Weaver

Heavy eyelids ... like small, brown, wrinkled egg-shells
    —Brian Glanville

Lids ... like furrows in deeply plowed soil —Anon

Lower lids as straight as ruler-edges —Dashiell Hammett

Eyelids flutter like butterflies that children have impaled alive on pins
    —Erich Maria Remarque

The thick red-lined lids hung over the eyeballs like blinds of which
    the cords are broken —Edith Wharton

Eye Movements

EYE MOVEMENTS

Blinked ... as if chasing a fly away —Aharon Megged

Blinking like a frightened cat —Dan Wakefield

Blinking like a mechanical toy —Peter Benchley

Eyeballs bulged like a lizard's —Paige Mitchell

Eyes ... beginning to bob like fishing corks on the sea
    —William Diehl

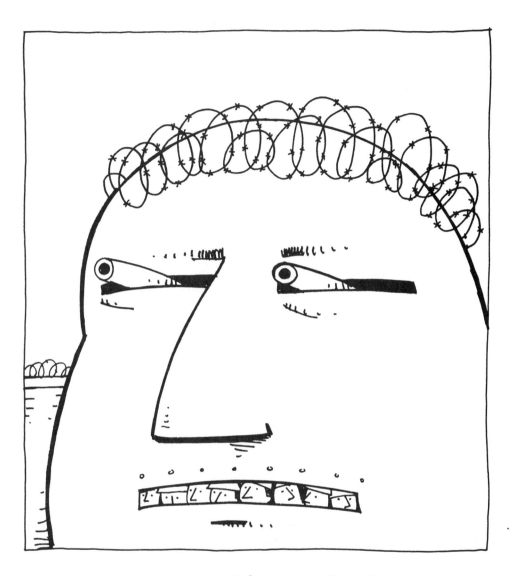

EYES NARROWED LIKE GUNSLITS

Eye Movements

Eyes bounce like marbles —Norman Mailer

Eyes closed, almost as if he was silently praying —John Fowles

Eyes darting like astonished fish —Brian Glanville

Eyes dart like a shoplifter's —Hilma Wolitzer

Eyes dart like swallows —Marge Piercy

Eyes did a dance like two flies looking for a place to light
    —Robert Campbell

(He nodded his head, but his) eyes didn't move, as if they were
    weighted in their sockets like the eyes of a doll —Jonathan Valin

Eyes dilated like an animal's caught in a trap —V. S. Pritchett

Eyes dilate like targets on a rifle range, and each word and gesture
    is emphasized by a blast of cigarette smoke that makes her look
    like she's walking in a cumulus cloud —Rex Reed
        The actress thus profiled by Reed is Bette Davis.

Eyes flashed and twinkled ... like the lamps of a lighthouse
    —Anthony Powell

Eyes flashing like magnifying glasses —H. E. Bates

Eyes flickered like uncertain lights —Ann Rice

Eyes flicker like leaves —Marge Piercy

Eyes fluttered around the room like moths —Donald McCaig

Eyes hovered about like mosquitoes —C. J. Koch

(Yonatan's) eyes narrowed like gunslits —Amos Oz

(Schwend's hurt) eyes opened like blooming peonies
    —Herbert Lieberman

Eyes opened like windows —Sharon Sheehe Stark

Eyes ... opened wide like a clairvoyant's —Anaïs Nin

Eyes roamed about like jellyfish —H. E. Bates

Eyes rolled in their sockets like loose marbles —Truman Capote

Eyes seemed to be clambering frantically, like a pair of blatant
    prisoners behind her heavy glasses —V. S. Pritchett

(His little) eyes snapped like two sparks. Like two sparks they
glowed in the smoulder of his bearded face
—Katherine Mansfield

In this example from her short story, *Ole Underwood*,
Katherine Mansfield demonstrates the effectiveness of
repeating a simile.

Eyes that kept winking and twinkling at each side of his inquisitive
nose, as if they were playing a perpetual game of peep-bo with
that feature —Charles Dickens

Eyes ... twirling around like fruit-flies —Jane Wagner

Eyes were closed like a man in violent prayer —William Styron

Furtive little eyes kept darting around in his head like rodents
—Thomas Wolfe

Languidly half closes his eyes, like a cat on a sofa —Anton Chekhov

Lowered her eyes like a nun beholding a statue —Honoré de Balzac

Narrowing his eyes like someone who knows there's a mouse in the
soup —Peter Meinke

Rapidly blinking eyes, as though he were caught in a constant
sandstorm —Daphne Merkin

Rolled his eyes like a pair of gambler's dice —Paige Mitchell

Tightly shutting her eyes like a shot pheasant falling out of the sky
—Kenzaburo Oë

Wide-spaced eyes floating like sea-slivers above his cheek bones
—Julia O'Faolain

FACE(S)
See also: BLUSHES; CHEEKS; EYEBROWS; EYELASHES; EYELIDS;
FACIAL COLOR; FACIAL DETAILS; FACIAL EXPRESSIONS,
BLANK; FACIAL EXPRESSIONS, MISCELLANEOUS; FACIAL
EXPRESSIONS, SERIOUS; FACIAL SHAPE; HAIR; LIPS; WRINKLES

Face like a bad orange —Joyce Cary

Face ... like a beaked bird —James Joyce

Face like a benediction —Miguel de Cervantes

Face like a butcher's block —Frank O'Connor

Face ... like a fiddle and everyone who sees him must love him
—Anon Irish saying
   Carl Sandburg who had a penchant for incorporating familiar similes into his work, quoted this in his poem, *New Hampshire Again.*

(A pale flat woman with a) face like a fillet of flounder
—Helen Hudson

Face like a knotty whorl in the bark of a hoary olive tree
—Amos Oz

Face ... like a mail-order ax —William H. Gass

A face like a Mediterranean Lolita —Carol Ascher

Face like an anemic cat's —Colette

Face like an old purse —Mary Hedin

(A little brown monkey of a man with) a face like a nut
—Ruth Rendell

Face like a peeled beet —Hanoch Bartov

Face like a picture of a knight, like one of that Round Table bunch
—O. Henry

Face ... like a piece of the out-of-doors come indoors: as holly-berries do —D. H. Lawrence

Face ... like a pillow that has been much but badly slept on
—Romain Gary

Face ... like a predatory bird, beaked, grim-lipped —Wallace Stegner

Face like a raisin cookie. Eyes set wide apart and shallow
—Donald McCaig

A face like a rock —Thomas Carlyle
   Carlyle thus described his publisher, Frederic Henry Hedge.

Face like a sack of flour —T. Coraghessan Boyle

Face like a sallow bust on a bracket in a university library
—Edith Wharton

Face like a shell —Ellen Gilchrist

Face like a slab of corned beef —Oakley Hall

Face like a small pale mask —William Faulkner

Face like a sodden pie —Edgar Lee Masters

A face like a very expensive cat —Josephine Tey

Face like a very ripe peach —Christopher Isherwood

Face like lean old glove leather —Richard Ford

Face ... like the cement in an old cellar, rough irregular lines lying
    thick and lumpy along a hard white surface —Charles Johnson

Face like the soul's awakening —P. G. Wodehouse

Her big powdered face was set like an egg in a cup in the frilly
    high-necked blouse —John Dos Passos

(He had) a face like the statue of some Victorian industrialist, heavy
    and firm and deeply lined, giving an impression of stern
    willingness —John Braine

A face like Walt Disney's idea of a grandfather
    —William McIlvanney

Face like warm baked clay —C. J. Koch

Face looked like a white blown-out paper bag —V. S. Pritchett

Face ... massive as a piece of sculpture —Harvey Swados

Face ravaged as the dimmest memories of the past ... creased and
    flabby, like an old bag —Kingsley Amis

Face red, swollen, like an overripe fruit —Graham Swift

Face sagged, as if its fleshy sub-structure had dried up
    —McKinlay Kantor

Faces bunched like fists —Irving Feldman

Faces harder than a rock —*The Holy Bible/Jeremiah*

Face shimmering and flat as the moon —Diane Wakoski

Face ... shines in the darkness like a thin moon
    —Erich Maria Remarque

Face short and blunt as a cat's —M. J. Farrell

Faces like dark boxes of secrets and desires ... locked safely, like old-fashioned caskets for the safe conduct of jewels on a voyage —Eudora Welty

(Young neat unscratched boys with) faces like the bottoms of new saucers —Charles Bukowski

Face like flint —*The Holy Bible/Isaiah*

Face smooth and intent like a man listening to music —Ross Macdonald

Face smooth and timeless as a portrait in a darkened gallery —T. Coraghessan Boyle

Face ... smooth, calculated, and precision-made, like an expensive baby doll —Ken Kesey

Face ... smooth like a balmy sky where there's peace —Helga Sandburg

Face ... soft and withered as an apple doll —Sue Grafton

Face so grimed with dirt it looked like a brown leather mask —John Dos Passos

Face ... so old that it looked as if the flesh had been polished away —Ellen Glasgow

Face sparkles like a diamond (at mention of favorite topic-collecting) —Honoré de Balzac

Faces ruddy and wrinkled like old apples —Margaret Bhatty

Faces shimmered like they were coming out of water —Jayne Anne Phillips

Face ... strong, like Greek statuary —Sue Grafton

Faces were like the faces of lions —*The Holy Bible/Kings*

A face that looked as if it had been left out on the fire escape for over half a century —Rex Stout

A face that resembled a diseased cauliflower —Miles Gibson

A face that seemed sometimes as intimidating as a clenched fist —Frank Tuohy

Face thin as a desert saint's —Z. Vance Wilson

Face thrust forward like a hatchet —Oakley Hall

Face twitched like a snapping rubber band —James Lee Burke

(The old woman's) face was like a worn rock at which all the waves
of life had smashed and beaten —Thomas Wolfe

Face was very like a crow —Lewis Carroll

Face ... wizened as an old potato —Ignazio Silone

(One day his) face would collapse, like that of a beautiful woman
who suddenly abandons the pretense and concedes defeat
—Harvey Swados

Face ... wound up like a spring —Alan Sillitoe

Features ... a little like a Roman emperor side-face —A. A. Milne

Features ... dark and indistinct, as if they'd been rubbed with a dirty
eraser —Alice McDermott

A flat face like an imprint in some thick, warm tar
—Robie Macauley

Flat white face, like a pillow with eyes —Richard Connell

Front face she was shapeless like poorly impressed sealing-wax
—Julia O'Faolain

Her face had filled out into two little puffs of vanity on either side
of her mouth, as if she were eating or were containing a yawn
—V. S. Pritchett

Her face had rounded with flesh that closed in about her eyes like a
dough doll's —Will Weaver

Her face, pinched from the cold, made her look like a young girl in
the Depression of the thirties —Penelope Gilliatt

Her face was like an old brown bowl —Thomas Wolfe

His countenance was like the countenance of an angel of God, very
terrible —*The Holy Bible/Judges*

His face was as ... the sun —*The Holy Bible/Revelation*

His face, with its thick crude lines ... and large mouth, gave him the
appearance of a slightly refined monkey —H. E. Bates

FACIAL COLOR
See also: BLUSHES, PALLOR, RED

A face like a raw steak —John Dos Passos

An extremely florid face, as if his blood pressure was about to pop
  —Peter Meinke

A bluish pallor had spread like a shadow over his face
  —Walter De La Mare

Carried a ruddy stain on either cheek, like a ripe apple
  —Robert Louis Stevenson

Cheeks and bunchy lips as red as they would have been if she had
  fallen into a pot of jam —Frank Swinnerton

Coloring as natural as a bird's egg or a leaf —Frank Tuohy

Coloring ... ss like the bloom of a ripe fruit, that nature in her
  seemed to have rivalled art —Italo Svevo

The color spread across his face like a bush fire —Mike Fredman

Face ... a curious, flat color, like the inside of a raw potato
  —Susan Hill

A face as white and almost as smooth as a bar of soap
  —Scott Spencer

Face dark with furious blood, dark as a plum —Guy Vanderhaeghe
    A variation by Gloria Norris: "Face ... turned purple as a
    plum."

Face ... dull red, as if baked by the heat of blazing towns
  —Stephen French Whitman

Face glows, spotty, like there's a tiny pink bulb burning behind each
  cheek —Sharon Sheehe Stark

(Marley's) face ... had a dismal light about it, like a bad lobster in a
  dark cellar —Charles Dickens

Face like a lobster —Robert Louis Stevenson

Face like a raw side of beef —Robert Campbell

Face ... like a strawberry —Mary Hedin
    In Hedin's short story, *The Secret*, the woman with the
    strawberry-like face had been bending over a stove.

(Passion has made his) face like pale ivory —Oscar Wilde

FLAT WHITE FACE, LIKE A PILLOW WITH EYES

Face pale and lined like a map —Hugh Walpole

Face ... pale as death and far more ghastly —Nathaniel Hawthorne

A face ... puffy and sallow, the color of old piano keys
—William Boyd
> In the novel, *An Ice-Cream War*, the author continues as follows: "As if he were just recovering from an illness or about to be seriously afflicted by one."

Face ... red as a parrot's —Dame Edith Sitwell

Face ... ruddy, flushed with blood, like a slaughterer's
—Isaac Bashevis Singer

Face shone red as a cock's comb —Rita Mae Brown

Faces red as steak —Sharon Olds

Faces stained by the cool night like wine —Dame Edith Sitwell

Faces white like paste —Hugh Walpole

Face the color and texture of kangaroo hide —Frank Ross

Face ... the color of cat's meat —James Thurber

Face turned to a dull white, like bread dough —Anon

Face went gray, like the mortar in the trough —Henry Van Dyke

Face yellow like ancient paper —Arthur A. Cohen

Great blushing face, like a Dutch cheese —Jilly Cooper

Her color had been pared away, like you pare an apple
—Donald McCaig

Her color was high, as though she had been sitting near a fire
—Geoffrey Wolff

Her face was ... white-powdered like a marshmallow —Frank Tuohy

A medium dark face, like antique gold under a black light
—Loren D. Estleman

Tanned as a hound's tooth —Robert Traver

Two spots of rouge like paper discs pasted on her cheekbones
—William Faulkner

Unnaturally red cheeks like varnished apples —Edith Wharton

FACIAL DETAILS

A blemish on the ridge of his nose stood out like a connecting point between his eyebrows, like a town on a map
—Bobbie Ann Mason

Blues under his eyes like chain links —Saul Bellow

The bones on his face stuck out like knobs under his skin
—Gloria Norris

Busted blood vessels in the nose and across his cheeks look like a precinct map of the city —Robert Campbell

The dimple in her chin is like a tiny keyhole —Joan Chase

Dimples that looked as if they had been poked into her cheeks by a mischievous finger —Rex Beach

Ears as sharp as a fox —MacDonald Harris
        A commonly used variation: "Ears like a fox."

Ears like bat's wings —Aharon Megged

Ears like jug handles —Borden Deal

Ears like pointed spears —David Ignatow

Ears ... pendulous scarlet ears that showed up like blobs of sealing wax on the pallor of his cheeks and were framed in wisps of silky white hair —Albert Camus

Ears sticking out like tabs he might be picked up and shaken by
—Eudora Welty

(Large) ears ... stuck out like wings —Leo Tolstoy

Freckled, as if she'd been sprinkled with nutmeg —Eudora Welty

(A mask of) freckles laid like a veil across his nose
—Ben Ames Williams

Freckles like rust spots —Willa Cather

Freckles like specks of nutmeg on his cheeks —Sharon Olds

(Nose bridged with) freckles like splotches of huge summer rain on the sidewalk —William Faulkner

Freckles lingered just below the skin, like a thin wash of gold
—Elizabeth Spencer

A gash as thick as a cigarette —T. Glen Coughlin

Facial Details

His nose was very short, just like a baby's, and he had a long blue upper lip, like a priest —Joyce Cary
See also: NOSES

A mole like a tiny cameo —Eudora Welty

(She brushed at the) mole that spotted her cheek like a tear —Truman Capote

Pimples big as candy corn —Ira Wood

Pimples ... shone like the sun trying to come out —Sharon Sheehe Stark

Red pimples spread across her forehead like strawberry jam —Alice McDermott
See also: FOREHEAD

Scars ... like claw marks —Louise Erdrich

A scar ... that twained his face from forehead to chin, like a portrait sliced in half —Davis Grubb

Scratches on his face like a cat had fought him hard for every one of its lives —O. Henry

The shadows under my eyes were like a pair of leathery wings —Jean Thompson

Facial Expressions, Blank

FACIAL EXPRESSIONS, BLANK
See also: EYE EXPRESSIONS, MISCELLANEOUS

Anonymous, like the faces one sees in a football crowd —Robert Traver

(Her face went as) blank as a chalkboard —Jonathan Valin

(The child's expression was) blank, as if her hair was drawn back and fastened so tightly that her facial muscles couldn't function —Margaret Millar

Countenance ... like a still, dark day, equally beamless and breezeless —Charlotte Brontë

Empty look ... like an actor without a part —John Le Carré

Expressionless as a smoked herring —Anon

Expressionless ... like a portrait of a great beauty by a not very great painter who had caught all the listed features, but not the living stir of loveliness —Elizabeth Taylor

Face ... cold and motionless, as of a man who is asleep —Mikhaïl P. Arzybashev

Face ... as blank as a target after a militia shooting-match —Mark Twain

Face ... as inanimate as a mask —Ellen Glasgow

Face as inscrutable as that of a snapping turtle —Arthur Train

A face as vacant as an untenanted house —Marcel Proust

Face, empty like that of a doll —Franz Werfel

Face had all the warmth, personality and individualism of an amoeba —Robert J. Serling

Face like a marble mask in which the lips were too rigid for speech —Edith Wharton

Face like one of those Easter Island stone carvings —Len Deighton

Face ... locked like a vault —T. Coraghessan Boyle

Face set in a fixed expression of friendly interest like a mask pulled over her skull —Frank Conroy

Face set into a stiff mask, like that of an acroterian —John Fowles

Faces that were as closed, as mysterious, and as mute as the faces of the dead who are possessed of a knowledge beyond the comprehension of the living —Joseph Conrad

Hardly ever smiling, with no cracks showing so no one could look in ... like an empty plate —Helen Hudson

Hopelessly blank, like the face of a blind man —Joseph Conrad

It [face] was blank, as though she no longer dwelt within her own skull, as though she had gone elsewhere —Margaret Laurence

His face was empty and impassive, shut tight as a graveyard gate —Nicholas Proffitt

Staring blankly ahead like a man with a fever —Mark Helprin

Wooden-faced as a cigar-store Indian —Raymond Chandler

This typifies the simile that outlives the relevancy of the comparison.

FACIAL EXPRESSIONS, MISCELLANEOUS
See also: EYE EXPRESSIONS, MISCELLANEOUS

Always had a ready smile, so that her face with its round rosy cheeks was more like something you could eat or lick; she reminded me of nothing so much as an apple fritter —Edna O'Brien

Anger on her cheeks like rouge —Truman Capote

Anxiety and annoyance chasing each other like the hands of a clock around his wide, flat face —Helen Hudson

Blinked ... like an owl surprised in daylight and annoyed at this interruption —John Galsworthy

Bright, inflamed look, as though she had just been crying or having her cheeks scrubbed by an angry nursegirl —Mary McCarthy

Face ... cold as a cameo —Barbara Howes

His countenance was like lightning —*The Holy Bible/Matthew*

Expression ... like a leopard who's just sighted a plump impala —Jilly Cooper

Expression like a stork that dropped a baby and broke it and is coming to explain to the parents —Mel Brooks

Face was wound up like a spring —Alan Sillitoe

Face ... cold, as though warmth and tenderness were dead in her —Jean Rhys

Face ... as calm as a mask —Ross Macdonald

Face ... as hard as ice —Roberta Allen

Face as welcoming as an open fire —William McIlvanney

Face becoming creased and flabby, like an old bag, with the strain of making it smile and show interest and speak its permitted few words —Kingsley Amis

Face bobbing anxiously like a man bidding at an auction —Derek Lambert

Face changed a little ... as if a headlight had flashed across it —Frank Tuohy

Face [of old man] crinkled into a laugh, so that it looked like a polished walnut —Lu Hsün

Face crumpled like a sheet of wadded paper —Pat M. Esslinger-Carr

Face ... delicate with fear, as if it might shatter like white china —Paul Theroux

Face had clenched like a pale wax-paper mask, into a ball of hate —Louise Erdrich

Face had fallen like a waffle —Frank O'Hara

Face harmoniously fixed, as if for a camera —Elizabeth Hardwick

Face harsh and wrung and savage beneath the springing tears like sweat —William Faulkner

Face is still calm, as though she had a cast made and painted to just the look she wanted —Ken Kesey

Face laced tight as a shoe —Lorrie Moore

(When he came ... her) face lighted up as if he had been sunshine —William Makepeace Thackeray

Face like a buttered scone, dripping complacency —Helen Hudson

Face lit up like a sunburst —Max Shulman

Face lit with a kind of radiant pain, as if she'd been bitten by a miracle —Sharon Sheehe Stark

(Icy anger tucked behind his) face, locked up like a store after hours —Lorrie Moore

Face looked all stiff, as if he were afraid the features would fall off —Helen Hudson

Face puckered and fierce and jowly and quizzical like a Boston bulldog —George Garrett

Face ... rigid, like the face of a man in the grip of a barely controlled rage —Wallace Stegner

(Tiny's) face sagged like an old pillow propped against a headboard —Harold Adams

Faces all knotted up like burls on oaks —William Carlos Williams

Faces became red and swollen as from an interior fire which flamed out from the clear holes of their eyes —Émile Zola

Faces chipped into expressions that never change, like flint arrowheads —Ken Kesey

(The sheriff's) face seems to melt like a plate of butter left too close to the fire —George Garrett

Face shining like a great sunflower —Aharon Megged

Face shone with a bright glow ... like the terrible glow of a fire on a dark night —Leo Tolstoy

Faces ... lifted up like flowers in a kind of rapt and mournful ecstasy —Thomas Wolfe

Face squinched up like a withered apple —Robert B. Parker

Faces with the word 'no' stamped like a coat of arms on them —V. S. Pritchett
>   The faces Pritchett describes belong to London landladies.

Face that looks as overworked as Gary Cooper trying to register an emotion —Wallace Stegner

Face twisted like a man who's accidentally swallowed a whole chili pepper —Gloria Norris

Face, vague like a shadow —Anatole France
See also: VAGUENESS

Face ... vigilant as some small cat's —Louise Erdrich

Face was set into an expression of intense attention, like a man listening to an important broadcast which might affect his course of action in some way —John Malcolm

Face went to pieces as if by its own weight —Ross Macdonald

Fearful expression ... like the fear of an animal which has been beaten and kicked for too long —Louis Bromfield

Features ... softening like wax too close to the flame —George Garrett

Fierce and variegated countenance, appeared like war personified —Nathaniel Hawthorne
See also: FEROCITY

A gentle, cowlike expression passed over her face like a cloud
—Colette

Grimaced, like a rubber Kewpie doll being squeezed in all the wrong
places —Paige Mitchell

The grin left his face and was replaced by the sort of amusement
that rings like a coin slapped on a bar —Jonathan Valin

Had a face like a requiem —Honoré de Balzac

Had an expression on his face as if he were listening for something,
so that one felt one couldn't disturb him —Ruth Prawer Jhabvala

(Her eyes were still red, but she) had the happy look of a child that
has outslept its grief —Edith Wharton

Had the mankind-loving look of a convert fresh from church
—Harold Adams

Hard, red face like a book of rules —Anthony Carson

Has a haunted, jumpy look, as if invisible alarm clocks were going
off throughout the day, to remind him of undone duties
—Christopher Isherwood

His fat face opened and smiled like a distorted, gold-toothed flower
—John Dickson Carr

His mangy little face lit up like a store window going on for the
night —Jonathan Valin

Like a peddler whose wares have been turned down all day, he
waited, with a look of patient expectation —Elizabeth Hardwick

Lips went white, like a person who has received a stunning blow
without warning and who, in the first moments of shock, does
not realize what has happened —Margaret Mitchell
See also: LIPS

(Every time he saw Conrad he) lit up like a fairground with hilarity
and self-satisfaction —A. Alvarez

A lonely face, pulled in like rain off the wild stretches
—Elizabeth Spencer

Look as startled as a hare —Joyce Cary

Looked smug ... like a messenger bringing the news of a battle won
—John Rechy

Looked wistful, like a kid who'd lost the magic penny
—Robert Campbell

Looking as miserable as sin —Penelope Gilliatt

Looking puzzled and dismayed, like a baby who's learned to pull
itself up on the sides of a crib, but hasn't figured out how to sit
down again —Sue Grafton

A look of intense mirth spread over Lily's face like water released
suddenly from a broken dam —Louis Bromfield

A look of surprise ... as if he'd just swallowed an ice cube
—T. Coraghessan Boyle
See also: SURPRISE

Looks perpetually surprised, but scared and insincere, like a play
actor —Jayne Anne Phillips

Looks puzzled and grieved, as if he can't believe his bad luck
—François Camoin

No pity or censure in her face, it was as immovable as a fact
—Margaret Millar

Official faces ... like death masks —Ross Macdonald

Old emotions, like old scars, savaged his face —Rita Mae Brown

One could see thoughts crossing his face like caravans of camels
lurching slowly across the seemingly endless Sahara
—Delmore Schwartz

Open-mouthed, like a fish —Anon

Pale astonishment in his face as if at a sudden accusation
—George Eliot

Pleading look, a beg for help like a message from a powerless
invaded country to the rest of the world
—Lynne Sharon Schwartz

Sensuality had been eroded from his face, nibbled away, as the sea
nibbles traces of meat from a shell —Julia O'Faolain

A set face, sad like a toy soldier's, wooden and clad with honor
—Z. Vance Wilson

(The other diners were listening with) shocked but rather smirking expressions, like good little boys who were going to hear the bad little boy told off —Jean Rhys

The compassionate look of a friendly dog —André Malraux

Their faces seemed unusually open, like so many windows —John Cheever

Tiredness and worry chasing one another like clouds across her face —Susan Hill

A tremor, as quick and delicate as a pulse, passed over her features ... so quickly it seemed a drop of rain had simply moved like a shadow across her face —Alice McDermott
See also: TREMBLING

His face [as he breaks into laughter] unfolds like a peony —Erich Maria Remarque

Your face is a book, where men may read strange matters —William Shakespeare

FACIAL EXPRESSIONS, SERIOUS
See also: EYE EXPRESSIONS, MISCELLANEOUS

Face all clouds, like a man in need of physic —George Garrett

A face as sad and featureless as a moon by day —George Garrett

Face austere as a hermit's —Lynne Sharon Schwartz

Face ... gloomy as an El Greco —John Fowles
Carlos Baker makes the El Greco comparison with 'Long,' which explains the meaning to include mood as well as physical shape.
See also: FACIAL SHAPE

Face grim as flu —Reynolds Price

Face like a clenched fist —Richard Condon

A face like a stomach cramp —Loren D. Estleman

Face like a vinegar bottle —Erich Maria Remarque

Face ... somber as a churchman's —Richard Ford

Face tightened up like a charley-horse —Raymond Chandler

Face was long, like a sheep's —W. Somerset Maugham
> The comparison is used to describe both sadness and a long-shaped face. To emphasize the psychological there's Daphne du Maurier's "Long and grave ... like a complaining sheep." To combine both meanings there's this by Margaret Atwood: "Face ... long and mournful, like a sheep's, but with the large full eyes of a dog, spaniel not terrier."

Grim as an ideological bigot —Frank Swinnerton

Had the face of a man suffering the awaited death of a loved one who's terminally ill —Mario Puzo

Had the look of a boy who had just lost his puppy to the county dogcatcher —Clive Cussler

He [Calvin Coolidge] looks as if he'd been weaned on a pickle —Alice Roosevelt Longworth

His long grim face, with the mouth running across its lower hem like a slipped thread in a linen sack, was as pitted as a battlefield —Cynthia Ozick

A long sad face like a cocker spaniel —George Garrett

Looked dismayed, like a child who's been used to hearing the same story with the same happy ending, and now the ending has been changed —Margaret Millar

Looked like a man being strapped into the electric chair while his wife French-kisses the D.A. in the hallway —T. Coraghessan Boyle

Looking as if the dentist had told him he'd have to have all his teeth pulled —Ross Macdonald

Looking as pensive as a monk in a spiritual crisis —Scott Spencer

Looking like a broody hen —Margaret Kennedy

(You) look like you just swallowed a bone —Charles Johnson

Sour and gray in the face, like a man who detests the food that keeps him alive; and must yet have it —Paul Horgan

Troubled face ... like a gravel parking lot —Ken Follett

Wore a permanently pinched look, as if he had just bitten into a piece of spoiled fish that he could neither swallow or spit out —Amos Oz

Worried look, like a bird dog uncertain of the scent —Elizabeth Spencer

FACIAL SHAPE

His flat face looked as if it were pressed against a window, except there was no window —Rebecca West

Big face, broad at the bottom, narrowed upward like a Dutch cheese —Saul Bellow

An enormous flat face like an unbaked pie —J. B. Priestly

Face as huge as the bowl of the sky —George Garrett

Face as long as his arm —Henry Van Dyke

Face, as round and white and incisively marked as the face of a clock —John Updike

Face ... as round as a skillet —James Lee Burke

Face broad and oval as a meat dish —Angela Carter

Face flat as a dough pan —James Lee Burke

Face, like a large tomato, was round and very red —Kenzaburo Oë

Face long as a fence line in flat country —Linda West Eckhardt

Face long as an El Greco —Carlos Baker

Face round as a full moon —James Crumley

Face ... round as a radar dish —John Updike

Faces as long as a wet week —H. E. Bates

Face shaped like a honeydew melon —Paige Mitchell

Face shaped like a shovel —Joyce Carol Oates

Face ... thin as a knife —Honoré de Balzac

A long face like a shoe —Christina Stead

A long narrow face cut like a tribal mask —Miles Gibson

Facial Shape

A round chubby face, like a soft beachball —John Rechy

Round face like the full moon —W. Somerset Maugham

Sharp-pointed face like a cat —Honoré de Balzac

A sparkling, triangular face like a cat —Pamela Frankau

A thin face shaped like the hatchet Lizzie Borden chopped up her mama with —Davis Dresser

Facts

FACTS

A fact is like a sack which won't stand up when it is empty —Luigi Pirandello

> In his play, *Six Characters in Search of an Author*, Pirandello expands upon the simile as follows: "In order that it may stand up, one has to put into it the reason and sentiment which have caused it to exist."

Facts apart from their relationships are like labels on empty bottles —Sven Halla

Facts fled before her like frightened forest things —Oscar Wilde

Statistics are like alienists, they will testify for either side —Fiorello H. La Guardia, *Liberty Magazine*, May, 1933

Use facts ... the way a carpenter uses nails —R. Wright Campbell

Use statistics as a drunken man uses lamp posts, for support rather than illumination —Andrew Lang

FAILURE
See: COLLAPSE, DISINTEGRATION

FAITH
See: BELIEF, RELIGION

FAITHFULNESS/FAITHLESSNESS
See: LOYALTY/DISLOYALTY

FALLING
See: COLLAPSE

FALSENESS
See: TRUENESS/FALSENESS

FAME
See: GREATNESS

FAMILIARITY
See also: COMMONPLACE

(The donors were as) anonymous as God —Herbert Gold

(Voice) as familiar as yesterday —Wallace Stegner

Everything reliable as the newly-wed suite in the Holiday Inn
    —Richard Ford
        The simile follows a description of a never-changing,
        always neat apartment in Ford's novel, *The Sportswriter.*

Familiar as an old mistake —Edward Arlington Robinson

Familiar as a town clock —Anon

(She became as snugly) familiar as his own armpit —Julia O'Faolain

Familiar ... as household words —William Shakespeare

Familiar as light or dark —Wallace Stegner

Familiar as luggage —Richard Ford

Familiar as one's own front door —Anon

Familiar as one's own face —Anon

Familiar as one's own spice shelf —Anon

Familiar as the contents of one's own broom closet —Anon

Familiar as the features of the President —Dorothea Straus

Familiar as the stars and stripes on the American flag —Anon

Familiar ... as the streets of our native town —W. H. Hudson

Familiar as the voice of a favorite broadcaster —Anon

Familiar ... as things are familiar in dreams, like the dreams of
    falling to one who has never climbed —William Faulkner

(The agony was as) familiar ... as waking to life —Paul Theroux

Familiar as warts or some birthmark —Derek Walcott

Familiar like an old tale —William Shakespeare

Familiarity

He knows my face. He reads it like a farmer reads the sky
—Marianne Hauser

Knew [her children's natures] as accurately as a bugler knows the notes of réveillé —Ouida

Know him like a book —Charles F. Briggs
> A variation that's become a popular daily expression is attributed to mystery writer, Margaret Millar, who used it in her novel, *The Weight of the Evidence:* "I know him like I know the back of my hand."

Know it [Boston] as an old inhabitant of a Cheshire knows his cheese —Oliver Wendell Holmes, Sr.

Know ... like a rabbit knows its warren —Frank Ross

(I got men that) know (these hills) like you know your wife's geography —Ross Macdonald

(A voice as) recognizable as a train whistle —Scott Simon about sports broadcaster, Harry Caray, National Public Radio, May 2, 1987

Recognized (every little curve and shadow) as he would have recognized, after half a life-time, the details of a room he had played in as a child —Edith Wharton

Sounds, familiar, like the roar of trees and crack of branches —Robert Frost

Standardized as boilerplate paragraphs in a law office —Anon

Standardized, as if put together with interchangeable parts —Philip Langdon, *The Atlantic*, December, 1985
> In an article entitled "Burger Shakes," Langdon used the simile to describe cities dotted with fast-food chains.

The stranger is like passing water in the drain —Margaret Laurence

Stylized as the annual report message to stockholders —Anon

FAMILY
See: RELATIONSHIPS

FASCINATION
See: ATTRACTIVENESS

FASHION
See: STYLE

FATE
See also: HELPLESSNESS

Chase destiny like a harpoonist —Edith Pearlman

Fate ... creeps like a rat —Elizabeth Bowen

The Fates, like an absent-minded printer, seldom allow a single line
    to stand perfect and unmarred —George Santayana

Fate treats me mercilessly, like a storm treats a small boat
    —Anton Chekhov

Like warp and woof all destinies are woven fast
    —John Greenleaf Whittier

Our lives carried us in our own dimensions, like people passing on
    different escalators —Mary Ladd Cavell

We're like dice thrown on the plains of destiny —Rita Mae Brown

FATNESS

Blew up like a poisoned dog —Rita Mae Brown
        The simile refers to a character in the novel, *Southern
        Discomfort*, who became fat after having a child.

Body ... encased in fat, like an insulated boiler —A. Alvarez

Body plump as a church rat's —Honoré de Balzac

Broad as a barn door —John Heywood's *Proverbs*
        A shorter, modern version: "Broad as a door."

(At the hips ... she was) broad as a sofa —Saul Bellow

Corpulent as a fire plug —Samuel Shem Fine

Fat and sleek: a dumpling —D. H. Lawrence

Fat as a balloon —Mark Twain

Fat as a duck —John Adams
        The man Adams compared to a duck was Aaron Burr.

Fat as a fool —John Lyly

Fat as an owl —Miles Gibson

Fat as a pig —John Cotgrave
> This is probably the most famous and often used "Fat as" comparison. Its earliest version "Fat as a pork hog" appeared in Sir Thomas Mallory's *Morte d'Arthur.* An offshoot, "Fat as a hen in the forehead," has been variously attributed to the playwrights Beaumont and Fletcher, and Jonathan Swift.

(I shall grow) fat as a porpoise —Jonathan Swift

Fat as a whale —Geoffrey Chaucer

Fat as butter —William Shakespeare
> A variation which has become an American colloquialism is "Fat as a butter-ball."

Fat as plenty —Hugh Ward

The fat on her was like loose-powdered dough —Carson McCullers

Fat overflowed not only from her jowl to her neck, but from her ankles to her shoes ... she looked like a pudding that had risen too high and run down the sides of the dish —Nadine Gordimer

(He was) fattening like a Christmas goose —Calder Willingham

Grew fat as a broiler —Kate Wheeler

He was fat, with a belly creased like a roll when he bent over —John Gunther

His stomach swells like a big cake baking —Carolyn Chute

I was square and looked like a refrigerator approaching —Jean Kerr
> Kerr likened herself to a refrigerator when she was pregnant.

Pudgy as a baby's hand —Jonathan Valin

Plump as an abbot —Robert Traver

Plump as a partridge —John Ray's *Proverbs*

She was round and plump as her favorite teapot —Peter De Vries

Stout as a stump —James Crumley

(Piglets) stout as jugs —W. D. Snodgrass

(A short man) wide as a door —Jessamyn West

A youngish plump little body, rather like a pigeon
    —Katherine Mansfield

FAULTFINDING
See: CRITICISM

FEAR
See: EMOTIONS, NERVOUSNESS

FEELINGS
See: EMOTIONS, PHYSICAL FEELINGS

FEET
See: LEGS

FEROCITY
See also: SCREAMS

Barked like an old sergeant —Frank Swinnerton

Fierce as a comet —John Milton

Fierce as a dog with tongue lapping for action —Carl Sandburg

Fierce as a fever —Anon

Fierce as a lobster making one last lunge out of the pot
    —Norman Mailer

Fierce as hunger —Babette Deutsch

Fierce as vengeance —John Greenleaf Whittier

Fierce as young bulls —William Shakespeare

Fiery as tiger eyes —Jessamyn West

Growled ... as a dog might do at a postman —Frank Swinnerton

Savage as a bear with a sore head —Frederick Marryat

Savage as a meat-ax
    —American colloquialism, attributed to Mid-south

(Hope) temptuous like a fire-cloud —Dante Gabriel Rossetti

(A fly is as) untamable as a hyena —Ralph Waldo Emerson

Ferocity

Wild as a monkey —Robert Silverberg

Wild as a starved cat —Elizabeth Spencer

Wild as the vultures' cry —Aeschylus

(Memories do not turn to dust. They live) wild as young colts
  —Elizabeth Spencer

(You're) wild ... just like a sea-bird —Clifford Odets

FERTILITY
See: GROWTH

FICKLENESS
See: LOYAL/DISLOYALTY

FICTION
See: STORIES

FIGHTING
See: ARGUMENTS

FINANCE
See: ECONOMICS

Fingers

FINGERS

Fingernails ... long as stilettos —T. Coraghessan Boyle

Fingernails that were long and curved and looked as tough as horn
  —Sue Grafton

Fingers are thin as ice —Marge Piercy

Fingers brown and hard as wood —Philip Levine

Fingers cool as gemstones —R. Wright Campbell

Fingers danced like midgets above a summer stream —O. Henry

Fingers fluttering ... like butterflies —William Goyen

Fingers fluttering like ribbons —Sharon Sheehe Stark

Fingers ... gnarled, like the roots of trees in an Arthur Rackham
  drawing —Antonia Fraser

Fingers ... hard and inactive, like the gnarled roots of a dead tree
  —Frank Swinnerton

Fingers ... like a bundle of broom straw, so thin and dry
—Louise Erdrich

Fingers like long wax candles —Cynthia Ozick

Fingers like pliers —Donald Seaman

(The woman's) fingers rustled like branches against her face
—Leigh Allison Wilson

Fingers spread apart like the talons of a predatory bird
—William March

Fingers spreading out like fans —Pat Conroy

Fingers tap like a lover's fondling a girl's hard little breasts
—Babette Deutsch

Fingers thick as sausages —James Crumley

Fingers tightly clenched, as if to check an involuntary gesture
—Edith Wharton

Fingers ... weighty as sandbags —Frank Conroy

Fingers were stiff as little darts —M. J. Farrell

Her fingers moved over his ribs gently as a harpist's
—Ross Macdonald
See also: SEXUAL INTERACTION

Knuckles ... like a row of little white onions —Roald Dahl
The white onion look is caused by a very hard hand grip.

(Hands crouched on the table before her, the) knuckles like miniature
snow-capped mountains —Marge Piercy

Knuckles [from gripping a table very hard] shone like white stones
—Mary Hedin

Long fingers arched like grapplehooks —William Carlos Williams

Long inquisitive fingers thrown out like antennae —Edith Wharton

Long thin fingers moving like knitting needles —Liam O'Flaherty

Long thin nails, like splinters —Elizabeth Spencer

My fingers fidget like ten idle brats —Wilfred Owens

Opening and closing his fingers like folding and unfolding a fan
—George Garrett

Pointed his finger like a revolver —Charles Johnson

Put his fingertips together thoughtfully, like a man preparing to pray
—Paul Theroux

Snapping his fingers together like a pair of scissors
—Margaret Atwood

Thumb like the butt of a pistol —Sterling Hayden

FIRE AND SMOKE
See: TOBACCO

FIRMNESS
See also: FLEXIBILITY/INFLEXIBILITY

(Bread ...) as hard as pumice —Mary Stewart

Be like a rocky head and on which the waves break incessantly, but
it stands fast and the waters sink to rest —Marcus Aurelius

(Continue) firm and unmoved as a column —James Boswell

Firm as alabaster —Henry James

Firm as a monkey's tail —Creole expression
Before Jean Claude Duvalier's Haitian regime toppled in
1983, he was quoted as saying, "I'm in control ... firm as
a monkey's tail."

[Figure] firm as an apple —H. E. Bates

(My heart is) firm as a stone —*The Holy Bible/Job*

Firm as morality —Thom Gunn

[A distant ridge] firm as solid crystal —William Wordsworth

Firm standing like a stone wall —Bernard Bee
The term "To stonewall" comes from Bee's simile about
Jackson at first battle of Bull Run.

Hard and dry as rustling corn —Dame Edith Sitwell

[A trained gangster] hard and solid, like a shark —John Malcolm

Hard as a billiard ball —Anon

(Soil) hard as a bowling alley —E. B. White

POINTED HIS FINGER LIKE A REVOLVER

Hard as a bulletproof vest
—Russell Baker, *New York Times*, May 21, 1986
To put this in full context: "Americans like their fish, and fish roe too, fried hard as a bulletproof vest."

Hard as a heavy-duty canvas fire-hose —Sharon Olds
In the poem from which this is taken, *Six-Year-Old Boy*, the fire-hose is used to describe a small boy waking up to urinate.

Hard as an egg at Easter —Michael Denham

(His body thin and stringy but) hard as armor plating
—Clive Cussler

Hard as a stone pillow —Anon
Back in the T'ang Dynasty chên or ceramic pillows were used during as well as after life as a means for keeping the eyes clear and preserving sight.

(The wheel of your life is ... as) hard as caked clay which nothing can grow in —Amy Lowell

(Words as) hard as cannon-balls —Ralph Waldo Emerson

Hard as corkwood —Miguel de Cervantes

(Felt as) hard as dried mud —James Crumley
The descriptive frame of reference is the face of a man who's been beaten up.

(Her breasts were small but looked) hard as green apples —Anon

Hard as the knots in a whip —Yehuda Amichai

Hard as nails —Charles Dickens
This now commonplace simile may well precede its appearance in Dickens' *Oliver Twist*. Other writers who've used it since have modified and extended it, e.g.: "Hard and sharp as nails," attributed to S. J. Weyman and "Hard as nails and sour as vinegar," attributed to George Beillairs.

Hard as steel —William Shakespeare

Hardened and set like concrete —Karl Shapiro

My ass ... was tight as a bull's in a thunderstorm
—Lael Tucker Wertenbaker

(His jaw was) rigid as a horseshoe —Flannery O'Connor

Rigid as a starfish —Joyce Cary

Rigid as bamboo —Diane Ackerman

Rigid as iron post —Marge Piercy

(He went as) rigid as Lenin's mummy —Joseph Wambaugh

Rigid as though bound and gagged —Eudora Welty

(Heat) solid as a hickory stick —Eudora Welty

Solid as a hill —William Boyd

Stand firm as a tower, which never shakes its top, no matter what
   winds are blowing —Dante Alighieri

Stiff as a garden hose left out in December —Will Weaver
         In Weaver's novel, *Red Earth, White Earth,* the comparison
         is used to describe the physical condition of a man who's
         had a stroke.

(His head,) stiff as a scarab —Theodore Roethke

Stiff as chessmen —Elizabeth Bowen

Stiff as icicles —Anon

Stiff as sticks —Dan Jacobson

[Bed sheet] stretched tight as a drumhead —Walker Percy

(Backside) sturdy as baking soda biscuits —Curtis White

Taut as a sail —Barbara Howes

Taut as a tent —Karl Shapiro

(Neck tendons) taut as banjo strings —Derek Walcott

Tight as a scout's knot —Lorrie Moore

FITTING
See: BELONGING

Flattery

As a wolf is like a dog, so is a flatterer like a friend
    —Thomas Fuller

Bang compliments backwards and forwards, like two asses scrubbing
    one another —Jonathan Swift

Bask in it [flattery] like a sunflower —Tennessee Williams

A compliment is something like a kiss through a veil —Victor Hugo

Compliments are like perfume, to be inhaled, not swallowed
    —Charles Clark Munn

Fawn like dogs —Percy Bysshe Shelley

Flattered me like a dog —William Shakespeare
        Shakespeare's simile from *King Lear* continues with, "And
        told me I had white hairs in my beard 'ere the black ones
        were there."

Flatterers, like cats, lick and then scratch —German proverb

Flatterers look like friends, as wolves like dogs —George Chapman

Flattering as a testimonial dinner —Anon

Flattery is like a cigarette; it is all right if you don't inhale
    —Adlai Stevenson

Flattery ... is like a qualmish liqueur in the midst of a bottle of wine
    —Benjamin Disraeli

Flattery is like champagne, it soon gets into the head
    —William Brown

Flattery is like cologne water, to be smelt of, not swallowed
    —Josh Billings
            Paraphrased from Billings' phonetic dialect which reads:
            "Flattery is like Kolone water, tew be smelt of, not
            swallowed."

Flattery is like friendship in show, but not in fruit —Socrates

Flattery is like wine, which exhilarates a man for a moment, but
    usually ends up going to his head and making him act foolish
    —Helen Rowland

(Twilight was) kind as candlelight to a bad face lift —Paige Mitchell

An overdose of praise is like ten lumps of sugar in coffee; only a very few people can swallow it —Emily Post

Praise, like gold and diamonds, owes its value only to its scarcity —Samuel Johnson

Some folks pay a compliment like they went down in their pocket for it —Kin Hubbard

FLAVOR
See: FOOD AND DRINK

FLAWS
See: ERRORS

FLEXIBILITY/INFLEXIBILITY
See also: HABIT

Adaptable as a Norwegian wharf rat —James Mills

Adjustable as prices of goods sold in a flea market —Anon

Adjust to as your eyes adjust to darkness or sudden light —Anon

Be pliable like a reed, not rigid like a cedar
    —Rabbi Simeon ben Eleazar

Elastic as a criminal's conscience —Anon

Elastic as a steel spring —Anon

Flexible as a diplomat's conscience —Anon

Flexible as figures in the hands of the statistician —Israel Zangwill

Flexible as silk —Ouida

Has as much give as a tree trunk —Jimmy Breslin

Implacable an adversary as a wife suing for alimony
    —William Wycherly

(Softly, unhurriedly but) implacably, like a great river flowing on and on —Harvey Swados

Inflexible as a marble pillar —Anon

Inflexible as steel —Ouida

Inflexible as the rings of hell —John Cheever

Intractable as a driven ghost —Sylvia Plath

Like all weak men he laid an exaggerated stress on not changing one's mind —W. Somerset Maugham

(The adolescent personality is as) malleable as infant flesh —Barbara Lazear Ascher, *New York Times*/Hers, October 23, 1986

The man who never alters his opinion is like standing water, and breeds reptiles of the mind —William Blake

Mind set like concrete —George Garrett

Pliable as wax —James Shirley

Pliant as cloth —Eugene Sue

Pliant as flesh —Linda Pastan

Rigidity yielding a little, like justice swayed by mercy, is the whole beauty of the earth —G. K. Chesterton

Set as a piece of sculpture —Charles Dickens

They made their hearts as an adamant stone
   —*The Holy Bible/Apocrypha*
         A variation from "Hearts firm as stone" and "Cold as stone" from the *Book of Job.*

Uncompromising as a policeman's club —Anon

Uncompromising as justice —William Lloyd Garrison

(There he was, as) unshakable as granite —Frank Swinnerton

FLIGHT
See: EXITS

FLIMSINESS
See: FRAGILITY

FOG

A churning mass of fog was welling up from the sea like a tidal wave —John Dos Passos

Fog closed in like a long sigh —George Garrett

Fog ... dissolving into the sky like milk in water —Ross Macdonald

The fog ... floated into the garden like gauze —Ludwig Bemelmans

Fog hung above the road like an alien intelligence —Charles Johnson

Foggy as London —Robert Traver

The fog rolled off the river like a woman rolling off a bed
    —Marianne Wiggins

The fog smothered sounds like an acoustical curtain
    —Margaret Millar

Fog that came like bitter smoke —Stephen Vincent Benét

(Pines ... wrapped with) fog that moved like bits of cloth in the
    wind —Shirley Ann Grau

A fog wandering like a pilgrim —Patricia Hampl

The fog was settling in and became rapidly denser. It was like
    wading about in dark milk soup —Erich Maria Remarque

The fog was thick and strangely white. Like wet bed sheets
    —Bertold Brecht

Haze ... like a thin smoke from slowly burning money
    —Ross Macdonald

Night fog thick as terry cloth —Maxine Kumin

Puffs of white fog which hung there like frozen cabbage
    —Donald McCaig

There's a fog at the waists of the trees, like a sash
    —William Matthews

Wreaths of white fog walked like ghosts in the haunted meadow
    —John Greenleaf Whittier

FOOD AND DRINK

Appetizing as a boiled cocktail —H. L. Mencken

Blackberries big as the ball of my thumb, and dumb as eyes
    —Sylvia Plath

A bottle of wine brings as much pleasure as the acquisition of a
    kingdom, and not unlike it in kind: the senses in both cases are
    confused and perverted —Walter Savage Landor

The brandy went to Whit's stomach like a saber cut —John Farris

Food and Drink

Cake ... beautiful as a palace—tall, shining and pink, outlined with balconies and battlements of white frosting
—Ruth Prawer Jhabvala

Cakes ... iced like the rock of Gibraltar —Penelope Gilliatt

A chocolate [birthday] cake ... lit up like an oil refinery
—Tom Robbins

Coffee ... black as the devil, hot as hell, pure as an angel, sweet as love —Charles de Talleyrand
> Talleyrand's description of good coffee once again illustrates how a simile which may sound trite by itself can gain muscle tone when appropriately combined with two or three others.

Coffee ... it tasted like swamp water —William Beechcroft

Coffee-pots breathing wisps of steam like old men talking in winter
—J. G. Farrell

Coffee should be black as Hell, strong as death, and sweet as love
—Turkish proverb

Coffee ... tasted like a third pressing —Derek Lambert

I consider supper as a turnpike through which one passes in order to get to bed —Oliver Edwards
> The inspiration for Edwards' simile was Samuel Johnson declaration that he never ate supper.

Cooking is like love. It should be entered into with abandon or not at all —Harriet Van Horn, *Vogue*, October 15, 1956

Croissants, light and warm as birds —Pat Conroy

The dining room table steamed [with hot food] like a caldron
—Dan Wakefield

A fish without bones is like an artichoke without leaves, a coconut without a shell, a lobster without a carapace —Anon item about an Idaho company's attempt to breed boneless fish, *New York Times*, November 5, 1986

Food is a narcotic in a way, like alcohol —Edna Ferber

Good coffee is like friendship: rich and warm and strong
—Slogan, Pan American Coffee Bureau, 1961

A good cook is like a sorceress who dispenses happiness
—Elsa Schiaparelli

[Soup] hot as an adulterous love —Erica Jong
This description from a poem entitled *Chinese Food* pertains to hot and sour soup. It is preceded by two other similes: "Dense as water ... sour as death."

Itt[beer] touched his stomach like petrol on live ashes —Caryl Phillips

It [water] was heavy, tepid, and savorless and like castor oil
—Vicki Baum

Lamb ... hard as a wood chip ... cold as Christmas —Richard Ford

Left their eggs up until the whites were glazed like plastic
—Daniela Gioseffi

Lettuces like garlands of faint green roses —Cynthia Ozick

The liquid [broth] went down my throat like bones —Maya Angelou

Margaritas flow like the Colorado River in March —Bryan Miller
reviewing a Mexican restaurant, *New York Times*, August 1, 1986

Martinis yellow as the rose and warm as summer rain —E. B. White

Pears ... like too many women their beauty condemns them to
uselessness —Bin Ramke

Pears ... shapely as violins —Babette Deutsch

Rice ... sticky as a snowball —Ira Wood

Roast beef, which tasted ... like the uppers of an old pair of pumps
—Shelby Hearon

A scrambled egg that tasted as if it had just hatched in the
refrigerator —Richard S. Prather

Sherry ... as thin and dry as benzine —Philip Levine

Slices the bread ... into thin volumes like poetry
—Sharon Sheehe Stark

Steam rose like incense from the bowl [of hot soup]
—Joanna Higgins

Stick as close to that kitchen [where a gourmet cook is in residence]
as the croûte to a pâté or the mayonnaise to an oeuf
—Angela Carter

Tea ... liquid and warm, like weeping —Margaret Drabble
> To expand upon the comparison, the author added, "It replaced the tears."

To drink a glass of sherry when you can get a dry martini is like taking a stagecoach when you can travel by the Orient Express —W. Somerset Maugham

Unripe oranges like dark-green golf balls —Ross Macdonald

The yolk of one of the eggs had leaked out onto the plate like a miniature pool of yellow blood —Ross Macdonald

FOOLISHNESS
See also: FUTILITY

A blockhead is as ridiculous when he talks as is a goose when it flies —Lord Halifax
> The words 'talks' and 'flies' have been modernized from the old English 'talketh' and 'flieth.'

Comparing them [American and Oriental women] is like comparing oven broilers and banties —Bobbie Ann Mason

Felt foolishness drag like excess flesh on his face —Sharon Sheehe Stark

Foolish as to cut off the head to preserve the hair —Anon
> An alternative to the cliche, "As foolish as to cut off your nose to spite your face."

Foolish as to judge a horse by its harness —Anon

A fool is like other men as long as he is silent —Jacob Cats

A fool ... says little, but that little said owes all its weight, like loaded dice, to lead —William Cowper

Gullible as geese —Anon

How foolish one would be to climb into the ring with love and try to trade blows with him, like a boxer —Sophocles

If all fools wore white caps, we should look like a flock of geese —Proverb

I'll not be a fool like the nightingale who is up till midnight without any ale —Dylan Thomas

Life's little suckers chirp like crickets while spending all on losing tickets —Ogden Nash

Lightheaded as a thistle —Mary Lavin

A man who commits suicide is like a man who longs for a gate to be opened and who cuts his throat before he reaches the gate —Dylan Thomas

Senseless ... it's like wearing a bulletproof vest with a hole over the heart —Senator John Heinz, December, 1985 news item

Unrealistic ... like someone who eats like a linebacker but yearns for the shape of a fashion model —Anon

FOOTBALL

The ball just skittered around in the backfield like a puck on ice —Jonathan Valin

The ball peeled his head like an onion
—Ken Stabler and Barry Stainback

Both players bounce up like toys —Richard Ford

My teammates were cringing in the huddle, like those scurvy hounds who live off garbage at county landfill projects —Pat Conroy

Passes faltered and tumbled like wounded ducks —James Crumley

Passes swerved like a diving duck —Y. A. Tittle, New York Giants quarterback, *New York Times*, January 12, 1987
> Tittle's simile dates back to 1962 when his team won the playoff game for the National Football League championship.

Pro football is like nuclear warfare. There are no winners, only survivors —Frank Gifford, *Sports Illustrated*, June 4, 1960

[Gary Anderson of the Miami Dolphins] runs like a locomotive — Craig James, Anderson's teammate, *New York Times*/Sports of the Times, September 10, 1986

Some of them [professional players] always look like brooding Pillsbury Doughboys and some of them look wizened from the start, middle-aged and beaten down, as if they'd never known what it was like to be young —Jonathan Valin

Football

To me football is like a day off. I grew up picking cotton on my daddy's farm and nobody asked for your autograph or put your name in the paper for that —Lee Roy Jordan

Treated his players as if he had bought them at auction with a ring in their noses and was trying not to notice they smelled bad —Jim Murray, about football coach Paul Brown, *Los Angeles Herald*, 1986

[Football] uniforms ... heavy as mattresses —Lael Tucker Wertenbaker

When you hit that line, it gave like a sponge, and when you tackled that big long Swede, he went down like he'd been hit by lightning —Sinclair Lewis

Without a network outlet, football will disappear like cigar smoke in the wind
—Harvey Meyerson, summation at NFL-USFL trial, 1986

Forehead

FOREHEAD

The artery in his forehead bulged like a snake —Richard Ford

Brow like masonry —Ted Hughes

Forehead ... as wrinkled as a washboard —Harvey Swados

Forehead like a bright new moon —*Arabian Nights*

(A slim girl with) a forehead which was shiny and protuberant, like a Bartlett pear —George Ade

Forehead, with wrinkles like lines drawn all over it —Ivan Turgenev

Her forehead shines like the gleam of morning —*Arabian Nights*

A high forehead with a soft vein running indirectly down the middle like an aimless trickle of water on a windowpane —John Hersey

His brows became contorted with thick frowns, like a bull's forehead —V. S. Pritchett

His brow swells out over his face like an eroded riverbank
—T. Coraghessan Boyle

His forehead bulged [with fury] as if he were horned
—Jonathan Valin
See also: ANGER

260

BROW LIKE MASONRY

His forehead rose like a gleaming dome towards the crown of his bald head —Alexander Solzhenitsyn

A pair of thin horizontal lines, like furrows in a meadow of snow, appeared on her forehead —Bill Pronzini

The skin [on a character's forehead] was wrinkled into long horizontal lines, like lines of inquiry —Dan Jacobson

FORGIVENESS

Forgiving the unrepentant is like drawing pictures in water —Japanese proverb

(God) pardons like a mother who kisses away the repentant tears of her child —Henry Ward Beecher

Forgiving without forgetting is like loving without liking —Anon

Overlooked as a favorite child's failings —Anon

FORLORNNESS
See: ABANDONMENT

FORMALITY/INFORMALITY

Formal and self-conscious as a football in a photograph —George Garrett

Formal as a Japanese print —Ramon Delgado

Formal as an undertaker —William McIlvanney

Informal as paper napkins —Dee Weber

Ordered ... like a nun's evening prayers —Charles Hanson Towne
This simile is extracted from the first stanza of Towne's poem, *The Best Road of All*, in which he writes about the best road being that which leads to God. In full context it reads: "I like ... a road that is an ordered road, like a nun's evening prayers."

FRAGILITY

As thin of substance as the air —William Shakespeare

(Laughter ... as) delicate and frail as new ice —Frederick Barthelme

(She was) delicate as a pig was not —Pat Conroy

Bones frail as a small bird's —George Garrett

Brittle as a dead tree —George Garrett

Brittle as dry wood —Miller Williams

Brittle as glass that breaks with a touch
    —Algernon Charles Swinburne

Brittle as straw —Ellen Glasgow

Brittle as twigs —Margaret Atwood

(Her own body seemed) fragile and empty like blown glass
    —Margaret Atwood

Fragile and rather beautiful, like a rare kind of mosquito
    —Lawrence Durrell

Fragile as a bird's egg —George Garrett

Fragile as a chrysalis —John Updike

Fragile as a coquillage bouquet —Truman Capote
        Capote's simile refers to Isak Dinesen.

Fragile as a cup —Reynolds Price

(Shoulder) fragile as a little bit of glass —Eudora Welty

Fragile as ancient lace or parchment —George Garrett

Fragile as a reed —Cornelia Otis Skinner

(Her conical breasts look) fragile as birds' eggs —R. V. Cassill

Fragile as snowflakes —Sharon Sheehe Stark

(She felt very weak and her plump body seemed, somehow, flat and)
    fragile, like a pressed leaf between the sheets —Helen Hudson

Fragile ... like a spider's web —John Fowles

Fragile like her good intentions —Marguerite Yourcenar

Fragile, like the skin on scalded milk —Sharon Sheehe Stark

Frail as a blade of grass —Belva Plain

(She felt as) frail as a cobweb —Jonathan Kellerman

Frail as a fading friendship —Anon

Frail as antique earthenware —Sylvia Plath
> Plath's simile describes the occupants of an old ladies' home.

Frail as April snow —Wallace Stevens

(Breasts rising) frail as blisters —Sharon Olds

Frail as flesh —Laman Blanchard

[School boys] frail, like thin-boned fledgling birds clamoring for food —Sylvia Berkman

I feel [fragile] like a poppy; one gust of wind and everything will blow away —Carla Lane, dialogue, "Solo," British sitcom, broadcast June 23, 1987
> The reason the character in Lane's script feels so fragile is that she is a woman in her fifties in a relationship with a much younger man.

I felt like a moth hanging on the windowpane —Jacqueline Kennedy, *Newsweek,* January 21, 1961
> The occasion being described was her first night in the White House.

Insubstantial ... like fake wedding cakes in a bakery window—lots of whipped cream rosettes and garlands surrounding a hollow middle —Michiko Kakutani, *New York Times*

Like a dry leaf closed into a book, he seemed frail and ready to crumble —Arthur A. Cohen

More frail than the shadows on glasses —Algernon Charles Swinburne

Promise as solid as a bundle of water —Hindu proverb

(Hair and garments) tenuous as gauze —W. D. Snodgrass

(You're so old) you're like a cup I could break in my hand —Paule Marshall

FRAUD
See: CRIME

FRECKLES
See: FACIAL DETAILS

FRESHNESS

(She looks as) clear as morning roses newly washed with dew
  —William Shakespeare

Fresh as a daisy —Slogan, June Dairy Products Co.

Fresh as an unveiled statue —Henry James

Fresh as any rose —John Lydgate
        The natural association between freshness and flowers has
        made this simile and its variants a common expression.
        The daisy rivals the rose as a popular comparison.

(Looking as) fresh as apple blossoms among the tender leaves of late
  spring —Frank Swinnerton

Fresh as April grass —Karl Shapiro

Fresh [in the face] as a rainwashed rose —Reynolds Price

Fresh as a spring morning —Slogan, Little America frozen foods

Fresh as hope —Susan Engberg

Fresh as paint —Francis Edward Smedley

Fresh as the dawn —Anon
        An extension used as a slogan by Pacific Egg Producers:
        "Fresh as dewy dawn."

Fresh as the month of May —Geoffrey Chaucer
        The above is modernized from, "As fresh as is the month
        of May."

Fresh as salt-drenched skin —Theodore Roethke

Fresh as the morning —Slogan, Campbell's corn flakes

Fresh as the morning wind that tatters the mist —Marge Piercy

Fresh as thyme or parsley —W. H. Auden

Fresh as tomorrow —James G. Huneker

Fresh as yesterday —Shelby Hearon
        In Hearon's novel, *A Small Town*, what's fresh is a family
        feud.

Fresh like frilled linen clean from a laundry —Virginia Woolf

Friendship, Defined

FRIENDSHIP, DEFINED

Acquaintances ... they're like weeds; they grow up around the real friends and choke them off —Christopher Isherwood

A broken friendship, like a broken cup, can be mended but it will never be perfect again —Anon
> This can be traced to the Latin proverb "A broken friendship may be soldered but will never be sound."

A cheerful friend is like a sunny day which spreads its brightness on all around —Sir John Lubbock

Choose your friends like your books, few but choice books —James Howell

The false friend is like the shadow of a sundial —French proverb

False friends, like birds, migrate in cold weather —Anon

The feeling of friendship is like that of being comfortably filled with roastbeef; love like being enlivened with champagne —Samuel Johnson

A friendless man is like a left hand without a right —Hebrew proverb

Friends are like fiddle-strings, they must not be screwed too tight —John Ray's *Proverbs*

Friends are like melons. Shall I tell you why? To find one good, you must a hundred try —Claude Mermet

Friendship is a disinterested commerce between equals; love, an abject intercourse between tyrants and slaves —Oliver Goldsmith

Friendship is a sheltering tree —Samuel Taylor Coleridge

Friendship is a single soul dwelling in two bodies —Aristotle

Friendship is like money, easier made than kept —Samuel Butler

Friendship is like a treasury; you cannot take from it more than you put into it —Benjamin Mandelstamm

Friendship is like two clocks keeping time —Anon

Friendship is love without his wings —Lord Byron

A friendship like a soft pillow that made her feel secure and
bolstered —Mary Gordon

Friendship, like credit, is highest where it is not used
—Elbert Hubbard

Friendship, like love, is destroyed by long absence, though it may be
increased by short intermission —Samuel Johnson

Friendship, like love, is but a name —John Gay

Friendship, like the immortality of the soul, is too good to be
believed —Ralph Waldo Emerson

The friendship of a great man is like the shadow of a bush soon
gone —French proverb

A group of good friends is like the relatives you wish you'd been
born with —Anon
> A twist in simile form of, "You can't pick your relatives,
> but you can pick your friends."

A hollow friendship is like a hollow tooth—it's always best to have
it out at once —*Punch*, 1862

I find friendship ... like wine, raw when new, ripened with age, the
true old man's milk and restorative cordial —Thomas Jefferson

An old friendship is like old wine; the longer it lasts the stronger it
grows —Antonio Perez

Old friendships are like meats served up repeatedly, cold, comfortless
and distasteful —William Hazlitt

Some friends are like the shadow; they follow us when our sun
shines —Moses Ephraim Kuh
> A variation of this attributed to Christian Nestell Bovee is,
> "False friends are like our shadow, keeping close to us
> while we walk in the sunshine, but leaving us the instant
> we cross into the shadow."

Some friends are like a sun-dial: useless when the sun sets
—Judah Jeiteles

An untried friend is like an uncracked nut —Russian proverb

Frustration

FRUSTRATION
See also: EMOTIONS

Feel so useless ... like a still life —Margaret Drabble

(I'm as) frustrated as a dog on a chain —Anton Chekhov

Frustrated [about career] ... as though she were peanut butter that was forced into a hypodermic syringe —Ann Jasperson

Frustration ... began to creep up his neck like a hot hand —Flannery O'Connor

Frustration lingered between her legs like an ache —Susan Lois

(The writing is becoming) more and more impossible ... I'm like a toad squashed by a paving stone, like a dog with its guts crushed out by a shit-wagon, like a clot of snot under a policeman's boot, etc. —Gustave Flaubert

(The reporters are still) running around like blind dogs in a meat house —James Reston, *New York Times*/The Changing Guard, February 22, 1987

FUN
See: PLEASURE

FURNITURE AND FURNISHINGS
See: ROOMS

Futility

FUTILITY

Being a producer around here is like trying to direct a Broadway show full of deaf-mutes —William Diehl

Charging like Don Quixote at the windmills —George Bernard Shaw

Cleaning your house while your kids are still growing is like shoveling the walk before it stops snowing —Phyllis Diller
> The twists on everyday life similes to describe ineffective actions are virtually without limit. A few more examples: effective "As using a sword against cobwebs," "As trying to plug a hole with Scotch tape," "As waxing a broken car."

Confronting Assistant Secretary of Defense Richard Perle with real arms control is like confronting Dracula with a silver cross: You expect him to make loud noises and thresh about
—*Wall Street Journal* editorial, March 25, 1986

Convincing her [to get an abortion] is like trying to convince her the moon's a yo-yo —Ann Beattie

Effective as redecorating a house over a corroding plumbing system —Anon

Explained to, cajoled, and bullied ... but he might as well have been boxing with a feather bolster —Lael Tucker Wertenbaker

Futile as an attempt to tattoo soap bubbles —Anon

Futile as regret —Edward Arlington Robinson

Futile as to attempt to dust cobwebs off the moon —Anon

Futile as to fight an earthquake with argument —Anon

Futile ... like a lacy valentine with a red heart which contains no message of love —Louis Auchincloss

Futile ... like emptying a cupful of ants into a butterfly nest for safekeeping —Beryl Bainbridge

Futile [to fight unfounded suspicions] ... like fighting with air, a mock battle with blank cartridges —August Strindberg

Futile like Samson pulling the roof down on the Philistines —George Garrett

Futile, like shoveling sand into the sea —Isabel Allende

Futile ... like talking to a lake, a chilled lake, no reaction, not a ripple —James Kirkwood

Lending to the feckless is like pelting a stray dog with dumplings —Chinese saying

Like a spent prisoner before the moment of execution, he knew that it was too late for protest —Dorothea Straus

Maintaining classical studies in 1987 is like *Cosmopolitan* magazine obstinately advertising bustles —Dennis O'Brien, *New York Times*/OpEd, February 12, 1987

O'Brien, a university president, used the comparison to support his argument that college should not be viewed as a product.

Might as well try to teach good manners to a wolf or a wild boar (as to bloody-minded soldiers who have lost whatever religion they may have had) —George Garrett

My efforts [to stir my husband out of a sense of doom] have been like so many waves, dashing against the Rock of Ages —Robert E. Sherwood
> Sherwood wrote this simile for the character of Mary Todd Lincoln in his play *Abe Lincoln in Illinois*.

(About as) pointless and inglorious as stepping in front of a bus —John Osborne

Pointless as throwing birdseed on the ground while snow still falls fast —Ann Beattie

The prophesying business is like writing fugues; it is fatal to everyone save the man of absolute genius —H. L. Mencken

Showing emotion [when with an uncommunicative father] was like having a snowball fight with a brick wall —Ann Jasperson

Speculating about it was like robbing last year's bee tree —Borden Deal

To argue with William is like arguing with Vesuvius —Delmore Schwartz
See also: ARGUMENT

FUTURE

Can see about as far ahead as a goat —Harold Adams

Doomed like a moth —Dame Edith Sitwell

A dreadful prospect, like losing your potency —Harvey Swados

The future comes like an unwelcome guest —Edmund Gosse

The future grows like a scar —Philip Levine

The future is an opaque mirror. Anyone who tries to look into it sees nothing but the dim outlines of an old and worried face — Jim Bishop, *New York Journal-American*, October 15, 1959

The future is like heaven; everyone exalts it but no one wants to go there now —James Baldwin

The future was like a sunny road that wandered through a wide-flung, wooden plain —W. Somersett Maugham

The future was rushing toward her like the jaws of a trap snapping shut —A. E. Maxwell

Great promise [of a brilliant career] ... faded like his imagination —Marguerite Young

He would fly, if he could, fly in search of a future like a sycamore seed —Louis MacNeice

The years stretched before her like some vast blank page spread out to receive the record of her toil —Edith Wharton

GAIETY
See also: CHEERFULNESS, LAUGHTER

As merry as a grig —Frank Swinnerton

As merry as a mouse in malt —George Garrett

As merry as forty beggars —Proverb

As merry as notes in a tune —Dame Edith Sitwell

As merry as the day is long —William Shakespeare
    Shakespeare used this in both *Much Ado About Nothing* and *The Life and Death of King John*. In daily conversation, 'cheerful' is often substituted for 'merry.'

Gay as the latest statistics on cancer or crime —Elyse Sommer

(Yours is) a spirit like a May-day song —Dorothy Parker

Blithe as the air is, and as free —Henry Wadsworth Longfellow

Cavorted like a mule let out to pasture —Borden Deal

Feeling like Fourth of July —Stephen Vincent Benét

The gaiety of life, like the beauty and the moral worth of life, is a saving grace, which to ignore is folly, and to destroy is a crime —Agnes Repplier

Gay as a funeral procession —Anon

As merry as a condemned man eating his last meal —Elyse Sommer

Gay as a honey-bee humming in June —Amy Lowell

Gay as a parade —Hilda Conklin

Gay as larks —Aesop
> The use of "gay as" and "merry as" comparisons to larks, crickets and just about any kind of humming or buzzing bird or insect abounds throughout the annals of literature as well as in daily speech.

Heart ... lighter than a flower —Elinor Wylie

Making merry like grasshoppers —Robinson Jeffers

A man without mirth is like a wagon without springs, in which one is caused disagreeably to jolt by every pebble over which it turns —Henry Ward Beecher
> Were Beecher alive today he might substitute "A car without shock absorbers" for "A wagon without springs."

(Everything went as) merrily as a marriage bell
—W. Somerset Maugham

A merry heart does good like a medicine —*The Holy Bible /Proverbs*
> The word 'doeth' has been modernized to 'does,' and the simile is often shortened to "A merry heart is like medicine."

Mirth is like a flash of lightning, that breaks through a loom of clouds, and glitters for a moment —Joseph Addison

GAIT
See: WALKING

GENIUS
See: GREATNESS

GENTLENESS

Gentle as a newborn colt —Rex Reed
> In Reed's novel, *Personal Effects*, the gentle behavior is that of a man making love.

(Looked as) gentle as a suckling dove —Arthur Train

Gently as a whisper —Slogan for door checks, Sargent & Co.

Tender as dusk —Jessamyn West

Tenderly as a mother —John Greenleaf Whittier

Tender as young love —Maxwell Anderson

GESTURES
See: HAND MOVEMENTS

GLIMMER
See: GLIMMER AND GLOSS

GLITTER AND GLOSS
See also: BRIGHTNESS, LIGHTING

Aglow, like fruit when it colors —William Canton

All ablaze like poppies in the sun —Ouida

All glittering like May sunshine on May leaves
     —Alfred, Lord Tennyson

Beams like flowers —Percy Bysshe Shelley

(Bright faces cast a thousand) beams upon me, like the sun
     —William Shakespeare

Blazing like a jewelled sun —W. S. Gilbert

Blinking like a digital display —Natascha Wodin

A dull sheen, like the white of a hard-boiled egg
     —T. Coraghessan Boyle

(Eyes) flashed like lightning —Honoré de Balzac

Flashy as the slot machines in a gambling casino —Anon

(Evening) flickers like the midnight sun —Karl Shapiro

Gleam and glitter ... like jewels in a dark velvet case
     —Louis Auchincloss

(His hair) gleamed like a freshly washed blackboard —Mavis Gallant

[A car] gleamed like a jewel in a box with an iridescent lining
     —Robin McCorquodale

(The Hyde Park Library, which was) gleaming like a chrome fender
     in the afternoon sun —Jonathan Valin

Gleaming like light on water —Beryl Markham

Gleaming like oil on water —Erica Jong

Gleaming like raw meat —James Crumley

Gleaming like water over moon-bright sand —Robert Penn Warren

Gleam like bone —Donald McCaig

Gleam like small change —Sylvia Plath

(The token woman) gleams like a gold molar in a toothless mouth
    —Marge Piercy

Gleams like a small coin —Philip Levine

Gleams like the cared-for brass of bank buildings —George Garrett

(The necklace) gleams, sharp as malice —Louise Erdrich

(Water) glimmered like a shower of diamonds in the broken
    moonlight —Joseph Sheridan Le Fanu

Glimmer ... like glow worms twinkling through the shade
    —Sir Walter Scott

Glimmer, sparkled like a matrix of platinum sequins laid over velvet
    —Richard Ford
        The sparkling place described is Oaxaca.

(Eyes ...) glinted ... like crumpled tinfoil —Susan Neville

(Helmets) glinted like nailheads —Derek Walcott

[Shoulders] glisten as silver —D. H. Lawrence

Glistened, like a globe of burnished gold —Edgar Allan Poe

Glistened like an oiled plum —Jerzy Kosinski
        The descriptive frame of reference in *The Painted Bird*, the
        novel from which this is taken, is a snake's head.

(The empty pavement that) glistened like a wet leather strap
    —Tadeusz Borowski

[A dog's coat] glistened like black velvet —Roald Dahl

(Her neck and shoulders) glistened like liquor in a crystal bottle
    —Paige Mitchell

(Peas) glistened like medieval enamels —Mark Helprin

Glistened like the sun in water —Henry Wadsworth Longfellow

(The van) glistening like opal —MacDonald Harris

Glistening like satin —Ouida

Glisten like melted butter —Marilyn Hacker

[Hair] glisten like sunshine —D. H. Lawrence

Glistens like the scaling of a snake —Mihail Lermontov
>In Lermontov's *A Hero of Our Time*, the comparison refers to a river.

(Eyes) glittered like a string of Christmas tree icicles
—Donald McCaig

Glittered like bracelets —Hans Christian Andersen

Glittered like confetti —Lawrence Durrell

Glittered like steel struck with a bright light —Honoré de Balzac

The glitter of the sea was like glass in my eyes —Steve Erickson

Glittering like armor —Frank O'Hara

[Fruit wet with mist] glowed like a globe of fire —Philip Levine

Glowed like painted glass —Lincoln Kirstein

Glowed like somebody had polished her —J. B. Priestly
>The narrator of Priestly's *Lost Empires* is describing a showgirl in her costume.

Glowed like the initials of an illuminated manuscript
—Edmund L. Pearson

(His head) glowing like a red sun —Bernard Malamud

Glow like a sunbeam —Alfred, Lord Tennyson

Glow, like moths by light attracted and repelled
—Percy Bysshe Shelley

(Water) glows ... like a crystal ball —Edward Hoagland

Glows like a drunk's nose —Hank Searls

Glows like a meteor in the distant North —William Blake

Lights glittering like Oz —Diane Ackerman

Polished like new boots —John Ciardi

Shimmered like the wing of a dragonfly —Eudora Welty

Shimmer like a vision —John Gardner

Sparkled like stars —Percy Bysshe Shelley

(Four tiny black-eyed girls ...) twinkling like Christmas trees
—Hart Crane

GLOOM
See also: BEHAVIOR; FACIAL EXPRESSIONS, SERIOUS; SADNESS

Bleak and uninviting as an empty hotel room —Jonathan Valin

Bleak as a winter hillside —F. van Wyck Mason

Brain which had become as inhospitable to the brighter side of life
as a house without windows is to cheerful lodgers
—Bertold Brecht

Brooded over ... misfortune, like Hamlet or a character in Ibsen
—Mary McCarthy

Brooding ... like a martyr —Paul Reidinger

Brooding like a woman unsatisfied —Joanne Selzer
The comparison as used by the author in a poem entitled
Summer Heat refers to the atmosphere after a heavy storm.
The simile in its full context begins as follows: "The air
hung heavy after the storm, brooding ... "

Brood like a ghost —Fannie Stearns Gifford

Cheerful as a turkey before Thanksgiving —Anon
Variants for changing seasons include: "Cheerful as a
rabbit before Easter" and "Cheerful as a goose before
Christmas."

Cold and gray ... like the mortuary —Mike Fredman

Dour as a wet cat —Warren Beck

Felt heavy as Sunday —John Braine

Gloom ... dark and stagnant like a bed of straw for sick livestock
—Kenzaburo Oë

Gloom, like a poisonous mist, fills the car —Ira Wood

Gloomy and melancholy, like ghosts —Mark Twain

Gloomy as a beach resort on a wet Sunday in July —Anon
> This may be inspired by a much-used, also unattributed simile, "Gloomy as a graveyard on a wet Sunday afternoon."

[A house] gloomy as a crypt —Michael Korda

Gloomy as a tick on Sunday —Grace Paley

Gloomy as a wet holiday —Anon

Gloomy as night —Homer

Glum as a gumboil, as sad as despair —Don Marquis

Glum as a student who's fallen hopelessly behind —John Gardner

Glum as a tongue-tied parrot —Joseph C. Lincoln

Grew clouded and closed, like the dense pallid sky —Sylvia Berkman
> See also: RESERVE

Ill-humor is like laziness, for it is a kind of laziness
> —Johann Wolfgang von Goethe

It was the kind of day that made suicide look like a reasonable proposition —Mike Fredman
> See also: DAY

Looked like he swallowed a lemon —William Diehl

Melancholy as a defeated politician —Herbert V. Prochnow

Melancholy as a gib [castrated] cat —William Shakespeare

Melancholy sound ... like the weeping of a solitary, deserted human heart —Guy de Maupassant
> See also: NOISE

Moping around like a chicken with the dropsy —Babs H. Deal

(The men grew silent and) morose like lumps of soft coal
> —Richard Ford

A sense of melancholy had enveloped her like a sheath
> —Charles Johnson

(My grandmother had) a permanently bleak outlook ... like one of those cartoon characters with a small cloud over their heads
> —Susan Walton, *New York Times*/Hers, June 25, 1987

Gloom

Somber and unreadable as Latin —Tony Ardizzone

Sour as port decanted too long —Truman Capote

Sulked like a bear —Anon

We [three motorists] drove out the lane like a funeral cortege
    —Ross Macdonald

GLOSSINESS
See: GLITTER AND GLOSS

GLUTTONY
See: GREED

GOD
See: FORGIVENESS, RELIGION

Golf

GOLF

Addressed his ball as if he were stroking a cat —P. G. Wodehouse
    Wodehouse, known for his humorous golf stories, not
    surprisingly coined many funny golf similes.

The ball breasting the hill like some untamed jack-rabbit of the
    California prairie —P. G. Wodehouse

Before making a shot, he would inspect his enormous bag of clubs
    and take out one after another, slowly, as if he were playing
    spillikens —P. G. Wodehouse

Brooded over each shot like one whose heart is bowed down by bad
    news from home —P. G. Wodehouse

Drove as if he were cracking a whip —P. G. Wodehouse

Golf is like a love affair: if you don't take it seriously, it's no fun. If
    you do take it seriously, it breaks your heart
    —Arnold Daly, *Reader's Digest*, November, 1933

He stood over his ball, pawing at it with his driving-iron like a cat
    investigating a tortoise —P. G. Wodehouse

He whiffed that baby [the ball] so bad he torqued like a licorice
    twist and found his head looking straight behind him like a
    cockatoo —Joseph Wambaugh

I'm playing like Tarzan and scoring like Jane —Chi Chi Rodriguez
quoted in the 1987 Masters tournament by Dick Schaap

A man ... with thirty-eight golfless years behind him ... loses all
sense of proportion [when he takes up the game] ... like a fly
that happens to be sitting on the wall of the dam just when the
crack comes —P. G. Wodehouse

Scooped with his mashie as if he were ladling soup
—P. G. Wodehouse

Stood addressing his ball [to tee off] like Lot's wife just after she
had been turned into a pillar of salt —P. G. Wodehouse

That poor golf ball ... perched on the tee, as naked as a quarterback
without a helmet —Dave Anderson, *New York Times*/Sports of
the Times, May 11, 1987

Wielded his midiron like one killing snakes —P. G. Wodehouse

With infinite caution, like one suspecting a trap of some kind, he
selected clubs from his bulging bag —P. G. Wodehouse

GOVERNMENT

An administration, like a machine, does not create. It carries on
—Antoine de Saint-Éxupéry

Any government, like any family, can for a year spend a little more
than it earns. But ... continuance of that habit means the
poorhouse —Franklin D. Roosevelt, July 30, 1932

The balance of power our founding fathers so brilliantly
contrived ... has functioned like a gyroscope to keep us from
plunging irretrievably into anarchy or despotism —John R.
Stockwell, *New York Times*/Op-Ed, December 14, 1986
    Stockwell's simile was part of his argument for open
    hearings on Colonel Oliver North.

The Constitution is an experiment, as all life is an experiment
—Oliver Wendell Holmes, Jr.

Democracy is like a raft. It never goes down but, dammit, your feet
are always wet —Fisher Ames

Government is like that old definition of a baby: an enormous
appetite at one end and no sense of responsibility at the other
—Ronald Reagan, 1986 speech

Government

Government ... like fire it is a dangerous servant and a fearful master; never for a moment should it be left to irresponsible action —George Washington

Governments are like men, more or less suspicious according to their temperaments —*Punch*, 1844

Governments, like clocks, go from the motions men give them, and as governments are made and moved by men, so by them they are ruined also —William Penn

A great empire, like a great cake, is most easily diminished at the edges —Benjamin Franklin

The life of governments is like that of man. The latter has a right to kill in case of natural defence: the former have a right to wage war for their own preservation
—Charles de Secondat Montesquieu

Like a funeral or a marriage, an administration in the making creates disparate relationships and revives forgotten alliances
—Maurice Edelman
Edelman put this simile into the mind of the fictional hero of his novel, *Disraeli Rising*.

Like clowns, they [royalty] amuse the people, even with their funerals —Marie, Queen of Romania

Like knights in search of the Holy Grail, lawmakers are always looking for painless ways to raise revenues —David E. Rosenbaum, *New York Times*/Op-Ed, March 5, 1986

A monarchy is like a man-of-war, bad shots between wind and water hurt it exceedingly; there is danger of capsizing. But democracy is a raft. You cannot easily overturn it —Joseph Cook

Monarchy is like a sleek craft, it sails along well until some bumbling captain runs it into the rocks —Fisher Ames, English Tory, former monarchist, quoted *Money Magazine*

A nation ... is like a body contained within a circle, having a common center, in which every radius meets; and that center is formed by representation —Thomas Paine

Nations are as a drop in a bucket —*The Holy Bible/Isaiah*

Nations are like olives. To gentle pressure they respond with sweet oil, to hard pressure with bitter oil —Ludwig Boerne

No nation can survive if government becomes like the man who in winter began to burn the wall boards of his house to keep warm until he had no house left —Ronald Reagan, on controlling government spending, annual address to annual conference of the International Monetary Fund and World Bank, September 30, 1986

States, like men, have their growth, their manhood, their decrepitude, their decay —Walter Savage Landor

States, like men, never protest their honor loudly unless they have a bad case to argue —Harold J. Laski

The superpowers often behave like two heavily armed blind men feeling their way around a room, each believing himself in mortal peril from the other whom he assumes to have perfect vision —Henry Kissinger

(It's all papers and forms,) the entire Civil Service is like a fortress made of papers, forms and red tape —Alexander Ostrovsky

GRACEFULNESS
See: AGILITY

GRACIOUSNESS
See: BEHAVIOR

GRAY
See also: GLOOM, HAIR COLOR, WEATHER

An ash-gray ... like that of the first thinning of the darkness after a rain-sodden night —Dan Jacobson

(His face was) faintly gray like newsprint —John Updike

(Eyes) gray as a goose —Geoffrey Chaucer

Gray as a vault —Elizabeth Spencer

Gray as bones —Martin Cruz Smith

Gray as cement —Philip Levine

(The weather had turned as) gray as concrete —Jean Thompson

Gray as flannel —Jonathan Valin
> In his novel, *Life's Work*, Valin thus describes what remains of a man's hair: "Bald on top, gray as flannel on the sides."

(Eyes) gray as glass —Geoffrey Chaucer
> Chaucer used the simile in *The Canterbury Tales* (*The Miller's Tale*) and Shakespeare used it in *Gentlemen of Verona*.

Gray as lava —D. H. Lawrence

(Skin) gray as lead —William Diehl

(Warships) gray as sharks —George Garrett

(Eyes ...) gray as storm clouds —Margaret Millar

(Max was) gray as the sky —Susan Fromberg Schaeffer

Gray like dust —Algernon Charles Swinburne

Gray [hair] like the last snows of winter —John Cheever

Gray like washed slate —John Updike

(Eyes had gone) icy gray, like winter frost —Andrew Kaplan

GREATNESS

Early genius is like a cabbage: it doesn't head well
> —Bartlett's *Dictionary of Americanisms*

A fine genius, in his own country, is like gold in the mine
> —Ben Franklin

Genius, in one respect, is like gold—numbers of persons are constantly writing bout both who have neither
> —Charles Caleb Colton

Genius is like a flint of many edges, but it is the edges that give the sparkle —Moritz Gottlieb Saphir

Genius, like humanity, rusts for want of use —William Hazlitt

Genius, like water, will find its level —Proverb

Genius must have talent as its complement and implement, just as, in like manner, imagination must have fancy
> —Samuel Taylor Coleridge
> > Coleridge built on this simile as follows: "In short, the higher intellectual powers can only act through a corresponding energy of the lower."

Genius without education is like silver in the mine
   —Benjamin Franklin

A genius without vices is like a race horse without a good jockey
   —Benjamin De Casseres

Great men are like mountains; we do not appreciate their magnitude
   while we are still close to them —Joseph Chamberlain

Great men are like meteors; they litter and are consumed to
   enlighten the world —Napoleon Bonaparte

Great men, like great epochs, are explosive material in whom
   tremendous energy has been accumulated —Friedrich Nietzsche
         The simile is sometimes quoted with the word 'ages'
         substituted for 'epochs.'

Great men stand like solitary towers in the city of God
   —William Wadsworth Longfellow

Great minds are like eagles, and build their nest in some lofty
   solitude —Arthur Schopenhauer

It is with rivers as it is with people: the greatest are not always the
   most agreeable nor the best to live with —Henry Van Dyke

Men of genius are like eagles, that live on what they kill, while men
   of talents are like crows, that live on what has been killed for
   them —Josh Billings
         In Billings' special phonetic dialect this reads: "Men ov
         genius ... tha live on what tha ... while men ov ... tha
         live on what haz bin killed for them."

GREED

(My) avarice cooled like lust in the chill grave
   —Ralph Waldo Emerson

Avarice is like a graveyard; it takes all that it can get and gives
   nothing back —Josh Billings

Avaricious ... like a pig which seeks its food in the mud, without
   caring where it comes from —Jean B. M. Vianney

The avaricious man is like the barren sandy ground of the desert
   which sucks in all the rain and dew with greediness, but yields
   no fruitful herbs or plants for the benefit of others —Zeno

Greed

Covetous persons are like sponges which greedily drink in water, but return very little until they are squeezed —G. S. Bowles

Greedy as a colt first loosed to pasture in the spring
—Ben Ames Williams

Greedy as a vulture —Tobias Smollett

He [Donald Trump] has an appetite [for property] like a Rocky Mountain vulture
—Alan Greenberg, *Wall Street Journal,* April 1, 1987

Kings, like hyenas, will always fall upon dead carcasses, although their bellies are full, and although they are conscious that in the end they will tear one another to pieces over them
—Walter Savage Landor

(Love surfeits not) lust like a glutton dies —William Shakespeare

Rapacious as a crocodile —Anon

Rapacious as a warlord —Sharon Sheehe Stark

Sucked him dry like a raw egg —Bertold Brecht

They're [the doctors] milking you like a cow —Molière

Green

GREEN

Bright green like a parrot's wing —Hugh Walpole

(Eyes as) deeply green as an Amazonian jungle —Ed McBain

Green and shiny as a frog come out of the swamp
—R. Wright Campbell

Green as a canker —V. S. Pritchett

Green ... as a well-watered palm —Mark Helprin

Green as jealousy —Vita Sackville-West

(Fields as) green as jellied mint —Malcolm Cowley

(Eyes) green as leeks —William Shakespeare

(The trees were) green as paper money —George Garrett

Green as spring —Beryl Markham

Green as St. Patrick's Day icing —Marge Piercy

(Eyes) green as wings of horseflies —Erica Jong

Greener than envy and money —George Garrett

GRIEF
See: SADNESS

GRINS
See also: LAUGHTER

Face ... cut wide open by a beautiful grin ... like pumpkins with candles shining out through their strong ivory teeth
    —Marge Piercy

Grin at each other as if we'd just completed a double steal
    —W. P. Kinsella

Grinning dreamily, like a man who has just had a final fix
    —James Crumley

A grin like a flash of dental lightning —Don Marquis

Grin like a German Shepherd —Rick Borsten

Grin like a kid caught smoking behind the barn —W. P. Kinsella

Grin like an apple slice —Julia O'Faolain

Grin like a salesman —Richard Ford

Grin like the moon, just barely there, and like the sun, getting ready to set —Hortense Calisher

Grinned at her like a six-year-old boy caught doing something he must charm his way out of —Niven Busch

Grinned at me very engagingly, like a daddy who has just finished explaining to his little boy how the new electric train works
    —Harvey Swados

Grinned, filling his cheeks, as if he had food in his mouth
    —Paul Theroux

Grinned just like a jackass chewing briars —George Garrett

Grinned like a hungry tiger —Harvey Swados

Grinned like a pumpkin —Marge Piercy

Grinned like a shark —T. Coraghessan Boyle

Grinned like a weasel in a chicken coop —T. Coraghessan Boyle

Grinning like a cageful of monkeys —Erich Maria Remarque

Grinning like a Death's-head —Loren D. Estleman

Grinned like beans —Rita Mae Brown

Grinning like egg-sucking foxes —John D. MacDonald

A grin of recognition spread across Bunty's face like a burn
    —Harvey Swados

Grins like a clown with a banjo —R.H.W. Dillard

Grin ... wide as a pumpkin's —Mary Hedin

His grin was like a big wrinkle among the small ones
    —Robert Campbell

A lop-sided grin, like he had a lemon in his mouth
    —Joseph C. Lincoln

GROANS AND WHISPERS
See also: SIGHS

The continuous moaning was a simple irritant, like the clanking of a
    radiator pipe —Mary McCarthy

Furious whispers which sounded like the hissing of snakes roused
    from a summer nap in some warm garden heap —Joyce Cary

Gasped like a big fish —Brian Moore

Groaning ... like the wind in the chimney —William Faulkner

Groan like a poleaxed steer —James Thurber

Grunted ... like a goat hit with a sledgehammer —William Moseley

Grunted like a man hit with a baseball bat —James Crumley

Grunt like a water-buffalo —O. Henry

Her husky whisper, gentle as a rain breeze, was like a tender caress
    —Cecilia Rosas

Hissed ... like the deadliest of adders —Joseph Heller

(Nola's) husky whisper had a thrill in it like the rattle of a snake
    —Wallace Stegner

Like the sound of water readying to boil were the whispers of his
    voice —Norman Mailer

Moan and pace like captured leopards —Diane Wakoski

Moaned ... deeply, like a cello —Martin Cruz Smith

Moaned ... like some baffled prowling beast —James Joyce

Moaning like a dumbstruck giant —Scott Spencer

Moans like a bedridden grandmother —T. Coraghessan Boyle

A moan that sounded as if it had been wrenched from her chest
    with a steel hook —James Crumley

Wail ... like wind outside a cabin window —Charles Johnson

(Felt my wrinkled heart) wheeze like a dog on a leash
    —Jayne Anne Phillips

Whimpering like a puppy just yanked from its mother and thrown
    onto the side of the road —Gloria Norris

Whimper like a well-trained pet wanting to be let out
    —George Garrett

A whispering moan like the rustle of wind in trees —James Stevens

Whispers dramatically, as though she were telling me a state secret
    —Daphne Merkin

Whisper softly as a girl's tear —Isaac Stern

Wince as if somebody had driven a red-hot spike into his head
    —P. G. Wodehouse

GROWTH
See also: SPREADING

Accumulate ... like acorns beneath the trees of a forest
    —Thomas H. Huxley

Accumulate like a pile of dead leaves drifting onto the pavement of
    August —Barbara Pym

Accumulate like wire coat hangers in a closet —Anon

Blooming as a bride —Anon

Blooming as spring —John Dryden

Bloom like wildflowers in moss —George Garrett

[A young girl] blossomed ... like a tree or a branch where every bud was breaking into flower —Rumer Godden

(Curiosity) blossomed like leprosy —Yehuda Amichai

(Life had) blossomed out like a flower in the sun —Ellen Glasgow

Blown up like a tumor —Ralph Waldo Emerson

Bred and nourished like a gardenia —Pat Conroy

Breed as quickly as cockroaches and are as difficult to stamp out —Bob Davis, in article about bugs in computer software, *Wall Street Journal*, January 28, 1987

Breed like cells under a microscope —Doris Lessing

Breeds like a rabbit —Jonathan Swift

(Ambassadors) cropped up like hay —W. S. Gilbert

(His belief ... came to the surface and) expanded like some delicate flower —E. M. Forster

Expanding like the shade of a cloud on sand —Wallace Stevens

Fertile like the divine creation —Victor Hugo

(The righteous shall) flourish as a branch —*The Holy Bible/Proverbs*

Flourishing like a weed —Stefan Zweig

Flourish like a cabbage rose —John Ashbery

Flourish like an herb —*The Holy Bible/Isaiah*

Going [a criminal investigation] like a grass shack fire —Harold Adams

Grew ... like a balloon being pumped full of gas —Myron Brinig

Grew like a larch —Emily Brontë

Grew like asparagus in May —W. S. Gilbert

[George Ade's popularity] grew like Jack's beanstalk —Lee Coyle

Grew like weeds in sand —Marge Piercy

Grow and grow like a maypole —Erica Jong

Grow like a summer pumpkin —W. P. Kinsella

(His notions) grow like a tropical forest —G. K. Chesterton

Grow like savages —William Shakespeare

(I watch our children) grow like stubborn weeds —George Garrett

Growth ... as fast as the light from polar regions —John Ashbery

Have grown like a bug from a bug out of the garden of Eden
    —Dylan Thomas

(In earth) like a man in a woman, I'll make food out of food
    —Daniela Gioseffi

A major advance ... it's like going from the propeller airplane to the
    jet —Dr. Bruce R. Baral, a dentist commenting on new cavity
    removal system, *New York Times*, December 31, 1986

(Disappointment) mounting higher every week, like a quick-growing
    hedge —Mazo De La Roche

Multiplies itself [ultimate truth about fellow men] like taxes
    —Ogden Nash

Multiplies like loaves and fishes —George Garrett

Multiply (thy seed) as the stars of the heaven, and as the sand
    which is upon the sea shore —*The Holy Bible/Genesis*

Multiply like fruitflies —Herbert Lieberman

Progress is like a merry-go-round. We get up on a speckled wooden
    horse ... we think we're travelling like the devil, but the man
    that doesn't care about the merry-go-round knows that we come
    back where we were —Finley Peter Dunne
        In Dunne's *Observations* by Mr. Dooley some words were
        in dialect ("Travellin' like the divvle but th' ... ").

Proliferate, like creditors at a bankruptcy —Mike Sommer

(Plots) ripen like fruit —O. Henry

Soaring like Halley's comet —Jane Wagner

Growth

As used in Jane Wagner's scenario for Lily Tomlin, *The Search for Signs of Intelligent Life*, soaring refers to a sharp increase, as in the teenage suicide rate.

(Poems) sprout like grain from quickened seeds —George Garrett

[Popularity] sprung up, like a grass fire —James Thurber

Stockpiled ... like grain in a grain elevator —Doug Feiden
> In Feiden's novel, *The Ten Million Dollar Getaway*, the people doing the stockpiling are mobsters and bodies are the frame of reference for the comparison.

Stretched out like a string released —Henri-Pierre Roche

Swelled like bullfrogs at mating time —R. V. Cassill
> Cassill's bullfrogs comparison is used by a character in *Hoyt's Child* to describe how policemen will fatten up their role if you let them in on your problems.

Swelling like a balloon —Robert Silverberg

Swelling up like blowfish —Peter De Vries

Unfolding like a tree —Philip Levine

We grow like a tree from the earth —Marge Piercy

GRUMBLING
See: CRITICISM

GUILT
See: CONSCIENCE

Habit

HABIT
See also: BEHAVIOR, FLEXIBILITY/INFLEXIBILITY

An annoying habit ... like the habit of people who take nonfattening sweeteners in their coffee, and order chocolate mousse —Marilyn Sharp

As the snow flakes gather, so our habits are formed —Jeremy Bentham

A bad custom is like a good cake, better broken than kept —Randle Cotgrave
> The word 'custom' is often interchanged with 'habit.'

Bad habits are like a comfortable bed; easy to get into, but hard to get out of —Rev. Watson C. Blake

The customs and fashions of men change like leaves on the bough, some of which go and others come —Dante Alighieri

(I like to) go tick-ticking along like a clock —Edith Wharton

Habit, like a crane, will bow its neck and dip its pulleyed cable, gathering me ... into the daylight —Harold Monro

(All will be well, we say; it is) a habit, like the rising of the sun —Edna St. Vincent Millay

The habit (of command) was already fitting him like a tailored suit —Ken Follett

Kept on along the narrow track of habit, like a traveler; climbing a road in a fog —Edith Wharton

Set in his ways as a chunk of concrete —F. Hopkinson Smith

Set in one's way, as elderly apple trees —Allison Lurie

Shook my wild habits from me ... like a worn-out cloak —O. Henry

Take for granted, like running water —Anon

Used to it, like a wart —Jonathan Kellerman

Using drugs like table salt —Jimmy Breslin

We are bagged in habit like clothes back from the cleaners —Marge Piercy

HAIR
See: BEARDS; HAIR COLOR; HAIR, CURLY; HAIR STYLES; HAIR TEXTURE; MUSTACHES

HAIR COLOR
See also: BLACK, BROWN, GRAY, RED

Black [hair] with only a few gray streaks like a timid motif running through it —Helen Hudson

Blond as a Zulu under the bleach —Raymond Chandler

Blond hair ... like long uncut grass but no color —Rosellen Brown

Hair Color

Braids, brown and shiny like a ripe hazelnut —Henry Van Dyke

A carroty mass of hair flaming round his cheeks and crown like a brush fire —T. Coraghessan Boyle

(Her long) chestnut hair was waving about like a curtain of silk —Francine du Plessix Gray

Gray hair ... like meringue —James Lee Burke

Gray hair that looks like the head of an old worn-out wet mop left out to dry and bleach in the sun —George Garrett

Gray hair, which he wore like a kind of silver beret —Robert Traver

Hair a fading mixture of black and gray, like an afternoon storm —Laura Furman

Hair ... artificially streaked, as though someone had emptied a bag of feathers over her head —Lynne Sharon Schwartz

Hair, as straight and red as ironed ketchup —Tom Robbins
> Redheads and their problems feature prominently in Robbins' *Life with Woodpecker,* and this is one of several similes about red hair.

Hair, black and shining like mica —Jean Garrigue

Hair, black as a seal's wet fur —Jean Garrigue

Hair ... bronze and silver like pear trees in full bloom —William Alfred

Hair ... dark and live as snakes —George Garrett

Hair ... had gray in it like streaks of milk —William Styron

Hair [red] ... like a fiery wick dipped in a well of incendiary sunlight —John Farris

Hair ... like Montana wheat planted in contours on a slope of hill —John Gunther

Hair looks as if it had been stained with blueberries —W. P. Kinsella

Hair, not just blonde, but radiating gold like a candleflame behind a window in winter —Stuart Dybek

Hair ... streaked like old piano keys —Reynolds Price

(His head and his) hair ... white like wool —St. John

Hair ... without definable color, as though it had very early begun to rehearse of its inevitable whiteness —Doris Grumbach

Her locks were yellow as gold —Samuel Taylor Coleridge

Her long hair was naturally a light brown, but the sun had bleached tawny streaks in it, like the stripes of a very old battle flag seen through imperfect glass —R. V. Cassill

His white hair stood out from his head like the fur of an Angora rabbit —Thomas McMahon

Long yellow hair like broken egg yolks spilling down all over her head —Helen Hudson

Pale auburn with a touch of gold ... like butter with paprika in it —John Gunther

Red hair ... all fluffed out, like her face lived in a pink cloud —Sharon Sheehe Stark

Red hair ... as glossy as plum-skins —Beverly Farmer

Red hair like a curtain that would draw down like a shade —Shirley Ann Grau

White hair ... flecked all over with little rust colored dashes, like India ink put on with a fine brush —Willa Cather

White hair like a cloud —Helen Hudson

White hair made her face look like a rose in snow —L. P. Hartley

White hair shone, like mountain snow —Percy Bysshe Shelley

White-headed as a mountain —Thomas Hardy

Yellow hair, like strands of gold
    —Anon line from early American ballad, "Locks and Bolts"

HAIR, CURLY
See also: HAIR STYLES

A circlet of crisp curly gray hair like a laurel wreath —Marge Piercy

Curled their hair so tightly that their heads looked like bunches of black grapes —Angela Carter

(Her gold) curls hang like lazy springs —Ira Wood

Curls like those of a young hyacinth —Edgar Allen Poe

Curls of yellow hair like pine shavings —Peter De Vries

(His dark) curls were flat, plastered over his head like a wet beret —Joan Hess

Curly, scented, black, stiff hair, like cock feathers —Janet Flanner

Hair ... as tightly curled as a poodle's —Margaret Millar
> A popular comparison with variations including the simplified as in "Hair ... curly as a poodle," and extensions like "Hair curled like a gilded poodle's." (T. Coraghessan Boyle's *Water Music*.)

Hair curled as rings of iron wire —Aharon Megged

Hair ... curled like the fruit on the trees —Dame Edith Sitwell

Hair ... curly as moss —Marge Piercy

Hair ... curly as the wool on a ram —George Garrett

Hair that curled naturally like very young leaves —Mollie Hardwick

Hair that sprang into ringlets like gold coins —Paige Mitchell

It [hair] covered either side of her thin face in curly muffs, like a poodle's ears —Jonathan Valin

Soft gray hair curled out of his skull like smoke —Miles Gibson

Towers of hair, curled like Indian temples —Joyce Cary

HAIR STYLES

Close-cropped head, cut so close to the scalp that the patches of gray are like a light stain —George Garrett

Hair ... almost as if ironed in place —H. E. Bates

Hair ... brushed straight back—like he was wearing a hairpiece or as though a small black beaver was lying on top of his skull —Donald McCaig

Hair ... cropped so short in back that he looked like a Marine in boot camp —Jonathan Valin

(Her chestnut) hair, cut short, closed about her neck like a choker —Arthur A. Cohen

Hair hanging down, straight, as if it were cut out of wood and painted —Rumer Godden

This is slightly modified from the dialect spoken by a character in Godden's story *No More Indians*: 'outa' and 'hangin' instead of 'out of' and 'hanging.'

Hair hanging ... like a brush across his forehead —Ella Leffland

Hair hanging like seaweed —John Updike

Hair ... hanging loose down to her shoulders, like a child's unbound for a party —Eudora Welty

Hair ... lay on her forehead like a ruffled crest —James Joyce

Hair parted from the middle of her forehead like the two panels of a curtain —Saul Bellow

Hair pulled back tight as if to punish it —Marge Piercy

Hair ... razor cut and blow-dried and sprayed so firmly into place that he looked like he was wearing a helmet —Robert B. Parker

Hair, so tightly braided it felt stitched on, showing her bare scalp like little seams all over her skull —Helen Hudson

Hair that grew long and thick around his face like ivy round a window —Helen Hudson

Hair ... twisted like a pastry into a knot —Patricia Henley

Hair was cut close to his scalp, like freshly mowed grass —Daphne Merkin

(Her white) hair was so permanently waved and arranged that it looked like concrete —Noël Coward

Her white hair ... stood high above her face like a chef's cap —Nancy Huddleston Packer

His hair ... covered half his forehead like a bowl —Reynolds Price

His hair ... cut short as that of a monk, seemed like a barber-college special —Thomas McGuane

His shiny brown hair was razor cut, wrapped like a scarf around his ears —Jonathan Valin

Pale fluffy hair whipped up beautifully on the top of her head like confectioner's cream —Elizabeth Bowen

Parted it [her hair] evenly, like the curtains of a neat house —Saul Bellow

Hair Styles

Short-cropped hair hugging her head like a bangle bracelet
—Arthur A. Cohen

Straight hair, cut like a little train to a point at the nape of her neck
—Eudora Welty

Wore her hair away from her forehead, like a cloud which a little wind in May peels off finely —Elizabeth Barrett Browning

Wore her hair nearly to her waist, in long pastel strands like the trailing branches of a weeping willow —Harvey Swados

Wore it [hair] as though he'd have thought it indecent exposure to have allowed anyone to catch even a glimpse of his eyebrows, his ears, or the back of his neck —George Bagby

Hair Texture

HAIR TEXTURE

Dead-looking hair ... as if it had been glued on —Willa Cather

Frizzy brown hair like short feathers —Marianne Hauser

A grand shock of hair, like the best type of sheepskin rug
—Phyllis Bottome
> *The Point of Vantage,* from which this is taken, leads off with a simile. Here it is in full context: "Teobaldo Kurt Dubrik was a large stout man with a grand shock of hair, like the best type of sheepskin rug."

Hair and mustache fluffy as down —Mark Helprin
See also: MUSTACHES

Hair as glossy as a blooded chestnut's coat —Elizabeth Spencer

Hair as sleek as a seal's fur —Sarah Bird

Hair ... black and dense and glossy, like boot polish
—Maeve Brennan

Hair ... coarse and slightly wavy, with just a trace of oil all over it, like a well-tossed salad —Roald Dahl

Hair, frizzy like unravelled rope —D. H. Lawrence

Hair ... like a coiled piece of copper —Laurie Colwin

Hair like a frizzled yellow sponge —Phyllis Bottome

Hair like blown-up gold and finer than gold —Joyce Carol Oates

HAIR WAS CUT CLOSE TO HIS SCALP, LIKE
FRESHLY MOWED GRASS

Hair like dirty cotton —Loren D. Estleman

Hair like fuzz on a tennis ball —Jean Thompson

Hair like moth-eaten fur —Ellen Glasgow

Hair like Persian lambs' fur —Saul Bellow

Hair like porcupine quills —Elizabeth Tallent

Hair ... like the raffia you had to soak before you could weave with it in a basket class —Saul Bellow

Hair ... matted and dry, like that of a sick animal —W. P. Kinsella

Hair ... tough as a rocking horse's —Penelope Gilliatt

Hair rich and dark, clustering thick as grapes or hyacinths —Elizabeth Spencer

Hair ... rough, like a mongrel dog's —Frank Tuohy

(Black,) shiny hair, hard as bristles —Ivan Turgenev

(His curly straw) hair shone like frail golden wires on his head —James Stern

Hair smooth as a cat's —Jayne Anne Phillips

Hair ... soft as milkweed silk —McKinlay Kantor

Hair ... straight as a string —Dorothy Canfield Fisher
> In her story *Married Children*, Fisher expands on this with, "She looks like a squaw."

Hair ... texture like damp thread —Anthony Powell

(A mane of black) hair that was as thick as a tow rope —Sumner Locke Elliott

Hair, thick and coarse as dune grass —Marge Piercy

Hair thick and glossy like fur —Martin Cruz Smith

Hair, thick as a cushion —Helen Hudson

Hair tough as a rocking horse's —Penelope Gilliatt

(Her pale red) hair was wispy and stuck out from her head like duckling down —Tama Janowitz

Her hair, after all the combing, shone like something Marco Polo
    might have brought back from Far Cathay to show the peasants
    —William Dieter

Her locks had been so frequently and drastically brightened and
    curled that to caress them ... would be rather like running one's
    fingers through julienne potatoes —Dorothy Parker

His fine dark hair looked more like a shadow than like real hair
    —Katherine Mansfield

Long coarse hair, like a mop —Rosa Guy

Straight shining hair like smooth straw —James Stern

Thick, bulging hair, like a bear's fur —Albert Moravia

HAND(S)
See: FINGERS, HAND MOVEMENTS, HANDSHAKE

HAND MOVEMENTS
See also: HANDSHAKE

Brushed at his forehead, like an insect had landed there
    —Donald McCaig

Clapped her hands like someone shooing pigeons
    —Sharon Sheehe Stark

Clapping as loudly as if their hands were wooden slats
    —Louis Auchincloss

Clapping her hands like cymbals —Ann Beattie

Clasped her hands behind her back like a child embarrassed at a
    social function, or stuck in the middle of a recitation
    —Peter De Vries

Cradled his hand in his lap, like it was a ruined bird
    —Donald McCaig

Flapped his hand like a flag —Mary Hedin

Flashing the palms of both hands like two headlights
    —Ludwig Bemelmans

Folding both hands in hhr lap like a reprimanded schoolgirl
    —Ed McBain

Hand Movements

(He flagged the car with ...) gestures like hoops —Eudora Welty

A hand, like a leaf, fell on his shoulder —Katherine Mansfield

Hands clasped like the hands of an old man round a stick
    —Sylvia Townsend Warner

Hands flapping like misshapen white moths —Joan Hess

Hands flew off the steering wheel like a pair of startled birds
    —Ed McBain

Hands fluttered like the fins of angel-fish —Frank Swinnerton

(Her delicate) hands ... flutter like birds —Phyllis McGinley

Hands gesticulating—flying through the air like two brown sparrows
    —Jonathan Kellerman

Hands jerked as if they were on wires —Dorothy Parker

Hands lifting out as if to smooth, like a sheet on a bed
    —John Updike

Hands rose and floated in the air, graceful and helpless as doves
    —Marge Piercy

Hands spread wide as calipers —Diane Ackerman

Hands were outspread as though he were leading an orchestra into a
    profound and final diminuendo —Ralph Ellison
        A plain and simple variation: "Raised his hand like an
        orchestra conductor."

Hasty, jerky gestures like a comedian in a silent movie
    —George Garrett

Held up her hand like a schoolgirl asking for permission to leave the
    room —Harvey Swados

Held up his hand like a traffic cop signaling stop —Ross Thomas

Kept rattling the ice in her glass, rattling her beads, rattling her
    bracelet like an impatient pony jingling its harness
    —Flannery O'Connor

Long thin hand ... floated like a scarf through the air
    —Marge Piercy

Nervous, tentative gesture, like someone making up his mind to
    stroke a dog that has the reputation of biting —Francis King

Opening and closing his fingers like a neon sign flickering at night
    —Ariel Dorfman

Passed her hand over her eyes as if to dispell a cloud
    —Robert Graves

Rearranges her hair like a horse shaking away a fly —W. P. Kinsella

Rubbing his hands together as if working tobacco for a pipe
    —Patrick White

Spread his hands in front of him, palms up, as if he intended to
    read in their lines the past as well as the future
    —Margaret Millar

Using his hands like a sculptor to shape the words he throws out
    —George Garrett

Wave as regal as Henry the Eighth's —Mary Hedin

HANDSHAKE

A grip like a trash compactor —Jonathan Valin

A grip like a weightlifter —Harvey Swados

Grip like iron —Walker Percy

A grip like pincers —Gerald Kersh

Hand gripped like bird claws —Wallace Stegner

(Your) hand grips mine like a railing on an icy night
    —Adrienne Rich

Hand ... pumping at mine as if he expected my fingertips to squirt
    milk or something —T. Coraghessan Boyle

Handshake like a bite —Leonard Michaels

Handshake like cold, cooked spaghetti —Mark Singer

Her hand was limp as a dead carp —Jay Parini

His fingers pressed my hand like pieces of wood —Aharon Megged

Shook hands ... like competitors before a match of some kind
    —Ross Macdonald

Shook hands like strangers —John Dos Passos

Handshake

Took it (the hand) cautiously, as if he were picking up a loathsome object preparatory to dropping it in the trash basket
—Evan Hunter

(She) took Jim's soft fingers and held them closely, until he felt that they had been drawn into a mangle —Frank Swinnerton

Handwriting

HANDWRITING

Handwriting ... like driven sleet —Peter De Vries

Handwriting looks as if a swarm of ants, escaping from an ink bottle, had walked over a sheet of paper without wiping their legs —Sydney Smith

HAPPINESS
See: CONTENTMENT, PLEASURE

HARDNESS
See: FIRMNESS, TOUGHNESS

HARD-HEARTEDNESS
See: CRUELTY

Harmlessness

HARMLESSNESS

As incapable of inflicting harm as a butterfly —Anon

Harmless and pleasant as the murmur of book and wind
—Robert Buchanan

Harmless as a Fuller Brush salesman —Raymond Chandler
Invariably topical or "brand name" similes either become obsolete or change when the name is no longer a household word. However, there's always a new name or catchword to take its place.

Harmless as a moth in a closet of Dacron —Anon

Harmless as an infant at play —William Cowper
Besides other variants meaning literally harmless ("Harmless as a baby," "Harmless as a sleeping infant"), there are also the more dramatic ones implying danger ("Harmless as an infant playing with knives/a box of pins/matches").

Harmless as a paper tiger —Chinese proverb

302

Harmless as doves —*The Holy Bible*
> Attribution for the simile is often given to Christina Rosetti's *Sonnet of Sonnets*, which contains this line: "She spread about her beauty for a snare, harmless as doves."

Harmless as leaves —Reynolds Price

Harmless as pigeons —Robinson Jeffers

Harmless as witches that have been robbed of their terror —Ellen Glasgow

HARSHNESS
See also: FIRMNESS

Austere ... as an aging virgin —Paige Mitchell

Corrosive as shame —Frank Swinnerton

Harsh as the bitterness of death —Algernon Charles Swinburne

Harsh as the yelping of jackals —Gustave Flaubert

(I will be ...) harsh as truth —William Lloyd

Rough as a cob and twice as corny
   —American colloquialism attributed to South

Shrill and active like a flight of gulls —George Garrett

Shrill as a whistling teapot with a head full of steam —Anon

(His nerves sang a song) shriller than a dog whistle
   —Douglas Adams

Shrill [voice] like a blade turning on a whetstone —Clifford Irving

Spoke sternly like a ward nurse to a familiar patient
   —Arthur A. Cohen

Strident as mustard —Marge Piercy

Threw orders around like lashes from a cat-o'nine-tails
   —Maya Angelou

HASTE
See: SPEED

HATRED

Hatred

Dislike ran round the table like electricity —Penelope Gilliatt

Exuded venom like a malicious old lady —Colette

The greatest hatred, like the greatest virtue and the worst dogs, is silent —Jean Paul Richter

Hate ... flowed like electric syrup through her veins —Marge Piercy

Hate is ptomaine, good-will is a panacea —Elbert Hubbard

Hating people is like burning down your own house to get rid of a rat —Harry Emerson Fosdick

Hatred fills my mouth like spit —Margaret Atwood

Hatred is a form of subjective involvement by which one is bound to the hated object —Lao Tzu

Hatred like fire; it makes even light rubbish deadly —George Elliott

Hatreds, like chickens, come home to roost —Joseph Shearing

He'll (a hated individual) be getting into your beer, like prussic acid; and blotting out your eyes, like a cataract; and screaming in your ears, like a brain tumor; and boiling around your heart, like melted lead; and ramping through your guts, like a cancer —Joyce Cary

I hate you like all-fire —Truman Capote

(Lady Charlotte would swallow back her hot feeling against Cynthia.) It [hate] was like a dark web within her, a fibrous tangle like the roots of plants in too small a pot —M. J. Farrell

My hate is like ripe fruit —Marvin Bell

The pleasure of hating, like a poisonous mineral, eats into the heart of religion and turns it to rankling spleen and bigotry —William Hazlitt

> In his essay, *The Pleasures of Hating,* Hazlitt continues to describe the effects of hatred: "It makes patriotism an excuse for carrying fire, pestilence, and famine into other lands; it leaves to virtue nothing but the spirit of censoriousness."

Promiscuous haters get religion as promiscuous lovers get clap
—Gerald Kersh

Spite may often see as clearly as charity —Lawrence Durrell

HEAD(S)
See: HEAD MOVEMENTS

HEAD MOVEMENTS

Bowed his head ... as if wishing to fall at her feet —Leo Tolstoy

Craned her head back and forth like a periscope, the way people do
when they are searching for a taxi at rush hour in Manhattan
—Daphne Merkin

Cranes his neck like a swan —Anton Chekhov

Drew his head into his shoulders like the bellows of an accordion
—Paul Olsen

Ducks his head, like a man someone has menaced and who has
barely gotten out of the way —Richard Ford

Gave a shake of his head, like a dazed boxer coming to
—Peter De Vries

Head, bobbing like a hollow ball —John Updike

(She was looking at her husband) head cocked like a setter bitch (as
if wondering, trying to remember who she had climbed into bed
with this time) —James Crumley

(The old man's) head had lowered itself into his collar like a turtle's
—Flannery O'Connor

Head moving like a prison search light —T. Glen Coughlin

Heads ... bent, like flowers following the sun or thrushes listening
for snails —Frank Swinnerton

Head sliding forward [while dozing] like an abandoned puppet
—T. Alan Broughton

(Little Nigel's) head snaps round like a weathervane in a gale
—John Le Carré

Head spun like a lazy susan —Jay Parini

Head Movements

Head thrust forward like a hungry hawk —Harold Adams

Head tilted to one side like a bib bird sitting on a branch of a tree —Harvey Swados

Head tilted to one side like a robin listening for worms —Jay McInerney

Head turning quickly from side to side, like an animal's —Eudora Welty

Head wagging like a mechanical toy —F. van Wyck Mason

Her head dropped like a soaked tea rose —Sharon Sheehe Stark

His head droops like a sun-flower —S. J. Perelman

His head hangs limp as a sock full of sand —Ira Wood

His head moved to and fro like a foolish kitten's after a swinging tangle of wool —Vicki Baum

His head rolled about his shoulders like a balloon that wanted to break its string —James Lee Burke

His head swung like a snake's as he talked, scanning anyone who chanced to come near —Donald MacKenzie

Holds up her head like a hen drinking —Scottish proverb

Lifted his big head like a listening deer —Zane Grey

Lifted up his head like a mouse sniffing the air —Isaac Babel

Lowered her head like a slow-witted schoolgirl trying to collect her thoughts in an effort to understand the teacher's question —Franz Werfel

Lowered his head to pray, like a martyr who believed the kingdom of heaven was at hand —Z. Vance Wilson

Made the convulsive movement of his head and neck, as if his tie were too tight —Leo Tolstoy
See also: NECK

A man with a small head is like a pin without any, very apt to get into things beyond his depth —Josh Billings

Nodded like a basking lizard —Derek Lambert

Nodded ... like a leaf —William McIlvanney

Nodded smartly —like a second lieutenant's salute—Jonathan Valin

Nodding his head like a pecking bird —Beryl Markham

Nods his head like a sage old trial judge —Richard Ford

Pulls back his head, like a turtle sensing danger —Rick Borsten

Shaking her head as if to get rid of a fly —Ruth Suckow

Shaking her head impatiently ... as if in a futile attempt to ease the chafing of an invisible collar —Carolyn Kizer

Shook his head like a wet retriever —Sharon Sheehe Stark

Shook his head like an overburdened professor —Martin Cruz

Shook my head back and forth like a silent, solid bell
—Richard S. Prather

Tossed her head with petulant violence, like a child who doesn't want her snarls combed out —John Updike

Turned her head ... cocking it a little, like a pretty canary in a cage
—Harvey Swados

Turning his head from side to side as though his necktie were too tight (and when he did that he usually clutched at his throat)
—Ivan Turgenev
> In a story entitled *Knock ... Knock ... Knock ...* Turgenev used this simile to describe a character who always felt cramped in the world.

Turns his head from side to side, like a turtle —Margaret Atwood

Wagged their heads like a company of cockatoos
—Katherine Mansfield

Waved her head here and there like a piece of wind-worried old orange-peel —F. Scott Fitzgerald

The way he moved his head from side to side made him seem like some sort of a little perky bird, a goldfinch, perhaps
—Roald Dahl

Withdrew his head like a scared tortoise —Donald MacKenzie

HEART(S)
See: AGITATION, HEARTBEAT

Heart(s)

Hard hearts, and cold, like weights of icy stone
—Percy Bysshe Shelley

The heart errs like the head —Anatole France

The heart (especially the Jewish heart) is a fiddle: you pull the strings, and out come songs, mostly plaintive —Sholom Aleichem

The heart is like the sky, a part of heaven, but changes night and day too, like the sky —Lord Byron

The heart is like a creeping plant, which withers unless it has something around which it can entwine —Charles James Apperley

The heart is like an instrument whose strings steal nobler music from Life's many frets —Gerald Massey

Heart like a child —Mary Hood

The heart of the wise, like a mirror, should reflect all objects, without being sullied by any —Confucius

Hearts isolated behind the bars of ribs and jumping around like monkeys —Yehuda Amichai

Hearts ... mellow as well-tilled soil in which good seed flourishes —Valdimir G. Korolenko

Hearts opening like jaws —Sharon Olds

Heart trembling a little like the door for Elijah the Prophet —Yehuda Amichai

A heart without affection is like a purse without money —Benjamin Mandelstamm

Her heart divided like two wings —Carson McCullers

Her heart sank like a wounded bird —Ellen Glasgow

His heart ached like Niagara Falls —Frank O'Hara

His heart is like a viper, hissing and spitting poison at God —Jonathan Edwards

His heart ... like the sea, ever open, brave and free —F. E. Weatherly

His heart sagged in its net of veins like a rock in a sling —George Garrett

His heart swelled up in his throat like a toad —Oakley Hall

His heart was open as the day —Anon ballad, "Old Grimes"

The human heart is like a ship on a stormy sea driven about by
    winds blowing from all four corners of heaven —Martin Luther

The human heart is like a millstone in a mill: when you put wheat
    under it, it turns and grinds and bruises the wheat to flour; if
    you put no wheat, it still grinds on, but then 'tis itself it grinds
    and wears away —Martin Luther

A man's heart is like a sponge, just soaked with emotion and
    sentiment of which he can squeeze a little bit out for every
    pretty woman —Helen Rowland

A man's heart, like an automobile, is always apt to skid and ditch
    him just at the psychological moment when he thinks he has it
    under perfect control —Helen Rowland

My heart clenched like a fist —Charles Johnson
        The fist comparison is also effective for describing a grim,
        pinched facial expression.
    See also: FACIAL EXPRESSIONS, SERIOUS

My heart is like an apple-tree whose boughs are bent with thick-set
    fruit —Christina Rossetti
        The first stanza of *A Birthday*, from which this is taken,
        contains yet another heart comparison: "My heart is like a
        rainbow shell that paddles in a halcyon sea."

My heart is like an outbound ship that at its anchor swings
    —John Greenleaf Whittier

My heart is like a singing bird —Christina Rossetti

My little heart pops out, like springs —Diane Wakoski
        This simile is the title of a poem which begins with yet
        another simile: "A little spirit in me that's wound up like a
        clock."

The heart is like a creeping plant, which withers unless it has
    something around which it can entwine —Charles James Apperley

Without a loved one my heart's like a beet root choked with
    chickweed —A Broken-Hearted Gardener, anonymous 19th
    century verse

HEARTBEAT
See also: AGITATION

Chest chiming like a cathedral gone berserk —Jonathan Gash

Feel his heart beating wildly inside his child's body, like a bird in a frail cage —Ruth Prawer Jhabvala

Heart banged like a drum —Katherine Mansfield

Heart beating like an African drum —Hugh Walpole

(Mrs. Arkin's) heart fluttered like a bird's wing —Gloria Norris

Heart jumping like a puppy —Anne Sexton

Heart noisy as a crockcrow —Walter de la Mare
See also: NOISE

Heart pulsing like a womb which has just given birth —Erica Jong

Heart ... running like a hamster on a wheel —Diane Ackerman

Hearts ... like muffled drums, are beating funeral marches to the grave —Henry Wadsworth Longfellow

A heart that ran up and down within the cage of ribs like a restless panther —Leonard Casper

Heart thumping like a June bug —Anne Sexton

Heart thumping like an outboard —Richard Ford

His heart ... beat high and fast like the ticking of a watch under a pillow —Frank Swinnerton

His heart began to give off tremendous explosions like a rifle —Eudora Welty

His heart beating, fiercely, like a small clock —Celia Dale

His heart flapped like a mass of furled banners —Bernard Malamud

His heart fluttered like that of a small bird about to be stoned —Alice Walker

My heart leaps forward like a hungry dog —Karl Shapiro

My heart pounds away, confident as a clock —Denise Levertov

My heart pounds down on itself like an anvil —Richard Ford

My heart staggers like a drunk —George Garrett

My heart was beating intolerably like a held bird —Reynolds Price

The noise that his heart valve produced sounded like two mechanical mice making love in a spoon drawer —Tom Robbins

Heart like a bass drum in her chest —Susan Richards Shreve

Heart [of a skylark] ... drumming like a motor —Ted Hughes

(In his ears his) heart sounded like jungle drums —Mary Hedin

HEARTINESS
See: EMOTIONS

HEAT
See: WEATHER

HEAVINESS

Feel heavy ... like a corpse —Penelope Gilliatt

Feel heavy like the September limbs of an apple tree
   —Diane Wakoski

The hand upon his shoulder weighed like a hand of lead
   —Oscar Wilde

Heavy and indistinct, like the consciousness of a man in a dream
   —Gustave Flaubert
   See also: VAGUENESS

Heavy as a lecher's kiss —Sylvia Plath

(A cold sky) heavy as a vault —Malcolm Cowley

(They are) heavy as dumplings —Henry David Thoreau
      To give added emphasis and specificity, there's "Heavy as overcooked dumplings," "Heavy as matzoh balls," "Heavy as latkes," "Heavy as wontons."

Heavy as guilt —Anon

Heavy as hard luck —Philip Larkin

Heavy as ingots —Diane Ackerman

(The glass mugs were) heavy as sin —Harvey Swados

[A suitcase] heavy as some icon —Cynthia Ozick

311

Heaviness

Heavy as the weight of dreams —Henry Wadsworth Longfellow

Leaden like a bullet —Ted Hughes

Helplessness

HELPLESSNESS

As defenseless [without a gun] as a tethered goat in a jungle
—Eric Ambler

Brutally as on a gag in her mouth, she choked on the sense of her
defenselessness —Dorothy Canfield Fisher

Chucked about like a cork —Nicholas Monsarrat

Feel like a card in a deck that is being constantly shuffled
—W. P. Kinsella

Feel like a rookie runner caught off base by a wily pitcher, hung up
in that vast area between first and second, fluttering back and
forth like a wounded bird who knows he's doomed
—W. P. Kinsella

Felt as a lost sailor on a sinking ship might feel, who throws his last
rope, and no saving hands to grasp it —Stella Benson

Felt [as result of being moved to another home by grandparents] as
if I was being kidnapped —Elizabeth Bishop

Felt helpless, like a rape victim —Rose Tremain

Felt helpless, as if he were involved in some disgraceful fraud
—Katherine Anne Porter

Felt helpless, like a dog that's been run over —Robert Lowry

Felt I was nothing but a husk blown this way and that way by the
winds of misfortune —Angela Carter

Felt like a beast in a trap, whose enemy would come upon him soon
—H. G. Wells

Felt like a bone between dogs —Julia O'Faolain

Felt like a man trapped in a swamp —Donald MacKenzie

Felt like a marionette, as though something outside her were jerking
the strings that forced her to scream and strike —Jean Rhys

Felt like a wounded fish who faced a larger hungry fish
—William Beechcroft

Felt more and more like a soldier being pitched into battle without proper orders —John Fowles

Felt ridiculous and out of control, like an engine breaking itself apart —Mark Helprin

Helpless and hopeful as a blade of grass —George Garrett
See also: HOPE

Get tossed like salad —Charles Bukowski

Helpless ... as a hooked fish swinging to land —Thomas Hardy

Helpless as a lion without teeth —F. Scott Fitzgerald

Helpless as an infant caterpillar in a nest of hungry ants —James Montgomery

Helpless as a plant without water —F. Hopkinson Smith

Helpless [against tide of emotions] as a swimmer swept away in a strong current —Margaret Kennedy

Helpless as a turtle on its back —O. Henry

Helpless as a writhing beetle on its back —Robert Traver

(I have become as) helpless as if the branch I seize and the one I stood upon both broke at the same time —Tamil

Helpless as shadows —Jean Garrigue

Helpless as the dead —W. S. Gilbert

Helpless as the owner of a sick goldfish —Kin Hubbard

Helpless ... like a man with a rumbling volcano in his pocket, trying to hold back the eruption with his naked hand —Irving Stone

Impotent yet defiant ... like a wild animal driven into a hole or fettered to a stake —Arthur Train

It was like being in an elevator cut loose at the top. Falling, falling, and not knowing when you will hit —Margaret Atwood

I was like a lamb or an ox that is brought to the slaughter —*The Holy Bible/Jeremiah*

Lame as a butterfly spread on a pin —Shirley Kaufman

Helplessness

Like elastic, stretched beyond its uttermost, his reason, will, faculties of calculation and resolve snapped to within him
—John Galsworthy

Looked like sheep looking for their shepherd
—W. Somerset Maugham

My will was a leaf in a gust of wind —Natascha Wodin

Powerless ... as a stone —Elizabeth Barrett Browning

Powerless as before a cataract —Simone de Beauvoir

Powerless as the wind —Percy Bysshe Shelley

The sense of being trapped ran through him like fire through dry grass —Ben Ames Williams

Sense of helplessness ... like a soft-shell crab that just shed its shell
—Kenzaburo Oë

Sinking under the leaden embrace of her affection like a swimmer in a drowning clutch —Edith Wharton

The situation [of tumbling stock market prices] is like being caught in the Bermuda Triangle
—Harvey P. Eisen, *New York Times*, January, 1986

Tossed about like an empty can in the sea —Romain Gary

Tossed about like cattle on a train —Ignazio Silone

Tossed about like twigs in an angry water —Willa Cather

Unable to do anything ... it was like watching a big cat thrash around in a cage and being helpless to free the beast
—May Sarton

Watching a friend fail ... it's like a bunch of lifeguards standing and watching their friend drown —Robin Williams, "Sixty Minutes" interview, September 21, 1986
> The comedian's comparison described how comedians feel when they watch one of their own fail on stage.

We're all drawn by wires like puppets, and the strongest wire pulls us in the direction in which we are meant to go —Ellen Glasgow

Without power, like a buzzing horsefly —George Garrett

Worked by strings, like a Japanese marionette —W. S. Gilbert

Wriggling helplessly, like a butterfly impaled by a pin
—Louis Bromfield

HISTORY
See also: PAST, THE

Americans treat history like a cookbook. Whenever they are uncertain what to do next, they turn to history and look up the proper recipe, invariably designated "The lesson of history"
—Russell Baker
See also: CHARACTERISTICS, NATIONAL

Carried his history with him like a tattooed sailor —Alice McDermott

History is a hill or a high point of vantage, from which alone men see the town in which they live or the age in which they are
—G. K. Chesterton
> Chesterton continues this simile as follows: "Without some such contrast or comparison, without some such shifting of the point of view, we should see nothing whatever of our own social surroundings. We should take them for granted, as the only possible social surroundings."

History is floated like a bond issue on the fat of banks
—Marge Piercy

History is written to order like the Sunday funnies —Marge Piercy
> This is one of several similes pertaining to history in Piercy's poem, *For Shoshana Rihm.*

History ... like some lump of viscid porridge sliding slowly down a sink —Lawrence Durrell

History passes like falling rocks in the dark —Robinson Jeffers

History [in narrator's view] ... sifting and seeping, piddling itself away as one wastes a Sunday —William H. Gass

History trails its meaning like old cobwebs caught in a cellar broom
—Robert Penn Warren

History was a trash bag of random coincidences torn open in a wind
—Joseph Heller

To the scientific eye all human history is a series of collective movements, destructions or migrations, like the massacre of flies in winter or the return of birds in spring —G. K. Chesterton

You can't escape history, or the needs and neuroses you've picked up like layers and layers of tartar on your teeth —Charles Johnson

HOME
See: ROOMS

HONESTY

Clean as a hound's hind leg —William Beechcroft

Honest as bread —Mollie Hardwick

Honesty is a compulsion swinging a heavy sword like loving —Marge Piercy

Honesty is like an icicle; if once it melts that is the end of it —Anon

Incorruptible as a statue —Jean Garrigue

Law-abiding as a cow —G. K. Chesterton

(I'm totally legit.) Legal as a Jesuit —Jay Parini

HONOR
See: REPUTATION

HOPE

As renewed as a baby born to middle life —Richard Ford

As spring flowers are promised by seed-sellers in their new catalogues, you too were once full of promise —Charles Simic

Carry hope like a tallow candle —Marge Piercy

Cold hopes swarm like worms within our living clay —Percy Bysshe Shelley

Every wish is like a prayer with God —Elizabeth Barrett

Full of inexpressible expectations, like a child running downstairs on Christmas morning, not knowing what wonderful things may be in the stocking —Harvey Swados

Had his hopes jerked back and forth like Pinocchio —
dialogue from "Hill Street Blues," television drama,
broadcast 1987

Hope dawned in the distance like a sail —Marguerite Yourcenar

Hope is like the setting of the sun. The brightness of our life is gone
—William Wadsworth Longfellow

(Nothing in the world is as) hopeful as knowing a woman you like
is somewhere thinking about only you —Richard Ford

Hopeful, like extras at an audition —Lawrence Durrell

Hope has as many lifes as a cat or a king
—Henry Wadsworth Longfellow

Hope is a kind of cheat: in the minute of our disappointment we are
angry; but upon the whole matter there is no pleasure without it
—Lord Halifax

Hope is like the sun, which, as we journey towards it, casts the
shadow of our burden behind us —Samuel Smiles

Hope is nearly as strong as despair, and greatly more pertinacious
and enduring —Walter Savage Landor

Hope is to a man as a bladder to a learning swimmer; it keeps him
from sinking ... but yet many times it makes him venture beyond
his height —Owen Feltham

Hope ... it's like a fire in the wind; the slightest breeze will diminish
it, but if I feed it the wind will make it blaze
—Richard Maynard

Hope's as cheap as despair —H. G. Bohn's *Handbook of Proverbs*

Hopes like a child —Randall Jarrell

Hope springing like a Jack-in-the-box —Alice McDermott

It was as though a great eraser had swept across Stern's mind, and
he was ready to start fresh again —Bruce Jay Friedman

Like our shadows, our wishes lengthen as our sun declines
—Edward Young

Living on hope is like living on an 800 calorie-a-day diet —Anon
This may have its origins in a Scottish proverb: "He who
lives on hope lives on a very lean diet."

Hope

Look at hopefully, like a bird with its beak opennwaiting for a nice juicy worm —Sara Woods

Plucked my spirits up like a hitchhiker who catches a ride when all hope was lost —Richard Ford

Through the sunset of hope like the shapes of a dream, what paradise islands of glory gleam —Percy Bysshe Shelley

Wishes, like painted landscape ... afar off they appear beautiful; but near they show their coarse and ordinary colors
—Thomas Yalden

Hospitality

HOSPITALITY

Giving a party is very much like having a baby; its conception is more fun than its completion —Anon

Hospitable as Welcome Wagoners —Lisa Harris
The hospitality described in Harris' book, *The World of a Hasidic Family*, is that of the Lubavitcher women in New York's Crown Heights section.

A host is like a general: it takes a mishap to reveal his genius —Horace

The service was as slow as the progress of a snail and a good-humored as Rip Van Winkle —O. Henry

318

ICICLES
See: SNOW

IDEALS
See: BELIEFS

IDLENESS
See: SITTING

IMITATION
See: SIMILARITY

IMMEDIACY
See: SPEED

IMMOBILITY
See: LYING, POSTURE, SITTING, STANDING

IMPASSIVENESS
See: RESERVE

IMPATIENCE
See: RESTLESSNESS

IMPERMANENCE
See: FRAGILITY

IMPETUOUSNESS
See: BEHAVIOR, NATURALNESS

IMPOSSIBILITY
See: FUTILITY, OPPORTUNITY

IMPROPRIETY
See: PROPRIETY/IMPROPRIETY

INACCURACY
See: ERRORS

INAPPROPRIATENESS
See: BELONGING

INCORRECTNESS
See: ERRORS

INCREASE
See: GROWTH

INDECISION
See: CHOICES

INDIFFERENCE
See: RESERVE

LAW-ABIDING AS A COW

INDISTINCTNESS
See: VAGUENESS

INDIVIDUALITY
See: ORIGINALITY

INEFFECTIVENESS
See: FUTILITY

INEXORABILITY
See: STEADINESS

INEXPENSIVENESS
See: COST

INFATUATION
See: LOVE

INFLATION
See: ECONOMICS

INFORMALITY
See: FORMALITY/INFORMALITY

INFORMATION
See: KNOWLEDGE

INHERITANCE
See: PAST, THE

INNOCENCE
See: HARMLESSNESS

INQUISITIVENESS
See: CURIOSITY

INSANITY
See: MADNESS

INSEPARABILITY
See: RELATIONSHIPS

INSIGHT
See: WISDOM

INSTINCTIVENESS
See: NATURALNESS

INTANGIBILITY
See: ELUSIVENESS

INTEMPERANCE
See: DRINKING

INTENSITY
See: STARES

INTIMACY
See: RELATIONSHIPS

IRREGULARITY
See: REGULARITY/IRREGULARITY

IRRITABLENESS
See: NERVOUSNESS

JOURNALISM
See: PROFESSIONS, WRITERS/WRITING

JOWLS
See: CHEEKS

JOY
See: CONTENTMENT, PLEASURE

JUDGMENTS
See: OPINIONS

JUMPING
See: LEAPING

KINDNESS
See: GENTLENESS, SWEETNESS

KISSES

Kisses

Batted them [breast nipples] over and over with my tongue like gum
    —Joe Coomer

Being kissed ... was something done to her, like the shampoos her
    mother used to give her at the kitchen sink —John Updike

He kissed her ... his neck arching forward, hers backward, like a pair
    of swans —T. H. White

Her lips grazed mine, cool, soft, and tremulous as the wings of a
    moth —Robert Traver

His kiss dropped on her like a cold smooth pebble —Edith Wharton

His [kisser's mouth] mouth was as soft as a flower and his breath as
    sweet —Ruth Prawer Jhabvala

It [kissing someone] was like putting your mouth against an
    automatic bank teller, where it swallows your credit card
    —John Updike

Kissed (the children) with an official air, as if she were conferring an honor, pinning on her kisses like orders —Rebecca West

Kisses are like confidences, one follows the other —Denis Diderot

Kisses are like grains of gold or silver found upon the ground, of no value themselves, but precious as showing that a mine is near —George Villiers

Kisses, like folks with diminutive souls, will manage to creep through the smallest of holes —J. G. Saxe

Kisses ... sticky like a child's —Flannery O'Connor

Kisses strong like wine —Algernon Charles Swinburne

Kiss ... felt like a drop of rain in the desert —John Updike

Kissing a person who's self-righteous and intolerant is like licking a mongoose's ass —Tom Robbins

Kissing a smoker is like licking an ashtray —Tom Robbins

Kissing her lips was like kissing warm but uncooked liver —Stephen King

Kissing her ... .was like playing post office with a dead and rotting whale —Truman Capote

Kissing him would be like kissing razor blades —David Brierly

Kissing is a good deal like eating; there is not much fun when person is hungry in standing by, and seeing it done by another fellow —Josh Billings

> Portions originally in the Billings phonetic dialect: "iz hungry ... it did bi anuther fellow."

A kiss without a mustache is like an egg without salt —Spanish proverb

Moved her head and face about under the kisses as if they were small attacking waves —Doris Lessing

One more such kiss and I am ready to be roasted upon a slow fire like any chicken or duckling —Delmore Schwartz

Pecks like chicken scratchings —Mary Morris

She dug her lips into my mouth like tiger's claws —Jaroslav Seifert

She kissed me as moistly as a little girl —John Braine

Kisses

She took kisses like so many coats of paint —Lawrence Durrell

They kissed like two old people going to bed after the clock has been wound and the cat put out —Derek Lambert

To kiss her would be like a Becket play to a college student: She would study it, dissect it, analyze it, appraise it and inject it with the serum of significance, until at last she transformed the simple touching of four lips into a Rosetta Stone that would give meaning to her life —Peter Benchley

When she kissed him, he melted like a lump of milk chocolate —Marge Piercy

KNEES
See: LEGS

Knowledge

KNOWLEDGE

A body without knowledge is like a house without a foundation —Hebrew proverb

The desire for knowledge, like the thirst of riches, increases ever with the acquisition of it —Laurence Sterne

Follow knowledge, like a sinking star, beyond the utmost bound of human thought —Alfred, Lord Tennyson

Gleaned bits of information like a mouse hoarding pellets of bran stolen from the feed manger —Rita Mae Brown

(There are no limits to his knowledge, on small subjects as well as great;) he is like a book in breeches
—Sydney Smith about Macaulay

In knowledge, as in swimming, he who flounders and splashes on the surface, makes more noise, and attracts more attention than the pearl-diver who quietly dives in quest of treasures to the bottom —Washington Irving

In science, as in life, learning and knowledge are distinct, and the study of things, and not of books is the source of the latter —Thomas H. Huxley

It's like swimming; once you learn it, you never forget it
—Miguel de Cervantes

Knowledgeable as a walking encyclopedia of universal knowledge
—Louisa May Alcott

Knowledge ... is like a fire, which must first be kindled by some
external agent, but which will afterwards propagate itself —
Samuel Johnson, letter to William Drummond, August 23, 1766

Knowledge ... like a rough diamond ... will never be worn or shine,
if it is not polished —Lord Chesterfield

Knowledge, like religion, must be "experienced" in order to be
known —Edwin Percy Whipple

The knowledge of man is like the waters, some descending from
above, and some springing from beneath; the one informed by
the light of nature, the other inspired by divine revelation
—Francis Bacon
>   Paraphrased from Bacon's "Knowledge of man is as the
>   waters."

Knowledge, when wisdom is too weak to guide her, is like a
headstrong horse that throws the rider —Francis Quarles

The right to know is like the right to live. It is fundamental and
unconditional in its assumption that knowledge, like life, is a
desirable thing —George Bernard Shaw

The struggle for knowledge has a pleasure in it like that of wrestling
with a fine woman —Lord Halifax
>   The original simile used 'hath' instead of 'has.'

The understanding, like the eyes, while it makes us see and perceive
all things, takes no notice of itself, and it requires art and pains
to set it at a distance and make it its own subject —John Locke
>   The fifth word is a modernization of the original, 'whilst.'

We deal our knowledge like a pack of cards —George Garrett

With informations we can go anywhere in the world, we are like
turtles, our houses always on our backs —John Le Carré
>   In his novel *A Perfect Spy*, Le Carré expands the simile as
>   follows: "You learn to paint, you can paint anywhere. A
>   sculptor, a musician, a painter, they need no permits. Only
>   their heads."

KNUCKLES
See: FINGERS

Language

LANGUAGE
See also: SPEAKING

Greek is like lace; every man gets as much as he can
— Samuel Johnson

It is with language as with manners: they are both established by the usage of people of fashion —Lord Chesterfield

Language, if it throws a veil over our ideas, adds a softness and refinement to them, like that which the atmosphere gives to naked objects —William Hazlitt

Language is a city, to the building of which every human being brings a stone —Ralph Waldo Emerson

Language is an art, like brewing or baking —Charles R. Darwin

Languages evolve like species. They can degenerate just as oysters and barnacles have lost their heads —F. L. Lucas

Languages, like our bodies, are in a perpetual flux, and stand in need of recruits to supply those words which are continually falling into disuse —C. C. Felton

Show them [Americans with a penchant for "fat" talk] a lean, plain word that cuts to the bones and watch them lard it with thick greasy syllables front and back until it wheezes and gasps for breath as it comes lumbering down upon some poor threadbare sentence like a sack of iron on a swayback horse —Russell Baker

Slang is English with its sleeves rolled up —Carl Sandburg, quoted by William Safire in series on English language, PBS, September, 1986

To write jargon is like perpetually shuffling around in the fog and cottonwool of abstract terms —Sir Arthur Quiller-Couch

Laughter

LAUGHTER
See also: GAIETY, GRINS

As the crackling of thorns under a pot, so is the laughter of a fool
— *The Holy Bible/Ecclesiastes*

326

Basically when you laugh you have to make a fool of yourself ... it's like sex —Robin Williams, "Sixty Minutes" interview, September 21, 1986

Chuckle ... it sounded like a trapped wasp —Jonathan Gash

Chuckles ... empty and round, like bubbles —Dan Jacobson

Chuckling like a jovial insurance salesman —James Crumley

Contralto laughter, like a violin obligato under trills of a flute —Carlos Baker

A dry crackle like leaves crushed underfoot —Louise Erdrich

Dry laughter like the cackle of crows or the crackling of fallen leaves underfoot —Margaret Laurence

Giggled ... like a naughty child which has unintentionally succeeded in amusing the grown-ups —Christopher Isherwood

(They kissed. And) giggled like cartoon mice —Tom Robbins

Giggle, like a child watching a Hollywood adventure film —Nadine Gordimer

A good laugh is sunshine in a house —William Makepeace Thackeray

Heavy, melodious laughter, like silver coins shaking in a bag —Aharon Megged

Her braying laugh rang out like the report of a shotgun —James Thurber

Her laugh broke like a dish —Cynthia Ozick

Her laugh crackled ... like a leap of electricity —Richard Francis

Her laugh pealed out like a raven escaping into the night —Donald McCaig

Her laugh rang like the jangling of bracelets —Derek Walcott

Her laughter hung in the air like sleigh bells on a winter night —Jay Parini

Her laughter was a titanic, passionate thing that seemed to pass up like a wave from her toes to her mouth —Pat Conroy

High laugh, like a dove cry—Eudora Welty

Laughter

A high laugh like a wicked witch —Carolyn Chute

His laughter thickened like a droning bell —James Wright

A hoarse, very small laugh, like a cat's cough —Frank Swinnerton

A horrifying derisive laugh, like rolling tin —Barry Hannah

Laugh ... as if a demon within him were exulting with gloating scorn
—Iris Murdoch

(Louisa's) laugh begins high and descends from there like a cascade
—Daphne Merkin

Laughed, a little drugged giggle, like chatter —Paul Theroux

Laughed contemptuously like a whore being offered too little money
—Gary Hart

Laughed, like a bowlful of jelly —Clement C. Moore

Laughed like a windup machine —John D. MacDonald

Laughed like monkeys —Richard Ford

Laughed like murmurs of the sea —W. B. Yeats

Laughed ... like the trill of a hedge-warbler —Frank Swinnerton

A laugh exploded out of me like a sneeze —Scott Spencer

Laughing, a sound like wind in the grass —T. Coraghessan Boyle

A laugh is just like sunshine —Anon rhyme
    The simile is the poem's repeat motif.

Laugh ... like the barking of a fox —Erich Maria Remarque

Laugh ... like a bird's carol on the sunrise breeze
—John Greenleaf Whittier

Laugh like a hyena —William Shakespeare
    This simile from *As You Like It* crops up in many a modern
    short story and novel.

Laugh ... like a spoon tinkling against a medicine glass
—Katherine Mansfield

Laugh ... like a thrush singing —Oscar Wilde

A laugh like clapboards being ripped off the side of a house
—Peter De Vries

Laughs [in a film] ... come out of despair like bits of green in a graveyard —Walter Goodman about the movie, *No Surrender, New York Times*, August 6, 1986

Laughs like a rhinoceros —Tom Davies
> The person Davies described was Samuel Johnson.

Laughs like little bells in light wind —George Garrett

Laughter ... checked by small clutches of muscle, like tiny fists, at the corners of his mouth —Leonard Michaels

Laughter crackling like a schoolgirl who has not experienced enough of the world to fear it —Ira Wood

Laughter cruel as barbed wire —George Garrett

Laughter falls like rain or tears —Dame Edith Sitwell

Laughter fell like a shower of coins —George Garrett

Laughter ... high and free and musical, like a happy soprano limbering up —Harvey Swados

Laughter hung smoke-like in the sudden stillness —Ralph Ellison

Laughter ... keeps coming like a poison that must be ejected —Nora Johnson

Laughter leaped suddenly from her throat ... then stopped, like something flung away and lost —Graham Swift

Laughter like hiccoughs —T. Coraghessan Boyle

Laughter, light and restrained like the clatter of rolling nuts —Yisrael Zarchi

Laughter lonelier than tears —Anonymous blurb preceding a humorous quote, *New York Times Book Review*/Noted With Pleasure, September 14, 1986

The laughter of a fool is like that of a horse —Welsh proverb
See also: FOOLISHNESS

Laughter roared through the spectators like wind through trees —Gerald Kersh

Laughter spilled out of his prodigious frame like gravel being unloaded from a dump truck —Pat Conroy

A laugh that rippled ... like the sound of a hidden brook
  —O. Henry

A laugh that rumbles like a freight train in the night —Michael
  Goodwin about sports broadcaster, Steve Zabriskie, *New York
  Times*/TV Sports, October 2, 1986

A laugh that unfolds like a head of lettuce —Antler

Let out a cackle of a laugh, like the sound a hen might make if the
  hen were mad about something —Larry McMurtry

Men who never laugh may have good hearts, but they are deep
  seated; like some springs, they have their inlet and outlet from
  below, and show no sparkling bubble on the brim —Josh Billings
    Words originally in Billings' phonetic dialect are: 'laff'
    (laugh), 'hav' (have), 'sum' (some).

A most pleasant laugh, bubbly and controlled, like fine champagne
  —Margaret Millar

Peal of laughter like the ringing of silvery bells
  —Nathaniel Hawthorne

A queer stage laugh, like the cackle of a baffled villain in a
  melodrama —Edith Wharton

(Boutin's mouth opened from ear to ear in) a roar of laughter, like
  the bursting of a mortar —Honoré de Balzac

She laughed, sounding like a small barking dog —Robert Campbell

She pursed her lips each time she laughed, making laughter seem a
  gesture of self-control —W. P. Kinsella

A silvery laugh, like a brook running out to meet the river
  —Mike Fredman

A slow ripple of laughter, like a scattering of autumn leaves
  —Robert Traver

A snort of a chuckle like a bull-frog —Lawrence Durrell

Some ... laugh just as a rat does, who has caught a steel trap, with
  his tail —Josh Billings
    In the original phonetic dialect this is: "Laff just az a rat
    duz, who haz caught a steel trap with his tale."

The sound [of laughter] was like the whirring of an old grandfather
  clock before it strikes —Frank Swinnerton

Stopped laughing as suddenly as if a set ring had been broken
—Loren D. Estleman

A sudden fizz of laughter like soda water —George Garrett

Tittering like a small bird —Beryl Markham

Twinkled like Old King Cole —Donald McCaig

When he laughed, a satyr-like quality suffused his face
—Nathaniel Benchley

When she does laugh ... it's like polished crystal, like a stream in the
Alps racing over a pebbly bed here below, like ... like another
simile —Hanoch Bartov
> For anyone interested in multiple similes ... here's the
> simile itself to round up a medley of comparisons.

When she laughed it was as if a wren sang —Frank Swinnerton

When she was about to laugh, her tone grew higher and melodious,
easing into the laugh like a singer easing from recitative to an
aria —Lynne Sharon Schwartz

Wrinkles of laughter leaped into sight on his face, like small friendly
insects running all over it —Romain Gary

LAW
See: LAWYERS

LAWBREAKING
See: CRIME

LAWYERS
See also: PROFESSIONS

A certain criminal lawyer, like a trapeze performer, is seldom more
than one step from an awful fate
—Paul O'Neil, *Life*, June 22, 1959

A countryman between two lawyers is like a fish between two cats
—Benjamin Franklin

The glory of lawyers, like that of men of science, is more corporate
than individual —Oliver Wendell Holmes, Sr., April 15, 1890

If you would wax thin and savage, like a half-fed spider, be a
lawyer —Oliver Wendell Holmes, Sr.

Holmes senior gave up the law for a career in medicine and literature. His son, on the other hand, enjoyed a distinguished legal career culminated by his appointment to the Supreme Court.

A lawyer's face always gives warning of an ambush. Like a blockhouse. Used to conceal the artillery —Joyce Cary

A lawyer awaiting a decision in a big case is like a murderer waiting for the jury to come out —Robert Traver
> In the novel, *Laughing Whitefish*, this comparison continues, "in both, wistful hope mingles inevitably with gloom and foreboding."

A lawyer deep in his case is like a man fallen in love. Whether shaving or bathing or plain old-fashioned knaving, in bed or out, always and forever he is obsessed by his goddam case —Robert Traver
> A variation of this from *People Versus Kirk* also appears in Traver's best known novel, *Anatomy of a Murder*.

A lawyer lacking a flock of law books is like a carpenter run out of nails —Robert Traver

A lawyer preparing for the trial of a difficult and complex case ... is like a man consulting a dictionary who winds up chasing everything but the word he needs —Robert Traver

Lawyers are just like physicians: what one says, the other contradicts —Sholom Aleichem

Lawyers, like bread, are best when they are young and new —Thomas Fuller

Lawyers on opposite sides of a case are like the two parts of shears; they cut what comes between them, but not each other —Daniel Webster

Like most corporate attorneys, he sat squarely on the fence with both ears to the ground —Anon

Years of practice had made them sensitive to every whimsy of emotion and taught them how to play upon the psychology of the jury as the careless zephyr softly draws its melody from the aeolian harp —Arthur Train

LEAPING

(The flashlight) leaped about like a will-o'-the-wisp —Brian Moore

Leaped from his chair as a runner leaps crouching, from the mark —Frank Swinnerton

Leaped like a fawn —Pat Conroy

Leaped like a high jumper —Frank Conroy

(Goats) leaped ... like arrows speeding from the bow —Willa Cather

Leaped like a spring released —John Updike

Leaped ... like a startled frog —Théophile Gautier

Leaped up like a little singed cat —O. Henry

Leaps like a buck in air —Caroline Finkelstein

Leaps like a flash —Maxwell Anderson and Laurence Stallings
> This is a line from the Anderson/Stallings play, *What Price Glory.*

(The pulse in his palm) leapt like a trout in a brook —Eudora Welty

Leaping through the air like a man released from gravity —Ed Bradley, about basketball star Michael Jordan, "Sixty Minutes," February 15, 1987

LEAVES

Aspen and poplar leaves covered the road like yellow snow —Susan Engberg

The dirty leaves were hanging down from the [rain-wet] trees like dead bats —Josephine Tey

Dry leaves blew across the sidewalk like arched spiders —Joan Hess

Dry leaves chatter like a children's brigade —Diane Ackerman

A few leaves had fallen and lay like neglected toys on the grass —Carolyn Slaughter

The forest leaves moved like small rustling animals over the moss —Hayden Carruth

The last leaves of some sultry September hung stiffly, like leaves pressed between the pages of an old catechism —Nelson Algren

Leaves

Leaves as light and agitated as swarms of little butterflies that hovered above the clover —Willa Cather

Leaves as limp as soiled money —George Garrett

Leaves delicately veined as a baby's hands —W. P. Kinsella

Leaves digest sun as men and women eat each other to love —Daniela Gioseffi

Leaves drooped (over white frame houses) like hands —James Reiss

Leaves fallen like wet rags —Bernard Malamud

The leaves ... fall off the branches by the hundreds, like paratroopers from their planes —David Ignatow

Leaves fell like notes from a piano —Derek Walcott

Leaves fell like rejected brown stars —John Rechy

The leaves fly up like birds —Conrad Aiken

Leaves hanging down like tongues —Jean Thompson

Leaves hissing and steaming like kettles —Philip Levine

Leaves ... hung lustreless, like drying tea-dregs —Julia O'Faolain

Leaves ... large as a lady's apron —Caroline Finkelstein

Leaves ... like a soggy blanket ... covered gutter, sidewalk, lawn, backyard, bushes and alley —Bernard Malamud

Leaves like green lace —George Garrett

Leaves like ruffled wavelets —Sylvia Berkman

Leaves like scarlet hands floated on the green slow water —Truman Capote

The leaves of the red maples glowed like fruit —Jean Thompson

The leaves paled and fell from the shedding trees like old wishes —George Garrett

Leaves peep out so fresh and green, so pure and bright, like young lives pushing shyly out into the bustling world —Jerome K. Jerome

Leaves rattled dryly together, like scales of metal —Aldous Huxley

Leaves scatter and point to every part of the sky, like famished fingers waving —Richard Wilbur

(A giant tree which bore) leaves shaped like fans —Anaïs Nin

The leaves sift down one by one like notes in music —May Sarton

The leaves that a few days before had been green now dropped like heat-withered cellophane —Wallace Stegner

The leaves turn and twist in the wind as if quarreling with one another —David Ignatow

The leaves were motionless on the trees, as if they were resting in the heat —Willis Johnson

Leaves, wrinkled or shiny like apples —Frank O'Hara

Some of its [a plant's] leaves had turned black and were curled up like charred Christmas ribbons —Margaret Millar

Yellow leaves like lamps of gold —John Greenleaf Whittier

The yellow leaves swam through the air as silently as fish —Jean Thompson

The young leaves were still soft and slack ... less like leaves than like petals, and drooping in the sweet forest-air like seaweeds in deep water —Isak Dinesen

LEGS

Ankles fine as an antelope's —Josephine Edgar

Ankles like door knobs —Anon

The calves of her legs were as taut and stiff as anchor chains —Mary Ellen Chase

Feet heavy as anchors —Richard Ford

Feet large as spades —Aharon Megged

Feet like canoes —Herbert Wilner

Feet ... swollen, driven through my shoes like devilled egg through a pastry bag —Ira Wood

Feet ... tripping like the feet of a restless pony —Adela Rogers St. John

Legs

(The fiddler's) feet were like the black hooves of a trotting horse that never seemed to touch the ground —Will Weaver
See also: DANCING

Her bony toes seemed as long and articulate as fingers —Thomas Williams

Her legs were shapeless ... like a fisherwoman's —H. E. Batess

His legs felt like two old rusted rain gutters —Flannery O'Connor

(She was a vast blonde girl, with) huge limbs like a piece of modern sculpture —Barbara Pym

Knees tuck out ... like two hard-boiled eggs —Anne Piper

Legs bowed like a wishbone —Ian MacMillan

Legs ... as heavy as sunken logs —Nolan Miller

Legs as shapeless and almost as thin as the lines in a child's drawing —Niven Busch

Legs as thick as newel posts —F. van Wyck Mason

Legs bent like monster springs —Richard S. Prather

Legs ... bowed, rickety, like bent pipes —George Garrett

Legs have gone mottled, like Roquefort cheese —Nadine Gordimer
Another simile to describe the effects of cellulite is "Thighs like cottage cheese."

Legs in motion like the hind parts of a dog —David Ignatow

Legs knotted and angular as whittled wood —George Garrett

Legs like a baseball bat —Delmore Schwartz

(A large man with) legs like a billiard table —Joyce Cary

Legs like an emaciated monkey's —Louis-Ferdinand Celine

Legs like redwood trees —Pat Conroy

Legs ... like two pillars —Bertold Brecht

Legs moving like the hammers of a grand piano —Paul Kuttner

Legs shaped like lion's paws —Jilly Cooper

Legs solid as tree trunks —Richard Deming

Legs ... stiff as a wooden soldier's legs —William Kotzwinkle,

Legs ... straight as a pair of poplar trees in a storm —Ariel Dorfman
    See also: STRAIGHTNESS

Legs were strong as old roots —Truman Capote

Legs that were too long, like a colt's —Beryl Markham

Long, thin legs like wading birds —Elizabeth Hardwick

My feet feel like balloons —Anthony Powell

(The young lady has) a pair of ankles like chianti bottles
    —George Jean Nathan

The pull of the tendons at his ankle like the taut ropes that control
    the sails of ships —Nadine Gordimer

She (a ballet dancer) has legs like a Fordham tackle —Irwin Shaw

Skinny legs, like the legs of a turkey gobbler —Ellen Glasgow

Swings his game leg like a gate, creaking on its hinges
    —Bette Howland

Thighs big as trees —John D. MacDonald

Thighs like a wild mare —Thomas Williams

Thighs like pillars of a temple —Peter De Vries

Thighs like twin portals —Paule Marshall

Thighs solid as poplars —Sharon Sheehe Stark

Thighs ... they look like they're made of steel —Jonathan Valin

Varicose veins crawled like fat blue worms under her stockings
    —Ross Macdonald

Veins like big ugly worms —James Crumley

LETTER-WRITING
See: CORRESPONDENCE

Lies/Liars

Falsehood, like poison, will generally be rejected when administered alone; but when blended with wholesome ingredients, may be swallowed unperceived —Richard Whately

Falsehood, like the dry rot, flourishes the more in proportion as air and light are excluded —Richard Whately

A great lie is like a great fish on dry land; it may fret and fling, and make a frightful bother, but it cannot hurt you. You have only to keep still and it will die of itself —George Crabbe

(He's as) honest as the cat when the meat's out of reach
—H. G. Bohn's *Handbook of Proverbs*

Lie as fast as a dog can lick a dish —John Ray's *Proverbs*

Lied as often and as badly as politicians —James Crumley

Lied like a fish —John Dos Passos

Lied like an Arab —Anaïs Nin

Lied like a rug —Anon
> In his novel, *private i*, Jimmy Sangster extends this with "Lying like a cheap carpet."

The lie fell as easily from his lips as a windfall apple
—Donald Seaman

A lie is like a snowball; the longer it is rolled, the larger it is
—Martin Luther

Lie like a trooper
—American colloquialism, attributed to New England

Lie like fish —Saul Bellow

Lies are as communicative as fleas —Walter Savage Landor

Lies as fast as a dog trots —John Ray's *Proverbs*

Lies as fast as a horse can trot —Danish proverb
> The comparison tends to change with use "As fast as a dog can trot" being one of the most frequently heard variants.

Lies ... buzz about the heads of some people, like flies about a horse's ears in summer —Jonathan Swift

Lies fall like flaxen thread from the skies —John Ashbery

Lies flew out of my mouth like moths —Susan Fromberg Schaeffer

Lies like a car-dealer —William McIlvanney

Lying like a book —Bertold Brecht

Lying like an accountant at an audit —A. E. Maxwell

Lying like stink —Angus Wilson

Lying to someone is like blindfolding him: you cannot see the other's eyes to see how he sees you and so you do not know how it stands with yourself —Walker Percy

The nimble lie is like the second-hand upon a clock; we see it fly, while the hour-hand of truth seems to stand still, and yet it moves unseen, and wins at last, for the clock will not strike till it has reached the goal —Henry Wadsworth Longfellow

(Our) one white lie sits like a little ghost (here on the threshold of our enterprise) —Alfred, Lord Tennyson

The prevaricator is like an idolater —Eleazar

The telling of a falsehood is like the cut of a sabre; for though the wound may heal, the scar of it will remain —Sadi

When the lie was said it had the effect of leaving her breathless, as if she had just crowned a steep rise —Nadine Gordimer

LIFE
See: LIFE, DEFINED; MANKIND

LIFE, DEFINED

The course of life is like the sea; men come and go; tides rise and fall; and that is all of history —Joaquin Miller

Each person's life is like a mountain. And each person has to climb that mountain top alone —Rosamund Pilcher
> Pilcher builds on the mountain simile by explaining that as a child you start in a warm and sunny valley, then you climb a somewhat steeper mountain with a wonderful view to make the end of the journey worthwhile.

Life, Defined

A human life is like a single letter in the alphabet. It can be meaningless. Or it can be part of a great meaning —essay by National Planning Committee of Jewish Theological Seminary for Rosh Hashan, September 5, 1956

Human life may be regarded as a succession of frontis pieces. The way to be satisfied is never to look back —William Hazlitt

Life ... a formless lump like cold tea leaves from which goodness and badness and even the last tang of bitterness have been stewed out —Gerald Kersh
> The life being compared to cold tea leaves in Kersh's novel, *The Angel and the Cuckoo*, is obviously one that is deteriorating.

Life is a big gambling game. Some are born lucky and some are born unlucky —Jack London

Life is a blister on top of a tumor, and a boil on top of that —Sholom Aleichem

Life is, after all, a kind of disaster through which we do what we can to keep each other's spirits up —Thomas Mallon, *New York Times Book Review*, October 12, 1986

Life is a kind of chess, in which we have often points to gain, and competitors or adversaries to contend with, and in which there is a vast variety of good and evil events that are, in some degree, the effect of prudence or the want of it —Benjamin Franklin

Life ... is a kind of stage play, where men come forth, disguised one in one array, and one in another, each playing his part —Erasmus

Life is a little like disease, with its crises and periods of quiescence, the daily improvements and setbacks —Italo Svevo
> In his novel, *Confessions of Zeno*, Svevo continues the simile as follows: "But unlike other diseases life is always mortal. It admits of no cure. It would be like trying to stop up the holes in our body, thinking them to be wounds. We should die of suffocation almost before we were cured."

Life is ... a long series of challenges, like hurdles in a race —Rosamund Pilcher

Life is a long strong twisted rope made up of a number of human relationships —Mary Borden

Life is an incurable disease —Abraham Cowley

Life is a public performance on the violin, in which you must learn the instrument as you go along —E. M. Forster

Life is a train constantly crossing the border from the past to the present —Susan Fromberg Schaeffer

Life is but a day; a fragile dew-drop on its perilous way from a tree's summit —John Keats

Life ... is like a beach covered with lots of pebbles, the faster we qualify ourselves to pick these pebbles the richer we will be —Evan A. Sholl

Life is like a beautiful and winding lane —George Augustus Sala
> The simile continues as follows: "On either side bright flowers, beautiful butterflies, and tempting fruits which we scarcely pause to admire and taste, so eager are we to hasten to an opening which we imagine will be more beautiful still. But by degrees, as we advance, the trees grow bleak, the flowers and butterflies frail, the fruits disappear, and we find we have arrived to reach a desert waste."

Life is like a B-picture script. It is that corny
—Kirk Douglas, *Look*, October 4, 1944
> To add emphasis to his simile, Douglas added: "If I had my life story offered to me to film, I'd turn it down."

Life is like a cash register, in that every account, every thought, every deed, like every sale, is registered and recorded
—Fulton J. Sheen

Life is like a cup of tea ... needing love to make it sweet
—Edward A. Guest
> To show that the same basic simile can have different meanings, there's this line from J. M. Barrie's *The Admirable Crichton*: 'Life, Crichton, is like a cup of tea; the more heartily we drink, the sooner we reach the dregs."

Life is like a dissected map. If I could live a hundred years ... I feel I could put the pieces together until they made a properly connected whole —Oliver Wendell Holmes, Sr.

Life is like a fire; it begins in smoke, and ends in ashes
—Arab proverb

Life is like a game of dice —Alexis

The comparison of life to the roll of the dice has been an irresistible simile throughout history. Variations include "Life is like a game of tables," dating back to B.C., and "Life is like a game of roulette."

Life is like a game of cards —Edgar Watson Howe
Howe built on the comparison as follows: "Reliability is the ace, industry the king, politeness the queen, thrift the jack. Common sense is playing to best advantage the cards you draw." A 1978 poem by Diane Wakoski used the simile for its title and theme.

Life ... is like a grapefruit ... sort of orangy-yellow and dimpled on the outside, wet and squidgy in the middle —Douglas Adams

Life is like a jigsaw puzzle with most of the pieces missing —Anon

Life is like a kiss that does not last long enough for a fellow to ascertain how good it is —Elbridge G. Dow Jr.

Life is like a mountain: after climbing up one side and sliding down the other, put up the sled —Josh Billings
The word 'is' has been changed from the dialect form 'iz.'

Life is like an onion, which one peels crying —French proverb

Life is like an onion: you peel off layer after layer and then you find there is nothing in it —James G. Huneker

Life is like a school of gladiators, where men live and fight with one another —Seneca The Elder

Life is like a scrambled egg —Don Marquis

Life is like a stew, you have to stir it frequently, or all the scum rises to the top —Tom Robbins

Life is like drunkenness: the pleasure passes away, but the headache remains —Persian proverb

Life is like music, it must be composed by ear, feeling and instinct, not by rule —Samuel Butler

Life is like playing a violin solo in public and learning the instrument as one goes on —Samuel Butler

Life is like that, a cake-walk —Clifford Odets
The simile is from Odets play, *Awake and Sing.*

Life is not a game of chess, the victory to the knowing; it is a game
    of cards, one's hand by skill to be made the best of
    —Jerome K. Jerome

Life is very much like an arms race, each side waiting for the other
    one to put his stick down first —Merle Shain

Life, like a dome of many-coloured glass, stains the white radiance of
    eternity —Percy Bysshe Shelley

Human life is like the petals that fall from the rose and lie soft and
    withering by the side of the vase —Anon Persian poem

The life of every man is a diary in which he means to write one
    story, and writes another, and his humblest hour is when he
    compares the volume as it is with what he vowed to make it
    —J. M. Barrie

The life of man is like a long journey with a heavy load on the
    back —Japanese proverb

Life's a library owned by an author. In it are a few books which he
    wrote but most of them were written for him
    —Harry Emerson Fosdick

Life seems to me like a Japanese picture which our imagination does
    not allow to end with the margin —Oliver Wendell Holmes, Jr.

Life's like a play: it's not the length but the excellence of the acting
    that matters —Seneca
        A variation made famous by the playwright Ben Jonson:
        "Our whole life is like a play."

Man's life is like a candle in the wind —Chinese proverb

The scenes of our life are like pictures done in rough
    mosaic ... There is nothing beautiful to be found in them, unless
    we stand some distance off —Arthur Schopenhauer

This mundane life is like a drink of salt water, which seems to
    quench, but actually inflames —Gaon Elijah

The way of life is like a path between two forbidding roads, one of
    fire and one of ice —Judah
        Judah built on the simile with this advice: "The slightest
        bend in either direction is fatal. Let him walk in the
        middle."

Life, Defined

A well-ordered life is like climbing a tower; the view halfway up is better than the view from the base, and it steadily becomes finer as the horizon expands —William Lyon Phelps

The whole of life of some people is a kind of partial death, a long lingering death-bed, so to speak, of stagnation and nonentity on which death is but the seal —Samuel Butler

Lighting

LIGHTING
See also: BRIGHTNESS

All lit up like warships in a foggy port —Amos Oz

Everything lit up like a disco on Saturday night —Loren D. Estleman

A glittering neon sign like wolves' eyes —Elizabeth Bowen

The gray light of the winter dawn lit the bedroom like a dreary fake impressionistic painting —Jerry Bumpus

The house [with all lights on] blazed like a stage set
—T. Coraghessan Boyle
See also: LIGHTING

Light as a paper airplane (and as elegant) —Marge Piercy

Lighted winnows [at dawn] were scattered like yellow diamonds on black velvet —Loren D. Estleman

Lighting streaked the snow. Like the urine of dogs by trees
—William H. Gass

(Offices ... in which) light is a kind of yellow fluid, like old shellac
—Scott Turow
> In his novel, *Presumed Innocent*, Scott Turow uses this comparison to paint a picture of the "Dickensenian" atmosphere in which the hero's fellow lawyers work.

The light seemed to be draining away like flood-water
—Kenneth Grahame

Lights glittered ... like a diamond necklace round the neck of a lovely signorina —Donald Seaman

Lights ... pouring over us like scalding milk —Ira Wood

The lights (of the bridge) were like strings of pearls hanging up in the air —Cornell Woolrich

The light was golden like the flesh of women —Thomas Wolfe

Like moons around Jupiter, pale moths revolved about a lone lamp
    —Vladimir Nabokov

(The big glass window was) lit like a stage —Frank Tuohy

(The place was) lit up like a birthday cake —Jayne Anne Phillips

Lit up like a midway —Tom Robbins

Lit up like a paper lantern —Willis Johnson

Lit up like a whorehouse on Saturday night —Loren D. Estleman

Lit up like skyscrapers or planes taking off —Marge Piercy

[A truck] plastered with lights like a beer-joint —Carlos Baker

Streetlights cast their shadows on the wall like a sharp, white
    condolence —Ariel Dorfman

The street lights shone like tiny beads on a string —David Huddle

When the lamps in the house are lighted it is like the flowering of
    lotus on the lake —Chinese proverb

Windows [of a building] glowing like those of a lighted card-board
    house under a Christmas tree —Willa Cather

LIKENESS
See: SIMILARITY

LIMBS
See: LEGS

LINGERING

Brooded over ... the way a plane caught in a fog hovers longingly
    over a blurred landing strip —Lynne Sharon Schwartz

(Haven't you got anything better to do than) hang around here like
    a prairie dog in heat —line from the movie, *Bronco Billy.*

Hang around like a rent collector or a man come to fix the faucet
    —Harvey Swados

Hang around like sullen clouds over the sun —John Ashberry

Hanging around like a fart in a phone box —Australian colloquialism

[An idea] hang over ... like a thunderstorm reluctant to break
—Gavin Lyall

[The smell of circus lions] hangs like August heat
—Delmore Schwartz

Hover like a moth intoxicated with light —John Galsworthy

Hover like butterflies —Lee Smith

Hover over like an ugly bird of prey —Anon

Hung around ... like a herd of sheep with no sheep dog
—Ignazio Silone

(The Fraziers had refused to leave his mind; they had stayed on,)
imposing themselves on his consciousness and his conscience like
the troubling memory of a drunken evening —Elizabeth Hardwick

Languish like a mist at noon —Herbert Read

Lingered like heat, like poppy petals, like desert sand —Kay Boyle

Lingered, like smoke after fire —Paul Kuttner

Lingering like an unloved guest —Percy Bysshe Shelley

Lingering like second thoughts —George Bradley

(Light) lingers like a lover's tongue —Bin Ramke
This simile concludes a poem entitled *What the Weather is Like.*

Lodged like a marble in a crack —James Crumley

Loitered like a school child —Jean Stafford

(A cold notion flew into my brain and) squatted there like a buzzard,
patient, in a tree —George Garrett

Stalling like a Scotchman in front of a pay toilet —Harold Adams

LIPS

An upper lip shaped like a circumflex accent —Eric Ambler

Drew her lips into a thin wiggly line like fish bait
—Sharon Sheehe Stark

Full lips like a French movie star —Ira Wood

Her lips glistened as if she'd just eaten a pound of vaseline
—Sarah Bird

Her lips looked ... delicious, as though if you bit them it would be like biting into a sweetmeat, one of those candies which are filled with a pleasant warming liquid —Ben Ames Williams

His lips, like those of all men who work, were puckered up like a bag with the string drawn tight —Honoré de Balzac

His lips were tightened in a thin line, as if he had them sewn together to keep from vomiting —Robert J. Serling

His lips were too red, as if he had a hangover —Louise Erdrich

His long lips tightened, as if he sought to conquer pain
—Frank Swinnerton

Lips always compressed as if to keep back a swarm of curses
—George Garrett

Lips as bloodless as lips of the slain —John Greenleaf Whittier

Lips ... as glossy as ripe cherries —Anton Chekhov

Lips delicate as peach-toned porcelain —Jayne Anne Phillips

Lips ... drawn in a tight line like the lips of a child not quite ready
  to take a dose of bad-tasting medicine —George Garrett

Lips ... dry and faint as her tea leaves —Shirley Ann Grau

Lips full as thighs —Lyn Lifshin

Lips like a thread of scarlet —*The Holy Bible/Song of Solomon*

Lips like lilies —*The Holy Bible/Song of Solomon*

Lips ... like pale velvet —Jimmy Sangster

Lips like sausages —John D. MacDonald

Lips ... like the petals of a red flower —Oscar Wilde

Lips like wet cherries —Virginia Woolf

Lips moved noisily, smacking like a three-day thirst
—Sharon Sheehe Stark

Lips ... red as two buds —Louise Erdrich

Lips

Lips ... set in exasperation, as if she had just been about to say something and found out her voice was snatched in death —Louise Erdrich

Lips ... shining like rain on night streets —Jayne Anne Phillips

Lips that, like a ventriloquist's, scarcely stirred —Katherine Bush

Lips that looked as if she were permanently whistling —Mike Fredman

Lips that shine wetly, just like a Cosmo girl —George Garrett

Lips that stand out from his skin like two thick weals —Aldous Huxley

Lips tighter than any knot —Tim O'Brien

Lips trembling like elastic stretched too taut —George Garrett

A long blue upper lip, like a priest —Joyce Cary

The muscles of her chapped lips were broken and loose like the snap of an old purse —Gerald Kersh

Pursed his lips as if he were just before receiving a terrible blow —Richard Ford

Set her lips as though she would never speak again —Dorothy Canfield Fisher

Sharp-pointed lips stretched out like a slingshot —Bobbie Ann Mason

She kept closing her lips over her teeth and then pursing her lips, so that she looked as though she were going to give somebody a little goodbye kiss —Maeve Brennan

Thick lips ... like lozenges of hard rubber —Jonnthan Valin

Thin lips fitted tightly together, as though they were parts of a very well-made piece of furniture —Aldous Huxley

An upper lip that twiched softly, like a cow's in a fly-ridden summer —Penelope Gilliatt

LITERATURE
See: BOOKS, WRITERS/WRITING

LIVELINESS
See: ENERGY

LOVE BURST OUT... ALL OVER
OUR BODIES, LIKE SWEAT

LOOSENESS

Looseness

(Muscle) lax as a broken shade —Diane Ackerman

(Face) lax as a wax work —Daniel Berrigan

(The gear worked) loose as a hound's shoulder —Elizabeth Spencer

Loose as a gossip's tongue —Anon

Loose as ashes —Anon

Loose as eggs in a nest —Walter Savage Landor

Loose as windblown sand —Mark Helprin

Slack as a toad —Barbara Howes

Sprawled ... lax as a drowned man —George Garrett

LOVE

Love

Absence in love is like waters upon fire; a little quickens, but much extinguishes it —Hannah More

All loving emotions, like plants, shoot up most rapidly in the tempestuous atmosphere of life —Jean Paul Richter

Amorous as Emma Bovary —James G. Huneker

Could love forever run like a river —Lord Byron

Falling in love is something you forget, like pain —Nina Bawden

Felt love like a lottery prize —Geoffrey Wolff

First and passionate love, it stands alone, like Adam's recollection of his fall —Lord Byron

The force of her love ... is bulky and hard to carry, like a package that keeps untying —Louise Erdrich

Going through life without love is like going through a good dinner without an appetite; everything seems flat and tasteless —Helen Rowland

350

Her love was like the swallow's, whose first thought is for its nest
—Italo Svevo

If love were what the rose is, and I were like the leaf, our lives
would grow together —Algernon Charles Swinburne

I love you as New Englanders love pie —Don Marquis

Infatuation like paralysis, is often all on one side —Helen Rowland

It [love] could, like grief, grow forgetful and weary and slowly wear
away —Alice Mc Dermott

Knew as much about love as a pig knows about St. Valentine's Day
—Harry Prince

Like the water of a deep stream, love is always too much
—Wendell Berry
> This line from a poem entitled *The Country of Marriage* is
> followed by: "We did not make it. Though we drink till we
> burst we cannot have it all, or want it all."

Love as an old man loves money, with no stomach
—William Shakespeare

Love burst out ... all over our bodies, like sweat —Yehuda Amichai

Love can die of truth as friendship of a lie —Abel Bonard

Love ... comes as a butterfly tipped with gold
—Algernon Charles Swinburne

Love comes into your being like a tidal wave ... sometimes it
withdraws like a wave, till there isn't such a thing as a pool left,
and every bit of your heart is as dry as seaweed beyond the
wave's reach —Phyllis Bottome

Love comforts like sunshine after rain —William Shakespeare
> The original simile as used in *Venus and Adonis* had the
> word 'comforts' spelled as 'comforteth.'

Love doesn't just sit there, like a stone, it has to be made, like
bread; re-made all the time, made new —Ursula K. Le Guin

Love ... entered the room like a miracle —Milan Kundera

Love had seized her as unexpectedly as would sudden death
—Elizabeth Taylor

(Our cook is in love.) Love hangs on the house like a mist
—Phyllis McGinley

Love hung still as crystal over the bed —Louis MacNeice

Love is fierce as death —*The Holy Bible/Song of Songs*

Love is flower-like —Samuel Taylor Coleridge

Love is ... fresh as dew when first it is new —British folk song,
"The Water Is Wide" (*The Good Times Songbook*, Abingdon Press,
1974)
> The complete refrain includes yet another simile: "Oh,
> love is sweet and love is fair, fresh as the dew when first it
> is new, but love grows old and waxeth cold, and fades
> away like morning dew."

Love is like the moon; when it does not increase it decreases
—Joseph Alexandre Pierre Segur

Love is ... lone as the sea, and deeper blue —Dorothy Parker

Love ... it makes him [the lover] fluent as a tin whistle, as limber as
a boy's watch chain, and as polite as a dancing master
—Josh Billings
> Parts originally in the Billing phonetic dialect: 'whissel'
> and 'perlite' as a 'dansing.'

Loveless as the multiplication table —Sylvia Plath

Love life ... just about as interesting as the love life of the desert
horned toad —William Saroyan

Love, like a tear, rises in the eye and falls upon the breast
—Publius Syrus

Love like chicken salad or restaurant hash, must be taken on blind
faith or it loses all its flavor —Helen Rowland

Love, like death, a universal leveller of mankind —William Congreve

Love, like death, changes everything —Kahlil Gibran

Love, like fire, cannot subsist without constant impulse; it ceases to
live from the moment it ceases to hope or to fear
—François, duc de La Rochefoucauld

Love, like money, is probably best kept in the family —William
Gaddis, *New York Times Book Review*, May 24, 1987

Gaddis used this simile to conclude his review of Saul
Bellow's novel, *More Die of Heartbreak.*

Love passed between them like a field of light —Ellen Gilchrist

Love ... pricks like a thorn —William Shakespeare

Love ... roots up the will like a leaf —Gustave Flaubert

Lovers are always in a hurry ... like a racing river
     —Ben Ames Williams

Lovers fail like seasons —F. D. Reeve

Love's dominion, like a king's, admits of no partition —Ovid

Love sometimes is like the flower of the wild poppy: you can't carry
     it home —Jaroslav Seifert

Love was a treadmill, like churchgoing —Elizabeth Hardwick

Love washes on me like rain on a dead man's shoes
     —Ellen Gilchrist

Love without grace is like a hook without bait —Anne de Lencos

Love without respect is cold as a boa constrictor —Marge Piercy
          In her poem, *Witnessing a Wedding,* Piercy continues with,
          "its caresses as choking."

Loving someone that much younger is like taking a trip to a foreign
     country —Ellen Gilchrist

Making love to a woman too many times is like scratching a place
     that doesn't itch any more —Anon, *Playboy,* 1965

A man in love may behave like a madman but not like a dunce
     —François, duc de La Rochefoucauld
          Man has been substituted for gentleman to give the simile
          a more modern tone.

The man who is not loved hovers like a vulture over the sweetheart
     of others —Victor Hugo

My heart simmered with angry love like chicken soup on grandma's
     stove —James Atlas

My love is like foliage in the woods. Time will change it as winter
     changes the trees —Emily Brönte
          The love described is Cathy's for Heathcliff in *Wuthering
          Heights.*

Once love is purged of vanity it is like a feeble convalescent, hardly capable of dragging itself around
—Sebastien Roch Nicolas de Chamfort

Our love is like our life; there's no man blest in either till his end
—Shackerley Marmion

Our love is like the misty rain that falls softly ... but floods the river
—African proverb

(What I want ... is something organic ...) potato love, natural as earth, scruffy and brown, clinging to your roots, helping you grow fit and firm —Daphne Merkin

Romance, like a ghost, eludes touching —G. W. Curtis

Romance, like alcohol, should be enjoyed but must not be swallowed to become necessary —Edgar Z. Friedenberg

Romantic love is ephemeral and occasionally unavoidable ... like the viral flu —Marcia Froelke Coburn, *New York Time Book Review*, September 14, 1986

A rush of love swamped her heart ... like a tide
—Vita Sackville-West

The science of love demands delicacy, perseverance, and practice, like the piano —Anatole France

The simple accident of falling in love is as beneficial as it is astonishing —Robert Louis Stevenson

(She was long married ... but she had recently) stepped out of the country of love; briskly, and without a backward glance, as if she had spent too much time in its steamy jungles —John Cheever

This was a game, like bridge, in which you said things instead of playing cards. Like bridge you had to pretend you were playing for money or playing for some stakes —Ernest Hemingway

Threw herself into love like a suicide into the river
—Guy De Maupassant

To love a woman who scorns you is like licking honey from a thorn
—Welsh proverb

To talk of honour in the mysteries of love, is like talking of Heaven or the Deity in an operation of witchcraft, just when you are employing the devil: it makes the charm impotent
—William Wycherley

Trapped in love ... like a great tortoise trapped in a heavy death-like shell —Joyce Carol Oates

It [being loved by affectionately possessive wife] was like being loved by a large moist sponge —Phyllis Bottome

Without love our life is ... unprofitable as a ship without a rudder ... like a body without a soul —Sholom Aleichem

With true loves as with ghosts: everyone speaks of them, but few have seen them —François, duc de La Rochefoucauld

(I) wore my heart like a wet, red stain on the breast of a velvet gown —Dorothy Parker

LOYALTY/DISLOYALTY
See also: LOVE

Always at her side like a Great Dane —Carlos Baker

As the rolling stone gathers no moss, so the roving heart gathers no affection —Anna Jameson

Devoted and caretaking as a cat with her kittens
—Katherine Anne Porter

(In the end, people's) devotion hung like rocks around your neck
—Alice Munro

Endless devotion ... like a straitjacket —Lynne Sharon Schwartz

Faithful (to each other) as the Canada goose, more or less
—Laurie Colwin

Fickle as spring sunlight —Carolyn Kizer

A heart true as steel —William Shakespeare
    Shakespeare gave this comparison from *Midsummer Night's Dream* a slight twist in *Romeo and Juliet:* 'My man's as true as steel.''

Like a woman in her first love affair, he insisted on unconditional commitment —Ariel Dorfman

Loyal, like a dog —Lynne Sharon Schwartz

Loyalty ... small and hard, like buckshot lodged in her stomach
—Sarah Litsey

To say that you can love one person all your life is just like saying that one candle will continue burning as lonngas you live —Leo Tolstoy

True to her husband as the dial to the sun —Henry Fielding

LUCIDITY
See: CLARITY

LUNACY
See: MADNESS

LUSHNESS
See: ABUNDANCE

LYING

See also: POSTURE, SITTING, STANDING

Lay ... as if chloroformed —Wallace Stegner

Lay as still as a fallen doll —George Garrett

Lay in bed like a tree stump —Charles Johnson

Lay lifeless as if spellbound —Herman Melville

Lay like an aimlessly flung sack of bones —Harvey Swados

Lay on his back ... rigid and ruined, like some stained window mannequin —Davis Grubb

Lay on the sofa like cast-off silk stockings —Delmore Schwartz
    In his journal entry Schwartz followed this with two additional comparisons: "Like fallen buildings ... like a car over turned." Had he been writing forty years later, he would have been apt to refer to pantyhose instead of silk stockings.
See also: ABANDONMENT

Lay perfectly still, as if dead with fear —D. H. Lawrence

Lay ... rigid, as if she were dead —Elizabeth Taylor

Lay rigidly still, as still as if he were in his coffin —Dorothy Canfield Fisher

Lay side by side like fish —Lawrence Durrell

(Fallen and helpless, he) lay there like a pine tree that has been torn up by the roots —Ellen Glasgow

Lay there ... stretched like a corpse —Hugh Walpole

Lay where she was for a few minutes like a flake of foam —Vicki Baum

(We'd) lie ... like two sticks in bed —Elizabeth Spencer

The lovers like great scissors lay —Delmore Schwartz
     See also: MEN AND WOMEN

Sprawled around ... like shepherds in a frieze —Julia O'Faolain

Sprawled like a man who had been threshed —Stephen Crane

Sprawling like an exhausted dog —Mary Hedin

MADNESS

As crazy as a baboon chasing shit around a tree
     —American colloquialism

As crazy as a loon —American colloquialism
     Popular variations include "Crazy as bats" and "Crazy as a bed bug," the latter said to make its first appearance in Ernest Hemingway's *For Whom the Bell Tolls*.

Crazy as owl shit —Pat Conroy

As mad as a brush —Julia O'Faolain

As mad as a March hare —English phrase
     Even though Lewis Carroll didn't coin the phrase as many people think, its appearance in *Alice in Wonderland* probably contributed towards its common and continued usage to describe irrationality. The same is true of "Mad as a hatter" which originally alluded to the symptoms of madness by workers in the hat industry caused by exposure to chemicals.

As mad as a serpent
     —Carolyn See, *New York Times*/Hers, July 3, 1986

As nutty as a fruitcake —American colloquialism

In vogue since around 1935 this has seeded such twists as "You're as nutty as a Mars bar" (Tom Robbins) and "Nuttier than a Hershey bar with almonds" (Ed Mc Bain). Departing from the candy and cake comparisons altogether, there's "As nutty as a squirrel's nest" (Mike Sommer).

MALICE
See: CRUELTY

MANKIND
See also: HELPLESSNESS

As the clay is in the potter's hand, to fashion at his pleasure: so man is in the hand of Him that made him
—*The Holy Bible/Apocrypha*

Every man is like his affliction —André Malraux

Extraordinary men, like the stones that are formed in the highest regions of the air, fall upon the earth only to be broken and cast into the furnace —Walter Savage Landor

He [man] bolts down all events, all creeds, and beliefs, and persuasions ... as an ostrich of potent digestion gobbles down bullets and gun flints —Herman Melville

Human as a kiss —Vance Thompson

Human beings are like timid punctuation marks sprinkled among the incomprehensible sentences of life —Jean Giraudoux

Humanity is like people packed in an automobile which is traveling down the highway without lights on a dark night at terrific speed and driven by a four-year old —Lord Dunsany

It is with men as with horses; those who do the most prancing make the least progress —Baron de Stassart

Like leaves on trees, the race of man is found, now green in youth, now withering on the ground —Homer

Like the hours in the day, people come in two classes: the happy and the sad —Bin Ramke

Like the irresponsible black waterbugs on summer ponds, they [people in cities] crawl and circle and hustle about idiotically, without aim or purpose —O. Henry

Man ... cometh up, and is cut down, like a flower
—*The Book of Common Prayer*

Man is a rope stretched between the animal and the Superman, a rope over an abyss —Friedrich Nietzsche

Man is as full of potentiality as he is of impotence
—George Santayana

Man is like a ball tossed betwixt the wind and the billows
—Friedrich von Schiller

A man is like a letter of the alphabet: to produce a word, it must combine with another —Benjamin Mandelstamm

A man is like all earth's fruit, you preserve him dry or pickled
—Hayden Carruth

Man is like a musical box. An imperceptible jolt, and he plays a different tune —Ludwig Boerne

Man is like a precious stone: cut and polished by morals, adorned by wisdom —Isaac Halevi Satanov

Mankind is like the Red Sea: the staff has scarcely parted the waves asunder, before they flow together again
—Johann Wolfgang von Goethe

A man like a watch is to be valued for his goings —Turkish proverb

Man's like a bird all the days of his breath, and pleasures are nets that allure him to death —Judah Al-Harizi

Man's like a candle in a candlestick made up tallow, and a little wick —John Bunyan

Men are like bricks, alike but placed high or low by chance
—John Webster

Men are like ciphers: they acquire their value merely from their position —Napoleon Bonaparte

Men are like ears of corn: the emptier the head the more and the lower they stoop —Moritz Gottlieb Saphir

Men are like nuts; you can't tell what they're like till they're broken
—Phyllis Bottome
> This simile marks the opening of Bottome's story, *A Lost Leader.*

Men are like plants; the goodness and flavor of the fruit proceeds from the peculiar soil and exposition in which they grow
—Michel Guillaume Jean de Crèvecoeur

Men are like the herbs of the field; while some are sprouting, others are withering —*Babylonian Talmud*

Men are like strange dogs ... walk right up to them, bold as life, and they're as gentle as ducks —Owen Johnson

Men are like the stars: some generate their own light while others reflect the brilliance they receive —José Marti

Men are like trees ... each one must put forth the leaf that is created in him —Henry Ward Beecher

Men are like weasels: weasels drag and lay up and know not for whom, and men save and hoard and know not for whom
—*Talmud*

Men, like peaches and pears, grow sweet a little while before they begin to decay —Oliver Wendell Holmes, Sr.

Others are to us like the 'characters' in fiction, eternal and incorrigible —Mary McCarthy

People are like planks of wood: soft until seasoned
—St. John De Chevecoeur

People are mostly layers of violence and tenderness, wrapped like bulbs —Eudora Welty

People are somewhat like novels, we operate on beginnings, middles, and ends —Charles Johnson
> In Johnson's novel, *Faith and the Good Thing*, the simile includes this parenthetical comment: "Don't make too much of that simile."

People are very much like flagstaffs. Some flagstaffs are very tall and prominent and some are small —Harry Emerson Fosdick

Fosdick's simile continued with the following observation: "But the glory of a flagstaff is not its size but the colors that it flies. A very small flagstaff flying the right colors is far more valuable than a very tall one with the wrong flag."

The race of men is like the race of leaves. As one generation flourishes another decays —Homer

Some individuals are like a brush heap, a helter-skelter, miscellaneous pile of twigs and branches —Harry Emerson Fosdick

Some men are like Einstein's theory of relativity; nobody at home understands them —Anon

Some men are like pyramids, which are very broad where they touch the ground, but grow narrow as they reach the sky
—Henry Ward Beecher

Some men are like rifles with plenty of powder but no bullet ... a great flow of language but no thought —Sylvanys Stall

So much of a man walks about dead ... like a pianoforte with half the notes mute —D. H. Lawrence

Strong men are made by opposition; like kites they go up against the wind —Frank Harris, *Reader's Digest,* June, 1936

The study of human nature is a good deal like the study of dissection: you find out a good many curious things, but it is a nasty job after all —Josh Billings
     Billings wrote this in dialect which read as follows: "The studdy ov huymin natur is a gooddeal like the studdy ov dessekshun, yu finde out a good menny curis things, aut it is nasty job after awl."

To the gods we are as flies to wanton boys —William Shakespeare

We are all like vessels tossed on the bottom of the deep
—Pietro Mestastasio
     The simile continues: "Our passions are the winds that sweep us impetuously onward; each pleasure is a rock; the whole of life is a wide ocean."

We are like sun that rises and sheds light upon things, and then falls and leaves them in darkness again —William Goyen

We run to and fro upon the earth like frightened sheep
—Robert Louis Stevenson

361

What a piece of work is a man! In action, how like an angel! In
apprehension, how like a god! —William Shakespeare

MANNERS
See: BEHAVIOR, PROPRIETY/IMPROPRIETY

MARRIAGE
See also: RELATIONSHIPS

Adultery in a house is like a worm in poppy seeds
—*Babylonian Talmud*

Adultery's like the common cold, if one bedfellow contracts it, his
companion automatically does —Robert Traver

Alimony is like buying oats for a dead horse
—Arthur Baer, *New York Journal American*

Bridesmaids in their flowery frocks bloom round the bride like
hollyhocks —Ogden Nash

The death of a man's wife is like cutting down an ancient oak that
has long shaded the family mansion —Alphonse de Lamartine

Divorced men are like marked-down clothes; you get them after the
season during which they would have made a sensation, and
there is less choice, but they're easier to acquire —Judith Martin

Divorce is like a side dish that nobody remembers having ordered
—Alexander King

For an artist to marry his model is as fatal as for a gourmet to
marry his cook: the one gets no sittings, and the other no
dinners —Oscar Wilde

For an old man to marry a young girl is like buying a new book for
somebody else to read —Anon

Getting married is like a healthy man going into a sickbed
—Isaac Bashevis Singer

Getting married is serious business. It's kinda formal, like funerals or
playing stud poker
—line from 1940 movie, *They Knew What They Wanted*
The actor voicing this was William Gargan.

HUSBANDS ARE LIKE FIRES, THEY GO OUT
WHEN UNATTENDED

He [husband of long-standing] is like an old coat, beautiful in texture, but easy and loose —Audrey Colvin, letter to *New York Times*/LI, July 17, 1986

A husband, like religion and medicine, must be taken with blind faith —Helen Rowland
> This has been modernized from "Like unto religion."

Husbands, like governments must never admit they are wrong —Honoré de Balzac

Husbands are like (motor) cars; all are good the first year —Channing Pollock

Husbands are like fires, they go out when unattended —Zsa Zsa Gabor

Husbands should be like Kleenex, soft, clean and disposable — Madeline Kahn, interview, television news program, December, 1985

A husband without ability is like a house without a roof —Spanish proverb

It [a second marriage] is the triumph of hope over experience —Samuel Johnson

It [marriage] resembles a pair of shears, so joined that they cannot be separated; often moving in opposite directions, yet always punishing any one who comes between them —Sydney Smith

It's [the permanence of marriage] like having siblings: you can't lose a brother or a sister. They're always there —Germaine Greer, *Playboy*, January, 1972

It [marriage and motherhood] was like being brainwashed, and afterward you went about numb as a slave in some private, totalitarian state —Sylvia Plath

Like suicide, divorce was something that had to be done on a thoughtless impulse, full speed ahead —R. V. Cassill

A man's wife should fit like a good, comfortable shoe —Ukrainian proverb

A man with a face that looks like someone had thrown it at him in anger nearly always marries before he is old enough to vote —Finley Peter Dunne

Many a marriage has commenced like the morning, red, and perished like a mushroom ... because the married pair neglected to be as agreeable to each other after their union as they were before it —Frederika Bremer

Marriage may be compared to a cage: the birds outside frantic to get in and those inside frantic to get out —Michel de Montaigne
> The simile also appeared in a play by a sixteenth century dramatist, John Webster, beginning "Marriage is just like a summer bird cage in a garden." See the French proverb below for yet another twist on the same theme.

Marriage from love, like vinegar from wine, a sad, sour, sober beverage —Lord Byron

Marriage is a good deal like a circus: there is not as much in it as is represented in the advertising —Edgar Watson Howe

Marriage is a hand grenade with the pin out. You hold your breath waiting for the explosion —Abraham Rothberg

Marriage is like a three-speed gearbox: affection, friendship, love —Peter Ustinov

Marriage is like a beleaguered fortress; those who are without want to get in, and those within want to get out —French proverb

Marriage is like a dull meal with the dessert at the beginning —dialogue from the movie, *Moulin Rouge*
> The dialogue was spoken by Jose Ferrer as Toulouse Lautrec.

Marriage is like a long trip in a tiny rowboat: if one passenger starts to rock the boat, the other has to steady it; otherwise they'll go to bottom together
—Dr. David R. Reuben, *Reader's Digest*, January, 1973

Marriage is like a river; it is easier to fall in than out —Anon

Marriage is like a ship; sometimes you just have to ride out the storm —"L. A. Law," television drama, 1987

Marriage is like buying something you've been admiring for a long time in a shop window ... you may love it when you get home but it doesn't always go with everything else in the house —Jean Kerr

Marriage is like life in this ... that it is a field of battle, and not a bed of roses —Robert Louis Stevenson

365

Marriage is like panty-hose; it all depends on what you put into it —Phyllis Schlafly

Marriage is like twirling a baton, turning handsprings or eating with chopsticks; it looks so easy till you try it —Helen Rowland

Marriage like death is nothing to worry about —Don Herod

Marriages are like diets. They can be ruined by having a little dish on the side —Earl Wilson

Marriages, like houses, need constant patching —Nancy Mairs, *New York Times*/Hers, July 30, 1987

> The simile was the highlighted blurb to capture reader attention. Actually it was a capsulized paraphrase from Ms. Mairs' own concluding words: "Marriages, like houses, haven't got 'ever afters'." The stucco chips off and the cat falls through the screen and the bathroom drain runs slow. If you don't want the house falling down around your ears, you must plan to learn to wield a trowel and a hammer and a plunger.

Marriages were breaking up as fast as tires blowing in a long race —Norman Mailer

A marriage that grew like a great book, filling twenty-five years with many thousands of elaborate and subtle details —Larry McMurtry

A (seventeen-year) marriage that had been patched like an old rubber tire gone too many miles on a treadmill —Paige Mitchell

(She had decided long before that) marriage was like breathing, as soon as you noticed the process, you stopped it at peril of your life —Laura Furman

A married man forms married habits and becomes dependent on marriage just as a sailor becomes dependent on the sea —George Bernard Shaw

Married so long ... like Siamese twins they infect each other's feelings —Mary Hedin

Marrying a daughter to a boor is like throwing her to a lion —*Babylonian Talmud*

Marrying a woman for her money is very much like setting a rat-trap, and baiting it with your own finger —Josh Billings

> In Billings' phonetic dialect: "munny is vera mutch like ... with yure own finger."

Matrimony, like a dip in the sea, first stimulates, then chills. But once out of the water the call of the ocean lures the bather to another plunge —Anon

Middle-aged marriages in which people seem stuck like flies caught in jelly —Norma Klein
See also: ENTRAPMENT

(I am as) monogamous as the North Star —Carolyn Kizer

The sickening cords of their marriage drying everything like an invisible paste —John Updike

A successful marriage is an edifice that must be rebuilt every day —Andre Maurois

They [bride and groom] looked as though they belonged on top of their own enormous cake —Paul Reidinger

Wartime marriage ... it's like being married on top of a volcano —H. E. Bates
See also: DANGER

Wedlock's like wine, not properly judged of till the second glass —Douglas Jerrold

Wife swapping is like a form of incest in which nobody's more guilty than anybody else —Germaine Greer, *Playboy*, January, 1972

MATHEMATCS AND SCIENCE

Arithmetic is where numbers fly like pigeons in and out of your head —Carl Sandburg

Every science, like a recurring decimal, has a beginning and no end —Anton Chekhov
> In his story, *On The Way*, Checkhov elaborates on this as follows: "Zoology has discovered thirty-five thousand five hundred different species of insects; chemistry can count sixty-five elements; if you were to add ten zeros to the right of each of these figures, zoology and chemistry would be no nearer the end of their labors than they are now."

Science is, like virtue, its own ... great reward —Charles Kingsley

Science is love with seeing eyes —Elbert Hubbard

Mathematcs and Science

The study of mathematics is like climbing up a steep and craggy mountain; when once you reach the top, it fully recompenses your trouble, by opening a fine, clear and extensive prospect —Tryon Edwards

MATRIMONY
See: MARRIAGE

Maxims, Proverbs and Sayings

MAXIMS, PROVERBS AND SAYINGS

Browsing through a book of proverb ... it's like taking a turn in a garden ... full of roses and fruit, where the bushes speak to you; and I come back rested, with smiles in my mind —Anatole France

Figures of speech are risky; for in art, as in arithmetic, many have no head for figures —G. K. Chesterton

Genuine proverbs are like good (kambrick) needles, short, sharp, and shiny —Josh Billings
    The first word was originally in Billings' phonetic dialect: 'ginowine.'

His sayings are generally like women's letters; all the pith is in the postscript —William Hazlitt
    The man with the pith in his postscripts was Charles Lamb.

Like many cliches, it has the ring of truth —Anon

A man of maxims only is like a Cyclops with one eye, and that eye placed in the back of his head —Samuel Taylor Coleridge

Maxims are like lawyers who must needs see but one side of the case —Gelett Burgess

Proverbs, like the sacred books of each nation, are the sanctuary of the intuitions —Ralph Waldo Emerson

A proverb without wisdom is like a body without a foot —Moses Ibn Ezra

Rustic sayings which she threw, like flowers, into the conversation —Anatole France

A saying is like a fruit; one has first to eat it ... before one can know its taste —Sholem Asch

Sayings by wise men ... they are like burning glasses, as they collect the diffused rays of wit and learning in authors, and make them point with warmth and quickness on the reader's imagination —Jonathan Swift

Sayings by wise men ... they are of great value, like the dust of gold, or the sparks of diamonds —John Tillotson

Similes are like songs on love: they much describe; they nothing prove —Matthew Prior

Similes dangle like baubles from me —William H. Gass

A word [that's been overused] ... lost its identity like an old coat in a second-hand shop —Anaïs Nin

MEANNESS
See: CRUELTY

MEEKNESS
See: MODESTY

MEETINGS

Come together as inevitably as the key to the magnet —Hugh Walpole

Converge like pulsars —Diane Ackerman

Face each other [across table] like partners at bridge —Thomas Pynchon

Like driftwood spars, which meet and pass upon the boundless ocean-plain, so on the sea of life, alas, man meets man, meets and quits again —Matthew Arnold

Like mountain streams we meet and part, each living in the other's heart —Oliver Wendell Holmes, Sr.

Like two doomed ships that pass in storm we had crossed each other's way —Oscar Wilde
> The simile, from *The Ballad of Reading Goal,* concludes as follows: "But we made no sign, we said no word, we had no word to say."

Met [briefly] ... like a couple of trucks, side-swiping each other —Robert E. Sherwood

Meetings

Meet like enemy generals, knocking your sabers against the table, bluffing each other —Scott Spencer

There are some meetings in life so useful, so truly wonderful, that they seem like visible interventions of Providence —Ernest Hello

MELANCHOLY
See: GLOOM

Memory

MEMORY
See also: PAST, THE

(I am) clean forgotten, as a dead man out of mind
—*Book of Common Prayer*

Could be forgotten as quickly and painlessly as a doubting of Jesus or a fear of death from the measles —Peter Taylor

[Memory] drifted into my mind like a bit of weed carried in a current and caught there, floating but fixed, refusing to be carried away —Katherine Anne Porter

Eventually I thought about him [a once close friend] only once a week or so, as if he were a relative who had died years ago —Richard Burgin

Faded memories worn as a buffalo head a nickel —A. D. Winans

Felt old memories stir in him like dead leaves —Helen Hudson

Fettered to a pack of useless memories like a living person to a corpse —Ouida

Follow one after the next like cars out on the street, memories, there is just no stopping them —Tony Ardizzone

For a person blessed with a memory as full of holes as an Iranscam scenario, life can be a continuous state of astonishment —Donald Henahan
>Henahan uses this simile to introduce his comments about a revival of the musical, *South Pacific*. The editorial blurb writer used a simile from the musical's lyrics, "As Corny as Kansas in August" to highlight the article.

Forgotten as quickly as warm days in winter or cool days in summer —Ellen Glasgow

Forgotten like a station passed through on a train
    —Elizabeth Spencer

(Be) forgotten like spilt wine —Algernon Charles Swinburne

Gather memories like dry twigs, thorns and thistles
    —Yehuda Amichai

The ghosts of our remembrances throng around us like dead leaves
    whirled in the autumn wind —Jerome K. Jerome

His memory could work like the slinging of a noose to catch a wild
    pony —Eudora Welty

His memory lifted its skirts ... and hurried convulsively, like an old
    lady picking her way barefoot across a shingly beach
    —Noël Coward

His memory was something like his appendix, a vestigial repository
    —John Cheever

(He never forgets a face.) His mind is like a video camera
    —Ilie Nastase

If only there could be an invention that bottled up memory, like a
    scent —Daphne du Maurier

The image [of remembered scene] ... is like a photograph on my
    memory —Richard Maynard

An incident would suddenly crop up in her memory, like a piece in
    a jigsaw puzzle that seemed to have come from the wrong box
    —Mary McCarthy

It isn't a thing one forgets overnight, like losing a pencil
    —Mary Stewart

It was as though an endless series of hangars had been shaken ajar
    in the air base of his memory and from each, like a young wasp
    emerging from its cell, arose the memory of a plane
    —Ralph Ellison

Like a dull actor ... I have forgot my part —William Shakespeare

Memories are like books; a few live in our hearts through life, and
    the rest, like the bills we pay, are read, and then forgotten
    —Gerald Bendall

Memories are like stones, time and distance erode them like acid
    —Ugo Betti

Memory

Memories ... began to play across the surface of his mind like movies on a screen —Richard McKenna

Memories bursting in her mind like forsythia buds on the first warm day of the year —B. S. Johnson

Memories [troublesome] ... flitted like unexplained shadows across her happier thoughts —George Eliot

Memories ... floated like gossamer through her thoughts —Frank Swinnerton

Memories ... like worms eating into the flesh —William Golding

Memory ... crawling to the surface like a fat worm after rain —Harvey Swados

The memory ... fell upon him like a weight of black water —Willa Cather

The memory [of a man] glimmered in her thoughts like a bright thread in the pattern of a tapestry —Mazo De La Roche

Memory is a rare ghost-raiser. Like a haunted house, its walls are ever echoing to unseen feet. (Through the broken casements we watch the flitting shadow of the dead, and the saddest shadows of them all are the shadows of our own dead selves) —Jerome K. Jerome

Memory is as full of chimerical as forgetfulness, deceptive as any other work of the imagination —Madison Smart Bell

Memory is like a noisy intruder being thrown out of the concert hall ... he will hang on the door and continue to disturb the concert —Theodore Reik, *Saturday Review*, January 11, 1958

Memory, is like a purse, if it's too full, it can't be shut, and everything will drop out of it —Thomas Fuller

Memory is like the moon ... it has its new, its full, and its wane —Duchess of Newcastle
    The word 'hath' has been modernized to 'has.'

The memory is salty, like sweat, like the emissions of love-making, like the sea —Lael Tucker Wertenbaker

Memory, like a drop that, night and day, falls cold and ceaseless, wore my heart away —Thomas Moore

Memory, like a horrible malady, was eating his soul away
  —Oscar Wilde

Memory, like a juggler, tosses its colored balls into the light, and
  again receives them into darkness —Conrad Aiken

Memory ... like an old musical box it will lie silent for long years;
  then a mere nothing, a jerk, a tremor, will start the spring, and
  from beneath its decent covering of dust it will talk to us of
  forgotten passion and desire —Thomas Burke

A memory like a powerful microchip —Anon

A memory like a telephone directory —William McIlvanney

A memory like flypaper —Nora Johnson

Memory, like sleep, has powers which dreams obey
  —William Wordsworth

Memory, like women, is usually unfaithful —Spanish proverb
      Depending upon who's talking, the comparison would be
      as appropriate if attributed to men.

The memory of our lost friends is welcome to us like the bitter taste
  in wine that is very old —Michel de Montaigne

The memory of past favors is like a rainbow, bright, vivid, and
  beautiful, but it soon fades away —Thomas Chandler Haliburton

Memory [of something unpleasant] ... pokes at him like a nightmare
  in the womb —T. Coraghessan Boyle

A memory, very beautiful and delicate like a flavor or a perfume
  —Ruth Prawer Jhabvala

Had a mind like a mainframe memory bank —William Beechcroft

The moment hung like crystal in Meredith's mind —Babs H. Deal

My memory is like camphor. It evaporates with time
  —Dominique Lapierre

My memory kicked in; one of those wonderful little mental jolts, like
  a quick electric shock when a plug's gone bad —Sue Grafton

My memory's like a policeman, never there when you want it
  —Ronald Harwood
      This line is spoken by the main character in Harwood's
      play *The Dresser.*

Picking over the shames and humiliations ... like an invalid mulling over a plate of unwanted food —Harvey Swados

Pulled up at it [gap in memory] as if his advance had been checked by a chasm in the pavement at his feet —Edith Wharton

Recollections ... collected like spit from an aging throat —Elizabeth Spencer

Recollections dropped over him like a noose —Laurie Colwin

Remembrance is a tripping stone in the path of hope —Kahlil Gibran

Remembrance ... tickles the end of his nose like the fingertips of a child —Hayden Carruth

(I have) a retentive memory, a mind like flypaper to which facts stick —Desmond Begley

Shameful memories grip me like an anchor —Delmore Schwartz

She sank from his consciousness like one of those poor people encased in concrete who are heaved over the side and plummet to the bottom of the sea —William Styron

MEN AND WOMEN
See also: LOVE, MARRIAGE, SEXUAL INTERACTION

Handle a small woman like she's made out of steel, and a big woman like she's made out of glass —Paige Mitchell
See also: ADVICE

The happiest women, like the happiest nations, have no history —George Eliot

He goes about the business of fondling you, like someone very tired at night having to put out the trash and bolt-lock the door —Lorrie Moore

He likes fat women the way a rat likes pumpkins —Rita Mae Brown

He ran through women like a child through growing hay —Louis MacNeice
> The same image from a conversation overheard on a bus describes the woman as the sexual predator: "She runs through men like a fever."

He regarded women in the way that little girls regard their dolls, as toys to be dressed and undressed —Frank Swinnerton

Her responsiveness was something that fed him as wood fed the fire
   —Paul Horgan

He swept through her like a great ragged hawk on its journey to another prey —John Le Carré

He thought she'd fall like a ripe apple —Rita Mae Brown

Making love to women is almost as old as chess —Robert Traver

A man is like a cat; chase him and he'll run ... sit still and ignore him and he'll come purring at your feet —Helen Rowland

Man without woman would be as stupid a game as playing checkers alone —Josh Billings

Men like to pursue an elusive woman, like a cake of wet soap in a bathtub; even men who hate baths —Gelett Burgess

A mistress should be like a little country retreat near the town; not to dwell in constantly, but only for a night and away
   —William Wycherly

My blood is singing in her system, like whisky —Irwin Shaw

Paired off like the animals in the ark —Ross Macdonald

She drained me like a fevered moon —Edgar Lee Masters

She leaned easily against his shoulder ... as if she had done herself up in a parcel, addressed to him, left on his doorstep, from now on, his responsibility —Elizabeth Taylor

She made the blood run round in my veins like horses on a track
   —Ross Macdonald

Sometimes being with her is like being caught in a tornado
   —Alvin Boretz, television drama, 1986

Some women learn, like slaves, to study men —Charles Johnson

Take them [women] away and his (man's) existence is as flat and secure as that of a moo-cow —H. L. Mencken

(They hugged ...) their hearts shook them, like two people pounding at the same time on both sides of a very thin door
   —Eudora Welty

To be intimate with a foolish man's like going to bed with a razor
   —Ben Franklin

Men and Women

A woman is like a salad: much depends on the dressing —Anon
> There's also a saying, "Clothes make the man," to prove that this simile has no gender limitation.

A woman moved is like a fountain troubled, muddy, ill-seeming, thick, bereft of beauty —William Shakespeare

A woman's heart, like the moon, is always changing, but there is always a man in it —*Punch*

A woman's preaching is something like a dog's walking on his hinder legs. It is not done well; but you are not surprised to find it done at all —Samuel Johnson
> Women preachers continue to make good newspaper copy—which prompted a *Wall Street Journal* reader to use the Johnson simile in response to a December 24, 1986 story on this subject.

A woman without a man is like a garden without a fence —German proverb

A woman without a man is like a wild rose which blooms fast and ... falls apart with the wind —Diane Wakoski

Women are always a touchstone ... like litmus paper or dogs before an earthquake —Iris Murdoch

Women are like flowers, a little dust or squeezing makes them the more fragrant —Josh Billings
> In Billings' dialect the first part of this read as follows: "Wimmin are like flowers, a little dust ov squeezing."

Women are like tricks to sleight of hand. Which to admire we should not understand —William Congreve

MERRIMENT
See: GAIETY

METHOD
See: PURPOSEFULNESS

MIND
See: MIND, DEFINED

Mind, Defined

MIND, DEFINED

The mind is a city like London, smoky and populous —Delmore Schwartz

This simile is a follow-up to a poem's title, *The Mind Is an Ancient and Famous Capital.*

As the fire-fly only shines when on the wing, so it is with the human mind; when at rest, it darkens —Letitia Landon

The brain is like the hand. It grows with using —Judge Louis D. Brandeis

The brain, like Rhenish wine, should be chilled, not iced to be at its best —A. J. Liebling

The brain of man is filled with passageways like the contours and multiple crossroads of a labyrinth ... in its curved folds like the imprint of thousands of images, recordings of millions of words —Anaïs Nin

Brains to the sluggard are like wings to the ant, or a torch to the blind, an added load of no use or aid —Jediah Bedersi

A brilliant mind without faith is like a beautiful face without eyes —Shalom Cohen

A child's mind is like a shallow brook which ripples and dances merrily over the stony course of its education, and reflects here a flower, there a bush and yonder a fleecy cloud —Helen Keller

The conscious mind may be compared to a fountain playing in the sun and falling back into the great subterranean pool of the subconscious from which it rises —Sigmund Freud

The cultivation of the mind is a kind of food supplied for the soul of man —Cicero

The human mind is kind of lie ... a piñata. When it breaks open, there's a lot of surprises inside —Jane Wagner

The human mind ... is like a pendulum, which the moment it has reached the limit of its swing in one direction goes inevitably back as far as the other side and so on forever —James Russell Lowell

The human mind should be like a good hotel ... open the year round —William Lyon Phelps

Many minds are like low-grade ores, there is gold in them, but it takes a vast deal of labor to get it out —John Alfred Spender

Mind, Defined

The mind is an iceberg ... it floats with only one-seventh of its bulk above water —Sigmund Freud, quoted in *New York Times* obituary, September 24, 1939

The mind is like a bow, the stronger for being unbent —Ben Jonson

The mind is like a mechanical instrument that plays a great variety of tunes, but it must play them in succession —William Hazlitt

The mind is like an ocean. The surface layers of the mind function actively while the deeper levels remain silent —Maharishi Mahesh Yogi

The mind is like a sheet of white paper ... the impressions it receives oftenest and retains the longest are black ones —Julius Charles and August William Hare

The mind is like a slate, one thing gets rubbed out for another —Sam Slick

The mind is like the stomach. It is not how much you put into it that counts, but how much it digests —Albert Jay Nook

The mind like any other oganism, gradually shapes itself to what surrounds it, and resents disturbance in the form which its life has assumed —Oliver Wendell Holmes, Sr.

The mind of man is like a clock that is always running down, and requires to be as constantly wound up —William Hazlitt

The mind of the people is like mud, from which arise strange and beautiful things —Walter J. Turner

Minds are like parachutes ... they only function when open —Lord Thomas Dewar

Minds, like bodies, will often fall into a pimpled, ill-conditioned state from mere excess of comfort —Charles Dickens

A mind without occupation is like a cat without a ball of yarn —Samuel Willoughby Duffield

Old minds are like old horses; you must exercise them if you wish to keep them in working order —John Adams

Our minds are like crows. They pick up everything that glitters no matter how uncomfortable our nets get with all that metal in them —Thomas Merton

Our minds are like our stomachs; they are whetted by the change of their food, and variety supplies both with fresh appetite —Quintilian

The shapes which the mind assumes are like those great forms, born of undifferentiated water, which assail or replace each other on the surface of the deep; each concept collapses, eventually, to merge with its opposite, like two waves breaking against each other only to subside into the same single line of white foam —Marguerite Yourcenar

Some minds are like concrete: thoroughly mixed and permanently set —Anon

The state of a man's mind is as much a fact as the state of his digestion —Baron Charles Synge Christopher Bowen
> The simile was used in reference to the legality of intent in an 1885 law case.

A weak mind is like a horoscope, which magnifies trifling things but cannot receive great ones —Lord Chesterfield
> The letter to Chesterfield's son from which this was culled addresses the question of taking a balanced view towards keeping track of expenditures. The comparison of the weak mind to a horoscope is used to underscore the author's statement that "A strong mind sees things in their true proportions."

MODESTY

As humbly as a guest who knows himself too late —Hart Crane

Humility is like underwear, essential but indecent if it shows
—Helen Nielsen, *Reader's Digest,* March, 1959

If you really were a hero ... you made it sound routine and
unglamorous, like shrugging off a ninety-yard touchdown run as
"Good luck and good blocking" —Dan Wakefield

I looked as if I were trying to melt into the scenery and become
invisible, like a giraffe standing motionless among sunlit leaves
—Christopher Isherwood

Modest as a flower —Ella Wheeler Wilcox

Modest as justice —William Shakespeare

Modesty is like virtue; suspected only when it is advertised
—Douglas Malloch

Modesty like a diver gathers pearls by keeping his head low —*Punch*

Modesty's at times its own reward, like virtue —Lord Byron

MONARCHY
See: GOVERNMENT

MONEY
See: COST, GREED

MONOTONY
See: DULLNESS, REPETITION

MOODINESS
See: GLOOM

MORALITY
See also: BELIEF

As moral as any elder of the church —Rumer Godden

Morality, like language, is an invented structure for conserving and
communicating order —Jane Rule

Morality without religion is a tree without roots
—George Bernard Shaw

Moral principles are like measles. They have to be caught
    —Aldous Huxley

Morals are an acquirement, like music, like a foreign language, like
    piety, poker, paralysis, no man is born with them —Mark Twain

The moral system of the universe is like a document written in
    alternate ciphers, which change frrm line to line —J. A. Froude

Turning the other cheek is a kind of moral jiu-jitsu
    —Gerald Stanley Lee

Wore her morality like long underwear —Delmore Schwartz
            Schwartz followed this entry in his journal with several
            alternative comparisons: "Fur coat, chemise, a rope of
            pearls."

MOTHERHOOD
See: CHILDREN, PARENTHOOD

MOTHERS-IN-LAW
See: PARENTHOOD

MOTIVATION
See also: PURPOSEFULNESS

Good intentions ... like very mellow and choice fruit, they are
    difficult to keep —G. Simmons

(I simply) ran out of motives, as a car runs out of gas —John Barth

The true motives of our actions, like the real pipes of an organ, are
    usually concealed —Charles Caleb Colton

MOUTH
See: CHIN; CHEEKS; MOUTH, OPEN/SHUT

MOUTH, OPEN/SHUT

Closed her mouth like a trap —Julia O'Faolain

Mouth comes open like a fish for air —Robert Penn Warren

Mouth slightly open, like an idiot's —D. H. Lawrence

(Uncle Harry's) mouth dropped open, as if either in the beginning of prayer or protest —H. E. Bates

Mouth gagged open ... as if the day had stuck in his throat —William McIlvanney

Mouth hanging open like a stove lid —Charles Johnson

Mouth ... open, black and wide as an attic —Louise Erdrich

Mouth opened like a dark hole —Jerry Bumpus

Mouth opened like a folding bed —Anon

Mouth round and open like a small empty cave —William Faulkner

Mouths came open like full moons —Will Weaver

(His huge brow furrowed, his gray eyes closed down to slits, his) mouth shut like a car door being slammed —Jonathan Valin

Mouth ... slightly open, as though it froze in the middle of an unspellable word —Louise Erdrich

(Don't sit there with your) mouth sprung open like a busted letter box —William Alfred

Opened and closed her narrow lips once or twice, like some beached shellfish gasping for the tide —Edith Wharton

Opening his mouth in a kind of snarling grimace, quite without ferocity, like an old lion in a cage —Christopher Isherwood

Small mouth hung open birdlike (as she sang) —MacDonald Harris

Mouth shut abruptly, like a puppet's —Jonathan Valin

Yawned like a menagerie lion —Gelett Burgess

A yawn like an unobtrusive earthquake —G. K. Chesterton

MOVEMENT
See also: LEAPING, RUNNING, TURNING AND TWISTING, WALKING

All her movements were soft as if timed to the sleeping of children —Ada Jack Carver

Charged across ... like a cat with a kerosened ass —Harold Adams

Crawled like a worm —Denis Diderot

MOUTH...OPEN, BLACK AND WIDE AS AN ATTIC

Creep and crawl ... stretching her fingers like a baby trying to climb the path —Eudora Welty

Creeping slowly toward him, like a lizard toward a bug —E. B. White

Crept like a man intent on crime —W. H. Auden

Crept ... like a spider on an endless thread of its own spinning —George Du Maurier

Darted about like a hummingbird —Rita Mae Brown

Darted like a bird about the room —John Steinbeck

Darting about and banging together like bubbles in soda water —Joyce Cary

Darting off this way and that, like the wax of a burning candle —Anon

Descended the stairs like a buffalo —Joe Coomer

Drifted north ... like a saddle tramp looking for a spring roundup —James Crumley

Float like a butterfly, sting like a bee —Bundini Brown
> The phrase describes Muhammed Ali and is often attributed to him. However, credit belongs to Brown, sometimes referred to as Ali's "jester-in-waiting."

Floated like a weed —Mavis Gallant

Folded herself up like a fresh-ironed shirt —Mary Hood

Glided as though on little wheels —Jules Renard, drama critic, about actress Sarah Bernhardt

Glide, like phantoms —John Keats

Glides to his meeting like a lover mumbling a secret, passionate message —Wallace Stevens

Go as if nine men pulled you and ten men held you —John Withal

Going (home) stealthily and unsteadily ... like a dissipated cat —Charles Dickens

Groped about like blind, cautious crabs —Ralph Ellison

He [a dog] dumped himself like a bag of bones —Robert Frost

He moved like a spring —Eudora Welty

He moves like a piece of darkness —Joe Coomer

His body waved like a flame in the breeze —TV obituary describing James Cagney's physical grace, 1986

Hurried with legs stretched out ahead of me like a horse —David Ignatow

Kicking and wriggling like a retriever pup —Walter Duranty

Lethargically, like sloth on the move —Kenzaburo Oë
    In the novel, *A Personal Matter*, the lethargy described is that of a man pedalling his bike.

Like a vein of gold I darted after you —Charles Simic

Like shoals of fish, they all headed one way —Elizabeth Taylor

Lowered herself [from bus] cautiously, like a climber —Elizabeth Bowen

A meandering pace that makes sweet Afton look like a white water stream —Helen Dudar, *New York Times Book Review*, September 21, 1986

Moved as smoothly as light wind across water —James Crumley

Moved by as if on a treadmill —Jonathan Kellerman
    See: RESTLESSNESS

Moved downhill [a street that lay on an incline] like rainwater. Like the twentieth century —Tom Robbins

Moved like a water bug, like a skipping stone, upon the glassy tense surface of his new life —John Updike

Moved like benign automata —Angela Carter

Moved passively with her head down, like a prisoner between guards —Ross Macdonald

Moved with funny little steps, like a chicken with an egg wedged up its legs —William Kotzwinkle

Move languidly ... like a hostess in her bathrobe emptying ashtrays on Sunday morning —Alice McDermott

Movement ... quick and quiet as a fish in deep water —Gerald Kersh

Move mindlessly, mechanically as a toy train through a Christmas tree town —Sharon Sheehe Stark

(Waiters) moving as deft and soft-footed as shadows —George Garrett

(Hand) moving imperceptibly like a marine plant —Marguerite Yourcenar

Moving listlessly back and forth, like a fish in an aquarium —Jill Ciment

Moving quick and light as a fairy —Dame Edith Sitwell

Moving ... slow and heavy as lead —Gerald Kersh

(The sun) moving up and down ... like a musical note —Saul Bellow

Paced around ... like a jaguar on the prowl —Jonathan Kellerman

Pace ... like impatient cats —Ira Wood

Pace like Socrates before the court —Charles Johnson

Passed like a circus —Wallace Stevens

People moved as if groping in the dimness of the subconscious for the memory of midday warmth that lingered faintly in the skin —Kenzaburo Oë

Prowled around like a dog that has forgotten where he put his bone —Raymond Chandler
See also: AIMLESSNESS

Rush sideways, like an excited crab —Jerome K. Jerome

Scampering about like frenzied ants —Brian Burland

Scamper like mice —Dame Edith Sitwell

Scuttling around it like a mouse trying to find a hole —Cornell Woolrich

Settled themselves, like chickens getting ready to roost —Christopher Isherwood

She got up and, like a vacuum cleaner with insomnia, roamed the room —Tom Robbins

Shied abruptly like a startled horse —Jack London

Shuffled about [text of a book] like a melancholy sheep in a pen
    —Mavis Gallant

Shuffles ... around like a deck of cards —Brian Burland

Slide like lizards —Anon

Sliding like a shadow among them —R. V. Cassill

The small procession moved ... slow and spaced out like a funeral
    —Ivo Andric

(I have seen thy waters) stealing onward, like the stream of life
    —Henry Wadsworth Longfellow

Step back as though I'd stepped on a snake
    —Dorothy Canfield Fisher

Steppin' high like a rooster in deep mud —American colloquialism

Stirred like a rustle of leaves —Maurice Edelman
        Edelman's simile is used to draw an image of whispers
        stirring up around the actions of the hero of his novel,
        Disraeli Rising.

Stomped back to bed, trying to make my footsteps sound like angry
    exclamation marks —Dorothy Francis

Straggled on back ... like tongue-dragging hounds —Thomas Zigal

Straightened up slowly, as if she were being raised
    —Marguerite Duras

Swept by like a spotlight —Donald McCaig

Tore through the black-and-gold town like a pair of scissors tearing
    through brocade —Katherine Mansfield

Tottering ... like a Chinese girl with bound feet
    —Jayne Anne Phillips

Travels unsteadily, as fogs do —David Ignatow

Twisted himself out like an eel —Sholom Aleichem

Twitched her shoulders like a bird shaking off water —Laura Furman

Wander like Alice —Karl Shapiro

Weave like a dreamer —John Barth

[Group of children] whirling off like autumn leaves, just as gay in their bright colors, and just as elusive —Beverly Mitchell

Wiggled like ribbons —R. V. Cassill

Wiggle [a tooth] like a loose picket in a fence —William Goyen

MURDER
See: CRIME

MUSCLES

The great muscles of his torso flickered and ran like the flank of a horse —Du Bose Heyward

Heavily defined pectoral muscles, on which the nipples stood out like pennies —Francis King

Muscled like a water buffalo —Gerald Kersh

Muscles [of leg] as big as a hill —Dylan Thomas

Muscles ... hard and ropy like the ones on the fantastic coursing dogs in the sad stone friezes of ancient Persia —Beryl Markham

Muscles ... hard as iron —Jack London

The muscles in his face seemed to pull together like a drawstring purse —Sue Grafton

The muscles in their arms bulge out like India rubber balls —Joanna M. Glass

Muscles in their backs rippled ... like fretted water over a stony bed —Beryl Markham

Muscles like armor plates pasted on his body —John Rechy

Muscles ... like blown-up balloons —François Camoin
    In his short story, *A Hunk of Burning Love*, Camoin completes the simile as follows: "Put a pipe in his mouth and he'd look like Popeye."

Muscles like marshmallows —Carlos Baker

The muscles of his arms and back stood out beneath his fair skin like the muscles of one of Rodin's bronze men —Louis Bromfield

Muscles of his forearms ... moved in ridges and hollows from a knot above his elbow, like pistons working from a cylinder —L. P. Hartley

Muscles of strength rose like a collar from his neck —Arthur A. Cohen

Muscles ... polished like metal, pure sculpture —Vita Sackville-West

Muscles pulled like cold rubber —Tony Ardizzone

Muscles rippled like stretching cats —Stephen Vincent Benét

Muscles stretched taut as cowhide stretched over a baseball —W. P. Kinsella

Muscles that flow like a mountain stream —Ogden Nash

Muscles twitching like the flesh of a horse stung by many flies —Ralph Ellison

Remember ... the rippling of bright muscles like a sea —Edith Sitwell

The ripple of muscles goes along him, like a cat's back arching —Margaret Atwood

Wore faded denims through which his clumsy muscles bulged like animals in a sack —Ross Macdonald

MUSIC
See also: SINGING

As music takes up the thread that language drops, so it is where Shakespeare ends that Beethoven began —Sidney Lanier

The band wound up the tune like a train rushing into a station —Donald McCaig

The cello is like a beautiful woman who has not grown older but younger with time, more slender, more supple, more graceful —Pablo Casals

Composing is like making love to the future —Lukas Foss

Composing is like organizing a meal. The different dishes must be so arranged as to rouse the appetite and renew the pleasure with each course —Moses Ibn Ezra

A concert is like a bullfight, the moment of truth —Artur Rubinstein

The conductor ... flapped his arms like a rooster about to crow
—Katherine Mansfield

Each musician looks like mumps from blowing umpah umpah umps
—Ogden Nash

Fiddles tuning up like cats in pain —Harvey Swados

Good music, like land and machines, had no people in sight
—Will Weaver
> In Weaver's novel, *Red Earth, White Earth,* this simile is
> used to explain a character's liking for music.

A great burst of music gushed up like a geyser —Mary Lavin

In came a fiddler, and tuned like fifty stomach aches
—Charles Dickens

In music as in love, pleasure is the waste product of creation
—Igor Stravinsky

It is like eating vanilla ice cream in Paradise, listening to beautiful
music —Camille Lemmonnier

Musical as the holes of a flute without the flute —O. Henry

Music as loud as the roar of traffic —Marge Piercy
See also: NOISE

The music rushed from the bow [of fiddle] like water from the rock
when Moses touched it —Henry Van Dyke

The music enchanted the air ... like the south wind, like a warm
night, like swelling sails beneath the stars
—Erich Maria Remarque

Music is a big sublime instinct, like genius of all kinds —Ouida

Music is a sort of dream architecture which passes in filmy clouds
and disappears in nothingness —Percy A. Scholes

Music is auditory intercourse without benefit of orgasm
—Aldous Huxley

Music is essentially useless, as life is —George Santayana

Music is like wine ... the less people know about it, the sweeter they
like it —Robertson Davies

Music is like a fickle, tantalizing mistress; one is rarely happy with her, but it is sheer tormented hell ever to be long away —Robert Traver

Music is ... like mathematics, very nearly a world by itself. It contains a whole gamut of experience, from sensuous elements to ultimate intellectual harmonies —George Santayana

Music is not water, but it moves like water; it is not fire, but it soars as warm as the sun —Delmore Schwartz

Music is the arithmetic of sounds as optics is the geometry of light —Claude Debussy

Music, like balm, eases grief's smarting wound —Samuel Pordage

(Drum, drum, drum, the) music like footsteps —T. Coraghessan Boyle

Music may be regarded as a thermometer that makes it possible to register the degree of sensibility of every people, according to the climate in which they live —André Ernest Grétry

Music throbbed like blood —T. Coraghessan Boyle

Music yearning like a god in pain —John Keats

Opera in English makes about as much sense as baseball in Italian —H. L. Mencken

The opera is like a husband with a foreign title: expensive to support, hard to understand, and therefore a supreme social challenge —Cleveland Amory

The orchestra sounds like fifty cats in agony —J. B. Priestly

Our musicians are like big canisters of gas. Light a match too close to them, and they will explode
—Yevgeny Svetlanov, *New York Times*, October 20, 1986
Svetlanov, the Moscow State Symphony conductor, thus described Russian musicians in an article by Bernard Holland.

The plaintive sound of saxophones moaning softly like a man who has just missed a short putt —P. G. Wodehouse

Playing 'bop' is like playing 'scrabble' with all the vowels missing — Duke Ellington, quoted in *New York Herald Tribune*, July 9, 1961

Pulled music from his violin as if he were lifting silk from a dressmaker's table —Pat Conroy

Music

Saxophones wailing like a litter of pigs —Lawrence Durrell

The string section sounded like cats in heat —Mary Hedin

(Wade and Beth could hear) the subterranean thudding of his rock music turned low, like a giant heart beating in a sub-cellar —John D. MacDonald

A symphony must be like the world, it must embrace everything —Gustav Mahler
>Mahler's comment was addressed to Jean Sibelius.

To some people music is like food; to others like medicines; to others like a fan —Arabian Nights

Tuneless and atonal, like the improvised songs of children caught up in frantic play —Robert Silverberg

The written note is like a strait jacket, whereas music like life itself is constant movement, continuous spontaneity, free from restriction —Pablo Casals

Mustaches

MUSTACHES
See also: BEARDS

Big mustaches that made him look like an animated mushroom —Arthur Train

A black mustache like the lowered wings of a crow —Carolyn Chute

A curled-up mustache, like two little rolls of barbed wire —Joyce Cary

A gray handlebar mustache with oiled points, like the long horns of an ox —Ira Wood

His mustache sags ... like a bat —Carolyn Chute

His white mustache, of thin separate hairs like glass threads —Joyce Cary

His yellow-to-brown mustache quivered and preened over his mouth like a sparrow's wing shaking off dust —Paul Horgan

The insignificant mustache trembled like a twig in a storm —Jonathan Kellerman

A light mustache that flourished upwards as if blown that way by the breath of a constant smile —Henry James

A little black mustache like an eyebrow —George Du Maurier

Little circumflex accent mustache ... like a black butterfly placed under his nose —Romain Gary

Little mustaches stiffened like a pointer's tail when he scents a bird —Arthur Train

A man without a mustache is like a woman with only one breast —M. M. Liberman

Mustache ... black as India ink and big as the switch on a cow's tail —James Crumley

Mustache ... black, like a charcoal smear on his upper lip —Paige Mitchell

Mustache bristled like intractable gorse —Frank Swinnerton

Mustache curling like a sultan's —Oliver Wendell Holmes, Sr.

Mustache cut short like a worn-out brush —Henry James

Mustache hanging heavy as a pelt —Carolyn Chute

Mustache like a soft black mouse —Ann Tyler

A mustache resting like a small white cloud beneath his undistinguished nose —F. Scott Fitzgerald

A mustache shadowing either side of his lip with a broad sweep, like a bird's wing —William Dean Howells

(The faded) mustaches hung like crossed pistols above his radiant smile —Eudora Welty

Mustache ... thick and neat as a bristle brush —Ira Wood

Mustache ... thin and straight like it was painted on —George Garrett

White mustache like a Viking's —Jo Bannister

NAILS
See: FINGERS

Names

NAMES

(Alex) acquired names as other women encrust themselves with jewels —Patrick White

Forgotten names sang through my head like forgotten scenes in dreams —Ralph Ellison

Fools' names like fools' faces, are often seen in public places —Thomas Fuller

Handed [told it to her] her his name as though he were extending a card on a copper salver —Harvey Swados

His name [a politician's] has become as institutionalized as a detergent —Robert Traver

It is with you as with the seas: the most varied names are given to what is in the end only salt water —Johann Wolfgang von Goethe

Lost their names like marbles on the schoolyard —George Garrett

Making fun of your name is like making fun of your nose —Willie Morris

Names and faces eluded him like ghosts —William Diehl

Patients ... they are as patient as their name —Randall Jarrell

Called me 'chéri' in such a way that it was a small fruit on her tongue —R. Wright Campbell

Some people have names like pitchforks, some people have names like cakes —Stephen Vincent Benét

Sounds like a name you'd see on a bracelet at Walgreen's —Richard Ford
> The character who thus expresses her discontent in the novel, *The Sportswriter*, happens to be named Vicki.

You carry your name forever, like a scepter alive with wings —Stephen Vincent Benét

Your name like a lozenge upon my tongue —Charles Wright

NATIONS
See: CHARACTERISTICS, NATIONAL; GOVERNMENT

NATURALNESS

(Her tight smile returned) as automatically as a gesundheit
   —Loren D. Estleman

(The doctor ... a man who listened to other people's hearts) as
   casually, as automatically, as he blew his own nose
   —Helen Hudson

As natural a part of her life as toothpaste —Julia Whedon

As natural as a vine grows —Babette Deutsch

(She was flushed, eager, and) as natural as daylight
   —Frank Swinnerton

As natural ... as the falling of leaves —Edith Wharton

(A faith ... as strong,) as natural, as irrational as the elements
   —Romain Gary

As natural as NutraSweet —Anon

(Had grown up believing that overcoming handicaps was) as natural
   as scratching your ear —Ira Berkow, *New York Times*/Sports of
   the Times, September 23, 1986
      Berkow's subject is Jim Plunkett, Raider quarterback.

As natural ... as the passion for air or food or drink
   —Stephen McKenna

As natural as the process of digestion —Walter De La Mare

He [Dr. Oliver Wendell Holmes] could no more stop it [wit flowing
   from him] than he could stop the blood flowing in his veins
   —Elizabeth Bowen

(His thoughts, his humor, his similes) rose as fast, as multitudinous,
   as irrepressible, as bubbles in the champagne, and nothing could
   prevent their coming to the surface —John T. Morse
      The man whose wit is the subject of the comparison is Dr.
      Oliver Wendell Holmes.

Spontaneous as a child's drawing —Anon

Spontaneous as a six-course sit-down dinner —Anon

Spontaneous as the song of a bird —W. H. Hudson

Spontaneous as the time of day
   —"St. Elsewhere," TV segment, December 16, 1986

Unconscious as an oak tree of its growth —Anon

Unconscious as the loyalty of bees to their queen —Lacfadio Hearn

Unconscious as you grow your fingernails —George Bernard Shaw

Unnatural as generosity to a miser —Elyse Sommer

Unthinkingly as a child heaping sand on its mother at the beach —Anatole Broyard, *New York Times Book Review*, January 16, 1986

NATURE
See: LEAVES, OCEAN/OCEANFRONT, PONDS AND STREAMS, RAIN, SNOW, STARS, WEATHER

NEATNESS
See: CLEANLINESS/UNCLEANLINESS

NECK
See also: CHEEKS, CHIN

Adam's apple bobbing like an eccentric toy —Robert Traver

Adam's apple bobbing like a fishing float —Andrew Kaplan

Adam's apple bobbing up and down like a prune seed in his throat —Calder Willingham

Adam's apple jumping up and down his throat like he got a ping-pong ball part way down and it got stuck —Carlos Baker

The Adam's apple of his thin, sinewy throat went up and down like a lift —Erich Maria Remarque

The cords in his [a man who's upset and angry] neck stick out like thumbs —Mary Hood

Her neck is like a stately tower —Thomas Lodge

Her neck rose [from folds of a shawl] like a column of slightly discolored Cararra marble —Arthur Train

His Adam's apple bulged so that when he drank it reminded Augustus of a snake with a frog stuck in its gullet —Larry McMurtry

His Adam's apple rippling up and down his skinny throat like a crazed mouse —James Crumley

His Adam's apple went up and down like an elevator
—Cornell Woolrich

Limp-necked like a faded daisy —Julia O'Faolain

A long neck built like a tower —Colette

The long, pale neck rising like a beam of light from his open shirt
—Helen Hudson

Neck ... as a tower of ivory —*The Holy Bible/Song of Solomon*

Neck as thick as a telephone pole —William Diehl

Neck like a steel truss —Jonathan Valin

Neck swiveled like a lazy susan —T. Coraghessan Boyle

Neck ... wrinkled like the wattles of some big bird —Anon
See also: WRINKLES

The sinews of his neck ... stood out like a cord of a hoist
—Arthur Train

The skin of his neck, flabby and wrinkled like a turkey's cockscomb
—Romain Gary

Thin neck like a goose —Jilly Cooper

Two rings of age on her neck looked like a cheap necklace
—V. S. Pritchett

The veins in his thin white neck stood out like cords —Leo Tolstoy

NEGLECT
See: ABANDONMENT, REJECTION

NEGLIGENCE
See: CARELESSNESS

NERVOUSNESS
See also: TREMBLING

All nervous and jerky like a windup toy or maybe a cockroach on its
back, waving its legs and trying to turn over —George Garrett

Clucked nervously, like a mongoose —Romain Gary

Excitable ... like a little rooster —Irwin Shaw

(Sat there open-mouthed,) feeling the nerves of his body twitter like so many sparrows perched upon his spinal column
—F. Scott Fitzgerald

Felt as if she were on the edge of a frozen pond, forced to go forward and not knowing how thick the ice was
—Donald MacKenzie

Felt as if someone had taken a vegetable peeler to my nerves
—T. Coraghessan Boyle

His nerves set themselves on edge like soured teeth —H. E. Bates

His stomach felt like a volcano about to erupt —Andrew Kaplan

It's (persistent feeling of impending insanity) like my head's in a vice and all the assholes of the world are turning the goddam handle
—Thomas Williams

Jumpy as a goat —James Thurber

Jumpy as a greyhound —Wallace Stegner

Jumpy as a jumping bean —Anon

Lived like an exposed nerve —Rita Mae Brown

Looked ... like a nervous rabbit nibbling the smell of a gun barrel
—Paul Theroux

Nerves burned like open sores on a dog's neck
—Hunter S. Thompson

Nerves like a bundle of firecrackers —Amy Lowell
> Lowell's poem, *Rosebud Wall-Paper*, from which this is taken was written in country dialogue, with 'of' written as 'o'.

Nerves like new thread —John Updike

Nerves tied in small, intricate knots, like embroidery stitching
—Jean Thompson

(In rapid motion, bright,) nervous as a butterfly —Marge Piercy

Nervous as a cat on a hot tin roof —Anon

In a television interview playwright Tennessee Williams stated that his father always used this phrase which became the title for one of his best known plays. It also served as a line for one of the leading characters, Maggie. During the interview Williams credited this and many other colorful phrases to Southern Blacks.

Nervous as a coyote in a pen —W. P. Kinsella

Nervous as a dog with a bone —Ben Hecht

Nervous as a hamster —Reynolds Price

Nervous as a kitten with a duck for a foster mother
    —Victor Canning

Nervous as a whore in church —American colloquialism

Nervous as a will o'-the-wisp —F. Scott Fitzgerald

On edge, like some restless night —Yasunari Kawabata

(They felt everything, feared everything, started back at the snapping
    of a twig, all their) senses strained like those of nervous explorers
    cautiously advancing, hand on cocked trigger, into an unknown
    jungle —Dorothy Canfield Fisher

Shuddering and wary, like horses bewildered by lightning
    —Ted Hughes
        Hughes' poem, *A Wind Flashes the Grass*, links the
        comparison of the wary horses to trees suddenly silent and
        motionless.

White and shaken, like a dry martini —P. G. Wodehouse

Wriggle nervously like captive fish —Margaret Millar

NEWNESS
See: FRESHNESS, TIMELINESS/UNTIMELINESS

NEWS
See also: KNOWLEDGE

As cold waters are to a faint soul, so is good news from a far
    country —*The Holy Bible/Proverbs*

Bad news travels fast like a bad shilling —line from British television
    program "Bless Me Father," 1986

News ... rose like a grenade across Washington
—Ellen Goodman, *Newsday*, December 2, 1986
> Goodman is contrasting the normalcy with which video shopping programs are working, with the scandal over arms shipments to Iran which exploded the sense of normalcy in the capital of the nation.

Share information like a basket lunch —Anon

NIGHT

The black night spread like glistening caviar —Diane Wakoski

The dark-blue velvet night hung like a curtain —Elizabeth Bowen

The darkness of night, like pain, is dumb; the darkness of dawn, like peace, is silent —Rabindranath Tagore

Dusk was falling like blue flakes —Truman Capote

The evenings and nights were like shutters opening and closing, no more than that —Dan Jacobson

Midnight shakes the memory as a madman shakes a dead geranium —T. S. Eliot

Night, bereft of dreams, is like a deserted railway station after hours —Robert Duncan

Night brings out stars as sorrow shows us truth —P. J. Bailey

Night comes like a blackout —John Rechy

The night dives down like one great crow —Richard Wilbur

Night falls like a dropped shutter —Beryl Markham

Night falls like fire —Algernon Charles Swinburne

The night feels like a gigantic Ferris wheel turning in blackness, very slowly —Margaret Laurence

Night had fallen like a black curtain —Colin Forbes

The night is as soft as milk —Albert Camus

The night is like flower petals, the air moist as a damp cloth —W. P. Kinsella

The night is soft and silent, warm as cashmere —W. P. Kinsella

The night roars on ... like an express train —Erich Maria Remarque

The night descended on her like a benediction —Joseph Conrad

The nights stick together like pages in an old book —John Ashberry

The night stretches before me like an endless checklist
    —Natascha Wodin

The night trickles on like liquid time —Natascha Wodin

The still night drifted deep like snow about me
    —Edna St. Vincent Millay

The summer night is like a perfection of thought —Wallace Stevens

The night, like ice, seemed to harden around her —William Dieter

NOISE

A clopping sound ... stung Lavinia's nerves like a box on the ears
    —L. P. Hartley

Creaked like a saddle when he shifted —Wallace Stegner

Creak like a rusty engine —Franz Werfel

A dissonant chord, as if somebody stepped on a cat
    —George Garrett

Door slam ... like the crack of a bat when the opposition has hit a
    homerun to beat the Mariners in the bottom of the ninth
    —Tom Robbins

(The phone's) dull ring ... like marbles rolling across a sheet of tin
    —Jean Thompson

Emitting throaty, explosive sounds like someone about to spit in
    someone else's face —Natascha Wodin

Fitful, hacking noise, like a dog coughing up a bone
    —William Styron

Footsteps echoing like gunfire in a well —T. Coraghessan Boyle

Growling away like an old mastiff with a sore throat
    —Charles Dickens

Growling like a fox in a trap —William Diehl

(Water) gulped and hissed like a dozen jacuzzis
—T. Coraghessan Boyle

Heels ticking on the parquet floor like the clock of a time bomb
—Margaret Millar

Her steps ... made tiny, sharp pecky sounds, kind of like Mother
drumming on the edge of the dinner table when Father tried to
promote himself a second piece of pie —Raymond Chandler

The hinges and springs [of a door] screech like a woman with a
hand over her mouth —Robert Campbell

Hissed like an adder —John D. MacDonald

(Tires) hissed like death —T. Coraghessan Boyle

(The sea) hissed like twenty thousand kettles —Joseph Conrad

Hisses and crackles like a doused campfire —Kate Wheeler

Hissing noise [as of crackling tissue paper] ... was like a nail on glass
to my nerves —Cornell Woolrich

Hum, like a devout crowd on its knees —Margaret Atwood

Like a log fire, the typewriter crackled —Delmore Schwartz
If Delmore Schwartz were alive and keeping a diary today,
instead of in 1944 when this entry was made, the crackling
might well be from a computer keyboard instead of a
typewriter.

(A beehive as) loud as an airfield —Maxine Kumin

Loud as gunfire —Reynolds Price

Loud as the last call of God —Harold Adams

A loud cracking sound, like a frozen river breaking up in spring
—Andrew Kaplan

Loud ... like a gun going off —Edith Wharton

Made a sound [in response to being kicked] like a sick cat
—Loren D. Estleman

(A printer that) makes noise like a mad elephant —Edward
Mendelson, reviewing computer products in *Yale Review*, 1985

Murmur like bees —Dame Edith Sitwell

(Through the audience went) a murmur, like the rustle of dead leaves —Henry Wadsworth Longfellow

The noise cracked like a whip in the still room —Margaret Mitchell
The noise Mitchell likened to the crack of a whip was made by Scarlett O'Hara when she slapped Ashley Wilkes' face in the famous scene from *Gone With the Wind* when he rejects her declaration of love.

Noise dwindling like a cut-back motor —Rosellen Brown

The noise level was deafening ... like some hideous unrelenting tape-loop of trains having sex
—Ben Hamper in article on changes at GM, *Mother Jones*, September, 1986

Noises rise and are lost in the air like balloons —Albert Camus

Noise [of continuous lightning] that sometimes burst like metal fireworks —Marguerite Duras

(The city by day was as) noisy and busy as a pack of children —Sinclair Lewis

(She would be as) noisy as a child at a playground —Helen Hudson

Noisy as a living skeleton having a fit on a hardwood floor —Leonard Washborn, reporting on 1880s baseball game for *Interocean* newspaper

Noisy as squirrels mating on a rooftop —Elyse Sommer

Noisy as the stock exchange —Augustine Bire

An occasional buzz [interrupting the silence] like an unheeded alarm clock —William Humphrey

Popping sounds, like hands clapped sharply together —W. P. Kinsella

[A typewriter] purrs like a seductive housecat —Tom Robbins

Rattling like a gong —Cynthia Ozick

Raucus whoop of children, spiteful and cruel like the sound of a lynch mob —Amos Oz
See also: CRUELTY, SCREAMS

Resounded like a gigantic trumpet —Émile Zola

Ring like bells of glass —Elinor Wylie

Rowdy as gulls —Marge Piercy

Rumble ... like a monster growl —Susan Minot

(The fiddle) screeched like a thing in pain —Elizabeth Bowen

Screeching with a noise like a buzz saw cutting through a knot
    —William Humphrey

Screech, like a car shifting gears on a dangerous uphill road
    —Yehuda Amichai

Sickening screech [of ripping metal] ... like the scream of a wounded
    beast —Richard Moran

Slammed the door after him like a six-gun salute —Cornell Woolrich

The slamming of the door sounded like the last crack of doom
    —Jimmy Sangster
        Sangster's comparison begins the prologue to his mystery
        novel, *private i*, with a literal and figurative bang.

Snorted like a horse —Geoffrey Chaucer

The sound ... filled the eardrums like wax —Wyatt Blassingame

Sound ... it seemed to fill the vast room as breath fills a toy balloon
    —Frank Trippett

Sound like rhinos crashing into trees —Pauline Kael

The sounds [of the city] broke over her like a wave
    —Marguerite Yourcenar

Sounds came to me dully, as if people were speaking through their
    handkerchiefs or with their hands over their mouths
    —Maya Angelou

Sounds faded to a muffled warble, like a stream over pebbles
    —CurttLeviant

Sounds ... grated and rumbled like a subway train —Norman Mailer

Sounds ... hurt his ear like the thrust of a knife —Ambrose Bierce

The sound was hollow like the hammer on a coconut
    —Carson McCullers

The [baseball] stands sounded like a gigantic drawerful of voices that
    had suddenly been pulled open —Bernard Malamud

STATIC CRACKLED ALONG THE LINE,
LIKE POPCORN POPPING

Static crackled along the line, like popcorn popping —William Diehl

The steady drone of the crowd, like bees humming —Anon

A steady murmur like the crowd noises made in a movie —Frank Conroy

Tapping and ticking like nervous fingers —Sylvia Plath

NONSENSE
See: FOOLISHNESS

NOSES
See also: FACIAL DETAILS

A fabulous outsized nose attached to his face like a sheltering of stone —Pat Conroy

A flattish nose like a prizefighter —Beryl Bainbridge

His nose made two twists from bridge to end, like the wriggle of a snake —O. Henry

His nose stuck out like the first joint of a thumb —Frederick O. Brien

His nostrils heaved like a pair of blacksmith's bellows —Isaac Babel

A large nose like a trumpet —Edward Lear

Little snub nose, like a bulldog's —Colette

A long narrow nose which clung against his face as if reluctant to leave it —MacKinlay Kantor

A long nose flattened as if it had been tied down —Willa Cather

A long pink nose like a crooked beckoning finger in the middle of his face —Sue Miller

Nose ... as big as an orange and the skin stretched over it was pebbled like an orange —François Camoin

Nose broad as a teacup —Carolyn Chute

Nose ... crackled with tiny veins, like the nose of a hardened boozer —Gavin Lyall

A nose like a Bartlett pear —James Whitcomb Riley

A nose like a battering ram —Ross Macdonald

Nose like a bone —Ivan Bunin

A nose like a boot —Michael Gilbert

Nose like a butcher's thumb —Mary Hedin

Nose like a delicate scythe —Mary Hedin

Nose like a duck's bill —Ivan Turgenev

Nose [of a heavy drinker] like a fire ball —Erich Maria Remarque

Nose like a gherkin —Jonathan Valin

Nose like a jungle-bird's —William H. Gass

Nose like a knife blade —R. Wright Campbell

Nose like a letter opener —Jonathan Valin

Nose [Julius Caesar's] like an elephant's trunk
    —George Bernard Shaw

Nose like an engorged purple potato —Sarah Bird

Nose like a parrot's beak —Honoré de Balzac

Nose like a scimitar —William H. Hallhan

A nose like a spear in youth, in middle age becomes more like a
    shield, and in old age a little bit of a thing that looks like a
    button —William Saroyan

Nose like a sponge —Maxim Gorky

Nose like a turkey's ass —Robert Campbell

Nose like the beak of a bird —Anton Chekhov
        A more specific variant by Donald MacKenzie: nose like a
        falcon's beak.

Nose ... long, like the nose in some old Italian pictures
    —Walter De La Mare

Nose ... sharp as a pen —William Shakespeare

Nose small and laid back with aboot as much loft as a light iron
    —P. G. Wodehouse

A nose that seemed to have been bent by a tire iron
    —Jimmy Breslin and Dick Schaap

Nose was like a wooden peg —Truman Capote

Nose was very short, just like a baby's —Joyce Cary

Nostrils flaring like a colt's in winter —Charles Johnson

Nostrils flaring like a trotter —Joan Hess

Nostrils heaving like a stallion's —T. Coraghessan Boyle

Nostrils ... shaped like the wings of a swallow —Oscar Wilde

Roman nose stuck up like the beak of a predatory bird
    —Carlos Baker

A straight nose, like a crusader modelled on a tomb —Antonia Fraser

An upturning nose like that of the Duchess in *Alice in Wonderland* —
    Frank Swinnerton

NOURISHMENT
See: MEMORY

NOVELS
See: BOOKS

NUMBNESS
See: RESERVE

OATH
See: PROMISE

OBESITY
See: FATNESS

OBJECTS, MISCELLANEOUS

Beach umbrellas, bright as lollipops ... like flowers grown grossly out
    of proportion in a garden —Stanley Elkin

Blankets and pillows ... like loving, hugging arms —Jean Stafford

(Bernard's) camera clicks like the gnashing of a lizard's tiny teeth
    —R. Wright Campbell

Canes like swords —John Dickson Carr

(Dangle) a long row of credit cards like the flags on the mast of a ship —George Garrett

Pennants steam from the twin copper peaks of the roof [of the golf course clubhouse] like a castle at tournament time —Walker Percy

The phone goes off like a shrill alarm —Jay McInerney

The plow bucked and staggered like a cow with a broken back —Will Weaver

Refrigerator as big as a garden shed —François Cammon

(Sometimes I think) TVs are like dollhouses but with real, little people inside —Will Weaver
> In his novel, *Red Earth, White Earth*, Weaver expands on this image as follows: "Close your eyes sometime, and put your ear right on the side of the T.V. It's like you're listening through a wall to the neighbors."

Transistor radio—one of those ghetto blasters that look like assorted pie plates glued to a masonry block —Jonathan Valin

A [very small] watch ... rode her bare wrist like a rubber band around a leg of lamb —Loren D. Estleman

Umbrellas, like faces, acquire a certain sympathy with the individual who carries them —J. W. Ferrier

OBLIVION
See: BLINDNESS

OBSCURITY
See: VAGUENESS

OBSOLESCENCE
See: TIMELINESS/UNTIMELINESS

OBVIOUSNESS
See also: CLARITY, VISIBILITY

(The magnificence of the Ambersons was) as conspicuous as a brass band at a funeral —Booth Tarkington

As conspicuous ... as a butterfly among moths —George Feifer

As conspicuous as a second nose —Mike Sommer

As conspicuous as two fleas in a glass of milk, and about as welcome —Rosa Guy

Blatant as a slammed door —George Garrett

Her face was as easy to read as a crooked optometrist's chart —Loren D. Estleman

It was written all over him [that he was prone to trouble] in letters like headlines —William Humphrey

Magnificence, like the size of a fortune, is always comparative —Booth Tarkington

Noticeable as perfume —Wallace Stegner

(The film has a payoff that's as) obvious as a cream pie in the face —Gene Siskel, television review, October 13, 1986

Obvious as a gesture —Stephen Crane

Obvious as an elephant's footprint —Anon

(Those two guys can't move around ... without being) obvious as turds on butcher blocks —Harold Adams

Obvious, like a poster forty feet high —J. B. Priestly

(Her thoughts and her emotions had all been) outspread ... like jewels —Edith Wharton

Plain as a pig on a sofa —Flannery O'Connor

(The case was as) plain as a pikestaff —Arthur Train

Plain as graffiti on a brick wall —Elyse Sommer

Plain as the nose on a man's face —Rabelais
      A variation by Robert Burton: "As clear and as manifest as the nose on a man's face."

Plain as the paint on a whore's face —Stephen Longstreet

Stick out like a pregnant woman's stomach —Anon

(He was) subtle as a salvo —Jonathan Gash

There's no one so transparent as the person who thinks he's devilish deep —W. Somerset Maugham

Transparent as water in a goldfish bowl —Anon

Unobtrusive as the roar of a lion —Erich Maria Remarque

OCEAN/OCEANFRONTS

The Alvin [a ship] ... moved through the dark sea like a robot fish
—Richard Moran

The beach is bare as the blue bowl of the sky —John Hall Wheelock

The beach was splattered with people like bright rags
—Nadine Gordimer

(Here in front of the summer hotel) the beach waits like an altar
—Anne Sexton

A beach, white and slender like a young moon —Louis Bromfield

A breaker ... roaring over the reef like a herd of crazed animals
running before a forest fire —Clive Cussler

The gentle surf crested in the quick darkness with swirling
phosphorous fringes of tiny animals like liquid silver
—James Crumley

Long blue rollers coming in ... each a neat and level line like an
ironed crease —George Garrett

The ocean frowns like elephant hide —Karl Shapiro

The ocean like sleek gray stone —Robinson Jeffers

The ocean looked like a wide lavender ribbon stitched up against a
pink-and-blue sky —Sue Grafton

The ocean rumbled like a train backing up —Anne Sexton

The ocean seemed to hover in the distance like a gray haze blending
into the gray of the sky —Sue Grafton

The rough white crests of waves walk as if in moccasins
—Diane Wakoski

The sea growled like a dog —John Mortimer

The sea has that oily sheen to it, like an empty swimming pool
—William Boyd

The sea is like a human being ... always moving, always something
deep in itself stirring it ... always wanting —Olive Shreiner

411

Ocean/
Oceanfronts

The sea [along the beach jetties] trembling among the stones like gelatin —Thomas McGuane

The sea whispered and hummed like a great shell held to the ear —Mary Stewart

The surf hisses like tambourines —Derek Walcott

The tide came in like ten thousand orgasms —Anne Sexton
See also: NOISE

The water ran over the sand, one wave covering another like the knitting of threads —Rachel Ingalls

Waves ... black as cypresses, clear as the water of a wishing well —Denise Levertov
See also: BLACK, CLARITY

Waves crashing with the sound as of breaking biscuits —Vita Sackville-West

Waves ... leaping like hounds up aatthe rocks —Josephine Jacobsen

Waves like small mountains rose with the shrieking wind into the black sky —James Stern

A wave like a vast castle —Arabian Nights

Waves, like blue animals stampeding —George Garrett

Waves like white feathers —George Garrett

The waves pulse ... like hearts —Sylvia Plath

A wave suddenly raged out like a mountain cat —Stephen Crane

Waves that rose like mountains —D. R. MacDonald

The waves were skidding in like big buildings that swayed drunkenly and then toppled over on their faces and splattered all over the hard sand —Arthur Miller
> Miller, best known for his plays, has also written short stories ... one of which, *I Don't Need You Any More,* is the source for this comparison.

When the surf is up its roaring fills you like a shell —Marge Piercy

The whole expanse of water ... glistened like a sheet of stretched blue silk —Robie Macauley

OCCUPATIONS
See: DOCTORS, LAWYERS, PROFESSIONS

OPAQUENESS
See: VAGUENESS

OPEN/SHUT

Closed [a newspaper] up like a surgeon closing an incision above an
   inoperable truth —Elizabeth Spencer

The door is closed like the shutter of a stalled-out camera
   —Thomas McGuane

It [a door] came [open] easy ... like a ghost had bown it open from
   inside —Jay Parini

Locked up tighter than Dick's hatband —Richard Ford
         Ford's simile used to describe a home business that's not
         open, is a takeoff on the American colloquialism generally
         linked with stinginess.

Open and shut as if cast from the shadow of a fallen angel's wing
   —Anon

(The elevator doors) opened suavely, like an expensive cream sliding
   smoothly on a flawless face —Judith Martin

(Let your mind) open like a clam when the waters slide back to feed
   it —Marge Piercy

Opens like a summer rose —George Garrett

(In love we) open wide as a house to a summer afternoon
   —Marge Piercy

(Wake up please) open yourself like a little umbrella —Donald Justice

(Our room was closed off and) sealed, like a grave inside a pyramid
   —Yehuda Amichai

[Emotions] sewn up tighter than a Victorian daughter's drawers
   —Roderic Jeffries

Shut down (the long Minnesota winter) like the white lid of a box
   —F. Scott Fitzgerald

Shut firmly in like a trunk locked up when the key is lost
   —Eibhlin Dhubh Ni Chonnaill

[Window-blinds] shut like an eye that sleeps —H. G. Wells

Shut tight as a drum —Anon

Shut up like a rabbit trap —Noel Streatfeild

(J. B's face) shut with a snap like a rat-trap —Gavin Lyall

(A world had opened and) was closing ... like a curtain being silently drawn —John McGahern

OPERA
See: MUSIC

OPINION

As men grow older, their opinions, like their diseases, grow chronic —Josh Billings
> In Billings' original dialect: Az men gro older their opinuns like thier diseazes, grow kronick.

Carried and opened this attitude like an umbrella —Delmore Schwartz

Observations ... are like children's cradles ... sometimes empty, sometimes full of noisy imbecility, and often lulling to sleep —Sydney Smith
> Smith modestly applied this simile to his own observations.

Of three minds, like a tree in which there are three blackbirds —Wallace Stevens

Opinion gathered like a cloud and danced and then seemed to freeze —H. E. Bates

Opinion is like a pendulum and obeys the same law. If it goes past the center of gravity on one side, it must go a like distance on the other —Arthur Schopenhauer
> Schopenhauer continued his simile like this: "And it is only after a certain time that it finds the true point at which it can remain at rest."

Opinion polls: polls are like sleeping pills designed to lull the public into sleeping on election day. You might call them "sleeping polls" —Harry S. Truman

Opinions, like showers, are generated in high places, but they invariably descend into lower ones, and ultimately flow down to the people, as rain unto the sea —Charles Caleb Colton

Opinions, like the temperaments, fell rapidly into pre-established categories —Marguerite Yourcenar

Opinions richocheted through the gathering like hyperactive pheromones —Susan Ferraro, *New York Times*/Hers, February 19, 1987

Opinions stout as oak —Phyllis McGinley

Passed opinions like gas —Rita Mae Brown

Played with our ideas like jacks, pressing our fingertips against their sharp points and round protuberances, testing how many we could scoop up at once —Lynne Sharon Schwartz

Public opinion in this country runs like a shower bath. We have no temperature between hot and cold —Heywood Broun
> Broun's public opinion simile is amongst the best known witticisms born at the famed Algonquin Round Table.

Sweeping judgments which are so common are meaningless ... like men who salute a whole crowd of people in the mass —Michel De Montaigne

The man who never alters his opinion is like standing water, and breeds reptiles of the mind —William Blake

The pressure of public opinion is like the pressure of the atmosphere; you can't see it—but, all the same, it is sixteen pounds to the square inch —James R. Lowell, interview with Julian Hawthorne, *New York Times*, April 2, 1922

The public buys its opinions as it buys its meat, or takes its milk, on the principle that it is cheaper to do this than to keep a cow. So it is, but the milk is more likely to be watered —Samuel Butler

Tosses off insights like the spray from a speedboat —Anon comment about an author's work
> Like many such complimentary similes, this one was later featured in an ad for the work thus praised.

To venture an opinion is like moving a piece at chess: it may be taken, but it forms the beginning of a game that is won —Johann Wolfgang von Goethe

OPPORTUNENESS
See: TIMELINESS/UNTIMELINESS

OPPORTUNITY

Opportunity

Life was opening up ... like an orchid in bloom
—T. Coraghessan Boyle

Opportunities, like eggs, don't come but one at a time —Josh Billings
In Billings' original dialect: "Oopportunitays ... kum but
one at a time."

Opportunity ... it fell like a lucky coin at his feet —George Garrett

Possibilities rising like new mountains —Richard Ford

Sometimes opportunity knocks like a loud windburst; more often it
arrives like a burglar and disappears before you realize it was
there —Elyse Sommer

OPTIMISM
See: CHEERFULNESS

ORATORY
See: SPEECHMAKING

ORDER/DISORDER
See: CLEANLINESS/UNCLEANLINESS

ORDINARINESS
See: COMMONPLACE

ORIGINALITY/UNORIGINALITY

**Originality/
Unoriginality**

As distinctive as a paper clip —Loren D. Estleman

As novel as teaching chickens to drive cars —Richard Ford

Blowing platitudes like bubbles through air —William Styron

The human mind can no more produce an original thought than a
tree can produce an original fruit —Jerome K. Jerome

Individualism is rather like innocence; there must be something
unconscious about it —Louis Kronenberger

Original as a xeroxed letter —Elyse Sommer

A platitude like a bad postcard of the Parthenon —Karl Shapiro

Unique as the suits worn to a banker's convention —Elyse Sommer

Unlike the rest of the family as wine from water —J. B. Priestly

Unoriginal as any rabbit —Robert Frost

Wondrous as the butterfly's birth from the worm —Alderman

Originality/
Unoriginality

OUT OF PLACE
See: BELONGING

PALLOR
See also: FACIAL COLOR, GRAY, RED, WHITE

Pallor

Pale as cardboard —Paige Mitchell

Pale as white wine —Sir Kenelm Digby

Blanch like conscious guilt personified —Charlotte Brontë

Bleached like the skeleton of a stranded walrus —Herman Melville

A face like paper —J. B. Priestly

Face like parchment —G. K. Chesterton

(His long, pendulous) face looked as if it had been dusted with
    white talc —Aharon Megged

Face ... pale as a Chinese mandarin's —Nadine Gordimer

Face ... pale as a dead man's —Ivan Turgenev

Face ... pale as a fish —T. Coraghessan Boyle

Face, pallid and simmering like a milk pudding over a slow flame
    —Julia O'Faolain

His waxy pallor was touched along the underside of his jaw with
    acne, like two brush burns —John Updike

Look [pale] like Yom Kippur before sunset —Isaac Bashevis Singer

Pale as a silkfish —Diane Ackerman

Pale and dirty as a pulled root —George Garrett

Pale as a birch —Louise Erdrich

(A scar) pale as a fishgut —Davis Grubb

417

Pale as a ghost with pernicious anemia —Anon
>A twist on the cliche, "Pale as a ghost."

Pale as a hyacinth grown in a cellar —Edith Wharton

(Looking as) pale as a magnolia blossom —Sarah Bird

Pale as a primrose —William Shakespeare

Pale [after donating a lot of blood] as a princess after a date with Dracula —Kenzaburo Oë

Pale as a prisoner —Carlos Baker

(Always cool and) pale as a root —Jayne Anne Phillips

Pale as a shell —James Wright

Pale as a smooth-sculptured stone —John Keats

Pale as a white rose —Nathaniel Hawthorne

Pale as bleached clay —Z. Vance Wilson

Pale as candles —Reynolds Price
>A more specific version by McKinlay Kantor is "Pale as a tallow candle."

Pale as china —Sylvia Plath

(The desert looks) pale as death —Henry Chettle
>According to Stevenson's *Book of Proverbs, Maxims, and Famous Phrases*, Chettle was the first to use the simile in his seventeenth century play, *Hoffman*. The earliest linkage to the complexion is variously attributed to Walter Scott's *Guy Mannering*, Thomas Hardy's *The Mayor of Casterbridge* and Henry James' *The Madonna of the Future*.

Pale as distemper —Miles Gibson

Pale as his shirt —William Shakespeare

Pale as ivory —Ouida

Pale as junket —Christina Stead

Pale as milk —William Shakespeare
>The similes from masters like the Bard are often used "as is" or with minor additions such as "Pale as cold milk" seen in Davis Grubb's novel, *The Golden Sickle*.

UNLIKE THE REST OF THE FAMILY
AS WINE FROM WATER

(Face) pale as sand —Stevie Smith

Pale as straw —William Evans

Pale as the bottom of a plate —Joseph Sheridan Le Fanu

Pale ... as the mist that hangs over the river —Oscar Wilde

Pale as the soap in the dish —Jean Thompson

Pale as the tenant of a tomb —Edgar Allen Poe

Pale as waxworks —Maxine Kumin

Paler than ashes —Algernon Charles Swinburne

Paler than grass in summer —Algernon Charles Swinburne

(Thighs) pale and soft as snow —Lyn Lifshin

So white she was almost transparent —Jonathan Gash

The transparent pallor of her skin was luminous like a sea-shell in green shadow of the pine-trees —Elinor Wylie

Turned white as a tablecloth —Rudyard Kipling

Wan as the Polar snows —Stephen Vincent Benét

PARENTAL LOVE
See: PARENTHOOD

PARENTHOOD

A childless person is like dead —Talmud

The honor due to parents is like the honor due to God
—*The Holy Bible/Exodus*

Children, grown up, now, and moved away ... though they had once occupied her like a house, possessing her to the fingertips —Helen Hudson

The ideal mother, like the ideal marriage, is a fiction
—Milton R. Sapirstein

(Maybe I've gt this secret kid. Chances are I have, 'cause) I probably got a sperm count like the national deficit —Jane Wagner

Love them [daughters] as sheep are loved by the shepherd
—Phyllis McGinley

Marriage without children ... like a garden without fruit
—Phyllis Bottome
> Compare this with the German proverb below, beginning with Wedlock.

Mother's virtues ... like a graft of a late fruit on an early apple or pear tree, do not ripen in her children until very late in the season —Oliver Wendell Holmes, Sr.

A mother-in-law and a daughter-in-law in one house are like two cats in a bag —Yiddish proverb

A mother-in-law is like the dry rot; far easier to get into a house than to get out again —*Punch*

Not to bear children ... was like a hen that did not lay eggs or a cow that was sterile or a tree that never came into blossom.
—H. E. Bates

Raising a child is like reading a very long mystery story; you have to wait for a generation to see how it turns out —Anon

Realized [after giving birth] the responsibility of launching the little creature labelled by name not of its own choosing, like launching a battleship, only instead of turrets and decks and guns she had to do with the miraculous tissue of flesh and brain
—Vita Sackville-West

Sharper than a serpent's tooth it is to have a thankless child
—William Shakespeare
> This is King Lear's famous lament.

The umbilical cord stretches like a nine-hundred-and-some-mile leash
—Peter De Vries

Wedlock without children [is like] a world without sun
—German proverb

A woman ... her heart is like an empty nest, if she has not a child
—Henry Van Dyke

PASSION
See also: LOVE

As passionate as shredded wheat —Lawrence Gilman

The echoes of passion in the emptiness of a lonely heart is like the urmurings of wind and water in the silence of the wilderness
—François Rene de Chateaubriand

Genuine passion is like a mountain stream; it admits of no impediment; it cannot go backward; it must go forward
—Christian Nestell Bovee

Hot as a forty-balled tomcat —Rita Mae Brown

Instant passion is like instant coffee; it's cheap and it's quick and it makes you wish you had a percolator —Carla Lane, dialogue for heroine of English television sit-com "Solo," broadcast April 7, 1987

Our passions are in truth, like the phoenix. The old one burns away, the new one rises out of its ashes at once
—Johann Wolfgang von Goethe

Our passions are like convulsion fits, which, though they make us stronger for the time, leave us the weaker ever after
—Jonathan Swift

Our world passions are like so many lawyers wrangling and brawling at a bar —Owen Feltham
> The comparison continues as follows: "Discretion is the lord-keeper of man that sits as judge, and moderation their contestations."

The passionate are like men standing on their heads; they see all things the wrong way —Plato

Passionate men, like fleet hounds, are apt to over-run the scent
—H. G. Bohn's *Handbook of Proverbs*

Passion burned through her like a sunrise —Ellen Glasgow

Passion is like crime; it does not thrive on the established order
—Thomas Mann

Passion is like genius: a miracle —Romain Rolland

Passionless as a clam —Gertrude Atherton

Passion ... like a fire on the prairie that devours everything around it
—W. Somerset Maugham

Passion ... like other violent excitements ... throws up not only what is best, but what is worst and smallest, in men's characters
—Robert Louis Stevenson

Passions and desires, like the two twists of a rope, mutually mix one with the other, and twine inextricably round the heart —Richard E. Burton

Passions are like fire and water, good servants but bad masters —Alexander Pope

Passions are like fire, useful in a thousand ways and dangerous only in one, through their excess —François duc de La Rochefoucauld

Passions are like the trout in a pond: one devours the others until only one fat old trout is left —Otto von Bismarck

A passion that had moved into his body, like a stranger —Arthur Miller

Passion ... went over him like an ocean wave —Jean Stafford
At another point in her novel, *The Mountain Lion*, Stafford used the ocean waves comparison to describe the powerful smell of flowers.

PAST, THE
See also: HISTORY

Events ... had receded so swiftly into the near-forgotten past, like a movie seen years before and dimly remembered —Harvey Swados

The events [of the past] were astir in me, like the loosening phlegm in an attack of bronchitis, waiting to come up —L. P. Hartley

Felt himself sliding ... back into a bumpy past where old humiliations still waited to confront him like hills grown taller with the dust of years —Helen Hudson

Going back is like lifting elephants with your teeth —Paul West

He [Sherwood Anderson] carried his childhood like a hurt warm bird held to his middle-aged breast —Herbert Gold

Her past years washed away like so many ridges of sand at high tide —Peter Meinke

Inheritance, like grace, is something you deserve —Hollis Summers
The inheritance being compared to grace is family achievement.

It was like those years were just a ghost town she'd walked through and then decided to forget —Lee Smith

Kept coming back like a song —J. W. Rider

Like a ball of wool that kittens have got at ... all the disposed-of process of my past unravelled on the floor —Louis MacNeice

The man who has not anything to boast of but his illustrious ancestors is like a potato ... the only good belonging to him is under ground —Sir Thomas Overbury

Our past ... clings to us like strange mystical lint —W. P. Kinsella

The past ... always affected her eyes like salt water. It filled her head as if she had stayed underwater too long —Susan Fromberg Schaeffer

The past, as steep as stone, wider than water, like all land and ocean stretches —Archibald MacLeish

Past and future lie joined like a lunatic serpent —Robert Silverberg

The past ... held him like a pain —Wallace Stegner

The past is a bucket of ashes —Carl Sandburg

The past is like a funeral gone by —Edmond Gosse

The past lies like an Alp upon the mind —Delmore Schwartz

Past ... like a burnt book —Lynne Sharon Schwartz

The past, like an inspired rhapsodist, fills the theatre of everlasting generations with her harmony —Percy Bysshe Shelley

The past was drumming, like a train coming nearer and nearer, in her head —V. S. Pritchett

A record as long as your arm —George Garrett
　　The simile is the title of a short story.

Rolled up his past like a carpet —Anon

The sense of accumulated riches of time and tradition pressed past him like a crowd moving in rank after rank, through unending centuries —G. K. Chesterton

Sometimes I want to go back to everything I had, as in a museum —Yehuda Amichai

She wears her past like other women wear perfume —Anon
　　ambassador about Nora Astorga of Nicaragua, *New York Times Magazine*, September 28, 1986

True to form, the simile was pulled out of the article and used as the caption for the main illustration.

Sloughed off my past ... like a skin that shuns the light of day
—Natascha Wodin

The thoughts of my past life rise like the ghosts of an unquiet dream —Percy Bysshe Shelley

Treated his past gingerly as if it were unfriendly to him
—Jean Garrigue

Where she has been, she drags behind her, heavy and slurred as the speech of the deaf —Lisa Ress

Worrying about the past is like trying to make birth control pills retroactive —Joey Adams

PATRIOTISM
See: BELIEFS

PAUNCHINESS
See: FATNESS, STOMACH

PAUSE
See also: CAUTION

Cease like a dropped watch —Henry James

Everybody froze with expectation like an orchestra when the conductor raises his baton —George Garrett

Faltered, chewing on his words sourly and fatuously, like an old cow
—William Styron

(We) froze [at seeing an unknown, staring man] as rabbits do
—Rumer Godden

Halted, suddenly trembling, like a person armed to defend himself against wild animals, but on meeting one face to face is immediately turned to stone —Jean Stafford
See also: TREMBLING

Hesitated like a cat testing an opening with its whiskers
—William McIlvanney

A pause, barely noticeable, like a sight between one word and another —Kent Nelson

Shrieked to a trembling stop like a dog on a yanked leash
——George Garrett

(Sky and earth did one last slow turn and) wobbled to a halt like a
coin coming to rest on a bartop ——Loren D. Estleman

Slowed down gradually, like a merry-go-round after a ride
——Eudora Welty

Stalled like a whale ——John Malcolm Brinnin

Stopped short, like a radio cut off on a crescendo ——Frank Tuohy

Stopped speaking for a moment, like a man walking who comes to a
brink ——John Fowles

Stopped there cold, like a man raking piles of dead leaves in his
yard who has turned up a severed hand ——W. D. Snodgrass

Stops [suddenly] as though shot in the back ——Erich Maria Remarque

Stumbled to a halt like sheep in a chute ——Will Weaver

Suddenly there was a lull in my mind, like the détente after a
retreating thunderstorm ——L. P. Hartley

Talk died ... as if the voices in the room were on tape and someone
had pulled the plug ——Will Weaver
See also: SPEAKING, SILENCE

PEACEFULNESS

(There was) an ease of mind that was like being alone in a boat at
sea ——Wallace Stevens
This is the first line of *Prologues to What is Possible,* a poem
studded with additional similes.

Had a certain peace, like a stone that wouldn't roll any more
——Paul Horgan

Inner serenity is a lot like grace under pressure except that it's all
going on inside where people might not notice and give you
credit ——Judith Viorst

Like a stone thrown into the smooth water of a spring, I had
disturbed their peace ——Mihail Lermontov

Like the course of the heavenly bodies, harmony in national life is a
resultant of the struggle between contending forces
——Justice Louis D. Brandeis

See also: AGREEMENT/DISAGREEMENT

A peace deep as death —Daniela Gioseffi

Peaceful as a breast —Kenneth Patchen

Peaceful as a church —Raymond Chandler

Peaceful as a leaf with its superhuman silence —Daniela Gioseffi

Peaceful as Socrates —Anon

Peaceful ... like a child asleep —Phyllis Roberts

Peaceful, like being in a time machine —Lee Smith

Peaceful like New Year's —Carlos Baker

Peaceful like warm Summer nights —Amy Lowell

Peace, like a mask, hides everything —Edwin Arlington Robinson

Peace, like charity, begins at home —Franklin D. Roosevelt

Peace, like war, can succeed only where there is a will to enforce it, and where there is available power to enforce it —Franklin D. Roosevelt, October 21, 1944 speech to Foreign Policy Association

Peacemaking is hard ... hard almost as war —Daniel Berrigan
> The simile comprises the title and first line of a poem.

Peace was over her ... like a mantle —Madeleine L'Engle

Peace will, like a broken limb united, grow stronger for the breaking —William Shakespeare

[A vacation] quiet and pleasant and womblike as a slow bath in a tub of warm water —Harvey Swados

Restful as a Rembrandt background —George Ade

Rest like lizards on rocks —Etheridge Knight

(Maybe it will emerge,) serene and smiling, like Daniel from the lion's den —Floyd K. Haskell, on tax reform, *New York Times*/Op-Ed, January 17, 1986

Serene as a snowman's smile —Julie Hayden

Serene as jade buddhas —Marge Piercy

Soothing ... as waves along a shore —John Gardner

Still and quiet, like a good conscience —Frank Swinnerton

Tranquility pushed their anxieties away, like a man finding a place for himself on a crowded bench —W. Somerset Maugham

Tranquilizing murmur [of voice] like the music of a dream —Elinor Wylie

Tranquilly like the rise and fall of sand dunes —Yukio Mishima

PENNANTS
See: OBJECTS, MISCELLANEOUS

PEOPLE, INTERACTION
See: CROWDS, RELATIONSHIPS

All her life she had looked for someone who would ... settle her in the proper place like a cushion on a couch —Helen Hudson

[Different types of people] all mixed up like vegetables in soup —Flannery O'Connor

All the hurtful ugly things that happened between us got somehow wrapped around the sweetness like a hard rind around a delicate rare fruit. Like a flower garden completely surrounded with tangles of barbed wire —Harryette Mullen

(Harris) always managed to make him feel ... like the character in the commercial who uses the wrong kind of deodorant soap —Andrew Kaplan

Avoid them like piranhas —Richard Ford
See also: ELUSIVENESS

Bitching patiently at each other like a couple married much too long —James Crumley
> The people doing the bitching in Crumley's novel, *The Wrong Case*, are two farmers in a bar.

Dealing with Valentine was like dealing with a king —Saul Bellow

Distance between them ... like the Persian Gulf —Robert Anderson

Faced each other like scruffy bookends —Jonathan Gash

Groups gathered a moment like flies —Bin Ramke

Guided him by one elbow [to a seat] like a tugboat turning a tanker
—Peter Benchley

Hoisted her up like a parcel —Henri-Pierre Roche

It was as if he could read my mind like an old tale he had learned
by heart —George Garrett

I want to lean into her [a daughter into her mother] the way wheat
leans into wind —Louise Erdrich

Lay side by side, like some old bronze Crusader and his lady on a
sarcophagus in the crypt of some ancient church
—MacDonald Harris

(Take her by the lily white hand and) lead her like a pigeon
—Anon American dance ballad, "Weevily Heart."
The ballad dates to the late eighteenth/early nineteenth
century.

Leaned on [another person] ... like a wounded man —George Garrett

Like the sun, his presence shone on her —Marge Piercy

Live together like brothers and do business like strangers —Arab
proverb

Loneliness sifted between us, like falling snow —Judith Rascoe

Our heart-strings were, like warp and woof in some firm fabric,
woven in and out —Edna St. Vincent Millay

People, like sheep, tend to follow a leader—occasionally in the right
direction —Alexander Chase

We seemed strangers [a group of three people sitting in room]
waiting in a station to take a train to another city
—Henry Van Dyke

People sat huddled together [on street benches] like dark grapes
clustered on a stalk —W. Somerset Maugham

Read him like a label on a beer can —William H. Hallhan

[Two men who don't like each other] recoiling from one another like
reversed magnets —Wyatt Blassingame

Responded to each other nervously, like a concord of music
—Lawrence Durrell

Sat ... like a pair of carefully-folded kid-gloves, bound up in each other —Charles Dickens

She could feel the distance between them like a patch of fog —Lynne Sharon Schwartz

She reads my silence like a page —Robert Campbell

Sitting like strangers thrown together by accident —Ross Macdonald

Something in her face spilled over me like light through a swinging door —Sue Grafton

Students, their faces like stone walls around him [a college professor] —Helen Hudson

[Many different kinds of people] swarmed around him like startled fish —Derek Lambert

Tangled together like badly cast fish lines —Katherine Anne Porter

They [a man and woman with child between them] lay like two slices of wheat bread with a peanut-butter center —Will Weaver

They needed each other's assistance, like a company, who, crossing a mountain stream, are compelled to cling close together, lest the current should be too powerful for any who are not thus supported —Sir Walter Scott

They were ... like two people holding on to the opposite ends of a string, each anxious to let go, or at least soon, without offending the other, yet each reluctant to drop the curling, lapsing bond between them —Hortense Calisher

Took me about like a roast [to make introductions] —Mark Helprin
This spotlights the importance of using a simile within an appropriate context. The character being taken about "like a roast" in Helprin's story, *Tamar,* is the last arrival at a dinner party. If someone were being introduced in a business setting, being passed around "Like a special report or a memo" might better suit the situation.

Touched him on the breast as though his finger were the fine point of a small sword —Charles Dickens

Treated him like crows treat a scarecrow: they ignored him and avoided him —William H. Hallhan
See also: REJECTION

Wanted me to share her pain like an orgasm, like lovers in poems who slit their wrists together —Max Apple

Watching each other like two cats; and then, as cats do, turn away again, indifferently, as if whatever was at stake between them had somehow faded out —L. P. Hartley

(The Heindricks) were making me feel like a specimen in a jar —Jonathan Gash
See also: DISCOMFORT

We sat half-turned toward one another like the arms of a parenthesis —Cornell Woolrich

You play my heart like a concertina —Harvey Fierstein

PERCEPTIVENESS
See: ALERTNESS

PERMANENCE
See: CONTINUITY

PERPLEXITY
See: BEWILDERMENT

PERSISTENCE
See: PURPOSEFULNESS

PERSONAL TRAITS
See: DULLNESS

PERSONALITY PROFILES

Elegant and remote ... like a statue carved in melancholy thought —Sylvia Berkman

A fascinating but sometimes uneasy presence ... as if he goes around with a black cloud over his head —Daniel Philips about fellow violinist Gidoa Kremer, *New York Times*, May 10, 1987

Handsome, proud, and ingrown, "like a toe-nail" —James Baldwin
The simile is an anonymous descriptions of Baldwin's father quoted in his essay, *Notes of a Native Son*.

He [Oliver Wendell Holmes] is a powerful battery, formed like a planting machine to gouge a deep self-beneficial groove through life —William James, letter to his brother Henry, July 5, 1876

He [Col. Gadhafi of Libya] is like a Bedouin in a sandstorm ... He [the Bedouin] bends over until it passes and then stands up strong as ever —Abdel Halim Abu Ghazala, defense minister of Egypt, *Wall Street Journal*, September 9, 1986

He [John McEnroe] is still more like a New York cab driver, with an opinion about everything —Peter Alfano, *New York Times*/Sports of the Times, August 6, 1986
> The simile is part of Alfano's speculation about the likelihood that McEnroe's will become a "laid-back Californian."

He [waiter upon being tipped and smiled at] looked as if he had shaken hands with God —Raymond Chandler

He looked as the dead do in dreams —Mavis Gallant

He looked businesslike, efficient, crew-cut and handsome, like a Midwestern professor just after giving a lecture on Shaw or Pinero —Harvey Swados

He looked hurried, as if he were catching a train or a boat —John Cheever

He looked like a cowboy in a cigarette ad —John D. MacDonald
> Preceding this from MacDonald's novel, *Free Fall in Crimson*, is this description: "A lean man with a deeply grooved face, an outdoor squint."

He [man in yellow suit, pinkish white shirt and greenish tie] looked like a friendly hound dog with light mange —Flannery O'Connor

He looked like a man secretly gnawed by a scarcely endurable pain —Margaret Mitchell

He looked like a man who had lost a penny and found a thousand pounds —Jimmy Sangster

He [Gordon Cooper, astronaut] looked like a man who played on a semi-pro football team because he wasn't big enough for the major leagues, and worked in a gas station the middle of the week —Norman Mailer

He looked like a mean mouse —Truman Capote

He looked like a piece of plot, standing there. An extra character, about to return to his mislaid car and his own life —Margaret Drabble

He looked like someone who had been long buried and then dug up again —W. Somerset Maugham

He somewhat resembled an owl, an angry, aging bird, recently balked of a field-mouse and looking about for another small animal to devour —Anthony Powell

He was a bundle of contradictions that clashed like cymbals —Irvin S. Cobb

He was a man around whom middle-age sat like a podium —William McIlvanney

He was like a monk who'd created his own order —James Mills
> Mills uses the comparison in *The Underground Empire* to describe a man who is difficult to work for.

His fifty-two years sat upon him like a finish which made youth appear crude —Edith Wharton

Horatio looked handsomely miserable, like Hamlet slipping on a piece of orange-peel —Charles Dickens

I am like a king of rainy country, wealthy but helpless, young and ripe with death —Charles Baudelaire

I am like a martini. The gin part is New York, the vermouth, Washington, and I'm not talking about the olive —Morton B. Zuckerman at party to celebrate new Washington restaurant attended by mostly Washingtonians and some New Yorkers, *New York Times* July 31, 1986

I look like a discouraged beetle battered by the rains of the Spring night —Colette

Innocent as milk and a build like a chocolate eclair —William Barry Furlon on Jack Nicklaus

It is as if he were in an incubator, breathing his own air —Mikhail Baryshnikov, about Fred Astaire, *Life* interview, January, 1980

Like people from Balzac, with their own individual characters and tastes —Janet Flanner
> Flanner's simile is from a letter to her friend Natalia Danesi Murray about some enjoyable people with whom she spent a weekend.

Like successful nuns, they [two older single women] had a slightly married air —Elizabeth Bowen

Like the [neglected] building ... she seemed to be a victim of overuse and neglect —Margaret Millar

Like the hypochondriac who discovers a tumor under his arm with a surge of fatalistic joy, he has had his worst suspicions confirmed —T. Coraghessan Boyle

(You are a bit ...) like the stars; happily incomprehensible, incapable of producing anxiety —Giuseppe di Lampedusa

Looked as if she had walked straight out of the ark —Sydney Smith

Looked as wholesome, stiff and unshakable as a bowl of tapioca —Rex Reed
> The stiff and unshakable man Reed describes is Robert Redford.

Looked ... firm and impassable as a good privet hedge —Reynolds Price

Looked, if not like a duke, at least like an actor of the old school who specialized in dukes' parts —W. Somerset Maugham

Looked like a beautiful and highly shockable nun —David Niven
> Niven used this simile to introduce his story about actress Mary Astor's sexual life which, at the time would indeed have shocked a nun.

(Dorothy Parker) looked like a bird at the mercy of every beast with teeth —Norman Mailer

Looked like a choirboy gone to seed —Pat Conroy

Looked like a man who had flown three and a half thousand miles with a hot coal in his mouth —Frank Ross

Looked like a runaway from a whiskey bottle —Rosa Guy

Looked like Lazarus risen from the dead —Mavis Gallant
> A slight variation seen in Ross Macdonald's *The Underground Man:* "He looked like Lazarus coming out of the tomb."

Looks like a demented stallion sniffling out a mare in estrus —T. Coraghessan Boyle

(Now he wears black horn-rims, and having lost weight and hair,) looks like an overworked insurance agent —Richard Ford

In his novel, *The Sportswriter*, Ford profiles a character who has changed from looking "Like a grinning tractor-trailer in a plastic helmet" in his ball-playing days, to the above description.

Looks middle-aged and respectable like someone's favorite uncle
—William Styron

Look strangely weary and solitary ... like a prospector preparing a meal in the midst of the wilderness —Christopher Isherwood

A man like an unmade bed —Angela Carter

A man of shifting contrasts, like watermarks on a desert horizon
—Rex Reed
The man of shifting contrasts is playwright Tennessee Williams.

Maturity, disappointment, decline of expectations had settled upon Palmer ... like the wrinkles caused by smiling
—Elizabeth Hardwick

A mind like a steel mousetrap and a heart like a twelve-minute egg
—Jay McInerney

Proceeded through life absented-mindedly, meditatively, as if considering some complex mathematical puzzle —Anne Tyler

She looked like a woman capable of plotting a President up from his cradle —James Patterson

She looks like a flower but she's as tough as a weed
—Robert Campbell

She made Narcissus look like Mother Teresa —Peter Benchley

She was like a beautiful flower which though its petals had not yet begun to drop, was already faded and without fragrance
—Leo Tolstoy

She [dimpled woman with conventional social responses] was like a musical box charged with popular airs —Edith Wharton

Spongy and spoiled like a child king —Wilfrid Sheed

Striped with good and evil like a giraffe —Delmore Schwartz

PHYSICAL APPEARANCE
See also: ATTRACTIVENESS, FATNESS, UNATTRACTIVENESS

As innocent of makeup as an apple he might have polished on his sleeve —John Yount

As straight as a stick and looked as brittle —V. S. Pritchett

Awful [looking] ... like an oil filter that should have been changed five thousand miles ago —Saul Bellow

Began to look like the last solitary frost-touched rose on a November bush —Honoré de Balzac

Looked like a sparrow fallen from its nest —Dominique Lapierre

Belly as bright ivory overlaid with sapphires ... legs are as pillars of marble —*The Holy Bible/Song of Solomon*

(He was) bowed and gnarled like an old tree
—W. Somerset Maugham

Chorus-line figure, but with a face like a racehorse —Richard Ford

Dry and bony, like a handsome tree withered by blight
—Louis Bromfield

Fragile-looking yet surprisingly voluptuous, she resembled a scaled-down ancient love goddess, the gilded plastic replica sold at museum shops —T. Gertler

Gnarled as a cyprus —Mary Lee Settle

Had a face like a barn owl. The heavy rolls of fat were covered with thick white powder and gave the appearance of a snow-covered mountain landscape. Her black eyes were like deep-set holes and she stared at Kern as though she might fly at him any moment with her claws —Erich Maria Remarque
> An example of a colorful portrait created with a string of similes, from Remarque's novel, *Flotsam*.

Had the aging body of a poet and the eyes of a starving panther
—Ellery Queen

Had the rough, blowsy and somewhat old-fashioned look of a whore of the Renoir period —Thomas Wolfe

Had the threadbare appearance of a worn-out litigant
—Sir Walter Scott

He'd been put together with care, his brown head and bullfighter's figure had an exactness, a perfection like an apple, an orange, something nature has made just right —Truman Capote

He had smooth skin and a thin moustache which made him look like the toy groom on a wedding cake —Andrew Kaplan

He looked like a goat. He had little raisin eyes and a string beard —Flannery O'Connor

(Up till then I'd assumed that "Gross" was the man's name, but it was his description.) He looked like something that had finally come up out of its cave because it has eaten the last phosphorescent little fish in the cold pool at the bottom of the cavern. He looked like something that better keep moving because if it stood still someone would drag it out back and bury it. He looked like a big white sponge with various diseases at work on the inside. He looked like something that couldn't get you if you held a crucifix up in front of you. He looked like the big fat soft white something you might find under a tomato plant leaf on a rainy day with a chill in the air —Donald E. Westlake

> A nice bit of comparative excess, something to be indulged in sparingly, which may account for the fact that Westlake's novel, *The Fugitive Pigeon,* contains few other similes.

He [Marvin Hamlish] looks at certain angles, like a cheeseburger with all the ingredients oozing awkwardly out of the bun —Rex Reed

Her anxious brown eyes and full, slightly drooping cheeks gave her the look of a worried hamster —Sheila Radley

Her face and hands were as white as though she had been drowned in a barrel of vinegar —O. Henry

Her great buttocks rolled like the swell on a heavy winter sea —Miles Gibson

He was handsome, in a brooding, archaic way, like a face from early Asiatic temple sculpture —Christopher Isherwood

He was like a piece of cinnamon bark, brown and thin and curled in on himself —David Brierley

He was ruddy as a ranch hand, and dressed like one —Joyce Reiser Kornblatt

His face and body had an evil swollen look as if they had grown stout on rotten meat —Ross Macdonald

His face and head had an unfinished look, like a sculpture an artist might have left under a damp cloth until he had time to work on it again —Dorothy Francis

(The guy didn't seem to have any neck at all.) His head rested on his shoulders like a bowling ball on a shelf —Jonathan Valin

(She is tall), homely as Lincoln —Alice McDermott

A huge ruin of a woman with a face like a broken statue —Edith Wharton

In appearance she was not unlike a sea cow —Larry McMurtry

A little gnarled fellow like the bleached root of a tree —Zane Grey

Look awful, all trembling and green about the gills, like a frog with shell shock —A. Alvarez

Looked and moved like an elderly gentleman with bowel problems —T. Coraghessan Boyle

[Old people] looked dry as a locust shell stuck on a pear tree —Anthony E. Stockanes

Looked like a pale spectre beneath the moon —Émile Zola

Looked like a bat ... had the ears and the snout and the gray pinched mouse-face, the hunched bony shoulders that were like folded wings —Paul Theroux

Looked like a man recuperating from a coronary or just about to have one —Jonathan Kellerman

Looked like a man who has stepped on the business end of a rake and given himself a good one, whack between the eyes —Stephen King

Looked like an animated skeleton —Jimmy Sangster

Looked like a pearl laid against black velvet —O. Henry

Looked like a seedy angel —William McIlvanney

Looking like a drooping and distracted hen —Patrick White

[Paul Newman in *The Color of Money*] looking like an only slightly worn Greek statue —Julie Salamon, *Wall Street Journal*, October 16, 1986

Look ... like a fine healthy apple —Katherine Anne Porter

Look like someone who's spent the night in a bus station —Anon

Looks as if when you touch her she'd crackle like cellophane
    —Harryette Mullen
    See also: FRAGILITY

Looks like a garage sale waiting for a place to happen
    —George V. Higgins

Looks like the ssie of a barn with the doors open
    —Ben Ames Williams

Managing with his mussed fair hair and mustache to look like a
    shopworn model for a cigarette advertisement —Derek Lambert

A man like a scarecrow, old and stormbeaten, with stiff, square, high
    shoulders, as if they were held up by a broomstick stuck through
    his sleeves —Vicki Baum

Men deteriorate without razors and clean shirts ... like potted plants
    that go to weed unless they are tended daily —Beryl Markham
        Markham makes this observation in her autobiography,
        West With the Night, when she lands her plane and is met
        by two unshaven hunters, adding this simile about one of
        them (Baron Von Blixen): "Blix, looking like an unkempt
        bear ... "

(Looks worse every time I see her, so) old and dried out, like a
    worn shoe —Jan Kubicki

Pink and glazed as a marzipan pig —Truman Capote about Henri
    Soule

A pinprick of a scarlet pimple glowed like blood against the very
    pale skin on the side of her nose. Her freshly washed gray hair
    was slightly askew, and she looked ... like that demented figure
    in the painting of Pickett's charge at Gettysburg —Joseph Heller

Plump and sweet as a candied yam —Marge Piercy

Potbellied, and bearded with extra chins like a middle-aged high
    school gym coach —Jonathan Valin

A profile and neck like a pharaoh's erotic dream
    —Loren D. Estleman

Raindrops sat on his white skin like sweat —Sue Miller

A regular old jelly ... sliding around like aspic on a hot plate
    —Joyce Cary

She is chipped like an old bit of china; she is frayed like a garment of last year's wearing. She is soft, crinkled like a fading rose
—Amy Lowell

She [a woman of sixty] looked like a lovely little winter apple
—Mary Lee Settle

She looked like a tree trunk ... her big gnarled hands seemed to protrude from her like branches —Marguerite Yourcenar

She looked, with her red-cherry cheeks and wide semicircle of smile, like something that might have briskly swung out of a weather-house predicting sunshine —Peter Kemp

She reminded him, in her limp dust-colored garments, of last year's moth shaken out of the curtains of an empty room
—Edith Wharton

She was gray as a wick and as thin —Patricia Hampl

She was heavy but not unattractive, like a German grandma
—Peter Meinke

She was in her mid-thirties ... faded, but still fruity, like a pear just beginning to go soft —Derek Lambert

She was like a fat little partridge with a mono-bosom
—Kate Wilhelm

She [mother dancing before narrator] was like a pretty kite that floated above my head —Maya Angelou

She was tall like a lily, carried herself like a queen ... was dressed like a rose —Hugh Walpole

A short woman, shaped nearly like a funeral urn
—Flannery O'Connor

Slender and tall as the great Eiffel Tower —W. H. Auden

Small, chinless and like an emasculated Eton boy —Dylan Thomas
The simile is a self portrait.

A smallish man who always looked dusty, as if he had been born and lived all his life in attics and store rooms —William Faulkner

Small, runty and rooty, she looks like a young edition of an old, gnarled tree —Laurie Colwin

Tall and flat like a paper doll —Elizabeth Bishop

Tan and wrinkled all over as if had been dipped and stained in
walnut juice —George Garrett

They [an old couple] were brown and shriveled, and like two little
walking peanuts —Carson McCullers

Thin and old-looking ... as if the frame she was strung on had
collapsed and the stuffing had shifted. Like a badly stuffed toy
after a month in the nursery —Josephine Tey

A thin man with a collarbone like a wire coathanger
—Penelope Gilliatt

Thin, white-whiskered ... like a consumptive Santa Claus
—Dashiell Hammett

With his longish head he looked like an Egyptian king
—Iris Murdoch

With his small dark eyes and jowly cheeks he looked like an
intelligent bulldog —Andrew Kaplan

PHYSICAL FEELINGS

The cold struck him like a blow from a fist —Bernard Malamud

Deep down within her she felt as though a fish moved its tail
—Sigrid Undset
> This lyrical simile describes the first stirrings of life in a
> pregnant woman.

Disembodied feeling, like going under an anaesthetic —Gavin Lyall

Feeling ... dizzy like someone who's been bound fast and is suddenly
free —Cornell Woolrich

(John sat there open-mouthed,) feeling the nerves of his body twitter
like so many sparrows perched upon his spinal column
—F. Scott Fitzgerald

(I am beginning to live a little, and) feel less like a sick oyster at
low tide —Louisa May Alcott

Feel my ribs and guts flattening together like leaves in a book
—Dashiell Hammett

Feels the arch of his eyebrows like drying paste on his forehead
—John Updike

Felt a chill like cold water at the roots of my hair
—Dorothy Canfield Fisher

Felt a pleasurable languor running through every limb as though all the blood in his body had turned to warm milk —Joseph Conrad

Felt a sudden dizziness, as though, from a mad flight through the couds and darkness, he had dropped to safety again, and the fall had stunned him —Edith Wharton

Felt giddy, as if I had come to the bottom of a staircase and found one more step than my feet expected —Mary Gordon

Felt his body ... settling down like furniture in a house at the end of a hot day —Frank Tuohy

Felt like a half-digested meal eaten in a greasy-spoon joint
—Raymond Chandler

Felt like a tree that had been struck by lightning —Richard Lourie

Felt like a Whoopee cushion sat on by a fat person —Peter Benchley

Felt like I'd eaten a pound of cold buttered popcorn and washed it down with bulk saccharin —Sue Grafton

A giddy feeling in his stomach, as though he were on a swing in the middle of its downward arc —John Yount

The great cold struck him like an icy douche —Émile Zola

The ground was shifting under his feet like the trick floors at sideshows —Shirley Ann Grau

Head [of main character] clears like a hazy morning giving way to noon —T. Coraghessan Boyle

Head feels like the inside of a soggy sandwich —François Camoin

His stomach was spinning like a stunting airplane over a cow pasture
—Elizabeth Spencer

Joints creak like a stiff shirt —Erich Maria Remarque

Joints ... stiff as dry sticks —Gloria Norris

Legs feel stiff, as if they are all bone —Gary Gildner

Legs felt like two old rusted rain gutters —Flannery O'Connor

Leg went to sleep ... it feels like a bag of nails —Thomas Williams

(Could feel all her) muscles shrinking like severed vines in the sun
—William Faulkner

My belly and behind were heavy as cold iron —Maya Angelou
See also: HEAVINESS

My face was sticky all over, like it wanted to sweat but it couldn't
—Lee Smith

My throat was as dry as ginned cotton —Borden Deal
See also: DRYNESS

Put my head between my legs and feel the blood rush around like a
herd of buffaloes trapped at the edge of a cliff —Tama Janowitz

Savoring the joy of rest as if she had twenty years' accumulation of
weariness to work off —Colette

Shivering fits, like rows of cold wet needles up and down my spine
—James Stern
See also: TREMBLING

My throat steams like a sewer —Marge Piercy

Stiff all over and felt like a sack of wet, chilly sand —Denis Johnson

The stillness soaked into her like a fine chill rain —Margaret Mitchell

Warmth ran through Bazely's body like a current of fire
—Phyllis Bottome

A wonderful feeling [of relief from pain after an injection] ... flowed
through him like some wonderful, gently warmed milk
—Heinrich Böll

PHYSICIANS
See: DOCTORS

PINK
See also: CHEEKS, FACIAL COLOR

Pink and sweet as a magnolia —Diane Ackerman

Pink as a new baby —George Garrett

Pink as an infant's skin —Charles Wright

(Flesh-coloured stockings seemed) pink as blush roses —Rebecca West

Pink

(Rosebuds) pink as girls' first lipsticks —Marge Piercy

(Belly) pink as strawberry ice cream —Marge Piercy

(Face) pink as wild roses —W. P. Kinsella

Pity

PITY

As fire drives out fire, so pity [drives out] pity
    —William Shakespeare

Collected sympathy like a street singer catching coins in a hat
    —Josephine Tey

Felt a positive gush of pity ... like the rising of a warm fountain
    —Rebecca West

Felt the dull old nagging pull of other people's trouble, like a
    toothache you can't leave alone —Ross Macdonald

Pity ... green as grain —E. E. Cummings

Ready sympathy that can be tapped like a vat
    —Sharon Sheehe Stark

Wanting pity like a cat wants the mange —John Farris

Wiped the pity away like cold sweat —James Crumley

Places

PLACES
See also: CITY/STREETSCAPES

(Some cities never sleep ...) Cincinnati sleeps each night like it's
    drugged —Jonathan Valin
        Cincinnati may sleep each night yet Valin manages to
        infuse plenty of action into his Cincinnati-based mystery
        novels.

Cities, like cats, will reveal themselves at night —Rupert Brooke

The city [San Francisco] acted in wartime [WWII] like an intelligent
    woman under siege. She gave what she couldn't with safety
    withhold, and secured those things which lay in her reach
    —Maya Angelou

The city [New York] is like poetry; it compresses all life, all races
    and breeds, into a small island and adds music and the
    accompaniment of internal engines —E. B. White

444

The city spawned ugliness like a predatory insect spewing out blood-hungry larva —David Niven

> Niven's simile from his autobiography *The Moon's a Balloon could probably be applied to any high-pressure place or industry.*

[London during the day] coated with crawling life, as a blossom with blight —Jerome K. Jerome

Coming to New York from the muted mistiness of London ... is like traveling from a monochrome antique shop to a Technicolor bazaar —Kenneth Tynan

Compared to the city, the country looks like the world without its clothes on —Douglas Jerrold

Comparing the Brooklyn that I know with Manhattan is like comparing a comfortable and complacent duenna to her more brilliant and neurotic sister —Carson McCullers

Dallas, a city that treated conspicuous consumption like an art form —Peter Applebome, *New York Times*, April 6, 1986

The danger and noise make it [New York or Chicago to a country person] seem like a permanent earthquake —William James

Detroit, city of lost industrial dreams, floats around us like a mirage of some sane and glaciated life —Richard Ford

Detroit lay across the river, a mile away, like a huge pincushion stuck full of lights —Eric Linklater

Each thought, each day, each life lies here [in Moscow] as on a laboratory table —Walter Benjamin

Fifth Avenue [at Christmas] shone like an enormous blue sugarplum revolving in a tutti-frutti rain of light —Hortense Calisher

> See also: GLITTER AND GLOSS

The gray cloud of Denver's smog humped over the horizon like a whale's back —James Crumley

Hollywood without Spiegel is like Tahiti without Gauguin —Billy Wilder

> Wilder's simile was coined in 1986 when Aaron Spiegel died.

Ice hard as iron bands bound the streets of New York —Robert S. Silverberg

I'm glad to be here in Pittsburgh because I feel a sense of kinship with the Pittsburgh Pirates. Like my candidacy, they were not given much chance in the spring
—John F. Kennedy, on the campaign trail

In great cities men are like a lot of stones thrown together in a bag; their jagged corners rubbed off till in the end they are smooth as marbles —W. Somerset Maugham

Ireland is something like the bottom of an aquarium, with little people in crannies like prawns —D. H. Lawrence

Italy is so tender, like cooked macaroni, yards and yards of soft tenderness, ravelled round everything —D. H. Lawrence

Japan offers as much novelty perhaps as an excursion to another planet —Isabella Bird

Leaving Los Angeles is like giving up heroin —David Puttnam

Life in Russia is like life at an English public school but with politics taking the place of sex —Isaiah Berlin

Like a resplendent chandelier, Paris in winter is made up of many parts —W. A. Poers

Like many picturesque neighborhoods, it has a chilling uniformity of character, as if the householders propped sternly in their lawn chairs or gazing out from the black space of a porch have been chosen and supplied to ornament their homes —Jonathan Valin

Living in England, provincial England, must be like being married to a stupid, but exquisitely beautiful wife —Margaret Halsey

(Looking down the wing I could see) the buildings of Manhattan, as tidy and neatly defined as an architect's model
—Madison Smart Bell

Moscow ... a city landscape wanting neon and city life, as if square miles of squat buildings had been abandoned at the first November snows —George Feifer

Most great cities (trail their own death around with them and) sleep, like John Donne, with one foot in the coffin —Jonathan Valin

New York ... a haven as cosy as toast, cool as an icebox and safe as skyscrapers —Dylan Thomas

New York fit him [Nolan Ryan, pitcher for the Astros, formerly the Mets] like a cheap suit
—Paul Daugherty, *Newsday*, October 9, 1986

New York ... looked like a pagan banner planted on a Christian rampart —Douglas Reed

New York's like a disco, but without the music —Elaine Stritch

Omaha is a little like Newark, without Newark's glamour
—Joan Rivers

Oaxaca sparkled like a matrix of platinum sequins laid over velvet
—Richard Ford

Paris was ... all little and bright and far away like a picture seen through the wrong end of a field glass —John Dos Passos

PLAINNESS
See: SIMPLICITY

PLANNING
See: PURPOSEFULNESS

PLEASURE
See also: GAIETY

As much fun as a newborn kitten —Mary Hood

As rewarding as a message from Billy Graham
—Anon blurb about a romantic novel

A decided pleasure ... as sweet as returning soldiers sometimes admit the act of killing to be —John Updike
> The simile from Updike's novel, *Roger's Version*, refers to the pleasure of affronting public opinion.

Enjoyed [the difficulties of a job] ... as a good fighter loves a battle
—Frank Swinnerton

Fun is like life insurance, the older you get the more it costs
—Abe Martin
> Frank McKinney Hubbard, also known as Kin Hubbard and Abe Martin, often wrote in country dialect. In the above simile, for example, he used 'git' instead of 'get.'

Pleasure

It's (talking on the telephone) as good as a warm bath and a glass of milk —Enid Nemy, quoting Hazel Duke's telephone habits, *New York Times*/ New Yorkers, August 24, 1986

It was marvelous, like seeing a capsized boat right itself, and knowing no serious damage had been done —John Fowles

Luxuriating like a fucked-out lion —John Updike

Pleased as a well tipped waiter —Anon

Pleased, like a young housewife going through her house and finding everything in good order —Isak Dinesen

Pleasure came like a lash —Julio Cortzar

Pleasure is frail like a dewdrop, while it laughs it dies —Sir Rabindranath Tagore

Pleasure is like a massive dose of vitamins —Anon

Pleasures are like poppies spread —Robert Burns

Pleasures are more beneficial than duties, because, like the quality of mercy, they are not strained, and they are twice blest —Robert Louis Stevenson

Pleasures are much like mushrooms. The right kind are fine, but you have to be on the lookout for the toadstools —*Boston Transcript*, May 21, 1921

Relish ... like a robin-redbreast —William Shakespeare

(She was as) satisfying as the morning breeze —Frank Swinnerton

Savor experience as naturally as he accepts the prismatic blessing of sunshine glancing through the glass he holds —Francis X. Clines, *New York Times*, October 19, 1986
    Clines' subject is television writer John Mortimer.

Snarl at pleasure like a stoic —Lord Chesterfield

Snatches a crumb of pleasure like a dog snapping up a bone amid a host of dangers —Honoré de Balzac

PLENTY
See: ABUNDANCE

448

POETS/POETRY
See also: WRITERS/WRITING

All good verses are like impromptus made at leisure —Joseph Joubert

Composed poetry ... like a dancer working at the barre, continually exercising the power of imagining, like a muscle that demanded flexing and stretching —Arthur A. Cohen

Explaining how you write poetry ... it's like going round explaining how you sleep with your wife —Phillip Larkin

He [the poet] approaches lucid ground warily, like a mariner who is determined not to scrape his bottom on anything solid. A poet's pleasure is to withhold a little of his meaning, to intensify by mystification —E. B. White

Like science, poetry must fix its thought in thing and symbol —Dilys Laing

Like a piece of ice on a hot stove the poem must ride on its own melting —Robert Frost

Like marijuana smoke are poet's verses —Jaroslav Seifert

Poems are like people ... there are not many authentic ones around —Robert Graves

The poet is like the prince of the clouds who rides the tempest ... exiled on the ground, amidst boos and insults, his giant's wings prevent his walking —Charles Baudelaire

Poetry is like light —Delmore Schwartz

Poetry is like painting; one piece takes your fancy if you stand close to it, another if you keep at some distance —Horace

Poetry ... is like spray blown by some wind from a heaving sea, or like sparks blown from a smouldering fire: a cry which the violence of circumstances wrings from some poor fellow —George Santayana

Poets ... are conductors of the senses of men, as teachers and preachers are the insulators —Karl Shapiro

> The simile is taken from a prose poem entitled *As You Say (not without sadness), Poets Don't See They Feel*. It contains another simile which sheds light on the poet as one who strips away insulation: "He pulls at the seams [of insulation] like a boy whose trousers are cutting him in half."

449

Poets/Poetry

Poets are like baseball pitchers. Both have their moments. The intervals are the tough things —Robert Frost

Publishing a volume of verse is like dropping a rose petal down the Grand Canyon and waiting for the echo —Don Marquis, *The Sun Dial*, 1878

Rhymes you as fast as a sailor will swear —Babette Deutsch
The simile is from a poem honoring John Skelton.

They [poets] are honored and ignored like famous dead Presidents —Delmore Schwartz

To try to read a poem with the eyes of the first reader who read it is like trying to see a landscape without the atmosphere that clothes it —W. Somerset Maugham

To write a lyric is like having a fit, you can't have one when you wish you could ... and you can't help having it when it comes itself —Oliver Wendell Holmes, Sr.

Writing free verse is like playing tennis with the net down —Robert Frost

Ponds and Streams

PONDS AND STREAMS

The black lake was shimmering like ink —Richard Russo

Light spread across the river like an oil spill —Jay Parini

Pond ... covered with rain like sequins or crinkled up with wind like a watered silk —Joyce Cary

River ... like a sheet of polished metal —Boris Pasternak

The river in evening like a dirty window —Delmore Schwartz

The river looked like an eye which for some reason or other was growing darker and darker as happens in love at the onset of ecstasy —Bertold Brecht

The river now all crinkled like tinfoil —Delmore Schwartz

The river raged by like a forest fire —Edward Hoagland

A river ran there as clear as the air itself, and the fish in it were like gold and silver —Hans Christian Anderson

The river ... smelled like a packing house for fish, but it looked like the melted, dark eyes of a million girls —Hortense Calisher

450

The river was brown and bubbly ... like cake icing —Lee Smith

The stream was like a silver magnet that pulled them across the
prairie —Dorothy Francis

POPULARITY

Favor, like disgrace, brings trouble with it —Lao Tzu

Hot as a pistol —Rex Reed
A variant to this is to be "Hot as a two dollar pistol."

(Nothing is as ...) popular as goodness —Michel de Montaigne

She looked as if her phone had been ringing continually ever since
she had reached puberty —J. D. Salinger
See also: PERSONALITY PROFILES

POSSIBILITY
See: OPPORTUNITY

POSTURE
See also: STRAIGHTNESS

Arched like a cavalry horse getting a whiff of the battlefield
—Katherine Anne Porter

A back like a marine drill instructor's ... straight as a rifle shot
—Loren D. Estleman

Bolt upright like drawn bayonets —Aharon Megged

Erect as a candle —Isak Dinesen
Dinesen used this simile in a short story, *The de Cats
Family*. Because many a simile is hard to establish as one
writer's creative invention, it should come as no surprise
that it also appeared in Ignazio Silone's novel, *The Secret of
Luca*.

Erect as a cavalry officer —Francine du Plessis Gray

Erect as a Grecian pillar —Anon

Held his shoulders back as though they were braced, and he sucked
in his stomach like a soldier —John Steinbeck

Her back is curved like a shell —Louise Erdrich

Her entire posture seemed to have bunched up like a fist
—Robert B. Parker

Her spine droops like a dying daisy —Ira Wood

Huddled up like a pale misshapen piece of pastry —Hugh Walpole

Hunched his shoulders like a fighter tensing for a blow
—Harvey Swados

Hunched like a cowboy that hears a rattler —Paul Theroux
Theroux's simile was particularly apt for the photographer-heroine of his novel, *Picture Palace.*

Hunched, like a man made lintel-shy by too many cracks on the head through adolescence —Harold Adams

Hunched over like an old turtle —Louise Erdrich

(Sit ...) hunched up like a crow —Elizabeth Spencer

Like a schoolmistress dealing with problem pupils, sat straight-backed —Dorothea Straus

Posture ... like an emaciated old man who once had been an athlete —Kenzaburo Oë

Posture ... rigid and stylized as a pair of bookends —George Garrett

Rigid as an effigy —Gavin Lambert
See also: FIRMNESS

(A sort of) savage stoop, like a bull lowering his horn
—G. K. Chesterton

Shoulders humped like a bull's —Mary Hedin

Shoulders sagged like empty sacks —James Crumley

Shoulders ... set like those of a man carrying a banner
—Hugh Walpole

Sits back, relaxed, as if she were watching an invisible TV and weeping over a soap opera —John J. Clayton

Slumped like a chimpanzee —Mary Morris

Slumped there like a bag of bones —Beryl Bainbridge

Slump ... like rags —Karl Shapiro

Slumps there like an outsized parenthesis —Marge Piercy

Standing to attention like a dead centurion at his post
—John Le Carré

Stands stiff as a bobby when the Queen appears —Maxine Kumin

Stands tall, straight and stern as an angel —Louise Erdrich

Stiff-backed as a cadet —George Garrett

Stood like a dart —Brian Merriman

Stood rigid as a carving —Madison Smartt Bell

Stood stiff as a marble statue —Johann Wolfgang von Goethe

Stood up very straight like somebody in opera —Rebecca West

Stooped, as though half-crouching under an expected blow
—Ben Ames Williams

Stooped like too tall visitors to an igloo —John Irving

Stooping like a decayed tree, he was so old —A. E. Coppard

Straightened like soldiers under review —Jay Parini

Tilted forward at the waist like a stickshift in third gear
—Rick Borsten

Upright as a palm tree —*The Holy Bible/Proverbs*
> Variations of this biblical simile link uprightness with a
> variety of other trees; for example, "Upright as a pine."

Upright like stalks —Aharon Megged

POVERTY
See also: ECONOMICS

Destitution, like a famished rat, begins by gnawing at the edges of
garments —Stefan Zweig

Her poverty was like a huge dream-mountain on which her feet
were fast rooted ... aching with the ache of the size of the thing
—Katherine Mansfield

(I felt as) poor as a Catholic without a sin for confession
—Harry Prince

Poor as a church mouse —Anon

Like Job, mice (and rats) have long been, and continue to be, proverbial comparisons for poverty. The writer most frequently credited with originating the simile is William Makepeace Thackeray who used it in *Vanity Fair.*

Poor as a couple of shithouse spiders —Leslie Thomas

Poor as Job —Anon
> A simile with a history dating back to the thirteenth century, and used by many illustrious writers. In *Henry IV*, Shakespeare extended it to, "Poor as Job ... but not so patient," while Sir Walter Scott in *The Fortunes of Nigel* made it, "Proud as Lucifer, and as poor as Job." A variation that was once a popular American colloquialism is "Poor as Job's turkey."

Poor as sin —F. Scott Fitzgerald

A poor man who oppresses the poor is like a sweeping rain which leaves no food —*The Holy Bible/Proverbs*
> The words 'oppresses' and 'leaves' have been modernized from 'oppresseth' and 'leaveth.'

Poverty is death in another form —Latin proverb

Poverty, like wealth, entails a ritual of adaptation —Arthur A. Cohen

Wearing squalor like a badge —Wilfrid Sheed

POWERLESSNESS
See: HELPLESSNESS

PRAISE
See: FLATTERY

PRAYER
See: RELIGION

PRECARIOUSNESS
See: DANGER

PRECISION
See: CORRECTNESS

PREDICAMENT
See: DANGER, PROBLEMS/SOLUTIONS

PREPAREDNESS

(I was) as unprepared to meet my mother as a sinner is reluctant to meet his Maker —Maya Angelou

Got ready like a depression fighter going into the main bout at the Garden on Friday night
—Norman Mailer, on preparing for a television appearance

He [the district attorney] prepares his cases as if he were laying the foundations of society —Ross Macdonald

In life, as in chess, forethought wins —Charles Buxton

Like a basketball coach in a close game, he looked poised to spring
—Fletcher Knebel

Poised like an acid-tipped arrow —Paige Mitchell

Prepare as though for a death
—Katherine Mansfield, on travel preparations

Prepared ... as healthy people are said to be prepared for death, in the sense of knowing it must come without in the least expecttng that it will —Edith Wharton

Prepared for combat [in business situation] like an ambitious and hungry heavyweight boxer before a fight —Andrew M. Greeley

Prepared like a porcupine for cold weather —Anon

Stands ... ready like a retriever —Erich Maria Remarque

Trained him like a race horse for academic success
—Robert L. Heilbroner
> The man whose educational upbringing Heilbrone likened
> to training a race horse is economist John Maynard
> Keynes.

PRESENT, THE

The present, like a note in music, is nothing but as it appertains to what is past and what is to come —Walter Savage Landor

The word 'now' is like a bomb through the window —Arthur Miller

PRESERVATION
See: PROTECTIVENESS

PROBLEMS/SOLUTIONS

Problems/ Solutions

As rust eats iron, so care eats the heart —Auguste Ricard

Being a new employee ... it's like picking up a screenplay and starting to act your part, only it's Act Three and you have not been in Acts One or Two
—Carol Clark, *New York Times*, July 28, 1986

Burdensome as a secret —French proverb

Carry your problems with you from place to place like a Santa Claus sack —George Garrett

Ceased to be an apparent problem ... the way crumbs swept under a rug cease to be an apparent problem —Rick Borsten

Difficulties strengthen the mind, as labor does the body
—Seneca, The Elder

(Doubt ...) dug at his peace of mind like a broken fingernail
—F. van Wyck Mason

(The electronics-crammed production booth is beginning to) resemble the bridge of a destroyer under air attack —Michael Cieply, writing about taping of a Bill Cosby television segment that ran into problems, *Wall Street Journal*, September 26, 1986

Face a problem with all the joy of a team preparing for a game it expects to lose —Anon

Felt speaking about one's personal problems was rather like talking about one's surgery scars ... a subject of consuming interest only to one's self —C.D.B. Bryan

Heading toward disaster, as certainly as a four-year-old behind the wheels of a Maserati
—Vincent Canby, *New York Times*, February 28, 1986

He was like a mathematician with an abstruse problem, worrying over it, but worrying very calmly and impersonally
—James Hilton

456

I am a man smothered with women and children, like a duck with onions —Sir Charles Napier
> Napier made these comparisons when he reflected on his life in England after retiring as commander of British forces in northern India.

An international crisis is like sex, as long as you keep talking about it, nothing happens
—Harold Coffin, *Reader's Digest*, September, 1961

It's [being on a losing streak] like a little time box that's going to explode —John Pennywell, football player on Columbia University's Lions, *New York Times*, November 8, 1986

(I was) living as if I were squeezed in an iron hand
—Honoré de Balzac

(The whole of) my life has passed like a razor ... in hot water or a scrape —Sydney Smith

(My immediate) problems ... as untouchable as a raw wound
—Norman Mailer

The problem stayed in the front of his mind like a sheer cliff he could not begin to climb —Ken Follett

Pry at the mousehole of a solution like a cat with infinite patience
—Bill Granger

Second-hand cares, like second-hand clothes, come easily on and off
—Charles Dickens

Sign of trouble ... like seeing a cannon muzzle poke out of the woods —James Sterngold, *New York Times*, March 22, 1986

The solution rushed on him like a fire storm —T. Coraghessan Boyle

They're [troubles] piled on my head like snows on a mountain top
—Bernard Malamud

They would gnaw on it for days like two puppies with a rubber bone —Charles Portis

Troubled as a plane with one wing —Anon

Trouble ... fell across her shoulders like a cloak. It was as if she had touched a single strand of a web, and felt the whole thing tremble and knew herself to be caught forever in its trembling
—Ellen Gilchrist

457

Troublesome as a wasp in one's ears —Thomas Fuller

Troubles visited from above like tornadoes —Marge Piercy

Weaponless deterrence is like bodiless sex. It gets you nowhere
—James Morrow

Women like to sit down with trouble as if it were knitting
—Ellen Glasgow

Work like an antitoxin ... before the complications come
—Clifford Odets

PROCRASTINATION
See: LINGERING

PROFANITY
See: CURSES

PROFESSIONS
See also: DOCTORS, LAWYERS

Archaeologists and historians ... they are like jewelers, examining
every tiny aspect of each valuable thing, with exactness and care
—Judith Martin

Business is a vocation. Philosophy is, or should be, an avocation
—Elbert Hubbard

A financier is a pawnbroker with imagination —Arthur W. Pinero

(I guess) getting into nunhood is about as hard as pro football
—Michael Malone

(In ordinary business, man can settle to routine. The journalist can't.)
He's [the journalist] like a robin, looking in all directions at once
—Frank Swinnerton

He who philosophizes is like a mirror that reflects objects that it
cannot see, like a cave that returns the echo of voices that it
does not hear —Kahlil Gibran

Journalism, like history, is certainly not an exact science
—John Gunther

The Notary Public, like the domestic dog, is found everywhere
—John Cadman Roper

PUNCTUAL AS DEATH

Professions

The philosopher is like a mountaineer who has with difficulty climbed a mountain for the sake of the surprise, and arriving at the top finds only fog; whereupon he wanders down again —W. Somerset Maugham

Philosophy is like the ocean: there are pearls in its depths, but many divers find nothing for all their exertion and perish in the attempt —Ha Yevani Zerahia

Police business ... it's a good deal like politics. It asks for the highest type of men, and there's nothing in it to attract the highest type of men —Raymond Chandler

Professors are just like actors. Actors got press agents that write things about them and they get so they believe it —Anon

Professors get to looking at their diplomas and get to believing what it says there —Will Rogers, radio broadcast, January 27, 1935

Psychoanalysis, like imagination, cannot be learned by rote —Theodor Reik

Psychology is like physics before Galileo's time, not a single elementary law yet caught a glimpse of —William James, letter to James Sully, 1890

Running a liberal paper is like feeding melted butter on the end of an awl to a wild cat —Oscar Ameringer, *Progressive*, January 17, 1942

Working journalists regularly chase wild geese. Like firemen, they answer alarms, many of them false —Richard Rovere

PROFUSION
See: ABUNDANCE

PROGRESS
See: GROWTH

PROLIFERATION
See: SPREADING

Promise

PROMISE

He promises like a merchant-man and pays like a man-of-war —Italian proverb

His promises are lighter than the breath that utters them
—John Ray's *Proverbs*

Lovers' oaths are thin as rain —Dorothy Parker

A pledge unpaid is like thunder without rain —Abraham Hasdai

Promise as solid as a bundle of water —Hindu proverb
    Modernized to non-sexist English from "A woman's word
    is like a bundle of water."

Promises are like pie-crusts —Danish proverb

The promises of authors are like the vows of lovers
    —Samuel Johnson
    See also: WRITERS/WRITING

When a man takes an oath, he's holding his own self in his own
    hands. Like water. And if he opens his fingers then, he needn't
    hope to find himself again —Robert Bolt

PROMPTNESS

Arrived on time, and left on time, like a European train
    —Laurie Colwin
    See also: ENTRANCES/EXITS

Punctual as a bride at a wedding —Honoré de Balzac

Punctual as a stage manager, watch in hand —Frank Swinnerton

Punctual as bills —Babette Deutsch

Punctual as death —Scott Spencer

Punctual as destiny —Edith Wharton

Punctual as lovers to the moment sworn —Edward Young

Punctually as a cuckoo in a Swiss clock —Edith Wharton

Punctually, as the tax collector —*Punch*, 1862
    Paraphrased from "Tax gatherer."

PRONUNCIATION
See: SPEECH PATTERNS

PROPRIETY/IMPROPRIETY

About as risqué as a bed in a hospital —George Jean Nathan

All wrong ... like a priest for whom one has a great respect
    suddenly taking his trousers off in church —Daphne du Maurier

Decorously as an old maid on the way to get her hair dyed blue
    —A. E. Maxwell

Improper as thumbing your nose at the pope —Anon

Prim as Hippolytus —Stevie Smith

(Girls, at sixteen, for all our strictures, are) proper as Puritans
    —Phyllis McGinley

Proper like the hostesses in restaurants frequented by women
    shoppers —Ludwig Bemelmans

PROSE
See: POETS/POETRY, WRITERS/WRITING

PROTECTIVENESS
See also: WATCHFULNESS

Guard [another person] like an armed sentry —Isak Dinesen

Mothers him like an old mare —Jilly Cooper

[Trees] preserved at all costs, like Grandpa's teeth —Elizabeth Bishop

Protective [of property] as a lion in winter —Anon
        This may have been inspired by James Goldman's play,
        The Lion in Winter, a simile from which can be found under
        AMBITION.

Protectively, like shepherd dogs —Harvey Swados

[Wife] watches over my reputation like a broody hen
    —Luigi Pirandello

PROTRUSION
See also: BELONGING, OBVIOUSNESS, VISIBILITY

Bulges out like bubble gum before popping —Tom Robbins

Protruding like a warning finger —Beryl Markham

[A church spire] standing out conspicuously like an indicating finger
   —MacDonald Harris

Standing out unnaturally, like a male harpist in an all-girl orchestra
   —William Safire

Stand out like a blind man at a tit show —William Diehl

Stand out like a polar bear in the desert —Andrew Kaplan

Stand out like a raisin on a coconut cake —Pat Conroy

Stands out like a blackberry in a pan of milk
   —American colloquialism, attributed to Vermont

Stick out like a bug on a butter knife —Loren D. Estleman

Sticks out like the belly of a pregnant woman —Robert Lowell

PROVERBS
See: MAXIMS, PROVERBS AND SAYINGS

PRUDENCE
See: CAUTION

PSYCHOLOGY
See: PROFESSIONS

PUBLIC OPINION
See: OPINION

PURITY

Incapable of taint as gold of rust —Aeschylus

Pure and white as Rainier's snows —Slogan, Mills flour

Pure as a salamander in the flames or wool among the brambles
   —Miguel de Cervantes

(I'm as) pure as driven slush —Tallulah Bankhead

Pure as snow —William Shakespeare

(I had grown) pure as the dawn and the dew
   —Algernon Charles Swinburne

Pure as the mountain air —Slogan, D. L. Clark candy

Pure as the sun —Stephen Vincent Benét

Purity

Pure in thought as angels —Samuel Rogers

She was as pure as snow and she drifted —Anon blurb for book, *New York Times Book Review*, November 2, 1986

Unblemished as the cloudless sky —Anne Morrow Lindbergh

Untouched as a nun —Wallace Stegner
> A variation on the same theme: "Pure as a nun" from Margaret Drabble's novel, *The Waterfall*.

Purposefulness

PURPOSEFULNESS

Came around ... deliberately like the gun turret of a great ship —Donald McCaig

Dedicated as a Japanese artist who has found the flower he must paint all his life —William McIlvanney

Deliberate as a bee taking honey —Molly Kean

Deliberate as a dog sniffing out a buried bone —Anon

Effort as conscious and deliberate as holding his breath under water —William Peden
> From a short story entitled *Night in Funland,* this refers to a character's effort to control his emotions.

Had a plan ... simple as Cain's —Alma and Paul Ellerbe

His time was organized, planned like the timetable of a battle maneuver —Arthur A. Cohen

Intent as a cannibal at breakfast —T. Coraghessan Boyle

Intent as a collector —W. H. Auden

Men, like nails, lose their usefulness when they lose their direction and begin to bend —Walter Savage Landor

Method is like packing things in a box; a good packer will get in half as much again as a bad one —Richard Cecil

Moved like a steamroller, in a straight line, crushing everything that was in her way —Margaret Millar

My will is like a long pencil, it must be sharpened —Delmore Schwartz

(I have always envied the man who found one single role and)
    played it [a role or life plan], clung and grew to it like a
    barnacle on a ship —George Garrett

Rehearsed her sensuality like a summa-cum student
    —Francine du Plessix Gray

(Somewhere in the earth is a drain of) resolution filling as a fresh
    teapot —Daniela Gioseffi

(He had) a resolution in him like an iron bar —Wallace Stegner

Schemed like Arabs —Thomas McGuane

(Ruthless and) singleminded as birds of prey —George Garrett

Used her charm like a tennis racket —Delmore Schwartz

Will without power is like children playing at soldiers
    —George Canning

PURSUIT

(He was) after her like a hound after a deer —Harriet Beecher Stowe

(He was) after it like a duck on a June bug
    —American colloquialism, attributed to the South
        A twist on the duck/bug comparison is to be after
        something, "Like a pet coon into the churn."

(He was) after it like the stink after onion
    —American colloquialism, attributed to the South

Chased him like a fox chases a turkey —Rosa Guy

Chased me ... like a kid after a fire truck —Irwin Shaw

Follow after me like an old weasel tracing a rat —John M. Synge
        In Synge's script for *The Playboy of the Western World*,
        'weasel' was spelled with the letter z.

Follow each other like lemmings over the cliffs of Dover —Richard
    Hicks, about discount book sellers, *Publishers' Weekly*, 1986

Follow every lead like a lawyer building a case —Anon

Followed her about like a little dog —William Makepeace Thackeray

Followed him like a trained sleuth —Shelby Hearon

Pursuit

Followed one another like insects going at dawn through the heavy grass —Eudora Welty

Follow you around like flies —Gavin Lyall

Haunted me like a passion —William Wordsworth

Held on his trail like an old hound after his last coon —James Crumley

Hounded him like bailiffs —Oakley Hall

Looked for ... like a bird looking for forage in a desert —Arthur A. Cohen

Pursue as wolves pursue sheep —William Reese, a rare book dealer, quoted in *Wall Street Journal article on how book collectors go after their finds, May 6, 1986*

[A disease] pursued him like a hobgoblin —Maurice Edelman

Pursue as a male dog goes after a bitch in heat —Anon

Pursuing him like a nemesis, like an unwanted, embarrassing relative —Donald McCaig

Slivered after him like mercury —Wilfrid Sheed

Sniff out like a terrier smells a rat —Basil Blackwell

Tagging along [behind character in story] like an anthropologist tags along behind his Indian —Deborah Eisenberg

Trailing ... like a cape before a bull —Lawrence Durrell

Trotting behind like a penny dog —Rita Mae Brown

Will run him down like a greyhound catching a hare —George Garrett

Would be on my back like a bad case of sunburn —Shelby Hearon

PUZZLEMENT
See: BEWILDERMENT

QUESTIONS/ANSWERS
See: PROBLEMS/SOLUTIONS

QUICKNESS
See: RUNNING, SPEED

466

RAIN
See also: WEATHER

As if a mask had been peeled off, the rain ended —Tim O'Brien

Big soft drops splash on people's hands and cheeks, immense warm drops like melted stars —Katherine Mansfield

Drizzle whispered upon Joseph's umbrella like muffled applause —Rick Borsten

Droplets fired upon our windows like bullets of tin —Ira Wood

The drops like bugs stuck on the pane —F. D. Reeve

A dull rain, like a tap left running —Jean Thompson

Fall rain as fine as spray from an atomizer —Harvey Swados

Felt the rain like cold tears on his hot face —James Crumley

The good rain, like a bad preacher, does not know when to leave off —Ralph Waldo Emerson

The gray rain continued to fall, stubbornly and insensibly, like a frozen madness —Amos Oz

Hiss in the gutter [the rain] like a thousand coiled snakes —T. Coraghessan Boyle

It seemed as if the lowering clouds, heavy with water had burst, emptying upon the earth ... melting it like sugar —Guy De Maupassant

Light rain fell around the big house and its trees like a veil —John McGahern

Light through which the slowing rain ran stitches like a sewing machine gone mad —Leslie A. Fiedler

The rain as thick as oil on the windows —Albert Camus

The rain beat down (on Paris) in endless steady sheets, straight down, like waterfalls —Sylvia Berkman
> A nice example of a simile to introduce a story and set its mood.

Rain ... beating down like a stampede of horses —Paige Mitchell

The rain bites like a whip across a prisoner's back —Anne Morrow Lindbergh

The rain came down like glass bead curtains —Joyce Cary

The rain came like an explosion in a glass factory
    —T. Coraghessan Boyle

The rain came sifting through the air, and settled like bloom on the
    fields —Mary Lavin
        Another rain simile to set a fictional scene, this one for
        Lavin's story, *Brigid.*

The rain came slowly and doggedly down, as if it had not even the
    spirit to pour —Charles Dickens

Rain comes down like the sky falling in skeins and yarny drifts
    —Marge Piercy

Raindrops ... as warm as the tears of a child not yet consoled
    —Marguerite Yourcenar

Rain drops down like worms from the trees —Anne Sexton

Raindrops hitting like bullets —Joyce Carol Oates

Raindrops, plump as Malaga grapes —Paul Kuttner

Raindrops pock the surface like a plague —T. Coraghessan Boyle

Raindrops sparkled like diamonds falling through sunshine
    —Rita Mae Brown

Raindrops tapped at our backs like insinuating fingers
    —T. Coraghessan Boyle

Raindrops that whined like bullets —Kenzaburo Oë

Rained like a cow pissing on a flat rock —American colloquialism

Rain falling just past the end of his nose like a curtain
    —Thomas McGuane

Rain ... fell like a silver veil from the dim grey sky
    —Mazo De La Roche

Rain ... fell like iron swords out of the black sky —Paul Theroux

Rain ... flowing in streaked silver patterns down the panes of the
    window nearby, like tears on the smooth shining face of a child
    —Bill Pronzini

Rain ... flying down like silver needles —Frank Swinnerton

Rain glimmered like silver threads being spun from the mist
—Paige Mitchell

Rain ... gold as the planet system —Dame Edith Sitwell

Rain hit the roof like pennies from heaven —T. Coraghessan Boyle

Rain keeps falling like a curse —Amos Oz

Rain knocked at the windows like a smirking voyeur
—T. Coraghessan Boyle

Rain ... like a river falling out of the sky —Donald Seaman

Rain ... like a deluge from heaven —W. Somerset Maugham

Rain, like dark-ruled lines on paper —Stephen Longstreet

The rain like pitchforks fell —Delmore Schwartz

Rain plastered the land till it was shining like hammered lead
—Ted Hughes

Rain poured down like a waterfall —Jilly Cooper

Rain ran from the roof like a sea —Irving Feldman

Rain ... rattling hard first on one side and then on the other like
someone nailing down a case —Saul Bellow

Rains drip like the slow beat of time —Dame Edith Sitwell

Rain sheeting down like a giant waterfall —Frank Swinnerton

The rains of summer's end were very like tears, falling warm and
gradually chilling where they fell —Lael Tucker Wertenbaker

Rain, so loud, like horses weeping —F. Scott Fitzgerald

Rainstorms that blacken like a headache —Amy Clampitt

The rain struck you so hard that it was like a warm gag in your
mouth —Louis-Ferdinand Celine

The rain stung like whips, and from underfoot the mud oozed up
over shoes and ankles like a live thing —Hugh Walpole

Rain ... swept the deck in angry gusts, like a nagging woman who
cannot leave a subject alone —W. Somerset Maugham

Rain thudded against the car like rotten fruit —Jean Thompson

469

Rain

The rain was blowing down the window glass like silk
—Paul Horgan

Showers ... drifting like scarves of gauze across the landscape
—Jules Romains

A slanted sheet of rain swept like a scythe across Placid Cove Trailer Park —John Lutz

> The scene being set with this simile is for a mystery story entitled *Ride the Lightning*.

The sound of rain seemed ... like the repeated attentions of a lover —John Cheever

A squall of rain driven around us in gusts like a wet veil
—Erich Maria Remarque

Through the mist it was as if fine threads of rain were being teased down slowly —John McGahern

Torrents of rain streamed through the darkness, like incessant floods of tears which threatened to devour the earth and drown it in a deluge of unquenchable grief —Vladimir G. Korolenko

The [rain] water was loud as a crowd hissing —Susan Minot

When it rains, there's a wonderful lush wooden wetness in the air, and you feel as refreshed as if you were the earth itself, drinking in the water —Christopher Isherwood

The wind-blown rain was smeared like jam on the glass [of the window] —Jonathan Valin

RANTING
See: SCREAMS

RAPIDITY
See: SPEED

RARITY
See: ORIGINALITY

RASHNESS
See: SPEED

READERS/READING
See: BOOKS

READINESS
See: PREPAREDNESS

REALIZATION

Awareness of failure plagued at him like a sword, twisting in his consciousness cruelly as though it had been lying in wait to murder his self-respect —Noël Coward

Began to see herself from the outside, as if she was a moving target in someone else's binoculars —Margaret Atwood

Flash of insight as pitiless as the late-autumn light
—Sharon Sheehe Stark

Horror ... burst upon him like an electric storm that throws a vivid light into the darkest shadow —Mazo De La Roche

It [realization] came to her slowly as a negative being developed
—Elizabeth Spencer

Knowledge penetrated my consciousness like a red-hot knife
—Stefan Zweig

Light burst on me as if a window of my memory had been suddenly flung open on a street in the city —Joseph Conrad

Like a lover or lecher, the awareness came to her at night. Every perception rejoices in itself like a fire catching fire through itself
—Delmore Schwartz

Like French women who can tell if a bottle of Cognac has been opened in the next room, Guido could tell what was happening at home as soon as he put his key in the lock —Laurie Colwin

Realization ... dawned ... like the sunrise —Donald Seaman

Realization came ... like a fist knocking the wind out of her
—David Leavitt

Realization grips them like a seizure —T. Coraghessan Boyle

The realization ... made the nape of my neck feel like I'd just applied an ice pack —Sue Grafton

Saw as one sees a landscape in a flash of lightning —Virginia Woolf

Saw it like a thunderbolt —Clifford Odets

See it all like a chart unrolled —John Greenleaf Whittier

Suddenly, as if a wet sheet had been thrown over her, the truth of the matter strikes her —T. Coraghessan Boyle

The knowledge sank like a plummet —Jean Stafford

A thousand things ... suddenly added up like a column of figures in her mind —William Humphrey

(Trifles ... like a spark falling upon tinder, can) throw a flame of light into the abyss of a mind —Stefan Zweig

The truth flared in his head like a marron —Miles Gibson

The truth popped out like a jack-in-the-box —George Garrett

Trying to find it [self-knowledge] in the bosom of a Mississippi family was like trying to find some object lost in a gigantic attic, when you really didn't know what you were looking for —Elizabeth Spencer

An uncomfortable truth had come to settle like a shroud over the ... investigation —Doug Feiden
> The comparison in Feiden's novel, *The $10,000,000 Getaway*, pertains to the investigation of a Lufthansa airline robbery.

Understanding fell across me like a velvet curtain —Russell Banks

REALNESS/UNREALNESS

Artificial like a piece of water in a French garden —W. Somerset Maugham

Abstract and decorative as a snowstorm in a glass paperweight —George Garrett

Artificial as a false mustache —Dorothea Straus

Blurred, unreal, like a picture in the newspaper —Katherine Mansfield

Distorted as the view through the wrong end of a telescope —Anon

False as waxworks —Karl Shapiro

(Sometimes I) feel like a figment of my own imagination —Lily Tomlin

Genuine as rain —J. B. Priestly

Had a squinty close view of the truth like a jeweler studying facets and flaws, like a man at a microscope —George Garrett

He could block out reality as easily as exposing a roll of film —Jonathan Kellerman

Real and insistent as a wound in one's body —Milovan Djilas

(The pain returned) real as a toothache —John Braine

Real as hunger —Anon

Real as several grain sacks thrown on top of each other —Flannery O'Connor

Real as the passing of time —Anon

(You and I are as) real at least as the people upstairs —James Merrill

Reality met him like a swung shovel —Sharon Sheehe Stark

(The room seemed as) unreal as a stage set —William McIlvanney

Real, like a punch on the nose —Stephen Longstreet

Unreal, as ghostly as the brushing of a leaf against his face —Katherine Anne Porter

Unreal as the emptiness of the air —Leonid Andreyev

Unreal, like a poorly-played drama on the stage —Ben Ames Williams

Unreal like mid-summer sunshine remembered at Christmas —Elizabeth Bowen

REAPPEARANCE

Always came back to me like a dog to his kennel —Nathan Shaham

(The day) began all over again, like a toothache, in her memory —Frank Swinnerton

[Kisses can ...] come back like ghosts —Carl Sandburg
> Sandburg used this simile to open and close a poem, as well as for its title. In between are several additional similes to illustrate that love does come to an end to be put away "Like a clock," "Like a violin," or "Like a summer day near fall time."

Double back like a fox eluding his pursuing hounds —Robert Traver

Keeps cropping up, like toadstools after a flood —Jonathan Kellerman

Like a repentant lover, I returned to that previous way of life
      —John Rechy

Recur like wind from a returning storm —Hallie Burnett

(Questions about her parentage) recurred like malaria
      —Rita Mae Brown

Recurring like a motif in music —G. K. Chesterton

(They were) returning again, like birds to their roosts
      —Graham Swift

Return like a bad penny —Anon

Return like a homing pigeon —Anon

Rolled like a stone back to where he'd started —Martin Cruz Smith

Turn up like an old arrest record —Marge Piercy

Turn up like a single boot after I finally threw the other away
      —Marge Piercy

[A deep-seated flaw] would surface like an aching wisdom tooth
      —James Lee Burke

RED
See also: BLUSHES, CHEEKS, LIPS

As red as any rose —William Shakespeare

Red as a matchtip —James Reiss

(Tongue) red as a pomegranate —Miles Gibson

Red as a radish —Anon

Red as a robin's breast —Anon

Red as a rooster's comb —Dorothy Canfield Fisher
            The simile from Canfield's *Sex Education* describes a face
            turned red with embarrassment.

Red as a strong man's heart —Robert Tristram Coffin
            The objects being compared are Vermont barns.

(Lips) red as a sun rising on the Atlantic and setting on the Pacific
      —Mary Morris

Red as a wound —Jon Silkin

[A cloak] red as blood —William Shakespeare
Similes linking the color red with blood abound
throughout literature as well as everyday speech.

(Hair) red as chili powder —Saul Bellow

Red as fire —William Shakespeare

(Lips) red as hell —Dame Edith Sitwell

(Fingernails) red as satin ribbons —Diane Ackerman

[Leather seats of a showy car] red as spilt blood —Saul Bellow

Red like poppies —Charlotte Brontë

Thin streaks of red, like veins in marble showed on his chalky teeth
—Wright Morris

REDUCTION
See: DECREASE

REGRET
See also: CONSCIENCE

Remorse is as the heart in which it grows —Samuel Taylor Coleridge
Coleridge's poem, *Remorse*, continues as follows: "If that
be gentle, it drops balmy dews of true repentance; but if
proud and gloomy, it is the poison tree, that pierces to the
inmost."

Repentance, like the sea, is always open to the ventures
—Shimoni Yalkut

Repentance, without amendment, is like continually pumping without
mending the leak —Lewis W. Dilwyn

Repentance follows crime ... as changes follow time
—Percy Bysshe Shelley

Regret is like a mountaintop from which we survey our dead life, a
mountaintop on which we pause and ponder, and very often
looking into the twilight we ask ourselves whether it would be
well to send a letter or some token —George Moore

The pang of regret, sharp as a sword thrust —L. P. Hartley

Regret is like tears seeping through closed eyelids —Galway Kinnell

(When I fall) let me fall without regret like a leaf —Wendell Berry

Remorseless as an alarm clock —Anon

REGULARITY/IRREGULARITY

Balance as a tail balances a kite —Anon

Balanced as the scales of justice —Anon

[A cat's purring] intermittent as a walkie-talkie —Lorrie Moore

Irregular as French verbs —Anon

Random, like love's choices —Patricia Hampl

Regular as a clock —Slogan for Serutan laxative, Healthaids, Inc.

Regular as a heartbeat —Mary Hedin

Regular as a metronome —Edward Hoagland

Regular as a motor boat —Lee Smith
> A more specific variation: "Regular as the chug-chug of a motor boat."

Regular as sun and tide —Wallace Stegner

Regular as the moon makes the tides —Henry James

Rhythmic as water —Amy Hempel
> In Hempel's story, *Beg, sl tog, Inc, Cont, Rep*, it's the sliding knitting needles that are likened to water.

Scattered like applause during a bad act —Anon

Steadily as a shell secretes its beating leagues of monotone —Hart Crane

Symmetrical as a doily —Betsy Wade, *New York Times*, May 2, 1986
> The descriptive frame of reference is a tree.

REJECTION
See also: ABANDONMENT

Cast away [anger] like spoiled milk —Marge Piercy

Discarded like outmoded customs —Elyse Sommer

Discarded (me) like yesterday's underpants —Sue Grafton

Dropped ... like a dead fish —T. Glen Coughlin

Dropped [from a list] ... like a hot rivet —Loren D. Estleman

He shook them [young women] off his back like a young stallion shaking off an unskilled rider —Russell Banks

Keep at a distance, like someone with an infectious disease —Anon
> The many twists on this usually refer to a specific diseases, whatever is most feared. Like so many phrases that have been mainstreamed into our language, this can be traced back to a line from Shakespeare, in this case: "Barred, like one infectious."

Push her away like a clinging dog —Daphne du Maurier

Push me aside like a kitchen chair —Philip Levine

Put (such thoughts) aside like chewed-up grapeskins —Bertold Brecht

Rejected [bad news] ... like a transplanted organ —Pat Conroy

Rejected [praise] like counterfeit money —William McIlvanney

Shoved aside like a row boat nosed away by a tanker
—Mary Gordon

Shun him like the plague —Charles Dickens

Some men, like spaniels, will only fawn the more when repulsed, but will pay little heed to a friendly caress —Abd-el-Kader

Spurn my passion like a worm —Jean Racine

Swept her aside as if she were a cobweb —Susan Kelly

They just dropped me ... like a bag of potatoes —Njabulo Ndebele

Threw aside everything ... like a contemptible burden —Heinrich Böll

RELATIONSHIPS
See also: MARRIAGE; PARENTHOOD

Charted his moods like a cartographer —Pat Conroy
> Conroy's simile from *The Great Santini* refers to the main character's understanding of and adjustment to his father's temperament.

Relationships

Families are a kind of closed system; like locked trunks, they are hard to penetrate from the outside —Daphne Merkin

Families are like wine. You get the old vintage that goes right off: goes weak as coloured water or old scent —Julia O'Faolain

A family, if it is large and well-connected, is like a religion —Paul Theroux
> In the novel, *Picture Palace*, from which this is taken, the author follows up the simile with the following explanation: "It serves the same purpose, to bewitch the believer with joy and offer him salvation; it consoles, it enchants, it purifies."

Getting to know someone is like opening a safe: you have to learn the unique combination of numbers —Delmore Schwartz
> Schwartz followed this entry into his journal with "No, this is not really true."

Her life was hung upon this relationship, like the cloth of a tent that would collapse into loose folds without the central post that supported it —Tennessee Williams

Human relations just aren't fixed in their orbits like the planets; they're more like galaxies, changing all the time, exploding into light for years, then dying away —May Sarton

The idea of a step-father is like a substitute host on a talk show —Bobbie Ann Mason

In the beginning of a relationship, if you're lucky enough to find wit at the right moments, it's like getting a cab in the rain —Steve Post, WNYC/FM, December 22, 1986

(There were Ben and his father, eye to eye, as) intimate as lovers —Pat Conroy

I was there for you, like an Eye-Beam ... any other beam would do —John Updike

Know each other's thoughts. Without words, as if traveling on connected bloodstreams —Mary Hedin

Know each other, crack and flaw, like two irregular stones that fit together —Adrienne Rich

Like the slowly tumbling arabesque of little cloud shapes drifting across the sand cliffs on a summer wind, neither [of two close sisters] was anything without the other —Wilbur Daniel Steele

478

Never got on ... like a couple of dogs not liking each other's smells
—Frank Swinnerton

Relationship ... as fragile as spindly bridges
—David Leavitt, *New York Times Book Review,* 1986
See also: FRAGILITY

The relationship bumps along like a car with three tires —Ira Wood

Relationship ... like two engines running at variance
—D. H. Lawrence

The relationship waxed, billowed like scenery on the breeze
—John Ashberry

Spread herself out like a cloak for the king to walk on
—Suzi Gablik, *New York Times Book Review,* 1986
> The simile is used to explain the relationship between the author of *My Life with Chagall* and the artist.

The string between you wore out ... like old elastic —Tess Slesinger

The sweet sorrow of loving a parent is as pure as the taste of a sourball when you are five —Norman Mailer

Their (a mother and daughter) connection had built-in tension and resiliency. Like the coiled telephone cord through which they communicated —Ellen Goodman

There was room for improvement [in relationship between two men] ... a sort of gap, like the Grand Canyon —J. F. Powers

Torn between them [warring parents] like a plot of land they both wanted to lay claim to —Ann Jasperson

Treated her like a twenty-carat diamond —Rita Mae Brown

Understand one another like thieves at a fair —Anatole France

(After half an hour ...) we were as familiar with one another as if we had unbosomed our whole life histories
—Erich Maria Remarque

RELIABILITY/UNRELIABILITY
See: FIRMNESS, STEADINESS

RELIEF
See: EMOTIONS

RELIGION
See also: BELIEF

As men's prayers are a disease of the will, so are their creeds a disease of the intellect —Ralph Waldo Emerson

As religious as any man who prays daily and hangs a rabbit's foot on his windshield —Harry Prince

Beautiful women without religion are like flowers without perfume —Heinrich Heine

Catholicism's a little too much like the gold standard: a fixed weight of piety translatable into a fixed exchange rate of grace —Michael M. Thomas

The Christian is like the ripening corn; the riper he grows, the more lowly he bends his head —Thomas Guthrie

Christianity is like electricity. It cannot enter a person unless it can pass through —Bishop Richard C. Raines

The church is a sort of hospital for men's souls, and as full of quackery as the hospitals for those bodies —Henry David Thoreau

A consistently godless world is like a picture without perspective —Franz Werfel

Faith ... a stiffening process, a sort of mental starch, which ought to be applied as sparingly as possible —E. M. Forster

Faith is like love: it cannot be forced —Arthur Schopenhauer

Faith without works is like a bird without wings —Francis Beaumont

Folded into his religion like a razor into its case —Anon

God's like a kid with too many toys to take care of —Sharon Sheehe Stark

People are born churchy or unchurchy, just as they are born with a tendency to arteriosclerosis, cancer or consumption —Anatole France

In religion, as in friendship, they who profess most are the least sincere —Richard Brinsley Sheridan

In religion as in politics it so happens that we have less charity for those who believe half our creed than for those who deny the whole of it —Charles Caleb Colton

Living without faith is like driving in a fog —Anon

The majority takes the creed [Calvinism] as a horse takes his collar; it slips by his ears, over his neck, he hardly knows how, but he finds himself in harness and jogs along as his fathers and forefathers before him —Oliver Wendell Holmes, Sr.

A man who writes of himself without speaking of God is like one who identifies himself without giving his address —Ben Hecht

Men's anger about religion is as if two men should quarrel for a lady they neither of them care for —Lord Halifax

Our faith ... runs as fast as feeling to embrace —William Alfred

Our faith is too often like the mercury in the weather-glass; it gets up high in fine weather; in rough weather it sinks proportionally low —Anon

Piety, like aristocracy, has its nobility —Johann Wolfgang von Goethe

Prayed like an orphan —Wendell Berry

Prayer is a force as real as terrestrial gravity —Alexis Carrel

Priestly mannerisms clung to him like the smell of candle-wax and incense —Peter Kemp

Religion is comparable to a childhood neurosis —Sigmund Freud

Religion is like love; it plays the devil with clear thinking
   —Rose Macaulay

Religion is like the breath of heaven; if it goes abroad in the open air, it scatters and dissolves —Jeremy Taylor

Religion, like water, may be free, but when they pipe it to you, you've got to help pay for the piping. And the piper
   —Muriel Spark

Religious as a lizard on a rock —Anon

Religious sense is like an esthetic sense. You're born with it or you aren't —P. D. James, *New York Times Magazine*, October 5, 1986

Sects and creeds of religion are like pocket compasses, good enough to point you in the direction, but the nearer the pole you get the worse they work —Josh Billings

In Billings' phonetic dialect: "Sekts and creeds of religion are like pocket compesses, good enuff tu point you inte the right direction, but the nearer the pole yu git the wuss tha wurk."

She fought off God like an unwelcome suitor —Nancy Evans about Emily Dickinson, "First Editions"/WNYC February 18, 1987

Some Christians are like soiled bank notes: while we acknowledge their value we wish them changed —William Lewis

Sometimes the curse of God comes like the caress of a woman's hand, and sometimes His blessing comes like a knife in the flesh —Amos Oz

The soul united to God is like a leaf united to the tree —Ignazio Silone

They treated their God like a desk clerk with whom they lodged requests and complaints —Helen Hudson

Without dogma a religion is like a body without skeleton. It can't stand —James G. Huneker

REMEDY
See: PROBLEMS/SOLUTIONS

REMEMBRANCE
See: PAST, THE

REMORSE
See: REGRET

REMOTENESS
See: RESERVE

REPETITION
See also: CONTINUITY, DULLNESS

Continue unceasingly like a drip from a leaking faucet —Anon

Iteration, like friction, is likely to generate heat instead of progress —George Eliot

Kept on repeating the words like a talisman —Edith Wharton

Life as repetitive as the seasons —J. B. Priestly

Like warmed-up cabbage served at each repast the repetition kills the wretch at last —Juvenal

Monotonous ... like a tap with a worn-out washer dripping ... in a kitchen sink —Gerald Kersch
> In Kersh's novel, *Repetition*, the dripping faucet image describes a character's voice.

Recited tirelessly as a language record —Marge Piercy
> In Piercy's poem, *A Cold and Married War*, the narrator is reciting her sins and errors.

(Rages ... which seemed to) recur in cycles, like menstruation —Ursule Molinaro

(Thought) repeated like a lesson —William H. Gass

Repeated like a rhyme —Amy Lowell

Repeats ... like an advertisement in neon —Marge Piercy

Repetitive as hieroglyphs —Derek Walcott

(Disembodied and) repetitive as the sea in a shell —Elizabeth Spencer

[The sweep hand of a clock] went around and around like a door-to-door salesman —Raymond Chandler

REPUTATION

As for taking a good man's name from him, you might as well undertake to pull goose-quills from the wings of an angel —Elbridge G. Dow, Jr.

A bad reputation in a woman allures like the signs of heat in a bitch —Aldous Huxley
> Huxley wrote *Point Counter Point* from which this is taken long before the women's movement raised our consciousness to gender-biased characterization.

Disgraces are like cherries: one draws another —George Herbert

A good name, like good will, is got by many actions and lost by one —Lord Francis Jeffrey

A good reputation is like the cypress; once cut, it never puts forth leaf again —Francesco Guicciardini

His record's as clean as a vestal virgin's —Dialogue from a 1967 movie, *The Deadly Affair*.

Honor is like a rocky island without a landing place; once we leave it we can't get it back —Nicolas Boileau

Honor is like the eye, which cannot suffer the least injury without damage; it is [like] a precious stone, the price of which is lessened by the least flaw —Jacques Bénigne Boussuet

Honor, like freedom, is a luxury for those with independent incomes —John Braine

Honors trailing away behind him like the tail of a comet —Vita Sackville-West

In scandal, as in robbery, the receiver is always as bad as the thief —Lord Chesterfield

A liar's reputation ... stuck with him like a cockleburr —Carlos Baker

A person's reputation is as fragile and vulnerable as human life itself —Robert Traver

To steal it [a person's honor] is like stealing your soul —William Diehl

RESERVE
See also: EMOTIONS

Animated as a department store mannequin —Anon

Apathy dropped from her like a garment —Edna Ferber

As excited as a mortician at a cheap funeral —Raymond Chandler

As much feeling as a sphinx
—Maureen Dowd, *New York Times*, 1985

(My father was) born without emotions like some people are born without little fingers —Pat Conroy

Buries her feelings as a dog buries a bone —Anon

Closed himself like a shellfish under attack —Kenzaburo Oë

Detached as a funeral director —Stanley Elkin

Detach oneself [as from a situation] like a zipout lining —Anon

(The sun is as) dispassionate as the hand of a man who greets you with his mind on other things —Beryl Markham

484

Drew a circle around herself, like the safe zone in a children's game
   where no pursuers may enter and no prisoners may leave
   —David Michael Kaplan

(I could) feel the armor, like a steel skin, slipping around me
   —William Diehl

The habit of reserve was like an iron mould —Ellen Glasgow
   See also: HABIT

Keep them [emotions] tucked away, and only produce them very
   occasionally, like special little pots of jam, when the people
   whom I love come to tea —Katherine Mansfield

Like a toothpaste ... gave only a little at a time —Donald Seaman

Lived inside herself as precisely as a walnut in its shell, nothing
   rattling, nothing wasting —Jessamyn West

(She had withdrawn into herself and) no longer projected anything,
   like an actor reaching the wings, the character falling like a cape
   to reveal the person beneath, innocuous
   —Lynne Sharon Schwartz

Numb as a broomstick —William Alfred

Persons extremely reserved are like old enamelled watches, which
   had painted covers that hindered your seeing what o'clock it was
   —Horace Walpole

A prudent reserve [about being open with other people] is as
   necessary as a seeming openness is prudent —Lord Chesterfield

Retreated into himself like a turtle —Carlos Fuentes

She was reserved ... like a picture so hung that it can be seen only
   at a certain angle; an angle known to no one but its possessor
   —Edith Wharton

Shrunk into herself as though she had been touched by something
   coarse —Anton Chekhov

Sit inside themselves like honey in a jar and just be
   —Elizabeth Janeway

Spiritless as corked champagne —James G. Huneker

Taught herself to control feelings ... the way an Indian fakir controls
   pain —Shana Alexander

Restlessness

Always fidgeting around to go, like a horse in an antbed
—Elmer Kelton

Fidgeted as though the skin on her back were as a plucked fowl's in a poulterer's shop window —Virginia Woolf

Fidgety as a child —Richard Wilbur

Fidgety, like a rabbit's nose —or a commuter—Don Marquis

Fitful as a cautery —Diane Ackerman

I'm as restless as a willow in a windstorm, I'm as jumpy as a puppet on a string —Oscar Hammerstein II, opening lines for "It Might As Well Be Spring" from *State Fair*
> "It Might As Well Be Spring" is a particularly outstanding example of Hammerstein's mastery of the light-hearted simile. The lyrics also compare a nightingale without a song to a feeling of discontentment, a spider to busyness and a baby on a swing to a feeling of giddiness.

As impatient as a wedding dick —American colloquialism

(It is a night like many another with the sky now a bit) impatient for today to be over like a bored salesgirl shifting from foot to stockinged foot —John Ashberry

Pacing up and down like an animal in a cage —Elizabeth Taylor

(Walking around) restless as a big animal in the lowering weather —Elizabeth Spencer

Restless as a rolling stone —Anon

Restless as sharp desire —Arthur C. Benson

Restless as Ulysses —William Makepeace Thackeray

Restless like a man running downhill who cannot keep on his legs unless he runs on, and will inevitably fall if he stops —Arthur Schopenhauer

A restless mind, like a rolling stone, gathers nothing but dirt and mire —John Balguy

Seemed always looking for a place, like one who goes to choose a grave —Stephen Crane

(Settled on the couch,) shifting and fluttering like birds in a nest —Peter Meinke

Squirming as though bitten by bugs —Bernard Malamud

Squirm like a country mule hitched beside the railroad track —American colloquialism, attributed to South

Tossed all night like a man running from himself —Paige Mitchell

Wriggling in her place, as if her chair was hot —Frank Swinnerton

RESTRAINT
See: EMOTIONS

RESULTS
See: CAUSE/EFFECT

RETREAT
See: EXITS

RETURN
See: PAST, THE; REAPPEARANCE

REVELRY
See: GAIETY

REVENGE
See: BITTERNESS

RHETORIC
See: SPEECHMAKING

RICHES
See: ABUNDANCE

RICHNESS

Rich as apricots in brandy —Robert D. McFadden

(Vellum) rich as country cream —Oliver Wendell Holmes, Sr.

Rich as memory —Marge Piercy

Rich as velvet brocade —Morris Philipson, describing the rich texture of language in a book, *New York Times Book Review,* April 12, 1987

RIDICULOUSNESS
See: FOOLISHNESS

RIGHTNESS
See: CORRECTNESS, TRUENESS/FALSENESS

Rising

RISING
See also: STANDING

Everything undulates like water weed —John Berger
Berger's simile appeared in his afterword for the published script of the movie, *Nineteen-Nineteen*.

Got up clumsily, cautiously, like one standing in a stalled Ferris wheel —Stanley Elkin

Lifts like a starting gate —Daniel Berrigan

Popped up ... like a released spring —Elizabeth Spencer

Raising himself in his seat like a panelist answering a question from the audience —Kingsley Amis

Reared like a seal —Erich Maria Remarque

(He felt his cock) rearing up like a kite —Jilly Cooper

Rise (from sleep) like driftwood out of surf —Karl Shapiro

(Smoke that) rises like birds —D. H. Lawrence

Rising gawkily like a tame goose trying to fly —Margaret Laurence

Rising like a north wind —Lawrence Durrell

Rising like a salmon against the bullnecked river —Louis MacNeice

Rising like cakes —Thomas Lux

Rising uncomfortably, like a schoolboy in the presence of a censuring teacher —Jan Kubicki

Rose like bubbles to the surface —Ivo Andric

Rose, like royalty —Edna Ferber

Rose ... slowly, like a statue coming reluctantly to life —James Crumley

Rose to go ... like a business man who has wasted a valuable twenty minutes on a prospective customer —Christopher Isherwood

Rose up like a flying swan —Stevie Smith

THE CARS CAME DOWN THEM
(LONDON STREETS) LIKE RATS

Scrambled back out of his chair like a foot soldier ducking a grenade
—Robert Lewis Taylor

Stood [up to go], like Cinderella hearing the stroke of midnight
—Eric Knight

Stood up, tawny and twinkling like a mobile in a breeze
—Dick Francis

Surfaced like a nugget on sinking soil —Derek Lambert

Surfaced like a trout that had spotted a dragonfly just above the water —Joan Hess
What surfaces in Hess' novel, *Strangled Prose*, is a character's alter ego.

RISK
See also: DANGER

About as risky as selling the farm to buy up blocks of Xerox in the early '60s —John Stravinsky about horse syndicate investments, *Wall Street Journal*, August 15, 1986

The art of gambling is like the art of painting. You've got to know when to stop —Maurice Edelman

Betting on Martin was like betting on an aging horse that lived on sourmash whiskey —Will Weaver

(Politics with a mass of people is as) chancy and fickle as a whore's heart —Robert Traver

Chancy as trying to catch a fish in the open hand
—Elizabeth Hardwick

It [the need to risk] was like statistics or gambling; you had to compute probabilities. And there was always the unforeseen, the little thing you overlooked that would catch you up in the end —Mary McCarthy

Precarious as wheat farming —Larry McMurtry
The profession McMurtry is likening to wheat farming is film making. He builds on the simile as follows: "He might raise a great crop of films ... then watch them all wither in the theater."

Risky ... It's like playing with a chemistry set without reading the directions —Vincent Canby, *New York Times*, January 22, 1986

The risky activity described is movie making by the inexperienced.

To remove the element of risk is like playing cards with a stacked deck —Stephen Gillers, *New York Times*/Op Ed, November 23, 1986

> Gillers, a law professor, used this simile to discuss the exposé of people in the financial world who had been taking the risk out of arbitrage by dealing on specially garnered or insider information.

RIVERS
See: PONDS AND STREAMS

ROAD SCENES

The cars come down them [London streets] like rats —V. S. Pritchett

Cars nestled around the place like puppies feeding off a giant tit —Dan Wakefield

Cars ... run along together like sticks on a stream —John Updike

Cars were flashing by [on highway] like toucans, bright red, hot pink and high yellow —Hortense Calisher

A dirt road that ran like string through some nearby woods —Wilfrid Sheed

The divided road looked like a striped gray snake curving across the brown landscape —A. E. Maxwell

Far off the highway ... lone lights signalled like boats anchored far at sea —Louise Erdrich

Gradually the landscape on either side of the road became like an embrace —Susan Engberg

Grunting taxicabs ... wallowing yellowly in the bright sun like panting porkers —Harvey Swados

The headlights of the cars in the deepening dusk were like a continuous stream of tracer-bullets aimed at anyone with temerity enough to cross their trajectory —Cornell Woolrich

The highway shimmers like a polished stove top —Mary Hedin

The interstate highway was like the ocean. It seemed to go on forever and was a similar color. Mirages of heat were shining in the distance like whitecaps —Bobbie Ann Mason

The lighted road seemed to shift like snow —Martin Cruz Smith

The motorway opened out before them like a black river, roaring —MacDonald Harris

The road, black as a ravine —Helen Hudson

The road dipped and rippled like a ribbon —Phyllis Naylor

The road lay straight as a spear —Terry Bisson

The road like a cat flattening its ears went into a straightaway —John Updike

Roads that never stopped ... but looped and turned with exquisite abandon, like a ball of yarn given infinite slack —Sharon Sheehe Stark

Road that looked as smooth as a tablecloth —Wallace Stegner

The road was tree-lined, the oaks arching over the roadway from either embankment like a canopy —Jonathan Valin

The road wound like a twisted snake —Stephen Vincent Benét

Saw the train pulled like a string of black beads over the horizon —Louise Erdrich

The searchlights [of cars on the highway] coursed ahead like elongated greyhounds —Erich Maria Remarque

The sound of the traffic is as faint as the roaring of a shell —John Cheever

Steely [railway] tracks ... like clean penstrokes —Dorothy Canfield Fisher

Traffic moved like flies through a sieve —Tom Robbins

ROARS
See also: SCREAMS

Ranting like a mad prophet —Amos Oz

Roar as loud as a howitzer —Norman Mailer

(The tiger) roaring like the sea —Dame Edith Sitwell

Roar like a jetport —T. Coraghessan Boyle

Roared like a tiger —Eudora Welty

Roar [of laughter] ... like a tractor backfiring —Raymond Chandler

Roar like a winter breeze —Cole Porter, from "I've Come to Wive It Wealthily In Padua," one of the lyrics for the musical, *Kiss Me Kate*, an adaptation of Shakespeare's *Taming of the Shrew*.

Roar like bears —*The Holy Bible/Isaiah*

Roars like a rhino (as she comes and comes) —Carolyn Kizer

We roar all like bears —*The Holy Bible/Isaiah*

A whoop like Yale making a touchdown against Princeton —Raymond Chandler

ROCKING AND ROLLING
See: MOVEMENT, UNSTEADINESS, VIBRATION

ROMANCE
See: LOVE

ROOMS

[An office] almost as severe as the cell of some medieval monk —J. D. McClatchy

Bathroom, mirrored like a discotheque —Diane Ackerman

Bedroom ... large as a football field and as cold —John Le Carré

Black bedroom with mirrors ... looks like a wet dream from Walt Disney —Richard North Patterson

The blue and white room was ... cold and hollow as an October mist —M. J. Farrell

The cramped space of the vestibule felt like the inside of a hooded cage —Kenzaburo Oë

[Small room] done up in moist red velvet, like the interior of a womb —Angela Carter

Dusty [a windowsill] as a literal Sahara —Tom Robbins

Entry hall ... as impersonal as a hotel lounge —John Braine

Rooms

Everything in the room was yellow ... it was a bit like having been swallowed by a butterfly —Pat M. Esslinger-Carr

[Wooden] floors as blonde as a movie star's hair —William Hamilton, National Public Radio, "Morning Edition," April 15, 1987

The floor [of room set aside for dancing] gleamed like egg yolk —Susan Fromberg Schaeffer

A hall that was cool and vaulted like a cloister —Ross Macdonald

(The little den was now) hideous as a torture-chamber —Stephen Crane

It [a room] is like a monastic cell —V. S. Pritchett

The living room was spacious and divided like Gaul into three parts —John Cheever

Oak floors shone like brown glass —Rebecca West

On the ceiling the reflection of the waves of the bay outside flickered on and on like conversation —Kate Grenville

The paint [on ceiling of room] peeling like the surface of the moon —Jilly Cooper

(In my gray) room, bare as a barn —Randall Jarrell

Room [small and narrow] ... friendly as Death Row —Gavin Lyall

The room glows like a field of forget-me-nots in the high country —Patricia Henley

A room is like a cast-off shoe, which holds the shape of its owner's unique foot —Paul Theroux

Room ... like a cell, except that there were no bars over the one small window —Dashiell Hammett

Room like a cupboard —Katherine Mansfield

The room [at a Howard Johnson's motel] ... sat like a young bride ... wanting only to please you —Max Apple

The room was as hot as the inside of a pig's stomach —Madison Smartt Bell

The room was as quiet and empty as a chapel —Wallace Stegner
See also: SILENCE

494

The room was filled like a pool with darkness —Josephine Jacobson

The [empty] room was like a fowl plucked clean —Jean Stafford

Room ... with nothing actually matching anything else but everything living happily together, like the random sowing of flowers —Rosamund Pilcher

Study ... like the returned-letter department of a post office, with stacks of paper everywhere, bills paid and unpaid, letters answered and unanswered, tax returns, pamphlets, leaflets. If by mistake we left the door open on a windy day, we came back to find papers flapping through the air like frightened birds —Mary Lavin

Twilight came drifting into the room like a shimmering cloud of powdered glass —Natascha Wodin

Walls white like a physician's consultation room —W. D. Snodgrass

RUNNING
See also: MOVEMENT, SPEED

Came running like a race —Lee Smith

A queer little hustling run, like a puppet jerked by wires —Ross Macdonald

Raced around ... like a migrant bird —Elizabeth Hardwick

Ran across the lawn towards us crookedly, like someone in an egg-and-spoon race —Kate Grenville

Ran after ... like a dog after its master —Isaac Babel
See also: PURSUIT

Ran down the steps as if the Devil was behind her —Donald Seaman

Ran in and out ... like a squirrel —Henry Van Dyke

Ran like a blind man —Stephen Crane

Ran like a stag —Jonathan Gash

Ran like a whirlwind —Thomas Macaulay
Another simile that has outlived its source, "The Battle of Lake Regillu," as a commonly used phrase.

Run ... like a blind sheep in a snowstorm —Borden Deal

Running

(A man comes up to them with a gun, they) run like antelopes
—Irwin Shaw

Run like a scalded dog —Rita Mae Brown

(Engineers and executives were) running around like ants in a
burning mound —Speer Morgan

Running around in circles like crazy sheepdogs —George Garrett

Running as if on fire —Bernard Malamud

Running ... like a leaf driven by the wind —Joseph Conrad

Running like a man who has jumped up in the dark and runs
listening between his footfalls for the reason of his still running
—Ted Hughes

[A rabbit] runs like a faucet —Marge Piercy

They [joggers] looked like an organized death march as they ran by
gasping, perspiring, stumbling, their faces contorted with pain
—Erma Bombeck

Trotted beside him like a frightened puppy beside an elephant
—Thomas Wolfe

RUTHLESSNESS
See: CRUELTY

Sadness

SADNESS
See also: EMOTIONS, GLOOM

As full of sorrow as the sea of sands —William Shakespeare

Could feel it [the sadness] pierce him like a foreign body in his heart
—Amos Oz

Crest-fallen as a dried pear —William Shakespeare

Crest-fallen as a spy who had been caught by a thief —Victor Hugo

Depressing as the last day of fishing —Robert Traver

A feeling of sadness that is not akin to pain, resembles sorrow only
as the mist resembles rain —Henry Wadsworth Longfellow

(Scarlett) felt bereft, as though she had sold one of her children
—Margaret Mitchell

496

The sadness which inspired the comparison was that experienced by the heroine of *Gone With the Wind* when she sold her lumber business.

Felt melancholy grip him, like a pain in the heart —Mary McCarthy

(I felt depressed,) filled to the neck with sadness like a carafe with bad wine —T. Coraghessan Boyle

His heart throbbed like a bruise in the sigh —Norman Mailer

His heart would sink down to his bowels like lead —Thomas Wolfe

Looked and acted like a man who had just driven home from a couple of heart-rending funerals —George Ade
See also: FACIAL EXPRESSIONS, SERIOUS

Melancholy as a discarded statesman —William Mountford

Melancholy as a fiddle with one string —Thomas Holcroft

My heart is within me as an ash in the fire
—Algernon Charles Swinburne

My heart was as lead —Jack London

Pathetic as all final efforts —Alice McDermott

Pathetic as an autumn leaf —George Moore

(A low call,) plaintive as a shepherd calling to sheep who need no strident invocation —Arthur A. Cohen

Sad as an eagle without wings, sad as a violin with only one string
—Jean Rhys

Sad as night —William Shakespeare

Sad as professional mourners —F. Scott Fitzgerald

Sad as twilight —George Eliot

Saddening as a forest fire —Robert Traver

Sad like graveyards —Terry Bisson

Sad ... like somebody who's pilot light got blown out a long time ago —Susan Kelly

Sadness ... gnawed like a rat at his mind —Roderic Jeffries

Sadness, like that inspired by a grave strain of music
—Joseph Conrad

Sadness that, over the years, had gathered in his chest like matter in a clogged drain —Joyce Reiser Kornblatt

There would come, like water washing over a sunken buoy, the little knell of sadness —Hortense Calisher
> Just as similes are used to give dramatic beginning to literary works, they can also be used to wind things up, as demonstrated by this final sentence from Calisher's novel, *Point of Departure.*

SAFETY
See also: DANGER, RISK

Feel as safe as a lone subway rider at 2 a.m. —Anon

Feel as safe as guarded by a charm —Elizabeth Barrett Browning

Looked as dangerous as a squirrel and much less nervous —Raymond Chandler

The man who looks for security, even in the mind, is like a man who would chop off his limbs in order to have artificial ones which will give him no pain or trouble —Henry Miller

Nothing as safe as simplicity —Edith Wharton

Safe and more or less invulnerable like sulky Achilles among Trojans —George Garrett

(I thought I was) safe as a good new boat —Reynolds Price

(They think they're) safe as angels —Dashiell Hammet

Safe as a nun in a roomful of eunuchs —Donald Seaman

Safe as a tank town —W. R. Burnett

Safe as houses —Mary Gordon

Safe as in a cradle —William Wordsworth

Safe as in God's pocket
—American colloquialism, attributed to New England

Safe as sunshine —Slogan R. E. Dietz Co.

Security ... tighter than the skin on a snake —William H. Hallhan

She's safe as a vault —Raymond Chandler

Squatting in safety like the yolk in an egg —Bertold Brecht

SATISFACTION
See: CONTENTMENT

SAYINGS
See: MAXIMS, PROVERBS AND SAYINGS

SCANDAL
See: REPUTATION

SCARS
See: FACIAL DETAILS

SCATTERING
See: DISPERSAL

SCIENCE
See: MATHEMATICS AND SCIENCE

SCREAMS
See also: ROARS

Bellowed like a locomotive —Marge Piercy

Bellowing like a wounded whale —William Diehl

Bellow, like an animal in pain —Jean Rhys

A broken shriek like a viola gone sour —T. Coraghessan Boyle

Cried out hoarsely like a bird warning the forest that a predator is
    on the loose —Derek Lambert

Cries ... shrill, like a pig having his throat cut
    —W. Somerset Maugham

Gave a short roar like a lion keeping in voice —Kingsley Amis

Gave a shriek like an engine —Joyce Cary

Gave a shrill scream like a wrung hen —Hugh Walpole

He bellered like a bull calf —William A. Owens

A high-pitched wail like a cat on fire —Peter Benchley

His scream sliced the night like a hatchet —William Diehl

Howled ... like a savage beast being goaded to death with knives and spears —Emily Brontë

Howling (through the streets) like an outcast dog —Erich Maria Remarque

Howl like dogs —Dante Alighieri

Howl like stabled wolves, or tigers at their prey —John Milton

A loud yell which rang through the lonely fields like the howl of an evil spirit —Charles Dickens

Screamed like a door creaking —Hugh Walpole

(Laughed and) screamed like herring gulls —Joan Aiken

Screamed like a horse in a fire —Gerald Kersh

Screamed ... like an eight-legged wildcat having a fit —Harold Adams

Screamed like gulls on stormy water —Saul Bellow

Screaming at the top of her lungs like a railroad whistle —Paige Mitchell

Screaming filled the air like an icy mist —Bertold Brecht

Screaming like a hawk making a long dive at a rabbit —W. P. Kinsella

Screaming ... like a saint sent to hell by mistake —Rosellen Brown

Scream like a peacock in heat —Tennessee Williams

Scream like a village of raped virgins —Clive Cussler
> In Cussler's novel, *Cyclops*, the simile refers to protests in Washington about a space shuttle in Russian hands.

Scream like sandstorms in the desert, like the death of the universe —T. Coraghessan Boyle

Scream ... like the death rattle of a slaughtered animal —Ignazio Silone

A scream of rage ... like a blast from hell —Fred Mustard Stewart

The scream rose like an aria —Larry McMurtry

Screams as if ice water is rippling down her back —Ira Wood

Screeched like a cage of mynas —Tony Ardizzone

Screeched like a dying pullet —Frank Ross

Screeched like a nighttime cat —Cynthia Ozick

(The women) screeching like bony parrots —H. E. Bates

Shout as demonstrative as a lizard —George Foy

Shrieked like an old screen door —Carolyn Kizer

Shrieking ... like she was at a fireman's picnic —John Dos Passos

Shriek like a knife in the heart —T. Coraghessan Boyle

A shriek like a needle-point —Elizabeth Bowen

Shriek like infuriated switch engines —Irvin S. Cobb

Shriek ... louder than the loud ocean —Lord Byron

Stormed and screamed like some shrill, wet hurricane about the
    house —Anita Desai

Talked and shouted for hours on end like a preacher
    —Ignazio Silone

Yelled ... as if I were being roasted alive —Natascha Wodin

Yelling and growling like savage but cowardly dogs
    —Lawrence Durrell

Yelping (at captain of waiters) like a terrier who had cornered some
    small defenseless animal —Ross Macdonald

Yowl like a tortured cat —Madison Smartt Bell

SCRUPULOUSNESS
See: CORRECTNESS

SEASCAPES
See: OCEAN/OCEANFRONT, PONDS AND STREAMS

SELF-CONSCIOUSNESS
See: DISCOMFORT, NATURALNESS

SENSATIONS
See: EMOTIONS

SERENITY
See: PEACEFULNESS

SERMONS
See: SPEECHMAKING

SEX
See: ATTRACTIVENESS, SEXUAL INTERACTION, RELATIONSHIPS

SEXUAL INTERACTION

Sexual Interaction

Attacked her with a loose and greedy mouth, like a man sucking at a torn fruit —Miles Gibson

Even when they made love ... it was perfunctory, as if he were listening for something else, a phone call, a footfall. He was like a man scratching himself. She was like his hand —Margaret Atwood

The first time that she spread her legs for him it had been like opening her jaw for the dentist —Tom Robbins

(She could only remember the times that he had lain with her,) fleeing into her body as if it were a refuge from his daily wage of fear and frustration —Davis Grubb

Fucking Barcaloo was like coupling with a shaggy dog —Robert Campbell

Fucking you is like stuffing sausage meat into a broiler. I'm always frightened I'll discover the giblets —Jilly Cooper

Gave her whole body to me, like something without a bone —Winston Graham

Gobbled her like a ripe peach —Peter De Vries

He aroused her so excruciatingly that she wanted to lie down right now for him in the middle of the muddy road and let him plough through her like a car —Julia O'Faolain

He fell into her with the ease and velocity of a stone dropping into the sea —MacDonald Harris

He fell on me like a wave. But like a wave he washed away, leaving no sign he'd been there —Louise Erdrich

He had never before made love like this ... as if he had found a twin whose body had been cast in the matching mold of his own —Amos Oz

He pulled up my clothes like a man unwrapping a parcel
—Graham Swift

Her touch moving over my body like pebbles in a stream
—Arthur A. Cohen

He slips into her like a thief entering a doorway —Hilma Wolitzer

He was like something washed ashore on her —Flannery O'Connor
This observation is prompted by an unsuccessful sexual
encounter.

His love making felt like having a tooth stopped by a singularly
incompetent dentist —Vicki Baum

His penis rising and throbbing like greedy fish to her bait
—Julia O'Faolain

It [sexual intercourse] was as if we'd been fused together, melting
into each other like amoebae but violently, like cars crashing
head on —John Braine

The lovemaking wasn't exactly by the numbers, but she did order
everything on the menu, like a teenage kid trying to impress his
date —Jonathan Valin

Made love like monkeys —Charles Johnson

Making love with Charlie was like being taken into a big warm
machine —Sue Grafton

(Harry) maneuvered her around like a load of wet wash
—R. Wright Campbell

Our body warmth flowed back and forth, coursing between us like
some underground hot spring —Harvey Swados

Our two bodies met like a thunderclap —Carolyn Kizer

Places her gently upon the bed like a newly pressed suit
—Roger McGough

She gave herself up to me like a condemned criminal —John Hagge

She snuggled into him like a kitten at the breast of its mother
—Rita Mae Brown

She stiffened on penetration and clung to him, relaxing as if
unlocked with his blunt key —Paul Theroux

Spills him off her body like a pile of sand —John Updike

Sexual Interaction

See also: REJECTION

Their touch together was like a miniature jolt of electricity —Paul Horgan

Undressed deliberately, slowly, as if she were unwrapping a gift —Graham Swift

We crashed against one another like waves on a breakwater —Sue Grafton

We ended up in bed together, sort of, spastic and looped, doomed for failure, like two senile inventors in an upstairs room, lonely as spoons —Lorrie Moore

We flowed together again like a stream that for an instant an island had separated —Truman Capote

We half walked half stumbled towards the bed, like uncertain dancers learning a new step —Peter De Vries

SHAME
See: BLUSHES

SHINING
See: BRIGHTNESS, GLITTER AND GLOSS

SHOCK
See: CAUSE/EFFECT, SURPRISE

SHOUTS
See: SCREAMS

SHRIEKS
See: SCREAMS

SHUT
See: OPEN/SHUT

Shyness

SHYNESS

Bashful as an egg at Easter —Sir John Denham
> This has expanded with the seasons to include "Bashful as a turkey at Thanksgiving or Christmas."

Demure as an African violet —Maya Angelou

Demure as an old whore at a christening —Thomas Fuller

Demure as if butter wouldn't melt in his mouth —Thomas Fuller

Shy as a squirrel —George Meredith

Shy as infants —Alice McDermott

Shy as rabbits —Anon

Shy, like a hospitable country hostess anxious to give pleasure, but afraid that she has not much to offer citizens of a larger world —Phyllis Bottome

A shy man is as a lonely man ... between him and his fellow-men there runs an impossible barrier ... a strong invisible wall —Jerome K. Jerome

SIDEBURNS
See: BEARDS

SIGHS
See also: GROANS AND WHISPERS

A collective sigh, like an escaping jet of steam —Robert Traver

Gave a deep sigh, like pain was a habit —Cornell Woolrich

Releasing a muffled sigh like a baby animal with a full belly —Kenzaburo Oë

Sighed, a rustling sound like wandering autumn leaves —Derek Lambert

Sighed like a long-suffering teacher —Ramsey Campbell

Sighed like a pair of bellows —William McIlvanney

Sighed like a poet in love —Beryl Markham

Sighed once with relief ... like a low note on a bagpipe —Sue Grafton

Sighed with pain, as if a knife had twisted deep inside —Louise Erdrich

Sighing, like a bagpipe's dying breath —Patrick White

Sighing like a punctured tire —Guy Bolton

Sighing like the night wind and sobbing like the rain
—Stephen Foster
> This is a line from the song, "Jeanie with the Light Brown Hair," which begins with yet another simile: "I dream of Jeanie with the light brown hair, borne like a vapor on the summer air."

Sigh like some sweet plaintive melody —William Motherwell

A sigh of relief escaped his lips like a long-needed crap —John Lennon

Sighs as if a mountain lay on her chest —Cora Sandel

Sigh ... tender and enchanting, like the wind outside a wood in the evening —Virginia Woolf

A sigh that was like a gust of sand raised and dropped suddenly by the wind —Flannery O'Connor

SILENCE

Quiet as a lady's fart —Harold Adams

Quiet as a lamb —William Langland

Quiet as a mouse —Anon

Quiet as an eel swimming in oil —Arthur Baer

Quiet as a nun —William Wordsworth
> English novelist Antonia Fraser borrowed Wordsworth's simile for a mystery novel about a nun.

(It was) quiet as a prayer —Mary Lee Settle

(The whole immense room ... was) quiet as a sepulchre —Walter De La Mare

Quiet as a stone —John Keats

Quiet as a street at night —Rupert Brooke

Quiet as a street of tombs in a buried city —John Ruskin

Quiet as a wasp in one's nose —John Ray's *Proverbs*

Quiet as a wooden-legged man on a tin roof —Anon
> This is one of many American folk similes incorporated by Carl Sandburg into his unique long poem, *The People, Yes.*

(The house was as) quiet as death, as the inside of a skull
—John Fowles

Quiet as dust —Ken Kesey

(Her mind was) quiet, as if a needle had been lifted from a
phonograph record —Ellen Gilchrist

(The town was all as) quiet as the hills —A. E. Coppard

Quiet as two tombs —Robert B. Parker

Quietly as a moth —Louis Bromfield

Quietly as smoke rising —Loren D. Estleman

Quiet ... pressed on her eardrums like a weight —Hortense Calisher

Silence grand as Versailles —Lorrie Moore

Silence heavy in the air like a threat —William Boyd

Silence ... hung in the air like a dead pheasant —Penelope Gilliatt

Silence is deep as eternity —Thomas Carlyle

Silence is his delight and instruction now ... as if a blessed quiet
came to him like water made into music —George Garrett

Silence ... like a great hand pressed across a mouth struggling to give
vent to a scream —Stephen French Whitman

Silence ... like an explosion —John Fowles

The silence like an ocean rolled, and broke against my ear
—Emily Dickinson

The silence of the place was like a sleep, so full of rest it seemed
—Henry Wadsworth Longfellow

Silence ... poured in between them like a drifting dune
—Lawrence Durrell

The silence ran between them like a fuse —William McIlvanney

Silence, rather like somebody had died —Elizabeth Spencer

Silence ... rich and winey, like a rest in music —Zona Gale

Silence rose like a mountain —Arthur A. Cohen

Silence settled on him like a mist —Frank Ross

Silence ... so intense that it was like a third presence in the room
—Antonia White

Silence so thick that he imagined he could cut a slice out of it, like a succulent melon —Ella Leffland

Silence ... steadily filling up the bare white room, like water rising in a tank —Christopher Isherwood

Silence stretched out like membrane on the point of tearing
—Ross Macdonald

Silence [in tension-filled room] stretched like a wire vibrating with impulses that were never heard —Hortense Calisher

Silence that falls between them ... like deep snow —Donald Justice

Silence that fell upon her like a restraining hand —Nadine Gordimer

Silence that made his own breathing seem like the breaking of distant surf —Mark Helprin

Silence walked beside them like the ghost of a dead man
—W. Somerset Maugham

The silence [in the room] was like an invasion, a possession by the great silent mountains —Gina Berriault

The silence was like a tranquilizer —Mignon F. Ballard

Silent as a burglar behind a curtain —Raymond Chandler

Silent as a cat on velvet —Reynolds Price

Silent as a country churchyard —Thomas Babington Macaulay

Silent as a ghost —Percy Bysshe Shelley

(Rooms) silent as a lantern —Daniela Gioseffi

Silent as a midnight thought —Anne Finch

Silent as a prisoner —Richard Ford

Silent as a snowflake settled on the ground —Donald Seaman

Silent as a standing pool —William Wordsworth

Silent as a stuffed sausage —Helen Hudson

Silent as a white shark —Diane Ackerman

QUIET AS DUST

Silent as despair —John Greenleaf Whittier

Silent as despairing love —William Blake
> A modern variant: "Silent as a breaking heart."

Silent as flight —Wendell Berry

(An object) silent as pillows —Diane Wakoski

Silent as rain or fleece —Lawrence Durrell

[Thoughts] silent ... as space —Lord George Byron
> Here is the complete simile as it appeared in *Don Juan:* "There was a depth of feeling to embrace ... thoughts, boundless, deep, but silent too as space."

Silent as the moon —John Milton
> Many writers continue to link the moon with silence, with frequent twists and extensions. Some examples from contemporary literature include: "She was as silent and distant as the moon" from a short story by Kate Wheeler and "Silent as the dark side of the moon" from *Water Music* by T. Coraghessan Boyle.

Soundless as any breeze —Dame Edith Sitwell

The sound of the silence was like the hum of her own nerves stretched taut —William Humphrey

Speechless as an anchorite —Lawrence Durrell

Speechless as though his tongue were paralyzed —Ouida

Stealthy silence as of a neatly executed crime —Joseph Conrad

(The house was) still as a bottomless well —Hugh Walpole

Still as a desert —Anon

Still as a mouse —Richard Flecknoe
> An extension of this by Sir Walter Scott: "Quiet as a mouse in a hole."

Still as a stone —*The Holy Bible/Exodus*

Still as mourners —Mark Strand

Still as the grave —William Shakespeare

Still like gulls —W. H. Auden

Stillness struck like a stopped guitar —Sharon Sheehe Stark

A sudden silence ... shook them like an inaudible explosion
    —Frank Tuohy

There seemed to be a lot of silence in the house, like something
    deep and sticky you had to wade through —Jane Rogers

There was absolute silence. It said as plainly as if silence were a
    language itself, "Go back." —Flannery O'Connor

(They walk close together,) silent as painted people —Julie Hayden

Tight-lipped as a Sioux —Charles Johnson

Tongues tight as immigrants —Daniel Berrigan

SILLINESS
See: FOOLISHNESS

SIMILARITY

As alike as buttons on a shirt —Anon

(We're almost) as alike as eggs —William Shakespeare
        Similes about things which tend to be uniform have and
        continue to inspire many "As alike as" comparisons. The
        other famous author most frequently credited for the
        "Alike as eggs" simile is Miguel de Cervantes with "As
        alike ... as one egg is like another" from *Don Quixote*.

As alike ... as grapes in a cluster —Edna Ferber

As alike as my finger is to my finger —William Shakespeare

As alike as two drops of water —James Miller
        This simile has become so common that no "As alike"
        introduction is needed, as illustrated by, "Just like two
        drops of water," used by Isaac Bashevis Singer in *The
        Family Moskat* to describe the resemblance between a
        mother and son.

As alike as two peas in a pod —Jack London

Even in an age where more peas make their way to the dinner table from frozen food packages than pods, this now commonplace expression shows no sign of diminishing use. The form shown here has supplanted older and now little used versions such as, "Alike as two peas to one another" and, "As like each other as two peas."

As like a hand to another hand —Robert Browning

As like as like can be —William Wordsworth

As like as rain to water —William Shakespeare

As undifferentiable ... as ballots in a ballot box —Richard Ford
> The simile as used by Ford in *The Sportswriter* describes modern parents whose lives are so lacking in mystery and difference that they are undifferentiated from their children.

[Pencilled doodles] identical as tracings —Margaret Millar

[TV commentators] looked alike as bowling pins
   —T. Coraghessan Boyle

Looked as alike ... as hair pins —Loren D. Estleman

Looked as much alike as blackbirds on a fence —John Yount

Resembled each other like waves —Gustave Flaubert

They're like as a row of pins —Rudyard Kipling

SIMILES
See: MAXIMS, PROVERBS AND SAYINGS

SIMPLICITY

As devoid of any taste for luxury as a stone-deaf person of the sense of hearing —Isak Dinesen

Crude as life among farming people —Daniel Berrigan

Great men, like nature, use simple language
   —Marquis de Luc de Clappiers Vauvenargues
   See also: SPEAKING

I am simple ... just like that broken bottle. I have no secrets
    —John Updike

Physically as plain as a pike —Charles Johnson
            A variation is to be "Plain as a pikestaff."

[Body as] plain as a cheap clothes-rack —Brian Moore

Plain as a pine door —Sumner Locke Elliott

Plain as black and white —Karl Shapiro

(Hands) plain as blank pages —Gerald A. Browne

Plain as English mutton —E. B. White

Simple as a bucket —Paul Theroux

Simple as a Hopper painting —Anon

Simple as chessboards —George Bernard Shaw

Simple as children's cradle songs —Adrienne Rich

(Words) simple as potatoes —Marge Piercy

Simple as rain —Theodore Dreiser

(Would that life were as) simple as sport —Rita Mae Brown

Simple as the golden rule —Anon

A very simple man ... like a tree that has not many roots, but one
    tap-root that goes down deep —Willa Cather

SINGING
See also: MUSIC

As anxious about his voice as a Don Juan about his sexual
    equipment: a roughness was the equivalent of a dose of clap,
    laryngitis of impotence —Francis King

Carry a tune as well as a mouse carries an elephant —Anon

His care for his voice was like that of a parent for a sickly and
    therefore abnormally cherished child —Francis King

Melody ... sweetened the air like raindrops —Paul Theroux

Most of them [sopranos] sound like they live on seaweed
    —Sir Thomas Beecham

Sang in a drone like a far-away tractor —Mary Ward Brown

Sang without passion, like a conscientious schoolgirl —Antonia White

Singing is as natural and common to all men as it is to speak high when they threaten in anger, or to speak low when they are dejected —William Law

Singing voice ... like a bee in a bottle, a melodious slightly adenoidal whine, wavering, full of sobs and breaks, and of a pitch like a boy's before the change of voice —William Humphrey

Sing like a lark —William Makepeace Thackeray

Sings as sweetly as a nightingale —William Shakespeare

Song ... old as air, and dark as doom —Mark Van Doren

Sopranos trilling loudly as if terrorized —Harvey Swados

(I tried to sing along but) the notes themselves kept sliding away from me like water drops dancing across a hot skillet
—A. E. Maxwell
See also: ELUSIVENESS

[A whistled] tune ... seemed to be pouring out of him as though he were a bird —James Baldwin

Tune ... that climbed and plummeted like a kite in the wind
—Lynne Sharon Schwartz

SITTING

Carefully lowered himself into the chair like someone entering a steaming hot bath —Andrew Kaplan

Grandly sitting like a great rock —John Ashbery

Hit his chair like a large rock —Rita Mae Brown

Hunkered down on our haunches like Indians —Stephen King

Just sits there ... like a sick cat —Niven Busch

Perched [on a stool] like a night owl —Jonathan Valin

[Eight matrons] perched like pigeons around two identical card tables
—Leigh Allison Wilson

Sank back [into chair] ... like a weighted diver into water
—Richard Moran

The diver comparison is particularly apt within the context of Moran's novel, *Cold Sea Rising*, with its many ocean scenes.

Sank into a chair like a stone sinking into water
—Lael Tucker Wertenbaker

Sat as still as a bird sleeping on a limb —James Crumley

Sat bolt upright, like a character in a work of cheap fiction
—Peter De Vries

Sat down heavily, like a farmer getting ready for Sunday dinner
—Harvey Swados

Sat like a bronze figure —William Brammer
> The variations on sitting, standing or being "Still as a statue" are virtually limitless.

Sat like a humped stone —Flannery O'Connor

Sat like a lump of lead —Erich Maria Remarque

Sat like granite —Walter Stone

Sat like half-folded shirts, arms out of the way and knees close together —Mary Ward Brown

Sat [silently] like someone who can't remember the punch-line
—William McIlvanney

Sat like some portent against the skies of the evening
—E. M. Forster

Sat like wood —Leslie Thomas

Sat silent, motionless, like guests waiting to be welcomed
—Helen Hudson

Sat stiff as a cockroach, waiting to spring to life —Miles Gibson

Sat stolidly, like an egg flattened on its bottom —David Ignatow

Sat there like a mountain —Eudora Welty

Sat up abruptly like a clockwork figure released by a spring
—Joyce Cary

Sat up and crossed his legs like a tailor. Like a tailor with no needle
—Sterling Hayden

Sitting

Sat up as if she'd been shot from a cannon —Jonathan Valin

Sat up —like a soldier at reveille—Jonathan Valin

Sat up like Lazarus —Ray Bradbury

She is dumped on the seat like a barrel of ashes —Malcolm Cowley

Sitting [on the floor] like a sack —Ivan Turgenev

Sit like a frog on a chopping block —John Ray's *Proverbs*

Sit like an umbrella —Bertold Brecht

Sit like fixed candlesticks —William Shakespeare

Stood there like a mannequin —T. Coraghessan Boyle

Sit silent and still as if they were in a photograph, slightly out of focus —George Garrett

Sits like a pile of dough —Lee Smith

Sits quietly with her hands in her lap, like a pregnant woman being driven to the delivery rooom —Alice McDermott

Sits up high like a job applicant —Richard Ford

Sitting like somebody found at Pompeii —William McIlvanney

Sitting motionless ... like a mother who affects not to notice the rude or awkward conduct of her children —Marcel Proust

(She straightened up,) sitting stiff and small, like a small mast against a storm —Elizabeth Spencer

Sitting there pop-eyed as a ventriloquist's dummy —Antonia White

You sit with your head like a carving in space —Wallace Stevens

SKEPTICISM
See: TRUST/MISTRUST

SKILLS
See: ACCOMPLISHMENT

SKIN
See: BALDNESS, FACIAL COLOR, FACIAL DETAILS, PALLOR, WRINKLES

SKY
See: SKY COLOR

SKY COLOR

The colors hanging suspended in midair like huge, floating ostrich plumes —Paul Kuttner

The edges of the sky had a yellowish tinge like cheap paper darkening in the sunlight —Ross Macdonald

Pale blue sky like some Stuka dive-bomber —Donald Seaman

A redness in the sky, like the flame at the back of a vast baker's oven —Saul Bellow

Skies are gray as tarn —Richard Ford

Sky blue as winter milk —Joyce Cary

The sky changed through several colors and became a soft crumbled gray. It was like walking under the roof of an enormous cave where hidden fires burned low —Ross Macdonald

Sky [at dusk] ... green as unripe apples —Erich Maria Remarque

The sky is gilded with red, as if intoxicated —Cora Sandel

Sky ... like terra cotta —Saul Bellow

Sky so pale blue and clear as a baby's eye —Joyce Cary

Sky the color of oiled steel —T. Coraghessan Boyle

The sky was a dome of gray, stretched evenly like parachute silk at full billow —Lael Tucker Wertenbaker

The sky was gray as a battleship —Mike Fredman

The sky was hard blue, like bright ink —James Stern

The sky was the color of dishwater —T. Coraghessan Boyle

The sky was yellow as brass —Erich Maria Remarque

SLEEP
See: SNORES

SLOPPINESS
See: CARELESSNESS

SLOWNESS
See also: MOVEMENT

Agonizingly slow like the gradual ripening of a peach on a limb
—Sue Grafton

By degrees, as lawyers go to heaven —Anon

[A locomotive] came slowly, like a bison —Saul Bellow

(An hour) crawled by like a sick cockroach —Raymond Chandler

Creeping like a snail —William Shakespeare

Dragged around ... like a dog with three legs —Shelby Hearon

[An endless journey] like crossing the Sahara by pogo stick
—Robert Silverberg

Gather slowly, like a storm that swirls at sea —Anon

Gradually, like a man entering a swimming pool slowly
—Michael Korda
> The gradual process being compared to entering a pool is a
> return to work.

Grew with such infinite slowness, like a stalactite —Lawrence Durrell

Happening in slow motion like a baseball replay —Maxine Kumin

Have all the speed and liquidity of a slug skating across salt —Erik
Sandberg-Diment, *New York Times*, January 18, 1987
> Diment's comparison refers to a word processing program.

It [the movie *Kangaroo]* moves like a slug climbing a cornstalk
—Rex Reed, 1987

It takes time ... like getting your hair curled —Carlos Baker

Leisurely as the drift of continents —T. Coraghessan Boyle

Life passed him as slowly as traffic on a main artery during the
evening rush hour —Anon

Moved as slow as paste —Paul Theroux

(My feet seemed deep in sand. I) moved like some heat-weary
animal —Theodore Roethke

Moved slowly, like a diver with heavy boots —Graham Swift

Moved slowly through her days, like a mermaid floating in a
translucent sea where all was calm, shadowy, and ambiguous
—Peter Meinke

(Here and there a herd of stray cows) moves as slowly as old men
    on their way to the graveyard —A. D. Winans

(The government) moves like a huge blob of molasses on a two-
    degree slope —John D. MacDonald
        An extension of the cliche, "Slow as molasses."

Moving about, slow as earthquake survivors —Brian Moore

A process about as slow and arduous as the building of the
    pyramids —Edith Wharton
        The process Wharton is describing is character building.

Pushes ahead; slow as a weight —Delmore Schwartz

Slow and silent, like old movies —Sharon Sheehe Stark
    See also: SILENCE

Slow as a dream —Robert Penn Warren

Slow as a hog on ice with his tail frozen
    —American colloquialism, attributed to Vermont
        The way Vermonters say it: "With his tail froze."

Slow as a tortoise —American colloquialism
        To add emphasis there's, "As old as an old tortoise."

Slow as dough —Sharon Sheehe Stark
        In a story entitled *The Horsehair*, the simile is used to draw
        a portrait of a dull, unambitious man.

Slow as molasses going uphill —Jamaican expression
        A variant of, "Slow as molasses."

Slow as the hands of a schoolroom clock —W. D. Snodgrass

Slow as the oak's growth —John Greenleaf Whittier

Slow-blooded, like a lizard in winter —Mary Hood

Slowly, like bodies being dragged —Ross Macdonald

Slowly, like turtles cooking in the sun, we rotated our heads
    —T. Coraghessan Boyle
    See also: HEAD MOVEMENTS

Slow-moving like an old woman with a walker —Anon

Slow reluctant process [a city's morning stirrings], like the waking of
    a heavy sleeper —Edith Wharton

Slowness

(Opened the case) with deliberate ceremonial slowness, as if breaking bread at a wedding banquet —Richard Lourie

SMELL
See: SWEAT

SMILES
See: BRIGHTNESS; FACIAL EXPRESSION, MISCELLANEOUS; GRINS; LAUGHTER

SMOKING
See: TOBACCO

Smoothness

SMOOTHNESS

(The syllables) flow like wind on water —T. Coraghessan Boyle

Glib as an auctioneer —James Crumley

Go down like milk and molasses —Russell Baker

Goes down like chopped hay —John Ray's *Proverbs*

It [a drink] was about as smooth as a rusty hacksaw
    —Harold Adams

(Cold,) polished as a marble column —Honoré de Balzac
        Balzac's description deftly characterizes Gosbeck, the main
        character in a short novel by that name.

Sleek and pretty as a new dime —Borden Deal

(Her breasts protruded from the suds wet and) sleek as seals
    —Jean Thompson

Slick as a button —American colloquialism
        Unlike "Smooth as glass" or "Smooth as alabaster" which
        usually describe texture, this generally applies to
        something easily done. Other widely used variations to
        describe a glib, shrewd person are "Slick as an eel" and
        "Slick as grease."

Slick as a cake of soap —Charles Wright

Slick as a pig —R. Wright Campbell

(Would make my life as) slick as a sonnet —Tallulah Bankhead

Slick as spit —James Lee Burke

Slick as a water snake —George Garrett

[Wet streets] slick as black satin —Paige Mitchell

Slick as black marble —Donald McCaig

[An icy roof] slick as cake icing —Davis Grubb

Slick as nail polish —Rosellen Brown

Slick as snot —Jonathan Kellerman

Slick as water —Terry Bisson

(Her glasses were) slippery as icicles —Cynthia Ozick

Smooth as a carpet —John Ray's *Proverbs*
> Still widely used ... or as one might say "Popular and enduring as a John Ray proverb."

Smooth as a kitten's ear —Slogan, Hammond Cedar Company

Smooth as a phantom —John Betjeman

(His movement was as) smooth as a ripple of water
   —Raymond Chandler

Smooth as a sage —Lawrence Durrell

(Her mind, clear and as) smooth as a sea stone beaten by the waves and elements for a millenium —Charles Johnson

Smooth as a suburbanized television professor —Harvey Swados

Smooth as corn syrup —Helen Hudson

(Her skin was as) smooth as glass —English ballad
> Probably one of the most frequently used "Smooth as" comparisons, with 'slick' and 'smooth' often used interchangeably, as in "The frozen lake was slick as a mirror," found in Mark Helprin's short story, *Ellis Island*.

Smooth as marbles —Anon

(Voice) smooth as mink oil —Linda Barnes

Smooth as monumental alabaster —William Shakespeare

Smooth as oil —William Shakespeare

(The sea was) smooth as pewter plate —Mazo De La Roche

Smoothness

Smooth as pine-nuts —Suzanne E. Berger

(Works as) smooth as sand running through an hour glass
—William Diehl

(Glasses) smooth as sea-washed stones —Ann Beattie

(Cheeks) smooth as silk —Juvenal
Though first used to describe complexion, the simile was expanded to broader use by O. Henry when he wrote "Everything goes smooth as silk."

Smooth as skin in oil —Reynolds Price

(The fellow was) smooth as soap —Jessamyn West

(Skin) smooth as stones on the shore —Mary Morris

Smooth as the inner lips of a shell —Sharon Olds
The shell comparison is used by poet Olds to describe the reddened, sun-swollen lips of the author's daughter.

Smooth as the nose of a moth —Karl Shapiro

Smooth as the road to ruin —Anon

(He shrugged and rolled up his sleeves. Both forearms were as) unmarked as a baby's bottom —Jonathan Valin

Worn smooth and slick as a chewed bone —George Garrett

Worn smooth as a tiger's eye —Sharon Sheehe Stark

Snores

SNORES

Snored as if all the frogs of spring were inside him —Eudora Welty

(Punctuated the air with a periodic) snore like the honk of geese
—Paige Mitchell

Snores go up and down like a zipper —Brad Leithauser

Snores like a diesel truck —Ira Wood

(Hoffman's) snores ... like muffled lamentations —Ross Macdonald

Snores ... like stones dropped on a polished surface
—T. Coraghessan Boyle

Snoring like a snare drum —John D. MacDonald

Snoring like a steamroller —Brian Burland

SNOW
See also: WEATHER

Big flakes ... floating like parachutes in the still air —Frank Ross

Drifts [of snow] heaping themselves like scaling-ladders against the walls —O. Henry

(Those) drifts of soft snow looked like featherbeds —Scott Spencer

A dry pellety snow hitting the sidewalk like uncooked grains of rice —Marge Piercy

Falling snow ... sinking into the ground as slowly as breadcrumbs thrown to fishes sink through water —Boris Pasternak

The fine snow had melted (on his hair and his eyelashes) and sparkled now like raindrops in a sunshower —Harvey Swados

Flakes ... bob and sail like moths across the driveway —Anon

The flakes fall like asterisks —James Reiss

Flakes of snow ... falling like feathers from the sky —Grimm Brothers

The flakes ... seemed thick as tarts —Peter De Vries

Flakes swarming around the streetlamps like soft, huge moths —George Garrett

The flakes were as large as an hour's circular tatting —O. Henry
The comparison is a vivid one but with tatting no longer a familiar pastime, a brief explanation would be needed for any but needlework aficionados.

Flakes were like feathers —Frank Swinnerton

(The sundial was) heaped with a foot-high frosting of snow like a tall, fantastic cake —Davis Grubb

(Snow was still falling,) heavy flakes like goose feathers —Jilly Cooper

(A row of) icicles like the crystal drops of a chandelier hung from the roof —H. E. Bates

Icicles like the teeth of fish —Saul Bellow

Icicles sparkling at the eaves like pendant blades of glass
  —William Styron

It [snow] fell like a great armistice, bringing all simple struggles to an
  end —Elizabeth Hardwick

It looks pretty in the garden [in the snow], like a living Christmas
  —Janet Flanner

A light fringe of snow lay like a cape on the shoulders of his
  overcoat and like toecaps on the toes of his galoshes
  —James Joyce

Lightly and whitely as wheat from the grain, thickly and quickly as
  thoughts through the brain, so fast and so dumb do the
  snowflakes come —Grace Denio Lichtfield

Like an army defeated, the snow has retreated —William Wordsworth

Long icicles, like crystal daggers —Oscar Wilde

(I looked down at the street ... at the) masses of snow like dirty
  suds —Saul Bellow

Melted [snow], leaving the gray grass like a pallet, closely pressed
  —Wallace Stevens

One of those brilliant, glittery snows that ought to emit some
  glorious sound with each crystal falling to earth, something
  transcendent like a Bach cantata —Lynne Sharon Schwartz
    The musical comparison is particularly appropriate to the
    novel, *Disturbances in the Field,* in which it appeared, as its
    main character is a classical musician.

The pilings of snow were like the white waves of a white sea
  —Truman Capote

(Her feet disperse the) powdery snow, that rises up like smoke
  —William Wordsworth

Snow as smooth to see as cake frosting and as light as powder
  —Ernest Hemingway

The snow at the roadside full of bubbles like white of egg beaten up
  —Joyce Cary

The snow began to spill down like quiet feathers —H. E. Bates

The snow came down last night like moths —Richard Wilbur
    A simile to begin a poem entitled *First Snow in Alsace.*

Snow ... came in thick tufts like new wool, washed before the weaver spins it —Leslie Silko

Snow ... comes down like lace —Marge Piercy

Snow ... decking the fields and trees with white as for a fairy wedding —Jerome K. Jerome

Snow ... driving him like a fusillade of frozen needles —T. Coraghessan Boyle

Snow fell in swift spirals, floating like gulls into the tree branches —Jean Stafford

Snowflakes dove at our window like fat moths —Donald McCaig

Snowflakes grew bigger and bigger, till at last they looked like big white chickens —Hans Christian Andersen

Snowflakes ... large as white carnations —Janet Flanner

Snow flakes shone ike silver —Hugh Walpole

Snowflakes sifting like crumbs into the yard —Paul Theroux

The [blindingly thick] snowflakes tormented him like a swarm of silver bees —G. K. Chesterton

The snow [during snow storm] flapped like an endless white blanket —Scott Spencer

Snow flying quick as thought —Adrienne Rich

Snow had begun to fall. It made the sidewalk a spotted hide, like leopard skin —Rosellen Brown

Snow had fallen like a fine dust —Martin Cruz Smith

The snow is now coming like dollar-sized confetti —John Wainwright

Snow ... it's like inebriation because it's very pleasing when it's coming, but very unpleasant when it's going —Ogden Nash

The snow lay soft like a down pillow —Thomas Mann

Snow lies like a down mattress over the earth —Lu Hsün

Snow ... lighted the streets like moonlight —Jean Stafford

Snow, like sheep's wool, only whiter —Gillian Tindall

Snow

The snow like the fuzz the morning after too much Stolichnaya
—Derek Lambert
> Lambert's suspense novel, *The Red House,* is set in Russia and so the reference to a Russian drink.

Snow poured down like salt —Helen Hudson

Snow ... settling like wool on the unmown grass —H. E. Bates

Snow smooth as the sky can shed —William Wordsworth

Snow ... soft as froth and easy as ashes —W. R. Rodgers

Snow sparkles like eyesight falling to earth —Wallace Stevens

Snow was falling in larger flakes, like a multitude of frozen moths
—Ellen Glasgow

The snow was yellow ... with orange seeping into its honey color like an aftertaste at sunset —Boris Pasternak

Snow will settle like a sheet over all live color —Frank O'Hara

Sociability/Unsociability

SOCIABILITY/UNSOCIABILITY
See also: BEHAVIOR

Antisocial as death —Mary McCarthy

(About as) chummy as a pair of panthers —James Forbes

Flung himself upon Arthur like a young bear
—Christopher Isherwood

Friendly as a letter from home —Slogan, wine advisory board

(He insisted on being) friendly, like a man running for sheriff
—Jay Parini

Greeted me like the morning sun that had deserted the skies
—Mike Fredman

The greeting I received (from Phoebe) was as damp as the weather outside —Mike Fredman

He was never alone. He wore other people like armour
—William McIlvanney

(The knocking was) hostile as a kick in the balls —Harold Adams

ANTISOCIAL AS DEATH

Similes can provide attention-getting openings for a story, as this one did for Adams' mystery novel, *The Fourth Widow.*

Pleasant as a smile —Anon

Snarled like a racoon (whenever she was pushed) —Miles Gibson

Unresponsive as a bag of wet laundry —David Leavitt

Affable as a wet dog —Alfred Henry Lewis

Society

SOCIETY

Civilization, like beauty, is in the eyes of the beholder —Anon

A good civilization spreads over us freely like a tree, varying and yielding because it is alive. A bad civilization stands up and sticks out above us like an umbrella —G. K. Chesterton

A community is like a ship; every one ought to be prepared to take the helm —Henrik Ibsen

Modern society is like a Calder mobile: disturb it here and it jiggles over there, too —George F. Will

Social life is a form of do-it-yourself theater
—Muriel Oxenberg Murphy, *New York Times* interview

Societies, like individuals, have their moral crises and their spiritual revolutions —Richard H. Tawney

Society is a kind of parent to its members. If it, and they, are to thrive, its values must be clear, coherent and generally acceptable —Milton R. Sapirstein

Society is a masked ball, where everyone hides his real character, and reveals it in hiding —Ralph Waldo Emerson

Society is like air; very high up, it is sublimated, too low down, a perfect choke-damp —Anon

Society is like a lawn, where every roughness is smoothed, every bramble eradicated, and where the eye is delighted by the smiling verdure of a velvet surface —Washington Irving

Society is like a wave. The wave moves onward, but the water of which it is composed does not —Ralph Waldo Emerson

Society is like the air, necessary to breathe, but insufficient to live on —George Santayana

SOLIDITY
See: FIRMNESS, STEADINESS

SOUL

Feel my soul rolling as if it were inside an empty barrel —Yehuda Amichai

The human soul is like a bird that is born in a cage. Nothing can deprive it of its natural longings or obliterate the mysterious remembrance of its heritage —Epes Sargent

The inner chambers of the soul are like the photographer's darkroom. Like a laboratory. One cannot stay there all the time or it becomes the solitary cell of the neurotic —Anaïs Nin

I thought that the soul went round like a Gladstone bag, never caring a damn for any particular station-rack or hotel cloakroom —Dylan Thomas

My soul is like a desert and the wind blows in its silent barren spaces —W. Somerset Maugham

My soul is like the oar that momentarily dies in a desperate stress beneath the wave, then glitters out again and sweeps the sea —Sidney Lanier

Some souls are like sponges. You cannot squeeze anything out of them except what they have sucked from you —Kahlil Gibran

Soul ... as disheveled as your apartment —Jay McInerney

A soul as white as heaven —Beaumont and Fletcher

The soul dwells in the body like a spider in its web —Anon Greek philosopher
> A variation from the same source: "The soul resides in the body like a sailor in a ship."

Soulless as apes. Spineless as mosquitoes or dandelions —Rick Borsten

The soul, like fire, abhors what it consumes —Derek Walcott

The soul of man is larger than the sky —Hartley Coleridge

Soul

A soul that, like an ample shield, can take in all, and verge enough for more —John Dryden

A soul through which the morning shines as through a leaf —Rainer Maria Rilke

Strong souls live like fire-hearted suns, to spend their strength in further striving action —George Eliot

The sweetest souls, like the sweetest flowers, soon canker in cities —Walter Savage Landor

Your soul was like a star, and dwelt apart —William Wordsworth
In Wordsworth's sonnet the first word was 'Thy.'

(Even if you're racked by troubles, and sick and poor and ugly,) you've got your soul to carry through life like a treasure on a platter —Alice Munro

Speaking

SPEAKING
See also: SPEECH PATTERNS

[A statement] came out flat as a sheet of onion-skin paper —Cornell Woolrich

Can speak as flashy as water runs —R. Wright Campbell

Cut short his speech, like a pang of pain —Joseph Conrad

The few sentences she uttered were like eternal judgments —Larry McMurtry

Had a habit ... of making a narrow remark which, like a plumber's snake, could work its way through the ear down the artery, halfway to my heart —Grace Paley

He [Peter O'Toole] doesn't just talk, he offers his words like presents, gift-wrapped —Robert Goldberg, *Wall Street Journal*, April 21, 1987

He was gathering toward speech, like a man about to rhumba, waiting to feel the beat —Leonard Michaels

His tongue [is] as a devouring fire —*The Holy Bible/Isaiah*

His rhetoric falls like a freight train over a bridge —David Brinkley about John L. Lewis

His talk was like a stream which runs with rapid changes from rock to roses —Winthrop Mackworth Praed

To illustrate the simile, the poem in which it appears continues with "It slipped from politics to puns; it passed from Mahomet to Moses."

If I open my mouth it's like pebbles rattling together —Albert Camus

Phrases ... looping out of her mouth like a backward spaghetti-eating process —Elizabeth Spencer

A remark thrown off like an idle dart —Sylvia Berkman

Said grimly ... like a man announcing that X-rated movies had been shown at the deacons' party —Stephen King

Said it flatly, like a tour guide reading from a Baedeker —Jonathan Valin

Sentences came ... fluently enough, even though they did sound rather like quotations from a phrase book —Christopher Isherwood

Sharpened their tongues like a serpent —*The Holy Bible/Psalms*

[Words] slipped out of me in a spasm of candor, like a sneeze —Paul Reidinger

Some men are like bagpipes, they can't speak till their belly's filled —Seamus MacManus

Speaking without thinking is like shooting without aiming —English proverb

Speak pleasantly ... like a stewardess in an airliner with only one wing and two engines, one of which is on fire —Douglas Adams

Spoke to them mildly as mid-May weather —Stephen Vincent Benét

Talked like birds, with a gentle malice —Dame Edith Sitwell

Talked like her eyes looked, like her eyes watching us and her voice talking to us did not belong to her. Like she was living somewhere else, waiting somewhere else —William Faulkner

Talking is like playing on the harp; there is as much in laying the hands on the strings to stop their vibrations as in twanging them to bring out the music —Oliver Wendell Holmes, Sr.

Talks like his tongue is in a cramp ... like he has adenoids as big as footballs ... and muscles to match —John Wainwright

Tough talk ... like whistling in a haunted house —John Wainwright

Voice stopped, like words written off the edge of a page
—Elizabeth Spencer

SPEECHMAKING

An after-dinner speech is like a love letter. Ideally, you should begin by not knowing what you are going to say, and end by not knowing what you've said —Lord Jowitt

Eloquence must flow like a stream that is fed by an abundant spring —Henry St. John, Viscount Bolinbroke

A good speech is like a pencil; it has to have a point like a breathless messenger's report —James Atlas

Great eloquence, like a flame, must have fuel to feed it, motion to excite it, and brightens by burning —Tacitus
> William Pitt the Younger is often credited with coining this simile, which was in fact a paraphrase from an unknown source: "It is with eloquence as with a flame; it requires fuel to feed it, motion to excite it, and brightens as it burns."

His speech was like a tangled chain; nothing impaired, but all disordered —William Shakespeare

Human speech is like a cracked tin kettle, on which we hammer out tunes to make tears dance when we long to move the stars —Gustave Flaubert

Make a speech that's like a long-horned steer, with a point here and there and a lot of bull in between —Norman Mailer

Oratory, like the drama, abhors lengthiness; like the drama, it must keep doing —Edward Bulwer-Lytton

Pompous words and long pauses which lie like a leaden pain over fever —Norman Mailer
> The pompous words and pauses were heard by Mailer at the 1960 Democratic convention.

Rhetoric without logic is like a tree with leaves and blossoms, but no root —John Selden

Sermons are like pie crusts, the shorter the better —Austin O'Malley

Speeches are like babies: easy to conceive, hard to deliver —Pat O'Malley

Speeches forgotten, like a maiden speech, which all men praise, but
none remember —Winthrop Mackworth Praed

A speech is like a love affair. Any fool can start it, but to end it
requires considerable skill
—Lord Mancroft, *Reader's Digest*, February, 1967

A speech is like an airplane engine. It may sound like hell but
you've got to go on —William Thomas Piper
Piper's involvement with airplanes makes this particularly
appropriate.

Speech is shallow as time —Thomas Carlyle

Speech is silver; silence is golden —Thomas Carlyle

The speech of men is like embroidered tapestries, since, like them, it
must be extended in order to display its patterns; but, when it is
rolled up, it conceals and distorts them —Plutarch

The speech ... took shape in his head as clearly and precisely as if it
were an official report —Leo Tolstoy

SPEECH PATTERNS

Accent ... almost as authentic as that of the white-jacketed medico
peddling hand cream to the TV millions —Harvey Swados

Accent ... thick as porridge —W. P. Kinsella

Diction ... each word distinct and unslurred, as if he were a
linguistics professor moderating a panel discussion on the future
of the language —T. Coraghessan Boyle

The doctor's English was perfect, pure Martha's Vineyard; he sounded
like Ted Kennedy's insurance salesman —T. Coraghessan Boyle

Dragging his words along like reluctant dogs on a string
—Edith Wharton

Had spoken the lines without expression, running them past,
uninspired, one behind the other like passing freight cars
—William Brammer

He [Edmund Wilson] spoke in a curiously strangled voice, with gaps
between his sentences, as if ideas jostled and thrashed about
inside him, getting in one another's way as they struggled to
emerge, which made for short bursts —Isaiah Berlin, *New York
Times Book Review*, April 12, 1987

Speech Patterns

His facile elocution ... which had so long charmed them, was now treated like warm gruel made to put cowards to sleep —Émile Zola

His statements are often preceded by stretches of silence as painful as the space between a stutterer's syllables, as he tries to translate his images into words —Ira Wood

Inflections that rise and fall with a tidal surge equal to that of the Bay of Fundy —Richard F. Shepard about comedian Jackie Mason, *New York Times*

Intoned monotonously like a sleep-walker —MacDonald Harris

Moouhing the words and nodding to himself like an actor memorizing his lines —Donald Seaman

Repeated slowly, as if he were sounding out syllables in a book —Jonathan Valin
See also: REPETITION

The rest of it [a remark] was delivered at a clipped, furious pace, like Morse code —Jonathan Valin

Said one word, carefully pursed in his mouth, spat out like a grape pip —John Fowles

The sentences were spoken like sentences from a judge summing up, bit by bit —V. S. Pritchett

Short brief staccato sentences like slaps —William Faulkner

Spaces her adjectives like little whiplashes —John Fowles

Spacing his words as if for a particularly stupid and stubborn person —Nancy Huddleston Packer

Spat out the words like orange seeds —Dorothy Francis

Speak falteringly, like an unrehearsed actor —Anon

Speaking [in a heavy tone] ... as if he were dropping words like molten lead —G. K. Chesterton

Speak like a death's head —William Shakespeare

Speak ... like a telegram —Dashiell Hammett

Spitting the word from her mouth ... as if it were a poisonous seed —Flannery O'Connor

Splutter and splash like a pig in a puddle —W. S. Gilbert

Spoke clearly, but in a low and hesitant voice, as if he were translating from Spanish as he went along —Norman Mailer

Spoke like a radio program —Ludwig Bemelmans

Spoke more slowly than ever before and with difficulty, like someone who fears a stammer —Dan Jacobson

Spoke slowly, with a kind of uniformity of emphasis that made his words stand out like the raised type for the blind —Edith Wharton

Spoke very slowly and deliberately, like a man reading aloud from a difficult text —Jonathan Valin

Sputtered out [words] like a wet fuse —Richard Moran

Stutter like a new-clipped crow —George Garrett

Talked flowingly like a medium —Anaïs Nin

Talked like she had bugs in her mouth —Madison Smartt Bell

Talked with commas, like a heavy novel —Raymond Chandler

(He had developed an unfortunate habit of) talking like a Chinese fortune cookie —John Cheever

(Tendency to) talk like a Sten gun —George F. Will about Hubert Humphrey

Used the English language with dictionary precision ... almost as if it were a foreign tongue he had learned perfectly —Lael Tucker Wertenbaker

Use her words cautiously, like weapons that might slip and inflict a wound —Edith Wharton

Words ... dragging out like words in an anthem —G. K. Chesterton

Words, each distinct and separate, like multicolored marbles —Francis King

Words leaped out of his mouth like machine-gun bullets —Frank Conroy

Words were being mouthed like signal flags —Norman Mailer

SPEED

See also: RUNNING

(Poems have become) as instant as coffee or onion soup mix
   —Donald Hall

(They'll whip her back ...) as quick as shit through a goose
   —Derek Lambert

As swift as meditation, or the thoughts of love
   —William Shakespeare

As swiftly as a reach of still water is crisped by the wind
   —Rudyard Kipling

Be not in a hurry, like the almond, first to blossom and last to ripen.
   Be rather like the mulberry, last to blossom and first to ripen
   —*The Holy Bible/Apocrypha*

The crowd was moving fast ... like a big spread ravelling, and the
   separate threads disappeared down the dark street
   —Flannery O'Connor

Drive [a car] like the hounds of hell —Rosamund Pilcher

Fast as a bird on the wing —Anon

Fast as a cat scurrying up a tree at the approach of a strange dog
   —Anon

Fast as a cook cracks eggs —Thomas Nash

Fast as a heartbeat —John D. MacDonald

Fast as a jet —Mark Helprin

Fast as a pickpocket —Anon

Fast as a propeller —Bertold Brecht

(Scrambles into the room,) fast as a spider —Robert Silverberg

Fast as greased lightning —American colloquialism

Fast as the blink of an eye —Anon

Fast-moving as the gray fox that climbs trees after squirrels
   —Marge Piercy

(Little and) fleet as a terrier running beside a bloodhound
   —Erich Maria Remarque

(To vanish,) fleet as days and months and years, fleet as the
    generations of mankind —William Wordsworth

Flying like ice in a sleet storm —Ben Ames Williams

Fly like a donkey with pepper up its behind —Aharon Megged

Galloped through [religious mass] like a man with witches after him
    —Edith Wharton

Goes like a ship-lash flicked across a horse's neck —Rudyard Kipling

Going like flames —Samuel Beckett

Going like sixty —F. D. Reeve

Go like a house afire —Anon
        One of many "Go like" similes that have worked their
        way into the American language mainstream since the late
        1830s. Some other examples: "Go like a shot," "Go like
        hell" and "Go like mad."

Go through like a dose of salts —American colloquialism
        While purgative salts are pretty much a thing of the past,
        the simile endures as a way to describe a very rapid pace.
        With the penchant for brand names, "Go through like Ex-
        Lax" has become a common alternative.

Go through them [reading materials] like a kid through potato chips
    —James Crumley

He rushed past her like a football tackle —James Thurber

(Wedding plans were) hurtling along like a train on tracks
    —Paul Reidinger

Insectlike swiftness —Saul Bellow

I must be done like lightning —Ben Jonson

Just a glance, like passing your eyes over the spines of books
    without being able to read the title ... that quick
    —Arthur A. Cohen

(Scurried off, his) legs going like a windmill —Paige Mitchell
    See also: MOVEMENT

Like a sunbeam, swift and bright —Sir Walter Scott

Move with the speed of a Grand Prix Racer —Anon

Moving fast as a train —Anon

My days are swifter than a weaver's shuttle —*The Holy Bible/Job*
> While this simile is not much used these days, it is the one that has seeded the many contemporary variations.

Quick and nimble, more like a bear than a squirrel —Henry G. Bohn's *Handbook of Proverbs*

Quick as a lizard —Anthony Trollope

Quick as an attack dog —Gloria Norris

(Acted) quick as a knife —Penelope Gilliatt

(The wolf ... ate her up as) quick as a slap —Anne Sexton

Quick as a striking snake —George Garrett

Quick as a weasel —Robert B. Parker

Quick as a wink —Anon
> While variations such as "Quick as dust" and "Quick as scat" have faded from the American vocabulary, "Quick as a wink" endures to the point of overuse.

(Goes) quick as light —Noël Coward, lyrics for "Chase Me Charlie"

Quick as lightning —Frances Sheridan
> The American adaption of the simile first used by Sheridan in a play named *Discovery* is "Quick as greased lightning."

Quick as mercury —Marguerite Yourcenar

(Slipped down) quick as minnows —Marge Piercy

(Barry's eye was as) quick as sound —Frank Swinnerton

Quicker than a crab underwater —John Updike

Quicker than boiling asparagus —Caesar Augustus
> According to Stevenson's *Proverbs, Maxims and Famous Sayings*, Augustus used this expression whenever he wanted anything to be done fast.

Quick on his feet as a running deer —Stephen Vincent Benét

(Lavella's brain) raced like a trapped rabbit —William Beechcroft

(Feet) rapid as the river —Henry Wadsworth Longfellow

Rash as fire —William Shakespeare

(Raleigh) rushed through (these hypotheses) like rosary beads
—Michael Malone

(Men) rushing like they were bolt out of a cannon —Richard Ford

Rushing wildly from room to room like a flustered hen
—Christopher Isherwood

Scurried like a crab —Michael Malone

She was so swift ... it was like having a small cute dog with you
—Isak Dinesen

Some people are too fast for their own good, like Asahel in the Book
of Samuel —Saul Bellow

Sped around like intergalactic missiles —Lisa Harris
        Harris's simile describes the activity of the Lubavitcher
        women in Crown Heights, the subject of her book *The
        World of a Hasidic Family.*

(The game) speeds along like a fast freight —W. P. Kinsella
        The game speeding along is baseball, the background for
        The Iowa Baseball Confederacy and other Kinsella novels.

Speedy as a steam roller —George Ade

Started for me (as to attack) like a streak of lightning —Rex Stout

Swift as a cloud between sea and sky —Percy Bysshe Shelley

Swift as a greyhound —Ouida

Swift as a mugger —David Leavitt

Swift as an arrow —Anon
        This has been attributed to numerous sources dating back
        to the early seventeenth century.

Swift as a plunging knife —Rudyard Kipling

Swift as a shadow —William Shakespeare

Swift as desire —Mary Pix

Swift as fear —Thomas Parnell

Swift as the eagle (flieth) —*The Holy Bible/Deuteronomy*

Swift as the waters —*The Holy Bible/Job*

Swift as thought —William Shakespeare

Swift as unbridled rage —Henry Abbey

Swifter than the wind —William Shakespeare

Swift in motion as a ball —William Shakespeare

(Fluttering her bristly black lashes as) swiftly as butterflies' wings
—Margaret Mitchell
> The girl fluttering her lashes is Scarlett O'Hara of *Gone
> with the Wind* fame.

Travelling fast as a wish —Elizabeth Bishop

(The race) went by like an express train —Enid Bagnold

(She dressed and) went off like a top with the whip behind it
—Vicki Baum

Went past ... like lightning past a hill —Jessamyn West

Went through it like a clown through a paper hoop —Temole Scott

Went through like shit through a tin horn —American colloquialism

SPOILAGE
See: DISINTEGRATION

SPONTANEITY
See: NATURALNESS

SPORTS
See: BOXING AND WRESTLING, FOOTBALL, GOLF

SPREADING
See also: GROWTH

(Anxiety was) as contagious as a yawn —Barbara Lazear Ascher, *New
York Times*/Hers, October 23, 1986

Blown up [with fever] like a tire —Elena Poniatowska

(Excuses) breaking out like pimples —Marge Piercy

Breed like guinea pigs —Raymond Chandler

Catch happiness as quickly as others catch colds —Storm Jameson

Catching like fire in dry grass —William Dean Howells

Contagious like the gladness of a happy child
—Edward Bulwer-Lytton

Excitement swept through Jalna [the estate which is the setting for a series of De La Roche novels] like a forest fire
—Mazo De La Roche

Expand like air in a pressure chamber —Penelope Gilliatt

Gather like dust on a windowsill —Anon

Multiply like troubles —Marge Piercy

Passed around [German measles] like a dish of cool figs at the first rehearsal —Reynolds Price

(Houses) popping up everywhere like the heat rash. Like pimples
—George Garrett

Spread a thought ... like butter on toast —Carlos Fuentes

(Feel her pleasure deepening and) spreading like a chord struck in all octaves at once, sustained, played, and then held and held till it slowly faded into its overtones —Marge Piercy

(She looked at me, recognition) spreading like a rash
—Sharon Sheehe Stark

(Pain) spreading like lava —John Braine

Spreading [throughout her system] ... like poison dye
—Margaret Millar

> In the mystery novel, *The Fiend*, the author uses the simile to describe a key character's growing alertness to dangerous situation.

(Affection ...) spread like an epidemic through the room
—Jean Stafford

Spread like an unconfirmed rumor —Elyse Sommer

Spread like a quenchless fire —Percy Bysshe Shelley

Spread ... like a tiny spray of ink on a piece of blotting paper
—Franz Werfel

Spread like butter under a knife —Lawrence Durrell

Spread like dandelions after spring rain —Marilyn Ross about growth of directories, *Publishers Weekly*, June 5, 1987

(But they cling and) spread like lichen —Elizabeth Bishop

Spread like mushrooms after a fresh spring rain —Anon
> Mushrooms have long lent themselves to quick growth comparisons. A variation: "Grow like toadstools."

Spread like mushrooms across an unsuspecting garden —Tom Robbins

Spread like pancake batter on a hot griddle —Elyse Sommer

Spread like the desert —Henry James

(Silence) spread ... like water that a pebble stirs —Dante Gabriel Rossetti

Spread out like a doily —Alma Stone

Spread out (the sun) like a jellyfish —John Steinbeck

(I saw the vineyards) spread out like wings —Eudora Welty

Spreads faster than panic in a plane —Donald Seaman

Spreads like a sigh —Anon

(Love that) spreads like a stain of ink in absorbent cloth —Diane Wakoski
> As poet Wakoski links the spreading stain with love in her poem, *My Little Heart Pops Out*, so W. H. Auden uses "Ruin spreading like a stain" in *Something Is Bound to Happen*.

Spreads like good news —Slogan for Satinwax, Economic Laboratory

Spread through like a clumsy, uninvited guest who is obese and eats too much —Lorrie Moore
> The descriptive frame of reference in Moore's novel, *Self-Help*, is cancer.

(Enemies ... are) sprouting (around me) like tulips —Peter Benchley

STALENESS
See also: TIMELINESS/UNTIMELINESS

As trite as the lyrics to a fifties hit —Hilma Wolitzer
> In her novel, *In the Palomar Arms*, Wolitzer compares the triteness of old song lyrics to what happens to the words spoken by someone once loved passionately.

Felt about as fresh as an old piece of chewing gum —Mike Fredman

Flat and cold as the muffins of this morning's breakfast
—Henry James
> In James' play, *Pyramus and Thisbe*, this describes
> personality traits grown stale with overuse and familiarity.

Flat as last night's beer —Louis Untermeyer

Stale as an old cigar —Wilfrid Sheed

Stale as yesterday's bread —Arthur A. Cohen

(But it was all unmeaningful to us, and all the proverbs seemed stiff
and) stale, like dusty labels on neglected antiquities
—G. K. Chesterton

Stale, like the butt of a dead cigar —Rudyard Kipling

Tired as a much-told joke —Anon

STANDING
See also: POSTURE

He was standing there with his arms at his sides like a wooden
soldier —Ann Beattie

(Mrs. Snow was) standing framed in the doorway like a faded vestal
virgin guarding a shrine —Ross Macdonald

Standing ... like a painted statue —Iris Murdoch

Stand like clockwork toys —W. S. Gilbert

Stands like the figurehead at a ship's prow —Stevie Smith
> A variation on the same theme: "Stood, like a carving on
> the prow of a ship."

Stood around like shadows —Maya Angelou

Stood as if thunderstruck —Joseph Conrad

Stood before us, huge and dark like a colossus —Margaret Drabble

Stood like a private before his colonel —Frank Swinnerton

Stood like lead —Wallace Irwin

Stood like stocks —Dorothy Canfield Fisher

Stood stiffly as a hanged man —Leigh Allison Wilson

Stood up and stretched like a sleepy cat —Gloria Norris

STARES

Dug his blue eyes into me, like nails —Jay Parini

(I've been feeling your) eyes boring into me like a pair of yellow
     jackets. She had a curiously intense stare, like a greedy child
     waiting for sweets —Beryl Bainbridge

Stared at each other quietly, like enemies —Robert Campbell

Stared at him, holding him, like the high point on a compass
     —Richard Ford

Stared at [a question] keenly as if it were a fly that he was waiting
     to swat when it came round again —V.S. Pritchett

Stared at me like blocks of wood —Donald Justice

Stared blankly at me like a dead fish —Joe Coomer

(Had no expression in his gray eyes. He) stared like a cat at an
     empty window —Bill Granger

Stared ... with the intensity of a man having a private audience with
     an angel —James Morrow

Stares at me like I'm dirt he intends to one day wipe off his shoes
     —Robert Campbell
     See also: CONTEMPT

Stares at my idea like a crystal vase suspended in his mind's rare
     ether —Richard Ford

(Powell's) stare seemed to pinch her like a pair of tongs
     —Flannery O'Connor

(Stood there) staring at him like a stunned ox —Oakley Hall

Staring at me with a studied air, as though measuring me
     —Kent Nelson

Staring into his face like a devotee before an idol
     —Elizabeth Spencer

Staring like rustics at a fair —Henry James

A way ... of staring at the wall or at the window like a detective at
     a murder scene, desperate for clues —Clive Barker

STARS

The dipper burned like a strand of diamonds on a sable cloak
—Joseph Wambaugh

The divisions between the rings [of Saturn] are furrows in which the
satellites rotate ... like sheepdogs running around the flock to
keep it compact —Italo Calvino

The evening star flickered like a lamp just lit —Willa Cather

In the dark vault of the sky, the stars hung like muted dots of
leaden silver —Heinrich Böll
This lovely simile is the first sentence of Böll's short story,
The Ration Runners.

Jupiter displays two equatorial stripes like a scarf decorated with
interwoven embroideries —Italo Calvino

A lovely star ... large as the full moon —Jaroslav Seifert

The Milky Way stands out so clearly that it looks as if it had been
polished and rubbed over for the holidays —Anton Chekhov

A star as bright as day
—Anon Christmas ballad, probably dating to Middle Ages

Starlight fell like rain —F. Scott Fitzgerald

Stars are dropping thick as stones —Sylvia Plath

(Tonight) the stars are like a crowd of faces moving round the sky
—Wallace Stevens

The stars burned steadily, like the lights of far-off ships
—Marjory Stoneman Douglas

The stars clung like snow crystals in the black sky —Ross Macdonald

Stars ... cold, like pieces of ice —Paige Mitchell

Stars ... dissolved like bubbles —Katherine Mansfield
The simile in full context: ''In the sky some tiny stars
floated for a moment and then they were gone—they were
dissolved like bubbles.''
See also: DISINTEGRATION

Stars gleamed and winked like searching fireflies —Robert Traver

Stars ... huge, like daisies —May Sarton

Stars large as asters —Mary Stewart

Stars

Stars ... like countless diamond lamps —Hans Christian Andersen

(At night) stars rise like the bubbles of the drowned
—Yehuda Amichai

The stars seemed to look down like a thousand winking eyes
—William Humphrey

The stars which at midnight looked like a spillway of broken pearls,
did not shine at this hour; they were holes of light, like eye
squints in black masks —Paul Theroux

Twinkle, twinkle, little star how I wonder what you are, up above
the world so high, like a diamond in the sky —Anne Taylor

STARTING AND STOPPING
See: PAUSE

STATISTICS
See: FACTS

Steadiness

STEADINESS
See also: FIRMNESS

(Believe in justice) inexorable as the decay of an isotope
—Marge Piercy

Solid as earthenware —Anne Sexton

Solid as the continent —Slogan, North American Life Insurance

Stayed steady as a castle —John Le Carré

(His touch is quick, sure,) steady as a laser —T. Coraghessan Boyle

Steady as the moonlight —Saul Bellow

(Hands as) steady as the murder rate —Loren D. Estleman

Steady as the stare of a glass eye —Arthur Baer

Steady as the water flowing from a hydrant —James G. Huneker

STIFFNESS
See: AWKWARDNESS, PHYSICAL FEELINGS

STILLNESS
See: PEACEFULNESS

STOMACH
See also: FATNESS

A beer gut like a beach ball —Rick Borsten

A belly like a huge alabaster bowl —Paule Marshall

Belly like a meadow —John D. MacDonald

Belly ... round as a tub —Will Weaver

Belly stuck out like a full moon —Carlos Baker

(My soft) belly that hangs over my shorts like the cap of a
     mushroom —Ira Wood

Belly tight as a drumhead —George Garrett

Big belly all puffed out in front like he took a tube in the morning
     and blew it up as far as it would go —George Garrett

A big belly that hung over his pants like a melon —Gloria Norris

Carried his paunch like something stolen and badly hidden beneath
     his shirt —John Irving

Her belly looked like a balloon —Tony Ardizzone

Her [pregnant] belly rises, tight as a beach ball —François Camoin

Her belly split like a backside by her caesarian scar
     —Alice McDermott

His abdomen looked like the carapace of a lobster, all rock-hard,
     etched, and segmented musculature —Jonathan Valin

His gut protruded like a basketball pumped to maximum pressure per
     square inch —Sue Grafton

The jowls of his belly crawl and swell like the sea —Karl Shapiro
          This vivid simile is the opening line of a poem entitled *The
          Glutton.*

Stomach ... hard as a cord of wood —Richard Ford

Stomach hard as a washboard —Cynthia Ozick

Stomach [of pregnant woman] like a globe —Ruth McLaughlin

Tight potbelly like a swallowed ball —Peter Matthiessen

STOP
See: PAUSE

Stories

STORIES
See also: BOOKS, WRITERS/WRITING

All circumstances in a tale answer one another like notes in music —Robert Louis Stevenson

Fiction is like a spider's web, attached ever so slightly perhaps, but still attached to life at all four corners —Virginia Woolf

A good story compels you like sexual hunger but the pace is more leisurely —Robert Hass

A good story is like a bitter pill with the sugar coating inside of it —O. Henry

A poor story is a good deal like a grist, the oftener it is told, the less there is of it —Josh Billings
    In Billings' dialect this reads: "The oftner it iz told, the less thare iz ov it."

Stories are like snapshots ... pictures snntched out of time with clean, hard edges —James Crumley

Stories, like whiskey, must be allowed to mature in the cask —Sean O'Faolain, *Atlantic Monthly*, December 1956

Stories that meandered along like lazy streams —George Garrett

A storyteller is like a ship's captain. He takes the passengers places where they might laugh or cry, but they always feel safe — Michael Parent, storyteller, *New York Times*, May 19, 1986

A story with a moral appended is like the bill of a mosquito. It bores you, and then injects a stinging drop to irritate your conscience —O. Henry

A tale without love is like beef without mustard —Anatole France

Straightness

STRAIGHTNESS
See also: POSTURE

Direct, like a guided torpedo —William Humphrey

Erect as compass in its curve —Anne Morrow Lindbergh

Even as a row of West Point cadets on parade —Arthur Baer

Even as a set of false teeth —Arthur Baer

(Noses ...) even as buttons on a tape —Beryl Markham

Straight as a column —Louis Adamic

Straight as a gun barrel (she carried her lengthy shadow up and down the golden sand) —Jean Stafford

(Walks) straight as a hoe —T. Coraghessan Boyle

(A woman) straight as a hunting knife —Stephen Vincent Benét

Straight as a line —Geoffrey Chaucer
> This is transcribed from Chaucer's Old English: "Streight as any lyne." An American folk variant said to originate in Maine is the much-used "Straight as a ramrod."

Straight as an arrow —Aphra Behn
> A simile much in use, both to describe physical and moral erectness. To emphasize the latter meaning there's "Straight as your sister" attributed to Jerome Barry.

(Teeth ...) straight as a picket fence —Susan Fromberg Schaeffer

Straight as a plumb line —Mike Sommer

Straight as a stick and looked as brittle —V. S. Pritchett

(I felt her to be) straight as a die —Colette

Straight as a fir tree —Henry Van Dyke

(The country road is wide, light gray,) straight as a ruler —Cora Sandel

[Lower eyelids] straight as ruler edges —Dashiell Hammett

Straight as the backbone of a herring —John Ray's *Proverbs*

Straight like a pine —Joseph Conrad

Straight ... like long rows of soldiers —Oscar Wilde

Straight, thin as a pencil —Miller Williams
> This marks the opening of a poem entitled *The Writer.*

(His two rifles as) upright as umbrellas —Edward Hoagland

STREAMS
See: PONDS AND STREAMS

STREETSCAPES
See: CITY/STREETSCAPES

STRENGTH
See: MUSCLES, TOUGHNESS

STRUGGLE
See also: BEHAVIOR, FUTILITY

(In his efforts with the numbing pain,) he was like a man wrestling with a creature of the air —Stephen Crane

Like the tiny coral insect, working deep under the dark waters, we strive and struggle, each for our own little ends
—Jerome K. Jerome

Struggle along ... stopping and starting like a blown newspaper
—J. G. Farrell

(The coalition Israelli government) struggled like two cats in a bag
—Ebra Ames

Struggle like a fish —Leo Tolstoy

Struggling like a fly trapped in a glass of water —Anon

Struggling like a moth to break its chrysalis —Rumer Godden

Struggling through life like a wearied swimmer trying to touch the horizon —Israel Zangwill

STUPIDITY
See: DULLNESS, FOOLISHNESS

STURDINESS
See: FIRMNESS

STYLE

Dress as if having been born in a clothing store —David Ignatow

Elegance stamped on her as by a die —Henry James

Elegant as a Cole Porter lyric
—Eric Pace, *New York Times*, December 1, 1986

Struggle

Style

Pace made this comparison about actor Cary Grant at the time of his death.

Elegant as a fifty-dollar whore —Raymond Chandler

Fashion is like a shadow: fly from it and it follows you; follow it and it flies from you —Anon

Had that elusive style some older women carry like blossom —Jonathan Gash

A man's style is intrinsic and private with him like his voice or his gesture, partly a matter of inheritance, partly of cultivation —Maurice Valency

Style, like the human body, is specially beautiful when the veins are not prominent and the bones cannot be counted —Tacitus

You can't get high aesthetic tastes, like trousers, ready-made —W. S. Gilbert

SUBTLETY
See: TACT

SUCCESS/FAILURE
See: GROWTH; PAST, THE

SUDDENNESS
See also: ENTRANCES/EXITS, SURPRISE

Abrupt as a sultry little thunder shower —Amy Leslie

Abruptly as string that snaps beneath the bow —Ernest William Hornung

Abruptly, like a summer rainstorm —Derek Lambert

Abrupt, startling shock, like the slap of a wet towel —Norman Mailer

All at once, like the wind dispersing storm clouds at a single puff —Lawrence Durrell

Appear suddenly as if out of a fold of the air —Iris Murdoch

Arbitrary as a cyclone —Anon

Burst into the room like a bullet crashing through a window —Guy De Maupassant

Didn't expect it ... like a storm on a very fine day —Ivan Turgenev

He was with them as suddenly as a gift, as if an arm had thrust in a bunch of roses or a telegram —Eudora Welty

(A reflex as) immediate as a sneeze —Leigh Allison Wilson
A common variation: "Sudden as a sneeze."

Steep as a broom handle —Elizabeth Spencer

Steep as hell's half acre —George MacDonald Fraser

Stopped all of a sudden, as if he had been shot
—William Makepeace Thackeray

Sudden and foolish as that almost silent fart —George Garrett
See also: FOOLISHNESS

Sudden as a burst of hiccuping —Anon
This and the entries that follow typify the simile that develops new twists from conversation to conversation, writer to writer.

Sudden as a dislocated joint slipping back into place —Anon

Sudden as a massacre —Anon

Sudden as a meteor shooting across the sky —Anon

Sudden as an epileptic seizure —Anon

Sudden as a stitch in your side —Anon

Sudden as a summer shower —Anon

Sudden as a tornado swooping down on a small town
—Alistair Cooke, Public Television, March 8, 1987
The comparison referring to the suddenness of the first World War was made during an introduction to an episode in the "Lost Empire" series.

[Call of a jaybird] sudden as conscience —Robert Penn Warren

Sudden as the stopping of breath —Mary Lee Settle

(The end was) sudden, like a foolish play —Karl Shapiro

Suddenly, as a train comes out of a tunnel —Virginia Woolf

Suddenly, like a pair of obscene words, (there appeared on the path two boys) —Truman Capote

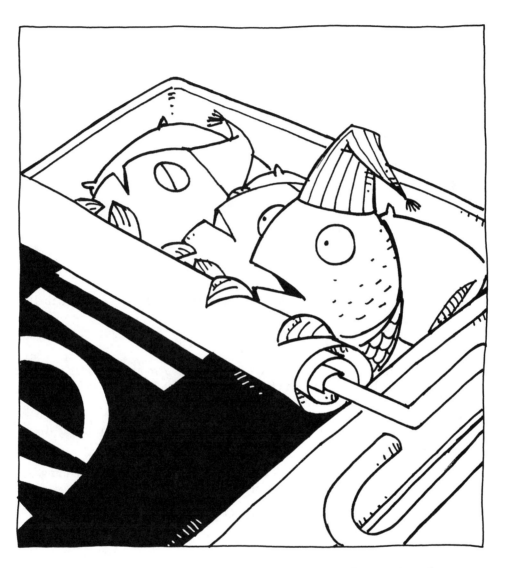

SURPRISED AS A SARDINE THAT WENT
TO SLEEP IN THE OCEAN AND WOKE UP IN
A DELICATESSEN STORE

Suddenness

Sudden resolutions, like the sudden rise of the mercury in the barometer, indicate little else than the changeableness of the weather —Julius Charles Hare and Augustus William Hare

Sudden, surprising ... it is like encountering a pun in a telephone directory —Karl E. Meyer

Too sudden ... like the lightning —William Shakespeare

SUN
See: SUNSET

Sunset

SUNSET

A huge sunset that drained away in the west like blood —William Styron

The sun ... drops like an angry brick at nightfall —Raymond Chandler

A sunset as thick as jam simmered in the sky —Isaac Babel

Sunset cast its colors through the leafless trees ... like panes of stained glass —Madison Smartt Bell

The (Montana) sunset lay between two mountains like a gigantic bruise from which dark arteries spread themselves over a poisoned sky —F. Scott Fitzgerald

The sunset looked like the fires of Hell were consuming it —Harry Prince

The sun was moving down slowly as if it were descending a ladder —Flannery O'Connor

The sun went down lopsided and wide as a rose on a stem —Eudora Welty

Surprise

SURPRISE
See also: SUDDENNESS

Crops up when you least expect it, like dandruff —Robin Worthington

(I read the note over several times with a kind of stupid) incredulity, like an unbelieving prisoner reading the formal sentence of his own execution —Robert Traver

Started [at sound of a sudden call] like a horse at the sound of the bugle —Stefan Zweig

(She) started like a quiet, lovely insect into which someone had suddenly stabbed a pin —Elizabeth Spencer

Startling as curves in a mountain road —Lorrie Moore

(The idea was as) startling ... as if in a blank wall before her a door had opened —Dorothy Canfield Fisher

(Perception as) startling as watching a feeling cross a face on Mount Rushmore —Paige Mitchell

Startling, like a face changing in front of you, from young to old, well to ill —Wilfrid Sheed

Surprised and shocked as if she had heard an explosion and seen her own shattered legs go flying across the floor —Rachel Ingalls

Surprised as a sardine that went to sleep in the ocean and woke up in a delicatessen store —Arthur Baer

Surprised [physical reaction] me as much as if I were a baby suddenly popped from the womb —Angela Carter

Surprise made me look like a goldfish —Rebecca West

Surprises keep us living: as when the first light surprised our infant eyes —Louis MacNeice

Surprising as a child's laugh rising higher, higher, higher —Babette Deutsch

(Sharp pain pierced his chest, as quick and) unexpected as the materialization of a hairline crack in bone —Paige Mitchell

Unexpected as aluminum siding in Buckingham Palace —Anon

Unexpected as best seller status for a book of Latin quotations —Anon

Unexpected as a heart attack —Anon

Unexpected as a heat wave in February —Anon

Unexpected as gourmet food in a second rate hotel —Anon

Unexpected as snow in July —Anon

Unexpectedly wonderful treat, like blue skies and warmth in a chilly spring —Janet Flanner

You never know what somebody's got in him: like the man with germs, suddenly he's down in bed with a crisis —Clifford Odets

SUSPICION
See: TRUST/MISTRUST

SWEARING
See: CURSES

SWEAT

Beads of perspiration, like seed pearls —Dorothea Straus

Beads of sweat gathered on his brow like tiny blisters —William Styron

Beads of sweat ... popped on his forehead like tiny, glistening prairie dogs —Joan Hess

Beads of sweat, tiny as dewdrops —Leigh Allison Wilson

(My forehead) bubbled sweat like a burning plastic bag —Ira Wood

Cold sweat burst from his pores, trickling down his back like ice water —Dorothy Canfield Fisher

A drop of it [sweat] hung like a Christmas tree ornament from the tip of his nose —Jonathan Valin

Feel the sweat like needles at my hair-roots —Randall Jarrell

Fine beads of sweat glistened [on a man's mustache] like little brilliants —Jessamyn West

Glistening with sweat like a circus seal —Ralph Ellison

Little pears of sweat had popped out like a corona around his shiny skull —Harvey Swados

Looked as if it would cost a thousand dollars to shake hands with him —Raymond Chandler

Small beads of sweat adorn his bald head like pearls on a bright dress —Erich Maria Remarque
See also: BALDNESS

Sweat clings like a crystal fixture to his receding brow —Mary Morris

Sweat collects in pores like ink does on fingerprints —Noel Behn

The sweat coming out on his face like somebody had squeezed it
    —Ernest Hemingway

Sweat crawling, like a procession of spiders and ants
    —George Garrett

Sweated like a coolie —Richard Wilbur

Sweated with self-consciousness and the effort to be suave, like a
    teen-ager dancing with a haughty girl —Derek Lambert

Sweating freely ... like a squeezed sponge —Ben Ames Williams

Sweating like a swamp rat —Norman Mailer

Sweating like a very fat man in a Turkish bath —Kingsley Amis

Sweating like Judas —Samuel Beckett

Sweat like black plates under his arms —Ian Kennedy Martin

Sweat poured out ... like a sprinkler —Andrew Kaplan

Sweat poured like rain —Ken Stabler, football quarterback and Berry
    Stainback, writer

Sweat ran down like water down a hill
    —American negro ballad "John Henry"
        In the original of this famous ballad 'water' was spelled
        'watah.'

The sweat ran over my back and down my arms and legs,
    branching, like an upside-down tree —Eudora Welty

Sweats like a mother of six, preparing lunch —Ira Wood

Sweat was pouring from his body like water coming out of a
    showerhead —Ann petry

Sweat was running down behind his ears and under his collar like
    cold, restless worms —Margaret Millar

Under each arm of his striped shirt there was a dark semicircle like
    a stain of secret guilt —Margaret Millar

SWEETNESS
See also: PLEASURE

Sweet as a chaplain —Elizabeth Hardwick

> 'Sweet' as a comparison dates way back probably beginning with Chaucer's "Sweet as the root of licorice" and Henry Buttes' 'Sweet as a nut." Variations continue to develop, or, to coin another simile, "Grow like the taste for sweet things."

Sweet as a first love affair —Isak Dinesen

(My tongue was) sweet as a fresh plum —George Garrett

Sweet as a kiss —Isak Dinesen

Sweet as a mountain lilac —Raymond Chandler

Sweet as apple cider —Eddie Cantor

> This simile was immortalized by singer-vaudevillian Eddie Cantor in his musical ode to his wife Ida: "Ida ... sweet as apple cidah!"

(The words) sweet as a reprieve —Delmore Schwartz

(We bit into life and life was) sweet as a ripe apple
    —George Garrett

Sweet as cream —Marge Piercy

Sweet as love, or the remembrance of a generous deed
    —William Wordsworth

Sweet as love songs —Slogan, Kerr butterscotch candy

Sweet as melancholy —Robert Burton

Sweet as new-mown hay —W. S. Gilbert

Sweet as pie —Anon

> The "Sweet as pie" continues in use, both in its literal sense and to describe someone's personality.

(Kisses as) sweet as sweet mountain dew —Langston Hughes

Sweet as the hope of Paradise —F. van Wyck Mason

Sweeter than honey from a rock —Christina Rossetti

Sweeter than perfume —William Shakespeare

Sweet like pineapple —Marge Piercy

SYMMETRY
See: REGULARITY/IRREGULARITY

SYMPATHY
See: PITY

TACT

Diplomacy, like politics, is the art of the possible —George W. Ball

A diplomatic note is like an anonymous letter. You can call a fellow anything you want, for nobody can find out exactly whose name was signed to it —Will Rogers

Discretion like a good priest —George Garrett

Had about as much finesse as a trained elephant doing the gavotte among ninepins —Cornell Woolrich

Subtle as fanfare —William McIlvanney

Subtle as snakes —Christina Rossetti

Subtle as the London blitz —T. Coraghessan Boyle

A tactless man is like an axe on an embroidery frame —Malay proverb

TALENT
See: ACCOMPLISHMENT

TALLNESS

I'm about as tall as a shotgun and just as noisy —Truman Capote

I towered over my parents like some big-footed freak of another species, like a cuckoo raised by sparrows —T. Coraghessan Boyle

Long and tall as a scarecrow —John Yount

Tall and gaunt as a hangman —Angela Carter

Tall as a building —Louise Erdrich

Tall as a crane —Dame Edith Sitwell

This is part of the opening and closing refrain of Dame Edith's *Aubade*, the full stanza reading, "Jane, Jane, tall as a crane, the morning light creaks down again." In the United States the "Tall as a crane" comparison can be traced back to an Arkansas railroad song in which the simile is used as follows: "He was six feet seven in his stocking feet and taller than any crane."

Tall as a stork —Angela Carter

Tall as a thunderstorm —Miles Gibson

(He was) tall as a tree in the middle of the night —Wallace Stevens

(Poppies as) tall as buildings —Arthur A. Cohen

Tall men are like houses of four stories, wherein commonly the uppermost room is worst furnished —James Howell

Tower over ... like the Washington Monument —James Thurber

TEARS
See also: CRYING

Could feel the tears, like fire, coming up —James Baldwin

Feel the tears brimming and sloshing in me like water in a glass that is unsteady and too full —Sylvia Plath

Generally men's tears, like the droppings of certain springs, only harden and petrify what they fall on —Walter Savage Landor

He [a weeping man] was like a sponge saturated with water, and then squeezed —Leonid Andreyev

Like a summer tempest came her tears —Lord Alfred Tennyson
This also appears as a chapter title in Kenneth Grahame's contemporary children's classic, *The Wind in the Willows.*

My tears like berries fell down —W. B. Yeats

Produce tears freely like a great actor —Erich Maria Remarque

Slow as the winter snow the tears have drifted to mine eyes —Elizabeth Barrett Browning

Suspended like shimmering icicles on Maxell's cheeks were tears —Arthur A. Cohen

A teardrop hung out of each blue eye, like a fat woman leaning out of a tenement window —Tom Robbins

Teardrops come a-splashin' down his cheeks like summer rain —Edward A. Guest

A tear had slipped down to dangle like sweat at the tip of a nostril —Truman Capote

A tear ran down her cheek, turning white with powder, like a tiny ball of snow —Jonathan Valin

Tears ... brightened her eyes and made them glitter like dark stars in a stormy sky —Frank Swinnerton

Tears died as laughter dies away —Dante Gabriel Rossetti

Tears fall like soft fruit juice —Rose Tremain

Tears fell like a plot —Stevie Smith

Tears fill up her eyes like a cup —Jessie Schell

Tears ... flailing my face like the torn ends of shattered rope —John Updike

Tears flooded out of his eyes like the floodwater over a levee —Pat Conroy

Tears ... flowed down upon him like a bower of willows —Arthur A. Cohen

Tears ... flowed like fountains —William Wordsworth
> A twist by Guy De Maupassant: "Wept like a fountain."

Tears flow ... like a swollen gutter gushing through the streets —Henry Fielding

Tears gathered like small· pools in the declivation of his eye cups —Arthur A. Cohen

Tears glittered in her eyes, deep down, like the sinking reflection of a well —Louise Erdrich

Tears glittered like rhinestones on her lashes —Ross Macdonald

Tears, like a stream, like a ceaselessly flowing fountain, flowed and flowed —Nikolai V. Gogol

Tears like bits of glass formed in his eyes —Leonard Michaels

Tears

Tears like molten lead surged in her eyes —Ruth Prawer Jhabvala

Tears ... like two little brooks —Carson McCullers

Tears ... made patterns on his cheeks, like wax trickling down a candle —Julia O'Faolain

Tears on his lashes, like silver drops of dew —Ruth Prawer Jhabvala

Tears rolled down like rain —Elizabeth Spencer

Tears ... roll one from each eye, like droplets on wax fruit —Ira Wood

Tears running down like lemonade —Anne Sexton

Tears rushed forth ... like mountain mists at length dissolved in rain —Lord Byron

> This simile from Byron's famous *Don Juan* has been slightly modernized and shortened. The original first line begins "The tears rush'd forth from her o'erclouded brain, like ... "

The tears seemed to cause the features of her face to melt and soften like hot wax —George Garrett

Tears, silent as a china egg —Marge Piercy

Tears, small as sequins, glinting in her narrowed eyes —Miles Gibson

Tears streamed down her cheeks, soft and bland like the sides of a Guernsey —John Updike

Tears that slipped like melting pellets of sleet down their grieved and angered cheeks —Alice Walker

Tears that streamed ceaselessly like a veil to keep her from seeing too clearly —Paul Horgan

Tears ... they deluge my heart like the rain —Emily Brontë

Tears welled up as freely as water from a drinking fountain —Jean Stafford

Though the tears had no healing power, they took off the edge of it [pain], like cold water on a burn —Margaret Drabble

A woman's tears, like a dog's limping, are seldom real —Russian proverb

TEDIUM
See: DULLNESS, REPETITION

TENDERNESS
See: AFFECTION, GENTLENESS, LOVE

TENSION
See: NERVOUSNESS

THICKNESS
See: ABUNDANCE

THIGHS
See: LEGS

THREATS
See: VIOLENCE

THROAT
See: NECK

THUNDER AND LIGHTNING
See: WEATHER

TIGHTNESS
See: FIRMNESS

TIME
See: DAY, NIGHT, SLOWNESS, SPEED

TIMELINESS/UNTIMELINESS
See also: STALENESS

As modern as tomorrow —Slogan, Royal Worcester Corset Co.

As out of date as the black stockings and high shoes worn by
    inmates of asylums that used to take up city blocks and loom
    large in the countryside
    —Eileen Simpson, *New York Times*/Op-Ed, May 1, 1987

As seasonable as snow in summer —John Ray's *Proverbs*

By the time they take place [dinner parties] the original impulse is
    lost ... like sending a Christmas card into space and hoping an
    alien finds it on the right date —Maxine Chernoff

Dated as a dodo, but who cares —Anon capsule review, television
    movie listings, *New York Times*, April, 1987

Dead as a failed product launch —Anon

Dead as an unsuccessful book —Henry James

Dead as Greek —Karl Shapiro

Dead as Sunday's paper on Tuesday morning —Anon
> Commonly used variations are "Dead as yesterday's front page news" and "Dead as last week's ticker tape."

Extinction, like a thing of beauty, is forever —Brad Leithauser, *New York Times Book Review*, June 7, 1987
> Another simile that was extracted from an article and featured as an attention-getting blurb.

Gone like the carriage-horse —Louis MacNeice
> Poet MacNeice precedes the simile with this question: "What's become of the squadron of butlers, valets, grooms and second housemaids?" Clearly, appropriate substitutions for the carriage-horse could give rise to as many similes beginning with "Gone like" as there are obsolete customs and objects. "Gone ... like five-cent candy and the drainboard on the sink" from a novel by Babs H. Deal offers just one possibility.

Good that comes too late is as good as nothing —Thomas Fuller

It's a little like being given the captaincy of the *Titanic* after it hit the ice floe —Senator Lawton Chiles of Florida, quoted in many newspapers on prospect of heading Senate budget committee, after November, 1986, Democratic victory
See also: FUTILITY

Like a punchline of a bad joke, the moment passed
—T. Coraghessan Boyle

(Conflicts as) new as each generation —Anon, jacket copy
> Because similes are so often pulled out from book jacket copy, the more one can appropriately include, the better; and so, this and the "Old as literature" comparison below were both featured on one book jacket.

New as tomorrow —Slogan, dictaphone company

(Passions and conflicts as) old as literature —Anon book jacket copy

No day is so dead as the day before yesterday
—W. Somerset Maugham

Obsolete as books in leather bindings —Louis MacNeice

Outdated like a last year's almanac —John Greenleaf Whittier

DEAD AS AN UNSUCCESSFUL BOOK

Timing ... as elegant as that of the Budapest String Quartet
—Karl Shapiro

(The reference library is quite) unfrequented ... like the mausoleum of
a once-proud family that has died out —Robert Barnard

TOBACCO

An acrid cigar held tightly in your teeth, you look like a banker or a
psychiatrist or both —Daniela Gioseffi

Ash flows like a breaking thundercloud from his clenched cigar
—Harvey Swados

Ashtray ... crammed with smoked cigarettes like dead bugs
—John Rechy

Blowing a cloud of coarse smoke [from pipe], like a steam roller
—Frank Swinnerton

(I lit) a cigar, a cheap twisted black thing like half a pepperoni
—T. Coraghessan Boyle

Cigarette coals dotted the room like watchfires —Thomas Pynchon

Cigarettes ... dangle from his lips like a second tongue
—Jonathan Valin

Cigarettes tasted like hot ashes —Anthony E. Stockanes

Cigars ... when lit, they exuded an overwhelming odor, like burning
manure from constipated giraffes —Richard S. Prather

A dead cigar which was always in his hand, seemed to belong there,
like a thumb or finger —Willa Cather

The glow in the bowl of his pipe went on and off like a firefly
—Jean Stafford

A good cigar is as great a comfort to a man as a good cry is to a
woman —Edward Bulwer-Lytton

His cheeks puffed [from smoking a cigar] like a bellows —Jay Parini

His cigar ... had become a natural appendage ... like a pipe stuck in
the face of a snowman —Robert Traver

It [tobacco] smells like Saturday, and consequently puts me in a
chronic holiday mood —Robert Benchley

It [cigarette] tasted like burning rope —F. Van Wyck Mason

Lit his stogy, which flared up like a burning bush —Arthur Train

My psyche felt as different without cigarettes as my body felt in moving from air to water —Norman Mailer

Removed his water-logged cigar, like a man calmly unscrewing his nose —Robert Traver

The smell of good tobacco ... heavy as incense in a church —Howard Spring

Smoked like a chimney —Richard Harris Barham

The smoke of cigars and ciigrettes like curtains before the lights —R. Wright Campbell

Smoking his clay pipe with the elegance of an Indian chief —André Malraux

Stubbed out the cigarette as if he were squashing a cockroach —Derek Lambert

The tip of his narrow cigarette danced like a tiny ballerina in the dark —Nelson Algren

Took another deep drag of his cigarette, letting the smoke curl up out of his mouth and around his head like ectoplasm —Margaret Millar

To smoke a cigar through a mouthpiece is the equivalent of kissing a lady through a respirator —Anon

TONGUE

Her tongue felt like a freshly painted shingle —Edwin L. Sabin

Her tongue hung out like a yard of red hall carpet —Wilson Mizener

Her tongue [as she kissed him] was like a kitten's, soft and rough, tasting of milk —Shirley W. Schoonover

His tongue darted in and out when he talked, as if he were keeping count of the words —Shelby Hearon

(A large dog lay panting,) his tongue unrolled like a carpet —Peter Meinke

My tongue is big as a liverwurst —Marge Piercy

Tongue

The tongue is like a race horse: the less weight it carries, the faster it runs —Joseph Addison
> This has been modernized from the original. "The tongue is like a race-horse, which runs the faster the lesser weight it carries."

Tongue like a pink dart —Joseph Conrad

The tongue ... like a stream, could run smooth music from the roughest stone —Elizabeth Barrett Browning

Your tongue curls up in your mouth like a cat lapping up cream —R. Wright Campbell

TOUGHNESS

Babies you about as much as Perry White babies Clark Kent —Peter H. Lewis describing a tough-to-master computer program, *New York Times*, 1985

(The man is as) hard as a cash register —Dialogue, "Miami Vice" television drama, broadcast January 7, 1986

(She can be) hard as a mineral —Philip Roth
> The "Hard as a mineral" lady is the mother of Nathan Zuckerman, hero of several Roth novels.

Hard as flint —Larry McMurtry

Hard as my fist —Tennessee Williams

Hard as a tortoise-shell —John Galsworthy

Hardboiled as a picnic egg —Edward E. Paramore

Resilient and tenacious as an amoeba —Natascha Wodin

She's [Genevieve Bujold] tough as a little green apple —Rex Reed

Tough and leathery as a jockey —John Mortimer

Tough and shrill as an old bird —H.E. Bates

Tough and hard-boiled as an Easter egg —Anon

Tough as a black oak —Dee Brown

Tough as a bone —W. S. Gilbert

Tough as a fast food steak —Tim McCarver, describing baseball player Dave Parker on television, January, 1987

Tough as a kibbutz woman —T. Coraghessan Boyle

(She was short and fat,) tough as a monkey —Rudolf Nassauer

Tough as an elephant's hide —Calder Willingham

(He was as) tough as a resistant bacterium —Patrick Suskind

Tough as a stale bagel —Anon

(Memories as) tough as a thorn —Babette Deutsch

Tough as boiled owls —Hubert H. Humphrey on his opponent for presidential election

(She's big as a damned barn and) tough as knife metal —Ken Kesey

Tough as marshmallows —Anon, *Forbes,* March 23, 1987
> The simile was used as a blurb to introduce an article about the government sounding tough but not following through.

(She was) a tough lady, like a military jeep rolling from place to place on thick tires —Harvey Jacobs

(She's as) tough as old boots —Mary Bridgman
> Around since 1870. A popular variant: "Tough as old shoe leather."

Tough as seaweed —Linda Pastan

Tough as teak —Bryan Forbes

Tough as tire treads —Lynn Haney
> The person being compared to tire treads is the late Edith Piaf.

TRANSIENCE
See also: BREVITY

About as fixed as liquid mercury
—Leslie Bennetts, *New York Times,* June 8, 1986

The brilliant passes like the dew at dawn
—Johann Wolfgang von Goethe
In *Faust,* from which this is taken, Goethe continues by presenting the other side of the coin: "The true endures for ages yet unborn."

Burnt like a faggot in a tempest —Willa Cather

Changed them like underwear —Paige Mitchell
In Mitchell's novel, *The Covenant,* law clerks are what are being so changed.

(His smile) comes and goes as quickly as snow —Robert Goldberg
about film maker Alain Resnais, *Wall Street Journal,* March 24, 1987
See also: ENTRANCES/EXITS

Disposable as extra income —Anon

Disposable as razor blades —Anon

Disposable as TV dinner containers —Anon

Enduring as a summer shower —Anon

Ephemeral as butterflies
—Susan Heller Anderson on literary magazines, *New York Times/* Column One, October 24, 1986

Ephemeral things, like movement, are manifestations of immortality
—Joanne Selzer
This is the closing line for a poem entitled *Prima Ballerina.*

Flare briefly like the candles upon a cake —Donald Justice

(Embrace ...) fleeting as a bird's poise —Edith Wharton

Fleeting as a dream of night lost in the garish day —Aeschylus

Fleeting as a raspberry season —Line from television drama, "St. Elsewhere," broadcast December 16, 1986

Fleeting as the estate of man —Marcus Aurelius

A fleeting gratification ... like alms thrown to the beggar, that keeps
   him alive today that his misery may be prolonged till the morrow
   —Lynne Sharon Schwartz

How fading are the joys we dote upon! Like apparitions seen and
   gone —John Norris

Like a rainbow, spectacular but short-lived —Anon
         A variation: "Like a shooting star—spectacular but short-
         lived."

Like water thrown on the sand: it [media campaign about energy
   crisis] left little trace —George F. Will

Mortality weights heavily on me like unwilling sleep —John Keats

(The moment of agitation) passed (from his gaze) like a cloud,
   leaving a clear blue sky —Christopher Isherwood

Passing through a certain stage, something rather like an illness
   —Thomas Mann

Permanent as a temporary price increase —Anon

Temporary as an idea in an empty head —Anon

Temporary as a wave —Anon

(Beauty is as) temporary as flowers —Anon

(His self-possession was) temporary, like a reflection in water that
   may be wiped out at the first swell —Saul Bellow

(His love was as) transient as the first golden streaks of dawn
   —Harry Prince

Transitory as childhood —Lawrence Durrell

Will last about as long as a snowball in hell —Anon

TRAVEL

Like a chastity belt, the package tour keeps you out of mischief but
   a bit restive for wondering what you missed —Peg Bracken

Like film critics, the guidebooks don't always see eye to eye
   —Peg Bracken

Like gin or plum pudding, travel is filling —Peg Bracken

Travel

One's travel life is basically as incommunicable as his sex life is
—Peg Bracken

A traveller without knowledge is a bird without wings —Sadi

Travel light, like the prayers of Jews —Yehuda Amichai

Travelling is almost like talking with men of three other centuries
—Rene Descartes

TREES
See: LEAVES

Trembling

TREMBLING
See also: VIBRATION

Body quivers like a dancing animal's —Maureen Howard

Felt a tremor ... like an earthquake in a swamp —William Getz
The tremor described is the shiver that goes through a
person.

(The handkerchief) flapped like a jib in a crosswind
—T. Coraghessan Boyle

(Ali's brain) flickered and wavered like a candle flame in a draft
—Gerald Kersh

(My tongue) fluttered like a dead leaf —George Garrett

Fluttered like paper in the wind —Gertrude Atherton

Fluttering around like birds in a thicket —Ariel Dorfman

Fluttering around ... like a yardful of hens —Harvey Swados

Fluttering in the wind, like a schooner in full rig —Anatole France
This referred to a feather fluttering on a hat, and while
feathered hats have not been in style for many years, the
comparison is not limited to this descriptive reference
point.

Fluttering like a white moth —O. Henry

Fluttering like pigeons —Christina Rossetti

Flutter like large butterflies —Oscar Wilde

Her hands and face shook like Jell-O —Joseph Heller

Trembling flesh and pudding make for vivid similes. Some variants: "Quivering all over ... like a dish of jelly on a rickety table" (Nikolay Leskov); "The whole huge torso, the shoulders, arms and breast and the great heaving belly, would shake and tremble like a hogshead full of jelly." (Thomas Wolfe)

His whole body was shaking and the more he tried to control it, the more violently it shook, as though the lines of communications between his brain and his muscles had been cut
—Margaret Millar

(Nostrils) pulse like a heart on fire —Gertrude Atherton

Quake like mice when the cat is mentioned —Honoré de Balzac

(His whole face) quivered convulsively as if pricked by pins and needles —Luigi Pirandello

[An evening gown] Quivered like a butterfly about to take wing —Dorothea Straus

Quivered like a pointer dog —Jonathan Gash

Quivered like a sob —Conrad Aiken

Quivered like forest-leaves —Dante Gabriel Rossetti

Quivering ... like a wounded bird —Leo Tolstoy

Quiver like a twig in a gale —L. P. Hartley

Quiver like tuning forks —Peter De Vries

(The Saab) rattled like a trayful of china —Scott Spencer

Shaking all over like someone attached to an electric reducing belt —Cornell Woolrich

Shaking like a dog shittin' peach pits —Ken Kesey

Shaking like a drunk the morning-after —Clarence Major

Shaking like a lamb led to slaughter —Sholom Aleichem

Shaking like an ague-fit —William Faulkner

Shaking like a piece of grass —Louise Erdrich

Shaking like a treed raccoon —Harvey Swados

Shaking like a wet spaniel —T. Coraghessan Boyle

(Her breath) shaking like turning leaves —Mary Hedin

Shiver as at the sight of a bug or a repulsively dirty man in the street —Colette

Shivered, like a swimmer who has tested the water with a toe and found it exceeding chill —Stefan Zweig

Shivering like a puppy —Ross Macdonald

Shivering like a whippet on a cold day —Jilly Cooper

Shiver like a flame —George Garrett

Shiver like ostriches in a zoo —Marge Piercy

Shivers like a fish in a net —George Garrett

Shook like a harpstring —Beryl Markham

[A hand that had been beaten] shook like a loose leaf in the air —James Joyce

Shook like an autumn leaf —Dante Gabriel Rossetti
> To "shake like an aspen leaf" is a familiar variant. "I shook like a leaf ... like a little leaf in a big storm" from a short story, *The Actor*, by Nunally Johnson exemplifies the simile extended.

(His whole body) shook like a thunder-stricken tree —Yisrael Zarchi

(His face was gray and) shook like a torn sail —Malcolm Cowley

Shook like a wet mutt [describing a dynamited building] —Tom Robbins

Shudder as if she were passing a cemetery —Elsa Schiaparelli

Shuddered all over, like a dog that recognizes the vet and smells its oncoming death —Frank Tuohy

Shuddered like a broken doll —Louise Erdrich

Shudders like an epileptic —T. Coraghessan Boyle

Shudders ... like a woman gently coming —Diane Ackerman

Shuddery like a hooked fish or a stallion —W. D. Snodgrass

Silently quivering like the waters of a lake when the wind blows off-shore —Yitzhak Shenhar

Swayed like the tail of a dog attempting to be friendly
    —F. van Wyck Mason

Sways like a broken stalk —Elizabeth Bishop

(Her body) sways like a willow in spring wind
    —Robert Penn Warren

Sways like tropical seaweed —Lawrence Durrell

Trembled like an adolescent —Robert Silverberg

Trembled tensely like a released harp-string —Joseph Conrad

Tremble like an aspirin —Ogden Nash

Trembling as if something were shaking him —Ben Hecht

Trembling like a colt —Lawrence Durrell

Trembling like an invalid —Mavis Gallant

Trembling like a string —Ivan Turgenev

(Knees) trembly like water —Peggy Bennett

Shudder as if she were passing a cemetery —Elsa Schiaparelli

Tremulous as a plant in a stream —Vita Sackville-West

Twitching like a hooked fish —Gerald Kersh

Twitching like a skate [fish] in a frying pan —Lawrence Durrell

An unexpected shudder rippled over her body, like a cold wind
    moving across water —Madeleine L'Engle

Wobble like a skittle —Graham Swift

TRITENESS
See: STALENESS

TROUBLES
See: PROBLEMS/SOLUTIONS

TRUENESS/FALSENESS

Deceptive as a cat's fur —Margaret Atwood

Deceptive as a Venus flytrap
—Vivian Raynor, *New York Times*, February 27, 1987
Ms. Raynor's simile refers to the fleeting and misleading resemblance of one artist's work to another's.

Deceptive as new paint on a second-hand car
—Herbert V. Prochnow

False as a lead coin —George Garrett

Falser than a weeping crocodile —John Dryden

Falser than malice in the mouth of envy —Mary Pin

Good and true as morning —Babs H. Deal

Right as rain —William Raymond
An older, less commonly used version from Shakespeare's *Richard III:* 'Right as snow in harvest.''

Ring as true as chapel bells on a windless morning —Anon

Ring true, like good china —Sylvia Plath

True as life itself —Louis Bromfield

True as the dial to the sun —Barton Booth

(I found him large as life and) true as the needle to the pole
—Henry James

True as the sky is blue —James Reiss

True as truth —Louis Bromfield

The true is stripped from the false like bone from meat
—George Garrett

TRUST/MISTRUST

Finding paranoia in your heart is like discovering a lump in your breast —just knowing it's there won't make it go away
—Jerry Bumpus

As confiding as a doe peeping between the tree trunks
—Vita Sackville-West

As suspicious of me as Hamlet was of his mother —Daphne Merkin

Carried years of suspicion strapped to her hip like a gun
—Ann Jasperson

Confidence in an unfaithful man in time of trouble is like a broken tooth, and a foot out of joint —*The Holy Bible/Proverbs*

Confidence (in their amorous destinies) like that of birds in their wings —William Faulkner

Confidence, like the soul, never returns, once it is gone —Publius Syrus

Doubt ... secret and gnawing like a worm —Joseph Conrad

Doubts seemed to steam like wet flies inside his own head —Julia O'Faolain

Head ... awhirl with doubts like a sky full of starlings —George Garrett

He was like a suspicion-caked old prospector —Ellery Queen

It [the thought that something was not right] was on the edge of her mind like a speck at the corner of your eye or fluff in your nostril —Julia O'Faolain

Lean on ... like a man on crutches —Ross Macdonald

Mistrust swells like a prune —Marge Piercy

No more to be trusted (with news) than a cat with a saucer of milk —Christopher Isherwood

Suspicion amongst thoughts are like bats amongst birds, they ever fly by twilight —Francis Bacon

Suspicion developed like a muscle —F. Scott Fitzgerald

Suspicious ... as a rat near strange bread —Patrick Kavanagh

Suspicious as a wild cat —Frank Swinnerton

Trust as I'd trust a rattlesnake —Anon

A trust, fierce and passionate, burning in her like a prayer —F. Scott Fitzgerald

Trust flourishes like a potato plant, mostly underground —Marge Piercy

As trusting to the future as a blind sky-diver —Richard Ford

Trust is like an egg and it's not like an egg. If you want to break an egg you have to do it from the outside. The only way to break up a trust is from the inside —O. Henry

Trustworthy as advice given by a cat to a mouse —Anon
     A simile with clear links to an Arabic proverb: "He gives advice such as a cat gives to a mouse."

Wearing doubt like a raincoat —Carlos Baker

TRUTH
See: HONESTY

TURNING AND TWISTING

Circling like polishing rags —Diane Ackerman

(His brain) spinning around and around like a ship's propeller —Graham Masterton

Spinning like a wind vane —William Faulkner

Spun like someone caught in a revolving door —William McIlvanney

(My whole house) spun around me like a crazy carnival ride —George Garrett

Swerving like a bird in mid-air —Lawrence Durrell

Swirling about like boiling milk —H. G. Wells

Sway like an elephant's trunk —Anon

(My senses) swivel like guns in their fixed sockets —Margaret Atwood

(We caught him red-handed and he) turned as easily as a trout in the pan —Bryan Forbes

Turned as a bucket turns in a well —Dante Gabriel Rossetti

Turning ... like a chicken on a spit —Enid Bagnold

Turning like a ghost across the road —Eudora Welty

Turning like a hand in water —Philip Levine

Turns and turns like a dog making a place to lie down —Maxine Kumin

Twisted like a caterpillar —Cornell Woolrich

Twisted like a desperate fish —Peter S. Beagle

(Ryan's mouth) twisted, like a key in a lock —Julia O'Faolain

Twisting his whole body as if his bones were made of rubber
    —Alexander Solzhenitsyn

Went around and around like the policeman and Charlie Chaplin,
    both intending to fall down —Eudora Welty

Wheeled like an ambushed cat —Nelson Algren

Whipped round like a steel spring —John Fowles

Whisking about like a swallow into its nest —O. Henry

(She was always) whisking about like a clean starched napkin
    —H. E. Bates

Wriggle ... like a snake —Mary Stewart

Writhing like a baited worm —Countee Cullen

UMBRELLAS
See: OBJECTS, MISCELLANEOUS

UNATTRACTIVENESS
See also: UNDESIRABILITY

As erotically stimulating as a mouthful of sardines —Ira Wood

As likable as a jaguar —William Beechcroft

Decorative as the scalps of an Indian brave —Frank Swinnerton

Disgusting, like moving cheese, like hills of ants or of flies
    —Ralph Waldo Emerson

Have all the charm of a black widow
    —Pia Lindstrom, television movie review, 1986

(Furniture) emanating bad taste like a cold draft —Milan Kundera

Lurid as a porcelain souvenir —Derek Walcott

(It sounded) obscene, like a rarely glimpsed body part —Lorrie Moore

Plain as cement sidewalks. Plain as bread crust —Jean Thompson

Ugly and fat as a maggot —Miles Gibson

Ugly and indestructible as the aluminum beer can —Stephen Minot

Ugly as a hairless monkey —Margaret Mitchell

Ugly as a hatful of assholes —Geoffrey Wolff

Ugly as a mud fence
  —American colloquialism, attributed to Southeast
      Southerners often elaborated on this as follows: "Ugly as a
      mud fence daubed with tadpoles."

(He was like most new babies as) ugly as an artichoke
  —Anne Sexton

Ugly as sin —Maria Edgeworth

Ugly ... like a great black spider —Rosamund Pilcher

Unappealing as a meringue with hardly any crust —Anon

UNAVAILABILITY
See: AVAILABILITY/UNAVAILABILITY

UNAWARENESS
See: BLINDNESS

UNCERTAINTY
See: FATE

UNCOMFORTABLENESS
See: DISCOMFORT

UNCONSCIOUSNESS
See: NATURALNESS

UNDEMONSTRATIVENESS
See: RESERVE

UNDERSTANDABILITY
See: CLARITY

UNDERSTANDING
See: KNOWLEDGE

UNDESIRABILITY

About as inviting as Lenin's tomb —Manuela Hoelterhoff, reporting on a large wall surrounding a new museum complex in Los Angeles, *Wall Street Journal*, December 15, 1986

About as pleasant as to have an umbrella jammed down your throat, and opened there, and pulled out open, so that the broken ribs lacerate your lungs, and beaten over the head with the handle —Don Marquis

About as thrilling as swimming lessons would be to a middle-aged goldfish —H. C. Witwer

As bad as marrying the devil's daughter and living with the old folks —G. L. Apperson

As bad as offering Satan a lost soul —Emily Brontë

As desirable as meeting a former lover during a honeymoon —Elyse Sommer

As much fun as a month in Gdansk —Joseph Wambaugh

(John Singer Sargent liked to make painting portraits sound) attractive as catching toads for a living —Manuela Hoeltershoff, introducing review of John Singer Sargent show at Whitney Museum, *Wall Street Journal*, October 15, 1986

Some like ill weather, unsent for —Brian Melbancke

(She was ...) desirable ... like a whore on a street corner —Derek Lambert

Disagreeable ... like a scent which raises fine hair on animals —John Updike

Gave him no pleasure ... it was like being invited to stretch himself out to be amputated, without an anesthetic —Storm Jameson

(Haggling about military bases) has all the joys of arm-wrestling on a sinking raft —*New York Times* editorial, March 23, 1987

Hates (publicity) the way Polly hates crackers —Arthur Baer

Have about as much pleasure ahead of us as a pig in a butcher shop —George Garrett

(Six years ago ... the idea of spending an afternoon at Shea Stadium) held about as much appeal as your basic monster traffic jam —Malcom Moran, *New York Times*, October 11, 1986

Jumped at the chance like a sardine leaps for the can —Anon

Liked ... about as much as I liked snakes or trunk murders
—T. Coraghessan Boyle

Like foul weather, you come unsent for, and troublesome when you
come —H. G. Bohn's *Handbook of Proverbs*

To love as a cat loves mustard —John Ray's *Proverbs*

Needed [an unpleasant scene] like a cover girl needs acne
—Loren D. Estleman

Position as enviable as that of a catcher on a javelin team —George
V. Higgins, on Rolland Smith's interaction with Mariette Hartley
on CBS-TV program, *Wall Street Journal*, January 19, 1987

To love as the devil loves holy water —John Ray's *Proverbs*

To love it as a dog loves a whip —John Ray's *Proverbs*

A trifle less welcome than something you would scrape off the
bottom of your shoe —C. W. Grafton

An unpleasant guest is as welcome as salt to a sore eye
—Danish proverb

Unsatisfying as a set compliment —Heywood Brrun

Unwelcome as a mouse in your shoe —Elyse Sommer

Wanted (to play baseball) like he wanted a third nostril
—Max Shulman

Welcome as a guest with sneakers at a Palm Beach party
—Tom Brokaw

Welcome as a mugger —Anon

Welcome as a painful and chronic disease —Elyse Sommer

Welcome as a storm —Thomas Fuller

Welcome as a tree falling across your Volkswagon
—"PM-TV Magazine"

Welcome as Satan —Alfred, Lord Tennyson

Welcome as snow at harvest time —John Ray's *Proverbs*

Welcome as the season's first snowstorm —Anon

AS DESIRABLE AS MEETING A FORMER LOVER
DURING A HONEYMOON

Undesirability

A skier or ski resort operator might look for this under the Desirability category.

(In the rarefied upper echelons of Japanese sumo wrestling, foreigners have been about as) welcome as Visigoths were at the gates of Rome —Clyde Haberman, about wrestler from Hawaii, *New York Times*, May 28, 1987

Welcome as water in a leaking ship —John Ray's *Proverbs*
> To tone down the image of disaster to common distress, there's another Ray proverb: "As welcome as water in one's shoes."

Welcomed ... the way a cardiac case does chest pains —William McIlvanney

UNEXPECTEDNESS
See: SUDDENNESS, SURPRISE

UNFRIENDLINESS
See: SOCIABILITY/UNSOCIABILITY

UNHAPPIIESS
See: DISCONTENT, GLOOM

UNIQUENESS
See: ORIGINALITY

UNKINDNESS
See: CRUELTY

UNNATURALNESS
See: NATURALNESS

UNOBTRUSIVENESS
See: OBVIOUSNESS

UNPREDICTABILITY
See: SURPRISE

UNPROFITABILITY
See: ADVANTAGEOUSNESS

UNREALITY
See: REALNESS/UNREALNESS

UNRESPONSIVENESS
See: RESERVE

UNSTEADINESS
See also: MOVEMENT

Flounder around like a fish on the beach —Anon
>A commonly used variation: "Flounder around like a beached whale."

Floundered like a waterlogged ship —James Hilton

Floundered like insects in yogurt
>—George F. Will, about those involved in Watergate crimes

Floundering like someone running in deep sand, blind without glasses, burdened with books —George Garrett

Flounder like a compass that's lost its needle —Anon
>A variation: "Flounder like a windup watch without a dial."

(Was solidly built but) gave the impression of not being very stable, like a building with imperfect foundations —MacDonald Harris

Reel like a leaf that's drawn to a water-wheel
>—Dante Gabriel Rossetti

Stagger like a drunken man —*The Holy Bible/The Psalms*

Staggers slightly ... like a carnival clown —Hilary Masters

Staggers to his feet like a battered middleweight coming out for the fifteenth round —T. Coraghessan Boyle

Stumbled ... like an old woman leaning on a cane that wasn't there
>—Ross Macdonald

Stumbled like fat sheep —Stephen Crane

Stumbling a little over his own feet like an adolescent not accustomed to his new growth —Margaret Millar

Tumbling ... like a moth blinded by sudden brightness
>—Jerzy Kosinski

Unconstant as the wind; as wavering as the weathercock
>—William Walker

Unstable as water —*The Holy Bible/Genesis*

(She seemed volatile right now,) unstable, like a vial of nitroglycerin
>—Sue Grafton

Unsteady like a pole balanced on the tip of one's finger
—Arthur Schopenhauer

Wavering as the wind —John Heywood's *Proverbs*
Modernized from the Old English: "Waueryng as the wynde."

Wobbled like an overfed penguin —Len Deighton

(His new English) wobbles like a first bicycle —Diane Ackerman

UNTIMELINESS
See: TIMELINESS/UNTIMELINESS

UNTRUTH
See: LIES/LIARS

UNWELCOMENESS
See: UNDESIRABILITY

UPRIGHTNESS
See: POSTURE, STRAIGHTNESS

UP-TO-DATENESS
See: TIMELINESS/UNTIMELINESS

VAGUENESS

(The image) blurred ... like something familiar seen beneath disturbed though clear water —William Faulkner

(The consonants) blur together like ink on a wet page —Sue Grafton

Clear as mud —Richard Harris Barham
This typifies the quick, humorous similes that were most often imported by New Englanders to add color to American speech.

Obscure as a bureaucrat's memorandum —Anon

Obscure as modesty —Sidney Lanier

(Eye ...) opaque as a muddy pool —F. Scott Fitzgerald

Opaque as a milk-glass bowl —Linda West Eckhardt

VARIETY
See: DIVERSENESS

VEHICLES
See: ROAD SCENES

VEHICLES, OPERATION OF

Drive like a nursemaid with a pramful of kids —Calder Willingham

Drove as if he were handling a hearse —Lael Tucker Wertenbaker

Drove silently, like a silent wind —Elizabeth Spencer

(Pulled out into traffic, his) engine cooking like grease on a cheap
    griddle —Loren D. Estleman

He [driver of car] took the curves like a bird
    —Erich Maria Remarque

Keeps that engine purrin' like a whore on a hundred-dollar date
    —John Farris

Touchdown [of airplane] was as smooth as arriving at the ground
    floor in a lift —Donald Seaman

VIBRATION
See also: TREMBLING

Body jerking like a fish —David Mamet, dialogue from "Hill Street
    Blues" television show, broadcast January 13, 1987

(Light ... came at him) throbbing like a drum —Mark Helprin

Jerking like a decked shark —Denis Johnson

A little ripple (went through her) like the commotion set up in a
    weeping willow by a puff of wind —O. Henry

Oscillate like a blancmange in an earthquake —John Wainwright

(Thoughts) rattle about ... like dried seeds in a pod —Ellen Glasgow

Rattle about [a large apartment] like dried peas in a pod
    —Janet Hobhouse

Rattled like a dicer's cup —Davis Grubb

(The King's heart) rattled like spook chains in a horror show
    —Tom Robbins

Rattling like a crockery shop in an earthquake —Arthur Baer

[A cough] shook me like a coconut tree in a tornado
—Dominique Lapierre

Throbbing like a heart —Marguerite Yourcenar

Throb like the heart of a coffee drinker —O. Henry

Vibrating like a dog's tail —Norman Mailer

Vibrating ... like a man with a high fever —Anon

VIGILANCE
See: ALERTNESS, WATCHFULNESS

VIOLENCE
See also: BEHAVIOR

Battered to and fro as a rat is shaken by a dog —Rudyard Kipling

Came after him like an antelope —William Diehl

Came at him like a kamikaze —T. Coraghessan Boyle

Cored him like an apple —John Yount

Dealt out blows with the precision of a punch press
—Natascha Wodin

Drove his fist straight in like a saber thrust —Joseph Wambaugh

Grabbed hold of me, as a cat grabs a mouse —George Garrett

Hit it [a man's chin] as if I was driving the last spike on the first
transcontinental railroad —Raymond Chandler

Hit like a tank —Ken Stabler and Berry Stainback

Howling and clawing at each other like wild beasts in heat
—Hunter S. Thompson

I can flatten him out like a crépe in a frying-pan —Henry Van Dyke

I could slice you down like cold meat before you could whisper
Mercy —Davis Grubb
> In Grubb's novel, *The Golden Sickle,* the man making this
> threat is wielding a knife.

I'll crush his ribs in like a rotten hazelnut —Emily Brontë

I'm gonna pop your eyes like busted eggs —William Kennedy

Knocked to the ground like a winged partridge
    —T. Coraghessan Boyle

Lunged [into the midst of group of people] like a whirlwind on a
    summer's day —Flannery O'Connor

[Mobster Sam Giancana, who) ordered killings as easily as he ordered
    linguini —Kitty Kelley

The propensity for violence exists like a layer of buried molten
    magma underlying all human topography —Robert Ardrey

Put me in an arm lock as easily as he might twist a soft pretzel
    —James Crumley

Showered her blows ... with the force and rapidity of a drummer
    beating his drum —Guy De Maupassant

Slapped her like a volleyball —Rochelle Ratner

Terrorism is a natural by-product of modern life. Like air pollution,
    family breakdown, excessively casual sexual promiscuity and
    exaltation of greed —Russell Baker, *New York Times*, 1986

Threw themselves at him like dogs at a bear —Mikhail Bulgakov

Violence and wrong are as a dream which rolls from steadfast truth,
    an unreturning stream —Percy Bysshe Shelley

Violence (was an inescapable factor of the heart ...) an ineradicable
    thing ... like a bad seed —William March

Violence in a house is like a worm on vegetables —Hebrew proverb

Violence is as American as cherry pie —Eldridge Cleaver

The violence of my impulses [to harm another person] was still
    within me, like the sharp end of a splinter improperly removed
    —Scott Spencer

Violence weighed him down like a pack —Harris Downey

Violent and ruthless as a puppy —James Mills

Violent death is like a monster. The closer you get to it, the more
    damage you sustain —Sue Grafton

Violent death leaves an aura, like an energy field that repels the
    observer —Sue Grafton

Was on him like a falling tree —Jerry Bumpus

A wound like a burst fruit —Jean Stafford

VIRTUE
See: ACCOMPLISHMENT, MORALITY, PURITY

VISIBILITY
See also: CLARITY, OBVIOUSNESS, PROTRUSION

Conspicuous, like giraffes —Karl Shapiro

(A trail as) faint as a whisp —Edward Hoagland

(The writing was as) faint as sparrow tracks in sand —Will Weaver

Hidden from view, like undeveloped negatives —Anon

Hide ... as a boat finds a cove until the storm passes
    —Mary Lee Settle

Hiding like tumors —Charles Johnson

Imperceptible as a spring breeze —Susan Richards Shreve

Imperceptible as grief —Emily Dickinson
        This is both the title and the first line of a poem.

Invisible as a city sparrow —Marge Piercy

Invisible as the web in a spider's belly —Marge Piercy

Invisible, like a bad odor —Stephen Longstreet

Just out of sight like stars in the noon sky —John Farris

Lurking beneath the surface like a nest of snakes —Anon article on
    drugs as the X factor in National Football League violence, *New
    York Times*, November 30, 1986

Noticeable as a fart in a hail storm —American colloquialism

Prominent as a fried egg stain on the front of a full dress vest
    —Arthur Baer

Protrude like hairs from an old man's nose —F. D. Reeve

(The scene in front of him remained) unclear, like a painting so
    encrusted with dirt and varnish its depths refuse the investigating
    eye —Clive Barker

Unnoticeable as a pore —Karl Shapiro

Unobtrusive as a thief —Paul Theroux

Unseen like our shadows —Margaret Atwood

Visible ... like a goldfish in a bowl —Cornell Woolrich

VIVIDNESS
See: BRIGHTNESS

VOCATION
See: PROFESSIONS

VOICE(S)
See: CRYING; GROANS AND WHISPERS; SINGING; VOICE, EFFECT OF;
VOICE, HARSH; VOICE, MONOTONOUS; VOICE, MUSIC-RELATED;
VOICE, SOFT; VOICE, WEAK

VOICE, EFFECT OF

Accent which tortured me as much as a fiddle with a soft G string
    or a clarinet reed blown through bubbles of saliva
    —Harvey Swados

Her low voice soothed him like honey in whiskey —Rita Mae Brown

Her voice curled around Melinda like a damp tongue
    —Jessamyn West

His father's voice entered Ben's ear like an icepick —Pat Conroy

His loud clear voice fell on her ears soft as snow —Margaret Millar

Loud voice that scrapes over our nerves like a brush
    —Erich Maria Remarque

The shrill voices stung her eardrums like sharp pebbles
    —Paul Kuttner

The sound of her voice drove itself into his senses like a spike
    —Kaatje Hurlbut

Voice ... irritating to the nerves like the pitiless clamour of the
    pneumatic drill —W. Somerset Maugham

Voices hitting the wall like stones —Maya Angelou

The voices were unnerving, like the dark come to life
—Martin Cruz Smith

The voice (of a platoon leader) would buzz against his ear like a passing insect, undefined and rather annoying —Norman Mailer

VOICE, HARSH
See also: HARSHNESS

A hard, crushing voice like stones smashing against each other
—Aharon Megged

Her voice ... creaked like the hinges of a rusty iron gate
—Stefan Zweig

Her voice flew around like pots and pans —Leonard Michaels

Her voice sounded as brittle and sharp as a broken sliver of glass
—Graham Masterton

High, irritating voice, like a razor blade —Caryl Phillips

His voice was harsh, like a great whirring mill saw
—T. Coraghessan Boyle

Hoarse bass voice like an echo in an empty house —Amos Oz

A hoarse voice ... like something broken —Romain Gary

A retching voice like a tin shovel scooping water off a concrete barn floor —Leonard Casper

A roughness in her voice like a grasshopper's —Virginia Woolf

[Voice] sounded like two shards of pottery being rubbed together
—Norman Mailer

Their voices slash like reeds —William Meredith

A thick, husky voice that sounded as if he'd swallowed too many years of fog —Margaret Millar

A voice as hard as the blade of a shovel —Raymond Chandler

Voice ... brittle as the first ice of autumn —Michael Gilbert

Voice ... brittle, like overdone candy cracking on a plate
—Pat M. Esslinger-Carr

Voice cracking like a trunk lid unopened for years —Patricia Henley

Voice ... croaky and tense and faintly honking, as if a metal tube were involved in its production —John Updike

Voice, cruel as a new knife —George Garrett

Voice ... deep, like crusted port wine —Donald Seaman

Voice flat and hard as a stove lid —James Crumley

Voice ... fringed and sharp like the edge of a saw
    —Carson McCullers

Voice ... hard as a nail on glass —William Beechcroft

Voice harsh and light as the scratching of dry leaves over the hard ground —Edna St. Vincent Millay

Voice harsh like tin and without heat like tin —William Faulkner

Voice ... hoarse as a rooster —John Farris

Voice like a chair scraping across a tiled floor —Roderic Jeffries

Voice like a fingernail scraping down a dry blackboard
    —Reynolds Price
        Modern usage favors 'chalkboard.'

Voice ... like a foghorn in foul weather —George Garrett

A voice like a howitzer
    —Thomas Carlyle about his publisher Frederic Henry Hedge

Voice ... like a pointer moving sharply on a map or blackboard
    —Mary McCarthy
        McCarthy's *Charmed Life* was written in the forties. As indicated in entry #28, the currently preferred word for 'blackboard' is 'chalkboard.'

Voice, like a rusty hinge —Margaret Mitchell

Voice like a slate-pencil squeak —Paul J. Wellman

Voice like a spoon scraping a cooking pot —Annette Sanford

Voice like a tight squeak —Anon, about Marilyn Monroe by Columbia Pictures when they fired her in 1948

Voice, like barbed wire —Helen Hudson

A voice like cracking glaciers —Elinor Wylie

A voice like frosted trees in the wind —Rolaine Hochstein

A voice like hot ashes —James Agee

Voice ... like sand —T. Coraghessan Boyle

Voice like scruffed gravel —Hortense Calisher

Voice like the cracked shriek of a desert wind —Phyllis Bottome

Voice ... reedy like a tall-legged, tall-necked bird —Carolyn Chute

Voice ... scratchily metallic as though it were being raked across miles of rusted roofing tin —Sharon Sheehe Stark

Voice ... sharp as a snowflake on a sunburned nose —Rex Reed, about Tennessee Williams

Voice ... sharp as porcupine quills —John Updike

Voice ... sharp, splintering, like dry kindling split by an ax. Voice like pebbles in a bucket —Carlos Baker

Voice so ruined it sounded like a wood rasp —John Yount

Voice sounded like a crow with a cold —Harold Adams

Voice ... sounds as if her throat is swollen shut —John Updike

Voices shrill as children's whistles —Marge Piercy

Voice that sounded like tires on a wet road —Richard Maynard

Voice ... with a hardness in it like struck steel —John Yount

Voice ... with an alluring crack in it, like some magisterial old woman who has smoked all her life —Lynne Sharon Schwartz

VOICE, MONOTONOUS

Drone on like a dull wind at night —James Stern

Voices grind on, like machines boring their way through tunnels —John Updike

Low monotonous voice like an absent-minded child haltingly reciting a lesson —Edith Wharton

No more inflection than a traffic light —John Updike

A noncommitttal noplace voice like a computer salesman, or somebody taking a poll, or an anchorman on TV —Lee Smith

Voice ... low and monotonous, like a voice that had never expressed any human passions —Henry James

Voices, fixed like leeches to their solitary subject —Jean Stafford

The voice went on, like the steady pressure of a surgeon's hand on a shrieking nerve —Edith Wharton

VOICE, MUSIC RELATED

Chimed in ... like a cracked bell —Angela Carter

Deep voice like a jovial bassoon —Willa Cather

His voice resonated like the bass in a barbershop quartet —Peter Meinke

Scratches in her soft voice like an old phonograph record —Wilfrid Sheed

Voice ... with a monotonous beat of syllables, like the rhythm of a wide and shallow drum pounding in the heart of a jungle night —Wilbur Daniel Steele

Voice ... clear and brassy, like a bugle —O. Henry

Voice ... deep as a gong —Rosamund Pilcher

Voice ... delicate and pleasant, like a reed pipe —Yuri Kazkov

A voice like a bassoon —Gerald Kersh

Voice like a cello solo —O. Henry

Voice like a church bell —George MacDonald Fraser

Voice like an aging church-choir soprano —Z. Vance Wilson

A voice like an old-fashioned wind instrument —Henry James

Voice like a sexual cello —Angela Carter

(Lift up thine) voice like a trumpet —*The Holy Bible/Isaiah*

Voice like a tuba —Charles Johnson

Voice ... like clarinets all ebony and silver —George Garrett

Voice like quiet music —Carlos Baker

Voice ... like someone relentlessly playing the kazoo during one of the more somber passages of a war requiem —Douglas Adams

Voice like the "D" string in a cello —Henry Van Dyke

Voice like the deepest woodwind —George Garrett

Voice ... off-key, like a neglected piano —Paige Mitchell

Voice rang like a great silver bell —O. Henry

Voice roared like an organ pipe —Joyce Cary

Voices like French horns —Margaret Millar

Voice soft, like the voice of a violin —Isak Dinesen

Voice sounds like an accordion played down at the end of a dark tunnel —Charles Baxter

Voice ... thin as a flute —Ross Macdonald

Voice ... vibrant as the tones of a crystal bell —Théophile Gautier

Voice ... refined and finicky, like a tenor's in a cathedral choir —Frank Tuohy

What a little piccolo voice she had, like a living character from a Walt Disney Cartoon —Tama Janowitz

VOICE, SOFT

A gentle, circling voice, as a warm hand is gentle circling the wrist —Kaatje Hurlbut

Her voice is a caress which strokes you like fingers —Jules Lemaître
Lemaître, a critic, was describing actress Sarah Bernhardt's voice.

His voice died in a frail wistful sigh, like wind through a shutter —William Styron

That beautiful voice which made everything she said sound like a caress —Virginia Woolf

Voice ... like a page of music —Pat Conroy

Voice like dark brown velvet —Josephine Tey

Voice like down feathers —William Diehl

Voice ... like liquid —Mark Helprin

Voice ... like melting honey —Jimmy Sangster

Voice like thick soup —Edith Wharton

Voices as soft and murmurous as wings —George Garrett

Voice soft and cool as a prison yard —Joseph Wambaugh

Voice soft and rich as that of a counselling angel —Henry James,
	letter to Thomas Sergeant Perry, November 1, 1863

Voice soft as maple syrup running into a glass container
	—F. Scott Fitzgerald

Voice ... soothing as running water —Dorothy Parker

When we spoke, it was softly, like TV cowboys expecting an ambush
	—Deborah Eisenberg

VOICE, WEAK

Forced little voice, wavering like a puff of smoke —Ivan Turgenev

Her voice came soft and faint, as though another person had aid the
	words first and she was merely passing them on
	—Harvey Swados

Her voice was small, as if she had to squeeze it up from the depths
	—Laura Furman

Little voice, that wavered like a thread of smoke —Ivan Turgenev

Voice as faint as the buzzing of a bee's wings —Kenzaburo Oë

Voice ... faded, thin away. Like a river diminishing to a stream and
	then to a trickle —Maya Angelou

Voice no bigger than a starling's —R. Wright Campbell

Voice ... thin as a sheet of Zig Zag —Arnold Sawislak

His voice [Tennesee Williams,] wavers unsteadily like old gray cigar
	smoke in a room with no ventilation, rising to a mad cackle like
	a wounded macaw, settling finally in a cross somewhere between
	Tallulah Bankhead and Everett Dirksen —Rex Reed

WALKING
See also: AWKWARDNESS, CAUTION, MOVEMENT, RUNNING

As fond of long walks as hairdressers are of fishing —Colette
	See also: PLEASURE

As she walked she lifted her knees high, her feet far out in front of her, like a drum majorette on parade —Nancy Huddleston Packer

A curiously modest gait, like a preoccupied steer —Cynthia Ozick

A heavy man who walked as though he was still a lean one
—Pat Conroy
See also: FATNESS

His feet strike at the trembling earth like a bailiff pounding a door with an iron bar —Angela Carter

His stride was a sort of ambulatory Rorschach test. One could project anything one fancied into it —James Morrow

His stride was light and long, like that of a man on the moon
—Mark Helprin

Light rapid steps ... like the hops of a bird —Paul Horgan

The men walked like scissors; the women trod like cats
—Katherine Mansfield

My steps became extravagantly buoyant, like those of a high-wire artist walking on a hidden trampoline —Robert Traver

Paced [from room to room] ... like a marathon runner cooling down
—Gerald A. Kersh

Paced the room like proctors at a college board examination
—Scott Spencer

Picked his way as if he were walking on an iceberg —Peggy Bennett

A shambling gait like a trained bear —William Faulkner

Stalked over ... like a traffic cop —James Thurber

Step as light as summer air —John Greenleaf Whittier
A popular variation: "Trod as lightly as if he were walking on air."

Stiffly, like a man walking the trunk of a tree that bridges a chasm, he began to walk —Anon

Strut like a crow in a gutter —John Ray's *Proverbs*

Strut like a fighting cock —George Garrett

Struts like a bandit —Diane Ackerman

Strutting ... like an Olympic shot putter —T. Coraghessan Boyle

(I still have) a trotting bounce to my walk, like a middle-aged coyote who lopes along avoiding the cougars and hedgehogs, though still feeling quite capable of snapping up rabbits and fawns —Edward Hoagland

Unsteady but purposeful walk, as if she were on a wheel that misguided her —Eudora Welty

Up and down he went, like a sailor with a limp —Wright Morris

Walked as a man might show off a garden, stopping here and there to pluck a flower —Lawrence Durrell

Walked as if a puppet master dangled her from a set of strings —Jay Parini

Walked as if he were completely alone, like an abdicated king —Beryl Markham

Walked high on his feet, like his shoes were hurting him —Donald McCaig

Walked like a man with a pain in his gut —William H. Hallhan

Walked like two snakes —Maeve Brennan

Walked neither fast nor slow, like a man going to work at a job he didn't enjoy —Harold Adams

Walked sedately, as though he were being watched —Helen Hudson

Walked very quickly, moving his arms as he walked like a tall thin bird flapping its wings —Jean Rhys

Walk ... like an invalid just liberated from the sedentary months of his sickbed —Frederick Exley

Walking sedately back and forth, like a plump abbot who has just found exquisite confirmation of his long-cherished view of paradise —Robert Traver

Walks like a stately yacht listing disconcertingly to starboard —Frank Rich, about Robert Mitchum's performance in television miniseries, *New York Times*, 1986

Walk slowly, like one accustomed to be alone —Karl Shapiro

Walk together, like prisoners out for exercise —W. D. Snodgrass

Wandering around like a tit in a trance —Carolyn Slaughter

When he walks, he moves like an engine —William Shakespeare

With those long strides he looks like an antelope when he runs
—Gary Thorn

WAR
See also: ARMY

The art of war is like the art of the courtesan; indeed, they might be
called sisters, since both are the slaves of desperation
—Pietro Aretino

The beginning of war is like the first days of peace: neither the
world nor our hearts know they are there —Jane Wagner

Being a soldier [in war time] was like being on a team in a sport
that drew no crowds, except for the players' own parents and
friends —Dan Wakefield

Great warriors, like great earthquakes, are principally remembered for
the mischief they have done —Christian Nestell Bovee

Marrying in wartime is like sowing among thorns —Ignazio Silone
See also: MARRIAGE

Success in war, like charity in religion, covers a multitude of sins
—Lord Napier

War is like an aging actress; more and more dangerous, and less and
less photogenic —Robert Capa

War will disappear, like the dinosaur, when changes in world
conditions have destroyed its survival value —Robert A. Millikan

Went to war with an air, as if they went to a ball
—Stephen Vincent Benét

WASTE

In delay we waste our lights in vain, like lamps by day
—William Shakespeare

Wasted his wealth like spittle —Stephen Vincent Benét

Wasted more money in a day than a Boeing 747 full of proverbial
welfare queens ccould have squandered in a century —Hodding
Carter III, *Wall Street Journal,* March 30, 1986

Carter's simile referred to new defense spending policies.

Wasteful as drunkenness at undue times —Robert Browning

Wasteful as regrets —Anon

WATCHFULNESS
See also: PROTECTIVENESS

Followed [by keeping eyes fixed on other person] ... like someone studying a historical figure —Lawrence Durrell

Had a way of looking around ... as if hidden cameras were photographing her —Ann Beattie

He watched her as a cat does a mouse —James Howell
Of all the comparisons linked to watchfulness this is probably the most famous and enduring, dating back to 1624. In Robert Louis Stevenson's *Kidnapped* it appears as "We sat at table like a cat and a mouse, each stealthily observing the other."

Hovering like an old bird over one egg —Eudora Welty

(Each evening I) peered surreptitiously through the kitchen curtains, like a spinster keeping tab on her neighbors —W. P. Kinsella

Vigilant as cat to steal cream —William Shakespeare

Watched as if from a cat's distance —Martin Cruz Smith

Watched him like musicians watching the conductor —Wilfrid Sheed

Watched ... like a warden —Anon
The warden comparison has gained considerable currency in the last decade or so. Two recent novels in which it appeared are *Disturbances in the Field*, by Lynne Sharon Schwartz: "Kept watch like a warden" and *Riders*, by Jilly Cooper: "Watching him like a warden."

Watched, like Indians at a corral —Etheridge Knight

Watched me like a fish hawk —James Crumley

Watched ... tensely, like a spider lying in wait for the fly's last drop of blood —Heinrich Böll

(My mother) watches me for signs of bloom and decay, like a plant —Daphne Merkin

Watchful as a ferret —R. Wright Campbell

Watching me like a bloodhound after a convict —Shelby Hearon

Watching [someone's looks and moves] ... with an attention as intense as if an ordeal involving my life depended on them —Joseph Sheridan Le Fanu

Watch (tensely) like a cat stationed near a bird feeder —Bobbie Ann Mason

Watch ... like a dead white moon —Ross Macdonald

Watch ... like a nursemaid —Nicholas Monsarrat

Watch like one who fears robbing —William Shakespeare

Watch like ravens on a tree branch —R. Wright Campbell

WATER
See: OCEAN/OCEANFRONT, PONDS AND STREAMS

WEAKNESS
See: HELPLESSNESS

WEATHER
See also: FOG, RAIN, SNOW

The chilly, drizzly June day smelled like a basement —Marge Piercy

The elements are but as qualities that change forever, like all things that have known generation —Dame Edith Sitwell

Frost made the sunny air seem like a bright keen knife —Howard Spring

Humidity ... dropped down over the city like a damp serge cloak —Carlos Baker

The humidity ... slapped me in the face like a mugger's glove —Loren D. Estleman

Rain and thaw took its [snow's] place, and now the world looks about as pleasing as a wet cat —John Wainwright

The storm crashes like god-wars —Hayden Carruth

The [hot] weather clings, like a low fever you cannot shake off —Angela Carter

HE WATCHED HER AS A CAT DOES A MOUSE

Weather ... cool and gray as wash water —George Garrett

Weather in towns is like a skylark in a counting-house, out of place and in the way —Jerome K. Jerome

The weather was like a waiter with a tray —Wallace Stevens

The whine of wind and rattle of rain and the thunder rolling terribly loud and near overhead like a thousand beer trucks roaring over the bridge —John Dos Passos

WEDDINGS
See: MARRIAGE

WEIGHT
See: HEAVINESS

WELCOMENESS
See: DESIRABILITY

WHISPERS
See: GROANS AND WHISPERS

WHITE
See also: PALLOR

(Face) more white than sin —Dame Edith Sitwell

Pure white as china door knobs —Reynolds Price

White and bare as a winter moon —George Garrett

White and clean as driftwood —George Garrett
    See also: CLEANLINESS

(A yacht) white and pretty as a birthday cake —George Garrett

White and wan, like the head and skin of a dying man
    —Percy Bysshe Shelley

(The desert is) white as a blind man's eye —Sylvia Plath

(He's as) white as a chicken —Honoré de Balzac

(Face) white as a bandage —Helen Hudson

White as a dog's bone —Anne Sexton

White as a foam-flower —Henry Van Dyke

(Ball) white as a leghorn egg —W. P. Kinsella

White as a lily —William Shakespeare

(In marble halls as) white as milk —Anon old English riddle
> Some variations to intensify the image: "White as new milk" by Dorothy Canfield Fisher and "Snow white as white milk from a white cow" by Eleanor Wylie.

White as a milk tooth —Charles Simic

(Body) white as an aspirin —Richard Ford

White as any bough that blooms in May —Geoffrey Chaucer

White as a peeled stick —Helen Hudson

(Moon) white as a sand dollar —Diane Ackerman

White as blanched almonds —Charles Cotton

(Teeth) white as detergent —Margaret Atwood

White as ermine —Dame Edith Sitwell

(Her neck and temples were) white as flour —T. Coraghessan Boyle

White as frost —G. K. Chesterton
> An extension of this opening line of Chesterton's poem, *The Mirror of Madmen,* is "White as hoarfrost."

White as ivory —Oscar Wilde
> An extension by a contemporary short story writer, Barry Targan: "White as polished ivory."

White as lightning —Cynthia Ozick
> The comparison is being used to describe the look of a woman in a nurse's uniform.

(The air blew white in my face,) white as my daughter's communion dress, white as a bridal veil —Elizabeth Spencer

(The little space between earth and sky was filled by a broken veil of drifting flakes as) white as pear blossoms —Phyllis Bottome

(Teeth,) white as peeled almonds —Gerald Kersh

(Veins) white as porkfat —Sylvia Plath

White as pulverized bone —T. Coraghessan Boyle

White as rice —Reynolds Price

White as sheets and blizzards —T. Coraghessan Boyle

White as snow —*The Holy Bible*
> Similes comparing the whiteness of complexions, hair and miscellaneous objects to snow can be found throughout literature as well as in our everyday language. Some well-known variations include: "White as driven snow" by William Shakespeare, "White as new-fallen snow" by William Wordsworth, "White as dead snow" by Algernon Charles Swinburne and "White as the snow on high hills" by Elizabeth Barrett Browning.

(Teeth) white as sun-cured bone —Beryl Markham

(Hand) white as talcum —Mavis Gallant

(Teeth) white as the petals of a daisy —Dan Jacobson

White as the sun —Henry Chettle

White as the surf —Oscar Wilde

(Face is) white as the wall —Daphne du Maurier

(Chest ...) white as wax —Patricia Henley

(Hair) white as whipped cream —W. P. Kinsella

(Face) white like a whitewashed fence —William Faulkner

White like May-blossom —Charlotte Brontë

White like salt —Aharon Megged

White like sea foam —Joan Chase

WILDNESS
See: FEROCITY

WIND
See: WEATHER

WISDOM
See also: KNOWLEDGE

Chewing over their combined worldly wisdom like so many puppies
with a shoe —Mary Ladd Cavell
> The wisdom in Cavell's story, *The Rotifer*, is being shared by three apartment mates.

The heart of the wise man lies quiet like limpid water
—Cameroonian proverb

The heart of the wise, like a mirror, should reflect all objects,
without being sullied —Confucius

If a man is as wise as a serpent, he can afford t be as harmless as
a dove —Josh Billings
This is an elaboration of "Harmless as a dove" which dates
back to the Bible. In Billings' phonetic dialect this reads,
"Iz az wize az a serpent."

Insight as keen as frosty star —William Wordsworth

A learned man is a tank; a wise man is a spring —William R. Alger

String of wise jests ... like gold links —Penelope Gilliatt

To learn a person's life ... like learning a language, you must start
with the little things, the little pictures
—Susan Fromberg Schaeffer

Wisdom and virtue are like two wheels of a cart —Japanese proverb

Wisdom in a poor man is like a diamond set in lead
—H. G. Bohn's *Handbook of Proverbs*

Wisdom is like fire: a little enlightens, much burns —Moses Ibn Ezra

Wisdom is like gold ore, mixed with stones and dust
—Moses Ibn Ezra

Wisdom, like life itself, appeared to me to be comprised of
continuing progress, of starting over again, of patience
—Marguerite Yourcenar

Wisdom, like perfume, rises out of its own essence —Norman Mailer

Wisdom shook itself like a drop off a dog (and he lost it)
—Cynthia Ozick

Wise as a wisp —George Garrett

Wise as heaven —Algernon Charles Swinburne

WIT
See also: WISDOM

As much wit as three folks, two fools and a madman
—Thomas Fuller

Wit

One wit, like a knuckle of ham in soup, gives a zest and flavor to the dish, but more than one serves only to spoil the pottage —Tobias Smollett

Satire is a sort of glass, wherein beholders do generally discover everybody's face but their own —Jonathan Swift

Sharp wits, like sharp knives, do often cut their owner's fingers —Aaron Arrowsmith

Wit and wisdom are like the seven stars, seldom seen together —Thomas Fuller

Wit is as infinite as love —Agnes Repplier
> Repplier built on her simile with "And a deal more lasting in its qualities."

Wit ... like a quick-flashing blade —Henry James

Wit ... like champagne, not only sparkles, but is sweet —Benjamin Disraeli

Wit, like money, bears an extra value when rung down as soon as it's wanted —Douglas Jerrold

Wit must grow like fingers —John Selden

Wit ... penetrates through the coldness and awkwardness of society, gradually bringing men nearer together, and, like the combined force of wine and oil, giving every man a glad heart and a shining countenance —Sydney Smith

Wit, without learning, is like a tree which bears no fruit —Aristippus

Wit, without wisdom, is like a song without sense; it does not please long —Josh Billings

WIVES
See: MARRIAGE

WORD(S)
See: SPEAKING; WORDS, DEFINED; WORDS, EFFECT OF; WRITERS/WRITING

Words, Defined

WORDS, DEFINED

The English language is like an enormous bank account —Robert Claiborne

The great man's word is like the elephant's tusk [i.e. not to be concealed or withdrawn] —Hindu saying

Long words, like long beards, are ooten the badge of charlatans —F. L. Lucas

Pithy sentences are like sharp nails which force the truth upon our memories —Denis Diderot

Technical terms ... are like red, white and blue poker chips. They stand for whatever the players agree upon —John B. Kerfoot

A word fitly spoken is like apples of gold in a setting of silver —*The Holy Bible/Proverbs*

A word is not a crystal transparent and unchanged; it is the skin of a living thought and may vary greatly in color and content according to the circumstances and the time in which it is used —Oliver Wendell Holmes, Sr.

Words are like bodies, and meanings like souls —Abraham Ibn Ezra

Words are like labels, or coins, or better, like swarming bees —Anne Sexton

Words are like leaves, some wither every year —Horace
Alexander Pope's variation of this reads as follows: "Words are like leaves and where they most abound, much fruit of sense beneath is rarely found."

Words are like money, not the worse for being common, but ... it is the stamp of custom alone that gives them circulation or value —William Hazlitt

Words are like money; there is nothing so useless, unless when in actual use —Samuel Butler

Words are like money, a medium of exchange; and the sureness with which they can be used varies not only with the character of the coins themselves, but also with the character of the things they buy, and that of the men who tender and receive them —Allen Upward

Words are like money; and when the current value of them is generally understood, no man is cheated by them —Sir Richard Steele
This and the next three entries rely on what follows the basic simile for individuality.

Words are loaded pistols —Jean-Paul Sartre

Words ... a syllable which sounds like a bumblebee breaking wind —Hortense Calisher

Words, like cavalry horses answering the bugle, group themselves automatically into familiar dreary patterns —George Orwell
> Orwell's simile was used to urge against re-using any phrase once it appears in print. Anyone following his advice would use this book strictly as a guide to phrase elimination.

The words of a man's mouth are as deep waters, and the wellsprings of wisdom as a flowing brook —*The Holy Bible /Proverbs*

A word without thought is like a foot without sinew —Moses Ibn Ezra

WORDS, EFFECT OF

Epithets, like pepper, give zest to what you write —Lewis Carroll
> Carroll expanded on the simile as follows: "And if you strew them sparely, they whet the appetite; but if you lay them on too thick, you spoil the matter quite!'

Everything you say is just like scraping a wound with a knife —Iris Murdoch

Hearing a word break like a wave on the shells of my ears —John Hersey

Her words pelted me like hail —Edith Wharton

Her words showered down upon us like little glass pellets —Saul Bellow

His words dropped in Spandarian's ear like pellets of ice —Derek Lambert

Like heavy hostile fists the words pounded on Andrew's incredulous ears —F. van Wyck Mason

Listening to The Weasel [an unpleasant person] was like having a dirty hand paw through your personal belongings, leaving them in confusion and so soiled that after the first look you were disgusted and tempted to throw them away, for they had changed —Ann Petry

HER WORDS PELTED ME LIKE HAIL

Words, Effect of

The sentences ... like toy life-buoys made of paper, they carried no weight or conviction —James Stern

That terrible word caused Flora's heart to slide like frozen snow —Frank Swinnerton

The word ... went through Morgan's heart like a poisoned spear —Noël Coward

The word pierced her side like a sharp horn —Z. Vance Wilson

The words beat on Gerty's brain like the sound of a language which had seemed familiar at a distance but on approaching is found to be unintelligible —Edith Wharton

Words cutting like diamonds —Frank Swinnerton

Words dig at her like fingers in clay —T. Coraghessan Boyle

The words drive home like separate blows from a mallet —T. Coraghessan Boyle

The words felt like a medicine ball to the stomach —T. Glen Coughlin

Words, like daggers, enter in my ears —William Shakespeare
> In *Hamlet* the words enter into "mine" not "my ears." Another Shakespearean dagger image from *Titus Andronicus:* 'These words are razors to my wounded heart."

Words ... rattle and roll like dice —George Garrett

The words shook her like a tempest —Edith Wharton

The words slid over her like water poured on stones —Ellen Gilchrist

Words that sting and creep like insects —Karl Shapiro

Words were like nails. Like little knives. —George Garrett

The words trickled through his mind like a warm and friendly brook, or a leak in a boat which filled it only slowly —MacDonald Harris

The word went home. It hit on his heart like a tennis ball in fast play —Vicki Baum

612

WORK
See: DOCTORS, LAWYERS, PROFESSIONS

WORLD

Our world is only a practical joke of God, like a bad day
    —Franz Kafka

This world is like Noah's Ark in which few men but many beasts
    embark —Samuel Butler

The universe is like a safe to which there is a combination, but the
    combination is locked up in the safe —Peter de Vries

The world is a gaming table so arranged that all who enter the
    casino must play and all must lose more or less heavily in the
    long run, though they win occasionally by the way
    —Samuel Butler

The world is a looking glass, and gives back to every man the
    reflection of his own face —William Makepeace Thackeray
        The looking glass comparison from *Vanity Fair* continues
        as follows: "Frown at it and it will in turn look sourly upon
        you; laugh at it and with it, and it is a jolly kind
        companion."

The world is a mirror: what looks in looks out. It returns only what
    you lend it —Ludwig Boerne

The world is an expensive hotel; you pay dearly for each pleasure
    —Israel Salanter Lipkin

The world is like a beautiful book, but of little use to anyone who
    cannot read it —Carolo Goldon
        The original simile used the word 'him' instead of
        'anyone.'

The world is like a board with holes in it, and the square men have
    got into the round holes, and the round into the square
    —Bishop George Berkeley

The world is like a cucumber, today it's in your hand, tomorrow up
    your arse —Arabic proverb

The world is like a drunken peasant. If you lift him into the saddle
    on one side, he will fall off on the other. One can't help him,
    no matter how one tries —Martin Luther

The world is like a fair: people gather for a while, then part; some profit and rejoice, others lose and grieve —Bahya

The world is like a fountain-wheel: the buckets ascend full and descend empty —*The Holy Bible/Exodus*
> The biblical passage concludes with "Who's rich today may not be so tomorrow."

The world is like a foyer leading to the world to come —Rabbi Jacob
> In the *Mishna,* this continues with "Prepare yourself in the foyer, so that you may enter into the inner chamber." Another version of this reads: "The world is like an antechamber to the next. Prepare yourself here that you may be admitted to the banquet hall there."

The world is like a great staircase, some go up and others go down —Hipponax

The world is like a house, with the sky as a ceiling, the earth spread out like a carpet, the stars arrayed like lamps ... and man its master —Bahya

The world is like a ladder: one goes up, another goes down —Immanuel of Rome

The world is like a map of antipathies ... in which everyone picks the symbolic color of his difference —Juan Ramon Jiménez

The world is like an enormous spider web and if you touch it, however lightly, at any point, the vibration ripples to the remotest perimeter —Robert Penn Warren

The world is like an old coquette who conceals her age —Voltaire

The world is like a pump-wheel, through which the full is emptied and the empty filled —Naham Bratzlav

The world like a cradle rises and falls on a wave of confetti and funerals —Louis MacNeice

The world waits to be made over by each man who inhabits it, and it is made over every morning like a bed —William Saroyan

A world where cliches fit like a gown by Edith Head —Tom Nolan, *New York Times Book Review,* November 9, 1986
> The comparison to a Hollywood designer's gowns was most appropriate as the book being reviewed had a Hollywood background.

WORRY
See: AGITATION

WRINKLES
See also: COMPLEXION, FOREHEAD

All the flesh of him that showed, had creases like miniature gullies in the skin —Paul Horgan

Deep lines that looked like dark parentheses around her lips —Alice McDermott

Face as creased as his trousers —Sumner Locke Elliott

Face as lined as an Indian squaw's —John Fowles

Face creased up like a fine soft handkerchief —Lawrence Durrell

A face crisscrossed with lines like an old paper bag —Margaret Millar

Face ... delicately wrinkled like a fine thin notepaper —Louise Erdrich

The face grows lined and wrinkled like a chart —Karl Shapiro

Face like a withered walnut —Edith Wharton

Face lined as soft leather —Sue Grafton

Face, lined like a much-folded map —Mollie Hardwick

Face lined like a river delta —T. Coraghessan Boyle

Face ... marked by a little cross-hatching of fine lines, as though his cheek had lain on corduroy —Harvey Swados

Face marked with gossamer lines like the craze of enamel —Samuel Yellen

Face ... savagely gouged, like the land after the passage of a fast-running rain that makes temporary rivers which plow the ground and leave sunbaked veins of rut afterward —Paul Horgan

Face so wrinkled that it was like a parchment loaded with hieroglyphics —G. K. Chesterton

Faces ... wrinkled by wind and sun like cured meat —George Garrett

Face wrinkled in deep furrows like the fissures in a red clay road after rain —Ellen Glasgow

Face ... wrinkled like the bark of the pine trees
—Susan Fromberg Schaeffer

Face ... wrinkling like a bent leather glove —Harvey Swados

Grooves like gashes ran from his nostrils to his mouth-corners
—Dashiell Hammett

Had a thousand wrinkles on her face, so that she looked most like
an aging Barbie doll —Shelby Hearon

Her face is etched all over with fine liies, as though her skin has
been caught under a butterfly net —Daphne Merkin

Her face was wrinkled like a roll-top desk —Arthur Baer

Her skin had a pattern all its own of numberless branching wrinkles
and as though a whole little tree stood in the middle of her
forehead —Eudora Welty

His neck all in wrinkles resembling cracks, criss-crossing one another,
as though his neck were made of cork —Ivan Bunin

His skin wrinkled up like crumpled butcher paper —Jonathan Valin

Jagged lines around his eyes, lines like scars from a broken bottle
—Richard Lourie

The lines deep graven in the soft skin about her eyes and mouth
were like rivers in a black-and-white map —Frank Swinnerton

Lines etched by age, like frost patterns on a windowpane
—Dorothea Straus

The lines on her forehead and neck were as if scored with a knife
—John Braine

Pink skin scored with wrinkles like the furrows of a corn field
—Carlos Fuentes

Shriveling like an overbaked potato —Ira Wood

Skin ... wrinkled like a wine-skin —W. Somerset Maugham

Skin wrinkled like an old paper bag —Margaret Millar

Skin wrinkles like paint —Derek Walcott

Stretch marks ... looked like streaky bacon held up to the light
—David Niven

(On my skin) the wrinkles branch out, overlapping like hair or
   feathers —Margaret Atwood

Thin long ines like the lines in cracked glass or within a cake of ice
   —Saul Bellow

A sheaf of fine wrinkles spread [from corners of eyes] like a fan
   —L. P. Hartley

Wary lines around the corners of his eyes, like sparrow's claws
   —Derek Lambert

Wrinkled as an iguana —Richard Ford

Wrinkled as a dry plum —Anon
   A much-used variation: "Wrinkled as a prune."

[A newborn baby] wrinkled as a head of lettuce —Charles Johnson

Wrinkled as a walnut —Dominique Lapierre

A wrinkled, wizened face, like that of an aged monkey
   —William Styron

Wrinkle like an apple left uneaten too long —Anon
   Simile makers are greatly drawn to comparisons between
   apples and wrinkled skin. Some examples from current
   literature: "Wrinkled as a roasted apple" (Desmond
   O'Grady); "Wrinkled like a stale apple" (Graham Greene);
   "Wrinkled like a winter apple" (Isak Dinesen); "Wrinkled
   like the skin of a winter-kept apple" (Wallace Stegner);
   "Wrinkles crept into it [a woman's face] like worms" (Erich
   Maria Remarque).

The wrinkles in her skin shone like a bright net —Eudora Welty

Wrinkles of delight appearing on the leathery skin like cracks in a
   shattered safety glass —Robert J. Serling

Wrinkles [in forehead] ... rush together like sentinels —Irving Stone

Wrinkling like a potato —W. D. Snodgrass

WRITERS/WRITING
See also: POETS/POETRY

The act of writing itself is done in secret, like masturbation
   —Stephen King

Alliteration is like ivy, some of it is poison —Delmore Schwartz

As a baker bakes more bread than brown; or as a tumbler tumbles up and down; so does our author, rummaging his brain, by various methods try to entertain —Henry Fielding

An author at work is like an oyster, clam-quiet and busy —Rumer Godden

An author introduced to people who have read, or who say they have read his books, always feels like a man taken for the first time to be shown to his future wife's relations —Jerome K. Jerome

An author is like a baker; it is for him to make the sweets, and others to buy and enjoy them —Leigh Hunt

Authors are like cattle going to a fair: those of the same field can never move on without butting one another —Walter Savage Landor

Authors, like coins, grow dear as they grow old; it is the rust we value, not the gold —Alexander Pope

An author who speaks of his own books is almost as bad as a mother who talks about her own children —Benjamin Disraeli

Being an author is like treading water in the middle of the ocean; you can never stop, you can never stop treading water —Delmore Schwartz

Being a writer in a library is rather like being a eunuch in a harem —John Braine, *New York Times*, Oct. 7, 1961

A biographer is like a contractor who builds roads: it's terribly messy, mud everywhere, and when you get done, people travel over the road at a fast clip —Arthur Wilson

Churn out books as though his days were numbered —Michiko Kakutani, *New York Times*, February 14, 1987
> In reviewing Anthony Burgess' autobiography, *Little Wilson and Big God*, Kakutani uses this simile to introduce heerrecounting the story of how Burgess began writing when he thought that his days were in fact numbered.

Clear writers, like fountains, do not seem so deep as they are —Walter Savage Landor
> The simile is followed by this about the less-than-clear: "The turbid look the most profound."

A collection of essays is a collection of variations
—Elizabeth Hardwick

The essayist is kind of poet in prose —Alexander Smith

Every author, however modest, keeps a most outrageous vanity
chained like a madman in the padded cell of his breast
—Logan Pearsall Smith

For the blocked or hesitant, the advent of the computer is like the
advent of spring: the frozen river surges, the hard earth flowers
—Edward Mendelson reporting on computers for writers, *Yale
Review*, 1985

Getting a book published without a literary agent is like swimming
dangerous waters without a shark repellent
—Rae Lawrence, *New York Times Magazine*, July 5, 1987
Lawrence's simile serves to introduce her experience in
finding and choosing a literary agent for her first novel.

Good writing is a kind of skating which carries off the performer
where he would not go —Ralph Waldo Emerson

Grammar is an art. Style is a gift. You are born with your style, just
as you are born with your voice —Anatole France

The great writer finds style as the mystic finds God, in his own soul
—Havelock Ellis

Hiring someone to write your autobiography is like hiring someone to
take a bath for you
—Mae West, quoted in *Bookviews*, February 11, 1977

I can get a kind of tension when I'm writing a short story [as
compared to a novel], like I'm pulling on a rope and know
where the rope is attached —Alice Munro, quoted *New York
Times Book Review*, September 14, 1986

I get a thing I call sentence-fever that must be like buck-fever; it's a
sort of intense literary self-consciousness that comes when I try to
force myself —F. Scott Fitzgerald

(I enjoy the hell out of writing because) it's [writing] like an Easter
egg hunt. Here's 50 pages and you say, "Oh, Christ, where is it?
Then on the 51st page, it'll work" —John D. MacDonald

Like thrifty French cooks, waste nothing —Leslie Garis, *New York
Times Magazine*, February 8, 1987

Garis used the simile to describe Joan Didion and John Gregory Dunne's extensive note taking.

A long preface to a short treatise is like a high hat crowning a low brow —Zevi Hirsh Somerhausen
> Paraphrased for more modern English usage from "Like a high hat crowning a low brow is a long preface to a short treatise."

Long sentences in a short composition are like large rooms in little houses —William Shenstone

Method in writing is like ceremony in living too often used to supply the want of better things —Thomas Killigrew

Minor characters [in scripts] are rather like knights in chess: limited in movement, but handy in their capacity for quick turns, for fixing situations —John Fowles

A narrative is like a room on whose walls a number of false doors have been painted; while within the narrative, we have many apparent choices of exit, but when the author leads us to one particular door, we know it is the right one because the door opens —John Updike

Nobody can write a real drama who hasn't smelled the grease paint; it's like somebody composing who's never played an instrument —Mary McCarthy

Novels, like human beings, usually have their beginnings in the dark —Rita Mae Brown

People who write books take as much punishment as prizefighters —Norman Mailer

A pin has as much head as some authors and a great deal more point —George D. Prentice

The profession of book-writing makes horse racing seem like a solid, stable business —John Steinbeck

The profession of writing is wrong, like smoking cigarettes, bad for your health, a diminisher of life expectancy —William Saroyan

Prose as smooth and burnished as well-oiled furniture
—A. R. Gurney Jr., *New York Times Book Review*, 1985
> The author of this smooth prose is Louis Auchincloss.

Prose consists of ... phrases tacked together like the sections of a prefabricated hen-house —George Orwell

Prose is like music, every word must be placed for sound, color and nuance —James G. Huneker

A sentence should read as if its author, had he held a plough instead of a pen, could have drawn a furrow deep and straight to the end —Henry David Thoreau

Sometimes writing a recipe takes me a whole day ... to communicate it correctly. It's like writing a little short story —Julia Child

To inclose him (a fictional character) as irradiantly as amber does the fly and yet the while to preserve every detail of his being has, of all tasks, ever been the dearest to me —Stefan Zweig
> In his foreword to a collection of stories and novelettes, Zweig used this simile to explain that he considers his short fiction as much an accomplishment as his more "spacious" works.

Typing your own manuscript for submission is a lot like dressing to see that old lover who left you five years ago —Ira Wood
> In his novel, *The Kitchen Man*, Wood expands the simile as follows: "Ready to walk out the door you stop one last time at the mirror, just to be sure they're going to regret what they walked out on. Well, maybe the belt is wrong, you think, throwing it on the bed, pulling out another. No, these old shoes won't do, too dowdy. After an hour, you're stripped to your socks and in tears, absolutely sure now that you are the perfect mess they said you were. And so your manuscript will be if you don't fight every urge to better every sentence."

A well-written life is almost as rare as a well-spent one —Thomas Carlyle

Words flowed from his pen like sparkling spring water —Yoko Ono, about husband John Lennon's writing

A writer may take to long words, as young men to beards, to impress —F. L. Lucas

Writers, like teeth, are divided into incisors and grinders —Walter Bagehot

The writer's work is a little like handwriting. It comes out to be you no matter what you do
—John Updike, *New York Times,* January 18, 1987

The writer who draws his material from a book is like one who borrows money only to lend it —Kahlil Gibran

Writes like a comrade, the kind of friend with whom it is a pleasure to dispute —Jacques Barzun about H. W. Fowler, the author of *Modern English Usage, New York Times Book Review*, December 12, 1986
> Reviewer John Gross in his turn applied the simile to Barzun's book, *A Word Or Two Before You Go.*

Writing a first draft is like groping one's way into a pitch dark room, or overhearing a faint conversation, or telling a joke whose punchline you've forgotten —Ted Solotaroff

Writing for a newspaper is like running a revolutionary war; you go into battle not when you are ready but when action offers itself —Norman Mailer

Writing for him was as hard work as catching fleas —Ivan Turgenev

Writing is akin to fortunetelling ... you look into someone's life, read where they have been and predict what will happen to them —Marcia Norman, quoted *New York Times Book Review*, May 24, 1987

Writing is like building a house —Ellen Gilchrist

Writing is like pulling the trigger of a gun: if you are not loaded, nothing happens —Henry Seidel

Writing is like religion. Every man who feels the call must work out his own salvation —George Horace Lorimer

Writing is like serving a jail sentence, you're not free until you've done time on the rock-heap —Paul Theroux

Writing is like writing a check ... it's easy to write a check if you have enough money in the bank, and writing comes more easily if you have something to say —Sholem Asch

Writing ... it is rather like building a house, every separate word is another brick laid into place, cemented to its fellows, and gradually you begin to see the wall beginning to rise, and you know that the rooms inside will take their shape as you intended —Vita Sackville-West

Writing without publishing gets to be like loving someone from afar, delicious for fantasies but thin gruel for a living —Ted Solotaroff

Wrote not without puzzlements and travail, nevertheless as naturally as birds —Cynthia Ozick

You become a good writer just as you become a good joiner: by planing down your sentences —Anatole France

Your article should be like a lady's skirt: long enough to cover the essentials, and short enough to be interesting —editorial advice to free lancers, *PhotoGraphic*, January 1987

YELLS
See: SCREAMS

YELLOW

Dun-yellow color, a color like that of old lions in the zoo —Harold Brodkey

Yellow and solid as lemons —Joyce Cary

(Hair) yellow as a dandelion —Anne Sexton

(Hair) yelloo as a full moon —George Garrett

Yellow as a marsh-marigold —Henry Van Dyke

Yellow as an old tooth —Howard Spring

(Dandelions ...) yellow as butter —Cynthia Ozick

(The field is) yellow as egg-bread dough —Randall Jarrell

(Hair) yellow as hay —Henry Wadsworth Longfellow

Yellow as mustard —Edna St. Vincent Millay

Yellow as the yolk of eggs —Marcel Proust

(Eyes) Yellow like amber —Isaac Bashevis Singer

Yellow like moldy linen —Sinclair Lewis

Yellow like ripe corn —Dante Gabriel Rossetti
    The point of reference is to the golden hair of the subject
    of Rossetti's famous poem, *The Blessed Damozel.*

Yellow like unburnished gold —Honoré de Balzac

Author Index

All references are to categories found within the text.

Algeh, William R.
Wisdom
Algren, Nelson
Blood; Disappearance; Dryness; Leaves;
Places; Tobacco; Turning and Twisting
Ali, Muhammed
Movement
Alighieri, Dante
Eye(s); Eyes, Bright; Collapse;
Firmness; Habit; Screams
Allen, Roberta
Facial Expressions, Miscellaneous
Allende, Isabel
Anger; Futility
Altringham, Lord
Commonplace
Alvarez, A.
Facial Expressions, Miscellaneous;
Fatness; Physical Appearance
Ambler, Eric
Eye(s); Helplessness; Lips
Ameringer, Oscar
Professions
Ames, Fisher
Dryness; Government
Ames, Ebra
Struggle
Amichai, Yehuda
Behavior; Breasts; Firmness; Growth;
Heart(s); Love; Men and Women;
Noise; Open/Shut; Past, The; Stars;
Travel
Amis, Kingsley
Breasts; Breathing; Collapse; Face(s);
Facial Expressions, Miscellaneous;
Personality Traits; Rising; Screams;
Soul; Sweat
Ammons, A. R.
Belief
Amory, Cleveland
Music
Andersen, Hans Christian
Birds; Clarity; Cloud Movements;
Glitter and Gloss; Ponds and Streams;
Snow; Stars
Anderson, Dave
Disintegration; Golf
Anderson, Maxwell
Body; Day; Gentleness; Leaping
Anderson, Sherwood
Disappointment
Anderson, Susan Heller
Transience
Andreyev, Leonid
Realness/Unrealness; Tears
Andric, Ivo
Movement; Rising
Angelou, Maya
Atmosphere; Conversation; Food and

Drink; Harshness; Noise; Physical
Appearance; Physical Feelings; Places;
Preparedness; Shyness; Standing;
Voice, Effect of; Voice, Weak
Anthony, Piers
Eye Color
Antler
Laughter
Apperley, Charles James
Heart(s)
Apperson, G.l.
Undesirability
Apple, Max
Chin; Cleanliness; Contentment;
Disappearance; Rooms
Applebome, Peter
Places
Arabian Nights
Agitation; Body; Brightness; Eyes,
Bright; Forehead; Oceans/Oceanfronts
Arcel, Ray
Boxing and Wrestling
Ardizzone, Tony
Breathing; Disintegration; Errors;
Gloom; Memory; Muscles; Screams;
Speed; Stomach
Ardrey, Robert
Violence
Aretino, Pietro
War
Aristippus
Wit
Aristotle
Friendship, Defined
Arnold, Matthew
Meetings
Arrowsmith, Aaron
Wit
Arzybashev, Mikhaïl P.
Anger; Facial Expressions, Blank
Asch, Sholem
Baldness; Maxims, Proverbs and
Sayings; Writers/Writing
Ascher, Barbara Lazear
Flexibility/Inflexibility; Spreading
Ascher, Carol
Breasts; Face(s)
Ashbery, John
Cleanliness; Dryness; Growth;
Lingering; Memory; Night;
Relationships; Restlessness; Sitting
Astaire, Fred
Age
Atherton, Gertrude
Passion; Trembling
Atlas, James
Love; Speechmaking
Atwood, Margaret
Brevity; Brightness; Collapse;

Wrestling; Breasts; Brown;
Contentment; Control; Embraces;
Emotions; Exits; Eye Movements;
Face(s); Facial Shape; Firmness; Hair
Styles; Legs; Marriage; Mouth,
Open/Shut; Nervousness; Opinions;
Pallor; Screams; Snow; Toughness;
Turning and Twisting

Bates, Lewis J.
Cruelty

Baudelaire, Charles
Personality Profiles; Poets/Poetry

Baum, Vicki
Breathing; Clothing Accessories;
Crowds; Discontent; Diverseness; Head
Movements; Lying; Physical
Appearance; Sexual Interaction; Speed;
Words, Effect of

Bawden, Nina
Conversation; Eye Color; Love

Baxter, Charles
Voice, Music Related

Beach, Rex
Facial Details; Personality Traits

Beagle, Peter S.
Turning and Twisting

Beattie, Ann
Caution; Clothing, Its Fit; Eye(s);
Futility; Hand Movements; Smoothness;
Standing

Beaumont, Francis
Blindness; Fatness; Religion; Soul;
Watchfulness

Beauvoir, Simone de
Helplessness

Beck, Warren
Gloom

Beckett, Samuel
Speed; Sweat

Bedersi, Jediah
Mind, Defined

Bee, Bernard
Firmness

Beecher, Henry Ward
Body; Forgiveness; Gaiety; Mankind

Beecham, Sir Thomas
Singing

Beechcroft, William
Body; Contentment; Dryness; Face(s);
Food and Drink; Helplessness;
Honesty; Memory; Speed;
Unattractiveness; Voice, Harsh

Beerbohm, Max
Moon

Begley, Desmond
Memory

Behn, Aphra
Straightness

Behn, Noel
Sweat

Bell, Madison Smartt
Body; Day; Embraces; Entrances/Exits;
Memory; Places; Posture; Rooms;
Screams; Speech Patterns; Sunset

Bell, Marvin
Hatred

Bellairs, George
Firmness

Bellamann, Henry
Memory

Belloc, Hilaire
Books

Bellow, Saul
Age; Anger; Attractiveness;
Awkwardness; Beards;
Beginnings/Endings; Behavior; Body
Organs; Brown; Cost; Disintegration;
Eyebrows; Facial Details; Facial Shape;
Fatness; Hair Styles; Hair Texture;
Looks; Movement; Physical
Appearance; Rain; Red; Screams; Sky
Color; Slowness; Snow; Speed;
Transience; Words, Effect of; Wrinkles

Bemelmans, Ludwig
Complexion; Eye(s); Fog; Hand
Movements; Propriety/Impropriety;
Speech Patterns; Steadiness

Benchley, Peter
Children; Eye Expressions,
Miscellaneous; Eye Movements; Kisses;
Laughter; Personality Profiles; Physical
Feelings; Screams; Spreading

Benchley, Robert
Tobacco

Bendall, Gerald
Memory

Benét, Stephen Vincent
Behavior; Bewilderment; Black;
Brightness; Cleanliness; Clothing
Accessories; Decrease; Dispersal;
Dryness; Eyes, Bright; Fog; Gaiety;
Muscles; Names; Pallor; Purity; Road
Scenes; Speaking; Speed; Straightness;
War; Waste

Benjamin, Park
Beginnings/Endings

Benjamin, Walter
Places

Bennett, Arnold
Clarity

Bennett, Peggy
Trembling; Walking

Bennetts, Leslie
Transience

Benson, Arthur C.
Restlessness

Benson, Stella
Dullness; Helplessness
Bentham, Jeremy
Affection; Habit
Berger, John
Rising
Berger, Suzanne E.
Smoothness
Bergman, Ingrid
Age
Berkeley, Bishop George
World
Berkman, Sylvia
Body; Cheerfulness; Crowds; Eyebrows;
Fragility; Gloom; Leaves; Personality
Profiles; Rain; Speaking
Berkow, Ira
Choices; Contempt; Naturalness
Berlin, Isaiah
Places; Speech Patterns
Berrigan, Daniel
Blindness; Eye Expressions,
Miscellaneous; Looseness; Peacefulness;
Rising; Simplicity
Berry, Wendell
Love; Regret; Religion
Berryman, John
Age; Breathing
Betjeman, John
Smoothness
Betti, Ugo
Memory
Bhagavad-gita
Actions
Bhatty, Margaret
Face(s)
Bible, The Holy
Age; Agreement/Disagreement; Anger;
Beauty, Defined; Bitterness; Black;
Breasts; Cheeks; Control; Cruelty; Day;
Death, Finality of; Disappearance;
Disintegration; Dispersal; Emotions;
Errors; Face(s); Facial Expressions,
Miscellaneous; Firmness;
Flexibility/Inflexibility; Gaiety;
Government; Growth; Harmlessness;
Helplessness; Laughter; Lips; Love;
Mankind; Neck; News; Parenthood;
Physical Appearance; Posture; Poverty;
Roars; Speaking; Speed; Trust/Mistrust;
Unsteadiness; Voice, Music Related;
White; Words, Defined; World
Bierce, Ambrose
Belief; Noise
Bierds, Linda
Birds
Billings, Josh (henry Wheeler Shaw)
Advantageousness; Advice; Credit;
Desirability; Flattery; Greatness; Greed;

Kisses; Laughter; Life, Defined; Love;
Mankind; Marriage; Maxims, Proverbs
and Sayings; Men and Women;
Opinions; Opportunity; Religion;
Slander; Stories; Wisdom
Bird, Isabella
Places
Bird, Sarah
Baldness; Hair Texture; Lips; Looks;
Noses; Pallor
Bire, Augustine
Noise
Bishop, Elizabeth
Behavior; Entrances/Exits; Helplessness;
Physical Appearance; Protectiveness;
Speed; Spreading; Trembling
Bishop, Jim
Future
Bismarck, Otto Von
Passion
Bisson, Terry
Eye Expressions, Miscellaneous; Road
Scenes; Sadness; Smoothness
Blackman, M. C.
Looks
Blackwell, Basil
Pursuit
Blake, Reverend Watson C.
Habit
Blake, William
Abundance; Contempt;
Flexibility/Inflexibility; Glitter and
Gloss; Moon; Opinions
Blanchard, Laman
Fragility
Blassingame, Wyatt
Noise
Blixen, Baroness Karen
See Dinesen, Isak
Boerne, Ludwig
Government; Mankind; World
Bohn, Henry G.'s *Handbook of Proverbs*
Behavior; Belonging; Desirability; Hope;
Passion; Speed; Undesirability; Wisdom
Boileau, Nicolas
Reputation
Böll, Heinrich
Blushes; Memory; Physical Feelings;
Rejection; Stars; Watchfulness
Bolt, Robert
Professions
Bolton, Guy
Sighs
Bombeck, Erma
Clothing, Its Fit
Bonard, Abel
Love
Book of Common Prayer
Mankind; Memory

Booth, Barton
Trueness/Falseness
Borden, Mary
Life, Defined
Boretz, Alvin
Accomplishment; Aimlessness;
Embraces; Men and Women
Borland, John C.
Economics
Borowski, Tadeusz
Glitter and Gloss
Borsten, Rick
Body; Grins; Head Movements;
Problems/Solutions; Rain; Soul;
Stomach
Bossuet, Jaques Benigne
Posture
Boswell, James
Firmness
Bottome, Phyllis
Anger; Cheeks; Danger; Hair Texture;
Love; Mankind; Moon; Parenthood;
Physical Feelings; Shyness; Voice,
Harsh; White
Boucicault, Dion
Affection
Bourne, Randolph S.
Conversation
Boussuet, Jaques Bénigne
Reputation
Bovee, Christian Nestell
Friendship, Defined; Passion; War
Bowen, Baron Charles Synge Christopher
Mind, Defined
Bowen, Elizabeth
Day; Disappearance; Eye Expressions,
Miscellaneous; Fate; Firmness; Hair
Styles; Lighting; Movement;
Naturalness; Night; Noise; Personality
Profiles; Realness/Unrealness; Screams
Bower, Hamilton
Conscience
Bowles, G. S.
Greed
Boyd, William
Baldness; Facial Color; Firmness;
Oceans/Oceanfronts
Boylan, Clare
Looks
Boyle, T. Coraghessan
Agility; Agitation; Alertness; Anger;
Atmosphere; Beards; Behavior; Bigness;
Black; Blue; Body; Breasts; Breathing;
Cheeks; Clothing, Its Fit; Collapse;
Crying; Curses; Dancing; Day;
Emotions; Energy; Eye(s); Eyebrows;
Eye Color; Eye Expressions,
Miscellaneous; Face(s); Facial
Expressions, Blank; Facial Expressions,

Miscellaneous; Facial Expressions,
Serious; Fingers; Glitter and Gloss;
Grins; Groans and Whispers; Hair
Color; Handshake; Laughter; Lighting;
Memory; Music; Neck; Nervousness;
Noise; Noses; Opportunity; Pallor;
Personality Profiles; Physical
Appearance; Physical Feelings;
Problems/Solutions; Purposefulness;
Rain; Realization; Roars; Sadness;
Screams; Screams; Silence; Similarity;
Sitting; Sky Color; Slowness;
Smoothness; Snores; Snow; Speech
Patterns; Steadiness; Straightness; Tact;
Tallness; Timeliness/Untimeliness;
Tobacco; Toughness; Trembling;
Undesirability; Unsteadiness; Violence;
Voice, Harsh; Walking; White; Words,
Effect of; Wrinkles
Boyle, Kay
Collapse; Eyebrows; Forehead;
Lingering
Bracken, Peg
Travel
Bradbury, Ray
Crying; Sitting
Bradley, Ed
Leaping
Bradley, George
Lingering
Braine, John
Cheerfulness; Embraces; Face(s);
Gloom; Kisses; Moon;
Realness/Unrealness; Reputation;
Rooms; Sexual Interaction; Spreading;
Wrinkles; Writers/Writing
Brammer, William
Beginnings/Endings; Bigness; Breasts;
Sitting; Speech Patterns
Brandeis, Judge Louis D.
Agreement/Disagreement; Mind,
Defined; Peacefulness
Brecht, Bertold
Connections; Disappearance; Fog;
Gloom; Greed; Legs; Ponds and
Streams; Rejection; Safety; Screams;
Sitting; Speed
Bremer, Frederika
Marriage
Brennan, Maeve
City/Streetscapes; Hair Texture; Lips;
Places; Walking
Breslin, Jimmy
Belief; Flexibility/Inflexibility; Habit;
Noses
Bridgman, Mary
Toughness
Brierley, David
Eye Color; Kisses; Physical Appearance

Briggs, Charles F.
  Familiarity
Brinig, Myron
  Collapse; Growth
Brinkley, David
  Speaking
Brinnin, John Malcolm
  Crying; Pause
Britt, Stewart Henderson
  Advertising
Brodkey, Harold
  Personality Traits; Yellow
Brokaw, Tom
  Undesirability
Brombeck, Erma
  Running
Bromfield, Louis
  Attractiveness; Disappearance; Eyes,
  Bright; Facial Expressions,
  Miscellaneous; Helplessness; Muscles;
  Oceans/Oceanfronts; Physical
  Appearance; Trueness/Falseness
Brontë, Charlotte
  Cause/Effect; Disappearance; Facial
  Expressions, Blank; Pallor; Red; White
Brontë, Emily
  Differences; Emotions; Growth; Love;
  Screams; Tears; Undesirability; Violence
Brooke, Rupert
  Places
Brookner, Anita
  Appreciation
Brooks, Mel
  Behavior; Facial Expressions,
  Miscellaneous
Brothers, Dr. Joyce
  Credit
Broughton, T. Alan
  Head Movements
Brown, Dee
  Toughness
Broun, Heywood
  Opinions; Undesirability
Brown, Mary Ward
  Drinking; Singing; Sitting
Brown, Rita Mae
  Alertness; Anger; Breasts; Cloud
  Movements; Criticism; Dancing;
  Danger; Exits; Eyes, Bright; Facial
  Color; Facial Expressions,
  Miscellaneous; Fatness; Grins;
  Knowledge; Men and Women;
  Movement; Nervousness; Opinions;
  Passion; Personality Traits; Pursuit;
  Rain; Reappearance; Relationships;
  Running; Simplicity; Sitting; Voice,
  Effect of
Brown, Rosellen
  Conversation; Hair Color; Looks;

Noise; Screams; Sexual Interaction;
Smoothness; Snow
Brown, William
  Flattery
Browne, Gerald A.
  Simplicity
Browning, Elizabeth Barrett
  Age; Bitterness; Dullness; Experience;
  Hair Styles; Helplessness; Hope;
  Safety; Silence; Tears; Tongue; White
Browning, Robert
  Blindness; Collapse; Cost; Eye Color;
  Similarity; Waste
Broyard, Anatole
  Naturalness
Bryan, C.d.b.
  Problems/Solutions
Buchanan, Robert
  Harmlessness
Buck, Pearl S.
  Disappearance
Buddha
  Errors
Bukowski, Charles
  Clothing, Its Fit; Embraces; Eye(s);
  Face(s); Helplessness
Bulgakov, Mikhail
  Violence
Bulwer-Lytton, Edward
  Age; Brightness; Speechmaking;
  Spreading; Tobacco
Bumpus, Jerry
  Day; Lighting; Mouth, Open/Shut;
  Trust/Mistrust; Violence
Bunin, Ivan
  Baldness; Eye(s); Noses; Wrinkles
Bunyan, John
  Mankind
Burgess, Gelett
  Maxims, Proverbs and Sayings; Men
  and Women
Burgin, Richard
  Memory
Burke, James Lee
  Errors; Eye(s); Face(s); Facial Shape;
  Hair Color; Head Movements;
  Reappearance; Smoothness
Burke, Thomas
  Drinking; Memory
Burland, Brian
  Movement; Snores
Burnett, Hallie
  Reappearance
Burnett, W. R.
  Safety
Burns, Robert
  Disappearance; Pleasure
Burt, Struthers
  Beauty, Defined

Burton, Richard E.
Passion
Burton, Robert
Caution; Obviousness; Sweetness
Busch, Niven
Grins; Legs; Sitting
Bush, Katherine
Lips
Butler, Samuel
Death, Defined; Death, Finality of;
Friendship, Defined; Life, Defined;
Opinions; Words, Defined; World
Butte, Henry
Sweetness
Buxton, Charles
Preparedness
Byron, Lord
Age; Anger; Bigness; Blue; Blushes;
Brightness; Crowds; Cruelty; Eye
Color; Eye Expressions, Miscellaneous;
Friendship, Defined; Love; Marriage;
Modesty; Screams; Tears
Cabanis, Pierre J. G.
Age
Caesar Augustus
Speed
Caine, Lynn
Emotions
Calisher, Hortense
Awkwardness; Children; Choices;
City/Streetscapes; Economics; Energy;
Face(s); Grins; Places; Ponds and
Streams; Sadness; Voice, Harsh; Words,
Defined
Calvino, Italo
Birds; History; Road Scenes; Stars
Camoin, François
Crying; Economics; Facial Expressions,
Miscellaneous; Muscles; Noses; Objects,
Miscellaneous; Physical Feelings;
Stomach
Campbell, Joseph
Age
Campbell, Robert
Anger; Belief; Body; Breasts; Chin;
Complexion; Crying; Eye(s); Eye
Movements; Facial Details; Facial
Expressions, Miscellaneous; Grins;
Laughter; Looks; Noses; Personality
Profiles; Stares
Campbell, R. Wright
Birds; Body Organs; Chin; Eyes, Bright;
Facts; Fingers; Looks; Names; Noise;
Noses; Objects, Miscellaneous; Sexual
Interaction; Smoothness; Speaking;
Tobacco; Tongue; Voice, Weak;
Watchfulness
Campion, Nardi Reeder
Eyebrows

Camus, Albert
Breathing; City/Streetscapes; Facial
Details; Night; Noise; Rain
Canby, Vincent
Cheerfulness; Complexity;
Problems/Solutions; Risk; Speaking
Canning, George
Purposefulness
Canning, Victor
Nervousness
Canton, William
Glitter and Gloss
Cantor, Eddie
Sweetness
Capa, Robert
War
Capote, Truman
Absorbabiity; Activeness; Blushes;
Brown; Cheeks; Clothing Accessories;
Conversation; Correspondence;
Eyebrows; Eye Color; Eyelashes;
Eyelids; Eye Movements; Facial Details;
Facial Expressions, Miscellaneous;
Fragility; Gloom; Hatred; Kisses;
Leaves; Legs; Night; Noses; Personality
Profiles; Physical Appearance; Places;
Snow; Suddenness; Tallness; Tears
Carlisle, Kitty
Age
Carlyle, Thomas
Abundance; Continuity; Face(s);
Speechmaking; Voice, Harsh;
Writers/Writing
Carman, Bliss
Anger
Carr, John Dickson
Facial Expressions, Miscellaneous;
Objects, Miscellaneous
Carrel, Alexis
Religion
Carriel, Jonathan
Vagueness
Carroll, Lewis
Black; Disappearance; Eyes, Bright;
Face(s); Madness; Words, Effect of
Carruth, Hayden
Leaves; Mankind; Memory; Moon;
Weather
Carson, Anthony
Facial Expressions, Miscellaneous
Carter, Angela
Birds; Body; Crying; Energy; Facial;
Food and Drink; Hair Color; Hair,
Curly; Helplessness; Movement; Noise;
Personality Profiles; Rooms; Surprise;
Tallness; Voice, Music Related;
Walking; Weather
Carter, Dyson
Age

Carter, Hodding
   Waste
Carvell, Professor Steven
   Advice
Carver, Ada Jack
   Movement
Cary, Joyce
   Breathing; Chin; Clothing Accessories; Collapse; Face(s); Facial Details; Facial Expressions, Miscellaneous; Firmness; Groans and Whispers; Hair Color; Hatred; Lawyers; Legs; Lips; Moon; Movement; Mustaches; Noses; Physical Appearance; Ponds and Streams; Rain; Screams; Sitting; Sky Color; Snow; Voice, Music Related; Yellow
Casals, Pablo
   Music
Casper, John
   Personality Traits
Casper, Leonard
   Heartbeat; Voice, Harsh
Casseres, Benjamin de
   Greatness
Cassill, R. V.
   Blushes; Day; Fragility; Growth; Hair Color; Marriage; Movement
Cather, Willa
   Birds; Body; Breathing; Cheerfulness; Emotions; Eye(s); Eyes, Bright; Face(s); Facial Details; Hair Color; Hair Texture; Helplessness; Leaping; Leaves; Lighting; Memory; Noses; Simplicity; Stars; Tobacco; Transience; Voice, Music Related
Cats, Jacob
   Foolishness
Cavell, Mary Ladd
   Fate; Personality Profiles; Wisdom
Cecil, Richard
   Purposefulness
Celine, Louis-Ferdinand
   Legs; Rain
Centlivre, Mrs.
   Behavior
Cervantes, Miguel de
   Beauty, Defined; Disintegration; Face(s); Firmness; Knowledge; Purity; Similarity
Chamberlain, Joseph
   Greatness
Chamfort, Sebastien Roch Nicolas de
   Love
Chandler, Raymond
   Abundance; Agility; Agreement/Disagreement; Baldness; Chin; Drinking; Dullness; Eye(s); Eye Expressions, Miscellaneous; Facial Expressions, Blank; Facial Expressions, Serious; Hair Color; Harmlessness;

Memory; Moon; Movement; Noise; Peacefulness; Personality Profiles; Physical Feelings; Professions; Repetition; Reserve; Roars; Safety; Slowness; Smoothness; Speech Patterns; Spreading; Style; Sunset; Sweat; Sweetness; Violence; Voice, Harsh
Chapman, George
   Flattery
Chase, Joan
   Day; Energy; Facial Details; White
Chase, Mary Ellen
   Legs
Chateaubriand, Francois Rene de
   Passion
Chatterton, Ruth
   Black
Chaucer, Geoffrey
   Activeness; Agility; Brightness; Brown; Fatness; Gray; Noise; Straightness; Sweetness; White
Cheever, John
   Beginnings/Endings; Body; Cause/Effect; Clarity; Eyebrows; Facial Expressions, Miscellaneous; Flexibility/Inflexibility; Gray; Love; Memory; Personality Profiles; Rain; Road Scenes; Rooms; Speech Patterns
Chekhov, Anton
   Abandonment; Believability; Body; Caution; Drinking; Elusiveness; Eye Movements; Fate; Frustration; Head Movements; Lips; Mathematics and Science; Moon; Noses; Reserve; Stars
Chernoff, Maxine
   Timeliness/Untimeliness
Chesterfield, Lord
   Knowledge; Language; Pleasure; Reputation; Reserve
Chesterton, G. K.
   Agility; Believability; Cheerfulness; Disintegration; Flexibility/Inflexibility; Growth; History; Honesty; Maxims, Proverbs and Sayings; Mind, Defined; Moon; Mouth, Open/Shut; Pallor; Past, The; Posture; Reappearance; Snow; Society; Speech Patterns; Staleness; White
Chettle, Henry
   Pallor; White
Chevecoeur, St. John de
   Mankind
Child, Julia
   Writers/Writing
Chiles, Senator Lawton
   Timeliness/Untimeliness
Chonnaill, Eibhlin Dhubh Ni
   Open/Shut

Dryness; Facial Expressions, Blank;
Moon; Night; Noise; Noses; Physical
Feelings; Realization; Running; Sadness;
Speaking; Standing; Straightness;
Tongue; Trembling; Trust/Mistrust

Conroy, Frank
Disappearance; Fingers; Leaping; Noise

Conroy, Pat
Abandonment; Activeness; Agitation;
Body; Breathing; Cause/Effect;
Contempt; Contentment; Dullness;
Energy; Facial Expressions, Blank;
Fingers; Food and Drink; Football;
Growth; Laughter; Leaping; Legs;
Madness; Moon; Music; Personality
Profiles; Protrusion; Rejection;
Relationships; Reserve; Speech Patterns;
Tears; Voice, Effect of; Voice, Soft;
Walking

Considine, Bob
Boxing and Wrestling; Fragility

Cook, Joseph
Government

Cooke, Alistair
Commonplace; Suddenness

Coolidge, Susan
Disappearance

Coomer, Joe
Kisses; Movement; Stares

Cooper, Jilly
Availability/Unavailability; Breasts;
Collapse; Complexion; Eyebrows; Facial
Color; Facial Expressions,
Miscellaneous; Legs; Moon; Neck;
Protectiveness; Rain; Rising; Rooms;
Sexual Interaction; Snow; Trembling;
Watchfulness

Coover, Robert
Agitation

Coppard, A. E.
Behavior; Posture

Cornwall, Barry
Brightness

Corrigan, E. Gerald
Economics

Cortázar, Julio
Crowds; Men and Women; Pleasure

Cotgrave, John
Fatness

Cotgrave, Randle
Habit

Cotton, Charles
White

Coughlin, T. Glen
Breasts; Facial Details; Head
Movements; Rejection; Words, Effect of

Coverdale, Miles
Clarity

Coward, Noël
Beginnings/Endings; Cleanliness; Hair
Styles; Memory; Realization; Speed;
Words, Effect of

Cowley, Abraham
Life, Defined

Cowley, Malcolm
Day; Green; Heaviness; Sitting;
Trembling

Cowper, William
Abundance; Conversation; Foolishness;
Harmlessness

Cox, Marcelene
Children

Cox, Palmer
Disappearance

Crane, Hart
Brightness; Glitter and Gloss; Modesty;
Regularity/Irregularity

Crane, Stephen
Bitterness; Collapse; Curses; Emotions;
Looks; Lying; Obviousness;
Oceans/Oceanfronts; Restlessness;
Rooms; Running; Struggle;
Unsteadiness

Crawford, F. Marion
Men and Women

Crèvecoeur, Michel Guillaume Jean de
Mankind

Crier, John
Exits

Croly, George
Dispersal

Cronyn, Hume
Age

Crumley, James
Agitation; Aimlessness; Awkwardness;
Beards; Bewilderment; Body Organs;
Breasts; Breathing; Cause/Effect;
Clothing, Its Fit; Collapse; Criticism;
Conversation; Crowds; Crying;
Disappearance; Drinking;
Entrances/Exits; Eyebrows; Eye Color;
Eye Expressions, Miscellaneous;
Eyelashes; Face(s); Facial Shape;
Fatness; Fingers; Firmness; Football;
Glitter and Gloss; Groans and
Whispers; Head Movements; Laughter;
Legs; Lingering; Men and Women;
Movement; Mustaches; Neck;
Oceans/Oceanfronts; Pity; Places;
Posture; Pursuit; Rain; Rising;
Smoothness; Speed; Stories; Violence;
Voice, Harsh; Watchfulness

Culff, Robert
Alertness; Desirability

Cullen, Countee
Turning and Twisting

Culross, Donald
  Children
Cummings, E. E.
  Moon; Pity
Cuomo, Mario M.
  Believability
Curley, Daniel
  Arm Movements; Looks
Currie, Ellen
  Availability/Unavailability; Habit
Curtis, G.w.
  Love
Cussler, Clive
  Body; Characteristics, National;
  Elusiveness; Entrances/Exits; Eye
  Expressions, Miscellaneous; Facial
  Expressions, Serious; Firmness;
  Oceans/Oceanfronts; Screams
Dahl, Roald
  Behavior; Caution; Clothing
  Accessories; Fingers; Glitter and Gloss;
  Hair Styles; Head Movements
Daly, Arnold
  Golf
Dancy, John
  Caution
Daniel, Samuel
  Beauty, Defined
Darwin, Charles R.
  Language
Daugherty, Paul
  Places
Davenant, Sir William
  Bigness
Davies, Robertson
  Disappointment; Men and Women;
  Music
Davies, Tom
  Laughter
Davis, Bob
  Growth
Day, Clarence
  Anger
Day, Edward Parsons
  Age; Books
Deal, Babs H.
  Gloom; Memory;
  Timeliness/Untimeliness;
  Trueness/Falseness
Deal, Borden
  Agitation; Contempt; Eye(s); Eye
  Expressions, Miscellaneous; Facial
  Details; Futility; Gaiety; Looks;
  Physical Feelings; Running; Smoothness
Debussy, Claude
  Music
Deighton, Len
  Facial Expressions, Blank; Unsteadiness

Dekker, Thomas
  Age; Black
de la Mare, Walter
  Breathing; Conversation; Experience;
  Heartbeat; Facial Color; Naturalness;
  Noses
de la Roche, Mazo
  Eye(s); Growth; Memory; Rain;
  Realization; Smoothness; Spreading
Delgado, Ramon
  Formality
Delmar, Viña
  Memory
Deming, Richard
  Legs
Demophilus
  Advice; Children
Denby, David
  City/Streetscapes; Men and Women;
  Places
Denham, Sir John
  Actions; Firmness; Shyness
Desai, Anita
  Screams
Descartes, Rene
  Books; Travel
De Tabley, Lord
  Clarity
Deutsch, Babette
  Age; Agility; Birds; Black;
  Conversation; Ferocity; Fingers; Food
  and Drink; Naturalness; Poets/Poetry;
  Promptness; Surprise; Toughness
De Vries, Peter
  Books; Brightness; Embraces; Eyebrows;
  Fatness; Growth; Hair Color; Hair,
  Curly; Hand Movements; Handwriting;
  Laughter; Legs; Parenthood; Sexual
  Interaction; Sitting; Snow; Trembling;
  World
Dewar, Lord Thomas
  Mind, Defined
Dexter, Timothy
  Appreciation
Dickens, Charles
  Age; Anger; Atmosphere; Behavior;
  Birds; Collapse; Crying; Disappearance;
  Dullness; Eye Movements;
  Flexibility/Inflexibility; Mind, Defined;
  Movement; Music; Noise; Personality
  Profiles; Problems/Solutions; Rain;
  Rejection; Screams
Dickey, James
  Actions; Brightness; Connections;
  Eyebrows; Facial Color; Silence
Dickinson, Emily
  Books; Visibility
Diderot, Denis
  Kisses; Movement; Vagueness; Words,

Fingers; Food and Drink; Hatred;
Rooms; Struggle

Farris, John
Agitation; Behavior; Body Organs;
Cloud Movements; Food and Drink;
Pity; Vehicles, Operation of; Visibility;
Voice, Harsh

Faulkner, William
Awkwardness; Black; Blindness; Clarity;
Clothing, Its Fit; Crowds; Crying;
Dryness; Eye(s); Eyes, Bright;
Eyebrows; Eye Color; Eye Expressions,
Miscellaneous; Face(s); Facial Color;
Facial Expressions, Miscellaneous;
Familiarity; Groans and Whispers;
Mouth, Open and Shut; Physical
Appearance; Physical Feelings;
Speaking; Speech Patterns; Trembling;
Trust/Mistrust; Turning and Twisting;
Vagueness; Voice, Harsh; Walking;
White

Feather, William
Age

Feder, Mike
Emotions

Feiden, Doug
Growth; Realization

Feifer, George
Obviousness; Places

Feldman, Irving
Enthusiasm; Face(s); Rain

Feltham, Owen
Discontent; Enthusiasm; Hope; Passion

Felton, C. C.
Language

Ferber, Edna
Arguments; Brightness; Food and
Drink; Places; Reserve; Rising;
Similarity

Ferguson, Patricia
Discomfort

Ferraro, Susan
Opinions

Ferrier, J.w.
Objects, Miscellaneous

Ferry, James
Children

Fiedler, Leslie A.
Rain

Fielding, Henry
Conversation; Loyalty/Disloyalty; Tears;
Writer/Writing

Fine, Samuel Shem
Fatness

Finkelstein, Caroline
Leaping; Leaves

Finney, Jack
City/Streetscapes

Fisher, Dorothy Canfield
Believability; Disappearance; Energy;
Face(s); Hair Texture; Helplessness;
Lips; Lying; Movement; Nervousness;
Red; Road Scenes; Standing; Surprise;
Sweat; White

Fitzgerald, Edward
Birth; Entrances/Exits

Fitzgerald, F. Scott
Age; Believability; Books; Choices;
Drinking; Head Movements;
Helplessness; Mustaches; Nervousness;
Open/Shut; Physical Feelings; Poverty;
Rain; Stars; Sunset; Trust/Mistrust;
Vagueness; Voice, Soft; Writers/Writing

Fitz-Gibbon, Bernice
Advertising

Flanner, Janet
Abundance; Agreement/Disagreement;
Blood; Carlessness; Enthusiasm; Hair
Color; Hair, Curly; Personality Profiles;
Snow; Surprise

Flaubert, Gustave
Commonplace; Dullness; Eye Color;
Frustration; Harshness; Heaviness;
Love; Similarity; Speechmaking

Fletcher, John
Blindness; Fatness; Soul

Fletcher, John Gould
Abandonment

Follett, Ken
Believability; Facial Expressions,
Serious; Habit; Problems/Solutions

Forbes, B.c.
Actions; Criticism

Forbes, Bryan
Toughness; Turning and Twisting

Forbes, Colin
Conversation; Dryness; Night

Forbes, James
Sociability/Unsociability

Ford, James L.
Complexity

Ford, Richard
Agility; Anger; Atmosphere; Bigness;
Blue; Boxing and Wrestling;
Conversation; Cruelty; Disappearance;
Drinking; Exits; Emotions; Facial
Expressions, Serious; Face(s);
Familiarity; Food and Drink; Football;
Forehead; Glitter and Gloss; Gloom;
Grins; Head Movements; Heartbeat;
Hope; Laughter; Legs; Lips; Names;
Open/Shut; Opportunity; Originality;
Personality Profiles; Physical
Appearance; Places; Similarity; Sitting;
Sky Color; Speed; Stares; Stomach;
Trust/Mistrust; White; Wrinkles

Expressions, Miscellaneous; Face(s);
Facial Expressions, Serious; Facial
Shape; Fingers; Flexibility/Inflexibility;
Fog; Formality; Fragility; Futility;
Gaiety; Gray; Green; Grins; Groans
and Whispers; Growth; Hair Color;
Hair, Curly; Hair Styles; Hand
Movements; Harshness; Heartbeat;
Helplessness; Knowledge; Laughter;
Leaves; Leaves; Legs; Lingering; Lips;
Looseness; Lying; Movement;
Mustaches; Names; Noise;
Obviousness; Oceans/Oceanfronts;
Open/Shut; Opportunity; Pallor; Past,
The; Pause; Personality Traits; Physical
Appearance; Pink; Posture;
Problems/Solutions; Purposefulness;
Pursuit; Speed; Realization;
Realness/Unrealness; Running; Safety;
Sitting; Smoothness; Snow; Speech
Patterns; Spreading; Stomach; Stories;
Suddenness; Sweat; Sweetness; Tact;
Tears; Trembling; Trueness/Falseness;
Trust/Mistrust; Undesirability;
Unsteadiness; Vagueness; Violence;
Voice, Harsh; Voice, Music Related;
Voice, Soft; Walking; Weather; White;
Wisdom; Words, Effect of; Yellow

Garrigue, Jean
Bewilderment; Eye Expressions,
Miscellaneous; Hair Color;
Helplessness; Honesty; Past, The;
Trembling; Turning and Twisting

Garrison, William Lloyd
Flexibility/Inflexibility

Gary, Romain
Entrances/Exits; Face(s); Helplessness;
Laughter; Mustaches; Naturalness;
Neck; Nervousness; Voice, Harsh

Gash, Jonathan
Drinking; Heartbeat; Laughter;
Obviousness; Pallor; Running; Style;
Trembling

Gass, William H.
Num; Anger; Bitterness; Collapse;
Conversation; Disintegration; Dispersal;
Face(s); History; Lighting; Maxims,
Proverbs and Sayings; Noses;
Repetition

Gazzo, Michael V.
Cruelty

Gautier, Théophile
Leaping; Voice, Music Related

Gay, John
Friendship, Defined

Gerard, Philip
Clothing, Its Fit

Gertler, T.
Physical Appearance

Getz, William
Trembling

Ghazala, Abdel Halim Abu
Personality Profiles

Gibbs, Woolcot
Face(s)

Gibran, Kahlil
Affection; Discontent; Economics;
Emotions; Enthusiasm; Love; Memory;
Professions; Writers/Writing

Gibson, Miles
Body; Breasts; Breathing;
Entrances/Exits; Eye(s); Eyes, Bright;
Face(s); Facial; Fatness; Hair Color;
Hair, Curly; Pallor; Physical
Appearance; Realization; Red;
Seascapes; Sexual Interaction; Sitting;
Soul; Sociability/Unsociability; Tallness;
Tears; Unattractiveness

Gide, André
Emotions

Gifford, Frank
Football

Gilbert, Michael
Voice, Harsh

Gilbert, W. S.
Abundance; Clothing, Its Fit; Cloud
Movements; Death, Finality of;
Discomfort; Dryness; Glitter and Gloss;
Growth; Helplessness; Noses; Speech
Patterns; Standing; Style; Sweetness;
Toughness

Gilchrist, Ellen
Abundance; Birds; Breathing; Face(s);
Love; Problems/Solutions; Words,
Effect of; Writers/Writing

Gildner, Gary
Physical Feelings

Giles, Molly
Brightness; Eyebrows

Gillers, Stephen
Risk

Gilliatt, Penelope
Body; Chin; Clothing, Its Fit;
Complexion; Contempt; Conversation;
Face(s); Facial Expressions,
Miscellaneous; Food and Drink; Hair
Texture; Hatred; Heaviness; Lips;
Physical Appearance; Speed; Spreading;
Wisdom

Gilman, Lawrence
Passion

Gioseffi, Daniela
Disintegration; Food and Drink;
Growth; Leaves; Peacefulness;
Purposefulness; Tobacco

Giraudoux, Jean
Characteristics, National; Mankind

Glanville, Brian
Eyelids; Eye Movements

Glanville, Joseph
Body

Glasgow, Ellen
Blue; Breathing; Disappearance;
Entrapment; Eye Expressions,
Miscellaneous; Face(s); Facial
Expressions, Blank; Fragility; Growth;
Hair Texture; Harmlessness; Legs;
Lying; Memory; Passion;
Problems/Solutions; Reserve; Snow;
Vibration; Wrinkles

Glass, Joanna M.
Muscles

Godden, Rumer
Arguments; Criticism; Dullness; Eye
Expressions, Miscellaneous; Growth;
Hair Styles; Morality; Pause; Struggle;
Writers/Writing

Godwin, Gail
Complexity

Goethe, Johann Wolfgang von
Behavior; Books; Differences;
Disappearance; Dispersal; Eye
Expressions, Miscellaneous; Gloom;
Mankind; Names; Opinions; Passion;
Posture; Religion; Transience

Gogol, Nikolai V.
Blue; Caution; Tears

Gold, Herbert
Body; Children; Conversation;
Familiarity; Past, The

Goldberg, Aaron
Enthusiasm

Goldberg, Robert
Speaking; Transience

Golding, William
Memory

Goldon, Carolo
World

Goldsmith, Oliver
Abandonment; Friendship, Defined

Goodman, Ellen
Economics; News; Relationships

Goodman, Walter
Conscience; Laughter

Goodwin, Michael
Laughter

Gordimer, Nadine
Blushes; Brightness; Conversation;
Crowds; Emotions; Eye Expressions,
Miscellaneous; Fatness; Laughter; Legs;
Lies/Liars; Oceans/Oceanfronts; Pallor

Gordon, Mary
Behavior; Cause/Effect; Cleanliness;
Clothing, Its Fit; Disappointment;
Energy; Friendship, Defined; Physical
Feelings; Rejection; Safety

Gore-Booth, Eva
Blindness

Gorky, Maxim
Dispersal; Eyebrows; Noses

Gornick, Vivian
Absorbabiity

Gosse, Edmond
Future; Past, The

Gould, Jack
Advertising

Goyen, William
Agitation; Blood; Fingers; Mankind
Movement

Gracian, Valtasar
Age; Control

Grafton, Sue
Beards; Body; Body Organs; Breasts;
Cause/Effect; Clarity; Crying; Death,
Finality of; Discomfort; Energy; Eye(s);
Face(s); Facial Expressions,
Miscellaneous; Fingers; Memory;
Muscles; Oceans/Oceanfronts; Physical
Feelings; Realization; Rejection; Sexual
Interaction; Slowness; Stomach;
Undesirability; Unsteadiness;
Vagueness; Violence; Wrinkles

Graham, Harry
Blushes

Graham, Winston
Sexual Interaction

Grahame, Kenneth
Crying; Lighting; Tears

Granger, Bill
Problems/Solutions; Stares

Grau, Shirley Ann
Eye(s); Eye Color; Fog; Hair Color;
Lips; Physical Feelings

Graves, Robert
Crowds; Drinking; Eye(s); Hand
Movements; Poets/Poetry

Gray, Francine Du Plessix
Breasts; Hair Color; Posture;
Purposefulness; Seascapes

Gray, Thomas
Dryness

Greeley, Andrew M.
Preparedness

Greenaway, Kate
Seascapes

Greenberg, Alan
Greed

Greene, Graham
Books; Eye Expressions, Miscellaneous

Greene, Robert
Breathing

Greer, Germaine
Marriage

Grenfell, Julian
Agility

Grenville, Kate
  Dryness; Rooms; Running
Grétry, André Ernest
  Music
Grey, Zane
  Head Movements; Physical Appearance
Grimm Brothers
  Snow
Gross, John
  Writers/Writing
Grubb, Davis
  Black; Danger; Disappearance;
  Emotions; Facial Details; Lying; Pallor;
  Sexual Interaction; Smoothness; Snow;
  Vibration; Violence
Grumbach, Doris
  Hair Color
Guerney, A. R., Jr.
  Crowds; Embraces; Writers/Writing
Guest, Edward A.
  Children; Life, Defined; Tears
Guicciardini, Francesco
  Reputation
Gunn, Thom
  Firmness
Gunther, John
  Fatness; Hair Color; Professions
Guthrie, Thomas
  Religion
Guy, Rosa
  Hair Texture; Obviousness; Personality
  Profiles; Pursuit
Habbington, William
  Blindness
Haberman, Clyde
  Undesirability
Hacker, Marilyn
  Bitterness; Glitter and Gloss
Hagge, John
  Sexual Interaction
Haliburton, Thomas Chandler
  Black
Halifax, Lord
  Foolishness; Hope; Knowledge; Religion
Hall, Captain Basil
  Places
Hall, Donald
  Speed
Hall, Oakley
  Collapse; Face(s); Pursuit; Stares
Halla, Sven
  Facts
Hallhan, William H.
  Embraces; Entrapment; Noses; Safety;
  Walking
Halsey, Margaret
  Places
Hamilton, Alexander
  Affection

Hamilton, William
  Rooms
Hammerstein, Oscar, I
  Cloud Movements; Commonplace;
  Restlessness
Hammett, Dashiell
  Black; Breathing; Disintegration; Eye(s);
  Eyelids; Physical Appearance; Physical
  Feelings; Rooms; Safety; Speech
  Patterns; Straightness; Wrinkles
Hamper, Ben
  Noise
Hampl, Patricia
  Fog; Physical Appearance;
  Regularity/Irregularity
Hannah, Barry
  Laughter
Hannon, Kent
  Control
Hansberry, Lorraine
  Clarity
Hardwick, Elizabeth
  Arguments; Collapse; Economics; Facial
  Expressions, Miscellaneous; Hair, Curly;
  Honesty; Legs; Lingering; Love;
  Personality Profiles; Risk; Running;
  Snow; Sweetness; Writers/Writing
Hardwick, Mollie
  Wrinkles
Hardy, Thomas
  Blue; Clarity; Eye(s); Hair Color;
  Helplessness; Pallor
Hare, Augustus
  Mind, Defined; Suddenness
Hare, Julius Charles
  Choices; Mind, Defined; Suddenness
Harris, Frank
  Mankind
Harris, Isa
  Hospitality; Speed
Harris, Macdonald
  Body; Breathing; Clothing, Its Fit;
  Facial Details; Glitter and Gloss;
  Mouth, Open/Shut; Protrusion; Road
  Scenes; Sexual Interaction; Speech
  Patterns; Unsteadiness; Words, Effect
  of
Hart, Gary
  Laughter
Hart, Lorenz
  Disappearance
Hartley, L. P.
  Clothing Accessories; Emotions; Hair
  Color; Muscles; Noise; Pause; Regret;
  Trembling; Wrinkles
Harwood, Ronald
  Memory
Hasdai, Abraham
  Promise

Haskel, Floyd K.
Peacefulness
Hass, Robert
Birds; Cleanliness; Day; Stories
Hauser, Marianne
Curses; Familiarity; Hair Texture
Hawthorne, Nathaniel
Clarity; Eyes, Bright; Facial Color;
Facial Expressions, Miscellaneous;
Laughter; Pallor
Hayden, Julie
Peacefulness; Silence
Hayden, Sterling
Body; Chin; Drinking; Entrapment;
Fingers; Sitting
Hayne, Paul Hamilton
Aimlessness
Hazlitt, William
Commonplace; Friendship, Defined;
Greatness; Hatred; Language; Maxims,
Proverbs and Sayings; Mind, Defined;
Words, Defined
Hearn, Lafcadio
Naturalness
Hearon, Shelby
Entrapment; Food and Drink;
Freshness; Pursuit; Silence; Slowness;
Tongue; Watchfulness; Wrinkles
Hecht, Ben
Arguments; Eye Expressions,
Miscellaneous; Nervousness; Religion;
Trembling
Hedin, Mary
Emotions; Eye(s); Eye Expressions,
Miscellaneous; Face(s); Facial Color;
Fingers; Grins; Hand Movements;
Heartbeat; Lying; Marriage; Noses;
Posture; Road Scenes;
Regularity/Irregularity; Relationships;
Trembling
Hedge, Frederic Henry
Voice, Harsh
Heilbroner, Robert L.
Preparedness
Heine, Heinrich
Actions; Books; Religion
Heine, Leonard M.
Caution
Heinz, Senator John
Foolishness
Heller, Joseph
Anger; Belonging; Breasts; Eye
Expressions, Miscellaneous; Face(s);
Groans and Whispers; History;
Physical Appearance; Trembling
Hello, Ernest
Meetings
Helps, Sir Arthur
Belief

Helprin, Mark
Blindness; Blushes; Breathing; Clarity;
Elusiveness; Facial Expressions, Blank;
Glitter and Gloss; Green; Hair Texture;
Helplessness; Looseness; Silence;
Smoothness; Speed; Vibration; Voice,
Soft; Walking
Hemingway, Ernest
Beards; Bigness; Body; Elusiveness;
Love; Snow; Sweat
Hempel, Amy
Bewilderment; Regularity/Irregularity
Henahan, Donald
Memory
Henderson, Leo
Economics
Henley, Patricia
Breasts; Brown; Dullness; Hair Styles;
Rooms; Voice, Harsh; White
Henry, Matthew
Anger
Henson, Robert
Contentment
Herbert, George
Advantageousness; Reputation
Herod, Dan P.
Marriage
Herrick, Robert
Day
Hersey, John
Forehead; Silence; Words, Effect of
Herzog, George
Actions
Hess, Joan
Death, Finality of; Eye Expressions,
Miscellaneous; Hair, Curly; Hand
Movements; Leaves; Noses; Rising;
Sweat
Hewlett, Maurice
Crying; Discomfort
Heyward, Du Bose
Muscles
Heywood, John
Agreement/Disagreement; Anger;
Fatness; Unsteadiness
Hicks, Richard
Pursuit
Higgins, Joanna
Food and Drink
Higgins, George V.
Physical Appearance; Undesirability
Hill, Susan
Facial Color; Facial Expressions,
Miscellaneous
Hillyer, Robert
Diverseness
Hilton, James
Memory; Problems/Solutions;
Unsteadiness

Leaves; Life, Defined; Memory;
Movement; Originality; Places;
Shyness; Snow; Struggle;
Writers/Writing

Jhabvala, Ruth Prawer
Breasts; Collapse; Disintegration;
Emotions; Eyebrows; Facial Expressions,
Miscellaneous; Food and Drink;
Heartbeat; Kisses; Memory; Tears

Jiménez, Juan Ramón
World

Jonson, Ben
Enthusiasm; Mind, Defined; Speed

Johnson, B. S.
Memory

Johnson, Charles
Agitation; Clarity; Energy; Face(s);
Facial Expressions, Serious; Fingers;
Fog; Gloom; Groans and Whispers;
History; Lying; Mankind; Men and
Women; Mouth, Open/Shut;
Movement; Noses; Sexual Interaction;
Silence; Simplicity; Smoothness;
Visibility; Voice, Music Related

Johnson, Denis
Brightness; Physical Feelings; Vibration

Johnson, Nora
Laughter; Memory

Johnson, Nunally
Trembling

Johnson, Owen
Mankind

Johnson, Pamela Hansford
Cheerfulness

Johnson, Samuel
Books; Contempt; Flattery; Food and
Drink; Friendship, Defined; Knowledge;
Language; Marriage; Men and Women;
Promise

Johnson, Willis
Beards; Body; Leaves; Lighting

Jong, Erica
Food and Drink; Glitter and Gloss;
Green; Growth; Heartbeat

Jordan, Lee Roy
Football

Joubert, Joseph
Cruelty; Poets/Poetry

Jowitt, Lord
Speechmaking

Joyce, James
Disintegration; Face(s); Groans and
Whispers; Hair Styles; Snow;
Trembling

Just, Ward
Eye Expressions, Miscellaneous

Justice, Donald
Commonplace; Open/Shut; Seascapes;
Silence; Stares; Transience

Juvenal
Repetition; Smoothness

Kael, Pauline
Noise

Kafka, Franz
World

Kahn, Madeline
Marriage

Kakutani, Michiko
Fragility; Writers/Writing

Kantor, Mackinlay
Face(s); Hair Texture; Noses

Kaplan, Andrew
Body; Collapse; Embraces; Eye
Expressions, Miscellaneous; Neck;
Noise; Physical Appearance; Protrusion;
Sitting; Sweat

Kaplan, David Michael
Breasts; Reserve; Sitting

Kappell, Frederick
Bigness

Kates, Joanne
Control; Men and Women

Kaufman, Shirley
Helplessness

Kavanagh, Patrick
Trust/Mistrust

Kawabata, Yasunari
Disintegration; Memory; Nervousness

Kazkov, Yuri
Voice, Music Related

Kean, Molly
Purposefulness

Keating, H. R. F.
Bigness

Keats, John
Clarity; Disappearance; Life, Defined;
Movement; Music; Pallor; Silence

Keifetz, Norman
Body Organs

Keller, Helen
Books; Mind, Defined

Kellerman, Jonathan
Awkwardness; Collapse; Eyelashes;
Fragility; Habit; Hand Movements;
Movement; Mustaches; Physical
Appearance; Realness/Unrealness;
Reappearance; Smoothness

Kelley, Kitty
Violence

Kelly, Susan
Rejection

Kelton, Elmer
Competition; Restlessness

Kemp, Peter
Personality Profiles; Religion

Ken Kesey
Bigness; Curses; Silence

Leviant, Curt
Noise
Levine, Philip
Anger; Body; City/Streetscapes;
Disintegration; Fingers; Food and
Drink; Futility; Glitter and Gloss; Gray;
Growth; Leaves; Rejection; Turning
and Twisting
Lewes, G.h.
Crime
Llewllyn, Richard
Baldness
Lewis, Alfred Henry
Sociability/Unsociability
Lewis, C. S.
Agility
Lewis, Peter H.
Toughness
Lewis, Sinclair
Beards; Football; Noise;
Writers/Writing
Lewis, William
Religion
Liberman, M. M.
Mustaches
Lichtenberg, Georg Christoph
Books
Lichtfield, Grace Denio
Snow
Lieberman, Herbert
Anger; Disappearance; Eye Movements;
Growth
Liebling, A.j.
Mind, Defined
Lifshin, Lyn
Lips; Memory; Pallor
Lincoln, Abraham
Arguments; Death, Defined
Lincoln, Joseph C.
Breathing; Gloom; Grins
Lindbergh, Anne Morrow
Birds; Conversation; Disappearance;
Protrusion; Rain; Straightness
Linklater, Eric
Places
Linley, George
Disappearance
Lipkin, Israel Salanter
World
Liston, Sonny
Boxing and Wrestling
Litsey, Sarah
Loyalty/Disloyalty
Lloyd, Donald
Conversation
Lloyd, William
Harshness
Llwellyn, Richard
Baldness

Locke, John
Knowledge
Lodge, Thomas
Neck
Logan, John
Connections
Lois, Susan
Breasts; Frustration
London, Jack
Blood; Curses; Eyes, Bright; Face(s);
Movement; Muscles; Sadness; Similarity
Longfellow, Henry Wadsworth
Age; Breathing; Brown; Clarity; Cloud
Movements; Disappearance; Dispersal;
Entrances/Exits; Gaiety; Glitter and
Gloss; Greatness; Heartbeat; Heat;
Heaviness; Hope; Lies/Liars;
Movement; Noise; Sadness; Silence;
Speed; Yellow
Longstreet, Stephen
Availability/Unavailability;
Cheerfulness; Danger; Disappearance;
Obviousness; Rain; Visibility
Longworth, Alice Roosevelt
Facial Expressions, Serious
Lopate, Phillip
Dullness; Style
Lorimer, George Horace
Writers/Writing
Lotta, Congressman Dale
Criticism
Lourie, Richard
Drinking; Physical Feelings; Slowness
Lowell, Amy
Breasts; Collapse; Crowds; Firmness;
Gaiety; Nervousness; Peacefulness;
Physical Appearance; Repetition
Lowell, James Russell
Language; Opinions
Lowell, Robert
Protrusion
Lowry, Robert
Helplessness
Lubbock, Sir John
Friendship, Defined
Lucas, E. V. (edward Verrall)
Blushes
Lucas, F. L.
Language; Words, Defined;
Writers/Writing
Luce, Clare Booth
Control
Lurie, Allison
Habit
Luther, Martin
Lies/Liars; World
Lutz, John
Rain

Lux, Thomas
Baldness; Commonplace; Rising

Lyall, Gavin
Brevity; Lingering; Noses; Open/Shut;
Physical Feelings; Pursuit; Rooms;
Seascapes

Lydgate, John
Freshness

Lyly, John
Fatness

Macauley, Robie
Cloud Movements; Face(s);
Oceans/Oceanfronts

Macaulay, Rose
Religion

Macdonald, D. R.
Oceans/Oceanfronts

MacDonald, John D.
Agitation; Baldness; Breasts; Choices;
Cruelty; Dullness; Grins; Laughter;
Legs; Lips; Music; Noise; Personality
Profiles; Slowness; Snores; Speed;
Stomach

MacDonald, Ross
Atmosphere; Awkwardness; Beards;
Behavior; Body; Chin;
City/Streetscapes; Clothing, Its Fit;
Collapse; Danger; Emotions;
Entrapment; Eye(s); Face(s); Facial
Expressions, Miscellaneous; Facial
Expressions, Serious; Familiarity;
Fingers; Fog; Fog; Food and Drink;
Gloom; Handshake; Legs; Men and
Women; Movement; Muscles; Noses;
Personality Profiles; Physical
Appearance; Pity; Preparedness;
Rooms; Running; Screams; Silence; Sky
Color; Slowness; Snores; Standing;
Stars; Tears; Trembling; Trust/Mistrust;
Unsteadiness; Voice, Music Related;
Watchfulness

MacKenzie, Donald
Behavior; Eye(s); Head Movements;
Helplessness; Nervousness; Noses

MacLeish, Archibald
Differences; Experience; Past, The

MacLeish, Rod
Differences

MacMahon, Thomas
Hair Color

MacManus, Seamus
Speaking

MacMillan, Ian
Legs

Macneice, Louis
Abandonment; Adversary; Futility;
Love; Men and Women; Past, The;
Rising; Silence; Surprise;
Timeliness/Untimeliness; World

MacNeil, Robert
Entrapment

Magnani, Anna
Children

Mahler, Gustav
Music

Mailer, Norman
Brightness; Conversation; Eye(s); Eyes,
Bright; Eye Expressions, Miscellaneous;
Eye Movements; Ferocity; Groans and
Whispers; Marriage; Memory; Noise;
Personality Profiles; Preparedness;
Problems/Solutions; Relationships;
Roars; Sadness; Speechmaking; Speech
Patterns; Suddenness; Sweat; Tobacco;
Vibration; Voice, Effect of; Voice,
Harsh; Wisdom; Writers/Writing

Mairs, Nancy
Marriage

Major, Clarence
Trembling

Malamud, Bernard
Abundance; Agitation; Arm
Movements; Birds; Breasts;
Disappearance; Dryness; Emotions; Eye
Color; Glitter and Gloss; Heartbeat;
Leaves; Noise; Problems/Solutions;
Restlessness; Running; Silence

Malcolm, John
Abandonment; Collapse; Facial
Expressions, Miscellaneous; Firmness

Malloch, Douglas
Modesty

Malone, Michael
Professions; Speed

Malraux, André
Facial Expressions, Miscellaneous;
Mankind; Tobacco

Mamet, David
Vibration

Mancrft, Lord
Speechmaking

Mandelstamm, Benjamin
Friendship, Defined; Mankind

Mann, Thomas
Beauty, Defined; Cloud Movements;
Passion; Snow; Transience

Mansfield, Katherine
Agitation; Day; Eye(s); Eye Movements;
Face(s); Hair Texture; Hand
Movements; Head Movements;
Heartbeat; Laughter; Men and Women;
Movement; Music; Posture;
Preparedness; Rain; Realization;
Reserve; Rooms; Silence; Stars;
Walking

March, William
Fingers; Violence

Marie, Queen of Romania
Government
Markham, Beryl
Anger; Blindness; Brightness; Clarity;
Cleanliness; Cruelty; Day;
Disappearance; Disintegration;
Dispersal; Energy; Glitter and Gloss;
Green; Head Movements; Laughter;
Legs; Muscles; Night; Physical
Appearance; Protrusion; Reserve; Sighs;
Straightness; Trembling; Walking;
White
Marmion, Shackerley
Love
Marquis, Don
Blue; Disappearance; Gloom; Grins;
Life, Defined; Love; Poets/Poetry;
Restlessness; Undesirability
Marryatt, Captain Frederick
Ferocity
Marsh, Edward
Face(s)
Marshall, Paule
Anger; Eyes, Bright; Fragility; Legs;
Stomach
Marti, José
Mankind
Martin, Abe
Pleasure
Martin, Ian Kennedy
Sweat
Martin, Judith
Collapse; Marriage; Open/Shut;
Professions
Marx, Groucho
Correspondence
Marx, Karl
Economics
Mascagni, Pietro
Danger
Mason, Bobbie Ann
Attractiveness; Awkwardness; Beards;
Breasts; Breathing; Complexion; Facial
Details; Foolishness; Lips;
Relationships; Road Scenes;
Watchfulness
Mason, F. van Wyck
Behavior; Body; Clothing Accessories;
Cloud Movements; Complexion;
Disappearance; Entrapment; Eye(s);
Gloom; Head Movements; Legs;
Problems/Solutions; Sweetness;
Tobacco; Trembling; Words, Effect of
Maspero, Francois
Crying
Massey, Gerald
Disappearance
Masters, Edgar Lee
Face(s); Men and Women; Silence

Masters, Hilary
Curses; Eyes, Bright; Unsteadiness
Masterton, Graham
Behavior; Belief; Drinking; Emotions;
Eye Expressions, Miscellaneous;
Turning and Twisting; Voice, Harsh
Matthews, William
Face(s); Fog
Matthiessen, Peter
Body; Stomach
Maucaulay, Thomas Babington
Silence
Maugham, W. Somerset
Abandonment; Behavior; Birds; Body;
Breasts; Brightness; Clarity;
Complexion; Conversation; Cruelty;
Day; Disintegration; Dullness;
Elusiveness; Energy; Eye(s); Facial
Expressions, Serious; Facial Shape;
Flexibility/Inflexibility; Food and Drink;
Futility; Gaiety; Helplessness;
Obviousness; Passion; Peacefulness;
Personality Profiles; Physical
Appearance; Places; Poets/Poetry;
Professions; Rain; Realness/Unrealness;
Screams; Seascapes; Silence; Soul;
Wrinkles; Timeliness/Untimeliness;
Voice, Effect of
Maupassant, Guy de
Anger; Attractiveness; Baldness; Belief;
Complexion; Correctness; Crying;
Gloom; Love; Rain; Suddenness;
Violence
Maurois, André
Conversation; Marriage; Silence
Maxwell, A. E.
Anticipation; Birds; Dullness; Eye(s);
Futility; Lies/Liars;
Propriety/Impropriety; Road Scenes;
Singing
Maynard, Richard
Body; Danger; Hope; Memory;
Seascapes; Voice, Harsh
Mcbain, Ed
Awkwardness; Behavior; Blue; Green;
Hand Movements; Madness; Vagueness
McCaig, Donald
Behavior; Emotions; Eye(s); Eye
Expressions, Miscellaneous; Eye
Movements; Face(s); Facial Color; Fog;
Glitter and Gloss; Hair Styles; Hand
Movements; Laughter; Movement;
Music; Purposefulness; Pursuit;
Smoothness; Snow
McCarthy, Eugene
Conversation
McCarthy, Mary
Activeness; Behavior; Brown; Danger;
Disappointment; Eye Color; Gloom;

Merman, Ethel
Dullness
Merriman, Brian
Posture
Merrill, James
Realness/Unrealness
Merton, Thomas
Mind, Defined
Mestastasio, Pietro
Mankind
Meyer, Karl E.
Suddenness
Meyerson, Harvey
Football
Michaels, Leonard
Clothing, Its Fit; Eyelids; Handshake;
Laughter; Speaking; Tears; Voice,
Harsh
Midrash, L'Olam
Anger
Millar, Margaret
Baldness; Behavior; Birds; Breathing;
Brown; City/Streetscapes; Clothing, Its
Fit; Connections; Entrapment; Eye(s);
Eye Color; Eye Expressions,
Miscellaneous; Face(s); Facial
Expressions, Blank; Facial Expressions,
Miscellaneous; Facial Expressions,
Serious; Familiarity; Fog; Gray; Hair,
Curly; Hand Movements; Laughter;
Leaves; Nervousness; Noise; Personality
Profiles; Purposefulness; Seascapes;
Silence; Similarity; Spreading; Sweat;
Tobacco; Trembling; Unsteadiness;
Voice, Effect of; Voice, Music Related;
Wrinkles
Millay, Edna St. Vincent
Clarity; Disappearance; Habit; Memory;
Night; Voice, Harsh; Yellow
Miller, Arthur
Eye(s); Oceans/Oceanfronts; Passion;
Present, The
Miller, Bryan
Eye Expressions, Miscellaneous; Food
and Drink
Miller, Henry
Crying; Safety
Miller, James
Similarity
Miller, Joaquin
Life, Defined
Miller, Nolan
Legs
Miller, Sue
Breasts; Noses; Physical Appearance
Millikan, Robert A.
War
Mills, James
Accomplishment; Flexibility/Inflexibility;

Personality Profiles; Violence
Milne, A. A.
Face(s)
Milton, John
Abundance; Believability; Children;
Ferocity; Screams; Silence
Minot, Susan
Chin; Noise; Rain
Minot, Stephen
Unattractiveness
Mishima, Yukio
Body; Exits; Peacefulness
Mitchell, Beverly
Movement
Mitchell, Donald G.
Abandonment
Mitchell, Margaret
Agility; Behavior; Eye Expressions,
Miscellaneous; Noise; Personality
Profiles; Physical Feelings; Sadness;
Speed; Unattractiveness; Voice, Harsh
Mitchell, Paige
Anger; Arguments; Beards; Behavior;
Clothing, Its Fit; Connections; Crowds;
Drinking; Emotions; Eyes, Bright;
Eyebrows; Eye Expressions,
Miscellaneous; Eye Movements; Facial
Expressions, Miscellaneous; Facial
Shape; Flattery; Glitter and Gloss;
Hair, Curly; Harshness; Marriage; Men
and Women; Mustaches; Pallor;
Preparedness; Rain; Restlessness;
Screams; Smoothness; Snores; Speed;
Stars; Surprise; Toughness; Voice,
Music Related
Mizener, Wilson
Tongue
Moir, D. M.
Curses
Molière
Greed
Molinaro, Ursule
Repetition
Monro, Harold
Habit
Monsarrat, Nicholas
Cruelty; Helplessness; Watchfulness
Montague, James J.
Dullness
Montague, Lady Mary Wortley
Characteristics, National
Montaigne, Michel de
Marriage; Memory; Opinions;
Popularity
Montesquieu, Charles de Secondat
Government
Montgomery, James
Disintegration; Helplessness

Moore, Brian
Agitation; Body; Cloud Movements;
Disappearance; Groans and Whispers;
Leaping; Simplicity; Slowness

Moore, Clement C.
Laughter

Moore, George
Alertness; Books; Regret; Sadness

Moore, Lorrie
Dullness; Facial Expressions,
Miscellaneous; Firmness; Men and
Women; Regularity/Irregularity; Sexual
Interaction; Silence; Spreading;
Surprise; Unattractiveness

Moore, Marianne
Personality Profiles

Moore, Thomas
Clarity; Decrease; Memory

Moran, Malcom
Undesirability

Moran, Richard
Breathing; Noise; Oceans/Oceanfronts;
Sitting; Speech Patterns

Moravia, Albert
Hair Texture

More, Hannah
Love

Morgan, Speer
Running

Morris, Herbert
Clothing, Its Fit

Morris, Mary
Kisses; Posture; Smoothness; Sweat

Morris, Willie
Names

Morris, William
Baldness; Names

Morris, Wright
Entrances/Exits; Eye Color; Red;
Walking

Morrow, James
Complexity; Problems/Solutions; Stares;
Walking

Morse, John T.
Naturalness

Mortimer, John
Availability; Clothing Accessories;
Oceans/Oceanfronts; Toughness

Moseley, William
Breathing; Groans and Whispers

Mosher, Howard Frank
Discontent

Motherwell, William
Sighs

Mountford, William
Sadness

Mullen, Harryette
Memory; Physical Appearance

Munn, Charles Clark
Flattery

Munro, Alice
Books; Emotions; Loyalty/Disloyalty;
Soul

Murdoch, Iris
Cheerfulness; Dispersal; Laughter;
Memory; Men and Women; Standing;
Suddenness; Words, Effect of

Murphy, Muriel Oxenberg
Society

Murray, Jim
Elusiveness; Football

Nabokov, Vladimir
Breasts; Lighting

Naham, Bratzlav
World

Najarian, Peter
Disappearance

Napier, Lord
Problems/Solutions; War

Napoleon Bonaparte
Greatness; Mankind

Narayan, R. K.
Breasts

Nash, Ogden
Attractiveness; Behavior; Body;
Conversation; Disappearance;
Foolishness; Growth; Marriage;
Muscles; Music; Snow; Speed;
Trembling

Nassauer, Rudolf
Toughness

Nastase, Ilie
Memory

Nathan, George Jean
Characteristics, National; Criticism;
Propriety/Impropriety

Naylor, Phyllis
Clothing, Its Fit; Conversation;
Embraces; Legs; Road Scenes

Ndebele, Njabulo
Cheeks; Embraces; Rejection

Nelson, Kent
Disintegration; Emotions; Pause; Stares

Nemerov, Howard
Drinking

Nemy, Enid
Pleasure

Netanyahu, Benjamin
Behavior

Neville, Susan
Arm Movements; Glitter and Gloss

Newcastle, Duchess of
Memory

Nielsen, Helen
Modesty

Nietzsche, Friedrich
Conscience; Greatness; Mankind

Movements; Bigness; Birds; Black; Body; Breasts; Brightness; City/Streetscapes; Correctness; Curiosity; Day; Disintegration; Dryness; Emotions; Energy; Eye Movements; Fingers; Firmness; Glitter and Gloss; Green; Grins; Growth; Hair, Curly; Hair Styles; Hair Texture; Hand Movements; Harshness; Hatred; History; Hope; Kisses; Lighting; Love; Music; Nervousness; Noise; Oceans/Oceanfronts; Open/Shut; Peacefulness; Physical Appearance; Pink; Problems/Solutions; Rain; Reappearance; Rejection; Repetition; Richness; Running; Screams; Simplicity; Snow; Speed; Spreading; Steadiness; Sweetness; Tears; Tongue; Trembling; Trust/Mistrust; Visibility; Voice, Harsh; Weather

Pilcher, Rosamund
Cleanliness; Life, Defined; Rooms; Speed; Unattractiveness; Voice, Music Related

Pin, Mary
Trueness/Falseness

Pinero, Arthur W.
Professions

Piper, Anne
Legs

Piper, William Thomas
Speechmaking

Pirandello, Luigi
Abandonment; Agility; Protectiveness; Trembling

Plain, Belva
Accomplishment; Dispersal; Emotions; Eye Color; Facts; Fragility

Pix, Mary
Speed

Plath, Sylvia
Birds; Cheeks; Clarity; Correctness; Curiosity; Death Defined; Decrease; Disappearance; Discomfort; Disintegration; Eye Color; Flexibility/Inflexibility; Food and Drink; Fragility; Glitter and Gloss; Heaviness; Love; Marriage; Noise; Oceans/Oceanfronts; Pallor; Silence; Stars; Tears; Trueness/Falseness; White

Plato
Body; Passion

Plautus
Disintegration

Plutarch
Speechmaking

Poe, Edgar Allen
Cloud Movements; Collapse; Control; Disappearance; Glitter and Gloss; Hair,

Curly; Pallor

Poers, W.a.
Places

Pollock, Channing
Marriage

Poniatowska, Elena
Spreading

Pope, Alexander
Age; Arguments; Passion; Words, Defined; Writers/Writing

Popkin, Joel
Economics

Pordage, Samuel
Music

Porter, Cole
Anger; Entrances/Exits; Roars

Porter, Katherine Anne
Affection; Breasts; Curses; Helplessness; Loyalty/Disloyalty; Memory; Noise; Physical Appearance; Posture; Realness/Unrealness

Porter, William Sydney
See O. Henry

Portis, Charles
Body; Problems/Solutions

Post, Emily
Flattery

Post, Steve
Relationships

Powell, Anthony
Body; Eye Movements; Hair Texture; Legs; Personality Profiles

Powers, J. F.
Relationships

Praed, Winthrop Mackworth
Speaking; Speechmaking

Prather, Richard S.
Eye Color; Food and Drink; Head Movements; Legs; Tobacco

Prentice, George D.
Writers/Writing

Price, Reynolds
Bitterness; Brightness; Brown; Dryness; Elusiveness; Facial Expressions, Serious; Fragility; Freshness; Hair Color; Hair Styles; Harmlessness; Heartbeat; Nervousness; Noise; Pallor; Personality Profiles; Safety; Silence; Smoothness; Spreading; Tallness; Voice, Harsh; White

Priest, William W.
Economics

Priestly, J. B.
Belief; Body Organs; Facial Shape; Glitter and Gloss; Music; Obviousness; Originality; Pallor; Repetition

Prince, Harry
Agitation; Awkwardness; Cheerfulness; Complexion; Differences; Face(s); Love;

Voice, Weak

Reese, William
Pursuit

Reeve, F. D.
Age; Black; Blindness; Discontent; Rain; Speed; Visibility

Reid, Alastair
Age

Reid, Barbara
Breathing; Day

Reidinger, Paul
Gloom; Marriage; Speaking; Speed

Reik, Theodore
Memory; Professions

Reiss, James
Leaves; Red; Snow; Trueness/Falseness

Remarque, Erich Maria
Age; Anger; Availability; Baldness; Behavior; Breasts; Collapse; Cruelty; Crying; Curiosity; Decrease; Dispersal; Eye(s); Eye Color; Eyelids; Face(s); Facial Expressions, Miscellaneous; Facial Expressions, Serious; Fog; Grins; Laughter; Memory; Music; Night; Obviousness; Pause; Physical Appearance; Physical Feelings; Preparedness; Rain; Relationships; Rising; Road Scenes; Sitting; Sky Color; Speed; Sweat; Tears; Voice, Effect of; Wrinkles

Renard, Jules
Movement

Rendell, Ruth
Face(s)

Repplier, Agnes
Gaiety; Wit

Ress, Lisa
Past, The

Reston, James
Characteristics, National; Energy; Frustration

Reuben, Dr. David R.
Marriage

Rheinheimer, Kurt
Collapse

Rhoden, William R.
Behavior

Rhys, Jean
Eye Color; Facial Expressions, Miscellaneous; Helplessness

Ricard, Auguste
Problems/Solutions

Rice, Ann
Eye Movements

Rice, Cale Young
Brevity

Rich, Adrienne
Awkwardness; Disintegration; Handshake; Relationships; Simplicity; Snow

Rich, Frank
Vagueness; Walking

Richter, Jean Paul
Cheerfulness; Hatred; Love

Rider, J. W.
Past, The

Riley, James Whitcomb
Cleanliness; Eyes, Bright

Rilke, Rainer Maria
Anticipation; Soul

Rivers, Joan
Places

Robbins, Tom
Behavior; Crime; Day; Eye Expressions, Miscellaneous; Food and Drink; Hair Color; Heartbeat; Kisses; Laughter; Life, Defined; Lighting; Madness; Movement; Noise; Protrusion; Road Scenes; Rooms; Spreading; Tears; Trembling; Vagueness; Vibration

Roberts, Phyllis
Birds; Peacefulness

Robertson, Don
Day

Robertson, William
Cleanliness

Robinson, Edward Arlington
Futility; Peacefulness

Robinson, Jill
Emotions

Robinson, Edwin Arlington
Behavior

Robison, James
Arm(s)

Roche, Henri-Pierre
Breathing; Growth; Men and Women

Rochefoucauld, François, duc de la
Age; Cruelty; Errors; Love; Passion

Rodgers, W. R.
Contempt; Snow

Rodrigue, Chi Chi
Golf

Roethke, Theodore
Crying; Firmness; Freshness

Rogers, Samuel
Purity

Rogers, Thomas
Advice

Rogers, Will
Belief; Professions; Tact

Rogers, Jane
Silence

Rolland, Romain
Passion

Romains, Jules
Rain

Rooney, Andy
Correspondence

Roosevelt, Franklin D.
  Government; Peacefulness
Roper, John Cadman
  Professions
Rosas, Cecilia
  Groans and Whispers
Rose, Daniel Asa
  Dullness
Rosenbaum, David E.
  Government
Ross, Frank
  Anger; Breathing; Collapse; Facial
  Color; Familiarity; Personality Profiles;
  Silence; Snow
Ross, Marilyn
  Spreading
Rossetti, Christina
  Blue; Breathing; Eyes, Bright;
  Harmlessness; Sweetness; Tact;
  Trembling
Rossetti, Dante Gabriel
  Aimlessness; Belief; Spreading; Tears;
  Unsteadiness; Yellow
Roth, Philip
  Alertness; Characteristics, National;
  Correspondence; Disappearance;
  Ferocity; Toughness; Trembling;
  Turning and Twisting
Rothberg, Abraham
  Eyes, Bright; Marriage
Rovere, Richard
  Professions
Rowland, Helen
  Flattery; Love; Marriage; Men and
  Women
Rowland, Henry C.
  Age
Rowley, Samuel
  Dullness
Rubinstein, Artur
  Music
Ruffini, Giovanni
  Curses
Rule, Jane
  Morality
Rule, Rebecca
  Bitterness
Ruskin, John
  Cause/Effect; Silence
Russell, Bertrand
  Discontent
Russell, John
  Decrease
Russo, Richard
  Disappearance; Ponds and Streams
Rybako, Anatoly
  Blushes
Sabin, Edwin L.
  Tongue

Sackville-West, Vita
  Agility; Cleanliness; Control; Green;
  Love; Muscles; Oceans/Oceanfronts;
  Parenthood; Poverty; Reputation;
  Trembling; Trust/Mistrust;
  Writers/Writing
Sadi
  Lies/Liars; Travel
Safer, Morley
  Age
Safire, William
  Protrusion
Sagan, Françoise
  Disappearance
St. John
  Hair Color
St. John, Henry, (viscount Bolinbroke)
  Characteristics, National
St. Johns, Adela Rogers
  Emotions; Legs
Sala, George Augustus
  Life, Defined
Salamon, Julie
  Personality Profiles; Physical
  Appearance
Salinger, J. D.
  Contempt; Popularity
Saltus, Edgar
  Affection
Sandberg-Diment, Erik
  Commonplace
Sandburg, Carl
  Brightness; Cleanliness; Entrances/Exits;
  Ferocity; Language; Mathematics and
  Science; Memory; Past, The;
  Reappearance; Silence; Slowness
Sandburg, Helga
  Cheeks; Face(s)
Sandel, Cora
  Sighs; Sky Color; Straightness
Sandler, Corey
  Awkwardness
Sandys, George
  Abundance
Sanford, Annette
  Breasts; Voice, Harsh
Sanger, David E.
  Decrease
Sangster, Jimmy
  Collapse; Cruelty; Eye(s); Face(s);
  Lies/Liars; Lips; Noise; Personality
  Profiles; Physical Appearance; Voice,
  Soft
Santayana, George
  Death, Defined; Disappearance; Fate;
  Mankind; Music; Personality Profiles;
  Poets/Poetry; Society
Saphir, Moritz Gottlieb
  Greatness; Mankind

Women; Movement; Night; Opinions;
Peacefulness; Sitting; Snow; Stars;
Tallness; Weather

Stevenson, Adlai
Flattery

Stevenson, Robert Louis
Activeness; City/Streetscapes;
Conversation; Cruelty; Eye(s); Face(s);
Facial Color; Health; Health; Love;
Mankind; Marriage; Passion; Pleasure;
Stories; Watchfulness

Stewart, Fred Mustard
Emotions

Stewart, Mary
Memory; Oceans/Oceanfronts; Stars;
Turning and Twisting

Stockanes, Anthony E.
Physical Appearance; Silence; Tobacco

Stockwell, John R.
Government

Stone, Alma
Spreading

Stone, Irving
Abandonment; Agitation

Stone, Robert
Embraces

Stone, Walter
Sitting

Stoughton, John
Books

Stout, Rex
Anger; Face(s); Speed

Stowe, Harriet Beecher
Cruelty; Pursuit

Strand, Mark
Silence

Straus, Dorothea
Awkwardness; Beards;
City/Streetscapes; Eye Expressions,
Miscellaneous; Familiarity; Futility;
Posture; Realness/Unrealness; Sweat;
Trembling; Wrinkles

Stravinsky, Igor
Music

Stravinsky, John
Risk

Streatfeild, Noel
Open/Shut

Strindberg, August
Futility

Stritch, Elaine
Places

Stuart, Jesse
Eyes, Bright

Sturm, Marian
Disintegration

Styron, William
Agitation; Black; Elusiveness; Eye(s);
Eye Movements; Memory; Noise;

Originality; Pause; Personality Profiles;
Silence; Snow; Sunset; Sweat; Voice,
Soft; Wrinkles

Suckling, Sir John
Face(s)

Suckow, Ruth
Entrances/Exits; Face(s); Head
Movements

Sue, Eugene
Flexibility/Inflexibility

Summers, Hollis
Contentment; Past, The

Suskind, Patrick
Clarity; Contentment; Toughness

Sutherland, Margaret
Advantageousness; Availability;
Contentment

Svetlanov, Yevgeny
Music

Svevo, Italo
Facial Color; Life, Defined; Love

Swados, Harvey
Actions; Anticipation; Arm Movements;
Beards; Blood; Blushes; Chin; Clothing,
Its Fit; Connections; Conversation;
Elusiveness; Entrances/Exits; Eye(s);
Eye Expressions, Miscellaneous; Face(s);
Flexibility/Inflexibility; Forehead;
Future; Grins; Hair Styles; Hand
Movements; Handshake; Head
Movements; Heaviness; Hope;
Laughter; Lingering; Lying; Memory;
Music; Names; Past, The; Peacefulness;
Personality Profiles; Posture;
Protectiveness; Rain; Road Scenes;
Silence; Singing; Sitting; Skin;
Smoothness; Snow; Speech Patterns;
Sweat; Tobacco; Trembling; Voice,
Effect of; Voice, Weak; Wrinkles

Swartz, Joshua
Books

Swenson, May
Exits

Swerdlow, Joel
Behavior

Swift, Graham
Arguments; Clothing Accessories;
Disintegration; Dispersal; Face(s);
Laughter; Reappearance; Slowness;
Trembling

Swift, Jonathan
Books; Clothing, Its Fit; Fatness;
Flattery; Growth; Lies/Liars; Maxims,
Proverbs and Sayings; Passion; Wit

Swinburne, Algernon Charles
Activeness; Age; Bitterness; Brightness;
Clarity; Connections; Cruelty;
Embraces; Fragility; Gray; Harshness;
Kisses; Love; Memory; Night; Pallor;

Purity; Silence; White; Wisdom

Swinnerton, Frank
Alertness; Anger; Beards; Blindness; Books; Breathing; Caution; Clarity; Complexion; Connections; Cruelty; Curiosity; Day; Emotions; Entrances/Exits; Exits; Eye(s); Eye Color; Eye Expressions, Miscellaneous; Eyelashes; Face(s); Facial Color; Facial Expressions, Serious; Ferocity; Fingers; Flexibility/Inflexibility; Freshness; Gaiety; Hand Movements; Handshake; Harshness; Head Movements; Heartbeat; Laughter; Leaping; Lips; Memory; Men and Women; Mustaches; Naturalness; Noses; Peacefulness; Pleasure; Professions; Promptness; Rain; Reappearance; Relationships; Restlessness; Snow; Speed; Standing; Tears; Tobacco; Trust/Mistrust; Unattractiveness; Words, Effect of; Wrinkles

Synge, John M.
Collapse; Pursuit

Syrus, Publilius
Love; Trust/Mistrust

Tabley, Lord De
Clarity

Tacitus
Speechmaking; Style

Tagore, Rabindranath
Night; Pleasure

Tallent, Elizabeth
Hair Texture

Talleyrand, Charles de
Food and Drink

Talmud
Mankind; Parenthood

Talmud, Babylonian
Death, Defined; Mankind; Marriage

Tamil
Helplessness

Targan, Barry
Belonging; Diverseness

Tarkington, Booth
Disappearance; Obviousness

Taubman, Philip
Emotions

Tawney, Richard H.
Society

Taylor, Anne
Stars

Taylor, Ellen Du Pois
Black

Taylor, Elizabeth
Clothing Accessories; Danger; Embraces; Facial Expressions, Blank; Love; Lying; Men and Women; Movement; Restlessness

Taylor, Fred
Danger

Taylor, Henry
Disappearance

Taylor, Jeremy
Religion

Taylor, Pat Ellis
Agitation

Taylor, Peter
Memory

Taylor, Robert Lewis
Rising

Teasdale, Sara
Belief

Temple, Sir William
Books

Tennyson, Alfred, Lord
Arguments; Brightness; Clarity; Desirability; Glitter and Gloss; Knowledge; Lies/Liars; Tears; Undesirability

Tey, Josephine
Body; Emotions; Face(s); Leaves; Pity; Voice, Soft

Thackeray, William Makepeace
Black; Facial Expressions, Miscellaneous; Laughter; Poverty; Pursuit; Restlessness; Singing; Suddenness; World

Theroux, Paul
Birds; Eyes, Bright; Facial Expressions, Miscellaneous; Familiarity; Fingers; Grins; Laughter; Nervousness; Physical Appearance; Posture; Rain; Relationships; Simplicity; Singing; Slowness; Snow; Stars; Visibility; Writers/Writing

Thomas, Dylan
Belief; Breasts; Choices; Correspondence; Foolishness; Growth; Muscles; Physical Appearance; Places; Rooms; Soul

Thomas, Leslie
Poverty; Sitting

Thomas, Michael M.
Religion

Thomas, Ross
Hand Movements

Thompson, H.w.
Black; Commonplace; Nervousness

Thompson, Hunter S.
Nervousness; Violence

Thompson, James
Cruelty

Thompson, Jean
Activeness; Cheeks; Disintegration; Embraces; Face(s); Facial Details; Gray; Hair Texture; Leaves; Nervousness; Noise; Pallor; Rain; Smoothness;

Bright; Eye Color; Eye Movements;
Face(s); Facial Expressions, Blank;
Facial Expressions, Miscellaneous;
Fatness; Football; Forehead; Gloom;
Gray; Hair, Curly; Hair Styles;
Head(s); Handshake; Head Movements;
Legs; Lips; Men and Women; Mouth,
Open/Shut; Neck; Noise; Noses;
Objects, Miscellaneous; Physical
Appearance; Places; Rain; Road Scenes;
Sitting; Smoothness; Speaking; Speech
Patterns; Stomach; Sweat; Tobacco;
Wrinkles

Vanderhaeghe, Guy
Abandonment; Birds; Facial Color

Van Doren, Mark
Singing

Van Dyke, Henry
Belonging; Black; Complexion;
Experience; Eye(s); Facial Color; Facial
Expressions, Serious; Greatness; Hair
Color; Music; Parenthood; Rooms;
Straightness; Violence; Voice, Music
Related; White; Yellow

Van Horn, Harriet
Food and Drink

Van Vechten, Carl
Activeness

Vaughan, M.e.
Age

**Vauvenargues, Marquis de Luc de
Clapiers**
Advice; Simplicity

Vianney, Jean B. M.
Greed

Villiers, George
Kisses

Viorst, Judith
Peacefulness

Voltaire
Aimlessness; Books; World

Wade, Betsy
Regularity/Irregularity

Wagner, Jane
Breathing; Eye Movements; Growth;
Mind, Defined; Parenthood; War

Wainwright, John
Disintegration; Dullness; Eye(s);
Speaking; Vibration; Weather

Wakefield, Dan
Clothing, Its Fit; Eye Movements; Food
and Drink; Memory; Modesty; Road
Scenes; Snow; War

Wakeman, Frederic
Brightness

Wakoski, Diane
Agility; Anger; Disappearance; Dryness;
Emotions; Energy; Face(s); Groans and
Whispers; Heaviness; Men and

Women; Night; Oceans/Oceanfronts;
Silence; Spreading

Walcott, Derek
Agitation; Caution; City/Streetscapes;
Familiarity; Firmness; Laughter; Leaves;
Oceans/Oceanfronts; Repetition; Soul;
Unattractiveness; Wrinkles

Walker, Alice
Body Organs; Entrances/Exits; Glitter
and Gloss; Heartbeat; Tears

Walker, William
Unsteadiness

Walpole, Hugh
Behavior; Birds; Brightness; Cloud
Movements; Commonplace; Cost; Facial
Color; Green; Head(s); Heartbeat;
Lying; Meetings; Physical Appearance;
Posture; Rain; Reserve; Silence; Snow

Walton, Susan
Gloom

Walworth, Clarence
Books

Wambaugh, Joseph
Age; Agitation; Body; Clarity;
Complexity; Elusiveness; Exits; Golf;
Stars; Undesirability; Violence; Voice,
Soft

Ward, Hugh
Fatness

Warner, Charles Dudley
Conversation

Warner, Sylvia Townsend
Hand Movements

Warren, Robert Penn
Aimlessness; Correctness;
Disappearance; Energy; Glitter and
Gloss; History; Mouth, Open/Shut;
Silence; Slowness; Suddenness;
Trembling; World

Washburn, Leonard
Eye(s); Noise

Washington, George
Clarity; Government

Watts, Isaac
Activeness

Weaver, Gordon
Memory

Weaver, Will
Breasts; Eyelids; Face(s); Firmness;
Legs; Men and Women; Mouth,
Open/Shut; Music; Objects,
Miscellaneous; Pause; Risk; Stomach;
Visibility

Webster, Daniel
Lawyers

Weber, Dee
Dullness; Formality

Webster, John
Bitterness; Mankind

Weigel, Henrietta
Emotions
Wellman, Paul J.
Face(s); Voice, Harsh
Wells, H. G.
Connections; Disappearance;
Helplessness; Open/Shut; Turning and
Twisting
Welty, Eudora
Abandonment; Activeness; Caution;
Cheeks; Collapse; Complexity;
Contentment; Danger; Differences;
Eye(s); Eyes, Bright; Eyebrows;
Eyelashes; Face(s); Facial Details;
Firmness; Fragility; Hair Styles; Hand
Movements; Head Movements;
Heartbeat; Laughter; Leaping; Mankind;
Memory; Men and Women; Movement;
Mustaches; Pause; Pursuit; Sitting;
Snores; Spreading; Suddenness;
Turning and Twisting; Walking
Werfel, Franz
Actions; Behavior; Facial Expressions,
Blank; Glitter and Gloss; Noise;
Religion; Roars; Spreading;
Watchfulness; Wrinkles
Wertenbaker, Lael Tucker
Agitation; Arguments; Behavior;
Blushes; Experience; Face(s); Firmness;
Head Movements; Memory; Rain;
Sitting; Sky Color; Speech Patterns;
Sunset; Sweat; Vehicles, Operation of
West, Jessamyn
Conversation; Day; Eye Color; Fatness;
Ferocity; Football; Futility; Gentleness;
Reserve; Smoothness; Speed; Sweat;
Voice, Effect of
West, Mae
Writers/Writing
West,paul
Past, The
West, Rebecca
Black; Cruelty; Facial Expressions,
Serious; Kisses; Pink; Pity; Places;
Posture; Rooms; Surprise
Westlake, Donald E.
Physical Appearance
Weyman, S. J.
Firmness
Weyman, Stanley
Anger
Wharton, Edith
Abandonment; Age; Arguments;
Behavior; Belief; Breathing; Cheeks;
Collapse; Connections; Control;
Correspondence; Crowds; Crying;
Decrease; Disappearance;
Disintegration; Dullness; Eye(s); Eye
Expressions, Miscellaneous; Eyelids;

Face(s); Facial Color; Facial
Expressions, Blank; Facial Expressions,
Miscellaneous; Familiarity; Fingers;
Future; Habit; Helplessness; Kisses;
Laughter; Memory; Mouth, Open/Shut;
Naturalness; Noise; Obviousness;
Pallor; Personality Profiles; Physical
Appearance; Physical Feelings;
Preparedness; Promptness; Repetition;
Reserve; Slowness; Speech Patterns;
Transience; Voice, Monotonous; Voice,
Soft; Words, Effect of; Wrinkles
Whateley, Richard
Lies/Liars
Whedon, Julia
Naturalness; Silence; Speech Patterns;
Speed
Wheelock, John Hall
Arguments; Belief; Cloud Movements;
Collapse; Decrease; Disappearance;
Oceans/Oceanfronts
Wheeler, Kate
Fatness; Noise; Silence
Whipple, Edwin Percy
Knowledge
Whitaker, Jack
Disappearance
White, Antonia
Behavior; Silence; Singing; Sitting
White, Curtis
Firmness
White, E. B.
Brevity; Firmness; Food and Drink;
Movement; Places; Poets/Poetry;
Simplicity
White, Patrick
Baldness; Cheeks; Clothing, Its Fit;
Names; Physical Appearance; Sighs
White, T. H.
Clarity; Eye Color; Kisses
Whitman, Stephen French
Facial Color; Silence
Whitman, Walt
Alertness
Whittier, John Greenleaf
Blue; Disappearance; Dispersal;
Emotions; Eyes, Bright; Fate; Ferocity;
Fog; Gentleness; Laughter; Leaves;
Lips; Realization; Silence; Slowness;
Timeliness/Untimeliness; Walking
Wiggins, Marianne
Dryness; Fog
Wilbur, Richard
Aimlessness; Awkwardness; Birds;
Leaves; Night; Noise; Restlessness;
Snow; Sweat
Wilcox, Ella Wheeler
Modesty

Wilde, Oscar
Actions; Agitation; Blushes; Body;
City/Streetscapes; Crying; Eye(s); Facial
Color; Facts; Heaviness; Laughter; Lips;
Marriage; Meetings; Men and Women;
Noses; Pallor; Snow; Straightness;
Trembling; White

Wilde, Percival
Baldness

Wilder, Billy
Places

Wilhelm, kate
Physical Appearance

Will, George F.
Anger; Society; Speech Patterns;
Transience; Unsteadiness

Williams, Ben Ames
Agitation; Cleanliness; Elusiveness;
Entrances/Exits; Facial Details; Greed;
Helplessness; Lips; Physical
Appearance; Posture;
Realness/Unrealness; Speed; Sweat

Williams, Joy
Activeness

Williams, Miller
Disappearance; Fragility; Straightness

Williams, Robin
Helplessness; Laughter

Williams, Tennessee
Cleanliness; Flattery; Relationships;
Toughness

Williams, Thomas
Curses; Legs; Nervousness; Physical
Feelings

Williams, William Carlos
Facial Expressions, Miscellaneous;
Fingers

Williamson, Joy
Clarity

Willingham, Calder
Alertness; Breasts; Disappointment;
Fatness; Neck; Toughness; Vehicles,
Operation of

Wilner, Herbert
Legs

Wilson, Angus
Lies/Liars

Wilson, Arthur
Writers/Writing

Wilson, C. P.
Brightness

Wilson, Earl
Marriage; Behavior; Blindness

Wilson, Leigh Allison
Agitation; Arm Movements; Fingers;
Sitting; Standing; Suddenness; Sweat

Wilson, Louis D.
Cause/Effect

Wilson, Woodrow
Characteristics, National

Wilson, Z. Vance
Breathing; Cheeks; Collapse; Crying;
Exits; Eye(s); Face(s); Facial
Expressions, Miscellaneous; Head
Movements; Pallor; Voice, Music
Related; Words, Effect of

Winans, A. D.
Crying; Memory; Slowness

Winter, William
Carlessness

Withal, John
Movement

Witwer, H. C.
Blushes

Wodehouse, P. G.
Adversary; Agitation; Dancing; Face(s);
Golf; Groans and Whispers; Men and
Women; Music; Nervousness; Noses;
Silence

Wodin, Natascha
Agility; Atmosphere; Clarity;
Conversation; Danger; Darkness;
Embraces; Eye(s); Glitter and Gloss;
Helplessness; Night; Noise; Past, The;
Rooms; Toughness; Vibration

Woiwode, Larry
Emotions

Wolcott, John
Conscience

Wolfe, Thomas
Age; Agility; Body; Complexion; Eye
Movements; Face(s); Facial Expressions,
Miscellaneous; Lighting; Physical
Appearance; Running; Trembling

Wolfe, Tom
Disappearance; Head(s)

Wolff, Geoffrey
Conversation; Eye(s); Facial Color;
Health; Love; Unattractiveness

Wolitzer, Hilma
Eye Movements; Men and Women;
Staleness

Wollaston, Nicholas
Places

Wood, Ira
Agitation; Anger; Body; Breasts;
Dullness; Embraces; Eye Color; Eye
Expressions, Miscellaneous; Facial
Details; Food and Drink; Gloom; Hair,
Curly; Head Movements; Laughter;
Legs; Lighting; Lips; Movement;
Mustaches; Posture; Rain;
Relationships; Snores; Speech Patterns;
Stomach; Sweat; Tears;
Unattractiveness; Wrinkles;
Writers/Writing